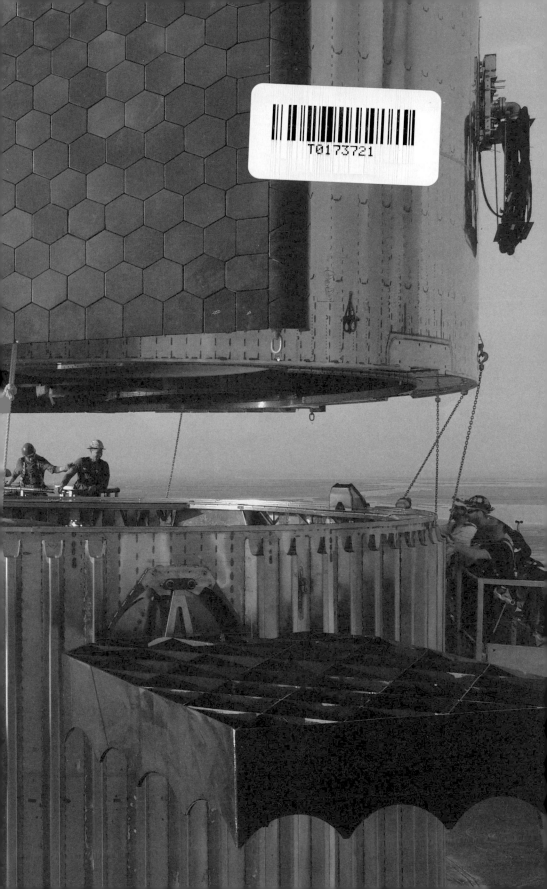

ELON MUSK

ALSO BY WALTER ISAACSON

The Code Breaker: Jennifer Doudna, Gene Editing,
and the Future of the Human Race

Leonardo da Vinci

The Innovators: How a Group of Hackers, Geniuses,
and Geeks Created the Digital Revolution

Steve Jobs

American Sketches

Einstein: His Life and Universe

Benjamin Franklin: An American Life

Kissinger: A Biography

The Wise Men: Six Friends and the World They Made
(with Evan Thomas)

Pro and Con

ELON MUSK

WALTER ISAACSON

**SIMON &
SCHUSTER**

London · New York · Sydney · Toronto · New Delhi

First published in the United States by Simon & Schuster,
an imprint of Simon & Schuster Inc., 2023
First published in Great Britain by Simon & Schuster UK Ltd, 2023

7 9 10 8 6

Simon & Schuster UK Ltd
1st Floor
222 Gray's Inn Road
London WC1X 8HB

www.simonandschuster.co.uk
www.simonandschuster.com.au
www.simonandschuster.co.in

Simon & Schuster Australia, Sydney
Simon & Schuster India, New Delhi

A CIP catalogue record for this book
is available from the British Library

Hardback ISBN: 978-1-3985-2749-2
eBook ISBN: 978-1-3985-2751-5

Printed and Bound in the UK using 100% Renewable
Electricity at CPI Group (UK) Ltd

To anyone I've offended, I just want to say, I reinvented electric cars and I'm sending people to Mars in a rocket ship. Did you think I was also going to be a chill, normal dude?

—Elon Musk, *Saturday Night Live*, May 8, 2021

The people who are crazy enough to think they can change the world are the ones who do.

—Steve Jobs

Contents

Muse of Fire

The playground

As a kid growing up in South Africa, Elon Musk knew pain and learned how to survive it.

When he was twelve, he was taken by bus to a wilderness survival camp, known as a *veldskool*. "It was a paramilitary *Lord of the Flies*," he recalls. The kids were each given small rations of food and water, and they were allowed—indeed encouraged—to fight over them. "Bullying was considered a virtue," his younger brother Kimbal says. The big kids quickly learned to punch the little ones in the face and take their stuff. Elon, who was small and emotionally awkward, got beaten up twice. He would end up losing ten pounds.

Near the end of the first week, the boys were divided into two groups and told to attack each other. "It was so insane, mind-blowing," Musk recalls. Every few years, one of the kids would die. The counselors would recount such stories as warnings. "Don't be stupid like that dumb fuck who died last year," they would say. "Don't be the weak dumb fuck."

The second time Elon went to *veldskool*, he was about to turn sixteen. He had gotten much bigger, bursting up to six feet with a bear-like frame, and had learned some judo. So *veldskool* wasn't so bad. "I realized by then that if someone bullied me, I could punch them very hard in the nose, and then they wouldn't bully me again. They might beat the shit out of me, but if I had punched them hard in the nose, they wouldn't come after me again."

South Africa in the 1980s was a violent place, with machine-gun attacks and knife killings common. Once, when Elon and Kimbal got off a train on their way to an anti-apartheid music concert, they had to wade through a pool of blood next to a dead person with a knife still sticking out of his brain. For the rest of the evening, the blood on the soles of their sneakers made a sticky sound against the pavement.

The Musk family kept German Shepherd dogs that were trained to attack anyone running by the house. When he was six, Elon was racing down the driveway and his favorite dog attacked him, taking a massive bite out of his back. In the emergency room, when they were preparing to stitch him up, he resisted being treated until he was promised that the dog would not be punished. "You're not going to kill him, are you?" Elon asked. They swore that they wouldn't. In recounting the story, Musk pauses and stares vacantly for a very long time. "Then they damn well shot the dog dead."

His most searing experiences came at school. For a long time, he was the youngest and smallest student in his class. He had trouble picking up social cues. Empathy did not come naturally, and he had neither the desire nor the instinct to be ingratiating. As a result, he was regularly picked on by bullies, who would come up and punch him in the face. "If you have never been punched in the nose, you have no idea how it affects you the rest of your life," he says.

At assembly one morning, a student who was horsing around with a gang of friends bumped into him. Elon pushed him back. Words were exchanged. The boy and his friends hunted Elon down at recess and found him eating a sandwich. They came up from behind, kicked him in the head, and pushed him down a set of concrete steps. "They sat on him and just kept beating the shit out of him and kicking him in the head," says Kimbal, who had been sitting with him. "When they got finished, I couldn't even recognize his face. It was such a swollen ball of flesh that you could barely see his eyes." He was taken to the hospital and was out of school for a week. Decades later, he was still getting corrective surgery to try to fix the tissues inside his nose.

But those scars were minor compared to the emotional ones inflicted by his father, Errol Musk, an engineer, rogue, and charismatic fantasist who to this day bedevils Elon. After the school fight, Errol sided with the kid who pummeled Elon's face. "The boy had just lost his father to suicide, and Elon had called him stupid," Errol says. "Elon had this tendency to call people stupid. How could I possibly blame that child?"

When Elon finally came home from the hospital, his father berated him. "I had to stand for an hour as he yelled at me and called me an idiot and told me that I was just worthless," Elon recalls. Kimbal, who had to watch the tirade, says it was the worst memory of his life. "My father just lost it, went ballistic, as he often did. He had zero compassion."

Both Elon and Kimbal, who no longer speak to their father, say his claim that Elon provoked the attack is unhinged and that the perpetrator ended up being sent to juvenile prison for it. They say their father is a volatile fabulist, regularly spinning tales that are larded with fantasies, sometimes calculated and at other times delusional. He has a Jekyll-and-Hyde nature, they say. One minute he would be friendly, the next he would launch into an hour or more of unrelenting abuse. He would end every tirade by telling Elon how pathetic he was. Elon would just have to stand there, not allowed to leave. "It was mental torture," Elon says, pausing for a long time and choking up slightly. "He sure knew how to make anything terrible."

When I call Errol, he talks to me for almost three hours and then follows up regularly with calls and texts over the next two years. He is eager to describe and send me photos of the nice things he provided to his kids, at least during the periods when his engineering business was doing well. At one point he drove a Rolls-Royce, built a wilderness lodge with his boys, and got raw emeralds from a mine owner in Zambia, until that business collapsed.

But he admits that he encouraged a physical and emotional toughness. "Their experiences with me would have made *veldskool* quite tame," he says, adding that violence was simply part of the learning experience in South Africa. "Two held you down while another pummeled your face with a log and so on. New boys were forced to fight the school thug on their first day at a new school." He proudly concedes that he exercised "an extremely stern streetwise autocracy" with his boys. Then he makes a point of adding, "Elon would later apply that same stern autocracy to himself and others."

"Adversity shaped me"

"Someone once said that every man is trying to live up to his father's expectations or make up for his father's mistakes," Barack Obama wrote in his memoirs, "and I suppose that may explain my particular malady." In Elon Musk's case, his father's impact on his psyche would linger, despite many attempts to banish him, both physically and psychologically. Elon's moods would cycle through light and dark, intense and goofy, detached and emotional, with occasional plunges into what those around him dreaded as "demon mode." Unlike his father, he would be caring with his kids, but in other ways, his behavior would hint at a danger that needed to be constantly battled: the specter that, as his mother put it, "he might become his father." It's one of the most resonant tropes in mythology. To what extent does the epic quest of the *Star Wars* hero require exorcising demons bequeathed by Darth Vader and wrestling with the dark side of the Force?

"With a childhood like his in South Africa, I think you have to shut yourself down emotionally in some ways," says his first wife Justine, the mother of five of his surviving ten children. "If your father is always calling you a moron and idiot, maybe the only response is to turn off anything inside that would've opened up an emotional dimension that he didn't have tools to deal with." This emotional shutoff valve could make him callous, but it also made him a risk-seeking innovator. "He learned to shut down fear," she says. "If you turn off fear, then maybe you have to turn off other things, like joy or empathy."

The PTSD from his childhood also instilled in him an aversion to contentment. "I just don't think he knows how to savor success and smell the flowers," says Claire Boucher, the artist known as Grimes, who is the mother of three of his other children. "I think he got conditioned in childhood that life is pain." Musk agrees. "Adversity shaped me," he says. "My pain threshold became very high."

During a particularly hellish period of his life in 2008, after the first three launches of his SpaceX rockets exploded and Tesla was about to go bankrupt, he would wake up thrashing and recount to Talulah Riley, who became his second wife, the horrendous things his father had once said. "I'd heard him use those phrases himself," she says. "It had a profound effect on how he operates." When he recalled these memories, he would zone out and seem to disappear behind his steel-colored eyes. "I think he wasn't conscious of how that still affected him, because he thought of it as something in his childhood," Riley says. "But he's retained a childlike, almost stunted side. Inside the man, he's still there as a child, a child standing in front of his dad."

Out of this cauldron, Musk developed an aura that made him seem, at times, like an alien, as if his Mars mission were an aspiration to return home and his desire to build humanoid robots were a quest for kinship. You'd not be totally shocked if he ripped off his shirt and you discovered that he had no navel and was not of this planet born. But his childhood also made him all too human, a tough yet vulnerable boy who decided to embark on epic quests.

He developed a fervor that cloaked his goofiness, and a goofiness that cloaked his fervor. Slightly uncomfortable in his own body, like a big man who was never an athlete, he would walk with the stride of a mission-driven bear and dance jigs that seemed taught by a robot. With the conviction of a prophet, he would speak about the need to nurture the flame of human consciousness, fathom the universe, and save our planet. At first I thought this was mainly role-playing, the team-boosting pep talks and podcast fantasies of a man-child who had read *The Hitchhiker's Guide to the Galaxy* once too often. But the more I encountered it, the more I came to believe that his sense of mission was part of what drove him. While other entrepreneurs struggled to develop a worldview, he developed a cosmic view.

His heritage and breeding, along with the hardwiring of his brain, made him at times callous and impulsive. It also led to an exceedingly high tolerance for risk. He could calculate it coldly and also embrace it feverishly. "Elon wants risk for its own sake," says Peter Thiel, who became his partner in the early days of PayPal. "He seems to enjoy it, indeed at times be addicted to it."

He became one of those people who feels most alive when a hurricane is coming. "I was born for a storm, and a calm does not suit me," Andrew Jackson once said. Likewise with Musk. He developed a siege mentality that included an attraction, sometimes a craving, for storm and drama, both at work and in the romantic relationships he struggled and failed to maintain. He thrived on crises, deadlines, and wild surges of work. When he faced tortuous challenges, the strain would often keep him awake at night and make him vomit. But it also energized him. "He is a drama magnet," says Kimbal. "That's his compulsion, the theme of his life."

When I was reporting on Steve Jobs, his partner Steve Wozniak said that the big question to ask was *Did he have to be so mean? So rough and cruel? So drama-addicted?* When I turned the question back to Woz at the end of my reporting, he said that if he had run Apple, he would have been kinder. He would have treated everyone there like family and not summarily fired people. Then he paused and added, "But if I had run Apple, we may never have made the Macintosh." And thus the question about Elon Musk: Could he have been more chill and still be the one launching us toward Mars and an electric-vehicle future?

At the beginning of 2022—after a year marked by SpaceX making thirty-one successful rocket launches, Tesla selling close to a million cars, and him becoming the richest man on Earth—Musk spoke ruefully about his compulsion to stir up dramas. "I need to shift my mindset away from being in crisis mode," he told me, "which it has been in for about fourteen years now, or arguably most of my life."

It was a wistful comment, not a New Year's resolution. Even as he made the pledge, he was secretly buying up shares of Twitter, the world's ultimate playground. That April, he snuck away to the Hawaiian house of his mentor Larry Ellison, founder of Oracle, accompanied by the actress Natasha Bassett, an occasional girlfriend. He had been offered a board seat at Twitter, but over the weekend he concluded that wasn't enough. It was in his nature to want total control. So he decided he would make a hostile bid to buy the company outright. Then he flew to Vancouver to meet Grimes. There he stayed up with her until 5 a.m. playing a new war-and-empire-building game, *Elden Ring*. Right after he finished, he pulled the trigger on his plan and went on Twitter. "I made an offer," he announced.

Over the years, whenever he was in a dark place or felt threatened, it took him back to the horrors of being bullied on the playground. Now he had the chance to own the playground.

1

Adventurers

Winnifred and Joshua Haldeman *(top left)*; Errol, Maye, Elon, Tosca, and
Kimbal Musk *(bottom left)*; Cora and Walter Musk *(right)*

Joshua and Winnifred Haldeman

Elon Musk's attraction to risk was a family trait. In that regard, he took after his maternal grandfather, Joshua Haldeman, a daredevil adventurer with strongly held opinions who was raised on a farm on the barren plains of central Canada. He studied chiropractic techniques in Iowa, then returned to his hometown near Moose Jaw, where he broke in horses and gave chiropractic adjustments in exchange for food and lodging.

He was eventually able to buy his own farm, but he lost it during the depression of the 1930s. For the next few years, he worked as a cowboy, rodeo performer, and construction hand. His one constant was a love for adventure. He married and divorced, traveled as a hobo on freight trains, and was a stowaway on an oceangoing ship.

The loss of his farm instilled in him a populism, and he became active in a movement known as the Social Credit Party, which advocated giving citizens free credit notes they could use like currency. The movement had a conservative fundamentalist streak tinged with anti-Semitism. Its first leader in Canada decried a "perversion of cultural ideals" because "a disproportionate number of Jews occupy positions of control." Haldeman rose to become chair of the party's national council.

He also enlisted in a movement called Technocracy, which believed that government should be run by technocrats rather than politicians. It was temporarily outlawed in Canada because of its opposition to the country's entry into World War II. Haldeman defied the ban by taking out a newspaper ad supporting the movement.

At one point he wanted to learn ballroom dancing, which is how he met Winnifred Fletcher, whose adventurous streak was equal to his. As a sixteen-year-old, she got a job at the Moose Jaw *Times Herald*, but she dreamed of being a dancer and actress. So she lit out by train to Chicago and then New York City. Upon her return, she opened a dance school in Moose Jaw, which is where Haldeman showed up for lessons. When he asked her to dinner, she replied, "I don't date my clients." So he quit the class and asked her out again.

A few months later, he asked, "When will you marry me?" She responded, "Tomorrow."

They had four children, including twin girls, Maye and Kaye, born in 1948. One day on a trip he spotted a For Sale sign on a single-engine Luscombe airplane sitting in a farmer's field. He had no cash, but he convinced the farmer to take his car in exchange. It was rather impetuous, since Haldeman did not know how to fly. He hired someone to fly him home and teach him how to pilot the plane.

The family came to be known as The Flying Haldemans, and he was described by a chiropractic trade journal as "perhaps the most remarkable figure in the history of flying chiropractors," a rather narrow, albeit accurate, accolade. They bought a larger single-engine plane, a Bellanca, when Maye and Kaye were three months old, and the toddlers became known as "the flying twins."

With his quirky conservative populist views, Haldeman came to believe that the Canadian government was usurping too much control over the lives of individuals and that the country had gone soft. So in 1950, he decided to move to South Africa, which was still ruled by a white apartheid regime. They took apart the Bellanca, crated it, and boarded a freighter for Cape Town. Haldeman decided he wanted to live inland, so they took off toward Johannesburg, where most of the white citizens spoke English rather than Afrikaans. But as they flew over nearby Pretoria, the lavender jacaranda flowers were in bloom, and Haldeman announced, "This is where we'll stay."

When Joshua and Winnifred were young, a charlatan named William Hunt, known (at least to himself) as "the Great Farini," came to Moose Jaw and told tales of an ancient "lost city" he had seen when crossing the Kalahari Desert in South Africa. "This fabulist showed my grandfather pictures that were obviously fake, but he became a believer and decided it was his mission to rediscover it," Musk says. Once in Africa, the Haldemans made a monthlong trek into the Kalahari every year to search for this legendary city. They hunted for their own food and slept with their guns so they could fend off lions.

The family adopted a motto: "Live dangerously—carefully." They embarked on long-distance flights to places such as Norway, tied for first place in the twelve-thousand-mile Cape Town–to–Algiers motor rally, and became the first to fly a single-engine plane from Africa to Australia. "They had to remove the back seats to put in gas tanks," Maye later recalled.

Joshua Haldeman's risk-taking eventually caught up with him. He was killed when a person he was teaching to fly hit a power line, causing the plane to flip and crash. His grandson Elon was three at the time. "He knew that real adventures involve risk," he says. "Risk energized him."

Haldeman imprinted that spirit onto one of his twin girls, Elon's mother, Maye. "I know that I can take a risk as long as I'm prepared," she says. As a young student, she did well in science and math. She was also strikingly good-looking. Tall and blue-eyed, with high cheekbones and sculpted chin, she began working at age fifteen as a model, doing department store runway shows on Saturday mornings.

Around that time, she met a boy in her neighborhood who was also strikingly good-looking, albeit in a smooth and caddish way.

Errol Musk

Errol Musk was an adventurer and wheeler-dealer, always on the lookout for the next opportunity. His mother, Cora, was from England, where she finished school at fourteen, worked at a factory making skins for fighter-bombers, then took a refugee ship to South Africa. There she met Walter Musk, a cryptographer and military intelligence officer who worked in Egypt on schemes to fool the Germans by deploying fake weapons and searchlights. After the war, he did little other than sit silently in an armchair, drink, and use his cryptology skills on crossword puzzles. So Cora left him, went back to England with their two sons, bought a Buick, and then returned to Pretoria. "She was the strongest person I ever met," Errol says.

Errol earned a degree in engineering and worked on building hotels, shopping centers, and factories. On the side, he liked restoring old cars and planes. He also dabbled in politics, defeating an Afrikaner member of the pro-apartheid National Party to become one of the few English-speaking members of the Pretoria City Council.

The *Pretoria News* for March 9, 1972, reported the election under the headline "Reaction against the Establishment."

Like the Haldemans, he loved flying. He bought a twin-engine Cessna Golden Eagle, which he used to ferry television crews to a lodge he had built in the bush. On one trip in 1986, when he was looking to sell the plane, he landed at an airstrip in Zambia where a Panamanian-Italian entrepreneur offered to buy it. They agreed on a price, and instead of taking a payment in cash, Errol was given a portion of the emeralds produced at three small mines that the entrepreneur owned in Zambia.

Zambia then had a postcolonial Black government, but there was no functioning bureaucracy, so the mine was not registered. "If you registered it, you would wind up with nothing, because the Blacks would take everything from you," Errol says. He criticizes Maye's family for being racist, which he insists he is not. "I don't have anything against the Blacks, but they are just different from what I am," he says in a rambling phone discourse.

Errol, who never had an ownership stake in the mine, expanded his trade by importing raw emeralds and having them cut in Johannesburg. "Many people came to me with stolen parcels," he says. "On trips overseas I would sell emeralds to jewelers. It was a cloak-and-dagger thing, because none of it was legal." After producing profits of roughly $210,000, his emerald business collapsed in the 1980s when the Russians created an artificial emerald in the lab. He lost all of his emerald earnings.

Their marriage

Errol Musk and Maye Haldeman began dating when they were young teenagers. From the start, their relationship was filled with drama. He repeatedly proposed to her, but she didn't trust him. When she discovered he was cheating on her, she became so upset that she cried for a week and couldn't eat. "Because of grief, I dropped ten pounds," she recalls; it helped her win a local beauty contest. She got $150 in cash plus ten tickets to a bowling alley and became a finalist in the Miss South Africa contest.

When Maye graduated from college, she moved to Cape Town to give talks about nutrition. Errol came to visit, brought an engagement ring, and proposed. He promised he would change his ways and be faithful once they were married. Maye had just broken off a relationship with another unfaithful boyfriend, gained a lot of weight, and begun to fear that she would never get married, so she agreed.

The night of the wedding, Errol and Maye took an inexpensive flight to Europe for their honeymoon. In France, he bought copies of *Playboy*, which was banned in South Africa, and lay on the small hotel bed looking at them, much to Maye's annoyance. Their fights turned bitter. When they got back to Pretoria, she thought of trying to get out of the marriage. But she soon became nauseated from morning sickness. She had become pregnant on the second night of their honeymoon, in the town of Nice. "It was clear that marrying him had been a mistake," she recalls, "but now it was impossible to undo."

2

A Mind of His Own

Pretoria, the 1970s

Elon and Maye Musk *(top left)*; Elon, Kimbal, and Tosca *(bottom left)*;
Elon ready for school *(right)*

Lonely and determined

At 7:30 on the morning of June 28, 1971, Maye Musk gave birth to an eight-pound, eight-ounce boy with a very large head.

At first she and Errol were going to name him Nice, after the town in France where he was conceived. History may have been different, or at least amused, if the boy had to go through life with the name Nice Musk. Instead, in the hope of making the Haldemans happy, Errol agreed that the boy would have names from that side of the family: Elon, after Maye's grandfather J. Elon Haldeman, and Reeve, the maiden name of Maye's maternal grandmother.

Errol liked the name Elon because it was biblical, and he later claimed that he had been prescient. As a child, he says, he heard about a science fiction book by the rocket scientist Wernher von Braun called *Project Mars*, which describes a colony on the planet run by an executive known as "the Elon."

Elon cried a lot, ate a lot, and slept little. At one point Maye decided to just let him cry until he fell asleep, but she changed her mind after neighbors called the police. His moods switched rapidly; when he wasn't crying, his mother says, he was really sweet.

Over the next two years, Maye had two more children, Kimbal and Tosca. She didn't coddle them. They were allowed to roam freely. There was no nanny, just a housekeeper who paid little attention when Elon began experimenting with rockets and explosives. He says he's surprised he made it through childhood with all of his fingers intact.

When he was three, his mother decided that because he was so intellectually curious he should be in nursery school. The principal tried to dissuade her, pointing out that being younger than anyone else in the class would present social challenges. They should wait another year. "I can't do that," Maye said. "He needs someone besides me to talk to. I really have this genius child." She prevailed.

It was a mistake. Elon had no friends, and by the time he was in second grade he was tuning out. "The teacher would come up to me and yell at me, but I would not really see or hear her," he says. His parents got called in to see the principal, who told them, "We have reason to believe that Elon is retarded." He spent most of his time in a trance, not listening, one of his teachers explained. "He looks out of the window all the time, and when I tell him to pay attention he says, 'The leaves are turning brown now.'" Errol replied that Elon was right, the leaves were turning brown.

The impasse was broken when his parents agreed that Elon's hearing should be tested, as if that might be the problem. "They decided it was an ear problem, so they took my adenoids out," he says. That calmed down the school officials, but it did nothing to change his tendency to zone out and retreat into his own world when thinking. "Ever since I was a kid, if I start to think about something hard, then all of my sensory systems turn off," he says. "I can't see or hear or anything. I'm using my brain to compute, not for incoming information." The other kids would jump up and down and wave their arms in his face to see if they could summon back his attention. But it didn't work. "It's best not to try to break through when he has that vacant stare," his mother says.

Compounding his social problems was his unwillingness to suffer politely those he considered fools. He used the word "stupid" often. "Once he started going to school, he became so lonely and sad," his mother says. "Kimbal and Tosca would make friends on the first day and bring them home, but Elon never brought friends home. He wanted to have friends, but he just didn't know how."

As a result, he was lonely, very lonely, and that pain remained seared into his soul. "When I was a child, there's one thing I said," he recalled in an interview with *Rolling Stone* during a tumultuous period in his love life in 2017. "'I never want to be alone.' That's what I would say. 'I don't want to be alone.'"

One day when he was five, one of his cousins was having a birthday party, but Elon was punished for getting into a fight and told to stay home. He was a very determined kid, and he decided to walk on his own to his cousin's house. The problem was that it was on the other side of Pretoria, a walk of almost two hours. Plus, he was too young to read the road signs. "I kind of knew what the route looked like because I had seen it from a car, and I was determined to get there, so I just started walking," he says. He managed to arrive just as the party was ending. When his mother saw him coming down the road, she freaked out. Fearing he would be punished again, he climbed a maple tree and refused to come down. Kimbal remembers standing beneath the tree and staring at his older brother in awe. "He has this fierce determination that blows your mind and was sometimes frightening, and still is."

When he was eight, he focused his determination on getting a motorcycle. Yes, at age eight. He would stand next to his father's chair and make his case, over and over. When his father picked up a newspaper and ordered him to be quiet, Elon would continue to stand there. "It just was extraordinary to watch," Kimbal says. "He would stand there silently, then resume his argument, then stand silent." This happened every evening for weeks. His father finally caved and got Elon a blue-and-gold 50cc Yamaha.

Elon also had a tendency to be spacey and wander off on his own, oblivious to what others were doing. On a family trip to Liverpool to see some of their relatives when he was eight, his parents left him and his brother in a park to play by themselves. It was not in his nature to stay put, so he started wandering the streets. "Some kid found me crying and took me to his mom, who gave me milk and biscuits and called the police," he recalls. When he was reunited with his parents at the police station, he was unaware that anything was amiss.

"It was insane to leave me and my brother alone in a park at that age," he says, "but my parents weren't overprotective like parents are today." Years later, I watched him at a solar roof construction site with his two-year-old boy, known as X. It was 10 p.m., and there were forklifts and other moving equipment lit by two spotlights that cast big shadows. Musk put X on the ground so the boy could explore on his own, which he did without fear. As he poked around amid the wires and cables, Musk glanced at him occasionally, but refrained from intervening. Finally, after X started to climb on a moving spotlight, Musk walked over and picked him up. X squirmed and squealed, unhappy about being restrained.

Musk would later talk about—even joke about—having Asperger's, a common name for a form of autism-spectrum disorder that can affect a person's social skills, relationships, emotional connectivity, and self-regulation. "He was never actually diagnosed as a kid," his mother says, "but he says he has Asperger's, and I'm sure he's right." The condition was exacerbated by his childhood traumas. Whenever he would later feel bullied or threatened, his close friend Antonio Gracias says, the PTSD from his childhood would hijack his limbic system, the part of the brain that controls emotional responses.

As a result, he was bad at picking up social cues. "I took people literally when they said something," he says, "and it was only by reading books that I began to learn that people did not always say what they really meant." He had a preference for things that were more precise, such as engineering, physics, and coding.

Like all psychological traits, Musk's were complex and individualized. He could be very emotional, especially about his own children, and he felt acutely the anxiety that comes from being alone. But he didn't have the emotional receptors that produce everyday kindness and warmth and a desire to be liked. He was not hardwired to have empathy. Or, to put it in less technical terms, he could be an asshole.

The divorce

Maye and Errol Musk were at an Oktoberfest celebration with three other couples, drinking beer and having fun, when a guy at another table whistled at Maye and called her sexy. Errol was furious, but not at the guy. The way Maye remembers it, he lunged and was about to hit her, and a friend had to restrain him. She fled to her mother's house. "Over time, he had gotten crazier," Maye later said. "He would hit me when the kids were around. I remember that Elon, who was five, would hit him on the backs of his knees to try to stop him."

Errol calls the accusations "absolute rubbish." He claims he adored Maye, and over the years he tried to win her back. "I've never laid a hand on a woman in my life, and certainly none of my wives," he says. "That's one of women's weapons is to cry that the man abused her, to cry and to lie. And a man's weapons are to buy and to sign."

On the morning after the Oktoberfest altercation, Errol came over to Maye's mother's house, apologized, and asked Maye to come back. "Don't you dare touch her again," Winnifred Haldeman said. "If you do, she's coming to live with me." Maye said that he never hit her after that, but his verbal abuse continued. He would tell her that she was "boring, stupid, and ugly." The marriage never recovered. Errol later admitted it was his fault. "I had a very pretty wife, but there were always prettier, younger girls," he said. "I really loved Maye, but I screwed up." They divorced when Elon was eight.

Maye and the children moved to a house on the coast near Durban, about 380 miles south of the Pretoria-Johannesburg area, where she juggled jobs as a model and dietician. There was little money. She bought her kids secondhand books and uniforms. On some weekends and holidays the boys (but usually not Tosca) would take the train to see their father in Pretoria. "He would send them back without any clothes or bags, so I had to buy them new clothes every time," she says. "He said that I would eventually return to him, because I would be so poverty-stricken and wouldn't be able to feed them."

Often she would have to travel on a modeling job or to give a nutrition lecture, leaving the kids at home. "I never felt guilty about working full-time, because I didn't have a choice," she says. "My children had to be responsible for themselves." The freedom taught them to be self-reliant. When they faced a problem, she had a stock response: "You'll figure it out." As Kimbal recalls, "Mom wasn't soft and cuddly, and she was always working, but that was a gift for us."

Elon developed into a night person, staying up until dawn reading books. When he saw his mother's light go on at 6 a.m., he would crawl into bed and fall asleep. That meant she had trouble getting him up in time for school, and on nights when she was away, he would sometimes not get to class until 10 a.m. After getting calls from the school, Errol launched a custody battle and had subpoenas issued for Elon's teachers, Maye's modeling agent, and their neighbors. Right before going to trial, Errol dropped the case. Every few years, he would initiate another court action and then drop it. When Tosca recounts these tales, she begins to cry. "I remember Mom just sitting there, sobbing on the couch. I didn't know what to do. All I could do was to hold her."

Maye and Errol were each drawn to dramatic intensity rather than domestic bliss, a trait they would pass on. After her divorce, Maye began dating another abusive man. The children hated him and would occasionally put tiny firecrackers in his cigarettes that would explode when he lit up. Soon after the man proposed marriage, he got another woman pregnant. "She had been a friend of mine," Maye says. "We had modeled together."

With broken tooth and scar

3

Life with Father

Pretoria, the 1980s

Elon pokes a tortoise and Errol watches *(top left)*; Kimbal and Elon with Peter and Russ Rive *(top right)*; the lodge in the Timbavati Game Reserve *(bottom)*

The move

At age ten, Musk made a fateful decision, one that he would later regret: he decided to move in with his father. He took the dangerous overnight train from Durban to Johannesburg on his own. When he spotted his father waiting for him at the station, he began "beaming with delight, like the sun," Errol says. "Hi Dad, let's get a hamburger!" he shouted. That night, he crawled into his father's bed and slept there.

Why did he decide to move in with his father? Elon sighs and stays silent for almost a minute when I ask this. "My dad was lonely, so lonely, and I felt I should keep him company," he finally says. "He used psychological wiles on me." He also adored his grandmother, Errol's mother Cora, known as Nana. She convinced him that it was unfair that his mother had all three children and his father had none.

In some ways, the move was not all that mysterious. Elon was ten, socially awkward, and had no friends. His mother was loving, but she was overworked, distracted, and vulnerable. His father, in contrast, was swaggering and manly, a big guy with large hands and a mesmerizing presence. His career had many ups and downs, but at that time he was feeling flush. He owned a gold-colored convertible Rolls-Royce Corniche and, more importantly, two sets of encyclopedias, lots of books, and a variety of engineering tools.

So Elon, still a small boy, chose to live with him. "It turned out to be a really bad idea," he says. "I didn't yet know how horrible he was." Four years later, Kimbal followed. "I didn't want to leave my brother alone with him," Kimbal says. "My dad guilted my brother into going to live with him. And then he guilted me."

"Why did he choose to go live with someone who inflicted pain?" Maye Musk asked forty years later. "Why didn't he prefer a happy home?" Then she paused for a moment. "Maybe that's just who he is."

After the boys moved in, they helped Errol build a lodge that he could rent to tourists in the Timbavati Game Reserve, a pristine stretch of bush about three hundred miles east of Pretoria. During construction, they slept around a fire at night, with Browning rifles to protect them against lions. The bricks were made of river sand and the roof was grass. As an engineer, Errol liked studying the properties of various materials, and he made the floors out of mica because it was a good thermal insulator. Elephants in search of water often uprooted the pipes, and monkeys regularly broke into the pavilions and pooped, so there was a lot of work for the boys to do.

Elon often accompanied visitors on hunts. Although he had only a .22 caliber rifle, it had a good scope and he became an expert shot. He even won a local skeet-shooting contest, though he was too young to accept the prize of a case of whiskey.

When Elon was nine, his father took him, Kimbal, and Tosca on a trip to America, where they drove from New York through the Midwest and then down to Florida. Elon became hooked on the coin-operated video games he found in the motel lobbies. "It was by far the most exciting thing," he said. "We didn't have that yet in South Africa." Errol displayed his mix of flamboyance and frugality: he rented a Thunderbird but they stayed in budget inns. "When we got to Orlando, my father refused to take us to Disney World because it was too expensive," Musk recalls. "I think we went to some water park instead." As is often the case, Errol spins a different tale, insisting that they went both to Disney World, where Elon liked the haunted house ride, and to Six Flags over Georgia. "I told them over and over on the trip, 'America is where you will come live someday.'"

Two years later, he took the three children to Hong Kong. "My father had some combination of legitimate business and hucksterism," Musk recalls. "He left us in the hotel, which was pretty grungy, and just gave us fifty bucks or something, and we didn't see him for two days." They watched Samurai movies and cartoons on the hotel TV. Leaving Tosca behind, Elon and Kimbal wandered the streets, going into electronics stores where they could play video games for free. "Nowadays someone would call the child-protection service if someone did what our dad did," Musk says, "but for us back then it was a wondrous experience."

A *confederacy of cousins*

After Elon and Kimbal moved in with their father in suburban Pretoria, Maye moved to nearby Johannesburg so the family could be closer together. On Fridays, she would drive to Errol's house to pick up the boys. They would then go see their grandmother, the indomitable Winnifred Haldeman, who cooked a chicken stew the kids hated so much that Maye would take them out for pizza afterward.

Elon and Kimbal usually spent the night at the house next door to their grandmother's, where Maye's sister Kaye Rive and her three boys lived. The five cousins—Elon and Kimbal Musk and Peter, Lyndon, and Russ Rive—became an adventurous and occasionally contentious bevy of bucks. Maye was more indulgent and less protective than her sister, so they would conspire with her when plotting an adventure. "If we wanted to do something like go to a concert in Johannesburg, she would say to her sister, I'm going to go take them to church camp this evening," says Kimbal. "Then she would drop us off and we would go do our mischief."

Those trips could be dangerous. "I remember once when the train stopped, there was an immense fight, and we watched a guy get stabbed through the head," says Peter Rive. "We were hiding inside the car, then the doors closed, and we were like moving on." Sometimes a gang would board the train to hunt down rivals, rampaging through the cars shooting machine guns. Some of the concerts were anti-apartheid protests, such as one in 1985 in Johannesburg that drew 100,000 people. Often brawls would break out. "We didn't try to hide from the violence, we became survivors of it," says Kimbal. "It taught us to not be afraid but also to not do crazy things."

Elon developed a reputation for being the most fearless. When the cousins went to a movie and people were making noise, he would be the one to go over and tell them to be quiet, even if they were much bigger. "It's a big theme for him to never have his decisions guided by fear," Peter recalls. "That was definitely present even when he was a child."

He was also the most competitive of the cousins. One time when they were riding their bicycles from Pretoria to Johannesburg, Elon was way out in front, pedaling fast. So the others pulled over and hitched a ride in a pickup truck. When Elon rejoined them, he was so angry that he started hitting them. It was a race, he said, and they had cheated.

Such fights were common. Often they would happen in public, the boys oblivious to their surroundings. One of the many that Elon and Kimbal had was at a country fair. "They were wrestling and punching each other in the dust," Peter recalls. "People were freaking out, and I had to say to the crowd, 'This is not a big deal. These guys are brothers.'" Although the fights were usually over small things, they could get vicious. "The way to win was to be the first person to punch or kick the other guy in the balls," Kimbal says. "That would end the fight because you can't continue if you get crunched in the balls."

The student

Musk was a good student, but not a superstar. When he was nine and ten, he got A's in English and Math. "He is quick to grasp new mathematical concepts," his teacher noted. But there was a constant refrain in the report card comments: "He works extremely slowly, either because he dreams or is doing what he should not." "He seldom finishes anything. Next year he must concentrate on his work and not daydream during class." "His compositions show a lively imagination, but he doesn't always finish in time." His average grade before he got to high school was 83 out of 100.

After he was bullied and beaten in his public high school, his father moved him to a private academy, Pretoria Boys High School. Based on the English model, it featured strict rules, caning, compulsory chapel, and uniforms. There he got excellent grades in all but two subjects: Afrikaans (he got a 61 out of 100 his final year) and religious instruction ("not extending himself," the teacher noted). "I wasn't really going to put a lot of effort into things I thought were meaningless," he says. "I would rather be reading or playing video games." He got an A in the physics part of his senior certificate exams, but somewhat surprisingly, only a B in the math part.

In his spare time, he liked to make small rockets and experiment with different mixtures—such as swimming-pool chlorine and brake fluid—to see what would make the biggest bang. He also learned magic tricks and how to hypnotize people, once convincing Tosca that she was a dog and getting her to eat raw bacon.

As they would later do in America, the cousins pursued various entrepreneurial ideas. One Easter, they made chocolate eggs, wrapped them in foil, and sold them door-to-door. Kimbal came up with an ingenious scheme. Instead of selling them cheaper than the Easter eggs at the store, they made them more expensive. "Some people would balk at the price," he says, "but we told them, 'You're actually supporting future capitalists.'"

Reading remained Musk's psychological retreat. Sometimes he would immerse himself in books all afternoon and most of the night, nine hours at a stretch. When the family went to someone's house, he would disappear into their host's library. When they went into town, he would wander off and later be found at a bookstore, sitting on the floor, in his own world. He was also deeply into comics. The single-minded passion of the superheroes impressed him. "They're always trying to save the world, with their underpants on the outside or these skin-tight iron suits, which is really pretty strange when you think about it," he says. "But they *are* trying to save the world."

Musk read both sets of his father's encyclopedias and became, to his doting mother and sister, a "genius boy." To other kids, however, he was an annoying nerd. "Look at the moon, it must be a million miles away," a cousin once exclaimed. Replied Elon, "No, it's like 239,000 miles, depending on the orbit."

One book that he found in his father's office described great inventions that would be made in the future. "I would come back from school and go to a side room in my father's office and read it over and over," he says. Among the ideas was a rocket propelled by an ion thruster, which would use particles rather than gas for thrust. Late one night at the control room of his rocket base in south Texas, Musk described the book at length to me, including how an ion thruster would work in a vacuum. "That book is what first made me think about going to other planets," he said.

Russ Rive, Elon, Kimbal, and Peter Rive

4

The Seeker

Pretoria, the 1980s

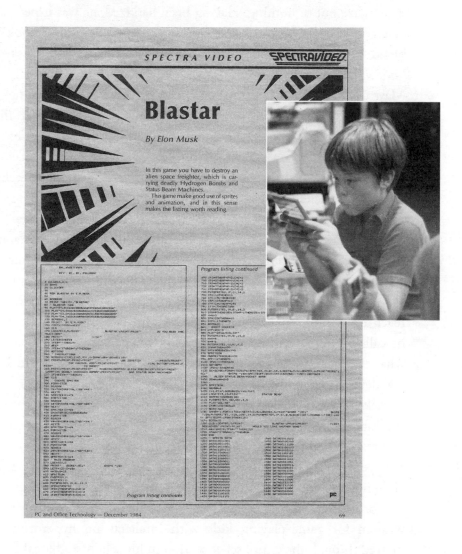

Existential crisis

When Musk was young, his mother started taking him to Sunday school at the local Anglican Church, where she was a teacher. It did not go well. She would tell her class stories from the Bible, and he would question them. "What do you mean, the waters parted?" he asked. "That's not possible." When she told the story of Jesus feeding the crowd with loaves and fishes, he countered that things cannot materialize out of nothing. Having been baptized, he was expected to take communion, but he began questioning that as well. "I took the blood and body of Christ, which is weird when you're a kid," he says. "I said, 'What the hell is this? Is this a weird metaphor for cannibalism?'" Maye decided to let Elon stay home and read on Sunday mornings.

His father, who was more God-fearing, told Elon that there were things that could not be known through our limited senses and minds. "There are no atheist pilots," he would say, and Elon would add, "There are no atheists at exam time." But Elon came to believe early on that science could explain things and so there was no need to conjure up a Creator or a deity that would intervene in our lives.

When he reached his teens, it began to gnaw at him that something was missing. Both the religious and the scientific explanations of existence, he says, did not address the really big questions, such as *Where did the universe come from, and why does it exist?* Physics could teach everything about the universe except why. That led to what he calls his adolescent existential crisis. "I began trying to figure out what the meaning of life and the universe was," he says. "And I got real depressed about it, like maybe life may have no meaning."

Like a good bookworm, he addressed these questions through reading. At first, he made the typical mistake of angsty adolescents and read existential philosophers, such as Nietzsche, Heidegger, and Schopenhauer. This had the effect of turning confusion into despair. "I do not recommend reading Nietzsche as a teenager," he says.

Fortunately, he was saved by science fiction, that wellspring of wisdom for game-playing kids with intellects on hyperdrive. He plowed through the entire sci-fi section in his school and local libraries, then pushed the librarians to order more.

One of his favorites was Robert Heinlein's *The Moon Is a Harsh Mistress*, a novel about a lunar penal colony. It is managed by a super-computer, nicknamed Mike, that is able to acquire self-awareness and a sense of humor. The computer sacrifices its life during a rebellion at the penal colony. The book explores an issue that would become central to Musk's life: Will artificial intelligence develop in ways that benefit and protect humanity, or will machines develop intentions of their own and become a threat to humans?

That topic is central to what became another of his favorites, Isaac Asimov's robot stories. The tales formulate laws of robotics that are designed to make sure robots do not get out of control. In the final scene of his 1985 novel *Robots and Empire*, Asimov expounds the most fundamental of these rules, dubbed the Zeroth Law: "A robot may not harm humanity, or, through inaction, allow humanity to come to harm." The heroes of Asimov's *Foundation* series of books develop a plan to send settlers to distant regions of the galaxy to preserve human consciousness in the face of an impending dark age.

More than thirty years later, Musk unleashed a random tweet about how these ideas motivated his quest to make humans a space-faring species and to harness artificial intelligence to be at the service of humans: "Foundation Series & Zeroth Law are fundamental to creation of SpaceX."

The Hitchhiker's Guide

The science fiction book that most influenced his wonder years was Douglas Adams's *The Hitchhiker's Guide to the Galaxy*. The jaunty and wry tale helped shape Musk's philosophy and added a dollop of droll humor to his serious mien. "*The Hitchhiker's Guide*," he says, "helped me out of my existential depression, and I soon realized it was amazingly funny in all sorts of subtle ways."

The story involves a human named Arthur Dent who is rescued by a passing spaceship seconds before the Earth is destroyed by an alien civilization that is building a hyperspace highway. Along with his alien rescuer, Dent explores various nooks and crannies of the galaxy, which is run by a two-headed president who "had turned unfathomability into an art form." The denizens of the galaxy are trying to figure out the "Answer to The Ultimate Question of Life, the Universe, and Everything." They build a supercomputer that after seven million years spouts out the answer: 42. When that provokes a befuddled howl, the computer replies, "That quite definitely is the answer. I think the problem, to be quite honest with you, is that you've never actually known what the question is." That lesson stuck with Musk. "I took from the book that we need to extend the scope of consciousness so that we are better able to ask the questions about the answer, which is the universe," he says.

The Hitchhiker's Guide, combined with Musk's later immersion into video and tabletop simulation games, led to a lifelong fascination with the tantalizing thought that we might merely be pawns in a simulation devised by some higher-order beings. As Douglas Adams writes, "There is a theory which states that if ever anyone discovers exactly what the Universe is for and why it is here, it will instantly disappear and be replaced by something even more bizarre and inexplicable. There is another theory which states that this has already happened."

Blastar

In the late 1970s, the role-playing game *Dungeons & Dragons* became a popular obsession among the global tribe of geeks. Elon, Kimbal, and their Rive cousins immersed themselves in the game, which involves sitting around a table and, guided by character sheets and the roll of dice, embarking on fantasy adventures. One of the players serves as the Dungeon Master, refereeing the action.

Elon usually played the Dungeon Master and, surprisingly, did it with gentleness. "Even as a kid, Elon had a whole bunch of different demeanors and moods," says his cousin Peter Rive. "As a Dungeon Master, he was incredibly patient, which is not, in my experience, always his default personality, if you know what I mean. It happens sometimes, and it's so beautiful when it does." Instead of pressuring his brother and cousins, he would turn very analytical to describe the options they had in each situation.

Together they entered a tournament in Johannesburg, at which they were the youngest players. The tournament's Dungeon Master assigned their mission: you have to save this woman by figuring out who in the game is the bad guy and killing him. Elon looked at the Dungeon Master and said, "I think you're the bad guy." And so they killed him. Elon was right, and the game, which was supposed to last a few hours, was over. The organizers accused them of somehow cheating and at first tried to deny them the prize. But Musk prevailed. "These guys were idiots," he says. "It was so obvious."

Musk saw his first computer around the time he turned eleven. He was in a shopping mall in Johannesburg, and he stood there for minutes just staring at it. "I had read computer magazines," he says, "but I had never actually seen a computer before." As with the motorcycle, he hounded his father to get him one. Errol was bizarrely averse to computers, claiming they were good only for time-wasting games, not engineering. So Elon saved his money from odd jobs and bought a Commodore VIC-20, one of the earliest personal computers. It could play games such as *Galaxian* and *Alpha Blaster*, in which a player attempts to protect Earth from alien invaders.

The computer came with a course in how to program in BASIC that involved sixty hours of lessons. "I did it in three days, barely sleeping," he remembers. A few months later, he tore out an ad for a conference on personal computers at a university and told his father he wanted to attend. Again, his father balked. It was an expensive seminar, about $400, and not meant for children. Elon replied that it was "essential" and just stood next to his father staring. Over the next few days, Elon would pull the ad out of his pocket and renew his demand. Finally his father was able to talk the university into giving a discounted price for Elon to stand in the back. When Errol came to pick him up at the end, he found Elon engaging with three of the professors. "This boy must get a new computer," one of them declared.

After he aced a programming skills test at his school, he got an IBM PC/XT and taught himself to program using Pascal and Turbo C++. At age thirteen, he was able to create a video game, which he named *Blastar*, using 123 lines of BASIC and some simple assembly language to get the graphics to work. He submitted it to *PC and Office Technology* magazine, and it appeared in the December 1984 issue with a short introduction explaining, "In this game, you have to destroy an alien space freighter, which is carrying deadly Hydrogen Bombs and Status Beam Machines." Although it's unclear what a Status Beam Machine is, the concept sounds cool. The magazine paid him $500, and he proceeded to sell it two other games, one like *Donkey Kong* and the other simulating roulette and blackjack.

Thus began a lifelong addiction to video games. "If you're playing with Elon, you play pretty much nonstop until finally you have to eat," Peter Rive says. On one trip to Durban, Elon figured out how to hack the games in a mall. He was able to hotwire the system so that they could play for hours without using any coins.

He then came up with a grander idea: the cousins could create a video-game arcade of their own. "We knew exactly which games were the most popular, so it seemed like a sure thing," Elon says. He figured out how the cash flow could finance the machines. But when the boys tried to get the city permits, they were told they needed someone over eighteen to sign the application. Kimbal, who had filled out the thirty pages of forms, decided that they couldn't ask Errol. "He was just too hard of a human," Kimbal says. "So we went to Russ and Pete's dad, and he flipped out. That basically shut the whole thing down."

5

Escape Velocity

Leaving South Africa, 1989

Jekyll and Hyde

At age seventeen, after seven years of living with his father, Elon realized that he would have to escape. Life with him had become increasingly unnerving.

There were times when Errol would be jovial and fun, but occasionally he would become dark, verbally abusive, and possessed by fantasies and conspiracies. "His mood could change on a dime," Tosca says. "Everything could be super, then within a second he would be vicious and spewing abuse." It was almost as if he had a split personality. "One minute he would be super friendly," Kimbal says, "and the next he would be screaming at you, lecturing you for hours—literally two or three hours while he forced you to just stand there—calling you worthless, pathetic, making scarring and evil comments, not allowing you to leave."

Elon's cousins became reluctant to visit. "You never knew what you were in for," Peter Rive says. "Sometimes Errol would be like, 'I just got us some new motorbikes so let's jump on them.' At other times he would be angry and threatening and, oh fuck, make you clean the toilets with a toothbrush." When Peter tells me this, he pauses for a moment and then, a bit hesitantly, notes that Elon sometimes has similar mood swings. "When Elon's in a good mood, it's like the coolest, funnest thing in the world. And when he's in a bad mood, he goes really dark, and you're just walking on eggshells."

One day Peter came over to the house and found Errol sitting in his underwear at the kitchen table with a plastic roulette wheel. He was trying to see whether microwaves could affect it. He would spin the wheel, mark down the result, then spin it and put it in a microwave oven and record the result. "It was nuts," Peter says. Errol had become convinced that he could find a system for beating the game. He dragged Elon to the Pretoria casino many times, dressing him up so that he looked older than sixteen, and had him write down the numbers while Errol used a calculator hidden under a betting card.

Elon went to the library and read a few books on roulette and even wrote a roulette simulation program on his computer. He then tried to convince his father that none of his schemes would work. But Errol believed that he had found a deeper truth about probability and, as he later described it to me, an "almost total solution to what is called randomness." When I asked him to explain it, he said, "There are no 'random events' or 'chance.' All events follow the Fibonacci Sequence, like the Mandelbrot Set. I went on to discover the relationship between 'chance' and the Fibonacci Sequence. This is the subject for a scientific paper. If I share it, all activities relying on 'chance' will be ruined, so I am in doubt as to doing that."

I'm not quite sure what all that means. Neither is Elon: "I don't know how he went from being great at engineering to believing in witchcraft. But he somehow made that evolution." Errol can be very forceful and occasionally convincing. "He changes reality around him," Kimbal says. "He will literally make up things, but he actually believes his own false reality."

Sometimes Errol would make sweeping assertions to his kids that were unconnected to facts, such as insisting that in the United States the president is considered divine and cannot be criticized. At other times he would weave fanciful tales that cast himself as either the hero or the victim. All would be asserted with such conviction that Elon and Kimbal would find themselves questioning their own view of reality. "Can you imagine growing up like that?" Kimbal asks. "It was mental torture, and it infects you. You end up asking, 'What is reality?'"

I found myself getting caught up in Errol's tangled web. In a series of calls and emails over the course of two years, he gave me varying accounts of his relationship with, and his feelings for, his kids, Maye, and his stepdaughter, with whom he would have two children (more on that later). "Elon and Kimbal have developed their own narrative about what I was like, and it doesn't accord with the facts," he claims. Their tales about him being psychologically abusive, he insists, are told to please their mother. But when I press him, he tells me to go with their version. "I don't care if they choose a different narrative, as long as they are happy. I have no desire for it to be my word versus theirs. Let them have the floor."

When talking about his father, Elon will sometimes let loose a laugh, a somewhat harsh and bitter one. It's similar to the laugh that his father has. Some of the words Elon uses, the way he stares, his sudden transitions from light to dark to light, remind his family members of the Errol simmering inside of him. "I would see shades of these horrible stories Elon told me surface in his own behavior," says Justine, Elon's first wife. "It made me realize how difficult it is not to be shaped by what we grew up with, even when that's not what we want." Every now and then, she dared to say something like "You're turning into your father." She explains, "It was our code phrase to warn him that he was going into the realm of darkness."

But Justine says that Elon, who was always emotionally invested in their children, is different from his father in a fundamental way: "With Errol, there was a sense that really bad things could happen around him. Whereas if the zombie apocalypse happened, you'd want to be on Elon's team, because he would figure out a way to get those zombies in line. He can be very harsh, but at the end of the day, you can trust him to find a way to prevail."

In order for that to happen, he had to move on. It was time to leave South Africa.

A one-way ticket

Musk began pushing both his mother and father, trying to convince them to move to the United States and take him and his siblings. Neither was interested. "So then I was like, 'Well, I'm just going to go by myself,'" he says.

He first tried to get U.S. citizenship on the grounds that his mother's father had been born in Minnesota, but that failed because his mother had been born in Canada and had never claimed U.S. citizenship. So he concluded that getting to Canada might be an easier first step. He went to the Canadian consulate on his own, got application forms for a passport, and filled them out not only for himself but for his mother, brother, and sister (but not father). The approvals came through in late May 1989.

"I would have left the next morning, but airline tickets were cheaper back then if you bought them fourteen days in advance," he says, "so I had to wait those two weeks." On June 11, 1989, about two weeks shy of his eighteenth birthday, he had dinner at Pretoria's finest restaurant, Cynthia's, with his father and siblings, who then drove him to the Johannesburg airport.

"You'll be back in a few months," Elon says his father told him contemptuously. "You'll never be successful."

As usual, Errol has his own version of the story, in which he was the action hero. According to him, Elon became seriously depressed during his senior year of high school. His despair reached a head on Republic Day, May 31, 1989. His family was preparing to watch the parade, but Elon refused to get out of bed. His father leaned against the big desk in Elon's room, with its well-used computer, and asked, "Do you want to go and study in America?" Elon perked up. "Yes," he answered. Errol claims, "It was my idea. Up until then, he had never said that he wanted to go to America. So I said, 'Well, tomorrow you should go and see the American cultural attaché,' who was a friend of mine from Rotary."

His father's account, Elon says, was just another of his elaborate fantasies casting him as the hero. In this case, it was provably false. By Republic Day 1989, Elon had already gotten a Canadian passport and purchased his airline ticket.

6

Canada

1989

At his cousin's barn in Saskatchewan and in his bedroom in Toronto

Immigrant

A myth has grown that Musk, because his father was on-and-off successful, arrived in North America in 1989 with a lot of money, perhaps pockets filled with emeralds. Errol at times encouraged that perception. But in fact, what Errol got from the Zambian emerald mine had become worthless years earlier. When Elon left South Africa, his father gave him $2,000 in traveler's checks and his mother provided him with another $2,000 by cashing out a stock account she had opened with the money she won in a beauty contest as a teenager. Otherwise, what he mainly had with him when he arrived in Montreal was a list of his mother's relatives he had never met.

He planned to call his mother's uncle, but discovered that he had left Montreal. So he went to a youth hostel, where he shared a room with five other people. "I was used to South Africa, where people will just rob and kill you," he says. "So I slept on my backpack until I realized that not everyone was a murderer." He wandered the town marveling that people did not have bars on their windows.

After a week, he bought a $100 Greyhound Discovery Pass that allowed him to travel by bus anywhere in Canada for six months. He had a second cousin his age, Mark Teulon, who lived on a farm in Saskatchewan province not far from Moose Jaw, where his grandparents had lived, so he headed there. It was more than 1,700 miles from Montreal.

The bus, which stopped at every hamlet, took days to wander across Canada. At one stop, he got off to find lunch and, just as the bus was leaving, ran to jump back on. Unfortunately, the driver had taken off his suitcase with his traveler's checks and clothes. All he had now was the knapsack of books he carried everywhere. The difficulty of getting traveler's checks replaced (it took weeks) was an early taste of how the financial payments system needed disruption.

When he got to the town near his cousin's farm, he used some of the change he had in his pocket to call. "Hey, it's Elon, your cousin from South Africa," he said. "I'm at the bus station." The cousin showed up with his father, took him to a Sizzler steak house, and invited him to stay at their wheat farm, where he was put to work cleaning grain bins and helping to raise a barn. There he celebrated his eighteenth birthday with a cake they baked with "Happy Birthday Elon" written in chocolate icing.

After six weeks, he got back on the bus and headed for Vancouver, another thousand miles away, to stay with his mother's half-brother. When he went to an employment office, he saw that most jobs paid $5 an hour. But there was one that paid $18 an hour, cleaning out the boilers in the lumber mill. This involved donning a hazmat suit and shimmying through a small tunnel that led to the chamber where the wood pulp was being boiled while shoveling out the lime that had caked on the walls. "If the person at the end of the tunnel didn't remove the goo fast enough, you would be trapped while sweating your guts out," he recalls. "It was like a Dickensian steampunk nightmare filled with dark pipes and the sound of jackhammers."

Maye and Tosca

While Elon was in Vancouver, Maye Musk flew from South Africa, having decided that she wanted to move as well. She sent back scouting reports to Tosca. Vancouver was too cold and rainy, she wrote. Montreal was exciting, but people there spoke French. Toronto, she concluded, was where they should go. Tosca promptly sold their house and furniture in South Africa, then she joined their mother in Toronto, where Elon also moved. Kimbal stayed behind in Pretoria to finish his last year in high school.

At first they all lived in a one-bedroom apartment, with Tosca and her mother sharing a bed while Elon slept on the couch. There was little money. Maye remembers crying when she spilled some milk because she didn't have enough to buy any more.

Tosca got a job at a hamburger joint, Elon as an intern in Microsoft's Toronto office, and Maye at the university, a modeling agency, and as a diet consultant. "I worked every day and also four nights a week," she says. "I took off one afternoon, Sunday, to do the laundry and get groceries. I didn't even know what my kids were doing, because I was hardly at home."

After a few months, they were making enough money to afford a rent-controlled three-bedroom apartment. It had felt wallpaper, which Maye insisted that Elon rip down, and a horrid carpet. They were going to buy a $200 replacement carpet, but Tosca insisted on a thicker one for $300 because Kimbal and their cousin Peter were coming over to join them and would sleep on the floor. Their second big purchase was a computer for Elon.

He had no friends or social life in Toronto, and he spent most of his time reading or working on the computer. Tosca, on the contrary, was a saucy teenager, eager to go out. "I'm coming with you," Elon would declare, not wanting to be lonely. "No you're not," she would reply. But when he insisted, she ordered, "You have to stay ten feet away from me at all times." He did. He would walk behind her and her friends, carrying a book to read whenever they went into a club or party.

Dancing with Kimbal in Toronto

7

Queen's

Kingston, Ontario, 1990–1991

With Navaid Farooq at Queen's and with his new suit

Industrial relations

Musk's college-admissions test scores were not especially notable. On his second round of the SAT tests, he got a 670 out of 800 on his verbal exam and a 730 on math. He narrowed his choices to two universities that were an easy drive from Toronto: Waterloo and Queen's. "Waterloo was definitely better for engineering, but it didn't seem great from a social standpoint," he says. "There were few girls there." He felt he knew computer science and engineering as well as any of the professors at both places, but he desperately desired a social life. "I didn't want to spend my undergraduate time with a bunch of dudes." So in the fall of 1990 he enrolled at Queen's.

He was placed on the "international floor" of one of the dorms, where, on the first day, he met a student named Navaid Farooq, who became his first real and lasting friend outside of his family. Farooq's father was Pakistani and his mother Canadian, and he was raised in Nigeria and Switzerland, where his parents worked for United Nations organizations. Like Elon, he had made no close friends in high school. At Queen's, he and Musk quickly bonded over their interests in computer and board games, obscure history, and science fiction. "For me and Elon," Farooq says, "it was probably the first place we were socially accepted and could be ourselves."

During his first year, Musk got A's in Business, Economics, Calculus, and Computer Programming, but he got B's in Accounting, Spanish, and Industrial Relations. The following year, he took another course in Industrial Relations, which studies the dealings between workers and management. Again, he got a B. He later told the Queen's alumni magazine that the most important thing he learned during his two years there was "how to work collaboratively with smart people and make use of the Socratic method to achieve commonality of purpose," a skill, like those of industrial relations, that future colleagues would notice had been only partly honed.

He was more interested in late-night philosophy discussions about the meaning of life. "I was really hungry for that," he says, "because until then I had no friends I could talk to about these things."

But most of all, he became immersed, with Farooq at his side, in the world of board and computer games.

Strategy games

"What you're doing is not rational," Musk explained in his flat monotone. "You're actually hurting yourself." He and Farooq were playing the strategy board game *Diplomacy* with friends in their dorm, and one of the players was allying himself with another against Musk. "If you do this, I will turn your allies against you and inflict pain on you." Musk tended to win, Farooq says, by being convincing in his negotiations and threats.

Musk had enjoyed all types of video games as a teenager in South Africa, including first-person shooters and adventure quests, but at college he became more focused on the genre known as strategy games, ones that involve two or more players competing to build an empire using high-level strategy, resource management, supply-chain logistics, and tactical thinking.

Strategy games—those played on a board and then those for computers—would become central to Musk's life. From *The Ancient Art of War*, which he played as a teen in South Africa, to his addiction to *The Battle of Polytopia* three decades later, he relished the complex planning and competitive management of resources that are required to prevail. Immersing himself in these games for hours became the way he relaxed, escaped stress, and honed his tactical skills and strategic thinking for business.

While he was at Queen's, the first great computer-based strategy game was released: *Civilization*. In it, players compete to build a society from prehistory to the present by choosing what technologies to develop and production facilities to build. Musk moved his desk so that he could sit on his bed and Farooq on a chair to face off and play the game. "We completely entered a zone for hours until we were exhausted," Farooq says. They moved on to *Warcraft: Orcs and Humans*, where a key part of the strategy is to develop a sustainable supply of resources, such as metals from mines. After hours of playing, they would take a break for a meal, and Elon would describe the moment in the game when he knew he was going to win. "I am wired for war," he told Farooq.

One class at Queen's used a strategy game in which teams competed in a simulation of growing a business. The players could decide the prices of their products, the amount spent on advertising, what profits to plow back into research, and other variables. Musk figured out how to reverse-engineer the logic that controlled the simulation, so he was able to win every time.

Bank trainee

When Kimbal moved to Canada and joined Elon as a student at Queen's, the brothers developed a routine. They would read the newspaper and pick out the person they found most interesting. Elon was not one of those eager-beaver types who liked to attract and charm mentors, so the more gregarious Kimbal took the lead in cold-calling the person. "If we were able to get through on the phone, they usually would have lunch with us," he says.

One they picked was Peter Nicholson, the executive in charge of strategic planning at Scotiabank. Nicholson was an engineer with a master's degree in physics and a PhD in math. When Kimbal got through to him, he agreed to have lunch with the boys. Their mother took them shopping at Eaton's department store, where the purchase of a $99 suit got you a free shirt and tie. At lunch they discussed philosophy and physics and the nature of the universe. Nicholson offered them summer jobs, inviting Elon to work directly with him on his three-person strategic planning team.

Nicholson, then forty-nine, and Elon had fun together solving math puzzles and weird equations. "I was interested in the philosophical side of physics and how it related to reality," Nicholson says. "I didn't have a lot of other people to talk to about these things." They also discussed what had become Musk's passion: space travel.

When Elon went with Nicholson's daughter, Christie, to a party one evening, his first question was "Do you ever think about electric cars?" As he later admitted, it was not the world's best come-on line.

One topic Musk researched for Nicholson was Latin American debt. Banks had made billions in loans to countries such as Brazil and Mexico that could not be repaid, and in 1989 the U.S. Treasury secretary, Nicholas Brady, packaged these debt obligations into tradable securities known as "Brady Bonds." Because these bonds were backed by the U.S. government, Musk believed that they would always be worth 50 cents on the dollar. However, some were selling as low as 20 cents.

Musk figured that Scotiabank could make billions by buying the bonds at that cheap price, and he called the Goldman Sachs trading desk in New York to make sure they were available. "Yeah, how much you want?" the gruff trader on the phone responded. "Would it be possible to get five million?" Musk asked, putting on a deep and serious voice. When the trader said that would be no problem, Musk quickly hung up. "I was like, 'Jackpot, no-lose proposition here,'" he says. "I ran to tell Peter about it and thought they would give me some money to do it." But the bank rejected the idea. The CEO said it already held too much Latin American debt. "Wow, this is just insane," Musk said to himself. "Is this how banks think?"

Nicholson says that Scotiabank was navigating the Latin American debt situation using its own methods, which worked better. "He came away with an impression that the bank was a lot dumber than in fact it was," Nicholson says. "But that was a good thing, because it gave him a healthy disrespect for the financial industry and the audacity to eventually start what became PayPal."

Musk also drew another lesson from his time at Scotiabank: he did not like, nor was he good at, working for other people. It was not in his nature to be deferential or to assume that others might know more than he did.

8

Penn

Philadelphia, 1992–1994

With Robin Ren at Penn; with cousin Peter Rive and Kimbal in Boston

Physics

Musk got bored at Queen's. It was beautiful, but not academically challenging. So when one of his classmates transferred to the University of Pennsylvania, he decided to see if he could do so as well.

Money was a problem. His father was providing no support, and his mother was juggling three jobs to make ends meet. But Penn offered him a $14,000 scholarship plus a student loan package, so in 1992 he transferred there for his junior year.

He decided to major in physics because, like his father, he was drawn to engineering. The essence of being an engineer, he felt, was to address any problem by drilling down to the most fundamental tenets of physics. He also decided to pursue a joint degree in business. "I was concerned that if I didn't study business, I would be forced to work for someone who did," he says. "My goal was to engineer products by having a feel for the physics and never have to work for a boss with a business degree."

Even though he was neither political nor gregarious, he ran for student assembly. One of his campaign pledges poked fun at those who sought student office in order to polish their résumés. The final promise of his campaign platform was "If this position ever appears on my résumé, to stand on [my] head and eat 50 copies of the offending document in a public place." Fortunately, he lost, which saved him from falling in with the student-government types, a world for which he was temperamentally unsuited. Instead, he fit comfortably into a crowd of geeks who liked making clever jokes involving scientific forces, playing *Dungeons & Dragons*, binging on video games, and writing computer code.

His closest friend in this crowd was Robin Ren, who had won a Physics Olympiad in his native China before coming to Penn. "He was the only person better than me at physics," Musk says. They became partners in the physics lab, where they studied how the properties of various materials change at extreme temperatures. At the end of one set of experiments, Musk took erasers from the ends of pencils, dropped them into a jar of super-cold liquid, then smashed them on the floor. He developed an interest in knowing, and being able to visualize, the properties of materials and alloys at different temperatures.

Ren recalls that Musk focused on the three areas that would shape his career. Whether he was calibrating the force of gravity or analyzing the properties of materials, he would discuss with Ren how the laws of physics applied to building rockets. "He kept talking about making a rocket that could go to Mars," Ren recalls. "Of course, I didn't pay much attention, because I thought he was fantasizing."

Musk also focused on electric cars. He and Ren would grab lunch from one of the food trucks and sit on the campus lawn, where Musk would read academic papers on batteries. California had just passed a requirement mandating that 10 percent of vehicles by 2003 had to be electric. "I want to go make that happen," Musk said.

Musk also became convinced that solar power, which in 1994 was just taking off, was the best path toward sustainable energy. His senior paper was titled "The Importance of Being Solar." He was motivated not just by the dangers of climate change but also by the fact that fossil fuel reserves would start to dwindle. "Society will soon have no option but to focus on renewable power sources," he wrote. His final page showed a "power station of the future," involving a satellite with mirrors that would concentrate sunlight onto solar panels and send the resulting electricity back to Earth via a microwave beam. The professor gave him a grade of 98, saying it was a "very interesting and well written paper, except the last figure that comes out of the blue."

Party animal

Throughout his life, Musk had three ways of escaping the emotional drama that he tended to generate. The first was the one that he shared with Navaid Farooq at Queen's: an ability to zone out on empire-building strategy games, such as *Civilization* and *Polytopia*. Robin Ren reflected another facet of Musk: the encyclopedia reader who liked to immerse himself in, as *The Hitchhiker's Guide* put it, "Life, the Universe, and Everything."

At Penn, he developed a third mode of relaxation—a taste for
partying—that drew him out of the lonely shell that had surrounded
him as a kid. His partner and enabler was a fun-loving social animal
named Adeo Ressi. A tall guy with a big head, laugh, and personality, Ressi was an Italian American from Manhattan who loved nightclubs. An offbeat character, he started an environmental newspaper
called *Green Times* and attempted to create his own major called
"Revolution" with copies of the newspaper as his senior thesis.

Like Musk, Ressi was a transfer student, so they were put in the
freshman dorm, where there were rules against parties and visitors
after 10 p.m. Neither of them liked following rules, so they rented a
house in a sketchy part of West Philadelphia.

Ressi came up with a scheme to throw big monthly parties. They
covered the windows and decorated the house with black lights and
phosphorescent posters. At one point Musk discovered that his desk
had been painted in lacquered glow-in-the-dark colors and nailed to
the wall by Ressi, who called it an art installation. Musk took it down
and declared that, no, it was a desk. At a junkyard they found a metal
sculpture of a horse's head and put a red light inside, so beams darted
out of its eyes. There was a band on one floor, a DJ on another, tables
with beer and Jell-O shots, and someone at the door to collect the $5
entrance fee. On some nights they would draw five hundred people,
which would easily pay the rent for a month.

When Maye visited, she was appalled. "I filled eight garbage bags
and swept the place, and I thought they would be grateful," she says.
"But they didn't even notice." At their party that night, they stationed
her in Elon's bedroom near the front door to check coats and guard
the money. She kept a pair of scissors in her hand, which she thought
she could use on anyone who tried to steal the cash box, and she
moved Elon's mattress next to one of the exterior walls. "The house
was shaking and bouncing so much from the music that I thought a
ceiling might collapse, so I figured if I was at the edge I'd be safer."

Although Elon loved the vibe of the parties, he never got fully immersed in them. "I was stone cold sober at the time," he says. "Adeo
would get wasted. I'd be banging on his door and say, like, 'Dude,

you've got to come up and manage the party.' I ended up being the one who had to keep an eye on things."

Ressi later marveled that Musk usually seemed a bit detached. "He enjoyed being around a party but not fully in it. The only thing he binged on was video games." Despite all of their partying, he understood that Musk was fundamentally alienated and withdrawn, like an observer from a different planet trying to learn the motions of sociability. "I wish Elon knew how to be a little happier," he says.

9

Go West

Silicon Valley, 1994–1995

July 1994

Summer intern

At Ivy League schools in the 1990s, ambitious students were tugged either east toward the gilded realms of Wall Street banking or west toward the tech utopianism and entrepreneurial zeal of Silicon Valley. At Penn, Musk received some internship offers from Wall Street, all lucrative, but finance did not interest him. He felt that bankers and lawyers did not contribute much to society. Besides, he disliked the students he met in business classes. Instead, he was drawn to Silicon Valley. It was the decade of rational exuberance, when one could just slap a *.com* onto any fantasy and wait for the thunder of Porsches to descend from Sand Hill Road with venture capitalists waving checks.

He got his opportunity in the summer of 1994, between his junior and senior years at Penn, when he scored two internships that allowed him to indulge his passions for electric vehicles, space, and video games.

By day he worked at Pinnacle Research Institute, a twenty-person group that had modest Defense Department contracts to study a "supercapacitor" developed by its founder. A capacitor is a device that can briefly hold an electric charge and discharge it quickly, and Pinnacle thought that it could make one that was powerful enough to provide energy for electric cars and space-based weapons. In a paper he wrote at the end of the summer, Musk declared, "It is important to note that the Ultracapacitor is not simply an incremental improvement, but a radically new technology."

In the evening he worked at a small Palo Alto company called Rocket Science, which made video games. When he showed up at their building one night and asked for a summer job, they gave him a problem they hadn't been able to solve: how to coax a computer to multitask by reading graphics that were stored on a CD-ROM while simultaneously moving an avatar on the screen. He went on internet message boards to ask other hackers how to bypass the BIOS and joystick reader using DOS. "None of the senior engineers had been able to solve this problem, and I solved it in two weeks," he says.

They were impressed and wanted him to work full-time, but he needed to graduate in order to get a U.S. work visa. In addition, he came to a realization: he had a fanatic love of video games and the skills to make money creating them, but that was not the best way to spend his life. "I wanted to have more impact," he says.

King of the road

One unfortunate trend in the 1980s was that cars and computers became tightly sealed appliances. It was possible to open up and fiddle with the innards of the Apple II that Steve Wozniak designed in the late 1970s, but you couldn't do that with the Macintosh, which Steve Jobs in 1984 made almost impossible to open. Similarly, kids in the 1970s and earlier grew up rummaging under the hoods of cars, tinkering with the carburetors, changing spark plugs, and souping up the engines. They had a fingertip-feel for valves and Valvoline. This hands-on imperative and Heathkit mindset even applied to radios and television sets; if you wanted, you could change the tubes and later the transistors and have a feel for how a circuit board worked.

This trend toward closed and sealed devices meant that most techies who came of age in the 1990s gravitated to software more than hardware. They never knew the sweet smell of a soldering iron, but they could code in ways that made circuits sing. Musk was different. He liked hardware as well as software. He could code, but he also had a feel for physical components, such as battery cells and capacitors, valves and combustion chambers, fuel pumps and fan belts.

In particular, Musk loved fiddling with cars. At the time, he owned a twenty-year-old BMW 300i, and he spent Saturdays rummaging around junkyards in Philadelphia to score the parts he needed to soup it up. It had a four-speed transmission, but he decided to upgrade it when BMW started making a five-speed. Borrowing the lift at a local repair shop, he was able, with a couple of shims and a little bit of grinding, to jam a five-speed transmission into what had been a four-speed car. "It was really able to haul ass," he recalls.

He and Kimbal drove the car from Palo Alto back to Philadelphia at the end of the summer of internships in 1994. "We both were, like, university sucks, there's no hurry to get back," Kimbal recalls, "so we did a three-week road trip." The car broke down repeatedly. On one occasion, they were able to get it to a dealership in Colorado Springs, but after the repairs it failed again. So they pushed it to a truck stop where Elon successfully reworked everything the professional mechanic had done.

Musk also took the BMW on a trip with his college girlfriend at the time, Jennifer Gwynne. Over Christmas break in 1994, they drove from Philadelphia to Queen's University, where Kimbal was still studying, and then to Toronto to see his mother. There he gave Jennifer a small gold necklace with a smooth green emerald. "His mom had a number of these necklaces in a case in her bedroom, and Elon told me they were from his father's emerald mine in South Africa—he pulled one from the case," Jennifer noted twenty-five years later, when she auctioned it online. In fact, the long-bankrupt mine had not been in South Africa and was not owned by his father, but at the time Musk didn't mind giving that impression.

When he graduated in the spring of 1995, Musk decided to take another cross-country trip to Silicon Valley. He brought along Robin Ren, after teaching him how to drive a stick shift. They stopped at the just-opened Denver airport because Musk wanted to see the baggage-handling system. "He was fascinated by how they designed the robotic machines to handle the luggage without human intervention," Ren says. But the system was a mess. Musk took away a lesson he would have to relearn when he built highly robotic Tesla factories. "It was over-automated, and they underestimated the complexity of what they were building," he says.

The internet wave

Musk planned to enroll at Stanford at the end of the summer to study material science as a graduate student. Still fascinated by capacitors, he wanted to research how they might power electric cars.

"The idea was to leverage advanced chip-making equipment to make a solid state ultracapacitor with enough energy density to give a car long range," he says. But as he got closer to enrolling, he began to worry. "I figured I could spend several years at Stanford, get a PhD, and my conclusion on capacitors would be that they aren't feasible," he says. "Most PhDs are irrelevant. The number that actually move the needle is almost none."

He had conceived by then a life vision that he would repeat like a mantra. "I thought about the things that will truly affect humanity," he says. "I came up with three: the internet, sustainable energy, and space travel." In the summer of 1995, it became clear to him that the first of these, the internet, was not going to wait for him to finish graduate school. The web had just been opened up for commercial use, and that August the browser startup Netscape went public, soaring within a day to a market value of $2.9 billion.

Musk had come up with an idea for an internet company during his final year at Penn, when an executive from NYNEX came to speak about the phone company's plans to launch an online version of the Yellow Pages. Dubbed "Big Yellow," it would have interactive features so that users could tailor the information to their personal needs, the executive said. Musk thought (correctly, as it turned out) that NYNEX had no clue how to make it truly interactive. "Why don't we do it ourselves?" he suggested to Kimbal, and he began writing code that could combine business listings with map data. They dubbed it the Virtual City Navigator.

Just before the enrollment deadline for Stanford, Musk went to Toronto to get advice from Peter Nicholson of Scotiabank. Should he pursue the idea for the Virtual City Navigator, or should he start the PhD program? Nicholson, who had a PhD from Stanford, did not equivocate. "The internet revolution only comes once in a lifetime, so strike while the iron is hot," he told Musk as they walked along the shore of Lake Ontario. "You will have lots of time to go to graduate school later if you're still interested." When Musk got back to Palo Alto, he told Ren he had made up his mind. "I need to put everything else on hold," he said. "I need to catch the internet wave."

He actually hedged his bets. He officially enrolled at Stanford and then immediately requested a deferral. "I've written some software with the first internet maps and Yellow Pages directory," he told Bill Nix, the material science professor. "I will probably fail, and if so I would like to come back." Nix said it would not be a problem for Musk to defer his studies, but he predicted that he would never come back.

May 1995

10

Zip2

Palo Alto, 1995–1999

Celebrating the sale of Zip2 with Maye and Kimbal;
taking delivery of the McLaren with Justine

Map quests

Some of the best innovations come from combining two previous innovations. The idea that Elon and Kimbal had in early 1995, just as the web was starting to grow exponentially, was simple: put a searchable directory of businesses online and combine it with map software that would give users directions to them. Not everyone saw the potential. When Kimbal had a meeting at the *Toronto Star*, which published the Yellow Pages in that city, the president picked up a thick edition of the directory and threw it at him. "Do you honestly think you're ever going to replace this?" he asked.

The brothers rented a tiny office in Palo Alto that had room for two desks and futons. For the first six months, they slept in the office and showered at the YMCA. Kimbal, who would later become a chef and restaurateur, got an electric coil and cooked meals occasionally. But mainly they ate at Jack in the Box, because it was cheap, open twenty-four hours, and just a block away. "I can still tell you every single menu item," Kimbal says. "It's just seared into my brain." Elon became a fan of the teriyaki bowl.

After a few months, they rented an unfurnished apartment that stayed that way. "All it had was two mattresses and lots of Cocoa Puffs boxes," says Tosca. Even after they moved in, Elon spent many nights in the office, crashing under his desk when he was exhausted from coding. "He had no pillow, he had no sleeping bag. I don't know how he did it," says Jim Ambras, an early employee. "Once in a while, if we had a customer meeting in the morning, I'd have to tell him to go home and shower."

Navaid Farooq came from Toronto to work with them, but he soon found himself in fights with Musk. "If you want your friendship to last," his wife Nyame told him, "this is not for you." So he quit after six weeks. "I knew that I could either be working with him or be his friend, but not both, and the latter seemed more enjoyable."

Errol Musk, not yet estranged from his sons, visited from South Africa and gave them $28,000 plus a beat-up car he bought for $500. Their mother, Maye, came from Toronto more often, bringing food and clothes. She gave them $10,000 and let them use her credit card because they had not been approved for one.

They got their first break when they visited Navteq, which had a database of maps. The company agreed to license it to the Musks for free until they started making a profit. Elon wrote a program that merged the maps with a listing of businesses in the area. "You could use your cursor and zoom in and move around the map," says Kimbal. "That stuff is totally normal today, but it was mind-blowing to see that at the time. I think Elon and I were the first humans to see it work on the internet." They named the company Zip2, as in "Zip to where you want to go."

Elon was granted a patent for the "interactive network directory service" that he had created. "The invention provides a network accessible service which integrates both a business directory and a map database," the patent stated.

For their first meeting with potential investors, they had to take a bus up Sand Hill Road because the car their dad had given them broke down. But after word spread about the company, the VCs were asking to come to them. They bought a big frame for a computer rack and put one of their small computers inside, so that visitors would think they had a giant server. They named it "The Machine That Goes Ping," after a *Monty Python* sketch. "Every time investors would come in, we showed them the tower," Kimbal says, "and we would laugh because it made them think we were doing hardcore stuff."

Maye flew from Toronto to help prepare for the meetings with venture capitalists, often staying up all night at Kinko's to print the presentations. "It was a dollar a page for color, which we could barely afford," she says. "We would all be exhausted except Elon. He was always up late doing the coding." When they got their first proposals from potential investors in early 1996, Maye took her boys to a nice restaurant to celebrate. "That's the last time we'll have to use my credit card," she said when she paid the bill.

And it was. They were soon astounded by an offer from Mohr Davidow Ventures to invest $3 million in the company. The final presentation to the firm was scheduled for a Monday, and that weekend Kimbal decided to make a quick trip to Toronto to fix their mother's computer, which had broken. "We love our mom," he explains. As he was leaving on Sunday to fly back to San Francisco, he got stopped by U.S. border officials at the airport who looked in his luggage and saw the pitch deck, business cards, and other documents for the company. Because he did not have a U.S. work visa, they wouldn't let him board the plane. He had a friend pick him up at the airport and drive him across the border, where he told a less vigilant border officer that they were heading down to see the David Letterman show. He managed to catch the late plane from Buffalo to San Francisco, and made it in time for the pitch.

Mohr Davidow loved the presentation and finalized the investment. The firm also found an immigration lawyer to help the two Musks get work visas and gave them each $30,000 to purchase cars. Elon bought a 1967 Jaguar E-type. As a kid in South Africa, he had seen a picture of the car in a book on the best convertibles ever made, and he had vowed to buy one if he ever struck it rich. "It was the most beautiful car you could imagine," he says, "but it broke down at least once a week."

The venture capitalists soon did what they often do: bring in adult supervision to take over from the young founders. It had happened to Steve Jobs at Apple and to Larry Page and Sergey Brin at Google. Rich Sorkin, who had run business development for an audio equipment company, was made the CEO of Zip2. Elon was moved aside to chief technology officer. At first, he thought the change would suit him; he could focus on building the product. But he learned a lesson. "I never wanted to be a CEO," he says, "but I learned that you could not truly be the chief technology or product officer unless you were the CEO."

With the changes came a new strategy. Instead of marketing its product directly to businesses and their customers, Zip2 focused on selling its software to big newspapers so they could make their own local directories. This made sense; newspapers already had sales forces that were knocking on the doors of businesses to sell them advertising and classifieds. Knight-Ridder, the *New York Times*, Pulitzer, and Hearst newspapers signed up. Executives from the first two joined the Zip2 board. *Editor & Publisher* magazine ran a cover story titled "Newspaperdom's New Superhero: Zip2," reporting that the company had created "a new suite of software structures that would enable individual newspapers to quickly mount large-scale city guide-type directories."

By 1997, Zip2 had been hired by 140 newspapers at licensing fees ranging from $1,000 to $10,000. The president of the *Toronto Star*, who had thrown a Yellow Pages book at Kimbal, called him to apologize and ask if Zip2 would be its partner. Kimbal said yes.

Hardcore

From the very beginning of his career, Musk was a demanding manager, contemptuous of the concept of work-life balance. At Zip2 and every subsequent company, he drove himself relentlessly all day and through much of the night, without vacations, and he expected others to do the same. His only indulgence was allowing breaks for intense video-game binges. The Zip2 team won second place in a national *Quake* competition. They would have come in first, he says, but one of them crashed his computer by pushing it too hard.

When the other engineers went home, Musk would sometimes take the code they were working on and rewrite it. With his weak empathy gene, he didn't realize or care that correcting someone publicly—or, as he put it, "fixing their fucking stupid code"—was not a path to endearment. He had never been a captain of a sports team or the leader of a gang of friends, and he lacked an instinct for camaraderie. Like Steve Jobs, he genuinely did not care if he offended or intimidated the people he worked with, as long as he drove them to accomplish feats they thought were impossible. "It's not your job to make people on your team love you," he said at a SpaceX executive session years later. "In fact, that's counterproductive."

He was toughest on Kimbal. "I love, love, love my brother very much, but working with him was hard," Kimbal says. Their disagreements often led to rolling-on-the-office-floor fights. They fought over major strategy, minor slights, and the name Zip2. (Kimbal and a marketing firm came up with it; Elon hated it.) "Growing up in South Africa, fighting was normal," Elon says. "It was part of the culture." They had no private offices, just cubicles, so everyone had to watch. In one of their worst fights, they wrestled to the floor and Elon seemed ready to punch Kimbal in the face, so Kimbal bit his hand and tore off a hunk of flesh. Elon had to go to the emergency room for stitches and a tetanus shot. "When we had intense stress, we just didn't notice anyone else around us," says Kimbal. He later admitted that Elon was right about Zip2. "It was a shitty name."

True product people have a compulsion to sell directly to consumers, without middlemen muddying things up. Musk was that way. He became frustrated by Zip2's strategy of relegating itself to being an unbranded vendor to the newspaper industry. "We wound up beholden to the papers," Musk says. He wanted to buy the domain name "city.com" and become a consumer destination again, competing with Yahoo and AOL.

The investors were also having second thoughts about their strategy. City guides and internet directories were proliferating by the fall of 1998, and none had shown a profit. So CEO Rich Sorkin decided to merge with one of them, CitySearch, in the hope that together they could succeed. But when Musk met with the CEO of CitySearch, the man made him uneasy. With the help of Kimbal and some of the engineers, Elon led a rebellion that scuttled the merger. He also demanded that he be made CEO again. Instead, the board removed him as chair and diminished his role.

"Great things will never happen with VCs or professional managers," Musk told *Inc. Magazine*. "They don't have the creativity or the insight." One of the Mohr Davidow partners, Derek Proudian, was installed as interim CEO and tasked with selling the company. "This is your first company," he told Musk. "Let's find an acquirer and make some money, so you can do your second, third, and fourth company."

The millionaire

In January 1999, less than four years after Elon and Kimbal launched Zip2, Proudian called them into his office and told them that Compaq Computer, which was seeking to juice up its AltaVista search engine, had offered $307 million in cash. The brothers had split their 12 percent ownership stake 60–40, so Elon at age twenty-seven walked away with $22 million and Kimbal with $15 million. Elon was astonished when the check arrived at his apartment. "My bank account went from, like, $5,000 to $22,005,000," he says.

The Musks gave their father $300,000 out of the proceeds and their mother $1 million. Elon bought an eighteen-hundred-square-foot condo and splurged on what for him was the ultimate indulgence: a $1 million McLaren F1 sports car, the fastest production car in existence. He agreed to allow CNN to film him taking delivery. "Just three years ago I was showering at the Y and sleeping on the office floor, and now I've got a million-dollar car," he said as he hopped around in the street while the car was unloaded from a truck.

After the impulsive outburst, he realized that the giddy display of his newfound taste for wealth was unseemly. "Some could interpret the purchase of this car as behavior characteristic of an imperialist brat," he admitted. "My values may have changed, but I'm not consciously aware of my values having changed."

Had they changed? His new wealth allowed his desires and impulses to be subject to fewer restraints, which was not always a pretty sight. But his earnest, mission-driven intensity remained intact.

The writer Michael Gross was in Silicon Valley reporting a piece for Tina Brown's glossy *Talk* magazine on newly rich techno-brats. "I was looking for an ostentatious lead character who might warrant skewering," Gross recalled years later. "But the Musk I met in 2000 was bursting with joie de vivre, too likable to skewer. He had the same insouciance and indifference to expectations he does now, but he was easy, open, charming, and funny."

Celebrity was enticing for a kid who had grown up with no friends. "I'd like to be on the cover of *Rolling Stone*," he told CNN.

But he would end up having a conflicted relationship with wealth. "I could go and buy one of the islands of the Bahamas and turn it into my personal fiefdom, but I am much more interested in trying to build and create a new company," he said. "I haven't spent all my winnings. I'm going to put almost all of it back to a new game."

11

Justine

Palo Alto, the 1990s

Justine, Elon, and Maye *(top)*; the family, with Errol and
Maye second and third from the right *(bottom)*

Romance drama

When Musk eased into the driver's seat of his new million-dollar McLaren, he said to the CNN reporter taping the scene, "The real payoff is the sense of satisfaction in having created a company." At that point a beautiful, willowy young woman who was his girlfriend put her arms around him. "Yes, yes, yes, but the car as well," she cooed. "The car. Let's be honest." Musk seemed slightly embarrassed and looked down to check the messages on his phone.

Her name was Justine Wilson, though when he first met her at Queen's University she was still using her more prosaic given name, Jennifer. Like Musk, she had been a bookworm as a kid, though her taste ran to dark fantasy novels rather than sci-fi. She had been raised in a small river town northeast of Toronto and fancied that she would become a writer. With flowing hair and a mysterious smile, she managed to be radiant and sultry at the same time, like a character out of the romance novel that she hoped to write someday.

She met Musk when she was a freshman and he was a sophomore at Queen's. After seeing her at a party, he asked her out for ice cream. She agreed to go with him the following Tuesday, but when he came by her room she was gone. "What's her favorite ice cream?" he asked a friend of hers. Vanilla-chocolate-chip, he was told. So he bought a cone and walked around campus until he found her studying a Spanish text in the student center. "I think this is your favorite flavor," he said, handing her the dripping cone.

"He's not a man who takes no for an answer," she says.

Justine at the time was breaking up with someone who seemed much cooler, a writer who sported a soul patch of hair on his chin. "I thought the soul patch was a dead giveaway that the guy was a douche," says Musk. "So I convinced her to go out with me." He told her, "You have a fire in your soul. I see myself in you."

She was impressed by his aspirations. "Unlike other ambitious people, he never talked about making money," she says. "He assumed that he would be either wealthy or broke, but nothing in between. What interested him were the problems he wanted to solve." His indomitable will—whether for making her date him or for building electric cars—mesmerized her. "Even when it seemed like crazy talk, you would believe him because he believed it."

They dated only sporadically before he left Queen's for Penn, but they stayed in touch, and he sometimes sent her roses. She spent a year teaching in Japan and jettisoned the name Jennifer "because it was far too common and the name of a lot of cheerleaders." When she returned to Canada, she told her sister, "If Elon ever calls me again, I think I'll go for it. I might have missed something there." The call came when he visited New York City to meet with the *Times* about Zip2. He asked her join to him there. The weekend went so well that he invited her to fly back with him to California. She did.

He had not yet sold Zip2, so they lived in his Palo Alto apartment with two housemates and a dachshund that wasn't housebroken named Bowie, after David. Most of the time she holed up in their bedroom writing and being antisocial. "Friends would not want to stay at my house because Justine was too grumpy," he says. Kimbal couldn't stand her. "If someone's insecure, they can be very mean," he says. When Musk asked his mother what she thought of Justine, she was typically blunt: "She has no redeeming feature."

But Musk, who liked edginess in his relationships, was smitten. One night over dinner, Justine recalls, he asked how many kids she wanted to have. "One or two," she answered, "although if I could afford nannies, I'd like to have four."

"That's the difference between you and me," he said. "I just assume that there will be nannies." Then he rocked his arms and said, "Baby." He was already a strong believer in having kids.

Shortly after that, he sold Zip2 and bought the McLaren. Suddenly there was money for nannies. She joked uneasily that maybe he would not dump her for a beautiful model. Instead, he got down on a bended knee on the sidewalk outside of their house, pulled out a ring, and proposed to her, just like out of a romance novel.

Both of them were energized by drama, and they thrived by fighting. "For somebody who was so amorous about me, he never hesitated to let me know that I was wrong about something," she says. "And I would fight back. I realized that I could say anything to him, and it just did not faze him." One day they were with a friend in a

McDonald's and started fighting loudly. "My friend was mortified, but Elon and I were used to having big arguments in public. There is a combative element to him. I don't think you can be in a relationship with Elon and not argue."

On a trip to Paris, they went to see the Lady and the Unicorn tapestries at the Musée de Cluny. Justine began describing what moved her, and she gave a spiritual interpretation involving the unicorn as a Christ-like figure. Musk called that "stupid." They began arguing furiously about Christian symbolism. "He was just so adamant and furious that I didn't know what I was talking about, that I was stupid and crazy," she says. "It was like the things he told me his father said to him."

The wedding

"When he told me he was going to marry her, I did an intervention," Kimbal says. "I was like, 'Don't, you must not, this is the wrong person for you.'" Navaid Farooq, who had been with Musk at the party when he first met Justine, tried to stop him as well. But Musk loved both Justine and the turmoil. The wedding was scheduled for a weekend in January 2000 on the Caribbean island of Saint Martin.

Musk flew in the day before with a prenuptial agreement his lawyers had written. He and Justine drove around the island looking for a notary who would witness it on a Friday evening, but they couldn't find one. She promised that she would sign it when they returned (she ended up doing so two weeks later), but the conversation sparked a lot of tension. "I think he felt very nervous about getting married and not having this thing signed," she says. That precipitated a fight, and Justine got out of the car and walked to find some of her friends. Later that night, they got back together in the villa but continued fighting. "The villas were open-air, so all of us could hear the row," Farooq says, "and we didn't know what to do about it." At one point Musk stalked out and told his mother that the wedding was off. She was relieved. "Now you won't be miserable," she told him. But then he changed his mind and returned to Justine.

The tension continued the next day. Kimbal and Farooq tried to convince Musk to let them whisk him away to the airport so he could escape. The more they insisted, the more intransigent he became. "No, I'm marrying her," he declared.

On the surface, the ceremony by the hotel swimming pool seemed joyous. Justine looked radiant in a sleeveless white dress and a tiara of white flowers, and Musk looked dapper in a tailored tuxedo. Both Maye and Errol were there, and they even posed for pictures together. After dinner, everyone joined in a conga line, then Elon and Justine took the first dance. He put both arms on her waist. She put her arms around his neck. They smiled and kissed. Then, as they danced, he whispered to her a reminder: "I am the alpha in this relationship."

12

X.com

Palo Alto, 1999–2000

With PayPal cofounder Peter Thiel

An all-in-one bank

When his cousin Peter Rive visited in early 1999, he found Musk poring over books about the banking system. "I'm trying to think about what to start next," he explained. His experience at Scotiabank had convinced him that the industry was ripe for disruption. So in March 1999, he founded X.com with a friend from the bank, Harris Fricker.

Musk now had the choice he had described to CNN: living like a multimillionaire or leaving his chips on the table to fund a new enterprise. The balance he struck was to invest $12 million in X.com, leaving about $4 million after taxes to spend on himself.

His concept for X.com was grand. It would be a one-stop everything-store for all financial needs: banking, digital purchases, checking, credit cards, investments, and loans. Transactions would be handled instantly, with no waiting for payments to clear. His insight was that money is simply an entry into a database, and he wanted to devise a way that all transactions were securely recorded in real time. "If you fix all the reasons why a consumer would take money out of the system," he says, "then it will be the place where all the money is, and that would make it a multitrillion-dollar company."

Some of his friends were skeptical that an online bank would inspire confidence if given a name that sounded like a porn site. But Musk loved the name X.com. Instead of being too clever, like Zip2, the name was simple, memorable, and easy to type. It also allowed him to have one of the coolest email addresses of the time: e@x.com. "X" would become his go-to letter for naming things, from companies to kids.

Musk's management style had not changed from Zip2, nor would it ever. His late-night coding binges followed by his mix of rudeness and detachment during the day led his cofounder Harris and their handful of coworkers to demand that Musk step down as CEO. At one point Musk responded with a very self-aware email. "I am by nature obsessive-compulsive," he wrote Fricker. "What matters to me is winning, and not in a small way. God knows why . . . it's probably rooted in some very disturbing psychoanalytical black hole or neural short circuit."

Because he held a controlling interest, Musk prevailed and Fricker quit, along with most of the employees. Despite the turmoil, Musk was able to entice the influential head of Sequoia Capital, Michael Moritz, to make a major investment in X.com. Moritz then facilitated a deal with Barclay's Bank and a community bank in Colorado to become partners, so that X.com could offer mutual funds, have a bank charter, and be FDIC-insured. At twenty-eight, Musk had become a startup celebrity. In an article titled "Elon Musk Is Poised to Become Silicon Valley's Next Big Thing," *Salon* called him "today's Silicon Valley It guy."

One of Musk's management tactics, then as later, was to set an insane deadline and drive colleagues to meet it. He did that in the fall of 1999 by announcing, in what one engineer called "a dick move," that X.com would launch to the public on Thanksgiving weekend. In the weeks leading up to that, Musk prowled the office each day, including Thanksgiving, in a nervous and nervous-making frenzy, and slept under his desk most nights. One of the engineers who went home at 2 a.m. Thanksgiving morning got a call from Musk at 11 a.m. asking him to come back in because another engineer had worked all night and was "not running on full thrusters anymore." Such behavior produced drama and resentments, but also success. When the product went live that weekend, all the employees marched to a nearby ATM, where Musk inserted an X.com debit card. Cash whirred out and the team celebrated.

Believing that Musk needed adult supervision, Moritz convinced him to step aside the following month and allow Bill Harris, the former head of Intuit, to become CEO. In a reprise of what had happened at Zip2, Musk remained as chief product officer and board chair, maintaining his frenzied intensity. After one meeting with investors, he went down to the cafeteria, where he had set up some arcade video games. "There were several of us playing *Street Fighter* with Elon," says Roelof Botha, the chief financial officer. "He was sweating, and you could see that he was a bundle of energy and intensity."

Musk developed viral marketing techniques, including bounties for users who signed up friends, and he had a vision of making X.com both a banking service and a social network. Like Steve Jobs, he had a passion for simplicity when it came to designing user interface screens. "I honed the user interface to get the fewest number of keystrokes to open an account," he says. Originally there were long forms to fill out, including providing a social security number and home address. "Why do we need that?" Musk kept asking. "Delete!" One important little breakthrough was that customers didn't need to have user names; their email address served that purpose.

One driver of growth was a feature that they originally thought was no big deal: the ability to send money by email. That became wildly popular, especially on the auction site eBay, where users were looking for an easy way to pay strangers for purchases.

Max Levchin and Peter Thiel

As Musk monitored the names of new customers signing up, one caught his eye: Peter Thiel. He was one of the founders of a company named Confinity that had been located in the same building as X.com and was now just down the street. Both Thiel and his primary cofounder Max Levchin were as intense as Musk, but they were more disciplined. Like X.com, their company offered a person-to-person payment service. Confinity's version was called PayPal.

By the beginning of 2000, amid the first signs that the air might be coming out of the internet bubble, X.com and PayPal were engaged in a race to sign up new customers. "It was this crazy competition where we both had insane dollar bonuses to get customers to sign up and refer friends," says Thiel. As Musk later put it, "It was a race to see who would run out of money last."

Musk was drawn to the fight with the intensity of a videogamer. Thiel, on the contrary, liked to coolly calculate and mitigate risk. It soon became clear to both of them that the network effect—whichever company got bigger first would then grow even faster—meant that only one would survive. So it made sense to merge rather than turning the competition into a game of *Mortal Kombat*.

Musk and his new CEO Bill Harris scheduled a meeting with Thiel and Levchin in the back room of Evvia, a Greek restaurant in Palo Alto. The two sides traded notes about how many users each had, with Musk engaging in some of his usual exaggerations. Thiel asked him how he envisioned potential merger terms. "We would own ninety percent of the merged company and you would own ten percent," Musk replied. Levchin was not quite sure what to make of Musk. Was he serious? They had roughly equal user bases. "He had an extremely serious I'm-not-joking look on his face, but underneath there seemed to be an ironic streak," Levchin says. As Musk later conceded, "We were playing a game."

After the PayPal team left the lunch, Levchin told Thiel, "This will never hunt, so let's move on." Thiel, however, was better at reading people. "This is just an opening," he told Levchin. "You just have to be patient with a guy like Elon."

The courtship continued through January 2000, causing Musk to postpone his honeymoon with Justine. Michael Moritz, X.com's primary investor, arranged a meeting of the two camps in his Sand Hill Road office. Thiel got a ride with Musk in his McLaren.

"So, what can this car do?" Thiel asked.

"Watch this," Musk replied, pulling into the fast lane and flooring the accelerator.

The rear axle broke and the car spun around, hit an embankment, and flew in the air like a flying saucer. Parts of the body shredded. Thiel, a practicing libertarian, was not wearing a seatbelt, but he emerged unscathed. He was able to hitch a ride up to the Sequoia offices. Musk, also unhurt, stayed behind for a half-hour to have his car towed away, then joined the meeting without telling Harris what had happened. Later, Musk was able to laugh and say, "At least it showed Peter I was unafraid of risks." Says Thiel, "Yeah, I realized he was a bit crazy."

Musk remained resistant to a merger. Even though both companies had about 200,000 customers signed up to make electronic payments on eBay, he believed that X.com was a more valuable company because it offered a broader array of banking services. That put him at odds with Harris, who at one point threatened to resign if Musk tried to scuttle merger talks. "If he quit, that would have been a disaster," Musk says, "because we were trying to raise more financing just as the internet market was weakening."

A break came when Musk had a bonding experience with Thiel and Levchin at another lunch, this one at Il Fornaio, a white-tablecloth Italian restaurant in Palo Alto. They had waited a long time without being served, so Harris barged into the kitchen to see what dishes he could extract. Musk, Thiel, and Levchin looked at each other and exchanged glances. "Here was this extreme extrovert business-development type acting like he had an S on his chest, and the three of us are all very nerdy," Levchin says. "We bonded over being the type of people who would never do what Bill did."

They agreed to a merger in which X.com would get 55 percent of the combined company, but Musk almost ruined things soon after by telling Levchin he was getting a steal. Infuriated, Levchin threatened to pull out. Harris drove to his home and helped him fold laundry as he calmed down. The terms were revised once again, to basically a 50-50 merger, but with X.com as the surviving corporate entity. In March 2000, the deal was consummated, and Musk, the largest stockholder, became the chairman. A few weeks later, he joined with Levchin to force Harris out and regain the role of CEO as well. Adult supervision was no longer welcome.

PayPal

The electronic payment systems of both companies were folded together and marketed under the brand name PayPal. That became the company's primary offering, and it continued to grow rapidly. But it was not in Musk's nature to make niche products. He wanted to remake entire industries. So he refocused on his original goal of creating a social network that would disrupt the whole banking industry. "We have to decide whether we are going to aim big," he told his troops. Some believed Musk's framing was flawed. "We had a vast amount of traction on eBay," says Reid Hoffman, an early employee who later cofounded LinkedIn. "Max and Peter thought we should focus entirely on that and become a master merchant service."

Musk insisted that the company's name should be X.com, with PayPal as merely one of its subsidiary brands. He even tried to rebrand the payment system X-PayPal. There was a lot of pushback, especially from Levchin. PayPal had become a trusted brand name, like a good pal who is helping you get paid. Focus groups showed that the name X.com, on the contrary, conjured up visions of a seedy site you would not talk about in polite company. But Musk was unwavering, and remains so to this day. "If you want to just be a niche payment system, PayPal is better," he said. "But if you want to take over the world's financial system, then X is the better name."

Musk and Michael Moritz went to New York to see if they could recruit Rudy Giuliani, who was just ending his tenure as mayor, to be a political fixer and guide them through the policy intricacies of being a bank. But as soon as they walked into his office, they knew it would not work. "It was like walking into a mob scene," Moritz says. "He was surrounded by goonish confidantes. He didn't have any idea whatsoever about Silicon Valley, but he and his henchmen were eager to line their pockets." They asked for 10 percent of the company, and that was the end of the meeting. "This guy occupies a different planet," Musk told Moritz.

Musk restructured the company so that there was not a separate engineering department. Instead, engineers would team up with product managers. It was a philosophy that he would carry through to Tesla, SpaceX, and then Twitter. Separating the design of a product from its engineering was a recipe for dysfunction. Designers had to feel the immediate pain if something they devised was hard to engineer. He also had a corollary that worked well for rockets but less so for Twitter: engineers rather than the product managers should lead the team.

Arm wrestling with Levchin

Peter Thiel drifted away from active involvement in the company, leaving his Confinity cofounder Max Levchin, a low-key and super-sharp Ukrainian-born software wizard, to be the chief technology officer and counterbalance to Musk. Levchin and Musk soon clashed on an issue that sounded technical but was also theological: whether to use Microsoft Windows or Unix as the main operating system. Musk admired Bill Gates, loved Windows NT, and thought Microsoft would be a more reliable partner. Levchin and his team were appalled, feeling that Windows NT was insecure, buggy, and uncool. They preferred using various flavors of Unix-like operating systems, including Solaris and the open-source Linux.

One night well after midnight, Levchin was working alone in a conference room when Musk walked in primed to continue the argument. "Eventually you will see it my way," Musk said. "I know how this movie ends."

"No, you're wrong," Levchin replied in his flat monotone. "It just isn't going to work in Microsoft."

"You know what," said Musk. "I will arm-wrestle you for it."

Levchin thought, correctly, that this was the stupidest imaginable way to settle a software-coding disagreement. Plus, Musk was almost twice his size. But he was loopy from working late hours and agreed to arm-wrestle. He put all his weight into it and promptly lost. "Just to be clear," Levchin told him, "I'm not going to use your physical weight as any sort of a technical decision input."

Musk laughed and said, "Yeah, I get it." But he prevailed. He spent a year having his own team of engineers rewrite the Unix coding that Levchin had written for Confinity. "We wasted a year doing these technical tap dances instead of building new features," Levchin says. The recoding effort also prevented the company from focusing on the growing amount of fraud that was plaguing the service. "The only reason we remained successful was because there were no other companies being funded during that time."

Levchin had trouble knowing what to make of Musk. Was his arm-wrestling gambit serious? Were his bouts of maniacal intensity punctuated by goofball humor and game-playing calculated or crazed? "There's irony in everything he does," says Levchin. "He operates on an irony setting that goes up to eleven but never goes below four."

One of Musk's powers was to entice other people into his irony circle so they could share an inside joke. "He turns on his irony flamethrower and creates this sense of exclusive Elon Club membership."

That didn't work well on Levchin, who was shielded from irony flamethrowers by his earnestness. He had a good radar for detecting Musk's exaggerations. During the merger, Musk kept insisting that X.com had close to twice as many users, and Levchin would check with its engineers and get the real number. "Elon didn't just exaggerate, he made it up," Levchin says. It was what his father would have done.

And yet, Levchin began to marvel at the counterexamples, such as when Musk astounded him by knowing things. At one point Levchin and his engineers were wrestling with a difficult problem involving the Oracle database they were using. Musk poked his head in the room and, even though his expertise was with Windows and not Oracle, immediately figured out the context of the conversation, gave a precise and technical answer, and walked out without waiting for confirmation. Levchin and his team went back to their Oracle manuals and looked up what Musk had described. "One by one, we all said, 'Shit, he's right,'" Levchin recalls. "Elon will say crazy stuff, but every once in a while, he'll surprise you by knowing way more than you do about your own specialty. I think a huge part of the way he motivates people are these displays of sharpness, which people just don't expect from him, because they mistake him for a bullshitter or goofball."

13

The Coup

PayPal, September 2000

The PayPal mafia *(top, left to right)*: Luke Nosek, Ken Howery, David Sacks, Peter Thiel, Keith Rope, Reid Hoffman, Max Levchin, Roelof Botha; Max Levchin *(bottom left)*; Michael Moritz *(bottom right)*

Street fight

By late summer of 2000, Levchin found Musk increasingly difficult to deal with. He wrote Musk long memos outlining how fraud was threatening to bankrupt the company (one of them incongruously titled "Fraud Is Love"), but all he got in response were terse dismissals. When Levchin developed the first commercial use of CAPTCHA technology to prevent automated fraud, Musk showed little interest. "It had an extremely depressive effect on me," Levchin says. He called his girlfriend to say, "I think I'm done."

Sitting in the lobby of a Palo Alto hotel where he was attending a conference, Levchin told a few colleagues of his plans to leave. They urged him instead to fight back. Others had similar frustrations. His close friends Peter Thiel and Luke Nosek had secretly commissioned a study that showed the PayPal brand was much more valuable than X.com's. Musk was furious and ordered the PayPal brand to be stripped from most of the company's website. By early September, all three, along with Reid Hoffman and David Sacks, had decided it was time to dethrone Musk.

Musk had married Justine eight months earlier, but he had not found time to go on a honeymoon. Fatefully, he decided to take one that September, just when his colleagues were plotting against him. He flew to Australia to attend the Olympics, with stops to meet potential investors in London and Singapore.

As soon as he left, Levchin telephoned Thiel and asked if he would come back as CEO, at least on a temporary basis. When Thiel said yes, the rebel group agreed to join hands and confront the board, enlisting other employees to sign a petition supporting their cause.

Thus armed and fortified, Thiel and Levchin and their compatriots caravanned up Sand Hill Road to Sequoia Capital's office to present their case to Michael Moritz. Moritz thumbed through the folder with the petition, then asked some specific questions about the software and fraud problems. He agreed that a change was necessary, but said he would support Thiel as CEO only if it was temporary; the company needed to begin a process of recruiting a seasoned top executive. The plotters agreed and headed off to a local dive bar, Antonio's Nut House, to celebrate.

Musk began to sense a problem during some of his phone calls from Australia. As usual, he would issue command decisions, but now his normally cowed lieutenants began pushing back. He figured out why four days into his trip, when he was copied on an email sent to the board by an employee who extolled Musk's leadership and denounced the plotters. Musk felt blindsided. "This whole thing is making me so sad that words fail me," he emailed. "I have given every last ounce of effort, almost all my cash from Zip2 and put my marriage on the rocks, and yet I stand accused of bad deeds to which I have not even been given an opportunity to respond."

Musk called Moritz to try to reverse his decision. "He described the coup as being 'heinous,'" says Moritz, who has a refined literary sensibility. "I remember, because most people don't use this word. He labeled it a heinous crime." When Moritz refused to back down, Musk quickly bought plane tickets—the only seats he and Justine could get were in coach—and headed home. When he got back to the X.com office, he huddled with some of his loyalists to figure out ways to fend off the coup. After a session that lasted late into the night, he retreated to the video-game consoles in the office and played round after round of *Street Fighter* by himself.

Thiel warned executives not to answer Musk's calls; he could be too persuasive or intimidating. But Reid Hoffman, the chief operating officer, felt he owed Musk a conversation. A bearlike entrepreneur with a jovial personality, Hoffman knew Musk's wiles. "He has reality-warp powers where people get sucked into his vision," he says. Nevertheless, he decided to meet Musk for lunch.

The lunch lasted three hours as Musk tried to persuade and cajole Hoffman. "I took all of my money and put it in this company," he said. "I have the right to run it." He also argued against the strategy of focusing just on electronic payments. "That should be only an opening act for creating a real digital bank." He had read Clayton Christensen's book *The Innovator's Dilemma*, and tried to convince Hoffman that the staid banking industry could be disrupted. Hoffman disagreed. "I told him that I believed his vision of a superbank was toxic, because we needed to focus on our payment service on eBay," he says. Musk then switched tacks: he tried to persuade Hoffman to become the CEO. Eager to end the lunch, Hoffman agreed to think about it, but quickly decided he wasn't interested. He was a Thiel loyalist.

When the board voted to remove Musk as CEO, he responded with a calm and grace that surprised those who had watched his feverish struggle to prevail. "I've decided that the time has come to bring in a seasoned CEO to take X.com to the next level," he wrote in an email to his fellow workers. "After that search is done, my plan is to take a sabbatical for about three to four months, think through a few ideas, and then start a new company."

Although a street fighter, Musk had an unexpected ability to be realistic in defeat. When Jeremy Stoppelman, a Musk acolyte who would later be a founder of Yelp, asked whether he and others should resign in protest, Musk said no. "The company was my baby, and like the mother in the Book of Solomon, I was willing to give it up so it could survive," Musk says. "I decided to work hard at repairing the relationship with Peter and Max."

The one remaining source of tension was Musk's desire, as he put it in his email, to "do some PR." He had been bitten by the celebrity bug, and he wanted to be a public face of the company. "I'm really the best spokesperson for the company," he told Thiel during a tense meeting in Moritz's office. When Thiel rejected the idea, Musk erupted. "I don't want to have my honor impugned," he shouted. "My honor is worth more than this company to me." Thiel was baffled about why this was a matter of honor. "He was very dramatic," Thiel recalls. "People don't usually talk with such a superheroic, almost Homeric kind of vibe in Silicon Valley." Musk remained the largest shareholder and a member of the board, but Thiel barred him from speaking for the company.

Risk seeker

For the second time in three years, Musk had been pushed out of a company. He was a visionary who didn't play well with others.

What struck his colleagues at PayPal, in addition to his relentless and rough personal style, was his willingness, even desire, to take risks. "Entrepreneurs are actually not risk takers," says Roelof Botha. "They're risk mitigators. They don't thrive on risk, they never seek to amplify it, instead they try to figure out the controllable variables and minimize their risk." But not Musk. "He was into amplifying risk and burning the boats so we could never retreat from it." To Botha, Musk's McLaren crash was like a metaphor: floor it and see how fast it goes.

That made Musk fundamentally different from Thiel, who always focused on limiting risks. He and Hoffman once planned to write a book on their experience at PayPal. The chapter on Musk was going to be titled "The Man Who Didn't Understand the Meaning of the Word 'Risk.'" Risk addiction can be useful when it comes to driving people to do what seems impossible. "He's amazingly successful getting people to march across a desert," Hoffman says. "He has a level of certainty that causes him to put all of his chips on the table."

That was more than just a metaphor. Many years later, Levchin was at a friend's bachelor pad hanging out with Musk. Some people were playing a high-stakes game of Texas Hold 'Em. Although Musk was not a card player, he pulled up to the table. "There were all these nerds and sharpsters who were good at memorizing cards and calculating odds," Levchin says. "Elon just proceeded to go all in on every hand and lose. Then he would buy more chips and double down. Eventually, after losing many hands, he went all in and won. Then he said, 'Right, fine, I'm done.'" It would be a theme in his life: avoid taking chips off the table; keep risking them.

That would turn out to be a good strategy. "Look at the two companies he went on to build, SpaceX and Tesla," says Thiel. "Silicon Valley wisdom would be that these were both incredibly crazy bets. But if two crazy companies work that everyone thought couldn't possibly work, then you say to yourself, 'I think Elon understands something about risk that everybody else doesn't.'"

PayPal went public in early 2002 and was acquired by eBay that July for $1.5 billion. Musk's payout was around $250 million. Afterward, he called up his nemesis Max Levchin and suggested they get together in the company parking lot. Levchin, a small and wiry guy who had occasionally harbored vague fears that Musk might one day beat him up, replied half-jokingly, "You want to have a fist fight behind the school?" But Musk was sincere. He sat on the curb looking sad and asked Levchin, "Why did you turn on me?"

"I honestly believed it was the right thing to do," Levchin replied. "You were completely wrong, the company was about to die, and I felt I had no other choice." Musk nodded. A few months later, they had dinner in Palo Alto. "Life's too short," Musk told him. "Let's move on." He did the same with Peter Thiel, David Sacks, and some of the other coup leaders.

"I was pretty angry at first," Musk told me in the summer of 2022. "I had thoughts of assassination running through my head. But eventually I realized that it was good I got couped. Otherwise I'd still be slaving away at PayPal." Then he paused for a few moments and let out a little laugh. "Of course, if I had stayed, PayPal would be a trillion-dollar company."

There was a coda. At the time of this conversation, Musk was in the midst of buying Twitter. As we walked in front of a high bay where his Starship rocket was being prepared for a test, he returned to the topic of what his grand vision for X.com had been. "That's what Twitter could become," he said. "If you combine a social network with a payments platform, you could create what I wanted X.com to be."

Malaria

Musk's ouster as PayPal CEO allowed him to have a true vacation, the first time that he had a weeklong holiday from work. It would also be the last time. He was not made for vacations.

Along with Justine and Kimbal, he went to Rio to see his cousin Russ Rive, who had moved there after marrying a Brazilian woman. From there they went to South Africa to attend the wedding of another relative. It was Musk's first time back after leaving the country eleven years earlier at age seventeen.

Justine had a tough time dealing with Elon's father and grand-mother, known as Nana. She had gotten a henna tattoo of a gecko on her leg while in Rio, and it had not yet faded. Nana told Elon that she was a "Jezebel," referring to the biblical woman whose name became associated with sexually promiscuous or controlling women. "That was the first time I'd ever even heard a woman refer to another woman as a Jezebel," Justine says. "I guess the tattoo of the gecko didn't help." They escaped Pretoria as soon as they could for a safari at a high-end game preserve.

After getting back to Palo Alto in January 2001, Musk started feeling dizzy. His ears were ringing, and he had recurring waves of chills. So he went to the Stanford Hospital emergency room, where he started throwing up. A spinal tap showed he had a high white blood cell count, which led the doctors to diagnose him with viral meningitis. It's generally not a severe disease, so the doctors rehy-drated him and sent him home.

Over the next few days he felt progressively worse and at one point was so weak he could barely stand. So he called a taxi and went to a doctor. When she tried to take his pulse, it was barely percepti-ble. So she called an ambulance, which took him to Sequoia Hospital in Redwood City. A doctor who was an expert in infectious diseases happened to walk past Musk's bed and realized that he had malaria, not meningitis. It turned out to be falciparum malaria, the most dan-gerous form, and they had caught it just in time. After symptoms be-come severe, as they had in Musk's case, patients often have only a day or so before the parasite becomes untreatable. He was put into intensive care, where doctors stabbed a needle into his chest for intra-venous infusions followed by massive doses of doxycycline.

The head of human resources at X.com went to visit Musk in the hospital and sort out his health insurance. "He was actually only hours from death," the executive wrote in an email to Thiel and Levchin. "His doctor had treated two cases of falciparum malaria prior to treating Elon—both patients died." Thiel remembers that he had a morbid conversation with the HR director after learning that Musk had taken out, on behalf of the company, a key-man life insur-ance policy for $100 million. "If he had died," Thiel says, "all of our financial problems were going to be solved." It was typical of Musk's outsized personality to take out such a large insurance policy. "We're happy that he survived and that gradually everything tracked for the company, so we didn't need the hundred million life insurance policy."

Musk remained in intensive care for ten days, and he did not fully recover for five months. He took two lessons from his near-death experience: "Vacations will kill you. Also, South Africa. That place is still trying to destroy me."

14

Mars

SpaceX, 2001

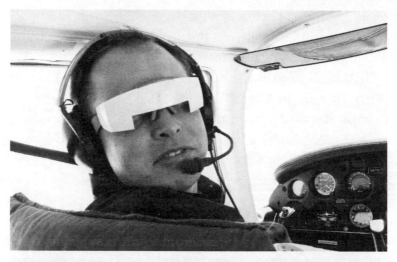

Learning to fly *(top)*; Adeo Ressi *(bottom)*

Flying

After his ouster from PayPal, Musk bought a single-engine turbo-prop and decided to learn how to fly, like his father and grandparents had done. In order to get his pilot's license, he needed fifty hours of training, which he crammed into two weeks. "I tend to do things very intensely," he says. He had an easy time with the Visual Flight Rules test, but he failed his first Instrument Flight Rules test. "You have a hood on, so you can't see outside, and you have half your instruments covered," he says. "Then they shut down one engine, and you have to land the plane. I landed it, but the instructor said, 'Not good enough. Fail.'" On the second try, he passed.

That emboldened him to take the crazy step of buying a Soviet Bloc military jet built in Czechoslovakia called the Aero L-39 Albatros. "It's what they used to train their fighter pilots, so it's incredibly acrobatic," he says. "But it's a bit dicey, even for me." At one point he and his trainer took it on a low-altitude flight over Nevada. "It was just like in *Top Gun*. You're no more than a couple of hundred feet above the ground, following the contour of the mountains. We did a vertical climb up the side of a mountain and then turned upside down."

The flying appealed to his daredevil gene. It also helped him visualize aerodynamics better. "It's not just a simple Bernoulli's principle," he says as he launches into an explanation of how wings lift a moving plane. After about five hundred hours of flying in the L-39 and other planes, he got a bit bored with it. But the allure of flight remained.

Red planet

On Labor Day weekend of 2001, soon after he had recovered from malaria, Musk went to visit his party pal from Penn, Adeo Ressi, in the Hamptons. Afterward, driving back to Manhattan on the Long Island Expressway, they talked about what Musk would do next. "I've always wanted to do something in space," he told Ressi, "but I don't think there's anything that an individual can do." It was too expensive, of course, for a private person to build a rocket.

Or was it? Exactly what were the basic physical requirements? All that was needed, Musk figured, was metal and fuel. Those didn't really cost that much. "By the time we reached the Midtown Tunnel," Ressi says, "we decided that it was possible."

When he got to his hotel that evening, Musk logged onto the NASA website to read about its plans for going to Mars. "I figured it had to be soon, because we went to the moon in 1969, so we must be about to go to Mars." When he couldn't find the schedule, he rummaged deeper on the site, until he realized that NASA had no plans for Mars. He was shocked.

In his Google searches for more information, he happened across an announcement for a dinner in Silicon Valley hosted by an organization called the Mars Society. That sounds cool, he said to Justine, and he bought a pair of $500 tickets. In fact, he ended up sending in a check for $5,000, which caught the attention of Robert Zubrin, the society's president. Zubrin sat Elon and Justine at his table, along with the film director James Cameron, who had directed the space-war thriller *Aliens* as well as *The Terminator* and *Titanic*. Justine sat next to him: "It was a big thrill for me because I was a huge fan, but he mainly talked to Elon about Mars and why humans would be doomed if they didn't colonize other planets."

Musk now had a new mission, one that was loftier than launching an internet bank or digital Yellow Pages. He went to the Palo Alto public library to read about rocket engineering and started calling experts, asking to borrow their old engine manuals.

At a gathering of PayPal alumni in Las Vegas, he sat in a cabana by the pool reading a tattered manual for a Russian rocket engine. When one of the alums, Mark Woolway, asked him what he planned to do next, Musk answered, "I'm going to colonize Mars. My mission in life is to make mankind a multiplanetary civilization." Woolway's reaction was unsurprising. "Dude, you're bananas."

Reid Hoffman, another PayPal veteran, had a similar reaction. After listening to Musk describe his plan to send rockets to Mars, Hoffman was puzzled. "How is this a business?" he asked. Later Hoffman would realize that Musk didn't think that way. "What I didn't appreciate is that Elon starts with a mission and later finds a way to backfill in order to make it work financially," he says. "That's what makes him a force of nature."

Why?

It's useful to pause for a moment and note how wild it was for a thirty-year-old entrepreneur who had been ousted from two tech startups to decide to build rockets that could go to Mars. What drove him, other than an aversion to vacations and a childlike love of rockets, sci-fi, and *A Hitchhiker's Guide to the Galaxy*? To his bemused friends at the time, and consistently in conversations over the ensuing years, he gave three reasons.

He found it surprising—and frightening—that technological progress was not inevitable. It could stop. It could even backslide. America had gone to the moon. But then came the grounding of the Shuttle missions and an end to progress. "Do we want to tell our children that going to the moon is the best we did, and then we gave up?" he asks. Ancient Egyptians learned how to build the pyramids, but then that knowledge was lost. The same happened to Rome, which built aqueducts and other wonders that were lost in the Dark Ages. Was that happening to America? "People are mistaken when they think that technology just automatically improves," he would say in a TED Talk a few years later. "It only improves if a lot of people work very hard to make it better."

Another motivation was that colonizing other planets would help ensure the survival of human civilization and consciousness in case something happened to our fragile planet. It may someday be destroyed by an asteroid or climate change or nuclear war. He had become fascinated by Fermi's Paradox, named after the Italian American physicist Enrico Fermi, who in a discussion of alien life in the universe said, "But where is everyone?" Mathematically it seemed logical there were other civilizations, but the lack of any evidence raised the uncomfortable possibility that the Earth's human species might be the only example of consciousness. "We've got this delicate candle of consciousness flickering here, and it may be the only instance of consciousness, so it's essential we preserve it," Musk says. "If we are able to go to other planets, the probable lifespan of human consciousness is going to be far greater than if we are stuck on one planet that could get hit by an asteroid or destroy its civilization."

His third motivation was more inspirational. It came from his heritage in a family of adventurers and his decision as a teenager to move to a country that had bred into its essence the spirit of pioneers. "The United States is literally a distillation of the human spirit of exploration," he says. "This is a land of adventurers." That spirit needed to be rekindled in America, he felt, and the best way to do that would be to embark on a mission to colonize Mars. "To have a base on Mars would be incredibly difficult, and people will probably die along the way, just as happened in the settling of the United States. But it will be incredibly inspiring, and we must have inspiring things in the world." Life cannot be merely about solving problems, he felt. It also had to be about pursuing great dreams. "That's what can get us up in the morning."

Faring to other planets would be, Musk believed, one of the significant advances in the story of humanity. "There are only a handful of really big milestones: single-celled life, multicellular life, differentiation of plants and animals, life extending from the oceans to land, mammals, consciousness," he says. "On that scale, the next important step is obvious: making life multiplanetary." There was something exhilarating, and also a bit unnerving, about Musk's ability to see his endeavors as having epoch-making significance. As Max Levchin drily puts it, "One of Elon's greatest skills is the ability to pass off his vision as a mandate from heaven."

Los Angeles

Musk decided that, if he wanted to start a rocket company, it was best to move to Los Angeles, which was home to most of the aerospace companies, including Lockheed and Boeing. "The probability of success for a rocket company was quite low, and it was even lower if I did not move to Southern California, where the critical mass of aerospace engineering talent was." He didn't explain the move to Justine, who thought it was because he was attracted to the celebrity glamour of the city. Because of their marriage, he was eligible to become a U.S. citizen, which he did in early 2002 at an oath-taking ceremony with thirty-five hundred other immigrants at the Los Angeles County Fairgrounds.

Musk began gathering rocket engineers for meetings at a hotel near the Los Angeles airport. "My initial thought was not to create a rocket company, but rather to have a philanthropic mission that would inspire the public and lead to more NASA funding."

His first plan was to build a small rocket to send mice to Mars. "But I became worried that we would end up with a tragicomic video of mice slowly dying on a tiny spaceship." That would not be good. "So then it came down to, 'Let's send a little greenhouse to Mars.'" The greenhouse would land on Mars and send back photographs of green plants growing on the red planet. The public would be so excited, the theory went, that it would clamor for more missions to Mars. The proposal was called Mars Oasis, and Musk estimated he could pull it off for less than $30 million.

He had the money. The biggest challenge was getting an affordable rocket that could take the greenhouse to Mars. There was, it turned out, a place where he might be able to get one cheaply, or so he thought. Through the Mars Society, Musk heard of a rocket engineer named Jim Cantrell, who had worked on a U.S.–Russian program to decommission missiles. A month after his Long Island Expressway ride with Adeo Ressi, Musk gave Cantrell a call.

Cantrell was driving in Utah with the top down on his convertible, "so all I could make out was that some guy named Ian Musk was saying that he was an internet millionaire and needed to talk to me," he later told *Esquire*. When Cantrell got home and was able to call him back, Musk explained his vision. "I want to change mankind's outlook on being a multiplanetary species," he said. "Can we meet this weekend?" Cantrell had been leading a cloak-and-dagger life because of his dealings with Russian authorities, so he wanted to meet

in a safe place without guns. He suggested they meet at the Delta
Air Lines club at the Salt Lake City airport. Musk brought Ressi,
and they came up with a plan to go to Russia to see if they could buy
some launch slots or rockets.

15

Rocket Man

SpaceX, 2002

With Adeo Ressi at a rocket facility and a dinner
with Russians in Moscow

Russia

The lunch in the back room of a drab Moscow restaurant consisted of small bites of food interspersed with large shots of vodka. Musk had arrived that morning with Adeo Ressi and Jim Cantrell on their quest to buy a used Russian rocket for their mission to Mars, and he was ragged after a late night of partying during a stopover in Paris. Plus, he was not an experienced drinker, so he didn't fare well. "I calculated the weight of the food and the weight of the vodka, and they were roughly equal," he recalls. After many toasts to friendship, the Russians gave the Americans gifts of vodka bottles with labels that had each person's image on a rendering of Mars. Musk, who was holding his head up with his hand, passed out, and his head slammed into the table. "I don't think I impressed the Russians," he says.

That evening, slightly recovered, Musk and his companions met with another group in Moscow that purported to be selling decommissioned missiles. That encounter turned out to be equally bizarre. The Russian in charge was missing a front tooth, so whenever he spoke loudly, which was often, spit would fly out in Musk's direction. At one point, when Musk started his talk about the need to make humans multiplanetary, the Russian got visibly upset. "This rocket was never meant for capitalists to use it for going to Mars on a bullshit mission," he shouted. "Who's your chief engineer?" Musk allowed that he was. At that point, Cantrell recalls, the Russian spit at them.

"Did he just spit on us?" Musk asked.

"Yeah, he did," Cantrell answered. "I think it's a sign of disrespect."

Despite the clown show, Musk and Cantrell decided to return to Russia in early 2002. Ressi didn't come, but Justine did. So did a new member of the team, Mike Griffin, an aerospace engineer who later became the administrator of NASA.

This time Musk focused on buying two Dnepr rockets, which were old missiles. The more he negotiated, the higher the price went. He finally thought he had a deal to pay $18 million for two Dneprs. But then they said no, it was $18 million for each. "I'm like, 'Dude, that's insane,'" he says. The Russians then suggested maybe it would be $21 million each. "They taunted him," Cantrell recalls. "They said, 'Oh, little boy, you don't have the money?'"

It was fortunate that the meetings went badly. It prodded Musk to think bigger. Rather than merely using a secondhand rocket to put a demonstration greenhouse on Mars, he would conceive a venture that was far more audacious, one of the most audacious of our times: privately building rockets that could launch satellites and then humans into orbit and eventually send them to Mars and beyond. "I was pretty mad, and when I get mad I try to reframe the problem."

First principles

As he stewed about the absurd price the Russians wanted to charge, he employed some first-principles thinking, drilling down to the basic physics of the situation and building up from there. This led him to develop what he called an "idiot index," which calculated how much more costly a finished product was than the cost of its basic materials. If a product had a high idiot index, its cost could be reduced significantly by devising more efficient manufacturing techniques.

Rockets had an extremely high idiot index. Musk began calculating the cost of carbon fiber, metal, fuel, and other materials that went into them. The finished product, using the current manufacturing methods, cost at least fifty times more than that.

If humanity was going to get to Mars, the technology of rockets must radically improve. And relying on used rockets, especially old ones from Russia, was not going to push the technology forward.

So on the flight home, he pulled out his computer and started making spreadsheets that detailed all of the materials and costs for building a midsize rocket. Cantrell and Griffin, sitting in the row behind him, ordered drinks and laughed. "What the fuck do you think that idiot-savant is doing up there?" Griffin asked Cantrell.

Musk turned around and gave them an answer. "Hey, guys," he said, showing them the spreadsheet, "I think we can build this rocket ourselves." When Cantrell looked at the numbers, he said to himself,

"I'll be damned—that's why he's been borrowing all my books." Then he asked the flight attendant for another drink.

SpaceX

When Musk decided he wanted to start his own rocket company, his friends did what true friends do in such a situation: they staged an intervention.

"Whoa, dude, 'I got screwed by the Russians' does not equal 'create a launch company,'" Adeo Ressi told him. Ressi made a highlight reel of dozens of rockets blowing up, and he corralled friends to fly to Los Angeles, where they gathered with Musk to talk him out of it. "They made me watch a reel of rockets exploding, because they wanted to convince me that I would lose all my money," Musk says.

The arguments about the risk served to strengthen Musk's resolve. He liked risk. "If you're trying to convince me this has a high probability of failure, I am already there," he told Ressi. "The likeliest outcome is that I will lose all my money. But what's the alternative? That there be no progress in space exploration? We've got to give this a shot, or we're stuck on Earth forever."

It was a rather grandiose mandate-from-heaven assessment of how indispensable he was to the progress of humankind. But like many of Musk's most laughable assertions, it contained a kernel of truth. "I wanted to hold out hope that humans could be a spacefaring civilization and be out there among the stars," he says. "And there was no chance of that unless a new company was started to create revolutionary rockets."

Musk's space adventure had begun as a nonprofit endeavor to inspire interest in a mission to Mars, but now he had the combination of motivations that would mark his career. He would do something audacious that was driven by a grand idea. But he also wanted it to be practical and profitable, so that it could sustain itself. That meant using the rockets to launch commercial and government satellites.

He decided to start with a smaller rocket that would not be too costly. "We're going to be doing dumb things, but let's just not do dumb things on a large scale," he told Cantrell. Instead of launching large payloads, as Lockheed and Boeing did, Musk would create a less expensive rocket for the smaller satellites that were being made possible by advances in microprocessors. He focused on one key metric: what it cost to get each pound of payload into orbit. That goal of maximizing boost for the buck would guide his obsession with increasing the thrust of the engines, reducing the mass of the rockets, and making them reusable.

Musk tried to recruit the two engineers who had accompanied him to Moscow. But Mike Griffin did not want to move to Los Angeles. He was working for In-Q-Tel, a CIA-funded venture firm based in the Washington, DC, area, and he was looking at a promising future in science policy. Indeed, President George W. Bush appointed him to be NASA administrator in 2005. Jim Cantrell considered joining, but he asked for a lot of job guarantees that Musk was unwilling to meet. So Musk ended up being, by default, the company's chief engineer.

Musk incorporated Space Exploration Technologies in May 2002. At first he called the company by its initials, SET. A few months later, he highlighted his favorite letter by moving to a more memorable moniker, SpaceX. Its goal, he said in an early presentation, was to launch its first rocket by September 2003 and to send an unmanned mission to Mars by 2010. Thus continued the tradition he had established at PayPal: setting unrealistic timelines that transformed his wild notions from being completely insane to being merely very late.

16

Fathers and Sons

Los Angeles, 2002

Errol, Kimbal, and Elon

Baby Nevada

Just as Elon was launching SpaceX in May 2002, Justine gave birth to their first child, a boy, named Nevada because he had been conceived at the annual Burning Man festival held in that state. When he was ten weeks old, the whole family went to Laguna Beach, just south of Los Angeles, for a cousin's wedding. During the reception, a manager at the hotel came in looking for the Musks. Something had happened to their baby, he said.

When they got back to the room, paramedics were intubating Nevada and giving him oxygen. The nanny explained that he had been sleeping in his crib, on his back, and at some point had stopped breathing. The cause was probably Sudden Infant Death Syndrome, an unexplained malady that is the leading cause of infant mortality in developed countries. "By the time the paramedics resuscitated him, he had been deprived of oxygen for so long that he was brain-dead," Justine later said.

Kimbal rode to the hospital with Elon, Justine, and the baby. Even though he had been declared brain-dead, Nevada was kept on life support for three days. When they finally made the decision to turn off the breathing machine, Elon felt his last heartbeat and Justine held him in her arms and felt his death rattle. Musk sobbed uncontrollably. "He cried like a wolf," his mother says. "Cried like a wolf."

Because Elon said he could not bear returning home, Kimbal arranged for them to stay at the Beverly Wilshire Hotel. The manager gave them the presidential suite. Elon asked him to get rid of Nevada's clothes and toys, which had been brought to the hotel. It was three weeks before Musk could bear to go home and see what had once been his son's room.

Musk processed his grief silently. Navaid Farooq, his friend from Queen's University, flew to Los Angeles and stayed with him right after he returned home. "Justine and I tried to draw him into conversations about what happened, but he did not want to talk about it," Farooq says. Instead, they watched movies and played video games. At one point, after a long silence, Farooq asked, "How are you feeling? How are you dealing with it?" Musk completely shut down the conversation. "I've known him long enough to read his face," Farooq says. "I could tell he was determined not to talk about it."

Justine, on the contrary, was very open about her emotions. "He wasn't very comfortable with me expressing my feelings over Nevada's death," she says. "He told me I was being emotionally manipulative, wearing my heart on my sleeve." She attributes his emotional repression to the defense mechanisms he developed during childhood. "He shuts down emotions when in dark places," she says. "I think it's a survival thing with him."

Errol arrives

When Nevada was born, Elon invited his father to fly from South Africa to see his grandson. It offered Elon a chance, thirteen years after he left South Africa, to reconcile with Errol, or at least to exorcise some demons. "Elon was Dad's first son, and maybe he had something to prove to him," Kimbal says.

Errol brought his new wife, their two young children, and his wife's three children from her previous marriage. Elon paid for all seven tickets. When they arrived in Raleigh, North Carolina, after the first leg of their flight from Johannesburg, Errol was paged by a Delta Air Lines representative. "We have some bad news," he was told. "Your son wants us to tell you that Nevada, your grandson, has died." Elon wanted to make sure the airline representative broke the news because he could not bear to speak the words himself.

When Errol got on the phone, Kimbal explained the situation and said, "Dad, you shouldn't come." He tried to convince him to turn around and fly back to South Africa. Errol refused. "No, we're already in the U.S., so we are coming to Los Angeles."

Errol remembers being astounded at the size of the penthouse at the Beverly Wilshire, "probably the most amazing thing I have ever seen." Elon seemed to be in a trance, but he was also very needy, in a complex way. He was uncomfortable having his blustery father see him in such a vulnerable state, but he also did not want him to leave. He ended up urging his father and his new family to stay in Los Angeles. "I don't want you to go back," he said. "I will buy you a house here."

Kimbal was appalled. "No, no, no, this is a bad idea," he told Elon. "You're forgetting that he's a dark human. Do not do this, do not do this to yourself." But the harder he tried to talk his brother out of it, the sadder Elon got. Years later, Kimbal wrestled with what yearnings were motivating his brother. "Watching his own son die, I think that that was what drove him to want his father near him," he told me.

Elon bought a house in Malibu for Errol and his brood, along with the biggest Land Rover he could find, and he arranged for the children to be put into good schools and chauffeured there each day. But things quickly got weird. Elon was getting concerned that Errol, who was then fifty-six, was becoming uncomfortably attentive to one of his stepdaughters, Jana, who was then fifteen.

Elon became furious at his father because of what he perceived as his inappropriate behavior, and he had developed a deep sympathy—and tugging sense of kinship—for Errol's stepchildren. He knew what they had to live with. So he offered to buy Errol a yacht to be harbored forty-five minutes from Malibu. If he agreed to live there on his own, he could see his family on weekends. That was not only a weird idea but also a bad one. It made the whole situation stranger. Errol's wife, who was nineteen years younger than he, began deferring to Elon. "She saw Elon now as the provider in her life and not me," Errol says, "and so it became a problematic situation."

One day when Errol was on the boat, he got a message from Elon. "This situation is not working," he said, and he asked Errol to go back to South Africa. Errol did. A few months later, his wife and family moved back as well. "I tried threats, rewards, and arguments to change my father for the better," Elon later said. "And he—" Musk breaks off for a long period of silence. "No way, it just got worse." Personal networks are more complex than digital ones.

17

Revving Up

SpaceX, 2002

Tom Mueller

Tom Mueller

As a kid growing up in rural Idaho, Tom Mueller loved playing with model rockets. "I made dozens. Of course, they didn't last long, because I'd always crash them or blow them up."

His hometown of Saint Maries (population 2,500) was a logging village about a hundred miles south of the Canadian border. His father worked as a lumberjack. "As a kid, I was always helping Dad work on his log truck, using the welders and other tools," Mueller says. "Being hands-on gave me a feel for what would work and what wouldn't."

Lanky and sinewy with a dimpled chin and jet-black hair, Mueller had the rough-hewn look of a future lumberjack. But inside he was studious like Musk. He immersed himself in the local library devouring science fiction. For a middle-school project, he put crickets inside a model rocket and blasted it off from his backyard to see what effect acceleration would have on them. He learned another lesson instead. The parachutes failed, the rocket smashed to Earth, and the crickets died.

At first, he bought rocket kits through the mail, but then he began making his own from scratch. When he was fourteen, he converted his father's welding torch into an engine. "I injected water into it to see what effect doing that had on its performance," he says. "That's kind of a crazy thing—adding water gives you more thrust."

The project won him second prize at a regional science fair, which qualified him to go to the international finals in Los Angeles. It was the first time he had been on an airplane. "I didn't come close to winning," he says. "There were robots and stuff that the other kids' fathers had built. At least I had done my project myself."

He worked his way through the University of Idaho by spending summers and weekends as a logger. When he graduated, he moved to Los Angeles to seek work in aerospace. His grades had not been great, but his enthusiasm was infectious, and that helped get him a job at TRW, which built the rocket engine that allowed astronauts to land on the moon. On weekends he would go to the Mojave Desert to test big homemade rockets with fellow members of the

Reaction Research Society, a club of rocket enthusiasts founded in 1943. There he partnered with a fellow member, John Garvey, to build what became the world's most powerful amateur rocket engine, weighing eighty pounds.

One Sunday in January 2002, while they were working in a rented warehouse on their amateur engine, Garvey mentioned to Mueller that an internet millionaire named Elon Musk wanted to meet him. When Musk arrived accompanied by Justine, Mueller was shouldering the suspended eighty-pound engine as he tried to bolt it to a frame. Musk began peppering him with questions. How much thrust did it have? Thirteen thousand pounds, Mueller answered. Have you ever made anything bigger? Mueller explained that at TRW he had been working on the TR-106, which had 650,000 pounds of thrust. What were its propellant fuels? Musk asked. Mueller finally quit bolting his engine so he could concentrate on Musk's rapid-shot questions.

Musk asked Mueller whether he could build an engine as big as TRW's TR-106 on his own. Mueller allowed that he had designed the injector and igniter himself, knew the pump system well, and with a team could figure out the rest. How much, Musk asked, would it cost? Mueller replied that TRW was doing it for $12 million. Musk repeated his question. How much would it cost? "Oh, my Lord, that's a tough one," answered Mueller, who was surprised by how fast the conversation had gotten into specifics.

At that point Justine, who was wearing a full-length leather coat, nudged Musk and said it was time to go. He asked Mueller if they could meet the following Sunday. Mueller was reluctant. "It was Super Bowl Sunday, and I had just gotten a widescreen TV and wanted to watch the game with some friends." But he sensed it was futile to resist, so he agreed to have Musk over.

"We watched like maybe one play, because we were so engaged in talking about building a launch vehicle," Mueller says. Along with a few other engineers there, they sketched plans for what became the first SpaceX rocket. The first stage, they decided, would be propelled by engines using liquid oxygen and kerosene. "I know how to make that work easy," Mueller said. Musk suggested hydrogen peroxide for the upper stage, which Mueller thought would be difficult to handle. He countered by suggesting nitrogen tetroxide, which Musk considered too expensive. They ended up agreeing to do liquid oxygen and kerosene on the second stage as well. The football game was forgotten. The rocket was more interesting.

Musk offered Mueller the job of head of propulsion, in charge of designing the rocket's engines. Mueller, who had been complaining about the risk-averse culture at TRW, consulted with his wife. "You'll kick yourself if you don't do this," she told him. Mueller thus became SpaceX's first hire.

One thing that Mueller insisted on was that Musk put two years' worth of compensation into escrow. He was not an internet millionaire, and he did not want to take the chance of being unpaid if the venture failed. Musk agreed. It did, however, cause him to consider Mueller an employee rather than a cofounder of SpaceX. It was a fight he had regarding PayPal and would have again involving Tesla. If you're unwilling to invest in a company, he felt, you shouldn't qualify as a founder. "You cannot ask for two years of salary in escrow and consider yourself a cofounder," he says. "There's got to be some combination of inspiration, perspiration, and risk to be a cofounder."

Ignition

Once Musk was able to enlist Mueller and a few other engineers, he needed a headquarters and factory. "We had been meeting in hotel conference rooms," Musk says, "so I started driving through the neighborhoods where most of the aerospace companies are, and I found an old warehouse right near the L.A. airport." (The SpaceX headquarters and the adjoining Tesla design studio are technically in Hawthorne, a town within Los Angeles County next to the airport, but I will refer to the location as Los Angeles.)

In laying out the factory, Musk followed his philosophy that the design, engineering, and manufacturing teams would all be clustered together. "The people on the assembly line should be able to immediately collar a designer or engineer and say, 'Why the fuck did you make it this way?'" he explained to Mueller. "If your hand is on a stove and it gets hot, you pull it right off, but if it's someone else's hand on the stove, it will take you longer to do something."

As his team grew, Musk infused it with his tolerance for risk and reality-bending willfulness. "If you were negative or thought something couldn't be done, you were not invited to the next meeting," Mueller recalls. "He just wanted people who would make things happen." It was a good way to drive people to do what they thought was impossible. But it was also a good way to become surrounded by people afraid to give you bad news or question a decision.

Musk and the other young engineers would work late into the night and then fire up a multiplayer shooter game, such as *Quake III Arena*, on their desktop computers, conference together their cell phones, and plunge into death matches that could last until 3 a.m. Musk's handle was Random9, and he was (of course) the most aggressive. "We'd be screaming and yelling at each other like a bunch of lunatics," said one employee. "And Elon was right there in the thick of it with us." He was usually triumphant. "He's alarmingly good at these games," said another. "He has insanely fast reactions and knew all the tricks and how to sneak up on people."

Musk named the rocket they were building Falcon 1, after the spacecraft from *Star Wars*. He left it to Mueller to name its engines. He wanted cool names, not just letters and numbers. An employee at one of the contractors was a falconer, and she listed the different species of that bird. Mueller picked "Merlin" for the engines on the first stage and "Kestrel" for those on the second stage.

18

Musk's Rules for Rocket-Building

SpaceX, 2002–2003

Test stand in McGregor, Texas

Question every cost

Musk was laser-focused on keeping down costs. It was not simply because his own money was on the line, though that was a factor. It was also because cost-effectiveness was critical for his ultimate goal, which was to colonize Mars. He challenged the prices that aerospace suppliers charged for components, which were usually ten times higher than similar parts in the auto industry.

His focus on cost, as well as his natural controlling instincts, led him to want to manufacture as many components as possible in-house, rather than buy them from suppliers, which was then the standard practice in the rocket and car industries. At one point SpaceX needed a valve, Mueller recalls, and the supplier said it would cost $250,000. Musk declared that insane and told Mueller they should make it themselves. They were able to do so in months at a fraction of the cost. Another supplier quoted a price of $120,000 for an actuator that would swivel the nozzle of the upper-stage engines. Musk declared it was not more complicated than a garage door opener, and he told one of his engineers to make it for $5,000. Jeremy Hollman, one of the young engineers working for Mueller, discovered that a valve that was used to mix liquids in a car wash system could be modified to work with rocket fuel.

After a supplier delivered some aluminum domes that go on top of the fuel tanks, it jacked up the price for the next batch. "It was like a painter who paints half your house for one price, then wants three times that for the rest," says Mark Juncosa, who became Musk's closest colleague at SpaceX. "That didn't make Elon too enthusiastic." Musk referred to it as "going Russian" on him, as the rocket hucksters in Moscow had done. "Let's go do this ourselves," he told Juncosa. So a new part of the assembly facility was added to build domes. After a few years, SpaceX was making in-house 70 percent of the components of its rockets.

When SpaceX began producing its first Merlin engines, Musk asked Mueller how much they weighed. "So if the Tesla engine is four times as heavy as your engine, why does yours cost so fucking much?"

One reason was that rocket components were subject to hundreds of specifications and requirements mandated by the military and NASA. At big aerospace companies, engineers followed these religiously. Musk did the opposite: he made his engineers question all specifications. This would later become step one in a five-point checklist, dubbed "the algorithm," that became his oft-repeated mantra when developing products. Whenever one of his engineers cited "a requirement" as a reason for doing something, Musk would grill them: Who made that requirement? And answering "The military" or "The legal department" was not good enough. Musk would insist that they know the name of the actual person who made the requirement. "We would talk about how we were going to qualify an engine or certify a fuel tank, and he would ask, 'Why do we have to do that?'" says Tim Buzza, a refugee from Boeing who would become SpaceX's vice president of launch and testing. "And we would say, 'There is a military specification that says it's a requirement.' And he'd reply, 'Who wrote that? Why does it make sense?'" All requirements should be treated as recommendations, he repeatedly instructed. The only immutable ones were those decreed by the laws of physics.

Have a maniacal sense of urgency

When Mueller was working on the Merlin engines, he presented an aggressive schedule for completing one of the versions. It wasn't aggressive enough for Musk. "How the fuck can it take so long?" he asked. "This is stupid. Cut it in half."

Mueller balked. "You can't just take a schedule that we already cut in half and then cut it in half again," he said. Musk looked at him coldly and told him to stay behind after the meeting. When they were alone, he asked Mueller whether he wanted to remain in charge of engines. When Mueller said he did, Musk replied, "Then when I ask for something, you fucking give it to me."

Mueller agreed and arbitrarily cut the schedule in half. "And guess what?" he says. "We ended up developing it in about the time that we had put in that original schedule." Sometimes Musk's insane schedules produced the impossible, sometimes they didn't. "I learned never to tell him no," Mueller says. "Just say you're going to try, then later explain why if it doesn't work out."

Musk insisted on setting unrealistic deadlines even when they weren't necessary, such as when he ordered test stands to be erected in weeks for rocket engines that had not yet been built. "A maniacal sense of urgency is our operating principle," he repeatedly declared. The sense of urgency was good for its own sake. It made his engineers engage in first-principles thinking. But as Mueller points out, it was also corrosive. "If you set an aggressive schedule that people think they might be able to make, they will try to put out extra effort," he says. "But if you give them a schedule that's physically impossible, engineers aren't stupid. You've demoralized them. It's Elon's biggest weakness."

Steve Jobs did something similar. His colleagues called it his reality-distortion field. He set unrealistic deadlines, and when people balked, he would stare at them without blinking and say, "Don't be afraid, you can do it." Although the practice demoralized people, they ended up accomplishing things that other companies couldn't. "Even though we failed to meet most schedules or cost targets that Elon laid out, we still beat all of our peers," Mueller admits. "We developed the lowest-cost, most awesome rockets in history, and we would end up feeling pretty good about it, even if Dad wasn't always happy with us."

Learn by failing

Musk took an iterative approach to design. Rockets and engines would be quickly prototyped, tested, blown up, revised, and tried again, until finally something worked. Move fast, blow things up, repeat. "It's not how well you avoid problems," Mueller says. "It's how fast you figure out what the problem is and fix it."

For example, there was a set of military specifications on how many hours each new version of an engine needed to be test-fired under a long list of different conditions. "It was a tedious approach and very expensive," Tim Buzza explains. "Elon told us just to build one engine and fire it up on the test stand; if it worked, put it on a rocket and fly it." Because SpaceX was a private company, and because Musk was willing to flout rules, it could take the risks it wanted. Buzza and Mueller pushed their engines until they broke, and then said, "Okay, now we know what the limits are."

This belief in iterative design meant that SpaceX needed a freewheeling place for testing. At first they considered the Mojave Air and Space Port, but a county board kept delaying a decision on SpaceX's application in late 2002. "We need to get the hell out of Mojave," Mueller told Musk. "California is difficult."

Musk gave a talk that December at Purdue, which has a renowned rocket-testing program, and he brought with him Mueller and Buzza. There they met an engineer who had worked for Beal Aerospace, one of the many private rocket companies that had gone bankrupt. He described Beal's abandoned test site outside of McGregor, Texas, about twenty-six miles east of Waco, and gave them the cell number of a former employee who still lived in the area.

Musk decided they should fly there that day. On the way, they called the former employee, Joe Allen, and reached him at Texas State Technical College, where he was studying computer coding after losing his job at Beal. Allen had never heard of Musk or SpaceX, but he agreed to meet them under a tripod on the old testing site. When they landed in Musk's jet, they had no trouble finding the tripod in the desert. It was 110 feet tall. At its base was Allen, standing next to his beat-up old Chevy pickup.

"Holy crap," Mueller muttered to Buzza as they walked the site. "Almost everything we need is here." There were test stands and water systems and a block house amid the scrubby grass. Buzza started to enthuse about how well the facility could work. Musk pulled him aside. "Stop saying how good all this is," he said. "You're making it more expensive." Musk ended up hiring Allen on the spot and was able to lease the McGregor site and its abandoned equipment for a mere $45,000 a year.

Thus began a buddy movie in which a platoon of die-hard rocket engineers, led by Mueller and Buzza with occasional visits by Musk, ignited engines and set off explosions, which they dubbed "rapid un-scheduled disassemblies," in a hardscrabble patch of concrete and rat-tlesnakes in the Texas desert.

The first test firing of a Merlin came on the night of Mueller's birthday, March 11, 2003. The kerosene and liquid oxygen was in-jected into the thrust chamber and burned for just half a second, which was all they needed to assure that the mechanisms worked. They celebrated with a $1,000 bottle of Rémy Martin cognac, which had been a gift to Musk for speaking at a space conference. His as-sistant, Mary Beth Brown, had given it to Mueller to use when a suitable cause for celebration arose. They polished it off from paper cups.

Improvise

Mueller and his team would spend twelve-hour days testing engines at McGregor, grab dinner at Outback Steakhouse, then have a late-night conference call with Musk, who peppered them with technical questions. Often he would erupt with the controlled yet searing fury of an engine burn when an engineer did not know an answer. With his tolerance for risk, Musk pushed them to find makeshift solutions. Using machine tools that Mueller had brought to Texas, they would try to make fixes on the spot.

One night lightning struck a test stand, knocking out the pres-surization system for a fuel tank. That led to a bulge and rip in one of the tank's membranes. In a normal aerospace company, that would have meant replacing the tanks, which would take months. "Nah, just fix it," Musk said. "Go up there with some hammers and just pound it back out, weld it, and we'll keep going." Buzza thought that was nuts, but he had learned to follow the boss's orders. So they went out to the test stand and pounded out the bulge. Musk jumped on his plane to make the three-hour flight to oversee things personally. "When he showed up, we began testing the tank with gas in it, and it held," Buzza says. "Elon believes that every situation is salvageable. That taught us a lot. And it actually was fun." It also saved SpaceX months in getting its initial rocket tested.

Of course that didn't always work. Musk tried a similar unconventional approach in late 2003 when cracks developed in the heat-diffusing material inside the thrust chambers of the engines. "First one, then two, then three of our first chambers cracked," Mueller recalls. "It was a disaster."

When Musk got the bad news, he ordered Mueller to find a way to fix them. "We can't throw them away," he said.

"There's no way to fix them," Mueller replied.

It was the type of statement that infuriated Musk. He told Mueller to put the three chambers on his jet and fly with them to the SpaceX factory in Los Angeles. His idea was to apply a layer of epoxy glue that would seep into the cracks and cure the problem. When Mueller told him that the idea was crazy, they got into a shouting match. Finally, Mueller relented. "He's the boss," he told the team.

When the chambers arrived at the factory, Musk was dressed in fine leather boots for a Christmas party he was planning to attend. He never got to the party. He spent all night helping to apply the epoxy and ruining his boots.

The gamble failed. As soon as pressure was applied, the epoxy came unstuck. The chambers had to be redesigned, and the schedule for launch slipped four months. But Musk's willingness to work all night at the factory pursuing the innovative idea inspired his engineers not to be afraid of trying offbeat fixes.

A pattern was set: try new ideas and be willing to blow things up. The residents in the area got used to explosions. The cows, however, did not. Like pioneers circling the wagons, they would run in a circle protecting the young calves in the center when a big bang happened. The engineers at McGregor set up what they called a "cow cam" so they could watch.

19

Mr. Musk Goes to Washington

SpaceX, 2002–2003

Gwynne Shotwell

Gwynne Shotwell

Musk does not naturally partner with people, either personally or professionally. At Zip2 and PayPal, he showed he could inspire, frighten, and sometime bully colleagues. But collegiality was not part of his skill set and deference not in his nature. He does not like to share power.

One of the few exceptions was his relationship with Gwynne Shotwell, who joined SpaceX in 2002 and eventually became its president. She has worked with Musk, sitting in a cubicle right next to his at SpaceX headquarters in Los Angeles, for more than twenty years, longer than anyone else.

Direct, sharp-spoken, and bold, she prides herself on being "mouthy" without crossing the line into disrespect, and she has the pleasant confidence of the high-school basketball player and cheerleading captain she once was. Her easygoing assertiveness allows her to speak honestly to Musk without rankling him and to push back against his excesses while not nannying him. She can treat him almost like a peer but still show deference, never forgetting that he's the founder and boss.

Born Gwynne Rowley, she grew up in a suburban village north of Chicago. When she was a sophomore in high school, she went with her mother to a panel of the Society of Women Engineers, where she became fascinated by a well-dressed mechanical engineer who had her own construction business. "I want to be like her," she said, and decided to apply to the engineering school at nearby Northwestern University. "I applied because of Northwestern's richness in other fields," she later told students there. "I was terrified of being tagged as a nerd. Now I'm super proud to be one."

As she was walking to a job interview with IBM's Chicago-area office in 1986, she stopped to watch a television in a store window that was broadcasting the launch of the Space Shuttle *Challenger* with teacher Christa McAuliffe aboard. What was supposed to be an inspirational moment turned to horror when the *Challenger* exploded a minute after takeoff. Shotwell was so shaken that she didn't get the job. "I must have really sucked eggs on the interview." Eventually she was hired by Chrysler in Detroit, then moved to California, where she became head of space systems sales for Microcosm Inc., a startup consulting firm in the same neighborhood as SpaceX.

At Microcosm she worked with an adventurous, rugged-faced German engineer named Hans Koenigsmann, who met Musk at one of the weekend gatherings of rocket-launching hobbyists in the Mojave Desert. Musk subsequently went to his house to recruit him, and in May 2002 he became SpaceX's fourth employee.

To help him celebrate, Shotwell took Koenigsmann to their favorite neighborhood lunch place, a bright-yellow Austrian restaurant called Chef Hannes. Then she drove Koenigsmann a few blocks down the street to drop him off at SpaceX. "Come on in," he told her. "You can meet Elon."

She found herself impressed with Musk's ideas for reducing the costs of rockets and making the parts in-house. "He knew the details," she says. But she thought the team was clueless about how to sell its services. "The guy you have doing discussions with possible customers is a loser," she told him bluntly.

The next day she got a call from Musk's assistant, who said that he wanted to talk to her about becoming vice president of business development. Shotwell had two kids, was going through a divorce, and was about to turn forty. The idea of joining a risky startup run by a mercurial millionaire did not have much appeal. She spent three weeks considering it before concluding that SpaceX had the potential to transform the sclerotic rocket industry into something that was innovative. "I've been a fucking idiot," she told him. "I'll take the job." She became the company's seventh employee.

Shotwell has a special insight that helps her when dealing with Musk. Her husband has the autism-spectrum disorder commonly called Asperger's. "People like Elon with Asperger's don't take social cues and don't naturally think about the impact of what they say on other people," she says. "Elon understands personalities very well, but as a study, not as an emotion."

Asperger's can make a person seem to lack empathy. "Elon is not an ass, and yet sometimes he will say things that are very assholey," she says. "He just doesn't think about the personal impact of what he's saying. He just wants to fulfill the mission." She does not try to change him, just salve people who get singed. "Part of my job is to tend to the wounded," she says.

It also helps that she is an engineer. "I'm not at his level, but I'm not an idiot. I understand the stuff he's saying," she says. "I listen hard, take him seriously, read his intentions, and try to achieve what he wants, even if what he is saying seems crazy initially." When she insists to me that "he tends to be right," it can sound as if she's a sycophant, but she actually isn't. She speaks her mind to him and gets annoyed at those who don't. She names a couple of them and says, "They work their asses off, but they are chickenshits around Elon."

Wooing NASA

A few months after she joined SpaceX in 2003, Shotwell and Musk traveled to Washington. Their goal was to win a contract from the Defense Department to launch a new breed of small tactical communications satellites, known as TacSat, that would allow commanders of ground forces to get imagery and other data quickly.

They went to a Chinese restaurant near the Pentagon, and Musk broke his tooth. Embarrassed, he kept putting his hand over his mouth, until she started laughing at him. "It was the funniest thing, watching him try to hide it." They were able to find a late-night dentist who made a temporary cap so that Musk would be presentable for their Pentagon meeting the next morning. There they sealed the contract, SpaceX's first, for $3.5 million.

To drum up public awareness about SpaceX, Musk in December 2003 brought a Falcon 1 rocket to Washington for a public event outside of the National Air and Space Museum. SpaceX built a special trailer with a bright blue cradle to haul the seven-story rocket from Los Angeles, and Musk ordered a production crunch with a crazy deadline to get a prototype of the rocket ready for the trip. To many of the company's engineers, this seemed like a mammoth distraction, but when the rocket was paraded up Independence Avenue with a police escort, it impressed Sean O'Keefe, the administrator of NASA. He dispatched one of his deputies, Liam Sarsfield, to California to assess the spunky startup. "SpaceX presents good products and solid potential," Sarsfield reported back. "NASA investment in this venture is well warranted."

Sarsfield admired Musk's hunger for information on highly technical issues, ranging from the docking system of the International Space Station to the ways that engines can overheat. They engaged in an extended email correspondence on these and other issues. But in February 2004, the exchange grew testy when NASA awarded a $227 million contract, without competitive bidding, to a rival private rocket company, Kistler Aerospace. The contract was for rockets that could resupply the International Space Station, something that Musk (rightly, as it turned out) thought SpaceX could do.

Sarsfield made the mistake of giving Musk an honest explanation. Kistler had been awarded the no-bid contract, he wrote, because its "financial arrangements are shaky" and NASA did not want it to go bankrupt. There would be other contracts for SpaceX to bid on, Sarsfield assured Musk. That infuriated Musk, who contended that NASA should be in the business of promoting innovation, not propping up companies.

Musk met with officials at NASA headquarters in May 2004 and, ignoring the advice of Shotwell, decided to sue them over the Kistler contract. "Everyone told me that it might mean we would never be able to work with NASA," Musk says. "But what they did was wrong and corrupt, so I sued." He even threw Sarsfield, his strongest advocate within NASA, under the bus by including in the lawsuit his friendly email explaining that the contract was meant to be a lifeline for Kistler.

SpaceX ended up winning the dispute, and NASA was ordered to open the project to competitive bidding. SpaceX was able to win a significant portion of it. "That was a huge upset—literally imagine, like, a ten-to-one odds underdog winning," Musk told the *Washington Post*'s Christian Davenport. "It blew everyone's mind."

Fixed-price contracts

The victory was crucial not only for SpaceX but for the American space program. It promoted an alternative to the "cost-plus" contracts that NASA and the Defense Department had generally been using. Under those contracts, the government kept control of a project—such as building a new rocket or engine or satellite—and issued detailed specifications of what it wanted done. It would then award contracts to big companies such as Boeing or Lockheed Martin, which would be paid all of their costs plus a guaranteed profit. This approach became standard during World War II to give the government complete control over the development of weapons and to prevent the perception that contractors were war-profiteering.

On his trip to Washington, Musk testified before a Senate committee and pushed a different approach. The problem with a cost-plus system, he argued, was that it stymied innovation. If the project went over budget, the contractor would get paid more. There was little incentive for the cozy club of cost-plus contractors to take risks, be creative, work fast, or cut costs. "Boeing and Lockheed just want their cost-plus gravy trains," he says. "You just can't get to Mars with that system. They have an incentive never to finish. If you never finish a cost-plus contract, then you suckle on the tit of the government forever."

SpaceX pioneered an alternative in which private companies bid on performing a specific task or mission, such as launching government payloads into orbit. The company risked its own capital, and it would be paid only if and when it delivered on certain milestones. This outcomes-based, fixed-price contracting allowed the private company to control, within broad parameters, how its rockets were designed and built. There was a lot of money to be made if it built a cost-efficient rocket that succeeded, and a lot of money to be lost if it failed. "It rewards results rather than waste," Musk says.

20

Founders

Tesla, 2003–2004

JB Straubel, with his scar; Martin Eberhard and Marc Tarpenning

JB Straubel

Jeffrey Brian Straubel—known as JB—was a corn-fed and clean-cut Wisconsin kid with a chipmunk-cheek smile who, as a thirteen-year-old car nerd, refurbished the motor of a golf cart and fell in love with electric vehicles. He also liked chemistry. In high school he did an experiment with hydrogen peroxide that blew up in his family basement, leaving a permanent scar on his otherwise cherubic face.

While studying energy systems at Stanford, he interned with a high-spirited and puckish New Orleans–born entrepreneur, Harold Rosen, who designed the geostationary satellite Syncom for Hughes Aircraft. Rosen and his brother Ben were trying to build a hybrid car with a flywheel that would generate electricity. Straubel tried something simpler. He converted an old Porsche into an all-electric vehicle powered by traditional lead-acid car batteries. It had head-snapping acceleration, but its range was only thirty miles.

After Rosen's electric car company failed, Straubel moved to Los Angeles. One night in the late summer of 2003, he played host to six exhausted and smelly students from Stanford's solar car team, who had just completed a Chicago-to–Los Angeles race in a car powered by solar panels.

They ended up talking most of the night, and their discussion turned to lithium-ion batteries, which were used in laptops. They packed a lot of power and could be strung together in large numbers. "What if we could put a thousand or ten thousand together?" Straubel asked. They figured out that a lightweight car with a half-ton of batteries might just be able to make it across America. As dawn broke, they went into the backyard with some lithium-ion cells and hit them with hammers so they would explode. It was a celebration of the future, and they made a pact. "We've got to do this," Straubel said.

Unfortunately, no one was interested in funding him. Until he met Elon Musk.

In October 2003, Straubel attended a seminar at Stanford where Musk, who had started SpaceX the year before, was a speaker. His talk touted the need for entrepreneurial space activities "led by the spirit of free enterprise." That prompted Straubel to push forward at the end and offer to arrange a meeting with Harold Rosen. "Harold was a legend in the space industry, so I invited them to come visit the SpaceX factory," Musk says.

The factory tour did not go well. Rosen, then seventy-seven, was jovial and self-assured as he pointed out the parts of Musk's design that would fail. When they went to lunch at a nearby McCormick and Schmick's seafood restaurant, Musk reciprocated by denouncing as "stupid" Rosen's latest idea, which was building electric drones to deliver internet service. "Elon is quick to form opinions," Straubel says. Musk remembers the intellectual sparring fondly. "It was a great conversation because Harold and JB are very interesting people, even though the idea was dumb."

Eager to keep the conversation going, Straubel changed the topic to his idea for building an electric vehicle using lithium-ion batteries. "I was looking for funding and being rather shameless," he says. Musk expressed surprise when Straubel explained how good the batteries had become. "I was going to work on high-density energy storage at Stanford," Musk told him. "I was trying to think of what would have the most effect on the world, and energy storage along with electric vehicles were high on my list." His eyes lit up as he processed Straubel's calculations. "Count me in," he said, committing to provide $10,000 in funding.

Straubel suggested that Musk talk to Tom Gage and Alan Cocconi, who had cofounded a small company, AC Propulsion, that was pursuing the same idea. They had built a fiberglass prototype, which they dubbed the tzero, and Straubel called to urge them to give Musk a ride. Sergey Brin, a cofounder of Google, also suggested that they talk to Musk. So in January 2004, Gage sent Musk an email. "Sergei Brin and JB Straubel both suggested you might be interested in driving our tzero sports car," he wrote. "We ran it against a Viper last Monday and it won 4 of 5 sprints on a ⅛ mile track. I lost one because I was carrying a 300 lb cameraman. Do you have time for me to bring it by?"

"Sure," Musk responded. "I would really enjoy seeing it. Don't think it could beat my McLaren (yet), though."

"Hmm, a McLaren, boy that would be a feather in my cap," Gage wrote back. "I can have it there on Feb 4th."

Musk was blown away by the tzero, even though it was a rough prototype without doors or a roof. "You have to turn this into a real product," he told Gage. "That could really change the world." But Gage wanted to start by building a cheaper, boxier, slower car. That made no sense to Musk. Any initial version of an electric car would be expensive to build, at least $70,000 apiece. "Nobody is going to pay anywhere near that for something that looks like crap," he argued. The way to get a car company started was to build a high-priced car first and later move to a mass-market model. "Gage and Cocconi were sort of madcap inventors," he laughs. "Common sense was not their strong suit."

For weeks Musk badgered them to build a fancy roadster. "Everyone thinks electric cars suck, but you can show that they don't," he implored. But Gage resisted. "Okay, if you guys don't want to commercialize tzero, do you mind if I do?" Musk asked.

Gage assented. He also made a fateful suggestion: Musk should partner with a pair of car enthusiasts down the street who had a similar idea. And that was how Musk ended up meeting with two people who had gone through a comparable experience with AC Propulsion and had decided to start their own car company, which they had registered under the name Tesla Motors.

Martin Eberhard

When Martin Eberhard, a lanky Silicon Valley entrepreneur with a lean face and high-voltage personality, was getting over a bad divorce in 2001, he decided he should, as he described it, "be like every other guy going through a midlife crisis and buy myself a sports car." He could afford a nice one because he had started and sold a company that made the first popular Kindle predecessor, the Rocket eBook. But he didn't want a car that burned gasoline. "Climate change had become real to me," he says, "plus I felt we kept fighting wars in the Middle East because of our need for oil."

Being methodical, he created a spreadsheet that calculated the energy efficiency of different types of cars, starting with the raw fuel source. He compared gasoline, diesel, natural gas, hydrogen, and electricity from various sources. "I worked through the exact math each step of the way, from when fuels come out of the ground to when they power the car."

He discovered that electric cars, even in places where the electricity was generated from coal, were the best for the environment. So he decided to buy one. But California had just gutted its mandate that auto companies offer some zero-emission vehicles, and General Motors quit making its EV1. "That really shook me up," he says.

Then he read about the tzero prototype made by Tom Gage and AC Propulsion. After seeing it, he told Gage he would invest $150,000 in the company if they would switch from lead-acid batteries to lithium-ion. The result was that Gage had a prototype tzero in September 2003 that could accelerate from zero to sixty in 3.6 seconds and had a range of three hundred miles.

Eberhard tried to convince Gage and the others at AC Propulsion to start manufacturing the car, or at least build him one. But they didn't. "They were smart people, but I soon realized that they were incapable of actually building cars," Eberhard says. "That's when I decided I had to start a car company of my own." He made a deal to license the electric motors and drivetrain from AC Propulsion.

He enlisted his friend Marc Tarpenning, a software engineer who had been his partner at Rocket eBook. They devised a plan to start with a high-end, open-body, two-seat roadster and later build cars for the mass market. "I wanted to make a sporty roadster that would absolutely change the way that people think about electric cars," Eberhard said, "and then use it to build a brand."

But what should that brand be? One night, while on a dinner-date at Disneyland, he was obsessing, somewhat unromantically, about what to name the new company. Because the car was going to use what was called an induction motor, he came up with the idea of naming it after the inventor of that device, Nikola Tesla. The next day, he had coffee with Tarpenning and asked his opinion. Tarpenning whipped out his laptop, went online, and registered the name. In July 2003, they incorporated the company.

Chairman Musk

Eberhard faced a problem. He had an idea and a name, but he had no funding. Then, in March 2004, he got a call from Tom Gage. The two had made an agreement that they would not compete for each other's investors. When it became clear that Musk was not going to invest in AC Propulsion, Gage offered him to Eberhard. "I'm giving up on Elon," he said. "You should give him a call."

Eberhard and Tarpenning had met Musk earlier, when they had gone to hear him speak at a Mars Society meeting in 2001. "I buttonholed him afterwards just to say hi, like a fanboy," Eberhard recalls.

He mentioned that encounter in an email to Musk asking for a meeting. "We would love to talk to you about Tesla Motors, particularly if you might be interested in investing," he wrote. "I believe that you have driven AC Propulsion's tzero car. If so, you already know that a high-performance electric car can be made. We would like to convince you that we can do so profitably."

That evening Musk replied, "Sure."

Eberhard came down from Palo Alto to Los Angeles that week, accompanied by a colleague, Ian Wright. The meeting, in Musk's cubicle at SpaceX, was supposed to last a half-hour, but Musk kept peppering them with questions while occasionally shouting over to his assistant to cancel his next meeting. For two hours they shared their visions for a supercharged electric car, discussing the details of everything from the drivetrain and motor to the business plan. At the end of the meeting, Musk said he would invest. When they got outside the SpaceX building, Eberhard and Wright exchanged high-fives. After a follow-up meeting that included Tarpenning, they agreed that Musk would lead the initial financing round with a $6.4 million investment and become chair of the board.

What struck Tarpenning was that Musk focused on the importance of the mission rather than the potential of the business: "He clearly had already come to the conclusion that to have a sustainable future we had to electrify cars." Musk had a couple of requests. The first was that the paperwork had to be done quickly, because his wife

Justine was pregnant with twins, and a C-section had been scheduled for a week later. He also asked Eberhard to get in touch with JB Straubel. Having invested in both Straubel's enterprise and Eberhard's, Musk thought they should work together.

Straubel, who had never heard of Eberhard or his fledgling Tesla enterprise, rode his bicycle over and came away skeptical. But Musk called him and urged him to join forces. "Come on, you've got to do this," Musk told him. "It will be a perfect fit."

The pieces thus came together for what would become the world's most valuable and transformative automobile company: Eberhard as CEO, Tarpenning as president, Straubel as chief technology officer, Wright as chief operating officer, and Musk as the chair of the board and primary funder. Years later, after many bitter disputes and a lawsuit, they agreed that all five of them would be called cofounders.

21

The Roadster

Tesla, 2004–2006

Straubel takes Governor Arnold Schwarzenegger for a
test drive in a Roadster

Cobbling together pieces

One of the most important decisions that Elon Musk made about Tesla—the defining imprint that led to its success and its impact on the auto industry—was that it should make its own key components, rather than piecing together a car with hundreds of components from independent suppliers. Tesla would control its own destiny—and quality and costs and supply chain—by being vertically integrated. Creating a good car was important. Even more important was creating the manufacturing processes and factories that could mass-produce them, from the battery cells to the body.

But that's not the way the company began. Just the opposite.

When producing their Rocket eBook, Martin Eberhard and Marc Tarpenning had outsourced the manufacturing process. Likewise, when it came time to make Tesla's first car, the Roadster, they decided to cobble it together from components made by outside suppliers. In a decision that would come to haunt Tesla, Eberhard decided that Tesla would get batteries in Asia and car bodies in England and drivetrains from AC Propulsion and a transmission from Detroit or Germany.

This was in line with the prevailing trends in the auto industry. In the early days of Henry Ford and other pioneers, carmakers did most of the work in-house. But beginning in the 1970s, the companies spun off their parts-makers and upped their reliance on suppliers. From 1970 to 2010, they went from producing 90 percent of the intellectual property in their vehicles to about 50 percent. That made them dependent on far-flung supply chains.

After Eberhard and Tarpenning decided to outsource the building of the car's body and chassis, they went to the Los Angeles Auto Show, invited themselves into the booth of the boutique British sports car maker Lotus, and cornered one of the executives. "He was a polite British guy and couldn't find a way to tell us to go away," Eberhard says. "When we were done, he was intrigued enough to invite us to the U.K." They eventually agreed to a deal in which Lotus would supply a slightly modified version of the body of its spritely

Elise roadster, and then Tesla would equip it with an electric engine and powertrain from AC Propulsion.

By January 2005, the eighteen engineers and mechanics at Tesla had cobbled together by hand what was known as a development mule, a vehicle that could be shown off and tested before being put into production. "To make a mule required a lot of hacking and slashing in order to jam our batteries and the AC Propulsion powertrain into a Lotus Elise," Musk says. "But at least we had a thing that looked like a real car. It actually had doors and a roof, unlike the tzero."

Straubel got to take the first test ride. When he touched the accelerator, it bolted forward like a startled horse, amazing even its engineers. Eberhard's turn came next, and tears came to his eyes as he gripped the wheel. After Musk took his turn zipping around and marveling at the car's super-quick but silent acceleration, he agreed to invest $9 million more in the company.

Whose company?

One issue with startups, especially those with multiple founders and funders, is who should be in charge. Sometimes the alpha male wins, as when Steve Jobs marginalized Steve Wozniak and when Bill Gates did the same to Paul Allen. At other times it's messier, especially when different players feel that they are the founder of a company.

Both Eberhard and Musk considered themselves to be the main founder of Tesla. In Eberhard's mind, he had come up with the idea, enlisted his friend Tarpenning, registered a company, chosen a name, and gone out and found funders. "Elon called himself the chief architect and all kinds of things, but he wasn't," Eberhard says. "He was just a board member and investor." But in Musk's mind, he was the one who put Eberhard together with Straubel and provided the funding needed to start the company. "When I met Eberhard and Wright and Tarpenning, they had no intellectual property, no employees, nothing. All they had was a shell corporation."

At first this difference in perspective was not a big problem. "I was running SpaceX," Musk says, "and I had no desire to also run Tesla." He was happy, at least initially, to be the board chair and let Eberhard be CEO. But as the person who owned most of the equity, Musk had ultimate authority, and it was not in his nature to defer. Especially when it came to engineering decisions, he became increasingly involved. Tesla's leadership team thus became an inherently unstable molecule.

For the first year or so, Musk and Eberhard got along. Eberhard handled the daily management of Tesla at its headquarters in Silicon Valley. Musk spent most of his time in Los Angeles and made visits only about once a month for board meetings or important design reviews. His questions tended to be technical, probing into the details of the battery pack, motor, and materials. He was not known for gushing emails, but one night early in their relationship, after working on a problem together, he sent one to Eberhard: "The number of great product people in the world is tiny and I think you are one of them." They talked most days, exchanged emails at night, and occasionally socialized. "I was never his drinking buddy," Eberhard says, "but we were in each other's houses every now and then and went out to eat."

Alas, they were too much alike for the buddy movie to last. Both were hard-driving, high-strung, detail-oriented engineers who could be brutally dismissive of those they considered fools. The problems began when Eberhard had a falling-out with Ian Wright, who had been part of the founding team. Their disagreements became so intense that each tried to convince Musk to fire the other. It was a tacit acknowledgment by Eberhard that Musk had the ultimate say. "Martin and Ian were telling me why the other one is a demon and needs to be thrown out," Musk says. "They are saying, 'Elon, you must make a choice.'"

Musk called Straubel for advice. "Okay, who should we pick here?" he asked. Straubel replied that neither choice was great, but when pressed he advised, "Maybe Martin is the lesser of two evils." Musk ended up firing Wright, but the situation deepened his doubts about Eberhard. It also prompted him to become more involved in the management of Tesla.

Design decisions

As Musk began to pay more attention to Tesla, he could not refrain from getting involved in design and engineering decisions. He would fly up from Los Angeles every couple of weeks, chair a design review meeting, inspect models, and suggest improvements. Being Musk, however, he did not consider his ideas to be mere suggestions. He bristled when they were not carried out. This was a problem, because the company's business plan called for cobbling together a body from Lotus and other suppliers without making major changes. "We had planned to do the minimal possible modifications," Tarpenning says, "at least until Elon got more involved."

Eberhard tried to resist most of Musk's suggestions, even if they would make the car better, because he knew they would increase costs and cause delays. But Musk argued that the only way to jump-start Tesla was to roll out a roadster that wowed customers. "We only get to release our first car once, so we want it to be as good as it can be," he told Eberhard. At one of the review meetings, Musk's face darkened, his stare turned cold, and he declared that the car looked cheap and ugly. "We couldn't have a crappy-looking car and sell it for around a hundred thousand dollars," he later said.

Although his expertise was computer software, not industrial design, he began putting a lot of time into the aesthetics of the Roadster. "I had never designed a car before, so I was studying every great car and trying to understand what made it special," he says. "I agonized over all the details." He would later proudly note that he was honored by the ArtCenter College of Design in Pasadena for his work on the Roadster.

One major design revision that Musk made was to insist that the door of the Roadster be enlarged. "In order to get in the car, you had to be a dwarf mountain climber or a master contortionist," he says. "It was insane, farcical." The six-foot-two-inch Musk found he had to swing his rather large butt into the seat, fold himself into nearly a fetal position, then try to swing his legs in. "If you're going on a date, how is a woman even going to get in the car?" he asked. So he ordered that the bottom of the door's frame be lowered three inches.

The resulting redesign of the chassis meant that Tesla could not use the crash-test certification that Lotus had, which added $2 million to the production costs. Like many of Musk's revisions, it was both correct and costly.

Musk also ordered that the seats be made wider. "My original idea was to use the same seat structures that Lotus used," Eberhard says. "Otherwise, we would have to redo all the testing. But Elon felt that the seats were too narrow for his wife's butt or something. I got a skinny butt, and I kind of miss the narrow seats."

Musk also decided that the original Lotus headlights were ugly because they had no cover or shield. "It made the car look bug-eyed," he says. "The lights are like the eyes of a car, and you have to have beautiful eyes." That change would add another $500,000 to the production costs, he was told. But he was adamant. "If you're buying a sports car, you're buying it because it's beautiful," he told the team. "So this is not a small deal."

Instead of the fiberglass composite material that Lotus used, Musk decided that the Roadster body should be made from stronger carbon fiber. That made it costlier to paint, but it also made it lighter while feeling more solid. Over the years, Musk was able to use techniques learned at SpaceX and apply them to Tesla, and vice versa. When Eberhard pushed back on the cost of carbon fiber, Musk sent him an email. "Dude, you could make the body panels for at least 500 cars worth per year if you bought the soft oven we have at SpaceX!" he wrote. "If someone tells you this is hard, they are full of shit. You can make high quality composites in the oven in your home."

No detail was too small to escape Musk's meddling. The Roadster originally had ordinary door handles, the kind that click open a latch. Musk insisted on electric handles that would operate with a simple touch. "Somebody who's buying a Tesla Roadster will buy it whether it has ordinary door latches or electric ones," Eberhard argued. "It's not going to add a single unit to our sales." It was an argument he had made about most of Musk's design changes. Musk prevailed, and electric door handles became a cool feature that helped define the magic of Tesla. But as Eberhard warned, it added yet another cost.

Eberhard finally got pushed to despair when, near the end of the design process, Musk decided that the dashboard was ugly. "This is a major issue and I'm deeply concerned that you do not recognize it as such," Musk wrote. Eberhard tried to put him off, begging that they deal with the issue later. "I just don't see a path—any path at all—to fixing it prior to start of production without a significant cost and schedule hit," he wrote. "I stay up at night worrying about simply getting the car into production sometime in 2007. . . . For my own sanity's sake and for the sanity of my team, I am not spending a lot of cycles thinking about the dashboard." Many people over the years would make similar pleas to Musk, few of them successfully. In this case, Musk relented. Improving the dashboard could wait until after the first cars entered production. But it didn't help Musk and Eberhard's relationship.

By modifying so many elements, Tesla lost the cost advantages that came from simply using a crash-tested Lotus Elise body. It also added to the supply-chain complexity. Instead of being able to rely on Lotus's existing suppliers, Tesla became responsible for finding new sources for hundreds of components, from the carbon fiber panels to the headlights. "I was driving the Lotus people crazy," Musk says. "They kept asking me why I was being so hardcore about every little curve of this car. And what I told them was, 'Because we have to make it beautiful.'"

Raising more capital

Musk's modifications may have made the car more beautiful, but they also burned through the company's cash. In addition, he repeatedly pushed Eberhard to hire more people so that the company could move faster. By May 2006, it had seventy employees, and it needed another round of financing from investors.

Tarpenning was acting as the company's chief financial officer, even though his expertise was in computer software and not finance. He had the unenviable task of telling Musk at a board meeting that they were running out of money. "This was sooner than we had originally planned, largely because we had been making these hires that Elon pushed for," Tarpenning recalls. "So Elon totally loses it."

During the tirade, Elon's brother Kimbal, who was on the board, reached into his satchel and looked through the budget presentations from the previous five meetings. "Elon," he quietly interjected, "if you take away the costs of the six unbudgeted new hires that you pushed for, then they would actually still be right on target." Musk paused, looked at the spreadsheets, and conceded the point. "Okay," he said, "I guess we should figure out how to raise more financing." Tarpenning says he felt like hugging Kimbal.

In Silicon Valley at the time, there was a tight-knit and hard-partying community of young entrepreneurs and tech bros who had become startup millionaires, and Musk had become one of its stars. He enlisted some of his friends to invest, including Antonio Gracias, Sergey Brin, Larry Page, Jeff Skoll, Nick Pritzker, and Steve Jurvetson. But board members encouraged him to broaden the network and seek financing from one of the major venture capital firms, such as those that gilded Palo Alto's Sand Hill Road. That would provide not just money but a stamp of legitimacy on Tesla.

First he approached Sequoia Capital, which had become king of the valley by being early backers of Atari, Apple, and Google. It was run by Michael Moritz, the wry and literate Welsh-born former journalist who had helped guide Musk and Thiel on the tumultuous ride of PayPal. Musk took him for a drive in a mocked-up Lotus prototype. "It was an absolutely bone-jarring ride with Elon at the wheel in this tiny car with no suspension that went from zero to sixty in less time than it takes to blink," Moritz says. "How much more terrifying can that be?" After Moritz recovered, he called Musk and said he wasn't going to invest. "I really admired that ride, but we're not going to compete against Toyota," he said. "It's mission impossible." Years later Moritz conceded, "I didn't appreciate the strength of Elon's determination."

Instead, Musk turned to VantagePoint Capital, led by Alan Salzman and Jim Marver. It became the lead investor in a $40 million financing round that closed in May 2006. "The duality of the management with Eberhard and Musk concerned me," Salzman says, "but I realized it was just the nature of this beast."

The duality was not evident in the press release announcing the funding round, which Musk did not see before it went out. It did not list Musk as one of the company's founders. "Tesla Motors was founded in June 2003 by Martin Eberhard and Marc Tarpenning," it declared. Eberhard was quoted politely thanking Musk for being an investor: "We are proud of Mr. Musk's continued confidence in Tesla Motors expressed through his strong participation in every round of financing and his leadership on the Board of Directors."

Getting credit

Musk, who had pushed to remain as spokesman for PayPal even after he had been ousted as CEO, had an enthusiastic but awkward attraction to publicity. He would never become an on-air pitchman for his products, like Lee Iacocca or Richard Branson, nor be a moth attracted to TV interviews. He would occasionally appear at conferences and sit still for magazine profiles, but he felt more comfortable spouting off on Twitter or holding court on a podcast. A master of memes, he had a clever instinct about how to garner free publicity by courting controversy and jousting on social media, though he could brood for years about slights.

One constant was his sensitivity about getting credit. His blood boiled if anyone falsely implied that he had succeeded because of inherited wealth or claimed that he didn't deserve to be called a founder of one of the companies he helped to start. That is what happened at PayPal and was now happening with Tesla, and both cases would lead to lawsuits.

Eberhard in 2006 had become a bit of a celebrity and enjoyed it. He was described in his frequent television interviews and conference appearances as Tesla's founder, and that year he appeared in an advertisement for the BlackBerry personal digital assistant (a precursor to the smartphone) which said that he "created the first electric sports car."

After the press release that May on Tesla's funding round, which referred only to Eberhard and Tarpenning as the company's founders, Musk moved forcefully to make sure that his own role was never again minimized. He began conducting interviews without clearing them with the company's public relations chief, Jessica Switzer, who had been hired by Eberhard. She found it problematic that Musk was making pronouncements about the strategy of the company. "Why is Elon doing these interviews?" she asked Eberhard one day when they were riding in a car. "You're the CEO."

"He wants to do them," Eberhard replied, "and I don't want to be arguing with him."

The unveiling

The issue came to a head in July 2006, when Tesla was ready to unveil a prototype of the Roadster. The team had hand-crafted a black one and a red one, each with the ability to go from zero to sixty in about four seconds. They still had not yet changed the skinny seats and ugly dashboard that Musk hated, but otherwise they were pretty close to what Tesla planned to put into production.

An important element in launching a new product, as Steve Jobs had shown with his dramatic announcement events, is creating a buzz that transforms it into an object of desire. This was especially true for an electric car, which needed to overcome the golf-cart image. Switzer came up with plans to hold a celebrity-studded party at the Santa Monica airport where guests would be given a ride in one of the prototypes.

Eberhard and Switzer flew down to Los Angeles to show Musk the plans. "Things went really badly," she recalls. "He went into every detail, including how much we planned to spend on catering. When I fought back, his whole body jerked away, and he stood up and walked out of the room." As Eberhard put it, "He shit all over her ideas and then told me to fire her."

Musk personally took over planning the event. He oversaw the guest list, chose the menu, and even approved the cost and design of the napkins. A smattering of celebrities showed up, including California governor Arnold Schwarzenegger, who was taken on a test drive by Straubel.

Both Eberhard and Musk spoke. "You can have a car that's quick, and you can have a car that's electric, but having one that's both is how you make electric cars popular," Eberhard said in his confident and polished talk. Musk was awkward, displaying his tendency to repeat words tentatively and stammer slightly. But his lack of slickness charmed the reporters. "Until today, all electric cars sucked," he declared. Buying the Roadster, he said, would help fund Tesla so that it could make a mass-market vehicle. "Tesla executives are not paid high salaries, and we don't issue dividends. All free cash flow goes completely into driving the technology to lower costs and make cars that are more affordable."

The event got glowing coverage. "This is not your father's electric car," the *Washington Post* raved. "The $100,000 vehicle, with its sports car looks, is more Ferrari than Prius—and more about testosterone than granola."

There was, however, one problem. Eberhard got almost all the credit. "He set out to build a sleek, battery-powered performance machine," *Wired* gushed about him in a lavishly illustrated story. "After reading biographies of John DeLorean and Preston Tucker, and reminding himself that launching a car company was a crazy idea, he did just that." Musk was mentioned as merely one of the investors Eberhard was able to enlist.

Musk sent a sharp email to Tesla's vice president, who had the misfortune of taking on the publicity portfolio from the fired Switzer. "The way that my role has been portrayed to date, where I am referred to merely as 'an early investor,' is outrageous," he wrote. "That would be like Martin being called an 'early employee.' My influence on the car itself runs from the headlights to the styling to the door sill to the trunk, and my strong interest in electric transport predates Tesla by a decade. Martin should certainly be the front and center guy, but the portrayal of my role to date has been incredibly insulting." He added that he would "like to talk with every major publication within reason."

The next day, the *New York Times* wrote a paean to Tesla, headlined "Zero to 60 in 4 Seconds," that did not even mention Musk. Worse yet, Eberhard was described as Tesla's chairman, and the only picture was one of him standing with Tarpenning. "I was incredibly insulted and embarrassed by the NY Times article," Musk wrote to Eberhard and to the public relations firm, PCGC, that they had hired. "I am not merely unmentioned, but Martin is actually referred to as the chairman. If anything like this happens again, please consider the PCGC relationship with Tesla to end immediately."

In an effort to assert his own central role, Musk published on Tesla's website a little essay that outlined the company's strategy. Cheekily titled "The Secret Tesla Motors Master Plan (just between you and me)," it declared:

> The overarching purpose of Tesla Motors (and the reason I am funding the company) is to help expedite the move from a mine-and-burn hydrocarbon economy towards a solar electric economy. . . . Critical to making that happen is an electric car without compromises, which is why the Tesla Roadster is designed to beat a gasoline sports car like a Porsche or Ferrari in a head-to-head showdown. . . . Some may question whether this actually does any good for the world. Are we really in need of another high-performance sports car? Will it actually make a difference to global carbon emissions? Well, the answers are no and not much. However, that misses the point, unless you understand the secret master plan alluded to above. Almost any new technology initially has high unit cost before it can be optimized, and this is no less true for electric cars. The strategy of Tesla is to enter at the high end of the market, where customers are prepared to pay a premium, and then drive down market as fast as possible to higher unit volume and lower prices with each successive model.

Musk also propelled himself toward celebrity by giving a tour of the SpaceX factory to the actor Robert Downey Jr. and director Jon Favreau, who were making the superhero movie *Iron Man*. Musk became a model for the title character Tony Stark, a celebrity industrialist and engineer who is able to transform himself into an iron man with a mechanized suit of armor he designed. "My mind is not easily blown, but this place and this guy were amazing," Downey later said. He asked that a Tesla Roadster be put in the movie set depicting Stark's workshop. Musk later appeared briefly as himself in *Iron Man 2*.

The prototype of the Roadster unveiled in 2006 accomplished the first step Musk had outlined: shattering the illusion that electric cars were destined to be boxy versions of a golf cart. Governor Schwarzenegger plunked down a $100,000 deposit for one, as did the actor George Clooney. Musk's neighbor in Los Angeles, Joe Francis, who produced the *Girls Gone Wild* television series, sent an armored truck with his $100,000 deposit in cash. Steve Jobs, who loved cars, showed a picture of a Roadster to one of his board members, Mickey Drexler, then the CEO of J.Crew. "Creating engineering this good is the beautiful part," Jobs said.

GM had recently discontinued its own lame version of an electric car, the EV1, and the filmmaker Chris Paine came out with a scathing documentary titled *Who Killed the Electric Car?* Now Musk and Eberhard and their plucky team at Tesla were poised to revive the future.

One evening, Eberhard was driving his Roadster around Silicon Valley when a kid in a super-pimped Audi pulled up beside him at a stoplight and revved his engine to challenge him to a drag. When the light changed, Eberhard left him in the dust. The same thing happened at the next two lights. Finally the kid rolled down his window and asked Eberhard what he was driving. "It's electric," Eberhard said. "There's no way you can beat it."

22

Kwaj

SpaceX, 2005–2006

Hans Koenigsmann and Omelek Island in the Kwajalein Atoll

Catch-22

Musk had planned to launch SpaceX's rockets from one of the most convenient possible locations: Vandenberg Air Force Base, a 100,000-acre facility on the California coast near Santa Barbara. Rockets and other equipment could easily be driven there from the SpaceX headquarters and factory in Los Angeles, about 160 miles to the south.

The problem was that the base was run by the Air Force, which treated rules and requirements as sacred. This did not sit well with Musk, who was instilling a culture based on questioning every rule and assuming that every requirement was dumb until proven otherwise. "The Air Force and us were such a mismatch," says Hans Koenigsmann, who was then SpaceX's chief launch engineer. "They had some requirements that Elon and I laughed about so hard that we would have to catch our breath." After a moment's reflection, he adds, "They probably laughed at us the same way."

Making matters worse, Vandenberg was scheduled to be used to launch a super-secret $1 billion spy satellite. In the spring of 2005, just as SpaceX's Falcon 1 was getting ready, the Air Force decreed that SpaceX would not be able to use its pad until the satellite was safely launched, and they could offer no timetable when that might happen.

SpaceX had no one covering its expenses. It did not have a cost-plus contract, and it got paid only when it launched or delivered on certain milestones. Lockheed, on the other hand, profited whenever there was a delay. After a conference call with the Air Force bureaucrats in May 2005, during which he realized that SpaceX would not get permission to launch anytime soon, Musk called Tim Buzza and told him to start packing. They were going to move the rocket to another site. Fortunately, they had one available. Unfortunately, it was as inconvenient as Vandenberg was convenient.

Gwynne Shotwell had scored for SpaceX a $6 million deal in 2003 to launch a communications satellite for Malaysia. The problem was the satellite was so heavy that it had to be launched near the equator, where the faster rotation of the Earth's surface would provide the extra thrust that was needed.

Shotwell invited Koenigsmann into her cubicle at SpaceX, spread out a map of the world, and moved her finger west along the equator. There was nothing to be found until halfway across the Pacific: the Marshall Islands, about forty-eight hundred miles from Los Angeles. It was near the international date line, but nothing else. Once a U.S. territory that was used as an atomic weapon and missile test site, the Marshall Islands had become an independent republic but remained closely aligned with the U.S., which maintained military bases there. One of them was on a string of tiny coral-and-sand islets known as the Kwajalein Atoll.

Kwajalein Island, known as Kwaj, is the largest speck in the atoll. It's home to a U.S. Army base with fraying hotel facilities that resemble dormitories and a landing strip that tries to pass for an airport. Three days a week, there was a flight from Honolulu. Factoring in layovers, it took close to twenty hours to get from Los Angeles to Kwaj.

When Shotwell researched Kwaj, she found that the facilities were run by the Army's Space and Missile Defense Command, headquartered in Huntsville, Alabama. The person in charge was Major Tim Mango, a name that made Musk laugh. "It's like something out of *Catch-22*," he says. "A person at the Pentagon decides to pick someone named Major Mango to run a tropical island base."

Musk called Mango out of the blue and explained that he had been a founder of PayPal and had gone into the rocket-launching business. Mango listened for a couple of minutes and hung up on him. "I thought he was nuts," Mango told Eric Berger of *Ars Technica*. Mango then did a Google search on Musk, saw a picture of him next to his million-dollar McLaren, read that he had started a company called SpaceX, and realized that he was for real. Scrolling through the SpaceX website, Mango found the company's phone number and dialed it. The same person with the slight South African accent answered. "Hey, did you just hang up on me?" Musk asked.

Mango agreed to visit Musk in Los Angeles. After they talked for a while in his cubicle, he invited Mango to a nice restaurant for dinner. Mango checked with his government ethics officer, who told him he would have to pick up the tab, so they went to Applebee's instead. Musk and some of his team reciprocated by flying a month later to

Huntsville to meet with Mango and his team. This time they ate better, going to a local roadside joint that featured catfish served fried with the head on. Musk ate one, along with some hush puppies. He wanted to make a deal.

So did Major Mango. His base at Kwaj, like many such installations, was expected to hustle for commercial contracts to cover up to half of their budget. "So Major Mango was rolling out the red carpet for us, while the Air Force was giving us the cold shoulder at Vandenberg," Musk says. On the flight from Huntsville, Musk told his team, "Let's go to Kwaj." A few weeks later, they flew on his jet to the remote atoll, took a tour in an open-door Huey helicopter, and decided to move their launch site there.

This side of paradise

Years later, Musk would admit that moving to Kwaj was a mistake. He should have waited for Vandenberg to become available. But that would have required patience, a virtue that he lacked. "I did not realize what a shitshow it would be dealing with the logistics and the salt air," he says of Kwaj. "Every now and then you shoot yourself in the foot. If you had to pick a path that reduced the probability of success, it would be to launch from an inaccessible tropical island." Then he laughs. Now that the scars have healed, he realizes that Kwaj was a memorable adventure. As his chief launch engineer Koenigsmann explains, "Those four years on Kwaj forged us, bonded us, and taught us to work as a team."

A hardy band of SpaceX engineers moved to the barracks on Kwajalein Island. The launch site itself was twenty miles away on an even tinier island in the atoll, known as Omelek. About seven hundred feet wide and uninhabited, it was accessible by a forty-five-minute catamaran ride, a trip that could cause a sunburn even through a T-shirt in the early morning. There the SpaceX team set up a double-wide trailer as an office and poured concrete for a launchpad.

After a few months, some of the crew decided it was easier to sleep on Omelek rather than make the trip across the lagoon each morning and night. They outfitted the trailer with mattresses, a small refrigerator, and a grill on which a jovial goateed SpaceX engineer from Turkey named Bülent Altan perfected a way to cook ground-beef-and-yogurt goulash. The atmosphere was a cross between *Gilligan's Island* and *Survivor*, but with a rocket pad. Each time a newbie stayed overnight, they were awarded a T-shirt imprinted with the mantra "Outsweat, Outdrink, Outlaunch."

At Musk's insistence, the crew devised ways to save money. Instead of paving the 150-yard path between the hangar and the launchpad, they rigged up a cradle on wheels to transport the rocket, laid pieces of plywood on the ground, rolled the rocket a few feet, then moved the plywood to smooth the way for rolling the next few feet.

How scrappy and non-Boeing-like were the crew on Kwaj? In early 2006, they planned to conduct a static fire test, one that ignites the engines briefly while the rocket stays attached to the launchpad. But when they began the test, they discovered that not enough electrical power was reaching the second stage. It turned out that the power boxes designed by Altan, the goulash-cooking engineer, had capacitors that could not handle the juiced-up voltage the launch team had decided to use. Altan was horrified because the window the Army had given them for the static test ended four days later. He scrambled to put together a save.

The capacitors were available in an electronics supply house in Minnesota. An intern in Texas was dispatched there. Meanwhile, Altan removed the power boxes from the rocket on Omelek, jumped on a boat to Kwaj, slept on a concrete slab outside of the airport waiting for the early-morning flight to Honolulu, and made the connection to Los Angeles, where he was picked up by his wife, who drove him to SpaceX headquarters. There he met the intern, who had arrived from Minnesota with the new capacitors. He swapped them into the faulty power boxes and rushed home to change clothes during the two hours it took for the boxes to be tested. Then he and Musk jumped into Musk's jet for the dash back to Kwaj, taking the intern with them as his reward. Altan hoped to sleep on the plane—he had been awake for most of forty hours—but Musk bombarded him with questions on every detail of the circuitry. A helicopter whisked them from the Kwaj airstrip to Omelek, where Altan put the repaired boxes onto the rocket. They worked. The three-second static fire test was a success, and the first full launch attempt of Falcon 1 was scheduled for a few weeks later.

23

Two Strikes

Kwaj, 2006–2007

Bülent Altan cooking goulash; Hans Koenigsmann,
Chris Thompson, and Anne Chinnery on Kwajalein

The first launch attempt

"Want to go for a bike ride?" Kimbal asked his brother when they woke at 6 a.m. They had flown to Kwaj for the scheduled launch day—March 24, 2006—when Elon hoped that the Falcon 1 rocket he had dreamed up four years earlier would make history.

"No, I need to go to the control center," Elon replied.

Kimbal pushed back. "The launch isn't until later. Let's go for a ride. It will be a stress reliever."

Elon relented, and they pedaled at their furious pace up a bluff where they could take in the sunrise. There Elon stood silently for a long time, staring into the distance, before heading to the control room. Wearing shorts and a black T-shirt, he paced amid the government-issued wooden desks. When Musk gets stressed, he often retreats into the future. He will surprise his engineers, who are focused on some impending major event, by peppering them with questions about the details of things that are years away: plans for Mars landings, "Robotaxis" without steering wheels, implanted brain chips that can connect to computers. At Tesla, amid the crises facing production of the Roadster, he would start quizzing his team about the status of parts for the next car he envisioned.

Now, on Kwaj, as the countdown for the first launch of the Falcon 1 entered its final hour, Musk was asking his engineers about the components needed for the Falcon 5, the future rocket that would have five Merlin engines. Had they ordered the new type of aluminum alloy for the fuel tanks? he asked a harried Chris Thompson, who was sitting at his console overseeing the countdown. When Thompson, one of SpaceX's first engineers, said no, Musk got angry. "We were right smack in the middle of a count, and he just wanted to have this deep, aggressive conversation about materials," Thompson later told Eric Berger. "I was absolutely dumbfounded that he was not even aware that we were trying to launch a rocket, and that I was the launch conductor, and responsible for basically calling out every single command that we're going to run. It just blew me away."

Only at the moment of launch did Musk again focus on the present. As the Falcon 1 lifted off the pad, and the engineers in the control room pumped their fists into the air, Musk stared at the video feed from a camera pointed down from the rocket's second stage. Twenty seconds into the flight, it showed the pristine beach and turquoise water of Omelek in the distance below. "It launched!" Kimbal said. "It really launched!"

Then, after five more seconds, Tom Mueller, who was looking at the data coming in, noticed a problem. "Oh, shit," he said. "We're losing thrust." Koenigsmann saw flames flickering around the outside of the engine. "Oh, shit," he said, echoing Mueller. "There's a fire, a leak."

For a moment, Musk hoped that the rocket would make it up high enough that the dwindling oxygen in the atmosphere would cause the flame to snuff out. Instead, it started to fall. On the video feed, Omelek began to come closer. Then the video went blank. Burning debris fell into the ocean. "My stomach wrenched," Musk says. An hour later, he and his top team—Mueller, Koenigsmann, Buzza, and Thompson—crammed into an Army helicopter to survey the wreckage.

That night, everyone gathered in the open-air bar on Kwaj and quietly sipped beer. A couple of the engineers cried. Musk brooded silently, his face like a stone and his eyes distant. Then he spoke, very softly. "When we started, we all knew we could fail on the first mission," he said. "But we will build another rocket and try again."

Musk and the rest of the SpaceX team were joined by local volunteers the next day as they walked the beach of Omelek and rode in small boats to collect the fragments. "We put the pieces in a hangar and pieced them together as we tried to figure out what went wrong," Koenigsmann says. Kimbal, a passionate foodie who trained as a chef after Zip2 was sold, tried to cheer everyone up that evening by cooking an outdoor meal that included a stew of meat, canned cannellini beans, and tomato, with a salad of bread, tomatoes, garlic, and anchovies.

As Musk and his top engineers flew on his jet back to Los Angeles, they studied the video. Mueller pointed out the moment when the flame broke out on the Merlin engine. It had clearly been caused by a fuel leak. Musk simmered, then exploded at Mueller: "Do you know how many people told me I should fire you?"

"Why don't you just fire me?" Mueller shot back.

"I didn't fucking fire you, did I?" Musk replied. "You're still fucking here." Then, to relieve tension, Musk put on the wacky action-film spoof *Team America: World Police*. As often happened with Musk, darkness gave way to silly humor.

Later that day he posted a statement: "SpaceX is in this for the long haul. Come hell or high water, we are going to make this work."

Musk has a rule about responsibility: every part, every process, and every specification needs to have a name attached. He can be quick to personalize blame when something goes wrong. In the case of the launch failure, it became evident that the leak had come from a small B-nut that secured a fuel line. Musk fingered an engineer named Jeremy Hollman, one of Mueller's first hires, who, the night before the launch, had removed and then reattached the nut in order to get access to a valve. At a public symposium a few days later, Musk described the mistake by "one of our most experienced technicians," and insiders knew he was referring to Hollman.

Hollman had stayed behind in Kwaj for two weeks to analyze the debris. On his flight from Honolulu to Los Angeles, he was reading news stories about the failure and was shocked to see that Musk had blamed him. As soon as he landed, he drove the two miles from the airport to SpaceX headquarters and barged into Musk's cubicle. A shouting match erupted, and both Shotwell and Mueller went over to try to calm things down. Hollman wanted the company to retract Musk's statement, and Mueller pressed for permission to do so. "I'm the CEO," Musk replied. "I'm the one that deals with the press, so stay out of it."

Hollman told Mueller he would stay at the company only if he never had to deal directly with Musk. He left SpaceX a year later. Musk says he doesn't remember the event, but he adds that Hollman was not a great engineer. Mueller disagrees: "We lost a good guy."

As it turned out, Hollman was not at fault. When the fuel line was found, part of the B-nut was still attached, but it was corroded and had cracked in half. The sea air of Kwaj was to blame.

The second attempt

After the failure of its first launch, SpaceX became more cautious. The team began testing carefully and recording the details of each of the hundreds of components in the rocket. For once, Musk did not push everyone to move at warp speed and sweep away caution.

Nevertheless, he did not try to eliminate all possible risks. That would make SpaceX rockets as costly and late as those built by the government's bloated cost-plus contractors. So he demanded a chart showing every component, the cost of its raw materials, the cost that SpaceX was paying suppliers for it, and the name of the engineer responsible for getting that cost down. At meetings he would sometimes show that he knew these numbers better than the engineers doing the presentation, which was not a pleasant experience. Review meetings could be brutal. But costs came down.

All of this meant taking calculated risks. For example, Musk had been the one who approved the use of cheap and light aluminum for the B-nut that corroded and doomed the first Falcon 1 flight.

Another example involved what are known as slosh baffles. As a rocket ascends, the fuel remaining in its tanks can slosh around. To prevent this, rigid metal rings can be attached to the inside wall of the tank. The engineers did that in the first stage of the Falcon 1, but adding mass to the upper stage was more of a problem because it had to be thrust all the way into orbit.

Koenigsmann's team ran a variety of computer simulations to test the risks from sloshing. Only in a tiny percentage of the models did it seem to be a problem. In the list they made of the top fifteen risks, number one was the possibility that the thin material they were using for the rocket shell might bend in flight. Second-stage sloshing was ranked number eleven. When Musk went over the list with Koenigsmann and his engineers, he decided they would accept some of the risks, including slosh. The likelihood of most of these risks could not be determined just by simulations. The risk of slosh would have to be tested in a real flight.

The test came in March 2007. As it had a year earlier, the launch started well. The countdown reached zero, the Merlin engine ignited, and the Falcon 1 lumbered toward space. This time Musk was watching from the control room at SpaceX headquarters in Los Angeles. "Yes, yes! We've made it," Mueller shouted, hugging him. As the second stage made its planned separation, Musk bit his lip, then started to smile.

"Congratulations," Musk said. "I'm going to watch that video for a long time."

For five full minutes, enough time to pop open a couple of bottles of champagne, there was jubilation. Then Mueller noticed something on the video. The second stage was beginning to wobble. The data feed confirmed his fears. "I knew right away it was slosh," he says.

On the video, it looked like the Earth was tumbling in a dryer, but it was actually the second stage spinning. "Catch it, catch it," an engineer yelled. But by then it was hopeless. At the eleven-minute mark, the feed went blank. The second stage and its payload were crashing back to Earth from 180 miles up. The rocket had reached outer space but had failed to get into orbit. The decision to accept the eleventh item on the risk list—to not incorporate slosh baffles—had come back to bite them. "From now on," Musk said to Koenigsmann, "we are going to have eleven items on our risk list, never just ten."

24

The SWAT Team

Tesla, 2006–2008

Antonio Gracias and Tim Watkins

Roadster costs

Designing a car is easy, Musk often said. The difficult part is manufacturing it. After the prototype of the Roadster was unveiled in July 2006, the hard part began.

The target cost of the Roadster had originally been about $50,000. But then came Musk's design changes as well as massive problems finding the right transmission system. By November 2006, the cost had swelled to $83,000.

That prompted Musk to do something unusual for a board chair: he flew to England to visit Lotus, the chassis supplier, without telling Martin Eberhard, his CEO. "I find this a rather awkward situation where Elon has asked for Lotus' own view of the production timing," one of the Lotus executives wrote Eberhard.

Musk got an earful in England. The Lotus team, which was dealing with rapidly shifting design specifications from Tesla, said that there was no way that they could start producing Roadster bodies until the end of 2007, at least eight months behind schedule. They presented him with a list of more than eight hundred problems that had arisen.

For example, there was a problem with the British company that Tesla had contracted to supply the customized carbon fiber panels, fenders, and doors. It was a Friday, and Musk impulsively decided to visit the supplier. "I hiked through the mud to this building, where I saw that the Lotus guys were right, the body tooling wasn't working," he says. "It was a total failure."

By the end of July 2007, the financial situation had worsened. The cost of materials for the first round of production was estimated to be $110,000 per car, and the company was projected to run out of cash within weeks. That's when Musk decided to call in a SWAT team.

Antonio Gracias

When Antonio Gracias was twelve years old, he asked for some Apple Computer for Christmas. Not the computer itself; he already had an early Apple II. He wanted the company's stock. His mother, who ran a small lingerie store in Grand Rapids, Michigan, spoke only Spanish, but she managed to buy him ten shares for $300. He still owns them. They are now worth about $490,000.

Among his first business ventures while a student at Georgetown University was buying condoms in bulk and shipping them to a friend in Russia to sell. That ended up not working well, so he had a huge inventory of condoms in his dorm room. He put them in matchboxes, sold advertising on the boxes, and distributed them at bars and fraternities.

He got a job at Goldman Sachs in New York, but quit to go to the University of Chicago Law School. Most law students, especially at a place like Chicago, find the work all-consuming, but Gracias was bored. On the side, he started a venture fund that bought small companies. One of them seemed particularly promising: a California firm that did electroplating. But it turned out to be a mess. Gracias found himself commuting to California to try to fix things at the factory, while a friend at law school named David Sacks took notes for him in class. (Remember these names, Antonio Gracias and David Sacks, because they will reemerge in the Twitter saga.)

Because Gracias spoke Spanish like most of the factory workers, he was able to learn from them where the problems were. "I realized that if you invest in a company, you should spend all your time on the shop floor," he says. When he asked how they could speed things up, one of the workers explained that having smaller vats for the nickel baths would make the plating go faster. Those and other worker-generated ideas succeeded so well that the factory began turning a profit, and Gracias started buying more troubled companies.

He learned one very big lesson from these ventures: "It's not the product that leads to success. It's the ability to make the product efficiently. It's about building the machine that builds the machine. In other words, how do you design the factory?" It was a guiding principle that Musk would make his own.

After law school, David Sacks had gone on to be a cofounder with Musk of PayPal. Gracias was an investor, and he and Musk were among the new millionaires who went to Las Vegas to celebrate Sacks's thirtieth birthday in May 2002.

Six of the partygoers were in a limousine when one of them, a friend from Stanford, threw up in the back seat. When the driver got them to the hotel, most of the others took off. "Elon and I looked at each other and said, we can't leave this poor driver with vomit in his car," Gracias recalls. So they rode with the driver to a 7-Eleven convenience store, bought paper towels and spray cleaner, and cleaned up the car. "Elon has Asperger's," Gracias says, "so he sometimes comes across as not emotional, but he actually can care."

Gracias and his venture capital firm, Valor Management, participated in four of Tesla's early funding rounds, and in May 2007 he joined the board. That was just when Musk was fathoming the depth of the production problems with the Roadster, and he asked Gracias to figure out what was wrong. For help, Gracias called on an eccentric partner who was a wizard at understanding factories.

Tim Watkins

After reviving his electroplating company, Gracias bought some similar companies, including one that had a small factory in Switzerland. When he flew there to inspect it, he was picked up at the airport by a ponytailed British robotics engineer named Tim Watkins, who was wearing a black T-shirt, jeans, and a black fanny pack. Whenever he took a new assignment, he would go to a local chain store and buy a ten-pack of T-shirts and jeans, which he would then shed like a molting lizard during his stay.

After a leisurely dinner, Watkins suggested that they go look at the factory. Gracias knew that it did not have a permit to run a night shift, so he was wary when Watkins and the plant manager drove him to a back alley of an industrial park. "I thought for a moment that they might rob me," Gracias admits. Watkins, with a flair for drama, threw open the back door. The lights were out, and it was pitch black, but there were sounds of high-speed stamping machines working. When Watkins turned on the lights, Gracias realized that they were whirring on their own, with no workers on the premises.

Swiss regulations decreed that workers could be on duty no more than sixteen hours per day. So Watkins had instituted a schedule of two eight-hour shifts separated by four-hour periods when machines would run on their own. He had devised a formula that predicted when every part of the process would need human intervention. "We could get twenty-four hours of production for sixteen hours of labor each day," he says. Gracias made Watkins a partner in his firm, and they became soul mates, even rooming together, as they developed a shared vision of how to swoop into manufacturing companies and make them more efficient. And that's what they set out to do for Musk and Tesla in 2007.

The supply-chain problem

The first task was to deal with the problem involving the British supplier of the carbon fiber panels, fenders, and doors. After Musk's visit to the company, he had some heated exchanges with its managers. A few months later, they called and said they were giving up. They couldn't deal with his demands, and they were canceling their contract.

As soon as Musk got the news, he called Watkins in Chicago. "I'm getting in my plane. I will pick you up in Chicago, and we'll go sort this out," he said. In England, they packed some of the machinery into the plane and flew it to France, where another company, Sotira Composites, had agreed to take on the work. Musk was worried that workers in France were not as dedicated as he was, so he gave them a pep talk. "Please don't strike or go on vacation right now, or Tesla will die," he pleaded. After a dinner at a Loire Valley chateau, he left Watkins behind to teach the French how to work with carbon fiber and make their production lines efficient.

The problem with the body panels prompted Musk to worry about other parts of the supply chain, so he asked Watkins to sort out the entire system. What he found was a nightmare. The process began in Japan, where the cells for the lithium-ion batteries were made. Seventy of these cells were glued together to form bricks, which were then shipped to a makeshift factory in the jungles of Thailand that once made barbecue grills. There they were assembled into a battery pack with a web of tubes as a cooling mechanism. These could not be flown by airplane, so they were shipped by boat to England and driven to the Lotus factory, where they were assembled into the Roadster chassis. The body panels came from the new supplier in France. The bodies with batteries would then be shipped across the Atlantic and through the Panama Canal to the Tesla assembly facility near Palo Alto. There a team was in charge of the final assembly, including the AC Propulsion motor and drivetrain. By the time the battery cells made their way into a customer's car, they had traveled around the world.

This presented not just a logistics nightmare but also a cash-flow problem. Each cell at the beginning of the journey cost $1.50. With labor, a full battery pack of nine thousand cells cost $15,000. Tesla had to pay for them up front, but it would be nine months before those packs made it around the world and could be sold in a car to consumers. Other parts going into the long supply process likewise burned cash. Outsourcing may save money, but it can hurt cash flow.

Compounding the problem was that the design of the car, partly because of Musk's fiddling, had gotten too complex. "It was just a flat-out burning dumpster fire of stupidity," Musk later admitted. The chassis had become 40 percent heavier and it had to be redesigned to fit the battery pack, which invalidated the crash testing Lotus had done. "In retrospect it would have been much smarter to start with a clean-sheet design and not try to modify the Lotus Elise," he says. As for the drivetrain, almost none of the AC Propulsion technology turned out to be viable for a production car. "We screwed the pooch six ways to Sunday," Musk says.

When Watkins got to Tesla's California headquarters to sort through this mess with Eberhard, he was shocked to discover that there was no bill of materials for the production of the Roadster. In other words, there was no comprehensive record of every part that went into the car and how much Tesla was paying for each. Eberhard explained that he was trying to move to an SAP system to manage such information, but he didn't have a chief financial officer to organize the transition. "You can't manufacture a product without a bill of materials," Watkins told him. "There are tens of thousands of components on a vehicle, and you are getting pecked to death by ducks."

When Watkins pieced together the true costs, he realized that things were worse than even the most pessimistic projections. The initial Roadsters off the assembly line would cost, including overhead, at least $140,000, and it would not fall much below $120,000 even after production increased. Even if they sold the car for $100,000, they would be hemorrhaging money.

Watkins and Gracias presented the grim findings to Musk. The cash-sucking supply chain and the cost of the car would bleed the company of all its money—including the deposits that had been made by customers to reserve a Roadster—before it could even begin selling the car at scale. "It was," Watkins says, "an oh-shit moment."

Gracias pulled Musk aside later. "This is not going to work," he said. "Eberhard is not being for real about the numbers."

25

Taking the Wheel

Tesla, 2007–2008

Martin Eberhard and the Roadster

Eberhard's ouster

Soon after he learned about Musk's secret trip to England, Eberhard asked him to dinner in Palo Alto. "Let's start a search to find someone who can replace me," he said. Later, Musk would be brutal about him, but that evening he was supportive. "Nobody will be able to take from you the importance of what you've done by being a founder of this company," he said. At a board meeting the next day, Eberhard described his plan to step aside, and everyone approved.

The search for a successor went slowly, mainly because Musk was not satisfied with any of the candidates. "Tesla's sheer number of problems was so high that it was nearly impossible to try to find a decent CEO," Musk says. "It's hard to find a buyer for a house that's on fire." By July 2007, they had not come close to finding one. That is when Gracias and Watkins came in with their report, and Musk's mood changed.

Musk called a meeting of the Tesla board for early August 2007. "What's your best estimate for the cost of the car?" he asked Eberhard. When Musk launches into such a grilling, it's not likely to end happily. Eberhard had trouble giving a precise answer, and Musk became convinced that he was lying. It's a word Musk uses a lot, often rather loosely. "He lied to me and said the cost would be no problem," Musk says.

"That's slanderous," Eberhard responds when I quote Musk's accusations. "I wouldn't lie to anybody. Why would I do that? The true cost is going to come out eventually." His voice rises in anger, but there is an undertone of pain and sorrow. He cannot figure out why Musk, after fifteen years, is still so fervent about disparaging him. "This is the richest man in the world beating on somebody who can't touch him." His original partner Marc Tarpenning admits that they badly miscalculated the pricing, but he defends Eberhard against Musk's allegation of lying. "Certainly, it wasn't deliberate," he says. "We were dealing with the pricing information that we had. We weren't lying."

A few days after the board meeting, Eberhard was on his way to a conference in Los Angeles when his phone rang. It was Musk, who informed him that he was being ousted as CEO immediately. "It was like getting hit by a brick on the side of the head, something I never saw coming," says Eberhard, who should have seen it coming. Even though he had suggested a search for a new CEO, he did not expect to be unceremoniously ousted before one was found. "They had had a meeting without me to vote me off the island."

He tried to reach some board members, but none would take his call. "It was unanimous board agreement that Martin had to go, including the members Martin had put on the board," Musk says. Tarpenning soon left as well.

Eberhard launched a little website called *Tesla Founders Blog*, where he vented his frustrations about Musk and accused the company of "trying to root out and destroy any of its heart that might still be beating." Board members asked him to tone it down, which didn't work, and then Tesla's lawyer threatened to withdraw his stock options, which did. There are certain people who occupy a demon's corner of Musk's headspace. They trigger him, turn him dark, and rouse a cold anger. His father is number one. But somewhat oddly, Martin Eberhard, who is hardly a household name, is second. "Getting involved with Eberhard was the worst mistake I ever made in my career," Musk says.

Musk unleashed a barrage of attacks on Eberhard in the summer of 2008, as Tesla's production woes mounted, and Eberhard responded by suing him for libel. "Musk has set out to re-write history," the lawsuit began. He still bristles at Musk's accusations that he lied. "What the fuck?" he says. "The company that Marc and I started turned him into the richest man in the world. Isn't that enough already?"

They finally reached an uneasy legal settlement in 2009 in which they agreed not to disparage each other and that henceforth both of them would be referred to as cofounders of Tesla, along with JB Straubel, Marc Tarpenning, and Ian Wright. In addition, Eberhard got a Roadster, which he had been promised. They each then issued nice statements about the other that they did not believe.

Despite the no-disparagement clause, Musk would not be able to stop himself from bursting out in anger every few months. In 2019, he tweeted, "Tesla is alive in spite of Eberhard, but he seeks credit constantly & fools give it him." The following year he declared, "He is literally the worst person I have ever worked with." Then in late 2021, "Founding story of Tesla as portrayed by Eberhard is patently false. I wish I had never met him."

Michael Marks and the asshole question

Musk should have learned by this point that he was not good at sharing power with a CEO. But he still resisted becoming Tesla's CEO himself. Sixteen years later, he would be the self-installed chief of five major companies, but in 2007 he thought that he should be like almost every other CEO and stick to one company, in his case SpaceX. So he tapped a Tesla investor, Michael Marks, to be interim CEO.

Marks had been the CEO of Flextronics, an electronics manufacturing services company, which he turned into a highly profitable industry leader by pushing a strategy that Musk liked: vertical integration. His company took end-to-end control of multiple steps in the process.

Musk and Marks got along well at first. Musk, who had the odd habit of being the world's wealthiest couch surfer, would stay at Marks's home when he visited Silicon Valley. "We'd have some wine and shoot the breeze," Marks said. But then, Marks made the mistake of believing he could steer the company rather than just carry out Musk's wishes.

The first clash came when Marks concluded that Musk's devotion to reality-defying schedules meant that supplies were ordered and paid for, even though there was no chance they would be used to build a car anytime soon. "Why are we bringing all these materials in?" Marks asked at one of his first meetings. A manager replied, "Because Elon keeps insisting that we will be shipping cars in January." The cash flow for these parts was bleeding Tesla's coffers, so Marks canceled most of the orders.

Marks also pushed back on Musk's harsh way of dealing with people. A naturally friendly person, Marks was known for his polite and respectful manner toward colleagues, from the janitor to top executives. "Elon is just not a very nice person and didn't treat people well," says Marks, who was appalled that Musk had not even read most of his wife Justine's novels. This wasn't just a matter of niceties, it was affecting Musk's ability to know where the problems were. "I told him that people won't tell him the truth, because he intimidates people," Marks says. "He could be a bully and brutal."

Marks still wrestles with whether Musk's brain wiring—his ingrained personality and what he calls his Asperger's—can explain or even excuse some of his behavior. Might it even be beneficial in some ways, when it comes to running companies where the mission is more important than individual sensitivities? "He's somewhere on the spectrum, so I think he honestly doesn't have any connection with people at all," Marks says.

Musk counters that being at the other extreme can be debilitating for a leader. Wanting to be everyone's friend, he told Marks, leads you to care too much about the emotions of the individual in front of you rather than caring about the success of the whole enterprise—an approach that can lead to a far greater number of people being hurt. "Michael Marks would not fire anyone," Musk says. "I would tell him, Michael, you can't tell people they have to get their shit together, and then when they don't get their shit together nothing happens to them."

A difference in strategy also emerged. Marks decided that Tesla should partner with an experienced automaker to handle the assembly of the Roadster. That flew in the face of Musk's fundamental instincts. He aspired to build Gigafactories where raw materials would go in one end and cars would come out the other.

During their debates over Marks's proposal to outsource assembly of the Tesla, Musk became increasingly angry, and he had no natural filter to restrain his responses. "That's just the stupidest thing I've ever heard," he said at a couple of meetings. That was a line that Steve Jobs used often. So did Bill Gates and Jeff Bezos. Their brutal honesty could be unnerving, even offensive. It could constrict rather than encourage honest dialogue. But it was also effective, at times, in creating what Jobs called a team of A players who didn't want to be around fuzzy thinkers.

Marks was too accomplished and proud to put up with Musk's

behavior. "He treated me like a child, and I'm not a child," he says. "I'm older than he is. I had also run a twenty-five-billion-dollar company." He soon left.

Marks concedes that Musk turned out to be right about the benefits of controlling all aspects of the manufacturing process. In a more conflicted way, he also wrestles with the core question about Musk: whether his bad behavior can be separated from the all-in drive that made him successful. "I've come to put him in the same category as Steve Jobs, which is that some people are just assholes, but they accomplish so much that I just have to sit back and say, 'That seems to be a package.'" Does that, I ask, excuse Musk's behavior? "Maybe if the price the world pays for this kind of accomplishment is a real asshole doing it, well, it's probably a price worth paying. That's how I've come to think about it, anyway." Then, after a pause, he adds, "But I wouldn't want to be that way."

When Marks left, Musk recruited a CEO he felt would be tougher: Ze'ev Drori, a combat-tested Israeli paratroop officer who had become a successful entrepreneur in the semiconductor business. "The only person who would actually agree to be CEO of Tesla was someone who was afraid of nothing, because there was a lot to be afraid of," Musk says. But Drori did not know anything about making cars. After a few months, a delegation of senior executives led by JB Straubel said that they would have trouble continuing to work for him, and Ira Ehrenpreis, a board member, helped convince Musk to take over himself. "I've got to have both hands on the steering wheel," Musk told Drori. "I can't have two of us driving." Drori gracefully stepped aside, and Musk became the official CEO of Tesla (and the fourth with that title in about a year) in October 2008.

26

Divorce

2008

Justine

After the death of their son Nevada, Justine and Elon decided to get pregnant again as soon as possible. They went to an in vitro fertilization clinic, and in 2004 she gave birth to twins, Griffin and Xavier. Two years later, again through IVF, they had triplets: Kai, Saxon, and Damian.

They had begun the marriage living together in a small apartment in Silicon Valley they shared with three roommates and a miniature dachshund who was not housebroken, Justine recalls, and now they were living in a six-thousand-square-foot mansion in the Bel Air hills section of Los Angeles with five quirky boys, a staff of five nannies and housekeepers, and a miniature dachshund who still was not housebroken.

Despite their tumultuous natures, there were times when their relationship was tender. They would walk to Kepler's Books near Palo Alto, arms around each other's waists, take their purchases to a café, and read over coffee. "I get choked up talking about it," Justine says. "There were moments of being just totally content, like totally."

Musk was awkward socially, but he liked to go to celebrity-studded parties and hang out until dawn. "We went to black-tie fundraisers and got the best tables at elite Hollywood nightclubs, with Paris Hilton and Leonardo DiCaprio partying next to us," Justine says. "When Google cofounder Larry Page got married on Richard Branson's private Caribbean island, we were there, hanging out in a villa with John Cusack and watching Bono pose with swarms of adoring women."

But through it all, they fought. He was addicted to storm and stress, and she was swept into the turbulence. During their worst arguments, Justine would express how much she hated him, and he would respond by saying such things as "If you were my employee, I would fire you." Sometimes he would call her "a moron" and "an idiot," chillingly channeling his father. "When I spent some time with Errol," Justine says, "I realized that's where he'd gotten the vocabulary."

Kimbal, who used to fight physically with his brother, found it difficult to watch him fight verbally with Justine. "Elon fights in a high-intensity way," Kimbal says. "And Justine could go to the mat as well. You watch it and you're like, holy moly, this is brutal. I ended up distancing myself from him for years because of Justine. I just could not be around it."

The entire unsettled lifestyle led to a downward spiral. "It was basically a massive cluster fuck of disruptive things," says Justine. She felt herself turning into, or being turned into, a "trophy wife," and, she says, "I sucked at it." He pushed her to dye her hair blonder. "Go platinum," he said. But she resisted and began retreating. "I met him when he didn't have much at all," she says. "The accumulation of wealth and fame changed the dynamic."

As he would do with his colleagues at work, Musk could flip instantly from light to dark to light. He would hurl some insults, pause, then his face would melt into an amused grin, and he would make some oddball jokes. "He's strong-willed and powerful, like a bear," Justine told *Esquire*'s Tom Junod. "He can be playful and funny and romp around with you, but in the end you're still dealing with a bear."

When Musk was focused on a work issue, he went into a zone, like he had back in grade school, where he was completely unresponsive. Later, when I recounted to Justine all the calamities at SpaceX and Tesla that were hitting him in 2008, she started to cry. "He didn't share these things with me," she says. "I don't think it occurred to him that maybe it would've been very helpful. He was in such a combative relationship with the world. All he had to do was clue me in."

The main thing she missed in him was empathy. "He's a great man in a lot of ways," she says, "but it's that lack of empathy that always gives me pause." During a drive one day, she tried to explain to him the concept of true empathy. He kept making it something cerebral, and he explained how, with his Asperger's, he had taught himself to be more psychologically astute. "No, it has nothing to do with thinking or analysis or reading the other person," she said. "It involves *feeling*. You *feel* the other person." He conceded that was important in relationships, but he suggested that his brain wiring was an advantage in running a high-performance company. "The strong will and emotional distance that makes him difficult as a husband," Justine concedes, "may be reasons for his success in running a business."

Elon would get annoyed when Justine pushed him to try psychotherapy. She had started going to a therapist after Nevada's death and developed a deep interest in the field. It led her, she says, to the insight that Elon's rough childhood and his brain wiring allowed him to shut down emotions. Intimacy was hard. "When you're from a dysfunctional background or have a brain wired like his," she says, "intensity takes the place of intimacy."

That's not exactly right. Especially with his kids, Musk can feel strongly and be emotionally needy. He craves having someone around, even former girlfriends. But it's true that what he lacks in daily intimacy he makes up for in intensity.

Justine's dissatisfaction with the marriage deepened her depression and made her angry. "She went from having some highs and lows to just being angry every day," Elon says. He blamed it on Adderall, a cognitive enhancer that her psychiatrist had prescribed, and he would go around the house throwing away the pills. Justine agrees that she was both depressed and reliant on Adderall. "I was diagnosed with Attention Deficit Disorder, and Adderall was an amazing help for me," she says. "But it wasn't the reason I was angry. I was angry because Elon shut me out."

In the spring of 2008, amid the exploding rockets and turmoil at Tesla, Justine was in a car accident. Afterward, she sat on their bed with her knees pulled up to her chest and tears in her eyes. She told Elon that their relationship had to change. "I didn't want to be a sideline player in the multimillion-dollar spectacle of my husband's life," she says. "I wanted to love and be loved, the way we had before he made all his millions."

Elon agreed to enter counseling, but after a month and three sessions, the marriage broke up. Justine's version is that Elon gave her an ultimatum: either she accept the marriage for what it was or he would file for divorce. His version is that she had repeatedly said she wanted to get divorced, and he finally said, "I'm willing to stay married, but you have to promise not to be mean to me all the time." When Justine made it clear that the current situation was unacceptable to her, he filed for divorce. "I felt numb," she recalls, "but strangely relieved."

27

Talulah

2008

With Talulah Riley in Hyde Park, London

In July 2008, after breaking up with Justine, Musk was scheduled to give a speech to the Royal Aeronautical Society in London. It was not a propitious time to be talking about rockets. Two of his had blown up, and the third attempt was supposed to launch in three weeks. Tesla's kludgy production chain was sucking up cash, and the early signs of a global economic meltdown were making new financing difficult. Plus his divorce wranglings with Justine threatened his ability to control his Tesla stock. Nevertheless, he went.

In his speech, he argued that commercial space ventures, such as SpaceX, were more innovative than government programs and were necessary if humans wanted to colonize other planets. He then went to visit the CEO of Aston Martin, who dumped all over the electric car movement and dismissed worries about climate change.

The next day, Musk awoke with stomach pains, which was not unusual. He can pretend to like stress, but his stomach can't. He was traveling with his friend Bill Lee, a successful entrepreneur, who took him to a clinic. When the doctor determined that he did not have appendicitis or anything worse, Lee insisted that they go let off some steam, and he called a friend, Nick House, who owned the hot nightclub Whisky Mist. "I was trying to snap Elon out of his mood," Lee says. Musk kept trying to leave, but House convinced them to come to a VIP room in the basement. A few moments later, an actress wearing an eye-catching evening gown walked in.

Talulah Riley, then twenty-two, grew up in a picture-book English village in Hertfordshire and, by the time she met Musk, had distinguished herself in some small but well-played roles, most notably as the tone-deaf middle Bennet sister, Mary, in an adaptation of Jane Austen's *Pride and Prejudice*. Tall and beautiful with long, flowing hair and a sharp mind and personality, she was very much Musk's type.

Introduced by Nick House and another friend, James Fabricant, she ended up sitting with Musk. "He seemed quite shy and slightly awkward," she says. "He was talking about rockets, and at first I didn't realize they were his rockets." At one point he asked, "May I put my hand on your knee?" She was a bit taken aback, but nodded her assent. At the end, he said to her, "I'm very bad at this, but please may I have your phone number because I would like to see you again."

Riley had only recently moved out of her parents' home, and she called the next morning to tell them about the man she had just met. As they were speaking, her father did a Google search. "This man is married and has five children," he reported. "You've been taken in by some playboy." Furious, she called her friend Fabricant, who calmed her down and assured her that Musk had broken up with his wife.

"We ended up having breakfast together," Riley says, "and at the end he said, 'I'd really like to see you for lunch.' And then after lunch that day, he said, 'Well, that was really wonderful. Now I'd like to see you for dinner.'" Over the next three days, they had almost every meal together and went shopping at Hamleys toy store to get gifts for his five kids. "They were love birds, holding hands the entire time," Lee says. At the end of the trip, he invited her to fly back to Los Angeles with him. She couldn't, because she had to go to Sicily for a photo shoot for a *Tatler* article about a movie she had just made, *St. Trinian's*. But from there she flew to Los Angeles.

Rather than moving in with Musk—which she believed was improper—she took a room for a week at the Peninsula Hotel. At the end of the visit, he proposed. "I'm really sorry I don't have a ring," he said. She suggested they shake hands on it, which they did. "I remember swimming around with him in the rooftop pool, very giddy, talking about how strange it was that we had known each other for about two weeks and were now engaged." Riley said she felt sure things would work out. "What's the worst that could happen to us?" she joked. Musk, suddenly in earnest mode, replied, "One of us could die." Somehow, in the moment, she found that very romantic.

When her parents flew from London to meet Musk a few weeks later, he asked her father if he could marry her. "I know my daughter very well, and I trust her judgment, so off you go," he replied. Maye flew to Los Angeles and, for once, approved of one of her son's partners. "She was an absolute delight, funny and loving and successful," she says. "And her parents were so nice, a really good English couple." But on the advice of his brother Kimbal, he decided, and Talulah concurred, that they should wait a couple of years before getting married.

28

Strike Three

Kwaj, August 3, 2008

Hans Koenigsmann with a Falcon 1

After two failed launches from the remote atoll of Kwajalein, the third attempt of the Falcon 1 rocket would make or break SpaceX, or at least that's what everyone, including Musk, thought. He told his team he had money for only three tries. "I believed that if we couldn't do it in three," he says, "we deserved to die."

For the second flight, SpaceX had not put a real satellite on top of the rocket because it did not want to lose a valuable payload if it crashed. But for this third attempt, Musk was all in, gambling on success. The rocket would carry an expensive 180-pound Air Force satellite, two smaller satellites from NASA, and the cremated remains of James Doohan, the actor who played Scotty on *Star Trek*.

The liftoff went beautifully, and the control room in Los Angeles, where Musk was watching, erupted in cheers as the rocket ascended. After two minutes and twenty seconds, the upper stage detached from the booster, as scheduled. The payload seemed to be headed for orbit. "Third time a charm!" one engineer shouted.

Then, once again, there was a gasp from Mueller seated in his usual spot next to Musk. One second after the booster started descending back to Earth, as it was supposed to do, it spurted up briefly and bumped into the second stage. The video feed went blank, and Musk and his team immediately knew that both stages, along with the remains of dear Scotty, were now crashing down.

The problem was that they had redesigned the cooling system for the Merlin engine, and that caused it to have a little bit of thrust even after it shut down. Mueller's team had tested the new system on the ground, and it worked fine under sea-level conditions. But in the vacuum of space, the tiny spurt of the residual fuel burn nudged the booster up a foot or so.

Musk had run out of money, Tesla was hemorrhaging cash, and SpaceX had crashed three rockets in a row. But he was not ready to give up. Instead, he would go for broke, literally. "SpaceX will not skip a beat in execution going forward," he announced a few hours after the failure. "There should be absolutely zero question that SpaceX will prevail in reaching orbit. I will never give up, and I mean never."

In the SpaceX conference room the next day, Musk got on a conference call with Koenigsmann, Buzza, and the launch team on Kwaj. They went over the data and figured out ways to allow more separation time so the bump would not happen again. Musk was in a somber mood. "It was the shittiest period of my life, given what was happening with my marriage, SpaceX, and Tesla," he says. "I didn't even have a house. Justine had it." The team worried that he would, as he often did, try to single out people to blame. They prepared for a cold eruption.

Instead, he told them that there were components for a fourth rocket in the Los Angeles factory. Build it, he said, and transport it to Kwaj as soon as possible. He gave them a deadline that was barely realistic: launch it in six weeks. "He told us to go for it," says Koenigsmann, "and it blew me away."

A jolt of optimism spread through headquarters. "I think most of us would have followed him into the gates of hell carrying suntan oil after that," says Dolly Singh, the human resources director. "Within moments, the energy of the building went from despair and defeat to a massive buzz of determination."

Carl Hoffman, a *Wired* reporter who had watched the failure of the second launch with Musk, reached him to ask how he maintained his optimism. "Optimism, pessimism, fuck that," Musk answered. "We're going to make it happen. As God is my bloody witness, I'm hell-bent on making it work."

29

On the Brink

Tesla and SpaceX, 2008

In the SpaceX control room

On February 1, 2008, an email went out to employees at Tesla headquarters. "P1 arriving now!" it announced. "P1" was the codename for the first Roadster to make it through the production process. Musk spoke briefly and then took the Roadster on a victory lap around Palo Alto.

This rollout of a few vehicles, which had all been fitted by hand, was only a small triumph. Many car companies, long bankrupt and forgotten, had done similar things. The next challenge was to have a manufacturing process that could churn out the cars profitably. In the past century, only one American car company (Ford) had managed to do that without going through bankruptcy.

At that moment, it was unclear that Tesla would become the second. A subprime mortgage meltdown had begun, which would lead to the most severe global recession since the Great Depression. Tesla's supply chain was unwieldy, and the company was running out of money. In addition, SpaceX had yet to get a rocket into orbit. "Even though I now had a Roadster," Musk says, "it was the beginning of the most painful year of my life."

Musk often skated close to the edge of legality. He kept Tesla afloat through the first half of 2008 by dipping into the deposits made by customers for Roadsters that had not yet been built. Some Tesla executives and board members felt that the deposits should have been kept in escrow rather than tapped for operating expense, but Musk insisted, "We either do this or we die."

As the situation got more desperate in the fall of 2008, Musk pleaded for money from friends and family to meet Tesla's payroll. Kimbal had lost most of his money in the recession and, like his brother, was close to bankruptcy. He had been clinging to $375,000 in Apple stock, which he said he needed to cover loans he had taken from his bank. "I need you to put it into Tesla," Elon said. Kimbal, ever supportive, sold the stock and did as Elon asked. He got an angry call from his banker at Colorado Capital warning that he was destroying his credit. "Sorry, but I have to do it," Kimbal replied. When the banker called again a few weeks later, Kimbal braced for an argument. But the banker cut him short with the news that Colorado Capital itself had just gone under. "That's how bad 2008 was," Kimbal says.

Musk's friend Bill Lee invested $2 million, Sergey Brin of Google invested $500,000, and even regular Tesla employees wrote checks. Musk borrowed personally to cover his expenses, which included paying $170,000 per month for his own divorce lawyers and (as California law requires of the wealthier spouse) those of Justine. "God bless Jeff Skoll, who gave Elon money to see him through," Talulah says of Musk's friend, who was the first president of eBay. Antonio Gracias also stepped up, loaning him $1 million. Even Talulah's parents offered to help. "I was very upset and called Mommy and Daddy, and they said they would remortgage their house and try to help," she recalls. That offer Musk declined. "Your parents shouldn't lose their house just because I put in everything I had," he told her.

Talulah watched in horror as, night after night, Musk had mumbling conversations with himself, sometimes flailing his arms and screaming. "I kept thinking he was going to have a heart attack," she says. "He was having night terrors and just screaming in his sleep and clawing at me. It was horrendous. I was really scared, and he was just desperate." Sometimes he would go to the bathroom and start vomiting. "It would go to his gut, and he would be screaming and retching," she says. "I would stand by the toilet and hold his head."

Musk's tolerance for stress is high, but 2008 almost pushed him past his limits. "I was working every day, all day and night, in a situation that required me to pull a rabbit out of the hat, now do it again, now do it again," he says. He gained a lot of weight, and then suddenly lost it all and more. His posture became hunched, and his toes stayed stiff when he walked. But he became energized and hyperfocused. The threat of the hangman's noose concentrated his mind.

There was one decision that everyone around Musk thought he would have to make. As 2008 careened toward a close, it seemed that he would have to choose between SpaceX and Tesla. If he focused his dwindling resources on one, he could be pretty sure it would survive. If he tried to split his resources, neither might. One day his high-spirited soulmate Mark Juncosa walked into his cubicle at SpaceX.

"Dude, why don't you fucking just give up on one of these two things?" he asked. "If SpaceX speaks to your heart, throw Tesla away."

"No," Musk said, "that would be another notch in the signpost of 'Electric cars don't work,' and we'd never get to sustainable energy." Nor could he abandon SpaceX. "We might then never be a multiplanetary species."

The more people pressed him to choose, the more he resisted. "For me emotionally, this was like, you got two kids and you're running out of food," he says. "You can give half to each kid, in which case they might both die, or give all the food to one kid and increase the chance that at least one kid survives. I couldn't bring myself to decide that one was going to die, so I decided I had to give my all to save both."

30

The Fourth Launch

Kwaj, August–September 2008

Musk in the control room and with engineers;
Koenigsmann pouring champagne on Kwaj

Founders to the rescue

Musk had budgeted for three launch attempts of the Falcon 1, and all had exploded before they could get to orbit. Facing personal bankruptcy and with Tesla in a financial crisis, it was hard to see how he was going to raise money for a fourth attempt. Then a surprising group came to the rescue: his fellow cofounders of PayPal, who had ejected him from the role of CEO eight years earlier.

Musk had taken his ouster with unusual calm, and he stayed friendly with the coup leaders, including Peter Thiel and Max Levchin. The old PayPal mafia, as they called themselves, were a tight-knit crowd. They helped finance their former colleague David Sacks—the friend who took notes for Antonio Gracias in law school—when he produced the satirical movie *Thank You for Smoking*. Thiel teamed up with two other PayPal alums, Ken Howery and Luke Nosek, to form the Founders Fund, which invested mainly in internet startups.

Thiel was, he says, "categorically skeptical about clean tech," so the fund had not invested in Tesla. Nosek, who had become close to Musk, suggested that they invest in SpaceX. Thiel agreed to a conference call with Musk to discuss the idea. "At one point I asked Elon whether we could speak to the company's chief rocket engineer," Thiel says, "and Elon replied, 'You're speaking to him right now.'" That did not reassure Thiel, but Nosek pushed hard to make the investment. "I argued that what Elon was trying to do was amazing, and we should be a part of it," he says.

Eventually Thiel relented and agreed that the fund could put in $20 million. "Part of my thinking was that it would be a way to patch things up from the PayPal saga," he says. The investment was announced on August 3, 2008, just after the third launch attempt failed. It served as a lifeline that allowed Musk to declare that he was going to fund a fourth launch.

"It was an interesting exercise in karma," Musk says. "After I got assassinated by the PayPal coup leaders, like Caesar being stabbed in the Senate, I could have said 'You guys, you suck.' But I didn't. If I'd done that, Founders Fund wouldn't have come through in 2008 and SpaceX would be dead. I'm not into astrology or shit like that. But karma may be real."

Crunch time

Musk had jolted his team, right after the third failed flight in August 2008, with his deadline of getting a new rocket to Kwaj in six weeks. That seemed like a Musk reality-distortion ploy. It had taken them twelve months between the first and second failed launches, and another seventeen months between the second and the third. But because the rocket did not need any fundamental design changes to correct the problems that caused the third failure, he calculated that a six-week deadline was doable and would energize his team. Also, given his rapid cash burn, he had no other choice.

SpaceX had components for that fourth rocket in its Los Angeles factory, but shipping it by sea to Kwaj would take four weeks. Tim Buzza, SpaceX's launch director, told Musk that the only way to meet his deadline would be to charter a C-17 transport plane from the Air Force. "Well, then, just do it," Musk replied. That's when Buzza knew that Musk was willing to put all his chips on the table.

Twenty SpaceX employees rode with the rocket in the hold of the C-17, strapped into jump seats along the wall. The mood was festive. The work-crazed crew members were about to pull off, they thought, a hardcore miracle.

As they flew over the Pacific, a young engineer named Trip Harriss pulled out a guitar and started playing. His parents were music professors from Tennessee, and he had trained to become a classical musician. But one Christmas, he was watching *Star Trek* and decided that he wanted to be a rocket scientist instead. "I ended up figuring out how to change my brain from doing music to doing engineering," which was not as much of a transition as he thought. After a year at Purdue, he was scrambling for a summer internship, but kept bombing interviews. He had resigned himself to working at a local Ace Hardware when his professor got a call from a friend at SpaceX saying it needed interns. Without waiting for any paperwork, Harriss got into his car the next morning, left his girlfriend behind, and drove from Indiana to Los Angeles.

As they started to descend for refueling in Hawaii, there was a loud popping sound. And another. "We're like looking at each other, like, this seems weird," Harriss says. "And then we get another bang, and we saw the side of the rocket tank crumpling like a Coke can." The rapid descent of the plane caused the pressure in the hold to increase, and the valves of the tank weren't letting in air fast enough to allow the pressure inside to equalize.

There was a mad scramble as the engineers pulled out their pocket knives and began cutting away the shrink wrapping and trying to open the valves. Bülent Altan ran to the cockpit to try to stop the descent. "Here's this big Turkish guy screaming at the Air Force pilots, who were the whitest Americans you have ever seen, to go back higher," Harriss says. Astonishingly, they did not dump the rocket, or Altan, into the ocean. Instead, they agreed to ascend, but warned Altan that they had only thirty minutes of fuel. That meant in ten minutes they would need to start descending again. One of the engineers climbed inside the dark area between the rocket's first and second stage, found the large pressurization line, and managed to twist it open, allowing air to rush into the rocket and equalize the pressure as the cargo plane again started to descend. The metal began popping back close to its original shape. But damage had been done. The exterior was dented, and one of the slosh baffles had been dislodged.

They called Musk in Los Angeles to tell him what happened and suggest that they bring the rocket back. "All of us standing there could just hear this pause," says Harriss. "He is silent for a minute. Then he's like, 'No, you're going to get it to Kwaj and fix it there.'" Harriss recalls that when they got to Kwaj their first reaction was, "Man, we're doomed." But after a day, the excitement kicked in. "We began telling ourselves, 'We're going to make this work.'"

Buzza and the chief of rocket structures, Chris Thompson, rustled up the equipment they needed at SpaceX headquarters, including new baffles to prevent slosh in the tanks, and loaded it onto Musk's jet for the trip from Los Angeles to Kwaj. There they found a hive of engineers scurrying around in the middle of the night working frantically on the stripped rocket, as if they were doctors in an emergency room trying to save a patient.

After SpaceX's first three failures, Musk had imposed more quality controls and risk-reduction procedures. "So we were now used to moving a little bit slower, with more documentation and checks," Buzza says. He told Musk that if they followed all these new requirements, it would take five weeks to repair the rocket. If they jettisoned the requirements, they could do it in five days. Musk made the expected decision. "Okay," he said. "Go as fast as you can."

Musk's decision to reverse his orders about quality controls taught Buzza two things: Musk could pivot when situations changed, and he was willing to take more risk than anyone. "This is something that we had to learn, which was that Elon would make a statement, but then time would go on and he would realize, 'Oh no, actually we can do it this other way,'" Buzza says.

As they scrambled in the brutal Kwaj sun, they were watched by an abnormally large coconut crab that was close to three feet long. They named it Elon, and under its gaze, they were able to complete the repairs in the allotted five days. "It was unlike anything that the bloated companies in the aerospace industry could possibly have imagined," Buzza says. "Sometimes his insane deadlines make sense."

"Fourth time's a charm!"

Unless this fourth launch attempt succeeded, it would be the end of SpaceX and probably of the wacky notion that space pioneering could be led by private entrepreneurs. It might also be the end of Tesla. "We wouldn't be able to get any new funding for Tesla," Musk says. "People would be like, 'Look at that guy whose rocket company failed, he's a loser.'"

The launch was scheduled for September 28, 2008, and Musk planned to watch from the command van at SpaceX headquarters in Los Angeles. To relieve tension, Kimbal suggested that they take their kids to Disneyland that morning. It was a crowded Sunday, and they had not arranged for VIP access, but waiting in the long lines was a blessing because it had a calming effect on Elon. Fittingly, they rode the Space Mountain roller coaster, which was such an obvious metaphor that it would seem trite were it not true.

Dressed in the beige polo shirt and faded jeans he had worn to Disneyland, Musk arrived at the command van just as the launch window was opening at 4 p.m. On one of the monitors, he could see the Falcon 1 on the Kwaj launchpad. There was silence in the control room as a woman's voice intoned the countdown.

When the rocket cleared the tower, the cheering began, but Musk stared silently at the data streaming onto his computer and at the monitor on the wall showing video from the rocket's cameras. After sixty seconds, the video showed the plume from the engine darkening. This was fine; it was because the rocket had reached more rarefied air with less oxygen. The islets of Kwajalein Atoll receded, looking like a strand of pearls in the turquoise sea.

After two minutes, it was time for the stages to separate. The booster engine shut down, and this time there was a five-second delay before the second stage was unleashed, to prevent the bumping that had doomed the third launch. When the second stage slowly pulled away, Musk finally allowed himself to let out a whoop of joy.

The Kestrel engine on the second stage performed perfectly. Its nozzle glowed a dull red from the heat, but Musk knew the material could get white-hot and survive. Finally, nine minutes after liftoff, the Kestrel engine cut off as planned and its payload was released into orbit. By now the cheers were deafening, and Musk was pumping his arms into the air. Kimbal, standing next to him, started to cry.

Falcon 1 had made history as the first privately built rocket to launch from the ground and reach orbit. Musk and his small crew of just five hundred employees (Boeing's comparable division had fifty thousand) had designed the system from the ground up and done all the construction on its own. Little had been outsourced. And the funding had also been private, largely out of Musk's pocket. SpaceX had contracts to perform missions for NASA and other clients, but they would get paid only if and when they succeeded. There were no subsidies or cost-plus contracts.

"That was frigging awesome," Musk yelled as he walked onto the factory floor. He did a little jig in front of cheering employees gathered near the canteen. "Fourth time's a charm!" As the cheers rose again, he began stuttering a bit more than usual. "My mind is kind of frazzled, so it's hard for me to say anything," he murmured. But then he pronounced his vision for the future: "This is just the first step of many. We're going to get Falcon 9 to orbit next year, get the Dragon spacecraft going, and take over from the Space Shuttle. We're going to do a lot of things, even getting to Mars."

Despite his stony appearance, Musk's stomach had been wrenched during the launch, almost to the point of throwing up. Even after the success, he had trouble feeling joy. "My cortisol levels, my stress hormones, the adrenaline, they were just so high that it was hard for me to feel happy," he says. "There was a sense of relief, like being spared from death, but no joy. I was way too stressed for that."

"ilovenasa"

The successful launch saved the future of entrepreneurial space endeavors. "Like Roger Bannister besting the four-minute mile, SpaceX made people recalibrate their sense of limitation when it came to getting to space," wrote the author Ashlee Vance.

That led to a major change in direction for NASA. The impending end of its Space Shuttle program meant that the U.S. would no longer have any capacity to send crews or cargo to the International Space Station. So the agency announced a competition for a contract to fly cargo missions there. The success of the fourth Falcon 1 flight allowed Musk and Gwynne Shotwell to fly to Houston in late 2008 to meet with NASA and push their case.

When they got off his jet, Musk pulled her aside for a chat on the tarmac. "NASA is worried that I have to split my time between SpaceX and Tesla," he told her. "I kind of need a partner." It was not an idea that came easily to him; he was better at commanding than partnering. Then he made her an offer. "Do you want to be president of SpaceX?" He would remain the CEO, and they would divide responsibilities. "I'll focus on engineering and product development," he said, "and I want you to focus on customer management, human resources, government affairs, and a lot of the finance." She accepted right away. "I love working with people, and he loves working with hardware and designs," she explains.

On December 22, as if to ring down the curtain on the horrible year of 2008, Musk got a call on his cell phone. NASA spaceflight chief Bill Gerstenmaier, who would later end up at SpaceX, gave him the news: SpaceX was going to be awarded a $1.6 billion contract to make twelve round trips to the Space Station. "I love NASA," Musk responded. "You guys rock." Then he changed his password for his computer login to "ilovenasa."

31

Saving Tesla

December 2008

An almost freakish love of risk: Braving a blindfolded
knife-thrower at one of his birthday parties

Tesla financing, December 2008

Musk could not savor the NASA contract for more than a few minutes. In fact, his stress level didn't abate at all. SpaceX may have gotten a Christmas reprieve, but Tesla was still careening toward bankruptcy at the end of 2008. It was due to run out of money on Christmas Eve. Neither the company nor Musk personally had enough in the bank to meet the next payroll.

Musk enlisted his existing investors to fund a new equity round of a mere $20 million. It would be just enough to enable Tesla to sputter forward for a few more months. But when he thought the plan was wrapped up, he discovered that one investor was balking: VantagePoint Capital, led by Alan Salzman. And in order for the new equity to be issued, all of the existing investors had to approve.

Salzman and Musk had spent the past few months disagreeing on strategy. At one point they got into a shouting match at Tesla's headquarters which could be overheard by employees. Salzman wanted Tesla to become a supplier of battery packs to other car companies, such as Chrysler. "It would help fund Tesla's growth," Salzman said. Musk thought that was nuts. "Salzman was trying to insist that we hitch our wagon to a legacy car company," he says, "and I'm like, that ship is literally sinking." Salzman was upset that Tesla was burning through the deposits made by Roadster customers, even though the cars had not been built. "People thought they put down a deposit, not an unsecured loan to fund the company. Morally, it was wrong." Musk was able to get outside counsel to provide an opinion that it was legal. Salzman also was repelled by Musk's behavior: "He was tough on people and needlessly insensitive. That was just part of his DNA. It didn't sit well with me."

On one unofficial board call with Kimbal listening in, Salzman tried to lay the ground for removing Musk as CEO. "I was furious at what these evil fools were trying to do to Elon," Kimbal says. "I started yelling, 'No way, no way, you're not doing this. You guys are fools.'" Antonio Gracias was also on the call. "Nope, we've got Elon's back," he said. Kimbal called his brother, who was able to block a board vote. He was in such a trancelike focus that he didn't even get angry.

Salzman and his partners insisted that Musk come to their office and detail Tesla's capital needs going forward. "He was trying to perform open-heart surgery, and we were trying to make sure that he wasn't putting in the wrong blood type," Salzman says. "When you have one person with inordinate control, and that person is under a lot of stress, that's a dicey situation."

Musk got angry. "We've got to do this right away or we'll miss payroll," he told Salzman. But Salzman insisted that they meet the following week. He also set the time for 7 a.m., further enraging Musk. "I'm a night owl, I'm like, oh man, this is fucked," he says. "Salzman was doing this to me because he is a dickhead." Musk felt that Salzman relished the chance to look him in the eye and say no, which is what happened.

Musk can be forgiving, as he showed by his reconciliation with his PayPal partners. But there are a few people who cause him to go ballistic, almost irrationally so. Martin Eberhart is one. And Alan Salzman became another. Musk thought he was intentionally trying to push Tesla into bankruptcy. "He is such a douche," Musk says. "When I say he is a douchebag, that is descriptive, not pejorative."

Salzman calmly denies Musk's allegations and seems sanguine about his insults. "We did not have any scheme to take over the company or force it into bankruptcy," he says. "That's absurd. Our role is simply to support a company and make sure its capital is spent wisely." Despite Musk's personal attacks on him, he actually expresses some admiration. "He has been a singular driving force behind the company, and I'll give him credit that it worked out. I doff my hat."

In order to get around Salzman's veto on a new equity round, Musk scrambled to restructure the financing so that it did not involve issuing more equity but instead taking on more debt. The make-or-break conference call came on Christmas Eve, two days after SpaceX was awarded its NASA contract. Musk was at Kimbal's house in Boulder, Colorado, along with Talulah Riley. "I was on the floor wrapping presents for the kids, and Elon was on the bed, on the phone, frantically trying to sort this thing out," she recalls. "Christmas for me is very important, so my priority was to buffer the kids from the situation. I kept saying, 'It's Christmas, there'll be some sort of miracle.'"

And there was. VantagePoint ended up supporting the plan, as did the other investors on the call. Musk broke down in tears. "Had it gone the other way, Tesla would have been dead," he says, "and maybe too the dream of electric cars for many years." At the time, all of the major U.S. car companies had quit making electric vehicles.

Government loans and a Daimler investment

Over the years, one criticism of Tesla has been that the company was "bailed out" or "subsidized" by the government in 2009. In fact, Tesla did not get money from the Treasury Department's Troubled Asset Relief Program (TARP), commonly known as "the bailout." Under that program, the government lent $18.4 billion to General Motors and Chrysler as they went through bankruptcy restructuring. Tesla did not apply for any TARP or stimulus package money.

What Tesla did get in June 2009 was $465 million in interest-bearing loans from a Department of Energy program. The Advanced Technology Vehicles Manufacturing Loan Program lent money to companies to make electric or fuel-efficient cars. Ford, Nissan, and Fisker Automotive also got loans.

The Energy Department's loan to Tesla was not an immediate infusion of cash. Unlike the bailout money to GM and Chrysler, the loan money was tied to actual expenses. "We had to spend money and then submit invoices to the government," Musk explains. So the first check did not come until early 2010. Three years later, Tesla repaid its loan along with $12 million interest. Nissan repaid in 2017, Fisker went bankrupt, and as of 2023 Ford still owed the money.

A more significant infusion for Tesla came from Daimler. In October 2008, amid Tesla's crisis and SpaceX's launch failures, Musk flew to the German company's Stuttgart headquarters. The Daimler executives told him that they were interested in creating an electric car, and they had a team that was planning to visit the U.S. in January 2009. They invited Tesla to show them a proposal for an electric version of Daimler's Smart car.

Upon his return, Musk told JB Straubel that they should scramble to put together an electric Smart car prototype by the time the

Daimler team arrived. They dispatched an employee to Mexico, where gasoline-powered Smart cars were available, to buy one and drive it to California. Then they put a Roadster electric motor and battery pack in it.

When the Daimler executives arrived at Tesla in January 2009, they seemed annoyed that they had been scheduled to meet with a small and cash-strapped company they had barely heard of. "I remember them being very grumpy and wanting to get out of there as soon as possible," Musk says. "They were expecting some lame PowerPoint presentation." Then Musk asked them if they wanted to drive the car. "What do you mean?" one of the Daimler team asked. Musk explained that they had created a working model.

They went to the parking lot, and the Daimler executives took a test drive. The car bolted forward in an instant and reached sixty miles per hour in about four seconds. It blew them away. "That Smart car hauled ass," Musk says. "You could do wheelies in that car." As a result, Daimler contracted with Tesla for battery packs and powertrains for Smart cars, an idea not so different from the one Salzman had suggested. Musk asked Daimler also to consider investing in the company. In May 2009, even before the Department of Energy loans were approved, Daimler agreed to take a $50 million equity stake in Tesla. "If Daimler had not invested in Tesla at that time we would have died," Musk says.

32

The Model S

Tesla, 2009

Drew Baglino and Musk with Franz von Holzhausen

Henrik Fisker

The Christmas 2008 financing round, Daimler investment, and government loan allowed Musk to proceed with a project that, if successful, would turn Tesla into a real automotive company that could lead the way into the electric-vehicle era: a mainstream four-door sedan, costing about $60,000, that would be mass-produced. It became known as the Model S.

Musk had spent a lot of time on the Roadster design, but he had a much harder time when he tried to help shape a four-door sedan. "In a sports car, the lines and proportions are like that of a supermodel, and it's relatively easy to make that good looking," he says. "But the proportions of a sedan are harder to make pleasing."

Tesla had originally contracted with Henrik Fisker, a Danish-born designer in Southern California who had produced the sensuous styling of the BMW Z8 and the Aston Martin DB9. Musk was not impressed with his ideas. The car "looks like a fucking egg on wheels," he said of one of Fisker's sketches. "Lower the roof."

Fisker tried to explain the problem to Musk. Because the battery pack would raise the floor of the car, the roof needed to bulge in order to provide enough headroom. Fisker went to a whiteboard and sketched the Aston Martin design that Musk liked. It was low and wide. But the Model S could not have the same sleek proportions because of its battery location. "Imagine you're at a fashion show with Giorgio Armani," Fisker explained. "A model who is six feet tall and weighs a hundred pounds comes in wearing a dress. You're with your wife and she is five feet tall and weighs a hundred fifty pounds, and you say to Armani, 'Make that dress for my wife.' It won't look the same."

Musk ordered dozens of changes, including to the shape of the headlights and the lines of the hood. Fisker, who considered himself an artist, told Musk why he didn't want to make some of them. "I don't care what you want," Musk replied at one point. "I'm ordering you to do these things." Fisker recalls Musk's chaotic intensity with a tone of weary amusement. "I'm not really a Musk type of guy," he says. "I'm pretty laid back." After nine months, Musk canceled his contract.

Franz von Holzhausen

Franz von Holzhausen was born in Connecticut and lived in Southern California but, true to his name, has a Euro-cool aura. He dresses in animal-free Technik-Leather jackets and tight jeans, and he has an ever-present half-smile that hints at both self-confidence and polite humility. After graduating from design school, he became a journeyman working stints at Volkswagen, GM, and then Mazda in California, where he found himself stuck in what he calls "a rinse-and-repeat cycle" of doing uninspired projects.

One of his passions was go-karting, and a fellow rider, who was working on opening Tesla's first showroom on Santa Monica Boulevard, gave his name to Musk during the brutal summer of 2008. Having canceled Fisker's contract, Musk was looking for someone to set up an in-house design studio at Tesla. When Musk called von Holzhausen, he agreed to come by that afternoon. Musk gave him a tour of SpaceX, which blew his mind. "Shit, he's launching rockets into space," von Holzhausen marveled. "Cars are easy compared to this."

They continued the conversation at the opening party that evening for the Santa Monica showroom. In a conference room away from the other partygoers, Musk showed him pictures of the work that Fisker had done on the Model S. "That is really no good," von Holzhausen declared. "I can make you something great." Musk started laughing. "Yes, let's do it," he said, hiring von Holzhausen on the spot. They would end up becoming a team, like Steve Jobs and Jony Ive, one of the few calming and nondramatic relationships Musk would have, professionally and personally.

Musk wanted the design studio to be near his cubicle at the SpaceX factory in Los Angeles, rather than at Tesla's office in Silicon Valley, but he did not have the money to build it. So he gave von Holzhausen a corner in the rear of the rocket factory, near where the nose cones were being assembled, and erected a tent to give his team some privacy.

The day after he arrived, von Holzhausen stood next to Gwynne Shotwell near the canteen of the SpaceX factory and watched on the monitors as the company made its August 2008 third launch attempt from Kwaj. That was the launch that failed when the booster, just after separation, lurched slightly and bumped the second stage. It dawned on him that he had left a cushy job at Mazda to work for a manic genius addicted to risk and drama. Both SpaceX and Tesla seemed to be spiraling into bankruptcy. "Armageddon was hitting," he says, "and there were days when I thought, man, we may not survive to even be able to show this cool car we're dreaming about."

Von Holzhausen wanted a sidekick, so he reached out to an auto-industry pal he had known for years, Dave Morris, a clay-modeler and engineer with a jolly fish-and-chips accent from his north London childhood. "Dave, you don't realize how bootstrap this organization is," von Holzhausen told him. "This is like a garage band. We may be going bankrupt." But when von Holzhausen took him through the rocket factory to the design studio area, Morris was hooked. "If he's this hardcore about rockets and he wants to do cars," Morris thought, "then I want to do this."

Musk eventually bought an old aircraft hangar next to the SpaceX factory to house von Holzhausen and his studio. He would drop by to talk almost every day, and he would spend an hour or two every Friday in an intensive design review session. Gradually a new version of the Model S took shape. After a few months of showing sketches and specification sheets, von Holzhausen realized that Musk was most comfortable responding to 3D models. So he and Morris worked with a couple of sculptors to make a full-scale model, which they continually updated. On Friday afternoons, when Musk came for his visits, they would push the model out of the studio and into a sunlit outside parking patio to get his reactions.

The battery pack

In order to keep the Model S from looking bulbous, Musk had to make its battery pack as thin as possible. That is because he wanted it to be underneath the floor of the car, unlike the Roadster, which had a boxy battery pack behind its two seats. Putting the battery low made the car easier to handle and almost impossible to tip over. "We spent a lot of time shaving millimeters from the battery pack so that we could ensure that you had enough headroom without making it a bubble car," Musk says.

The person he put in charge of the battery was a recent Stanford graduate named Drew Baglino. More personable than the average engineer, with an easy laugh, Baglino would rise to the top ranks of Tesla over the years, but his career almost ended at his first meeting with Musk. "How many battery cells do we need to get to our range target?" Musk asked him. Baglino and the rest of the powertrain team had been analyzing that question for weeks. "We had run dozens of models, looking at how good the aerodynamics could be, how efficient we could get the drivetrain, and how energy dense we could make each of the cells," he says. And the answer they came up with was that the battery pack would need about 8,400 cells.

"No," Musk replied. "Do it with 7,200 cells."

Baglino thought that was impossible, but he caught himself before blurting that out. He had heard the tales of Musk's anger when challenged. Nevertheless, he found himself several times after that on the receiving end of Musk's blowtorch. "He was really harsh," Baglino recalls. "He likes to challenge the messenger, which isn't always the best approach. He began attacking me."

Baglino told his boss, Tesla's cofounder JB Straubel, how shaken he was: "I never want to be in another meeting with Elon." Straubel, who had been through many such sessions, surprised him by declaring it had been a "great" meeting. "That's the kind of feedback we need," Straubel said. "You just have to learn how to deal with his demands. Figure out what his goal is, and keep giving him information. That's how he gets the best outcomes."

In the case of the battery cells, Baglino ended up being surprised. "The crazy thing about his 7,200 target was we indeed ended up with 7,200 cells," he says. "It was a gut calculus, but he nailed it."

Once he got the cell number reduced, Musk focused on how low the battery pack could be positioned. Putting it in the floor pan meant that it needed to be protected from being pierced by rocks or debris. That led to many showdowns with the more cautious members of his team, who wanted a thick plate under the battery. Sometimes the meetings erupted into shouting matches. "Elon would get personal and the engineers would freak out," Straubel says. "They'd feel that they were being asked to do something unsafe." When they dug in their heels, it was like waving a red cape in front of a bull. "Elon is a hypercompetitive guy, and challenging him means that a meeting can go to hell."

To be the chief engineer for the Model S, Musk hired Peter Rawlinson, a genteel Englishman who had worked on car bodies for Lotus and Land Rover. Together they came up with a way to do more than merely place the battery pack under the floor of the car. They engineered it so that the pack became an element of the car's structure.

It was an example of Musk's policy that the designers sketching the shape of the car should work hand in glove with the engineers who were determining how the car would be built. "At other places I worked," von Holzhausen says, "there was this throw-it-over-the-fence mentality, where a designer would have an idea and then send it to an engineer, who sat in a different building or in a different country." Musk put the engineers and designers in the same room. "The vision was that we would create designers who thought like engineers and engineers who thought like designers," von Holzhausen says.

This followed the principle that Steve Jobs and Jony Ive had instilled at Apple: design is not just about aesthetics; true industrial design must connect the looks of a product to its engineering. "In most people's vocabularies, design means veneer," Jobs once explained. "Nothing could be further from the meaning of design. Design is the fundamental soul of a man-made creation that ends up expressing itself in successive outer layers."

Friendly design

There was another principle that came out of Apple's design studio. When Jony Ive conceived the candy-colored, friendly iMac in 1998, he included a recessed handle. It was not very functional, because the iMac was a desktop computer that was not meant to be carried around. But it sent a signal of friendliness. "If there's this handle on it, it makes a relationship possible," Ive explained. "It's approachable. It gives you permission to touch."

Likewise, von Holzhausen sketched a way to do door handles that were flush to the car and popped out and lit up like a happy handshake when the driver approached with a key. It did not add any great functionality. A regular extruding door handle would work just as well. But Musk immediately embraced the idea. It would send a chirpy signal of friendliness. "The handle senses your approach, lights up, pops out to greet you, and it's magical," he says.

The engineers and production teams fought the idea. There was little space inside the door for the mechanisms, which would have to work thousands of times in various weather conditions. One of the engineers flung back at Musk one of his favorite words: "stupid." But Musk persisted. "Stop fighting me on this," he ordered. It ended up being a signature feature of the cars, one that sealed an emotional bond with the owner.

Musk had a resistance to regulations. He did not like to play by other people's rules. As the Model S neared completion, he got in the car one day and pulled down the passenger-side visor. "What the fuck is this?" he asked, pointing to the government-mandated warning label about air bags and how to disable them when a child is in the passenger seat. Dave Morris explained that the government required them. "Get rid of them," Musk ordered. "People aren't stupid. These stickers are stupid."

In order to get around the requirements, Tesla designed a system to suppress airbag deployments when it detected that a child was in the passenger seat. But that did not satisfy the government, and Musk didn't back down. Over the years, Tesla would engage in a back-and-forth with the National Highway Traffic Safety Administration, which sporadically issued recall notices for Tesla cars without the warning sticker.

Musk wanted the Model S to have a large touchscreen at the driver's fingertips. He and von Holzhausen spent hours kicking around ideas for the size, shape, and positioning of the screen. It turned out to be a game-changer for the auto industry. It gave the driver easier control over the lights, temperature, seat positions, suspension levels, and almost everything in the car except opening the glove compartment (which, for some reason, government regulations required have a physical button). It also allowed more fun, including video games, fart sounds for the passenger seat, different horn sounds, and Easter egg jokes hidden in the interfaces.

Most importantly, regarding the car as a piece of software rather than just hardware allowed it to be continuously upgraded. New features could be delivered over the air. "We were amazed at how we could add tons of functionality over the years, including more acceleration," Musk says. "It allowed the car to get better than when you originally bought it."

33

Private Space

SpaceX, 2009–2010

At Cape Canaveral with President Obama, 2010

Falcon 9, Dragon, and Pad 40

When SpaceX won the NASA contract to send cargo to the International Space Station, it came with a challenge. It would require a rocket that was much more powerful than the Falcon 1.

Musk initially planned that this next rocket would have five engines rather than one, and thus be called the Falcon 5. It would also need a more powerful engine. But Tom Mueller worried that it would take too long to build a new engine, and he persuaded Musk to accept a revised idea: a rocket with nine of the original Merlin engines. Thus was born the Falcon 9, a rocket that would become the workhorse of SpaceX for more than a decade. At 157 feet, it was more than twice as tall as the Falcon 1, ten times more powerful, and twelve times heavier.

In addition to the new rocket, they needed a space capsule, the module that is launched atop the rocket and carries a payload of cargo (or astronauts) into orbit and can dock with the Space Station and return back to Earth. Musk worked with his engineers in a series of Saturday-morning meetings to design one from scratch, which he dubbed Dragon, after *Puff the Magic Dragon*.

And finally, they needed a place—not Kwaj!—where they could regularly launch the new rocket. It would be too hard to ship the big Falcon 9 halfway across the Pacific. Instead, SpaceX made a deal to use part of the Kennedy Space Center at Cape Canaveral, which has close to seven hundred buildings, pads, and launch complexes spread out over 144,000 acres on Florida's Atlantic coast. SpaceX leased Launchpad 40, which since the 1960s had been used for the Air Force's Titan rocket launches.

To rebuild the complex, Musk hired an engineer named Brian Mosdell, who worked for the Lockheed-Boeing joint venture United Launch Alliance. Musk's job interviews can be disconcerting. He multitasks, stares blankly, and sometimes pauses silently for a full minute or more. (Applicants are warned in advance to just sit there and not try to fill the silence.) But when he is engaged and wants to truly get a bead on an applicant, he dives into detailed technical discussions. What were the scientific reasons to use helium rather than nitrogen? What were the best methods to do pump shaft seals and labyrinth purges? "I have a good neural net when it comes to assessing with just a few questions a person's ability to perform," Musk says. Mosdell got the job.

Regularly prodded by Musk, Mosdell rebuilt the area in SpaceX's typical scrappy way, literally. He and his boss, Tim Buzza, scavenged for components that could be cheaply repurposed. Buzza was driving down a road at Cape Canaveral and saw an old liquid oxygen tank. "I asked the general if we could buy it," he says, "and we got a $1.5 million pressure vessel for scrap. It's still at Pad 40."

Musk also saved money by questioning requirements. When he asked his team why it would cost $2 million to build a pair of cranes to lift the Falcon 9, he was shown all the safety regulations imposed by the Air Force. Most were obsolete, and Mosdell was able to convince the military to revise them. The cranes ended up costing $300,000.

Decades of cost-plus contracts had made aerospace flabby. A valve in a rocket would cost thirty times more than a similar valve in a car, so Musk constantly pressed his team to source components from non-aerospace companies. The latches used by NASA in the Space Station cost $1,500 each. A SpaceX engineer was able to modify a latch used in a bathroom stall and create a locking mechanism that cost $30. When an engineer came to Musk's cubicle and told him that the air-cooling system for the payload bay of the Falcon 9 would cost more than $3 million, he shouted over to Gwynne Shotwell in her adjacent cubicle to ask what an air-conditioning system for a house cost. About $6,000, she said. So the SpaceX team bought some commercial air-conditioning units and modified their pumps so they could work atop the rocket.

When Mosdell worked for Lockheed and Boeing, he rebuilt a launchpad complex at the Cape for the Delta IV rocket. The similar one he built for the Falcon 9 cost one-tenth as much. SpaceX was not only privatizing space; it was upending its cost structure.

Obama at SpaceX

"I've been told we should extend the Space Shuttle program. Is that right?" Barack Obama asked his campaign advisor on space issues, Lori Garver, in early September 2008.

"No," she answered. "The private sector should do this." It was a risky piece of advice. SpaceX had failed three times to launch a satellite into orbit and was just about to make what might be its final attempt.

Garver, a NASA veteran, was trying to convince the Democratic nominee for president that America's approach to rocket-building needed to change. NASA was planning to ground the Space Shuttle and hoped to replace it with a new rocket program it called Constellation. It was being run in the traditional way: NASA awarded cost-plus contracts to the Lockheed-Boeing United Launch Alliance to build most of the components. But the projected cost of the program had more than doubled, and it was nowhere near completion. Garver recommended that Obama scuttle it and instead allow private companies, such as SpaceX, to develop rockets that could take astronauts into space.

That is why she, like Musk, had a lot riding on the fourth launch attempt of the Falcon 1 from Kwaj that September. When it was a success, she received congratulatory calls from Obama's top staffers, and Obama ended up appointing her the deputy administrator of NASA.

Unfortunately for Garver, Obama chose as her boss Charlie Bolden, a former Marine Corps pilot and NASA astronaut, who did not share her enthusiasm for partnering with the commercial sector. "I was not an ideologue like many around me who felt that all we need to do is take NASA's budget, take everything for human space-flight, and give it to Elon Musk and SpaceX," Bolden says.

Garver also had to fight those in Congress who had Boeing facilities in their states and, despite being Republicans, were opposed to private enterprise taking over what they felt should be run by a government bureaucracy. "Senior industry and government officials took pleasure deriding SpaceX and Elon," Garver says. "It didn't help that Elon was younger and richer than they were, with a Silicon Valley disrupter mentality and lack of deference toward the traditional industry."

Garver won the argument at the end of 2009. Obama canceled NASA's Constellation program after his science advisor and budget director said that it was "over budget, behind schedule, off course, and unexecutable." NASA traditionalists, including the revered astronaut Neil Armstrong, denounced the decision. "The president's proposed NASA budget begins the death march for the future of U.S. human spaceflight," said Senator Richard Shelby of Alabama. Former NASA administrator Michael Griffin, who had traveled with Musk to Russia seven years earlier, charged, "Essentially the U.S. has decided that they're not going to be a significant player in human space flight." They were wrong. Over the next decade, relying mainly on SpaceX, the U.S. would send more astronauts, satellites, and cargo to space than any other country.

Obama decided to travel to Cape Canaveral in April 2010 to make the case that relying on private companies such as SpaceX did not mean that the U.S. was abandoning space exploration. "Some have said it is unfeasible or unwise to work with the private sector in this way," he said in his speech. "I disagree. By buying the services of space transportation—rather than the vehicles themselves—we can continue to ensure rigorous safety standards are met. But we will also accelerate the pace of innovations as companies—from young startups to established leaders—compete to design and build and launch new means of carrying people and materials out of our atmosphere."

The president's team had decided that he would go to one of the launchpads after the speech and have a photo op in front of a rocket. The way the story was reported, the president planned to go to a pad used by the United Launch Alliance, but it was preparing to launch a secret intelligence satellite, so that idea was nixed. Lori Garver says that wasn't the true story: "All of us at the White House were in agreement that we wanted to go to the SpaceX pad."

The televised image was priceless for both Obama and Musk: the young president, who was born the year that John Kennedy pledged

America would send a man to the moon, walking alongside the risk-taking entrepreneur, chatting casually as they circled the gleaming Falcon 9. Musk liked Obama. "I thought he was a moderate but also someone willing to force change," he says. He got the impression that Obama was trying to size him up. "I think he wanted to get a sense if I was dependable or a little nuts."

34

Falcon 9 Liftoff

Cape Canaveral, 2010

Marc Juncosa, center, leading a toast to the Falcon 9 liftoff

Into orbit . . .

Musk's chance to prove that he was not "a little nuts," or at least that he was also dependable, came two months later, in June 2010, when Falcon 9 attempted its first unmanned test voyage into orbit. The Falcon 1 had failed three times before being successful, and this rocket was far bigger and more complex. Musk thought it was unlikely to succeed on its first try, but there was a lot of pressure now that the president had made it America's policy to depend on such commercial launches. As the *Wall Street Journal* wrote, "A dramatic launch failure could further undercut an already faltering campaign by the White House to persuade Congress to spend billions to help SpaceX and perhaps two other rivals to develop commercial replacements for NASA's retiring Space Shuttle fleet."

The chances for success were not helped when a storm rolled in and soaked the rocket. "Our antenna got wet," Buzza recalls, "and we weren't getting a good telemetry signal." They lowered the rocket from the launchpad, and Musk came out with Buzza to inspect the damage. Bülent Altan, the goulash-cooking hero of Kwaj, climbed a ladder, looked at the antennas, and confirmed that they were too wet to work. A typical SpaceX fix was improvised: they fetched a hair dryer, and Altan waved it over the antennas until the moisture was gone. "You think it is good enough to fly tomorrow?" Musk asked him. Altan replied, "It should do the trick." Musk stared at him silently for a while, assessing him and his answer, then said, "Okay, let's do it."

The next morning, the radio frequency checks were still not perfect. "It wasn't the right sort of pattern," Buzza says. So he told Musk there might be another delay. Musk looked at the data. As usual, he was willing to tolerate more risk than others. "It's good enough," he said. "Let's launch." Buzza assented. "The important thing with Elon," he says, "is that if you told him the risks and showed him the engineering data, he would make a quick assessment and let the responsibility shift from your shoulders to his."

The launch went perfectly. Musk, who joined his jubilant team at an all-night party on Cocoa Beach pier, called it "a vindication of what the president has proposed." It was also a vindication of SpaceX. Less than eight years from its founding, and two years from facing bankruptcy, it was now the most successful private rocket company in the world.

. . . and return

The next big test, scheduled for later in 2010, was to show that SpaceX could not only launch an unmanned capsule into orbit but also return it to Earth safely. No private company had done that. In fact, only three governments had: the United States, Russia, and China.

Once again, Musk showed a willingness, bordering on the reckless, to take the risks that separated his programs from those run by NASA. The day before the planned December launch, a final pad inspection revealed two small cracks in the engine skirt of the rocket's second stage. "Everyone at NASA assumed we'd be standing down from the launch for a few weeks," says Garver. "The usual plan would have been to replace the entire engine."

"What if we just cut the skirt?" Musk asked his team. "Like, literally cut around it?" In other words, why not just trim off a tiny bit of the bottom that had the two cracks? The shorter skirt would mean the engine would have slightly less thrust, one engineer warned, but Musk calculated that there would still be enough to do the mission. It took less than an hour to make the decision. Using a big pair of shears, the skirt was trimmed, and the rocket launched on its critical mission the next day, as planned. "NASA couldn't do anything but accept SpaceX's decisions and watch in disbelief," Garver recalls.

The rocket was able, as Musk predicted, to lift the Dragon capsule into orbit. It then performed its assigned maneuvers and fired its braking rockets so that it would return to Earth, parachuting gently down to the water just off the coast of California.

As awesome as it was, Musk had a sobering realization. The Mercury program had accomplished similar feats fifty years earlier, before either he or Obama had been born. America was just catching up with its older self.

SpaceX repeatedly proved that it could be nimbler than NASA. One example came during a mission to the Space Station in March 2013, when one of the valves in the engine of the Dragon capsule stuck shut. The SpaceX team started scrambling to figure out how to abort the mission and return the capsule safely before it crashed. Then they came up with a risky idea. Perhaps they could build up the pressure in front of the valve to a very high level. Then if they suddenly released the pressure, it might cause the valve to burp open. "It's like the spacecraft equivalent of the Heimlich maneuver," Musk later told the *Washington Post*'s Christian Davenport.

The top two NASA officials in the control room stood back and watched as the young SpaceX engineers hatched the plan. One of SpaceX's software engineers churned out the code that would instruct the capsule to build up pressure, and they transmitted it as if it were a software update for a Tesla car.

Boom, pop. It worked. The valve burped open. Dragon docked with the Space Station and then returned home safely.

That paved the way for SpaceX's next great challenge, one even grander and riskier. Prodded by Garver, the Obama administration decided that, once the Space Shuttle was retired, the U.S. would rely on private companies, most notably SpaceX, to launch not only cargo but humans into orbit. Musk was prepared for that. He had already told the SpaceX engineers to build into the Dragon capsule an element that was not necessary for the transport of cargo: a window.

35

Marrying Talulah

September 2010

With Talulah at the Kentucky Derby

"I can take a hard path"

Musk had proposed to Talulah Riley weeks after they met in the summer of 2008, but they both agreed they should wait about two years before they actually got married.

Musk's emotional settings range from callous to needy to exuberant, the last one most evident when he falls in love. Riley went back to England in July 2009 to star in *St. Trinian's 2*, a sequel to the girls'-boarding-school comedy she had done two years earlier, and on her first day of filming, at a manor house near her childhood home north of London, she received five hundred roses from Musk. "When he's angry, he's angry, and when he's joyful, he's joyful, and he's almost childlike in his enthusiasms," she says. "He can be very cold, but he feels things in a very pure way, with a depth that most people don't get."

What struck Riley most was what she calls "the child within the man." When he's happy, this childlike inner self can manifest in a manic way. "When we went to the cinema, he would get so caught up with a silly movie that he would stare in rapture at the screen with his mouth slightly open laughing, then he would actually end up on the floor rolling around, holding his belly."

But she also noticed that the child within the man could be expressed in a darker way. Early on in their relationship, he would stay up late at night and tell Riley about his father. "I remember one of those nights, he began crying, and it was really horrendous for him," she says.

During those conversations, Musk would sometimes lapse into a trancelike state and recount things that his father used to say. "He was almost not conscious, not in the room with me, when he told me these things," she recalls. Hearing the phrases that Errol had used in berating Elon shocked her, not only because they were brutal but because she had heard Elon use some of the same phrases when he was angry.

A quiet and polite girl from the bucolic English countryside, she knew that marriage to Musk would be challenging. He was thrilling and mesmerizing, but also brooding and encrusted with layers of complexity. "Being with me can be difficult," he told her. "This will be a hard path."

She decided to go along for the ride. "Okay," she told him one day. "I can take a hard path."

They wed in September 2010 at Dornoch Cathedral, a thirteenth-century church in the Scottish Highlands. "I'm Christian, and Elon is not, but he very kindly agreed to get married in a cathedral," Riley says. She wore a "full-on princess dress from Vera Wang," and she gave Musk a top hat and cane so he could dance around like Fred Astaire, whose movies she had turned him on to. His five boys, dressed in tailor-made tuxedos, were supposed to share the duties of ring bearer and attendants, but Saxon, his autistic son, bowed out, the other boys began fighting, and only Griffin actually made it to the end of the aisle. But the drama added to the fun, Riley recalled.

The party afterward was at nearby Skibo Castle, also built in the thirteenth century. When Riley asked Musk what he wanted, he replied, "There shall be hovercraft and eels." It was a reference to a Monty Python skit in which John Cleese plays a Hungarian who tries to speak English using a flawed phrasebook and tells a shopkeeper, "My hovercraft is full of eels." (It's actually funnier than I've made it sound.) "It was quite difficult," Riley says, "because you need permits to transport eels between England and Scotland, but in the end we did have an amphibious little hovercraft and eels." There was also an armed personnel carrier that Musk and his friends used to crush three junked cars. "We all got to be young boys again," Navaid Farooq says.

The Orient Express

Riley liked to throw creative parties, and Musk, despite being socially awkward (or perhaps because of it), had an odd enthusiasm for them. They allowed him to let loose, especially during times of tension, which, for him, were most of the time. "So I used to throw very theatrical parties just to keep him entertained," she says.

The most lavish was for his fortieth birthday in June 2011, less than a year after their wedding. Along with three dozen friends, he and Talulah rented cars on the Orient Express train from Paris to Venice.

They met at the Hotel Costes, an opulent establishment near the Place Vendôme. A few of them, led by Elon and Kimbal, went to a fine restaurant, and as they were heading back to the hotel they decided on a lark to rent some bicycles and dash around the town. They biked until 2 a.m., then bribed the hotel to keep the bar open for them. After an hour of drinking, they got back on the bikes and ended up at an underground lounge called Le Magnifique, where they stayed until 5 a.m.

They didn't get up until 3 p.m. the next day, just in time to catch the train. Dressed in tuxedos, they had a formal dinner on the Orient Express, with caviar and champagne, followed by their own private entertainment by the Lucent Dossier Experience, a steampunky performance troupe featuring avant-garde music, aerial arts, and fire, somewhat like Cirque du Soleil, but more erotic. "People were hanging from the ceiling," Kimbal says, "which was a bizarre scene in the very traditional Orient Express train car." Riley would sometimes privately sing to Elon a song called "My Name Is Tallulah" from the movie *Bugsy Malone*. He said his one wish for his birthday was that she would perform it for the whole party. "I don't really sing, so it was traumatic for me, but I did it for him," she says.

Musk did not have many stable and grounded relationships, nor did he have many stable and grounded periods in his life. No doubt those two things were related. Among his few such relationships was the one he had with Riley, and the years he would spend with her— from their meeting in 2008 to their second divorce in 2016—would end up being the longest stretch of relative stability in his life. If he had liked stability more than storm and drama, she would have been perfect for him.

36

Manufacturing

Tesla, 2010–2013

With Griffin, Talulah, and Xavier celebrating ringing the
NASDAQ opening bell, June 2010; with Marques Brownlee
at the Tesla Fremont factory

Fremont

Beginning with the theology of globalization in the 1980s, and relentlessly driven by cost-cutting CEOs and their activist investors, American companies shut down domestic factories and offshored manufacturing. The trend accelerated in the early 2000s, when Tesla was getting started. Between 2000 and 2010, the U.S. lost one-third of its manufacturing jobs. By sending their factories abroad, American companies saved labor costs, but they lost the daily feel for ways to improve their products.

Musk bucked this trend, largely because he wanted to have tight control of the manufacturing process. He believed that designing the factory to build a car—"the machine that builds the machine"—was as important as designing the car itself. Tesla's design-manufacturing feedback loop gave it a competitive advantage, allowing it to innovate on a daily basis.

Oracle founder Larry Ellison joined only two corporate boards, Apple and Tesla, and he became close friends with Jobs and Musk. He said they both had beneficial cases of obsessive-compulsive disorder. "OCD is one of the reasons for their success, because they obsessed on solving a problem until they did," he says. What set them apart is that Musk, unlike Jobs, applied that obsession not just to the design of a product but also to the underlying science, engineering, and manufacturing. "Steve just had to get the conception and software right, but the manufacturing was outsourced," Ellison says. "Elon took on the manufacturing, the materials, the huge factories." Jobs loved to walk through Apple's design studio on a daily basis, but he never visited his factories in China. Musk, in contrast, spent more time walking assembly lines than he did walking around the design studio. "The brain strain of designing the car is tiny compared to the brain strain of designing the factory," he says.

Musk's approach came together in May 2010, when Toyota was looking to sell a factory that it had once shared with GM in Fremont, California, on the fringe of Silicon Valley, a half-hour drive from Tesla's headquarters in Palo Alto. Musk invited Toyota's president, Akio Toyoda, to his Los Angeles home and drove him around in a

Roadster. He was able to get the mothballed factory, which at one point had been worth $1 billion, for $42 million. In addition, Toyota agreed to invest $50 million in Tesla.

When redesigning the factory, Musk put the cubicles for the engineers right on the edge of the assembly lines, so they would see the flashing lights and hear the complaints whenever one of their design elements caused a slowdown. Musk often corralled the engineers to walk up and down the lines with him. His own open desk was in the middle of it all, with no walls around him, and it had a pillow underneath so he could spend the night when he wanted.

The month after Tesla bought the factory, Musk was able to take the company public, the first IPO by an American carmaker since Ford's in 1956. He traveled with Talulah and two of his sons to ring the opening bell at the NASDAQ stock exchange on Times Square. By the end of the day, the stock market had fallen, but Tesla's stock rose more than 40 percent, providing $266 million in financing for the company. That evening, Musk flew west to the Fremont factory, where he made a pithy toast. "Fuck oil," he said. Tesla was almost dead at the end of 2008. Now, just eighteen months later, it had become America's hottest new company.

Production quality

When the first Model S cars rolled off the Fremont assembly line in June 2012, hundreds of people, including California governor Jerry Brown, showed up for the celebration. Many of the workers waved American flags. Some cried. What had once been a bankrupt factory that had laid off all its workers now had two thousand employees and was leading the way to an electric-vehicle future.

But a few days later, when Musk was delivered his own Model S from the production line, he was not happy. More precisely, he declared that it sucked. He asked von Holzhausen to come to his house, and they spent two hours going over the vehicle. "Jesus Christ, is this the best we can do?" Musk asked. "The panel gap finish is crap. The paint quality is crap. Why aren't we getting the same production quality as Mercedes and BMW?"

When Musk gets angry, he is quick to pull the trigger. He fired three production quality chiefs in quick succession. One day that August, von Holzhausen was with him on his plane and asked how he could help. He should have been careful about making such an offer. Musk asked him to move to Fremont for a year to be the new production quality chief.

Von Holzhausen and his deputy Dave Morris, who accompanied him to Fremont, would sometimes walk the factory's assembly lines until two in the morning. It was an interesting experience for a designer. "It taught me how all the things you create on the drawing board have an effect at the other end, on the assembly line," von Holzhausen says. Musk joined them two or three nights a week. His focus was on root causes. What in the design was to blame for a production-line problem?

One of Musk's favorite words—and concepts—was "hardcore." He used it to describe the workplace culture he wanted when he founded Zip2, and he would use it almost thirty years later when he upended the nurturing culture at Twitter. As the Model S production line ramped up, he spelled out his creed in a quintessential email to employees, titled "Ultra hardcore." It read, "Please prepare yourself for a level of intensity that is greater than anything most of you have experienced before. Revolutionizing industries is not for the faint of heart."

The validation came at the end of 2012, when *Motor Trend Magazine* picked its car of the year. The headline: "Tesla Model S, Shocking Winner: Proof Positive That America Can Still Make (Great) Things." The review itself was so breathtaking that it surprised even Musk. "It drives like a sports car, eager and agile and instantly responsive. But it's also as smoothly effortless as a Rolls-Royce, can carry almost as much stuff as a Chevy Equinox, and is more efficient than a Toyota Prius. Oh, and it'll sashay up to the valet at a luxury hotel like a supermodel working a Paris catwalk." The article ended by mentioning "the astonishing inflection point the Model S represents": it was the first time that the award had gone to an electric vehicle.

The Nevada battery Gigafactory

The idea that Musk proposed in 2013 was audacious: build a gigan-tic battery factory in the U.S., with an output greater than all other battery factories in the world combined. "It was a completely wacky idea," says JB Straubel, the battery wiz who was one of Tesla's co-founders. "It seemed like science fiction crazy."

To Musk, it was a matter of first principles. The Model S was using about 10 percent of the world's batteries. The new models that Tesla had on the drawing board—an SUV called the Model X and a mass-market sedan that would become the Model 3—would require ten times the number of batteries. "What began as a show-stopper problem," Straubel says, "became a really fun blue-sky wacky brainstorming opportunity to say, 'Wow, this is actually a chance to do something unique.'"

There was one problem, Straubel recalls. "We had no clue how to build a battery factory."

So Musk and Straubel decided to pursue a partnership with their battery supplier, Panasonic. Together they would build a facility where Panasonic would make the battery cells and then Tesla would turn them into battery packs for cars. The 10-million-square-foot factory would cost $5 billion, and Panasonic would finance $2 billion of it. But Panasonic's top leaders were hesitant. They had never had that type of partnership, and Musk (understandably) did not strike them as an easy guy to dance with.

To prod Panasonic, Musk and Straubel came up with a charade. At a site near Reno, Nevada, they set up lights and sent in bulldozers to start preparing for construction. Then Straubel invited his coun-terpart at Panasonic to join him on a viewing platform to watch the work. The message was clear: Tesla was forging ahead with the fac-tory. Did Panasonic want to be left behind?

It worked. Musk and Straubel were invited to Japan by Pana-sonic's new young president Kazuhiro Tsuga. "It was a come-to-Jesus session where we had to make him truly commit that we were going to build the insane Gigafactory together," Straubel says.

The dinner was a formal, multicourse affair at a traditional low-table Japanese restaurant. Straubel was fearful about how Musk would behave. "Elon can be so much hell and brimstone in meetings and just unpredictable as all get out," he says. "But I've also seen him flip a switch and suddenly be this incredibly effective, charismatic, high-emotional-intelligence business person, when he has to do it." At the Panasonic dinner, the charming Musk appeared. He sketched out his vision for moving the world to electric vehicles and why the two companies should do it together. "I was mildly shocked and impressed, because, whoa, this is not like how Elon usually was on other days," says Straubel. "He's a person who's all over the map, and you don't know what he's going to say or do. And then, all of a sudden, he pulls it all together."

At the dinner, Tsuga agreed to be a 40 percent partner in the Gigafactory. When asked why Panasonic decided to do the deal, he replied, "We are too conservative. We are a ninety-five-year-old company. We have to change. We have to use some of Elon's thinking."

37

Musk and Bezos

SpaceX, 2013–2014

Having dinner in 2004

Jeff Bezos

Jeff Bezos, the supercharged Amazon billionaire with a boisterous laugh and boyish enthusiasms, pursues his passions with a talent for being, at the same time, both exuberant and methodical. Like Musk, he was a childhood addict of science fiction, racing through the shelves of Isaac Asimov and Robert Heinlein books at his local library.

As a five-year-old in July 1969, he watched television coverage of the Apollo 11 mission that culminated with Neil Armstrong walking on the moon. He calls it "a seminal moment" for him. Later, he would fund a series of missions that recovered from the Atlantic Ocean an Apollo 11 engine, which he installed in a niche off the living room of his house in Washington, DC.

His exhilaration about space turned him into one of those hard-core *Star Trek* fans who knows every episode. As the valedictorian of his high-school class, his speech was about how to colonize planets, build space hotels, and save our planet by finding other places to do manufacturing. "Space, the final frontier, meet me there!" he concluded.

In 2000, after making Amazon the world's dominant online retailer, Bezos quietly launched a company called Blue Origin, named after the pale blue planet where humans originated. Like Musk, he focused on the idea of building reusable rockets. "How is the situation in the year 2000 different from 1960?" he asks. "What's different is computer sensors, cameras, software. Being able to land vertically is the kind of problem that can be addressed by technologies that didn't exist in 1960."

Like Musk, he embarked on space endeavors as a missionary rather than a mercenary. There are easier ways to make money. Human civilization, he felt, will soon strain the resources of our small planet. That will confront us with a choice: accept static growth or expand to places beyond Earth. "I don't think stasis is compatible with liberty," he says. "We can fix that problem in exactly one way: by moving out into the solar system."

They met in 2004 when Bezos accepted Musk's invitation to take a tour of SpaceX. Afterward, he was surprised to get a somewhat curt email from Musk expressing annoyance that Bezos had not reciprocated by inviting him to Seattle to see Blue Origin's factory, so Bezos promptly did. Musk flew up with Justine, toured Blue Origin, then they had dinner with Bezos and his wife MacKenzie. Musk was filled with advice, expressed with his usual intensity. He warned Bezos that he was heading down the wrong path with one idea: "Dude, we tried that and that turned out to be really dumb, so I'm telling you don't do the dumb thing we did." Bezos recalls feeling that Musk was a bit too sure of himself, given that he had not yet successfully launched a rocket. The following year, Musk asked Bezos to have Amazon do a review of Justine's new book, an urban horror thriller about demon-human hybrids. Bezos explained that he did not tell Amazon what to review, but said that he would personally post a customer review. Musk sent back a brusque reply, but Bezos posted a nice personal review anyway.

Pad 39A

Beginning in 2011, SpaceX won a series of contracts from NASA to develop rockets that could take humans to the International Space Station, a task made crucial by the retirement of the Space Shuttle. To fulfill that mission, it needed to add to its facilities at Cape Canaveral's Pad 40, and Musk set his sights on leasing the most storied launch facility there, Pad 39A.

Pad 39A had been center stage for America's Space Age dreams, burned into the memories of a television generation that held its collective breath when the countdowns got to "Ten, nine, eight . . ." Neil Armstrong's mission to the moon that Bezos watched as a kid blasted off from Pad 39A in 1969, as did the last manned moon mission, in 1972. So did the first Space Shuttle mission, in 1981, and the last, in 2011.

But by 2013, with the Shuttle program grounded and America's half-century of space aspirations ending with bangs and whimpers, Pad 39A was rusting away and vines were sprouting through its flame trench. NASA was eager to lease it. The obvious customer was Musk, whose Falcon 9 rockets had already launched on cargo missions from the nearby Pad 40, where Obama had visited. But when the lease was put out for bids, Jeff Bezos—for both sentimental and practical reasons—decided to compete for it.

When NASA ended up awarding the lease to SpaceX, Bezos sued. Musk was furious, declaring that it was ridiculous for Blue Origin to contest the lease "when they haven't even gotten so much as a toothpick to orbit." He ridiculed Bezos's rockets, pointing out that they were capable only of popping up to the edge of space and then falling back; they lacked the far greater thrust necessary to break the Earth's gravity and go into orbit. "If they do somehow show up in the next five years with a vehicle qualified to NASA's human rating standards that can dock with the Space Station, which is what Pad 39A is meant to do, we will gladly accommodate their needs," Musk said. "Frankly, I think we are more likely to discover unicorns dancing in the flame duct."

The battle of the sci-fi barons had blasted off. One SpaceX employee bought dozens of inflatable toy unicorns and photographed them in the pad's flame duct.

Bezos was eventually able to lease a nearby launch complex at Cape Canaveral, Pad 36, which had been the origin of missions to Mars and Venus. So the competition of the boyish billionaires was set to continue. The transfer of these hallowed pads represented, both symbolically and in practice, John F. Kennedy's torch of space exploration being passed from government to the private sector—from a once-glorious but now sclerotic NASA to a new breed of mission-driven pioneers.

Reusable rockets

Both Musk and Bezos had a vision for what would make space travel feasible: rockets that were reusable. Bezos's focus was on creating the sensors and software to guide a rocket to a soft landing on Earth. But that was only part of the challenge. The greater difficulty was to put all of those features on a rocket that was still light enough, and whose engines had enough thrust, to make it into orbit. Musk focused obsessively on this physics problem. He liked to muse, half-jokingly, that we Earthlings live in a gamelike simulation created by clever overlords with a sense of humor. They made gravity on Mars and the moon weak enough that launching into orbit would be easy. But on Earth, the gravity seems perversely calibrated to make reaching orbit just barely possible.

Like a mountain climber paring the contents of his knapsack, Musk obsessed over reducing the weight of his rockets. That has a multiplier effect: removing a bit of weight—by deleting a part, using a lighter material, making simpler welds—results in less fuel needed, which further reduces the mass the engines have to lift. When he walked through SpaceX's assembly lines, Musk would pause at each station, stare silently, and challenge the team to delete or trim some part. At almost every encounter, he maniacally hammered home the message: "A fully reusable rocket is the difference between being a single-planet civilization and being a multiplanet one."

Musk brought this message to the 2014 annual black-tie dinner of the century-old Explorers Club in New York City, where he was given the President's Award. He shared the stage with Bezos, who accepted an award for the work of his team in recovering the engine of Neil Armstrong's Apollo 11 spacecraft. The dinner featured dishes designed to appeal to the overly adventurous, such as scorpions, maggot-covered strawberries, sweet-and-sour cow penis, goat-eyeball martinis, and whole alligators carved tableside.

Musk was introduced with a video showing his successful rocket launches. "You are kind enough not to show our first three launches," he said. "We'll have to have a blooper reel at some point." Then he gave his sermon about the need for a fully reusable rocket. "That's the thing that will allow us to establish life on Mars," he said. "Our upcoming launch will have landing legs on the rocket for the first time." Reusable rockets could someday get the cost of taking a person to Mars down to $500,000. Most people would not make the trip, he conceded, "but I suspect there are people in this room who would."

Bezos applauded, but at that moment he was quietly pursuing an unexpected attack. He and Blue Origin had applied for a U.S. patent titled "Sea landing of space launch vehicles," and a few weeks after the dinner it was granted. The ten-page application described "methods for landing and recovering a booster stage and/or other portions thereof on a platform at sea." Musk was livid. The idea of landing on ships at sea "is something that's been discussed for, like, half a century," he said. "It's in fictional movies; it's in multiple proposals; there's so much prior art, it's crazy. So, trying to patent something that people have been discussing for half a century is obviously ridiculous."

The following year, after SpaceX sued, Bezos agreed to have the patent canceled. But the dispute heightened the rivalry between the two rocket entrepreneurs.

38

The Falcon Hears the Falconer

SpaceX, 2014–2015

Viewing a landed booster

Grasshopper

Musk's quest to build a reusable rocket led to the development of an experimental Falcon 9 prototype dubbed "Grasshopper." It had landing legs and steerable grid fins and could take slow hops up and down to about three thousand feet at the SpaceX test facility in McGregor, Texas. Excited by the progress they were making, Musk invited the SpaceX board there in August 2014 to see the future in action.

It was the second day on the job for Sam Teller, a 240-volt Harvard grad and venture seeker, who had signed on to be Musk's de facto chief of staff. With a trimmed beard that accentuated his wide smile and alert eyes, he had the emotional receptors and eagerness to please that were missing in his boss. As a former business manager of *The Harvard Lampoon*, he knew how to harness Musk's humor and manic intensity (and even brought Musk to a party at the *Lampoon*'s castle soon after going to work for him).

At its meeting at the McGregor test facility, the SpaceX board discussed designs for the space suits the company was developing, even though they were years away from flying humans. "They're sitting around seriously discussing plans to build a city on Mars and what people will wear there," Teller later marveled, "and everyone's just acting like this is a totally normal conversation."

The main event for the board was watching the test of a Falcon 9 landing. It was a sun-blasted August day in the Texas desert, with giant crickets swarming, and the board members huddled under a small tent. The rocket was supposed to rise to about three thousand feet, activate its reentry rockets, hover above a pad, and then land erect. But it didn't. Shortly after liftoff, one of the three engines malfunctioned and the rocket exploded.

After a few moments of silence, Musk reverted to adventure-boy mode. He told the site manager to get the van so they could drive over to the smoldering debris. "You can't," the manager said. "Too dangerous."

"We're going," Musk said. "If it's going to explode, we might as well walk through burning debris. How often do you get to do that?"

Everyone laughed nervously and followed along. It was like a set from a Ridley Scott movie, with craters in the ground, the scrub grass on fire, and charred pieces of metal. Steve Jurvetson asked Musk if they could grab some pieces as souvenirs. "Sure," he said, collecting some himself. Antonio Gracias tried to cheer everyone up by saying how the best lessons in life come from failures. "Given the options," Musk replied, "I prefer to learn from success."

It was the beginning of a bad stretch not just for SpaceX but for the entire industry. A rocket made by Orbital Sciences exploded on a mission to deliver cargo to the Space Station. Then a Russian cargo mission failed. The astronauts on the Space Station were in danger of running out of food and supplies. So a lot was riding on SpaceX's Falcon 9 cargo mission scheduled for June 28, 2015, Musk's forty-fourth birthday.

But two minutes after liftoff, a strut in the second stage that held a helium tank buckled, and the rocket exploded. After seven years of successful launches, it was the first time that a Falcon 9 failed.

In the meantime, Bezos was making some progress. In November 2015, he launched a rocket on an eleven-minute, sixty-two-mile up-and-down hop to the altitude that is considered the beginning of outer space. Guided by a GPS system and steering fins, the rocket returned to Earth and its booster engine reignited to slow the descent. With its landing legs deployed, it hovered just above the ground, adjusted its coordinates, and landed gently.

Bezos announced the success on a press call the next day. "Full reuse is a game changer," he said. Then he unleashed his first-ever tweet: "The rarest of beasts—a used rocket. Controlled landing not easy but done right can look easy."

Musk was annoyed. It was, he felt, just a suborbital hop, not what he considered the true holy grail of launching a payload into orbit. So he unleashed a rejoinder on Twitter: "@JeffBezos Not quite 'rarest.' SpaceX Grasshopper rocket did 6 suborbital flights 3 years ago & is still around."

In fact, the Grasshopper had flown only about three thousand feet up, which was one-hundredth as far as Blue Origin's rocket. But Musk was right in the distinction he made. Rockets that could hop up and back to the edge of space might be fun for space tourists, but it would take rockets with the power of the Falcon 9 to do missions such as launching satellites and reaching the International Space Station. Landing and reusing such a rocket would be an accomplishment of a different order of magnitude.

"The Falcon has landed"

Musk's opportunity to do that came on December 21, 2015, just four weeks after Bezos's suborbital flight.

In his relentless quest to conquer gravity, Musk had redesigned the Falcon 9. The new version packed more liquid oxygen fuel onto the rocket by supercooling it to minus 350 degrees Fahrenheit, which made it much more dense. As always, he was looking for every way possible to cram more power into a rocket without significantly increasing its size or mass. "Elon kept hammering at us to eke out a tiny percent more efficiency by chilling down the fuel more and more," says Mark Juncosa. "It was ingenious, but it was giving us a real pain in the ass." A few times Juncosa pushed back, saying it would present challenges with valves and leaks, but Musk was unrelenting. "There is no first-principles reason this can't work," he said. "It's extraordinarily difficult, I know, but you just have to muscle through."

"I was just crapping in my pants during the countdown," Juncosa says. Suddenly he noticed something worrisome on the video feed from the cavity between the first and second stages. There were some drips, and he didn't know whether they were liquid nitrogen, which would be okay, or liquid oxygen from the supercooled tank, which might be a problem. "I was scared as hell," Juncosa recalls. "If it was my company, I would have shut it down."

"You got to call this one," Juncosa told Musk as the countdown got down to the final minute.

Musk paused for a few seconds. How risky would it be if there was some liquid oxygen in the interstage? Risky, but only a small risk. "Fuck it," he said. "Let's just go."

Years later, Juncosa watched footage of the moment Musk made that decision. "I thought he had done some complex quick calculations to decide what to do, but in fact he just shrugged his shoulders and gave the order. He had an intuition of what the physics were."

He was right. The liftoff went flawlessly.

Then came the ten-minute wait to see if the booster would return and land safely on the landing pad that SpaceX had built about a mile from Pad 39A. Just after the second stage separated, the booster fired its thrusters to flip around, head back toward the Cape, point its bottom downward, and slow its descent. With its GPS and sensors guiding it and its grid fins helping to steer, it eased down toward the landing pad. (Pause for a second and think how amazing all that is.)

Musk bolted out of the control room and ran across the highway, staring into the dark to watch the rocket reappear. "Come on down, come on down slowly," he whispered as he stood by the highway, arms akimbo. Then there was a boom. "Oh shit," he said, turning around and walking dejectedly back across the highway.

But inside the control room, there were loud cheers. The monitors were showing the rocket erect on the pad, and the launch announcer echoed the words that had been used by Neil Armstrong on the moon: "The Falcon has landed." The loud sound, it turned out, was the sonic boom from the rocket's reentry into the upper atmosphere.

One of the flight engineers ran out of the control room with the news. "It's standing on the pad!" she shouted. Musk turned around and did his fast lumber back toward the pad. "Holy fucking shit," he kept saying to himself. "Holy fucking shit."

That night, they all went to a waterfront bar called Fishlips to party. Musk hoisted a beer. "We just launched and landed the biggest rocket in the world!" he shouted to the hundred or so employees and other amazed onlookers. As the crowd chanted "USA, USA," he jumped up and down, pumping his fists into the air.

"Congrats @SpaceX on landing Falcon's suborbital booster stage," Bezos wrote in a tweet. "Welcome to the club!" Swaddled in his gauze of graciousness was a stiletto jab: the claim that the booster SpaceX landed was "suborbital," putting it in the same club as the booster that Blue Origin had landed. Technically he was right. The SpaceX booster had never gone into orbit itself, just boosted a payload that did. But Musk was furious. The ability to send a payload into orbit put the SpaceX rocket, he believed, in a different league.

39

The Talulah Roller Coaster

2012–2015

Taking on a Sumo wrestler *(top left)*; with Talulah *(top right)*;
with Navaid Farooq *(bottom)*

When Talulah Riley married Musk in 2010, she moved to California and pretty much gave up her acting career. An only child, she had dreamed of having many children, and in the pictures she drew there were always twin blond boys. "When I met Elon, he had five children and the oldest were these gorgeous little blond-haired twins that felt like they jumped up out of my imagination." But cautious about their relationship, she decided not to have kids of her own with him.

She continued to choreograph parties for Musk, as she had done in Scotland for their wedding and on the Orient Express for his fortieth birthday. For his forty-first, she rented a stately home in the English countryside and used as the theme *Flying Down to Rio*, based on the 1933 film that first paired Fred Astaire and Ginger Rogers and culminates with a dance sequence on the wings of an airplane. She hired the Breitling Wingwalkers, and guests were taught how to wingwalk on a biplane.

But Musk missed most of the party and instead spent time in his room on the phone dealing with various issues at Tesla and SpaceX. He liked to focus on work. At times he treated the rest of life as an unpleasant distraction. "The sheer amount of time that I spent at work was so extreme that any relationship was very difficult to maintain," he admits. "SpaceX and Tesla were difficult individually. Doing them both at the same time was almost impossible. So it was just all work all the time."

Maye Musk sympathized with Talulah. "She would invite me for dinner, and Elon wouldn't show because he's working late," she says. "She loved him to bits, but she understandably got tired of being treated that way."

When his mind was on work, which was most of the time, Talulah didn't know how to get through to him. He always seemed to be in a death struggle over some issue, which was such a contrast to life in her hometown English village, where everyone at the pub and church were so friendly. "I felt this was not the life I should be living," she says. "I hated Los Angeles and I was terribly homesick for England."

So in 2012, she filed for divorce and moved to an apartment in Santa Monica while their lawyers worked out a settlement. But when they met in court four months later to sign the agreement, the story took a cinematic twist. "I saw Elon there, standing in front of the judge, and he sort of asked, 'What the hell are we doing,' and then we started kissing," she says. "I think the judge thought we were crazy." Musk asked her to come back to his house and see the boys. "They've been wondering where you are." And so she did.

They went through with the divorce, but she ended up moving back in with him. To celebrate they took a road trip in a new Model S with the five kids. He also brought her to lunch with the *Esquire* writer Tom Junod. Her main job, she told Junod, was keeping Musk from going king-crazy. "You've never heard that term?" she asked. "It means that people become king, and then they go crazy."

For his forty-second birthday, in June 2013, Talulah rented an ersatz castle in Tarrytown, New York, just north of New York City, and invited forty friends. The theme this time was Japanese steampunk, and Musk and the other men were dressed as samurai warriors. There was a performance of Gilbert and Sullivan's *The Mikado*, which had been rewritten slightly to feature Musk as the Japanese emperor, and a demonstration by a knife-thrower. Musk, never one to avoid risks, even needless ones, put a pink balloon just underneath his groin for the knife-thrower to target while blindfolded.

The culmination was a demonstration of Sumo wrestling. At the end, the group's 350-pound champion invited Musk into the ring. "I went full strength at him to try a judo throw, because I thought he was trying to take it easy on me," Musk says. "I decided to see if I could throw this guy, and I did. But I also blew out a disc at the base of my neck."

Ever since, Musk has suffered severe bouts of back and neck pain; he would end up having three operations to try to repair his C5-C6 intervertebral disc. During meetings at the Tesla or SpaceX factories, he would sometimes lie flat on the floor with an ice pack at the base of his neck.

A few weeks after the Tarrytown party, in July 2013, he and Talulah decided to remarry. This time it was a very low-key affair in their dining room. Not all fairy tales, however, end happily ever after. Musk's obsession with work continued to plague their relationship. "So the same thing happened again, and I wanted to go back home," she says. She restarted her film career by writing, directing, and star-ring in a comedy called *Scottish Mussel* about a hapless criminal who decides to poach pearl mussels from rivers. When Musk and the boys came to visit her during the filming, she told him she wanted to stay in England and get divorced again.

After some hesitations and reconciliations, she made the final decision on her thirtieth birthday, in September 2015. She finished filming the HBO series *Westworld* in Los Angeles, then moved back to England for good. But she made him a promise. "You're my Mr. Rochester," she said, referring to the brooding husband in Charlotte Brontë's novel *Jane Eyre*. "And if Thornfield Hall burns down and you are blind, I'll come to you and take care of you."

40

Artificial Intelligence

OpenAI, 2012–2015

With Sam Altman

Peter Thiel, the PayPal cofounder who had invested in SpaceX, holds a conference each year with the leaders of companies financed by his Founders Fund. At the 2012 gathering, Musk met Demis Hassabis, a neuroscientist, video-game designer, and artificial intelligence researcher with a courteous manner that conceals a competitive mind. A chess prodigy at age four, he became the five-time champion of an international Mind Sports Olympiad that includes competition in chess, poker, *Mastermind*, and backgammon.

In his modern London office is an original edition of Alan Turing's seminal 1950 paper, "Computing Machinery and Intelligence," which proposed an "imitation game" that would pit a human against a ChatGPT–like machine. If the responses of the two were indistinguishable, he wrote, then it would be reasonable to say that machines could "think." Influenced by Turing's argument, Hassabis cofounded a company called DeepMind that sought to design computer-based neural networks that could achieve artificial general intelligence. In other words, it sought to make machines that could learn how to think like humans.

"Elon and I hit it off right away, and I went to visit him at his rocket factory," Hassabis says. While sitting in the canteen overlooking the assembly lines, Musk explained that his reason for building rockets that could go to Mars was that it might be a way to preserve human consciousness in the event of a world war, asteroid strike, or civilization collapse. Hassabis added another potential threat to the list: artificial intelligence. Machines could become superintelligent and surpass us mere mortals, perhaps even decide to dispose of us. Musk paused silently for almost a minute as he processed this possibility. During such trancelike periods, he says, he runs visual simulations about the ways that multiple factors may play out over the years. He decided that Hassabis might be right about the danger of AI, and he invested $5 million in DeepMind as a way to monitor what it was doing.

A few weeks after his conversations with Hassabis, Musk described DeepMind to Google's Larry Page. They had known each other for more than a decade, and Musk often stayed at Page's Palo Alto house. The potential dangers of artificial intelligence became a topic that Musk would raise, almost obsessively, during their late-night conversations. Page was dismissive.

At Musk's 2013 birthday party in Napa Valley, they got into a passionate debate in front of the other guests, including Luke Nosek and Reid Hoffman. Musk argued that unless we built in safeguards, artificial intelligence systems might replace humans, making our species irrelevant or even extinct.

Page pushed back. Why would it matter, he asked, if machines someday surpassed humans in intelligence, even consciousness? It would simply be the next stage of evolution.

Human consciousness, Musk retorted, was a precious flicker of light in the universe, and we should not let it be extinguished. Page considered that sentimental nonsense. If consciousness could be replicated in a machine, why would that not be just as valuable? Perhaps we might even be able someday to upload our own consciousness into a machine. He accused Musk of being a "specist," someone who was biased in favor of their own species. "Well, yes, I am pro-human," Musk responded. "I fucking like humanity, dude."

Musk was therefore dismayed when he heard at the end of 2013 that Page and Google were planning to buy DeepMind. Musk and his friend Luke Nosek tried to put together financing to stop the deal. At a party in Los Angeles, they went to an upstairs closet for an hour-long Skype call with Hassabis. "The future of AI should not be controlled by Larry," Musk told him.

The effort failed, and Google's acquisition of DeepMind was announced in January 2014. Page initially agreed to create a "safety council," with Musk as a member. The first and only meeting was held at SpaceX. Page, Hassabis, and Google chair Eric Schmidt attended, along with Reid Hoffman and a few others. "Elon's takeaway was the council was basically bullshit," says Sam Teller, then his chief of staff. "These Google guys have no intention of focusing on AI safety or doing anything that would limit their power."

Musk proceeded to publicly warn of the danger. "Our biggest existential threat," he told a 2014 symposium at MIT, "is probably artificial intelligence." When Amazon announced its chatbot digital assistant, Alexa, that year, followed by a similar product from Google,

Musk began to warn about what would happen when these systems became smarter than humans. They could surpass us and begin treating us as pets. "I don't love the idea of being a house cat," he said. The best way to prevent a problem was to ensure that AI remained tightly aligned and partnered with humans. "The danger comes when artificial intelligence is decoupled from human will."

So Musk began hosting a series of dinner discussions that included members of his old PayPal mafia, including Thiel and Hoffman, on ways to counter Google and promote AI safety. He even reached out to President Obama, who agreed to a one-on-one meeting in May 2015. Musk explained the risk and suggested that it be regulated. "Obama got it," Musk says. "But I realized that it was not going to rise to the level of something that he would do anything about."

Musk then turned to Sam Altman, a tightly bundled software entrepreneur, sports car enthusiast, and survivalist who, behind his polished veneer, had a Musk-like intensity. Altman had met Musk a few years earlier and spent three hours with him in conversation as they toured the SpaceX factory. "It was funny how some of the engineers would scatter or look away when they saw Elon coming," Altman says. "They were afraid of him. But I was impressed by how much detail he understood about every little piece of the rocket."

At a small dinner in Palo Alto, Altman and Musk decided to cofound a nonprofit artificial intelligence research lab, which they named OpenAI. It would make its software open-source and try to counter Google's growing dominance of the field. Thiel and Hoffman joined Musk in putting up the money. "We wanted to have something like a Linux version of AI that was not controlled by any one person or corporation," Musk says. "The goal was to increase the probability that AI would develop in a safe way that would be beneficial to humanity."

One question they discussed at dinner was what would be safer: a small number of AI systems that were controlled by big corporations or a large number of independent systems? They concluded that a large number of competing systems, providing checks and balances on each other, was better. Just as humans work collectively to stop evil actors, so too would a large collection of independent AI bots work to stop bad bots. For Musk, this was the reason to make OpenAI truly *open*, so that lots of people could build systems based on its source code. "I think the best defense against the misuse of AI is to empower as many people as possible to have AI," he told *Wired*'s Steven Levy at the time.

One goal that Musk and Altman discussed at length, which would become a hot topic in 2023 after OpenAI launched a chatbot called ChatGPT, was known as "AI alignment." It aims to make sure that AI systems are aligned with human goals and values, just as Isaac Asimov set forth rules to prevent the robots in his novels from harming humanity. Think of the computer Hal that runs amok and battles its human creators in *2001: A Space Odyssey*. What guardrails and kill switches can we humans put on AI systems so that they remain aligned with our interests, and who among us should get to determine what those interests are?

One way to assure AI alignment, Musk felt, was to tie the bots closely to humans. They should be an extension of the will of individuals, rather than systems that could go rogue and develop their own goals and intentions. That would become one of the rationales for Neuralink, the company he would found to create chips that could connect human brains directly to computers.

He also realized that success in the field of artificial intelligence would come from having access to huge amounts of real-world data that the bots could learn from. One such gold mine, he realized at the time, was Tesla, which collected millions of frames of video each day of drivers handling different situations. "Probably Tesla will have more real-world data than any other company in the world," he said. Another trove of data, he would later come to realize, was Twitter, which by 2023 was processing 500 million posts per day from humans.

Among those at the dinners with Musk and Altman was a research engineer at Google, Ilya Sutskever. They were able to lure him away, with a $1.9 million salary and starting bonus, to be the chief scientist of the new lab. Page was furious. Not only was his erstwhile friend and houseguest starting a rival lab; he was poaching Google's top scientists. After the launch of OpenAI at the end of 2015, they barely spoke again. "Larry felt betrayed and was really mad at me for personally recruiting Ilya, and he refused to hang out with me anymore," Musk says. "And I was like, 'Larry, if you just hadn't been so cavalier about AI safety then it wouldn't really be necessary to have some countervailing force.'"

Musk's interest in artificial intelligence would lead him to launch an array of related projects. These include Neuralink, which aims to plant microchips in human brains; Optimus, a humanlike robot; and Dojo, a supercomputer that can use millions of videos to train an artificial neural network to simulate a human brain. It also spurred him to become obsessed with pushing to make Tesla cars self-driving. At first these endeavors were rather independent, but eventually Musk would tie them all together, along with a new chatbot company he founded called X.AI, to pursue the goal of artificial general intelligence.

Musk's determination to develop artificial intelligence capabilities at his own companies caused a break with OpenAI in 2018. He tried to convince Altman that OpenAI, which he thought was falling behind Google, should be folded into Tesla. The OpenAI team rejected that idea, and Altman stepped in as president of the lab, starting a for-profit arm that was able to raise equity funding.

So Musk decided to forge ahead with building a rival AI team to work on Tesla Autopilot. Even as he was struggling with the production hell surges in Nevada and Fremont, he recruited Andrej Karpathy, a specialist in deep learning and computer vision, away from OpenAI. "We realized that Tesla was going to become an AI company and would be competing for the same talent as OpenAI," Altman says. "It pissed some of our team off, but I fully understood what was happening." Altman would turn the tables in 2023 by hiring Karpathy back after he became exhausted working for Musk.

41

The Launch of Autopilot

Tesla, 2014–2016

Franz von Holzhausen with an early "Robotaxi"

Radar

Musk had discussed with Larry Page the possibility of Tesla and Google working together to build an autopilot system that would allow cars to be self-driving. But their falling-out over artificial intelligence spurred Musk to accelerate plans for Tesla to build a system on its own.

Google's autopilot program, eventually named Waymo, used a laser-radar device known as LiDAR, an acronym for "light detection and ranging." Musk resisted the use of LiDAR and other radar-like instruments, insisting that a self-driving system should use only visual data from cameras. It was a case of first principles: humans drove using only visual data; therefore machines should be able to. It was also an issue of cost. As always, Musk focused not just on the design of a product but also on how it would be manufactured in large numbers. "The problem with Google's approach is that the sensor system is too expensive," he said in 2013. "It's better to have an optical system, basically cameras with software that is able to figure out what's going on just by looking at things."

Over the next decade, Musk would engage in a tug-of-war with his engineers, many of whom wanted to include some form of radar in Tesla's self-driving cars. Dhaval Shroff, a sparky young engineer from Mumbai who joined Tesla's Autopilot team in 2014 after graduating from Carnegie Mellon, remembers one of his first meetings with Musk. "Back then we had radar hardware in the car, and we told Elon that it was best safety-wise to use it," says Shroff. "He agreed to let us keep radar in, but it was clear that he thought we should eventually be able to rely on camera vision only."

By 2015, Musk was spending hours each week working with the Autopilot team. He would drive from his home in the Bel Air neighborhood of Los Angeles to the SpaceX headquarters near the airport, where they would discuss the problems his Autopilot system encountered. "Every meeting started with Elon saying, 'Why can't the car drive itself from my home to work?'" says Drew Baglino, one of Tesla's senior vice presidents.

This sometimes led the Tesla team to do some Keystone Kops

scrambling. There was a curve on Interstate 405 that always caused Musk trouble because the lane markings were faded. The Autopilot would swerve out of the lane and almost hit oncoming cars. Musk would come into the office furious. "Do something to program this right," he kept demanding. This went on for months as the team tried to improve the Autopilot software.

In desperation, Sam Teller and others came up with a simpler solution: ask the transportation department to repaint the lanes of that section of the highway. When they got no response, they came up with a more audacious plan. They decided to rent a line-painting machine of their own, go out at 3 a.m., shut the highway down for an hour, and redo the lanes. They had gone as far as tracking down a line-painting machine when someone finally got through to a person at the transportation department who was a Musk fan. He agreed to have the lines repainted if he and a few others at the department could get a tour of SpaceX. Teller gave them a tour, they posed for a picture, and the highway lines got repainted. After that, Musk's Autopilot handled the curve well.

Baglino was among the Tesla engineers who wanted to continue to use radar to supplement camera vision. "There was just such a gulf between Elon's goal and the possible," says Baglino. "He just wasn't aware enough of the challenges." At one point Baglino's team did an analysis of the distance perception an autopilot system would need for situations such as at a stop sign. How far left and right did the car need to see in order to know when it could safely cross? "We're trying to have those conversations with Elon to establish what the sensors would need to do," Baglino says. "And they were really difficult conversations, because he kept coming back to the fact that people have just two eyes and they can drive the car. But those eyes are attached to a neck, and the neck can move, and people can position those eyes all over the place."

Musk relented for the time being. Each new Model S, he conceded, would be equipped not only with eight cameras but also with twelve ultrasonic sensors plus a forward-facing radar that was able to see through rain and fog. "Together, this system provides a view of the world that a driver alone cannot access, seeing in every direction simultaneously and on wavelengths that go far beyond the human senses," the Tesla website announced in 2016. But even as Musk made this concession, it was clear that he would not give up pushing to make a camera-only system work.

Accidents

As Musk pursued his autonomous-vehicle ideas, he stubbornly and repeatedly exaggerated the Autopilot capability of Tesla cars. That was dangerous; it led some drivers to think they could ride in a Tesla without paying much attention. Even as Musk was making his grand promises in 2016, Tesla was being dropped by one of its camera suppliers, Mobileye. Tesla was "pushing the envelope in terms of safety," its chairman said.

It was inevitable that there would be some fatal accidents involving Autopilot, just as there were without Autopilot. Musk insisted that the system should be judged not on whether it prevented accidents but instead on whether it led to fewer accidents. It was a logical stance, but it ignored the emotional reality that a person killed by an Autopilot system would provoke a lot more horror than a hundred deaths caused by driver error.

The first reported case of a fatal accident involving Autopilot in the U.S. came in May 2016. A driver was killed in Florida when a tractor-trailer truck made a left turn in front of his Tesla. "Neither Autopilot nor the driver noticed the white side of the tractor-trailer against a brightly lit sky, so the brake was not applied," Tesla said in a statement. Investigators found evidence that, at the time of the crash, the driver was watching a Harry Potter movie on a computer propped on the dashboard. The National Transportation Safety Board concluded that "the driver neglected to maintain complete control of the Tesla leading up to the crash." Tesla had oversold its Autopilot capabilities, and the driver likely surmised that he did not have to pay close attention. There were reports of another fatal accident, involving a Tesla that was probably in Autopilot mode, that had occurred in China earlier that year.

The news about the Florida crash broke when Musk was on his

first visit back to South Africa in sixteen years. He immediately flew back to the United States, but he did not make any public statement. He had the mind of an engineer rather than a feel for human emotions. He could not understand why one or two deaths caused by Tesla Autopilot created an outcry when there were more than 1.3 million traffic deaths annually. Nobody was tallying the accidents prevented and lives saved by Autopilot. Nor were they assessing whether driving with Autopilot was safer than driving without it.

Musk held a conference call with reporters in October 2016, and he got angry when the first questions were about the two deaths. If they wrote stories that dissuaded people from using autonomous driving systems, or regulators from approving them, "then you are killing people." He paused and then barked, "Next question."

Promises, promises

Musk's grand vision—sometimes akin to a mirage that kept receding into the horizon—was that Tesla would build a completely autonomous car that would drive itself without any human intervention. He believed that would transform our daily lives as well as make Tesla the world's most valuable company. "Full Self-Driving," as Tesla began to call it, would be able to function, Musk promised, not only on highways but also on city streets with pedestrians, cyclists, and complex intersections.

As with his other mission-driven obsessions, including travel to Mars, he made what would turn out to be absurd predictions about timing. On his October 2016 call with reporters, he declared that by the end of the following year, a Tesla would be able to drive from Los Angeles to New York "without the need for a single touch" on the wheel. "When you want your car to return, tap Summon on your phone," he said. "It will eventually find you even if you are on the other side of the country."

This could have been dismissed as an amusing fantasy, except that he began pushing the engineers working on Tesla's Model 3 and Model Y to design versions that had no steering wheel and no pedals for acceleration and braking. Von Holzhausen pretended to comply.

Beginning in late 2016, there would always be pictures and physical models of "Robotaxis" for Musk to see when he walked through the design studio. "He was convinced that by the time we got Model Y into production it would be a full-on Robotaxi, fully autonomous," von Holzhausen says.

Almost every year, Musk would make another prediction that Full Self-Driving was just a year or two away. "When will someone be able to buy one of your cars and literally just take the hands off the wheel and go to sleep and wake up and find that they've arrived?" Chris Anderson asked him at a TED Talk in May 2017. "That's about two years," Musk replied. In an interview with Kara Swisher at a Code Conference at the end of 2018, he said Tesla was "on track to do it next year." In early 2019, he doubled down. "I think we will be feature complete, Full Self-Driving, this year," he declared on a podcast with ARK Invest. "I would say I am certain of that. That is not a question mark."

"If he lets up and admits that it's going to take a long time," von Holzhausen said at the end of 2022, "then nobody will rally around it and we won't design vehicles that require autonomy." On an earnings call with analysts that year, Musk admitted that the process had been harder than he expected back in 2016. "Ultimately, what it comes down to," he said, "is that to solve Full Self-Driving, you actually have to solve real-world artificial intelligence."

42

Solar

Tesla Energy, 2004–2016

Lyndon and Peter Rive

Burning Man

"I want to start a new business," Musk's cousin Lyndon Rive said as they were driving in an RV to Burning Man, the annual art-and-tech rave in the Nevada desert, at the end of the summer of 2004. "One that can help humanity and address climate change."

"Get into the solar industry," Musk replied.

Lyndon recalls that the answer felt like "my marching orders." With his brother Peter, he started work on creating a company that would become SolarCity. "Elon provided most of the initial funding," Peter recalls. "He gave us one clear piece of guidance: get to a scale that would have an impact as fast as possible."

Musk's three Rive cousins—Lyndon, Peter, and Russ—were the sons of Maye Musk's twin sister, and they had grown up with Elon and Kimbal, riding bikes and fighting and plotting ways to make money. Like Elon, they headed to America to pursue their entrepreneurial dreams as soon as they could leave South Africa. The whole clan, Peter says, followed the same maxim: "Risk is a type of fuel."

Lyndon, the youngest, was especially tenacious. His passion was playing underwater hockey, which may be the ultimate tenacity-testing sport, and he had come to America as a member of the South African national team. He stayed in Elon's apartment, liked the vibe in Silicon Valley, and took the lead in forming with his brothers a computer support company. They would zip around Santa Cruz on skateboards making service calls. Eventually they came up with their own software to automate many of the tasks, which helped them sell the company to Dell Computers.

After Elon suggested they go into the solar-panel business, Lyndon and Peter tried to figure out why so few people were buying them. The answer was easy. "We realized that the consumer experience was horrible and the high upfront cost was a massive barrier," Peter says. So they came up with a plan to simplify the process. A customer would call a toll-free number, a sales team would use satellite imagery to gauge the size of the roof and how much sunlight it got, and then the company would offer a contract specifying the cost, utility savings, and financing terms. If a customer agreed, the company would dispatch a team in green uniforms to install the panels and apply for government rebates. The goal was to create a nation-wide consumer brand. Musk invested $10 million to get the company started. On July 4, 2006—just when Tesla was about to reveal the Roadster—they launched SolarCity, with Musk as chairman of the board.

Buying SolarCity

For a while, SolarCity did pretty well. By 2015, it accounted for a quarter of all solar installations not done by a utility company. But it struggled to find a business model. At first it leased the solar panels to customers with no upfront cost. This led to mounting debt for the company, and the stock declined from a high of $85 per share in 2014 to about $20 a share in mid-2016.

Musk became increasingly frustrated with the company's practices, especially the way it relied on an aggressive sales force that was compensated by commissions. "Their sales tactics became like those schemes that go door to door selling you boxes of knives or something crappy like that," Musk says. His instincts had always been just the opposite. He never put much effort into sales and marketing, and instead believed that if you made a great product, the sales would follow.

Musk began hounding his cousins. "Are you a sales company or a product company?" he kept asking. They couldn't quite understand his fixation on product. "We would be kicking ass on market share," Peter says, "and Elon would be questioning aesthetic things and pointing out something like the look of the clips and get angry and say they were ugly." Musk became so frustrated that at one point he threatened to resign as chairman. Kimbal talked him out of it. Instead, in February 2016, he phoned his cousins and told them that he wanted Tesla to buy SolarCity.

After opening its Nevada battery factory, Tesla had begun making a refrigerator-size battery for the home, called the Powerwall. It could be connected to solar panels, such as those installed by SolarCity. The concept helped Musk avoid the mistake made by many corporate leaders of defining their business too narrowly. "Tesla is not just an automotive company," he said when the Powerwall was announced in April 2015. "It's an energy innovation company."

With a solar roof connected to a home battery and to a Tesla in the garage, people could free themselves from dependency on big utilities and oil companies. The combined offerings could enable Tesla to do more to fight climate change than any other company— perhaps any other entity—in the world. There was, however, a problem with Musk's integrated energy concept: his cousins' solar business was not part of Tesla. Having Tesla buy SolarCity would accomplish two things: allow him to integrate the home energy business and save his cousins' foundering enterprise.

At first the board of Tesla balked, which was unusual. They were normally very deferential to Musk. The proposed deal seemed like a bailout of Musk's cousins and Musk's SolarCity investment at a time when Tesla was suffering its own production problems. But the board approved the idea four months later, after SolarCity's financial condition worsened. Tesla would offer a rather high 25 percent premium for the purchase of SolarCity's stock, of which Musk was the largest holder. Musk recused himself from a few of the board votes, but he participated in many of the private discussions with his cousins at SolarCity.

When Musk announced the deal in June 2016, he called it a "no-brainer" that was "legally and morally correct." The acquisition fit with his original "master plan" for Tesla, which he had written in 2006: "The overarching purpose of Tesla Motors is to help expedite the move from a mine-and-burn hydrocarbon economy towards a solar electric economy."

It also fit with Musk's instinct to have end-to-end control of all his endeavors. "Elon made us realize that you've got to have solar and battery combined," says his cousin Peter. "We really wanted to offer an integrated product, but it was difficult when the engineers were at two different companies."

The deal received approval by 85 percent of "disinterested" shareholders (meaning Musk couldn't vote his shares) of both Tesla and SolarCity. Nevertheless, some Tesla shareholders sued. "Elon caused

Tesla's servile Board to approve the acquisition of an insolvent Solar-City at a patently unfair price, in order to bail out his (and other family members') foundering investment," they charged. In 2022, a Delaware chancery court ruled in Musk's favor: "The acquisition marked a vital step forward for a company that had for years made clear to the market and its stockholders that it intended to expand from an electric car manufacturer to an alternative energy company."

"This is shit"

On a call with SolarCity investors in August 2016, just before the shareholder votes that would finalize the merger with Tesla, Musk hinted at a new product that would transform the industry. "What if we can offer you a roof that looks way better than a normal roof? That lasts far longer than a normal roof? Different ballgame."

The idea that he and his Rive cousins were working on was a "solar roof" rather than solar panels that could be installed on top of a regular roof. It would be made of tiles that had solar cells embedded inside them. The solar tiles could replace the existing roof or be laid on top of it. Either way it would look like a roof rather than a bunch of solar panels mounted on a roof.

The solar roof project caused enormous friction between Musk and his cousins. In August 2016, around the time he was teasing the new product, Peter Rive invited Musk to inspect a version that the company had installed on a customer's roof. It was a standing-seam metal roof, meaning the solar cells were embedded in sheets of metal rather than tiles.

When Musk drove up, Peter and fifteen people were standing in front of the house. "But as often happened," Peter recalled, "Elon showed up late and then sat in the car looking at his phone while we all just waited very nervously for him to get out." When he did, it was clear that he was furious. "This is shit," Musk explained. "Total fucking shit. Horrible. What were you thinking?" Peter explained that it was the best they could do in a short time to make a version that was installable. That meant they had to compromise on aesthetics. Musk ordered them to focus instead on solar tiles rather than a metal roof.

Working around the clock, the Rives and their SolarCity team were able to mock up some solar tiles, and Musk scheduled a public unveiling for October. It was held on the Universal Studios Hollywood lot, where the solar roof options were mounted on a set of homes that had been used in the *Desperate Housewives* TV series. There were four versions, including those that looked like French slate and Tuscan barrel tiles, along with a house that featured the metal roof that Musk hated. When Musk visited two days before the scheduled event and saw the metal version, he erupted. "What part of 'I fucking hate this product' don't you understand?" One of the engineers pushed back, saying it looked okay to him and that it was the easiest to install. Musk pulled Peter aside and told him, "I don't think this guy should be on the team." Peter fired the engineer and had the metal roof removed before the public event.

Two hundred people showed up at Universal Studios for the presentation. Musk began by talking about rising carbon dioxide levels and the threat of climate change. "Save us, Elon!" someone shouted. At that point Musk pointed behind him. "The houses you see around you are all solar houses," he said. "Did you notice?"

Inside each of the garages was an upgraded version of Tesla's Powerwall along with a Tesla car. The solar tiles would generate electricity that could be stored in the Powerwall and in the battery of the car. "This is the integrated future," he said. "We can solve the whole energy equation."

It was a lofty vision, but it came at a personal cost. Within a year, both Peter and Lyndon Rive would leave the company.

43

The Boring Company

2016

On a trip to Hong Kong in late 2016, Musk had a jammed day of meetings and, as was often the case, needed some minutes of down time when he could recharge, check his phone, and just stare blankly. He was doing that stare when Jon McNeill, Tesla's president of sales and marketing, came over to break him out of his trance. "Did you ever notice that cities are built in 3-D, but the roads are only built in 2-D?" Musk finally said. McNeill looked puzzled. "You could build roads in 3-D by building tunnels under cities," Musk explained. He called Steve Davis, a trusted engineer at SpaceX. It was 2 a.m. in California, but Davis agreed to study ways to build tunnels quickly and inexpensively.

"Okay," Musk said, "I will call you back in three hours."

When Musk called back, Davis had figured out a few ideas for using a standard tunneling machine to bore a simple forty-foot-diameter round hole and not have to reinforce it with concrete. "How much do these machines cost?" Musk asked. Davis told him $5 million. Buy two of them, Musk said, and have them when I return.

When he arrived back in Los Angeles a few days later, Musk found himself stuck in traffic. So he started tweeting. "Traffic is driving me nuts," he wrote. "Am going to build a tunnel boring machine and just start digging." He toyed with various names for a new company, including Tunnels R Us and American Tubes & Tunnels. But then he struck on a name that appealed to his Monty Python sense of humor. As he tweeted an hour later, "It shall be called 'The Boring Company.' Boring, it's what we do."

Musk had come up with an even more audacious idea a few years earlier, which was to build a pneumatic-like tube with electromagnetically accelerated pods to propel people at close to supersonic speeds between cities. He called it Hyperloop. In an unusual show of restraint, he thought better of attempting to build one and instead set up a design competition for students. He built a mile-long vacuum-chamber tube alongside SpaceX headquarters for them to demonstrate their ideas. The first Hyperloop student competition was scheduled for a Sunday in January 2017, and student groups from as far away as the Netherlands and Germany were planning to come and show off their experimental pods.

Mayor Eric Garcetti and other officials would be there, so Musk decided it would be a good opportunity to announce his tunnel-boring idea. At a meeting that Friday morning, he asked how long it would take to begin digging a tunnel in the lot next to the Hyperloop experiment tube. About two weeks, he was told. "Get started today," he ordered. "I want as big of a hole as we can by Sunday." His assistant Elissa Butterfield scrambled to get Tesla workers to move their cars out of the lot, and within three hours the two tunneling machines Davis had bought were digging away. By Sunday, there was a gaping fifty-foot-wide hole leading down to the beginning of a tunnel.

Musk invested $100 million of his own money to get The Boring Company started, and over the next two years would frequently cross the street from SpaceX to check on progress. How can we move faster? What are the impediments? "He spent a lot of time giving us lessons about the importance of deleting steps and simplifying," says Joe Kuhn, a young engineer from Chicago who designed the way vehicles would get through the tunnel. For example, they were drilling a vertical shaft at the beginning of the tunnel to lower in the tunneling machine. "The gopher in my yard doesn't do that," Musk said. They ended up redesigning the tunneling machine so that it could simply be aimed nose down and start burrowing into the ground.

When the one-mile-long prototype tunnel was almost finished at the end of December 2018, Musk came by late one night with two of his sons and his girlfriend Claire Boucher, known as Grimes.

They piled into a Tesla with custom wheels, and then a large elevator dropped them down forty feet into the tunnel. "Let's go as fast as we can!" he said to Kuhn, who was driving. Grimes protested a bit, asking that they take it easy. Musk reverted to engineer mode, explaining why "the probability of longitudinal impact is extremely low." And so Kuhn gunned it. "This is crazy," Musk exulted. "This is going to change everything."

It didn't change everything. In fact, it became an example of a Musk idea that was overhyped. The Boring Company completed a 1.7-mile tunnel in Las Vegas in 2021 that transported riders in Teslas from the airport and through the convention center, and it began negotiations for projects in other cities. But by 2023, none of them had gotten underway.

44

Rocky Relationships

2016–2017

With Amber Heard, who left a kiss mark on his cheek;
with Donald Trump; Errol Musk

Trump

Musk had never been very political. Like many techies, he was liberal on social issues but with a dollop of libertarian resistance to regulations and political correctness. He contributed to the presidential campaigns of Barack Obama and then Hillary Clinton, and he was a vocal critic of Donald Trump in the 2016 election. "He doesn't seem to have the sort of character that reflects well on the United States," he told CNBC.

But after Trump won, Musk became cautiously optimistic that he might govern as a renegade independent rather than a resentful right-winger. "I thought that maybe some of the crazier stuff he said during the campaign was just a performance and he would land in a more sensible place," he says. So at the urging of his friend Peter Thiel, a Trump supporter, Musk agreed to join a gathering of tech CEOs who were meeting with the president-elect in New York in December 2016.

On the morning of the meeting, Musk visited the editorial boards of the *New York Times* and *Wall Street Journal* and then, because traffic was bad, took the Lexington Avenue subway to Trump Tower. In addition to Thiel, the two dozen tech CEOs at the meeting included Larry Page of Google, Satya Nadella of Microsoft, Jeff Bezos of Amazon, and Tim Cook of Apple.

Afterward, Musk stayed for a private meeting with Trump. A friend had given him a Tesla, Trump said, but he'd never driven it. This baffled Musk, who said nothing. Trump then declared that he "really wanted to get NASA going again." This baffled Musk even more. He urged Trump to set big goals—most notably sending humans to Mars—and let companies compete to fulfill them. Trump seemed amazed at the idea of sending people to Mars, then reiterated that he wanted "to get NASA going again." Musk thought the meeting was odd, but he found Trump to be friendly. "He seems kind of nuts," he said afterward, "but he may turn out okay."

Later, Trump told CNBC's Joe Kernen that he was impressed by Musk. "He likes rockets, and he does good at rockets, too, by the way," Trump told him, then lapsed into Trumpian babble. "I never saw where the engines come down with no wings, no anything, and they're landing, and I said, 'I've never seen that before,' and I was worried about him, because he's one of our great geniuses, and we have to protect our genius, you know we have to protect Thomas Edison and we have to protect all of these people that came up with originally the light bulb and the wheel and all of these things."

Juleanna Glover, a well-connected government-affairs consultant, helped set up some other meetings while they were in Trump Tower, including with vice president–elect Mike Pence and national security aides Michael Flynn and K. T. McFarland. The only one who impressed Musk was Newt Gingrich, who was a space buff and shared his enthusiasm for letting private companies bid for missions.

On Trump's first day as president, Musk went to the White House to be part of a roundtable of top CEOs, and he returned two weeks later for a similar session. He concluded that Trump as president was no different than he was as a candidate. The buffoonery was not just an act. "Trump might be one of the world's best bullshitters ever," he says. "Like my dad. Bullshitting can sometimes baffle the brain. If you just think of Trump as sort of a con-man performance, then his behavior sort of makes sense." When the president pulled the U.S. out of the Paris Accord, an international agreement to fight climate change, Musk resigned from the presidential councils.

Amber Heard

Musk was not bred for domestic tranquility. Most of his romantic relationships involve psychological turmoil. The most agonizing of them all was with the actress Amber Heard, who drew him into a dark vortex that lasted more than a year and produced a deep-seated pain that lingers to this day. "It was brutal," he says.

Their relationship began after she made an action movie in 2012 called *Machete Kills*, which features an inventor who wants to create a society on an orbiting space station. Musk agreed to be a consultant because he wanted to meet her, but that didn't happen until a year later, when she asked if she could come visit SpaceX. "I guess I could be called a geek for someone who can also be called a hot chick," she says jokingly. Musk took her for a ride in a Tesla, and she decided that he looked attractive for a rocket engineer.

She next saw him when they were in line to walk the red carpet at New York's Metropolitan Museum gala in May 2016. Heard, then thirty, was on the brink of an explosive divorce from Johnny Depp. She and Musk talked at the dinner and then the afterparty. Reeling from her relationship with Depp, she felt that Musk was a breath of fresh air.

A few weeks later, she was working in Miami and Musk came to visit. They stayed at a poolside villa he had rented at Miami Beach's Delano Hotel, and then he flew her and her sister up to Cape Canaveral, where a Falcon 9 launch was scheduled. She thought it was the most interesting date she had been on.

For his birthday that June, she decided to surprise him by traveling from Italy, where she was working, to the Fremont Tesla factory. As she got near, she pulled to the side of the road and picked some wild flowers. Working with his security team, she hid in the back of a Tesla and popped out with the flowers when he approached.

Their relationship deepened in April 2017 when he flew to be with her in Australia, where she was filming *Aquaman*, in which she played the princess-warrior lover of a superhero trying to save the world. They walked holding hands through a wildlife sanctuary and did the treetop rope course, after which Heard planted a kiss mark on his cheek. He told her that she reminded him of Mercy, his favorite character in the video game *Overwatch*, so she spent two months designing and commissioning a head-to-toe costume so she could role-play for him.

Her playfulness, however, was accompanied by the type of turmoil that attracted Musk. His brother and friends hated her with a passion that made their distaste for Justine pale. "She was just so toxic," Kimbal says. "A nightmare." Musk's chief of staff Sam Teller compares her to a comic-book villain. "She was like the Joker in *Batman*," he says. "She didn't have a goal or aim other than chaos. She thrives on destabilizing everything." She and Musk would stay up all night fighting, and then he would not be able to get up until the afternoon.

They broke up in July 2017, but then got back together for another five tumultuous months. The end finally came after a wild trip to Rio de Janeiro that December with Kimbal and his wife and some of the kids. When they got to the hotel, Elon and Amber had another of their flamethrowing fights. She locked herself in the room and started yelling that she was afraid she would be attacked and that Elon had taken her passport. The security guards and Kimbal's wife all tried to convince her that she was safe, her passport was in her bag, and she could and should leave whenever she wanted. "She really is a very good actress, so she will say things that you're like, 'Wow, maybe she's telling you the truth,' but she isn't," Kimbal says. "The way she can create her own reality reminds me of my dad." (Let that sink in.)

Amber concedes they had an argument and that she got rather dramatic. But she says that they resolved the fight that evening, which was New Year's Eve. They went to a party and celebrated the ringing in of the new year standing on a balcony overlooking Rio, she in a low-cut white linen dress, he in a partly unbuttoned white linen shirt. Kimbal and his wife were there, along with their cousin Russ Rive and his wife. To show that they had made up, Amber sent me pictures and videos of the evening. In one of them, Elon wishes her a happy new year and kisses her passionately on the lips.

She came to the conclusion that Musk cultivated drama because he needed a lot of stimuli to keep him invigorated. Even after they broke up for good, the embers endured. "I love him very much," she says. She also understands him well. "Elon loves fire," she says, "and sometimes it burns him."

The fact that Elon was attracted to Amber was part of a pattern. "It's really sad that he falls in love with these people who are really mean to him," Kimbal says. "They're beautiful, no question, but they have a very dark side and Elon knows that they're toxic."

So why does he do it? When I ask Elon, he lets out his large laugh. "Because I'm just a fool for love," he says. "I am often a fool, but especially for love."

Errol and Jana

Elon had not seen his father since the end of 2002, when Errol and his family visited after baby Nevada's death. During that stay, Elon had become uncomfortable about Errol's fondness for his then fifteen-year-old stepdaughter Jana, and Elon pressured him to go back to South Africa.

But in 2016, Elon and Kimbal planned a trip with their families to South Africa, and they decided that they should see their father, who was now divorced and had been having heart problems. Elon shares some things with his father, probably more than he would like to admit, including a birthday: June 28. So they scheduled a lunch to try to reconcile, at least briefly, on their birthdays, Elon's forty-fifth and Errol's seventieth.

They met at a restaurant in Cape Town, where Errol was then living. The group included Kimbal and his new wife Christiana, and Elon and the actress Natasha Bassett, whom he was occasionally dating. Justine had asked that their children, who were on the trip, not be exposed to Errol, so they left the restaurant just before Errol arrived. Antonio Gracias was on the trip and asked if he should leave as well. "Elon put his hand on my leg and said, 'please stay,'" Gracias recalls. "It was the only time I had ever seen Elon's hands shaking." When Errol walked into the restaurant, he loudly praised Elon for how beautiful Natasha was, which made everyone uncomfortable. "Elon and Kimbal were totally shut down, silent," Christiana says. After an hour, they said it was time to leave.

Elon had planned to take Kimbal, Christiana, Natasha, and the kids to Pretoria to see where he had grown up. But after the meeting with his father, he was not in the mood. He abruptly cut short the trip and flew back to the U.S., telling them and himself that he needed to get back to deal with the news of the death of the Florida driver who was using Tesla Autopilot.

The visit, though brief, seemed to herald a détente with his father that could, perhaps, have helped Elon tame some of the demons still haunting him. But that was not to be. Later in 2016, not long after

Elon left, Errol got Jana, then thirty, pregnant. "We were lonely, lost people," Errol later said. "One thing led to another—you can call it God's plan or nature's plan."

When Elon and his siblings found out, they were creeped out and furious. "I was actually slowly making amends with my father," Kimbal says, "but then he had a child with Jana and I said, 'You're done, you're out. I never want to speak to you again.' And I haven't spoken to him since."

Just after he heard the news in the summer of 2017, Musk was scheduled to give an interview to Neil Strauss for a *Rolling Stone* cover story. Strauss began with a question about Tesla's Model 3. As often happened, Musk just sat there silently. He was brooding about Amber Heard and about his father. Without much explanation, he got up and left.

After more than five minutes, Teller went to retrieve him. When Musk returned, he explained to Strauss, "I just broke up with my girlfriend. I was really in love, and it hurt bad." Later in the interview, he unloaded about his father, but without mentioning the child Errol had just had with Jana. "He was such a terrible human being," Musk said, starting to cry. "My dad will have a carefully thought-out plan of evil. He will plan evil. Almost every crime you can possibly think of, he has done. Almost every evil thing you could possibly think of, he has done." In his profile, Strauss noted that Musk would not go into specifics. "There is clearly something Musk wants to share, but he can't bring himself to utter the words."

45

Descent into the Dark

2017

Examining a battery pack with Omead Afshar (*far left*)

Are you bipolar?

Devastated by the breakup with Amber Heard and the news that his father had a child with the woman he had raised as his stepdaughter, Musk went through periods when he oscillated between depression, stupor, giddiness, and manic energy. He would fall into foul moods that led to almost catatonic trances and depressive paralysis. Then, as if a switch flipped, he would become giddy and replay old Monty Python skits of silly walks and wacky debates, breaking into his stuttering laugh. Professionally and emotionally, the summer of 2017 through the fall of 2018 would be the most hellacious period of his life, even worse than the crises of 2008. "That was the time of most concentrated pain I've ever had," he says. "Eighteen months of unrelenting insanity. It was mind-bogglingly painful."

At one point in late 2017, he was scheduled to be on a Tesla earnings call with Wall Street analysts. Jon McNeill, who was then Tesla's president, found him lying on the floor of the conference room with the lights off. McNeill went over and lay down next to him in the corner. "Hey, pal," McNeill said. "We've got an earnings call to do."

"I can't do it," Musk said.

"You have to," McNeill replied.

It took McNeill a half-hour to get him moving. "He came from a comatose state to a place where we could actually get him in the chair, get other people in the room, get him through his opening statement, and then cover for him," McNeill recalls. Once it was over, Musk said, "I've got to lay down, I've got to shut off the lights. I just need some time alone." McNeill said the same scene played out five or six times, including once when he had to lie on the conference room floor next to Musk to get his approval for a new website design.

Around that time, Musk was asked by a user on Twitter if he was bipolar. "Yeah," he answered. But he added that he had not been medically diagnosed. "Bad feelings correlate to bad events, so maybe the real problem is getting carried away for what I sign up for." One day, when they were sitting in the Tesla conference room after one of Musk's spells, McNeill asked him directly whether he was bipolar. When Musk said probably yes, McNeill pushed his chair back from the table and turned to talk to Musk eye to eye. "Look, I have a relative who is bipolar," McNeill said. "I've had close experience with this. If you get good treatment and your meds dialed right, you can get back to who you are. The world needs you." It was a healthy conversation, McNeill says, and Musk seemed to have a clear desire to get out of his messed-up headspace.

But it didn't happen. His way of dealing with his mental problems, he says when I ask, "is just take the pain and make sure you really care about what you're doing."

"Welcome to production hell!"

When the Model 3 began rolling off the production line in July 2017—miraculously meeting the insane deadline Musk had set— Tesla held a raucous event at the Fremont factory to celebrate. Before going onstage, he was scheduled to go into a small room and take questions from a handful of journalists. But something was wrong. He had been in a morbid mood all day, belting down a couple of Red Bulls to keep himself going, then trying to meditate, something he never had seriously done before.

Franz von Holzhausen and JB Straubel tried to break him out of his stupor with a pep talk. But Musk seemed unresponsive, blank-faced, depressed. "I've been in severe emotional pain for the last few weeks," he later said. "Severe. It took every ounce of will to be able to do the Model 3 event and not look like the most depressed guy around." Finally, he steeled himself to go into the press conference. He appeared irritated, then distracted. "Sorry for being a little dry," he told the reporters. "Got a lot on my mind right now."

Then it was time to appear in front of two hundred screaming fans and employees. He tried to put on a good show, at least at first. He drove a new red Model 3 onstage, jumped out, and raised his arms to the sky. "The whole point of this company was to make a really great, affordable electric car," he said, "and we finally have."

But his talk soon took on an eerie tone. Even those in the audience could tell that, despite his attempt to look joyful, he was in a very dark place. Instead of celebrating, he warned about tough times ahead. "The major challenge for us over the next six to nine months is how do we build a huge number of cars," he said haltingly. "Frankly we're going to be in production hell." Then he started giggling maniacally. "Welcome! Welcome! Welcome to production hell! That's where we are going to be for at least six months."

That prospect, like all hellish dramas, seemed to fill him with dark energy. "I look forward to working alongside you journeying through hell," he told his startled audience. "As the saying goes, if you're going through hell, just keep going."

He was: And he did.

Giga Nevada hell

In times of emotional darkness, Musk throws himself into his work, maniacally. And he did so after the July 2017 event marking the beginning of Model 3 production.

He had one primary focus: ramping up production so that Tesla was churning out five thousand Model 3s per week. He had done the calculations of the company's costs, overhead, and cash flow. If it hit that rate, Tesla would survive. If not, it would run out of money. He repeated that like a mantra to every executive, and he installed monitors at the factory showing the up-to-the-minute output of cars and components.

Reaching five thousand cars per week would be a huge challenge. By the end of 2017, Tesla was making cars at only half that rate. Musk decided he had to move himself, literally, to the factory floors and lead an all-in surge. It was a tactic—personally surging into the breach 24/7 with an all-hands-on-deck cadre of fellow fanatics—that came to define the maniacal intensity that he demanded at his companies.

He began with the Gigafactory in Nevada, where Tesla made batteries. The person who designed the line there told Musk that making five thousand battery packs a week was insane. At most they could make eighteen hundred. "If you're right, Tesla is dead," Musk told him. "We either have five thousand cars a week or we can't cover our costs." Building more lines would take another year, the executive said. Musk moved him out and brought in a new captain, Brian Dow, who had the gung-ho mentality Musk liked.

Musk took charge of the factory floor, playing the role of a feverish field marshal. "It was a frenzy of insanity," he says. "We were getting four or five hours' sleep, often on the floor. I remember thinking, 'I'm like on the ragged edge of sanity.'" His colleagues agreed.

Musk called in reinforcements, including his most loyal lieutenants: Mark Juncosa, his engineering sidekick at SpaceX, and Steve Davis, who headed The Boring Company. He even enlisted his young cousin James Musk, son of Errol's younger brother, who had just graduated from Berkeley and joined the Tesla Autopilot team as a coder. "I got a call from Elon saying be at the Van Nuys airstrip in an hour," he says. "We flew to Reno and I ended up staying there four months."

"There were a billion problems," Juncosa says. "A third of the cells were fucked up, and a third of the workstations were fucked up." They fanned out to work on different sections of the battery line, going station to station and troubleshooting any process that was slowing things down. "When we got too exhausted, we'd go crash at the motel for four hours, then head back," Juncosa says.

Omead Afshar, a biomedical engineer who had minored in poetry, had just been hired to join Sam Teller as an aide-de-camp to Musk. Growing up in Los Angeles, he carried a briefcase to grade school because he wanted to be like his father, an Iranian-born engineer. He worked for a few years setting up facilities for a medical equipment manufacturer, and he quickly bonded with Musk after joining Tesla. They both spoke with a soft stutter that cloaked an engineering mindset. On his first day on the job, after renting an apartment near Tesla's Silicon Valley headquarters, he was swept up in the surge and spent the next three months working at the Nevada battery Gigafactory and crashing at a $20-a-night motel nearby. Seven days a week, he would get up at 5 a.m., have a cup of coffee with the manufacturing guru Tim Watkins, work at the factory until 10 p.m., and then have a glass of wine with Watkins before crashing.

At one point Musk noticed that the assembly line was being slowed at a station where strips of fiberglass were glued to the battery packs by an expensive but slow robot. The robot's suction cups kept dropping the strip and it applied too much glue. "I realized that the first error was trying to automate the process, which was my fault because I pushed for a lot of automation," he says.

After much frustration, Musk finally asked a basic question: "What the hell are these strips for?" He was trying to visualize why fiberglass pieces were needed between the battery and the floor pan. The engineering team told him that it had been specified by the noise reduction team to cut down on vibration. So he called the noise reduction team, which told him that the specification came from the engineering team to reduce the risk of fire. "It was like being in a *Dilbert* cartoon," Musk says. So he ordered them to record the sound inside a car without the fiberglass and then with the fiberglass. "See if you can tell the difference," he told them. They couldn't.

"Step one should be to question the requirements," he says. "Make them less wrong and dumb, because all requirements are somewhat wrong and dumb. And then delete, delete, delete."

The same approach worked even on the smallest details. For example, when the battery packs were completed in Nevada, little plastic caps were put on the prongs that would plug it into the car. When the battery got to the Fremont car-assembly factory, the plastic caps were removed and discarded. Sometimes, they would run out of caps in Nevada and have to hold up shipment of the batteries. When Musk asked why the caps existed, he was told they had been specified to make sure the pins did not get bent. "Who specified that requirement?" he asked. The factory team scrambled to find out, but they weren't able to come up with a name. "So delete them," Musk said. They did, and it turned out they never had a problem with bent pins.

Although there was an esprit de corps among Musk's posse, he could be cold and rough on others. At 10 p.m. one Saturday, he became angry about a robotic arm that installed a cooling tube into a battery. The robot's alignment was off, which was holding up the process. A young manufacturing engineer named Gage Coffin was summoned. He was excited about the chance to meet Musk. He had been working for Tesla for two years and had spent the previous eleven months living out of a suitcase and working seven days a week at the factory. It was his first full-time job, and he loved it. When he arrived, Musk barked, "Hey, this doesn't line up. Did you do this?" Coffin responded haltingly by asking Musk what he was referring to. The coding? The design? The tooling? Musk kept asking, "Did you fucking do this?" Coffin, flummoxed and frightened, kept fumbling to figure out the question. That made Musk even more combative. "You're an idiot," he said. "Get the hell out and don't come back." His project manager pulled him aside a few minutes later and told him that Musk had ordered him fired. He received his termination papers that Monday. "My manager was fired a week after me, and his manager the week after that," Coffin says. "At least Elon knew their names."

"When Elon gets upset, he lashes out, often at junior people," says Jon McNeill. "Gage's story was fairly typical of his behavior where he just couldn't really process his frustration in a productive way." JB Straubel, Musk's kinder and gentler cofounder, cringed at Musk's behavior. "In retrospect it may seem like great war stories," he says, "but in the middle of it, it was absolutely horrific. He was making us fire people who had been personal friends for a very long time, which was super painful."

Musk says in response that people such as Straubel and McNeill were too reluctant to fire people. In that area of the factory, things had not been working well. Parts were piling up by the workstations, and the line wasn't moving. "By trying to be nice to the people," Musk says, "you're actually not being nice to the dozens of other people who are doing their jobs well and will get hurt if I don't fix the problem spots."

He spent that Thanksgiving Day at the factory, along with a few of his sons, because he had requested workers to come in. Any day that the factory was not making batteries would set back the number of cars that Tesla could produce.

De-automation

Ever since the development of assembly lines in the early 1900s, most factories have been designed in two steps. First, the line is set up with workers doing specific tasks at each station. Then, when the kinks are worked out, robots and other machines are gradually introduced to take over some of the work. Musk did the reverse. In his vision for a modern "alien dreadnought" factory, he *began* by automating every task possible. "We had this enormously automated production line that used tons of robots," says Straubel. "There was one problem. It didn't work."

One night, Musk was walking through the Nevada battery pack factory with his posse—Omead Afshar, Antonio Gracias, and Tim Watkins—and they noticed a delay at a workstation where a robotic arm was sticking cells to a tube. The machine had a problem gripping the material and getting aligned. Watkins and Gracias went over to a table and tried to do the process by hand. They could do it more reliably. They called Musk over and calculated how many humans it would take to get rid of the machine. Workers were hired to replace the robot, and the assembly line moved more quickly.

Musk flipped from being an apostle of automation to a new mission he pursued with similar zeal: find any part of the line where there was a holdup and see if de-automation would make it go faster. "We began sawing robots out of the production line and throwing them into the parking lot," Straubel says. On one weekend, they marched through the factory painting marks on machinery to be jettisoned. "We put a hole in the side of the building just to remove all that equipment," Musk says.

The experience became a lesson that would become part of Musk's production algorithm. Always wait until the end of designing a process—after you have questioned all the requirements and deleted unnecessary parts—before you introduce automation.

By April 2018, the Nevada factory was working better. The weather had warmed up a bit, so Musk decided he would sleep on the factory roof instead of driving to a motel. His assistant bought a few tents, and his friend Bill Lee and Sam Teller joined him. After inspecting the module and pack assembly lines until close to 1 a.m. one night, they went up to the roof, lit a little portable fire pit, and talked about the next challenge. Musk was ready to turn his attention to Fremont.

In the Jupiter conference room in Fremont in 2008, watching a launch and the Tesla production numbers

46

Fremont Factory Hell

Tesla, 2018

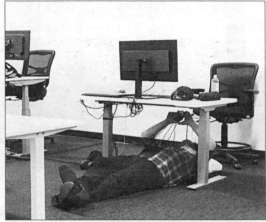

On the line and resting under his desk at the Fremont factory

Short-sellers

As the bottlenecks in the Nevada battery factory eased in the spring of 2018, Musk shifted his focus to the Fremont car-assembly factory, located on the fraying industrial fringe of Silicon Valley across San Francisco Bay from Palo Alto. By the beginning of April, it was producing only two thousand Model 3s per week. There seemed to be no way that the laws of physics would allow him to juice the plant's assembly lines into producing his magic number of five thousand per week, which he was now promising Wall Street would happen by the end of June.

Musk put a stake in the ground by telling all managers to order enough parts and materials to make that number. These had to be paid for, but if they were not turned into finished cars, Tesla would have cash-flow problems that would lead to a death spiral. The result was another one of those frenzied fire drills of activity that Musk called a surge.

Tesla stock was hovering near its all-time high in early 2018, making it more valuable than General Motors, even though GM had sold 10 million cars for a $12 billion profit the previous year, while Tesla had sold 100,000 cars and lost $2.2 billion. Those numbers, and skepticism about Musk's five-thousand-cars-per-week pledge, made Tesla stock a magnet for short-sellers, who make money if the stock price falls. By 2018, Tesla had become the most shorted stock in history.

This infuriated Musk. He believed that short-sellers were not merely skeptics but evil: "They are leeches on the neck of business." The short-sellers publicly attacked Tesla and Musk personally. He would scroll through his Twitter feed seething about the false information. Even worse was the true information. "They had up-to-date data from sources in the company and drones that flew over our factory giving them numbers in real time," he says. "They organized themselves into a shorty ground force and a shorty air force. The degree of inside information they had was insane."

That would eventually lead to their undoing. The short-sellers had hard numbers about how many cars could possibly be produced on the two assembly lines at Fremont, and it led them to conclude that there was no way Tesla could reach five thousand cars per week by mid-2018. "We think the deception is about to catch up to TSLA," wrote one of the shorts, David Einhorn. "Elon Musk's erratic behavior suggests that he sees it the same way." And the most prominent short-seller, Jim Chanos, publicly declared that Tesla stock was basically worthless.

Around that time, Musk made the opposite bet. The Tesla board granted him the boldest pay package in American history, one that would pay him nothing if the stock price did not rise dramatically but that had the potential to pay out $100 billion or more if the company achieved an extraordinarily aggressive set of targets, including a leap in the production numbers, revenue, and stock price. There was widespread skepticism that he could reach the targets. "Mr. Musk will be paid only if he reaches a series of jaw-dropping milestones based on the company's market value and operations," Andrew Ross Sorkin wrote in the *New York Times*. "Otherwise, he will be paid nothing." The payout would top out, Sorkin wrote, only "if Mr. Musk were somehow to increase the value of Tesla to $650 billion—a figure many experts would contend is laughably impossible."

Walk to the red

In the middle of the Fremont factory is the main conference room, known as Jupiter. Musk used it as his office, meeting space, haven from mental torments, and sometimes a place to sleep. An array of screens, blinking and updating like stock displays, tracked in real time the total output of the factory and of each workstation.

Musk had come to realize that designing a good factory was like designing a microchip. It was important to create, in each patch, the right density, flow, and processes. So he paid the most attention to a monitor that showed each station on the assembly line with a green or red light indicating whether it was flowing properly. There were also green and red lights at the stations themselves, so Musk was able to walk the floor and home in on trouble spots. His team called it "walk to the red."

The surge at Fremont began the first week of April 2018. That Monday, he began walking the floor with his fast bearlike gait, heading to any red light he saw. *What's the problem?* A part was missing. *Who's in charge of that part? Get him over here.* A sensor keeps tripping. *Who calibrated it? Find someone who can open the console. Can we adjust the settings? Why do we even need that fucking sensor?*

The process was paused that afternoon because SpaceX was launching a critical cargo supply mission to the Space Station. So Musk went back to the Jupiter conference room to watch it on one of the monitors. But even then, his eyes kept darting to the screens showing the production numbers and bottlenecks on the Tesla line. Sam Teller ordered Thai takeout, then Musk resumed his procession through the factory, looking for the red lights. At 2:30 a.m., he was with the night shift underneath a car being moved on a rack watching bolts being installed. *Why do we have four bolts there? Who set that specification? Can we do it with two? Try it.*

Throughout the spring and early summer of 2018, he prowled the factory floor, like he had in Nevada, making decisions on the fly. "Elon was going completely apeshit, marching from station to station," says Juncosa. Musk calculated that on a good day he made a hundred command decisions as he walked the floor. "At least twenty percent are going to be wrong, and we're going to alter them later," he said. "But if I don't make decisions, we die."

One day Lars Moravy, a valued top executive, was working at Tesla's executive headquarters a few miles away in Palo Alto. He got an urgent call from Omead Afshar asking him to come to the factory. There he found Musk sitting cross-legged underneath the elevated conveyor moving car bodies down the line. Again he was struck by the number of bolts that had been specified. "Why are there six here?" he asked, pointing.

"To make it stable in a crash," Moravy replied.

"No, the main crash load would come through this rail," Musk explained. He had visualized where all the pressure points would be and started rattling off the tolerance numbers at each spot. Moravy sent it back to the engineers to be redesigned and tested.

At another of the stations, the partially completed auto bodies were bolted to a skid that moved them through the final assembly process. The robotic arms tightening the bolts were, Musk thought, moving too slowly. "Even I could do it faster," he said. He told the workers to see what the settings were for the bolt drivers. But nobody knew how to open the control console. "Okay," he said, "I'm just going to just stand here until we find someone who can bring up that console." Finally a technician was found who knew how to access the robot's controls. Musk discovered that the robot was set to 20 percent of its maximum speed and that the default settings instructed the arm to turn the bolt backward twice before spinning it forward to tighten. "Factory settings are always idiotic," he said. So he quickly rewrote the code to delete the backward turns. Then he set the speed to 100 percent capacity. That started to strip the threads, so he dialed it back to 70 percent. It worked fine and cut the time it took to bolt the cars to the skids by more than half.

One part of the painting process, an electrocoat bath, involved dipping the shell of the car into a tank. Areas of the car shell have small holes so that the cavities will drain after the dipping. These holes are then plugged with patches made of synthetic rubber, known as butyl patches. "Why are we applying these?" Musk asked one of the line managers, who replied that it had been specified by the vehicle structures department. So Musk summoned the head of that department. "What the hell are these for?" he demanded. "They're slowing the whole damn line." He was told that in a flood, if the water is higher than the floorboards, the butyl patches help prevent the floor from getting too wet. "That's insane," Musk responded. "Once in ten years there will be such a flood. When it happens, the floor mats can get wet." The patches were deleted.

The production lines often halted when safety sensors were triggered. Musk decided they were too sensitive, tripping when there was no real problem. He tested some of them to see if something small like a piece of paper falling past the sensor could trigger a stoppage. This led to a crusade to weed out sensors in both Tesla cars and SpaceX rockets. "Unless a sensor is absolutely needed to start an engine or safely stop an engine before it explodes, it must be deleted," he wrote in an email to SpaceX engineers. "Going forward, anyone who puts a sensor (or anything) on the engine that isn't obviously critical will be asked to leave."

Some of the managers objected. They felt that Musk was compromising safety and quality in order to rush production. The senior director for production quality left. A group of current and former employees told CNBC that they were "pressured to take shortcuts to hit aggressive Model 3 production goals." They also said they were pushed to make patchwork fixes, such as repairing cracked plastic brackets with electrical tape. The *New York Times* reported that workers felt pressure to work ten-hour days. "It's a constant 'How many cars have we built so far?'—a constant pressure to build," one worker told the paper. There was some truth to the complaints. Tesla's injury rate was 30 percent higher than the rest of the industry.

Robot removal

During his push to ramp up production at the Nevada battery factory, Musk had learned that there are certain tasks, sometimes very simple ones, that humans do better than robots. We can use our eyes to look around a room and find just the right tool we need. Then we can weave our way over, pick it up with our fingers and thumb, eyeball the right spot to use it, and guide it there with our arm. Easy, right? Not for a robot, however good its cameras. At Fremont, where each assembly line had twelve hundred robotic devices, Musk came to the same realization he had in Nevada about the perils of pursuing automation too relentlessly.

Near the end of the final assembly line were robotic arms trying to adjust the little seals around the windows. They were having a hard time. One day, after standing silently in front of the balky robotics for a few minutes, Musk tried doing the task with his own hands. It was easy for a human. He issued an order, similar to the one he had given in Nevada. "You have seventy-two hours to remove every unnecessary machine," he declared.

The robot removal started grimly. People had a lot vested in the machines. But then it became like a game. Musk started walking down the conveyor line, wielding a can of orange spray paint. "Go or stay?" he would ask Nick Kalayjian, his vice president for engineering, or others. If the answer was "go," the piece would be marked with an orange X, and workers would tear it off the line. "Soon he was laughing, like with childlike humor," Kalayjian says.

Musk took responsibility for the over-automation. He even announced it publicly. "Excessive automation at Tesla was a mistake," he tweeted. "To be precise, my mistake. Humans are underrated."

After the de-automation and other improvements, the juiced-up Fremont plant was churning out thirty-five hundred Model 3 sedans per week by late May 2018. That was impressive, but it was far short of the five thousand per week that Musk had promised for the end of June. The short-sellers, with their spies and drones, determined that there was no way the factory, with its two assembly lines, could get to that number. They also knew that there was no way for Tesla to build another factory, or even get a permit to do so, for at least a year. "The shorts thought they had perfect information," Musk says, "and they were all gloating online that, 'Hah, Tesla is screwed.'"

The tent

Musk likes military history, especially the tales of warplane development. At a meeting at the Fremont factory on May 22, he recounted a story about World War II. When the government needed to rush the making of bombers, it set up production lines in the parking lots of the aerospace companies in California. He discussed the idea with Jerome Guillen, whom he would soon promote to being Tesla's president of automotive, and they decided that they could do something similar.

There was a provision in the Fremont zoning code for something called "a temporary vehicle repair facility." It was intended to allow gas stations to set up tents where they could change tires or mufflers. But the regulations did not specify a maximum size. "Get one of those permits and start building a huge tent," he told Guillen. "We'll have to pay a fine later."

That afternoon, Tesla workers began clearing away the rubble that covered an old parking lot behind the factory. There was not time to pave over the cracked concrete, so they simply paved a long strip and began erecting a tent around it. One of Musk's ace facilities builders, Rodney Westmoreland, flew in to coordinate the construction, and Teller rounded up some ice-cream trucks to hand out treats to those working in the hot sun. In two weeks, they were able to complete a tented facility that was 1,000 feet long and 150 feet wide, big enough to accommodate a makeshift assembly line. Instead of robots, there were humans at each station.

One problem was that they did not have a conveyor belt to move the unfinished cars through the tent. All they had was an old system for moving parts, but it was not powerful enough to move car bodies. "So we put it on a slight slope, and gravity meant it had enough power to move the cars at the right speed," Musk says.

At just after 4 p.m. on June 16, just three weeks after Musk came up with the idea, the new assembly line was rolling Model 3 sedans out of the makeshift tent. Neal Boudette of the *New York Times* had come to Fremont to report on Musk in action, and he was able to see the tent going up in the parking lot. "If conventional thinking makes your mission impossible," Musk told him, "then unconventional thinking is necessary."

Birthday celebration

Musk's forty-seventh birthday, on June 28, 2018, came just before the deadline he had promised for reaching five thousand cars per week. He spent most of the day in the paint shop of the main factory. *Why is it backing up?* he would ask each time there was a slowdown, and then he would walk over to the choke point and stand there until engineers came and fixed the situation.

Amber Heard called to wish him a happy birthday, after which he dropped his phone and it broke, so he was not in a good mood. But Teller was able to get him to take a break just after 2 p.m. for a quick celebration in the conference room. "Enjoy year 48 in the simulation!" read the icing on the ice-cream cake that Teller bought. There were no knives or forks, so they ate it with their hands.

Twelve hours later, just after 2:30 a.m., Musk finally left the factory floor and returned to the conference room. But it would be another hour before he would fall asleep there. Instead, he watched on one of the monitors the launch of a SpaceX rocket at Cape Canaveral. It was carrying a robotic assistant along with supplies that included sixty packets of super-caffeinated Death Wish Coffee for the astronauts on the International Space Station. The launch went flawlessly, making it the fifteenth successful cargo mission SpaceX had flown for NASA.

June 30, the deadline Musk had promised for reaching the goal of five thousand cars per week, was a Saturday, and when Musk woke up on the conference room couch that morning and looked at the monitors, he realized they would succeed. He worked for a few hours on the paint line, then rushed from the factory, still wearing protective sleeves, to his airplane to make it to Spain in time to be the best man at Kimbal's wedding in a medieval Catalonian village.

At 1:53 a.m. on Sunday, July 1, a black Model 3 was disgorged from the factory with a paper banner across its windshield reading "5000th." When Musk received a photograph of it on his iPhone, he sent a message to all Tesla workers: "We did it!! . . . Created entirely new solutions that were thought impossible. Intense in tents. Whatever. It worked. . . . I think we just became a real car company."

The algorithm

At any given production meeting, whether at Tesla or SpaceX, there is a nontrivial chance that Musk will intone, like a mantra, what he calls "the algorithm." It was shaped by the lessons he learned during the production hell surges at the Nevada and Fremont factories. His executives sometimes move their lips and mouth the words, like they would chant the liturgy along with their priest. "I became a broken record on the algorithm," Musk says. "But I think it's helpful to say it to an annoying degree." It had five commandments:

1. Question every requirement. Each should come with the name of the person who made it. You should never accept that a requirement came from a department, such as from "the legal department" or "the safety department." You need to know the name

of the real person who made that requirement. Then you should question it, no matter how smart that person is. Requirements from smart people are the most dangerous, because people are less likely to question them. Always do so, even if the requirement came from me. Then make the requirements less dumb.

2. Delete any part or process you can. You may have to add them back later. In fact, if you do not end up adding back at least 10% of them, then you didn't delete enough.

3. Simplify and optimize. This should come after step two. A common mistake is to simplify and optimize a part or a process that should not exist.

4. Accelerate cycle time. Every process can be speeded up. But only do this after you have followed the first three steps. In the Tesla factory, I mistakenly spent a lot of time accelerating processes that I later realized should have been deleted.

5. Automate. That comes last. The big mistake in Nevada and at Fremont was that I began by trying to automate every step. We should have waited until all the requirements had been questioned, parts and processes deleted, and the bugs were shaken out.

The algorithm was sometimes accompanied by a few corollaries, among them:

All technical managers must have hands-on experience. For example, managers of software teams must spend at least 20% of their time coding. Solar roof managers must spend time on the roofs doing installations. Otherwise, they are like a cavalry leader who can't ride a horse or a general who can't use a sword.

Comradery is dangerous. It makes it hard for people to challenge each other's work. There is a tendency to not want to throw a colleague under the bus. That needs to be avoided.

It's OK to be wrong. Just don't be confident and wrong.

Never ask your troops to do something you're not willing to do.

Whenever there are problems to solve, don't just meet with your managers. Do a skip level, where you meet with the level right below your managers.

When hiring, look for people with the right attitude. Skills can be taught. Attitude changes require a brain transplant.

A maniacal sense of urgency is our operating principle.

The only rules are the ones dictated by the laws of physics. Everything else is a recommendation.

On the assembly line

47

Open-Loop Warning

2018

With the Prime Minister of Thailand inspecting the mini-sub;
preparing to enter the cave with the trapped boys

Pedo guy

While Kimbal Musk was on his honeymoon in early July 2018, he got an email from Antonio Gracias, Elon's longtime friend and board member. "Sorry, dude, I know you want to be with your wife, but you have to come back right away," Gracias wrote. "Elon is having a meltdown."

The success of his production push should have made Musk happy. Tesla had hit its goal of producing five thousand Model 3 cars per week and was heading to a profitable quarter. SpaceX had completed fifty-six successful launches, with only one flight failure, and was now regularly landing its boosters so they could be reused. It was sending more payload into orbit than any other company or country, including China and the U.S. If Musk had been the type of person who could pause and savor success, he would have noticed that he had just brought the world into the era of electric vehicles, commercial space flight, and reusable rockets. Each was a big deal.

But for Musk, good times are unsettling. He began lashing out about what should have been small matters, such as an employee at the Nevada battery factory leaking about how much scrap material was being discarded. It was the beginning of a psychological tailspin, which lasted from July through October 2018, in which Musk was buffeted by his impetuous impulses and craving for storms. "It was another example of him being a drama magnet," Kimbal says.

The new dramas began just after Tesla hit its five-thousand-cars-per-week milestone. Musk was scrolling through Twitter and stumbled across a message from an unknown user with very few followers saying, "Hi sir, if possible can you assist in any way to get the twelve Thailand boys and their coach out of the cave?" He was referring to a dozen Thai soccer players who had been trapped by a flood while exploring a cave.

"I suspect that the Thai govt has this under control, but I'm happy to help if there is a way to do so," Musk tweeted.

Then his action-hero impulse kicked in. Working with engineers at SpaceX and The Boring Company, he began building a pod-like mini-submarine that, he thought, could be sent into the flooded cave to rescue the boys. Sam Teller got a friend to let them use a school swimming pool for testing that weekend, and Musk began tweeting pictures of the device.

The saga became a global news story, some criticizing Musk for grandstanding. Early on Sunday morning, July 8, he checked with a leader of the rescue team in Thailand to make sure that what he was building might be useful. "I have one of the world's best engineering teams who usually design spaceships and spacesuits working on this thing 24 hours a day," he emailed. "If it isn't needed or won't help, that would be great to know." The rescue team leader replied, "It is absolutely worth continuing."

Later that day, Musk and seven engineers crammed into his jet along with the mini-sub and piles of equipment. They arrived in northern Thailand at 11:30 p.m. and were greeted by the prime minister, who donned a SpaceX hat and took them through the forest to the cave. Shortly after 2 a.m., Musk and his security guards and engineers, wearing headlamps, waded through waist-deep water into the dark cave.

Once the mini-sub had been delivered to the cave site, Musk flew to Shanghai, where he was signing a deal to open another Tesla Gigafactory. By that time a rescue operation using scuba divers was underway, and Musk's sub was not needed. The boys and their coach were safe. There the story would have ended, except that a sixty-three-year-old English cave explorer named Vernon Unsworth, who had advised Thai rescuers on the scene, gave an interview to CNN dissing Musk's efforts as "just a PR stunt" that "had absolutely no chance of working." Unsworth suggested, with a giggle, that "he can stick his submarine where it hurts."

Trolls and detractors fling insults at Musk every hour, and occasionally one sends him into orbit. He responded with a barrage of tweets attacking Unsworth, concluding one of them with "Sorry pedo guy, you really did ask for it." When another user asked Musk if he was calling Unsworth a pedophile, he responded, "Bet ya a signed dollar it's true."

Tesla stock fell 3.5 percent.

Musk had no evidence for his allegations. Teller, Gracias, and Tesla's general counsel scrambled to convince him to retract his statement, apologize, and stay off Twitter for a while. After Teller sent him an email with a proposed apology statement, Musk fired back, "I'm not happy about the suggested approach. . . . We need to stop panicking." But a few hours later, Teller and others convinced him to tweet a retraction. "My words were spoken in anger after Mr. Unsworth said several untruths & suggested I engage in a sexual act with the mini-sub, which had been built as an act of kindness & according to specifications from the dive team leader. . . . Nonetheless, his actions against me do not justify my actions against him, and for that I apologize to Mr. Unsworth."

Once again, if Musk had then been content to leave bad enough alone, things may have ended there. But in August he responded to a Twitter user who chided him over calling Unsworth a pedo by saying, "You don't think it's strange he hasn't sued me? He was offered free legal services." Even one of his biggest fans on Twitter, Johnna Crider, advised him, "Yo Elon, don't feed into the drama bro thats what they want."

By that point Unsworth had hired a lawyer, Lin Wood (who would later become infamous as a conspiracy theorist trying to overturn the 2020 election). He sent a letter warning that he was filing a lawsuit on behalf of Unsworth for defamation. When Ryan Mac of *BuzzFeed* asked Musk for a comment, Musk prefaced his email response by saying it was "off the record." But *BuzzFeed* had never agreed to that stipulation and so printed the barrage that followed. "I suggest that you call people you know in Thailand, find out what's actually going on and stop defending child rapists, you fucking asshole," Musk began. "He's an old, single white guy from England who's been traveling to or living in Thailand for 30 to 40 years, mostly Pattaya Beach, until moving to Chiang Rai for a child bride who was about 12 years old at the time. There's only one reason people go to Pattaya Beach. It isn't where you'd go for caves, but it is where you'd go for something else. Chiang Rai is renowned for child sex-trafficking." The statement about Unsworth's wife was untrue, and Musk's allegation did not help bolster his claim that the phrase "pedo guy" was simply a random insult rather than a specific accusation.*

Tesla's major investors expressed concern. "He was kind of losing it," says Joe Fath of T. Rowe Price, who telephoned after the pedo tweets. "This stuff has got to stop," he told Musk, comparing his behavior to that of Lindsay Lohan, an actress who around that time was spinning out of control. "You're doing major damage to the brand." Their talk lasted for forty-five minutes, and Musk seemed to listen. But his destructive behavior continued.

Kimbal believed that Musk's turmoil was partly triggered by his continuing anguish, after almost a year, over his breakup with Amber Heard. "I definitely think that 2018 tailspin was not just Tesla related," Kimbal says. "It was a result of him just being in awful grief around Amber."

Musk's friends began referring to his crises as his going "open-loop." The term is used for an object, such as a bullet as opposed to a guided missile, that has no feedback mechanism to provide it with guidance. "Whenever our friends become open-loop, meaning that they don't have iterative feedback and don't seem to care about the outcomes, we take it upon ourselves to let each other know," Kimbal says. So after the pedo-tweet situation escalated, Kimbal said to his brother, "Okay, open-loop warning." It was a phrase he would use four years later when Musk was dealing with his purchase of Twitter.

Take private

At the end of July, Musk met in the Jupiter conference room of the Fremont factory with leaders of Saudi Arabia's government investment fund, who told him that they had quietly accumulated almost 5 percent of Tesla's shares. As they had in previous meetings, Musk

---

* The defamation suit, which included the *BuzzFeed* emails, went to trial in Los Angeles in 2019. Musk in his testimony apologized and said he did not believe the cave explorer was a pedophile. The jury found Musk not liable.

and the fund's leader, Yasir Al-Rumayyan, discussed the possibility of taking Tesla private. The notion appealed to Musk. He hated having the value of the company determined by speculators and short-sellers, and he chafed at the regulations that came with being traded on a stock exchange. Al-Rumayyan left the matter in Musk's hands, saying that he would "like to listen more" and would support a "reasonable" plan to take the company private.

Two days later, Tesla stock shot up 16 percent when it announced good second-quarter results, which included hitting the five-thousand-car-per-week output. Musk worried that if the stock kept rising, it would become too expensive to take the company private. So that night he sent his board of directors a memo: he wanted to take the company private as soon as possible, and he offered to do it at $420 a share. His original calculation set the price at $419, but he liked the number 420 because it was slang for smoking marijuana. "It seemed like better karma at four-twenty than at four-nineteen," he says. "But I was not on weed, to be clear. Weed is not helpful for pro-ductivity. There's a reason for the word 'stoned.'" He later admitted to the Securities and Exchange Commission that choosing a price as a dope joke was not a wise move.

The board did not make any public announcement as it considered Musk's suggestion. But on the morning of August 7, as he was rid-ing to the private air terminal in Los Angeles, he unleashed a fateful tweet. "Am considering taking Tesla private at $420. Funding secured."

The stock shot up 7 percent before stock exchange officials temporarily halted trading. One rule for public companies is that executives must warn the stock exchange ten minutes before any an-nouncement that might cause market volatility. Musk did not pay at-tention to rules. The SEC promptly opened an investigation.

The board and top management at Tesla were caught off guard. When the company's head of investor relations saw Musk's tweet, he texted Teller, asking, "Was this text legit?" Gracias called Musk to of-ficially express the board's concern and ask him to stop tweeting until the matter had been discussed.

Musk was unfazed by the flurry his tweet caused. He flew to the Nevada Gigafactory, where he joked with managers about how "420" was a marijuana reference, and worked for the rest of the day on the battery assembly line. In the evening, he flew to the Fremont factory, where he held meetings late into the night.

By this point the Saudis were expressing discomfort that their discussions about taking Tesla private had been inflated into a "funding secured" tweet. Al-Rumayyan, the head of the fund, told *Bloomberg News* that they were "in talks" with Musk. When Musk saw the article, he texted Al-Rumayyan, "This is an extremely weak statement and does not reflect the conversation we had. You said you were definitely interested in taking Tesla private and had wanted to do so since 2016. You are throwing me under the bus." He added that if Al-Rumayyan did not issue a stronger public statement, "We will never speak again. Never."

"It takes two to tango," Al-Rumayyan replied. "We haven't received anything yet. . . . We cannot approve something that we don't have sufficient information on."

Musk threatened to cut off discussions with the Saudis. "I'm sorry, but we cannot work together," he told Al-Rumayyan.

Facing push back from institutional investors, on August 23 Musk rescinded his proposal to take the company private. "Given the feedback I've received, it's apparent that most of Tesla's existing shareholders believe we are better off as a public company," he said in a statement.

The blowback was brutal. "This is classic, extreme bipolar behavior risk-taking," CNBC's Jim Cramer said on air. "I'm talking about behavior that is obviously being examined by many psychiatrists who are saying classic risk-taking, this is not what a CEO should be doing." In the *New York Times*, columnist James Stewart wrote that the "take private" tweet "was so impulsive, potentially inaccurate, poorly worded and thought out, and with such potentially dire consequences for himself, Tesla and its shareholders, that the board now must ask a sensitive but vital question: What was Mr. Musk's state of mind when he wrote it?"

In order to avoid a federal lawsuit for misleading investors, Musk's lawyers worked on a deal with the SEC to settle the charges. He would remain CEO of Tesla, step down as chairman, pay a $40 million fine, and put two independent directors on his board. Another proviso destined to become an irritant: Musk would not be allowed to make public comments or tweets about any material information without getting clearance from a company monitor. Gracias, and Tesla's CFO Deepak Ahuja pushed hard for him to accept these terms and put the controversy—and perhaps his months of meltdown—behind him. But Musk surprised them by abruptly rejecting the proposed deal. On the night of September 26, the SEC filed a lawsuit seeking to ban him for life from running Tesla or any other public company.

Sitting at Tesla's Fremont headquarters the next day, Musk clutched a bottle of water and stared at a large monitor tuned to CNBC. "SEC charges Tesla Founder & CEO Elon Musk with Fraud," the chyron read. A big chart came on the screen, announcing, "Tesla stock tumbles." It was down 17 percent. All that day, Musk's lawyers, along with Antonio and Kimbal and Deepak, pushed him to change his mind and make a settlement. Reluctantly, he agreed to take the pragmatic course and accepted the SEC deal. The stock went back up.

Musk believed that he had done nothing wrong. He was forced to make a deal, he says, because otherwise Tesla would have gone bankrupt. "So that's like having a gun to your child's head. I was forced to concede to the SEC unlawfully. Those bastards." He began joking about what SEC stood for, suggesting that the middle word was "Elon's."

He was partially vindicated in 2023 when he won a case against a group of shareholders who claimed they lost money based on his tweet. A jury unanimously decided that he was not liable for their losses. His hot-shot lawyer Alex Spiro argued to the jury, "Elon Musk is just an impulsive kid with a terrible Twitter habit." It was an effective defense strategy that had the added virtue of being true.

48

Fallout

2018

On the Joe Rogan show *(top)*; Kimbal *(bottom)*

"Are you OK?"

David Gelles, a business reporter at the *New York Times*, was one of many reporters pursuing the story of Musk's 2018 dramas. "He has to talk to us," he told a person who worked with Musk. Late on the afternoon of Thursday, August 16, Gelles got a call. "What do you want to know?" Musk asked him.

"Were you on drugs when you sent that tweet?"

"No," Musk answered. He did say he had used the prescription sleep medicine Ambien. Some of his board worried that he was overusing it.

Gelles could tell Musk was exhausted. Instead of peppering him with tough questions, he decided to try to draw him out. "Elon, how are you doing?" he asked. "Are you OK?"

The conversation went on for an hour.

"It's not been great, actually," Musk said. "I've had friends come by who are really concerned." Then he paused for a long time, overcome by emotion. "There were times when I didn't leave the factory for three or four days—days when I didn't go outside," he said. "This has really come at the expense of seeing my kids."

The *Times* had been told that Musk had worked with disgraced financier Jeffrey Epstein, who would later be convicted of child sex-trafficking charges. Musk denied it. Indeed, he had no connections with Epstein, other than the fact that Epstein's enabler Ghislaine Maxwell, whom Musk didn't know, had once photo-bombed him by standing behind him at the Met Gala.

Gelles asked whether things were improving. Yes, for Tesla, Musk said. "But from a personal pain standpoint, the worst is yet to come." He began to choke up. There were long pauses as he tried to regain his composure. As Gelles later noted, "In all the conversations I've had with business leaders over the years, not until Elon Musk got on the phone had an executive revealed such vulnerability."

"Elon Musk Details 'Excruciating' Personal Toll of Tesla Turmoil," the headline read. The story reported how he had choked up during the interview. "Mr. Musk alternated between laughter and tears," Gelles and his colleagues wrote. "He said he had been working up to 120 hours a week recently . . . [and] not taken more than a week off since 2001, when he was bedridden with malaria." Other organizations picked up the story. "Erratic NYT Interview Raises Alarm about Tesla Chief's Health," was the headline on *Bloomberg*.

The next morning, Tesla stocked plunged 9 percent.

The Joe Rogan show

In the wake of the stories about his precarious psychological condition, Musk's public relations consultant, Juleanna Glover, recommended that he clear up the issue by giving a long interview. "We just need to kill this nonsense speculation around your mental state," she wrote. She said she would come up with "options that present you at length—leading the companies, in charge, droll and self-aware." She added a warning: "In no universe is it OK for you to continue to contemplate the sexual predilections of a Thai diver who insulted you."

The venue Musk chose to quash the speculations that he had gone loopy was the video-streamed podcast of Joe Rogan, a knowledgeable and sharp-witted pundit, comedian, and (a bit too appropriately) Ultimate Fighting Championship color commentator, who likes to meander through minefields with his guests, flouting political correctness and courting controversy. Rogan lets his guests ramble on, and Musk did, for more than two and a half hours. He described how to create a snakelike exoskeleton when building tunnels. He ruminated about the threat of artificial intelligence, whether robots would take revenge on us, and how Neuralink could create a direct high-bandwidth connection between our minds and our machines. And they discussed how humans might be unwitting avatars in a video-game simulation devised by a higher intelligence.

These ruminations may not have seemed the perfect way for Musk to convince institutional investors that he had a firm grip on base reality, but the interview at least seemed like it would do no harm. But then, Rogan lit up a big "marijuana inside of tobacco" joint and offered Musk a toke.

"You probably can't because of stockholders, right?" Rogan said, giving Musk an out.

"I mean, it's legal right?" Musk replied. They were in California.

"Totally legal," said Rogan, handing over the spliff. Musk took a tentative puff, mischievously.

A few moments later, when they were talking about the role of geniuses in furthering civilization, Musk turned to look at his phone. "You getting text messages from chicks?" asked Rogan.

Musk shook his head. "I'm getting text messages from friends saying, 'What the hell are you doing smoking weed?'"

The front page of the next day's *Wall Street Journal* looked like no other the paper had ever run. It had a very big picture of Musk, with glassy eyes and a crooked smirk, holding the fat joint in his left hand with a cloud of smoke wafting around his head. "Tesla Inc.'s share price sank to near its lowest point for the year Friday after the electric-car maker lost more executives and Chief Executive Elon Musk appeared to smoke marijuana during an interview streamed on the web," reporter Tim Higgins wrote.

Musk may not have broken state law, but in addition to further rattling investors, he appeared to have broken federal regulations, leading to an investigation by NASA. "SpaceX was a NASA contractor, and they are big believers in the law," Musk says. "So I had to be subjected to random drug tests for a couple of years. Fortunately, I really don't like doing illegal drugs."

Flamethrower

Musk had come to the Joe Rogan studio bearing a gift for his podcast host: a plastic flamethrower with The Boring Company logo on it. Together they played with the toy, gleefully shooting its short propane flame as Sam Teller and the studio staff dodged and laughed.

The flamethrower was a good metaphor for Musk himself. He took glee in blurting out eyebrow-singeing comments. The idea came after the company merchandised "Boring Company" hats and sold out fifteen thousand of them. "What's next?" Musk asked. Someone suggested a toy flamethrower. "Oh my God, let's do it," Musk responded. He was a fan of the movie *Spaceballs*, a Mel Brooks parody of *Star Wars* that has a scene in which a Yoda-like character touts the movie's merchandise for sale, culminating with the line "Take home the flamethrower." Musk's kids loved that line.

Steve Davis, who ran The Boring Company, found a relatively safe prototype that could melt snow and singe weeds but was technically not hot enough to be regulated as a flamethrower. They began marketing it, tongue in cheek, as "not a flamethrower" to avoid running afoul of the law. The terms and conditions declared:

> *I will not use this in a house*
> *I will not point this at my spouse*
> *I will not use this in an unsafe way*
> *The best use is creme brulee . . .*
> *. . . and that exhausts our rhyming ability.*

They priced it at $500 (it now goes for twice that on eBay) and within four days had sold out twenty thousand of them, grossing $10 million.

Musk's goofy mode is the flip side of his demon mode. When he is in the darkest of places, he often cycles between anger and cackling laughter.

His humor has many levels. The lowest is his puerile affection for poop emojis, fart sounds programmed into the Tesla, and other discharges of bathroom humor. Say the voice command "Open Butthole" to the console in a Tesla, and it opens the electric charging port at the rear of the vehicle.

He also has a mordant, ironic strand of humor, demonstrated by a poster on the wall of his cubicle at SpaceX. It shows a twinkling dark blue sky with a shooting star. "When you wish upon a falling star, your dreams can come true," it reads. "Unless it's really a meteor hurtling to the Earth which will destroy all life. Then you're pretty much hosed, no matter what you wish for. Unless it's death by meteorite."

The most deeply ingrained strand of his humor is a metaphysical science-geek droll cleverness that he absorbed when he read and reread Douglas Adams's *The Hitchhiker's Guide to the Galaxy*. In the midst of his turmoil in 2018, he decided to launch his old cherry-red Tesla Roadster into deep space on an orbit that would, after four years, take it near Mars. He did it on the first launch of his new Falcon Heavy, a twenty-seven-engine rocket made by strapping together three Falcon 9 boosters. The Tesla had a copy of *The Hitchhiker's Guide* in the glove compartment and a sign on the dashboard with the "DON'T PANIC!" injunction from the novel.

Kimbal rupture

During their rough childhoods and as partners in Zip2, Kimbal and Elon had often fought ferociously with each other. But through it all, Kimbal had been Elon's closest compatriot, the one who understood him and would stick by him, even while telling him uncomfortable truths.

After Antonio Gracias summoned him back from his honeymoon in July, Kimbal worked almost full-time at Tesla, ignoring the farm-to-table restaurant business he had started in Colorado. During the SEC crisis, he was one of the strongest voices urging Elon to settle. And when Elon became fearful that some of his board might be plotting against him, Kimbal flew down to Los Angeles to stay with him. During one tense Saturday meeting at Elon's house, Kimbal did what he had done after the Falcon launch failure in Kwaj and many other times, which was to relieve the tension by cooking. This time he made salmon with peas and a potato-onion casserole.

But Kimbal's frustration with his brother had been building, especially when it took outsiders to convince him to settle with the SEC. A breaking point came in October. His restaurant group was having financing problems, and he needed to raise more money. "So I called Elon and I said, 'Look, I need you to help fund my business.'" The round was going to be about $40 million, and Kimbal needed Elon to do $10 million as a loan. Elon initially agreed. "I remember," says Kimbal, "writing down in my journal, 'unconditional love for Elon.'" But when Kimbal reached out to get the money transferred, Elon had changed his mind. His personal financial manager, Jared Birchall, had gone over the numbers and advised Elon that Kimbal's business was not sustainable. "The money Elon was putting into it was getting poured down the drain," Birchall told me. So Elon gave Kimbal the bad news: "I had my finance guy look at it, and the restaurants are struggling. I think they should die."

"What did you just say?" Kimbal yelled. "Fuck you. Fuck you! This is not how it works." He reminded Elon, forcefully, that when Tesla's finances were struggling, he had come to work by his brother's side and provided him financing. "If you would've looked at Tesla finance, it should have died as well," Kimbal said. "So this is not how this works."

Elon eventually relented. "I basically strong-armed him into putting in five million," says Kimbal. The restaurants survived. But the incident nevertheless caused a rupture. "I was absolutely furious with Elon and didn't speak to him," he says. "I felt like I lost my brother. That experience at Tesla had taken him to a place where he lost his mind. At that point I was like, 'I'm done with you.'"

After six weeks of silence, Kimbal reached out to heal the rift. "I decided to go back to being Elon's brother because I didn't want to lose him," he says. "I missed my brother." I asked how Elon reacted when he reached out to him. "He responded as if nothing had happened," Kimbal said. "That's how Elon is."

JB Straubel exits

Not surprisingly, many of Musk's top executives fled during the 2018 production hell and accompanying turmoil. Jon McNeill, who was Tesla's president overseeing sales and marketing, had taken on the role of helping Musk through his bouts of mental anguish, including when he was lying on the conference room floor. "It was becoming absolutely exhausting for me," he says. He went to Musk in January 2018, urged him to get psychological help, and said, "I love you, but I can't do this anymore."

Doug Field, the senior vice president of engineering, was considered a possible future CEO of Tesla. But Musk lost confidence in him at the outset of the production hell surge and stripped him of his role overseeing manufacturing. He left to go to Apple and then Ford.

The most important departure, at least symbolically and emotionally, was that of JB Straubel, the cheery cofounder who had stuck by Musk for sixteen years, ever since their 2003 dinner where Straubel had extolled the possibility of using lithium-ion batteries to make electric cars. At the end of 2018, he took a long vacation, his first real one in fifteen years. "My percent happiness level was low and trending downward," he says. He was getting much more pleasure from a side venture he had founded, Redwood Materials, which aimed to recycle lithium-ion car batteries. Another factor was Musk's mind-space at the time. "He was struggling, and that made him more mercurial than even the normal," Straubel says. "I felt terrible for him and tried to help him as a friend, but couldn't really."

Musk is usually not sentimental about people leaving. He likes fresh blood. He is more concerned with a phenomenon he calls "phoning in rich," meaning people who have worked at the company for a long time and, because they have enough money and vacation homes, no longer hunger to stay all night on the factory floor. But in the case of Straubel, Musk felt a personal affection as well as professional trust. "I was a little surprised at Elon's reluctance to have me leave," says Straubel.

Throughout early 2019, they had several conversations, and Straubel experienced Musk's erratic emotional oscillations. "He can flip, usually without warning, between being quite emotional and human to being literally zero percent of that," Straubel says. "Sometimes he can feel extremely loving and caring, shockingly so, and you're like, 'Oh my gosh, yeah, we've been through incredible hardship together and have this deep bond and I love you, man.' But then it becomes mixed with that blank stare, where it feels like he's seeing straight through you and not registering any emotion at all."

The plan they came up with was to announce Straubel's departure at Tesla's June 2019 annual meeting, to be held at the Computer History Museum near Palo Alto. Given the venue, it would be a chance to walk through the history of Tesla, from a dream sixteen years earlier to the now-profitable pathfinder into the era of electric vehicles. They would then introduce Straubel's successor Drew Baglino, a twelve-year company veteran. Straubel and Baglino had the same lanky aw-shucks body language and manner, and their affection ran deep.

In the greenroom just before the event, Musk had second thoughts about announcing Straubel's departure. "I've got a bad feeling about this," he said. "I don't think we should do it today." Straubel was secretly relieved. Facing his departure was emotionally hard.

Musk did the first part of the presentation alone. "It's been a hell of a year," he began, a phrase that was true on many levels. The Model 3 was now outselling all competitors combined—gasoline or electric—in the luxury car category, and it was the highest-selling by revenue of *any* car in the U.S. "Ten years ago, nobody would've believed that could happen," he said. His giddy humor flashed on for a moment. He began giggling about the "fart app" that allowed Tesla drivers to hit a button so the passenger seat would emit a fart sound when someone sat on it. "It's like perhaps my finest piece of work," he said.

He also, as always, promised that self-driving Teslas were just around the corner. "We expect to be feature complete with autonomy by the end of this year," he said, adding 2019 to the years this had been promised. "It should be able to go from your home garage to your parking space at work without intervention." An audience member went to the microphone and challenged him, saying that his previous promises about self-driving had not come true. Musk laughed, knowing the questioner was right. "Yeah, I'm sometimes a little too optimistic about time frames," he said. "It's time you knew that, yeah. But would I be doing this if I wasn't optimistic? Geez." The audience applauded. They were down with the joke.

When he invited Straubel and Baglino to the stage, there were loud cheers. Among Tesla fans, they were beloved stars. Straubel said with genuine affection, "Drew joined my team when it was a tiny, tiny team of five or ten of us a couple years after the company got started, and he's been my right-hand person involved in almost every key initiative that I've done at the company." This was the point when Straubel had planned to announce his retirement. Instead, Straubel and Musk took the opportunity to reminisce. "I trace Tesla back to 2003, with JB and me having lunch with Harold Rosen," Musk said. "Yeah, that was a good conversation."

"We didn't exactly envision how this would unfold," Straubel added.

"I believed we for sure would fail," said Musk. "Back in 2003, people thought electric cars were the stupidest thing ever, bad in every way, something like a golf cart."

"But it needed to be done," Straubel said.

During an earnings call a few weeks later, Musk casually dropped the news that Straubel was departing. But Musk's respect for him endured. In 2023, he would invite Straubel to join the board of Tesla.

49

Grimes

2018

Claire Boucher, known as Grimes, dressed for a performance;
with Musk at the Metropolitan Museum gala

EM+CB

Every now and then, often at the most complex of times, the Creators of Our Simulation—those rascals who conjure up what we are led to believe is reality—drop in a sparky new element, one that creates chaotic new subplots. And thus into Musk's life in the spring of 2018, amid the emotional tsunami caused by his breakup with Amber Heard, came a waiflike weaver of sounds, Claire Boucher, known as Grimes, a smart and spellbinding performance artist whose appearance would lead to three new children, on-and-off domesticity, and even a public battle with an unhinged rapper.

Born in Vancouver, Grimes had produced four albums by the time she started dating Musk. Drawing on science fiction themes and memes, her mesmerizing music combined sonic texture with elements of dream pop and electronica. She had an adventuresome intellectual curiosity that led her to become interested in eclectic ideas, such as a thought experiment known as Roko's basilisk, which posits that artificial intelligence could get out of control and torture any human who had not helped it gain power. These are the types of things that she and Musk worry about. When Musk wanted to tweet a pun about it, he Google-searched to find an image, and he discovered that Grimes had made it an element of her 2015 music video "Flesh without Blood." She and Musk got into a Twitter exchange that led, in the modern way, to direct-messaging and texting.

They had met before and, ironically, it was when Musk was in an elevator with Amber Heard. "Remember that elevator meeting?" Grimes asked during a late-night conversation I had with her and Musk. "I mean that was super weird."

"Of all the times to meet," Musk agreed. "You were staring at me very intensely."

"No," she corrected, "you were the one giving me a weird stare."

After they met again through the Roko's basilisk exchange on Twitter, Musk invited her to fly up to Fremont to visit his factory, his idea of a good date. It was the end of March 2018, amid the crazed push to make five thousand cars per week. "We just walked the floor all night, and I watched him try to fix things," Grimes says. The next night, while driving her to a restaurant, he showed how fast the car accelerated, then took his hands off the wheel, covered his eyes, and let her experience Autopilot. "I was like, oh shit, this guy is fucking crazy," she says. "The car was signaling and changing lanes by itself. It felt like a scene out of a Marvel movie." At the restaurant, he carved "EM+CB" on the wall.

When she compared his powers to those of Gandalf, he gave her a rapid-fire trivia test on *Lord of the Rings*. He wanted to see whether she was truly a faithful fan. She passed. "That mattered to me," Musk says. As a gift, she gave him a box of animal bones she had collected. In the evenings, they listened to Dan Carlin's *Hardcore History* and other history podcasts and audiobooks. "The only way I could be in a serious relationship is if the person I'm dating can also listen to an hour of, like, war history before bed," she says. "Elon and I have gone through so many topics, like ancient Greece and Napoleon and the military strategies of World War One."

This was all happening as Musk was going through his mental and work-related tailspins of 2018. "Man, you seem like you're in a really rough headspace," she said to him. "Do you want me to bring my music stuff over and I can work at your house?" He said he would like that. He did not want to be lonely. She figured that she would stay with him for a few weeks, until his emotional turmoil settled down. "But the storm just sort of never stopped, and then you're just on the ship and on the ride, and I just stayed there."

She accompanied him to the factory some nights when he was in battle mode. "He's always looking out for what's wrong with the motor, what's wrong with the engine, the heat shield, the liquid oxygen valve," she says. One night they went out to dinner, and Musk suddenly went silent, thinking. After a minute or two, he asked if she had a pen. She pulled an eyeliner out of her purse. He took it and began to draw on his napkin an idea for modifying an engine heat shield. "I realized that even when I was with him, there would be times when his mind would go somewhere else, usually to an issue at work," she says.

In May, taking a brief break from the Tesla factory production hell, he flew with her to New York to attend the Metropolitan

Museum's annual gala, a glittery extravaganza featuring just-over-the-top fashion and costumes. Musk suggested ideas for her outfit, a medieval-punk black-and-white ensemble with a hard glass corset and a necklace made of spikes that resembled the Tesla logo. He even had someone from the Tesla design team help execute it. He wore a white shirt with clerical collar and a pure-white tuxedo jacket with the faint inscription *novus ordo seclorum*, a Latin phrase heralding a new order of the ages.

Rap battle

Despite wanting to help him through his turmoil, Grimes was not a calming influence. The intensity that made her an edgy artist brought with it a messy lifestyle. She stayed up most of the night and slept most of the day. She was demanding and distrustful of Musk's household staff, and she had a difficult relationship with his mother.

Musk was a drama addict, and Grimes had a companion trait: she was a drama magnet. Whether she intended to or not, she attracted it. Just when the Thai cave incident and the turmoil about taking Tesla private were spinning out of control in August 2018, Grimes invited the rapper Azealia Banks to stay with her at Musk's house and collaborate on some music. She had forgotten that she and Musk had made plans to visit Kimbal in Boulder. Grimes told Banks she could stay at the guesthouse for the weekend. On that Friday morning, three days after his "take private" tweet, Musk got up, did a workout, made a few calls, and caught a short glimpse of Banks in his house. When he's focused on other things, he doesn't pay much attention to the things around him. He wasn't quite sure who she was, other than a friend of Grimes.

Upset that Grimes blew off their recording session so she could be with Musk, Banks unleashed a torrent of abuse on her well-followed Instagram. "I waited around all weekend while grimes coddled her boyfriend for being too stupid to know not to go on twitter while on acid," she posted. This was false (Musk never used acid), but it understandably piqued the interest of not only the press but also the SEC. Banks's postings about Grimes and Musk got progressively crazier:

LOL, Elon musk is better off hiring an escort. At least an escort would have kept her mouth shut about his business. He's got some dirty-sneaker-inbred-out of the woods Pabst beer pussy methhead-junkie running around town telling EVERYONE EVERYTHING ABOUT HIM. All because he needed a date to the Met Gala to hide his shrinking dick from Amber Heard LOL. . . . He's on the Down syndrome spectrum. There's something not quite right about that man. I wouldn't give him the credit of calling him an alien. He's a mutant. . . . Fucking crackers. The last time I try working with a white bitch.

When *Business Insider* did a phone interview with her, Banks connected the situation to Musk's pledge to take Tesla private, which made matters legally worse. "I saw him in the kitchen tucking his tail in between his legs scrounging for investors to cover his ass after that tweet," she said. "He was stressed and red in the face."

By then, wacky stories involving Musk had a short shelf life. The story was a tabloid sensation for about a week, then died down after Banks posted a letter of apology. Grimes was able to turn the tale into grist for her music. She released a song in 2021 titled "100% Tragedy," which she said was about "having to defeat Azealia Banks when she tried to destroy my life."

Many shades of Musk

Despite such dramas, Grimes was a good partner for Musk. Like Amber Heard (and Musk himself), she was inclined toward chaos, but unlike Amber, hers was a chaos that was undergirded by kindness and even sweetness. "My *Dungeons and Dragons* alignment would be chaotic good," she says, "whereas Amber's is probably chaotic evil." She realized that's what made Amber enticing to Musk. "He's attracted to chaotic evil. It's about his father and what he grew up with, and he's quick to fall back into being treated badly. He associates love with being mean or abusive. There's an Errol-Amber through line."

She enjoyed his intensity. One evening they went to see the 3D movie *Alita: Battle Angel*, but they arrived after all the 3D glasses were gone. Musk insisted they stay and watch it anyway, even though it was completely blurry. When Grimes was doing the voice recordings for the cyborg pop-star she played in the video game *Cyberpunk 2077*, he showed up at the studio wielding a two-hundred-year-old gun and insisted that they give him a cameo. "The studio guys were like sweating," Grimes says. Adds Musk, "I told them that I was armed but not dangerous." They relented. The cybernetic implants in the game were a sci-fi version of what he was doing at Neuralink. "It hit close to home," he says.

Her basic insight on Musk was that he was wired differently than others. "Asperger's makes you a very difficult person," she says. "He's not good at reading the room. His emotional comprehension is just very different from the average human." People should keep his psychological makeup in mind when judging him, she argues. "If someone has depression or anxiety, we sympathize. But if they have Asperger's we say he's an asshole."

She learned to navigate the many modes of his personalities. "He has numerous minds and many fairly distinct personalities," she says. "He moves between them at a very rapid pace. You just feel the air in the room change, and suddenly the whole situation is just transferred over to his other state." She noticed that his different personalities had different tastes, even in music and décor. "My favorite version of E is the one who's down for Burning Man and will sleep on a couch, eat canned soup, and be chill." Her bête noire is the Elon that's in what she calls demon mode. "Demon mode is when he goes dark and retreats inside the storm in his brain."

One night, when they were at dinner with a group, I watched as the clouds gathered and Musk's mood shifted. Grimes edged away from him. "When we hang out, I make sure I'm with the right Elon," she later explained. "There are guys in that head who don't like me, and I don't like them."

Sometimes one of the Elon versions will seem not to remember what another one has done. "You will say stuff to him and then he'll just have no memory of it whatsoever, because he was in a brain space," Grimes says. "If he's focused on a particular thing, he will not get stimulation, not consume any inputs from the outside world.

Stuff can be right in front of his eyes and he won't see it." Just like what happened when he was in grade school.

During the 2018 emotional turmoil at Tesla, she tried to coax him to relax. "Everything doesn't need to suck," she told him one night. "You don't need to feel stoked about everything all the time." But she also understood, in ways that others did not, that his restlessness was a driver of his success. So, too, was his demon mode, though that took her a little longer to appreciate. "Demon mode causes a lot of chaos," she says, "but it also gets shit done."

50

Shanghai

Tesla, 2015–2019

With Robin Ren in Shanghai

Robin Ren, the Shanghai-born Physics Olympiad winner who had been Musk's lab partner at Penn, did not know much about cars. In fact, almost all he knew came from the cross-country road trip that he had taken with Musk when they graduated in 1995. Musk had taught him how to deal with a broken-down BMW and how to drive a stick shift, skills he had not subsequently needed after becoming chief technology officer at Dell Computer's flash-drive subsidiary. That is why he was surprised by the request Musk made twenty years later when he asked him to lunch in Palo Alto.

Selling cars in China was key to Tesla's global ambitions, but things were not going well. Musk had fired two successive China managers and, after the company sold only 120 cars there one month, he was preparing to fire his whole top China-based team. "How do I fix Tesla's business in China?" he asked Ren at the lunch. Ren expressed his ignorance of the auto industry and simply gave a few high-level thoughts about how to do business in China. "I'm going to China next week to meet the vice premier," Musk said as they were getting up to leave. "Can you come with me?"

Ren demurred. He had just come back from a business trip to China. But he felt the tug to be part of Musk's mission, so he emailed the next morning to say he was ready to go. They had a cordial meeting with the vice premier. Afterward, they met with a former official and other advisors, who told them that in order to succeed in selling cars in China, Tesla would have to manufacture cars there. According to Chinese law, that would require forming a joint venture with a Chinese company.

Musk was allergic to joint ventures. He didn't share control well. So he emphasized, deploying his silly-humor mode, that Tesla did not want to get married. "Tesla is too young," he said. "Like, we are barely a baby. Now you want to marry?" He got up and mimicked two toddlers walking down a wedding aisle, then laughed his signature cackle. Everyone else in the room laughed, the Chinese a bit hesitantly.

On the flight back on Musk's jet, he and Ren reminisced about college and shared fun facts about physics. It was only after the jet landed, as they were walking down the stairs, that Musk popped the question: "Will you join Tesla?" Ren said yes.

Ren's big challenge was to find a way to do manufacturing in China. He could either wear down Musk's resistance and have Tesla form a joint venture, which is what every other car company had done, or he could convince China's top leaders to change a law that had defined Chinese manufacturing growth for three decades. He discovered that the latter was easier. Month after month, he lobbied the Chinese government. Musk himself went back in April 2017 to meet with Chinese leaders again. "We kept explaining why it would help China to have Tesla build an auto factory, even if it wasn't a joint venture," Ren says.

As part of President Xi Jinping's plans to make China a clean-energy innovation center, China finally agreed in early 2018 to let Tesla build a factory without having to enter into a joint venture. Ren and his team were able to negotiate a deal for more than two hundred acres near Shanghai along with low-interest loans.

Ren flew back to the U.S. to discuss the deal with Musk in February 2018. Unfortunately, that was in the midst of Musk's production hell at the Nevada battery factory, and he was in such a frenzy walking the floor that Ren could not corner him. They flew to Los Angeles together late that night, but it was only after they landed that Ren got a chance to talk to him. Ren started to go through a slide deck with maps, financing commitments, and deal terms, but Musk did not look at them. Instead, he stared out of the window of his plane for almost a full minute. Then he looked Ren directly in the eye. "Do you believe this is the right thing?" Ren was so taken aback that he paused for a few seconds before saying yes. "Okay, let's do it," Musk said and left the plane.

The formal signing ceremony with the Chinese leaders came on July 10, 2018. Musk arrived in Shanghai directly from being waist-deep in water in a Thai cave after delivering the mini-sub he had built to rescue the stranded young soccer players. He changed into a dark suit and stood stiffly in a red-draped banquet hall as they all exchanged toasts. The first Teslas began rolling out of the factory in October 2019. Within two years, China would be making more than half of Tesla's vehicles.

51

Cybertruck

Tesla, 2018–2019

With Franz von Holzhausen discussing Cybertruck design, 2018

Steel

On almost every Friday afternoon since he created Tesla's design studio in 2008, Musk held a product review session with his chief designer Franz von Holzhausen. These sessions, usually in the quiet white-floored design studio showroom just behind SpaceX headquarters in Los Angeles, were a calming respite, especially after tumultuous weeks. Musk and von Holzhausen would slowly meander the hangar-like room stroking prototypes and clay models of the vehicles that they envisioned for Tesla's future.

Beginning in early 2017, they began kicking around ideas for a Tesla pickup truck.

Von Holzhausen started with traditional designs, using a Chevrolet Silverado as a model. One was placed in the middle of the studio, and they studied its proportions and components. Musk said he wanted something more exciting, perhaps even surprising. So they looked at historical vehicles with a cool vibe, most notably the El Camino, a retro-futuristic coupé made by Chevrolet in the 1960s. Von Holzhausen designed a pickup truck with a similar vibe, but as they walked around the model they agreed that it felt too soft. "It was too curved," von Holzhausen says. "It didn't have the authority of a pickup truck."

Musk then added another design reference that inspired him: the Lotus Esprit of the late 1970s, a pointy, wedge-nosed British sports car. Specifically, he was enamored with a version that appeared in the 1977 James Bond movie *The Spy Who Loved Me*. Musk bought the one that was used in the movie for close to $1 million and displayed it in the Tesla design studio.

The brainstorming was fun, but it still did not lead to a concept that excited them. For inspiration, they visited the Petersen Automotive Museum, where they noticed something surprising. "We realized," von Holzhausen says, "that pickup trucks basically haven't changed in their form or their manufacturing process in eighty years."

That led Musk to shift his focus to something more basic: What material should they use to build the truck's body? By rethinking the materials and even the physics of the vehicle's structure, it could open up the possibility of wildly new designs.

"Originally we were thinking aluminum," von Holzhausen says. "We also kicked around titanium, because durability was really important." But around that time, Musk became enthralled by the possibility of making a rocket ship out of glistening stainless steel. That might also work for a pickup truck, he realized. A stainless steel body would not need painting and could bear some of the vehicle's structural load. It was a truly out-of-the-box idea, a way to rethink what a vehicle could be. One Friday afternoon, after a few weeks of discussion, Musk came in and simply announced, "We are going to do this whole thing in stainless steel."

Charles Kuehmann was the VP for materials engineering at both Tesla and SpaceX. One of the advantages that Musk had was that his companies could share engineering knowledge. Kuehmann developed an ultra-hard stainless steel alloy that was "cold rolled" rather than requiring heat treatments, which Tesla patented. It was strong enough and cheap enough to use for both trucks and rockets.

The decision to use stainless steel for the Cybertruck had a major implication for the engineering of the vehicle. A steel body could serve as the load-bearing structure of the vehicle, rather than making the chassis play that role. "Let's make the strength on the outside, make it an exoskeleton, and hang everything else from the inside of it," Musk suggested.

The use of stainless steel also opened up new possibilities for the look of the truck. Instead of using stamping machines that would sculpt carbon fiber into body panels with subtle curves and shapes, stainless steel would favor straight planes and sharp angles. That allowed—and in some ways forced—the design team to explore ideas that were more futuristic, edgier, even jarring.

"Don't resist me"

In the fall of 2018, Musk was just emerging from Nevada and Fremont factory hell, the pedophile and "take private" tweets, and the mental turmoil of what he called the most agonizing year of his life. In times of challenge, one of his refuges is to focus on a future project. That is what he did in the serene haven of the design studio on

October 5, when he turned his regular Friday visit into a brainstorming session on the design of the pickup truck.

The Chevy Silverado was still on the showroom floor for reference. In front of it were three large display boards with pictures of a wide variety of vehicles, including ones from video games and sci-fi movies. They ranged from retro to futuristic, sleek to jagged, curvaceous to jarring. With his hands casually in his pockets, von Holzhausen had the easygoing and loose-limbed manner of a surfer looking for the right wave. Musk, arms akimbo, was coiled like a bear searching for prey. After a while, Dave Morris and then a few other designers wandered in.

As he looked at the pictures on the display boards, Musk gravitated to the ones that had a futuristic, cyber look. They had recently settled on the design for the Model Y, a crossover version of the Model 3, and Musk had been talked out of some of his more radical and unconventional suggestions. Having played it safe with the Model Y, he did not want that to happen with the design of the pickup truck. "Let's be bold," he said. "Let's surprise people."

Every time someone would point to a picture that was more conventional, Musk would push back and point to the car from the video game *Halo* or in the trailer for the forthcoming game *Cyberpunk 2077* or from Ridley Scott's movie *Blade Runner*. His son Saxon, who is autistic, had recently asked an offbeat question that resonated: "Why doesn't the future look like the future?" Musk would quote Saxon's question repeatedly. As he said to the design team that Friday, "I want the future to look like the future."

There were a few dissenting voices suggesting that something too futuristic would not sell. After all, this was a pickup truck. "I don't care if no one buys it," he said at the end of the session. "We're not doing a traditional boring truck. We can always do that later. I want to build something that's cool. Like, don't resist me."

By July 2019, von Holzhausen and Morris had built a full-size mockup of a futuristic, jarring, cyber design with sharp angles and diamond facets. One Friday they surprised Musk, who had not yet seen it, by putting it in the middle of the showroom floor next to the more traditional model they had been considering. When Musk walked in the door leading from the SpaceX factory, his reaction was instantaneous. "That's it!" he exclaimed. "I love it. We are doing that. Yes, this is what we are going to do! Yes, okay, done."

It became known as the Cybertruck.

"A majority of people in this studio hated it," says von Holzhausen. "They were like, 'You can't be serious.' They didn't want to have anything to do with it. It was just too weird." Some of the engineers started working secretly on an alternative version. Von Holzhausen, who is as gentle as Musk is brusque, spent time listening carefully to their concerns. "If you don't have buy-in from the people around you, it's hard to get things done," he says. Musk was less patient. When some designers pushed him to at least do some market testing, Musk replied, "I don't do focus groups."

When the design of the truck was finished in August 2019, Musk told the team he wanted to reveal a working prototype publicly that November—in three months rather than the nine months it normally takes to make a running prototype. "We won't be able to have one that we can actually drive by then," von Holzhausen said. Musk replied, "Yes, we will." His unrealistic deadlines usually do not pan out, but in some cases they do. "It forced the team to come together, work twenty-four-seven, and rally around that date," von Holzhausen says.

On November 21, 2019, the truck was driven onto a stage in the design studio for a presentation to the press and invited guests. There were gasps. "Many in the crowd clearly couldn't believe that this was actually the vehicle they'd come to see," CNN reported. "The Cybertruck looks like a large metal trapezoid on wheels, more like an art piece than a truck." There was also an unexpected surprise when von Holzhausen tried to show the toughness of the truck. He swung at the body with a sledgehammer, which didn't make a dent. Then he threw a metal ball at one of the "armor glass" windows, to show it wouldn't break. To his surprise, it cracked. "Oh my fucking God!" Musk said. "Well, maybe that was a little too hard."

Overall, the presentation was not a great success. Tesla stock dropped 6 percent the next day. But Musk was satisfied. "Trucks have been the same for a very long time, like for a hundred years," he told the crowd. "We want to try something different."

Afterward, he took Grimes for a spin in the prototype to Nobu restaurant, where the valet parkers just stared at it without touching. On the way out, pursued by paparazzi, he drove over a pylon in the parking lot with a "No Left Turn" sign and turned left.

52

Starlink

SpaceX, 2015–2018

An internet in low-Earth orbit

When Musk launched SpaceX back in 2002, he conceived it as an endeavor to get humanity to Mars. Every week, amid all the technical meetings on engine and rocket design, he held one very otherworldly meeting called "Mars Colonizer." There he imagined what a Mars colony would look like and how it should be governed. "We tried to avoid ever skipping Mars Colonizer, because that was the most fun meeting for him and always put him in a good mood," his former assistant Elissa Butterfield says.

Getting to Mars would cost serious money. So Musk combined, as he often did, an aspirational mission with a practical business plan. There were many revenue opportunities he could pursue, including space tourism (like Bezos and Branson) and satellite launches for the U.S. and other countries and companies. In late 2014, he turned his attention to what was a much bigger pot of gold: providing internet service to paying customers. SpaceX would make and launch its own communications satellites, in effect rebuilding the internet in outer space. "Internet revenue is about one trillion dollars a year," he says. "If we can serve three percent, that's $30 billion, which is more than NASA's budget. That was the inspiration for Starlink, to fund getting to Mars." He pauses, then adds for emphasis, "The lens of getting to Mars has motivated *every* SpaceX decision."

To pursue this mission, Musk announced in January 2015 the creation of a new division of SpaceX, based near Seattle, called Starlink. The plan was to send satellites into low-Earth orbit, about 340 miles high, so that the latency of the signals would not be as bad as systems that depended on geosynchronous satellites, which orbit 22,000 miles above the Earth. From their low altitude, Starlink's beams cannot cover nearly as much ground, so many more are needed. Starlink's goal was to eventually create a megaconstellation of forty thousand satellites.

Mark Juncosa

In the midst of the hellacious summer of 2018, Musk was having a Spidey sense that something was amiss at Starlink. Its satellites were too big, expensive, and difficult to manufacture. In order to reach a profitable scale, they would have to be made at one-tenth the cost and ten times faster. But the Starlink team did not seem to feel much urgency, a cardinal sin for Musk.

So one Sunday night that June, without much warning, he flew to Seattle to fire the entire top Starlink team. He brought with him eight of his most senior SpaceX rocket engineers. None knew much about satellites, but they all knew how to solve engineering problems and apply Musk's algorithm.

The engineer he tapped to take over was Mark Juncosa, who was already in charge of structural engineering at SpaceX. That had the advantage of integrating the design and manufacture of all SpaceX products, from the boosters to the satellites, under one manager. It also had the advantage of that person being Juncosa, a feverishly brilliant engineer who could mind-meld with Musk.

Juncosa grew up as a lanky surfer dude in Southern California, deeply loving the weather, culture, and vibe, but without falling prey to the laid-back languidness. He uses his iPhone as a fidget spinner, whipping it around his thumb and index finger with the magic of a plate spinner at a circus, and he speaks in a rapid scattershot of exclamations studded with "you know" and "like" and "wow, dude."

He went to Cornell, where he joined the college's Formula One racing team. His initial job was fabricating the car bodies, which used his skill at making surfboards, and then he was drawn into the engineering work. "I really, like, fell in love with it, you know, and felt, like, wow, man, this is what I was built to do," he says.

On a visit to Cornell in 2004, Musk sent a note to some engineering professors inviting them to bring one or two of their favorite students to lunch. "It was like, you know, do you want a free lunch on this rich guy?" Juncosa says. "Hell yeah, I'm into that for sure." When Musk described what he was doing at SpaceX, Juncosa thought, "Man, this guy is crazy as hell, and I think he's going to lose all his money, but he seems super smart and motivated and I like his style." When Musk offered him a job, he accepted immediately.

Juncosa impressed Musk with his risk-taking, rule-breaking attitude. When he was overseeing the development of the Dragon capsule that carries the Falcon 9 payload into orbit, he was repeatedly chided by SpaceX's quality-assurance manager for not filing the proper paperwork. Juncosa's team was designing the capsule all day and then spending most of the night building it themselves. "I told the dude that we didn't have time to paper our work orders and quality checks, we were just going to build it and test it at the very end," he says. "The quality dude was pretty mad, rightly, so we ended up in Elon's cubicle arguing it out." Musk got fired up and started berating the quality-assurance manager. "It was pretty edgy, but he and I were hell-bent on getting this capsule done because we risked running out of money," says Juncosa.

Improved Starlinks

When Juncosa took over at Starlink, he threw away the existing design and started back at a first-principles level, questioning every requirement based on fundamental physics. The goal was to make the simplest communications satellite possible, and later add bells and whistles. "We had marathon meetings, and Elon pushed on every little thing," says Juncosa.

For example, the satellite's antennas were on a separate structure from the flight computer. The engineers had decreed that they be thermally isolated from one another. Juncosa kept asking why. When told that the antennas might overheat, Juncosa asked to see the test data. "By the time that I asked 'Why?' five times," Juncosa says, "people were like, 'Shit, maybe we should just make this one integrated component.'"

By the end of the design process, Juncosa had turned a rat's nest into what was now a simple flat satellite. It had the potential to be an order of magnitude cheaper. More than twice as many could be packed into the nose cone of a Falcon 9, doubling the number each flight could deploy. "I was, like, pretty happy with it," Juncosa says. "I'm sitting there thinking how clever I had been."

But Musk was still picking over each detail. When they were launched on a Falcon 9, there were connections holding each satellite down so that they could be released one at a time and not bump into each other. "Why not release them all at once?" he asked. That initially struck Juncosa and the other engineers as crazy. They were afraid of collisions. But Musk said the motion of the spaceship would cause them to separate naturally. If they did happen to bump, it would be very slow and harmless. So they got rid of the connectors, saving a little bit of cost, complexity, and mass. "Life got way easier because we culled those parts," Juncosa says. "I was too chicken to propose that, but Elon made us try it."

By May 2019, the design of the simplified Starlink was complete and the Falcon 9 rocket began launching them into orbit. When they became operational four months later, Musk was at his south Texas house and went on Twitter. "Sending this tweet through space via Starlink satellite," he wrote. He was now able to tweet on an internet that he owned.

53

Starship

SpaceX, 2018–2019

Musk's living room and backyard in Boca Chica;
Bill Riley and Mark Juncosa

Big F Rocket

If Musk's goal had been to create a profitable rocket company, he could have allowed himself to collect his winnings and relax after surviving 2018. His reusable workhorse Falcon 9 had become the world's most efficient and reliable rocket, and he had developed his own communications satellites that would eventually produce a gusher of revenue.

But his goal was not merely to be a space entrepreneur. It was to get humanity to Mars. And that could not be done on a Falcon 9 or its beefed-up sibling, the Falcon Heavy. Falcons can fly only so high. "I could have made a lot of money, but I could not have made life multiplanetary," he says.

That is why he announced in September 2017 that SpaceX would develop a much bigger reusable rocket, the tallest and most powerful ever built. He code-named the big rocket the BFR. A year later, he sent out a tweet: "Renaming BFR to Starship."

The Starship system would have a first-stage booster and a second-stage spacecraft that together stacked to be 390 feet high, 50 percent taller than the Falcon 9 and thirty feet taller than the Saturn V rocket that was used in NASA's Apollo program in the 1970s. Outfitted with thirty-three booster engines, it would be capable of launching more than a hundred tons of payload into orbit, four times more than the Falcon 9. And someday it would be able to carry a hundred passengers to Mars. Even as he was wrestling with the Nevada and Fremont Tesla factories, Musk found time each week to look at the renderings of the type of amenities and accommodations that Starship would have for passengers on a nine-month trip to Mars.

Stainless steel, again

From his childhood days hanging around his father's engineering office in Pretoria, Musk had a feel for the properties of building materials. In Tesla and SpaceX meetings, he would focus on the various options for battery cathodes and anodes, engine valves, vehicle frames, rocket structures, and the body of a pickup truck. He could (and very often did) discourse at length on lithium, iron, cobalt, Inconel and other nickel-and-chromium alloys, plastic composites, grades of aluminum, and alloys of steel. By 2018, he was falling in love with one very common alloy that, he realized, would work equally well for a rocket as it would for the Cybertruck: stainless steel. "Stainless steel and I should go get a room somewhere," he joked to his team.

Working with him on Starship was a cheerfully humble engineer named Bill Riley. He had been a member of the fabled Cornell car racing team and helped coach Mark Juncosa, who later lured him to SpaceX. Riley and Musk bonded over a love of military history—especially air warfare in World Wars I and II—and material science.

One day in late 2018, they were visiting the Starship production facility, which was then located near the Port of Los Angeles about fifteen miles south of the SpaceX factory and headquarters. Riley explained that they were having problems with the carbon fiber material they were using. The sheets were developing wrinkles. Also, the process was slow and expensive. "If we keep going with carbon fiber, we're doomed," Musk said. "This extrapolates to death. I'll never be able to get to Mars." Cost-plus contractors don't think that way.

Musk knew that the early Atlas rockets, which in the early 1960s boosted the first four Americans into orbit, had been made of stainless steel, and he had decided to use that material for the body of the Cybertruck. At the end of his walk around the facility, he got very quiet and stared at the ships coming into the port. "Guys, we've got to change course," he said. "We are never going to build rockets fast enough with this process. What about going with stainless steel?"

Initially there was resistance, even a bit of incredulity. When he met with his executive team in the conference room at SpaceX a few days later, they argued that a rocket of stainless steel would likely be heavier than one built of carbon fiber or the aluminum-lithium alloy used for the Falcon 9. Musk's instincts said otherwise. "Run the numbers," he told the team. "Run the numbers." When they did so, they determined that steel could, in fact, turn out to be lighter in the conditions that Starship would face. At very cold temperatures, the strength of stainless steel increases by 50 percent, which meant it would be stronger when holding the supercooled liquid oxygen fuel.

In addition, the high melting point of stainless steel would eliminate the need for a heat shield on Starship's space-facing side, reducing the overall weight of the rocket. A final advantage was that it was simple to weld together pieces of stainless steel. The aluminum-lithium of the Falcon 9 required a process called stir welding that needed to be done in a pristine environment. But stainless steel could be welded in big tents or even outdoors, making it easier to do in Texas or Florida, near the launch sites. "With stainless steel, you can smoke a cigar next to it as you weld it," Musk says.

The switch to stainless steel allowed SpaceX to hire builders without the specialized expertise needed for fabricating carbon fiber. At its engine test site in McGregor, Texas, it contracted with a company that erected stainless steel water towers. Musk told Riley to reach out to them for help. One question was how thick the Starship's walls should be. Musk talked to some of the workers—those actually doing the welding rather than the company's executives—and asked what they thought was safe. "One of Elon's rules is 'Go as close to the source as possible for information,'" Riley says. The line workers said they thought the tank walls could get as thin as 4.8 millimeters. "What about four?" Musk asked.

"That would make us pretty nervous," one of the workers replied.

"Okay," Musk said, "let's do four millimeters. Let's give it a try."

It worked.

Within just a few months, they had a prototype, known as Starhopper, ready to test with low-altitude hops. It had three legs designed to test how Starship might be able to land safely after a flight and be reused. By July 2019, it was doing an eighty-foot-high test hop.

Musk was so pleased with the concept of Starship that one afternoon, during a meeting in the SpaceX conference room, he impulsively decided to deploy his burn-the-boats strategy. Cancel the Falcon Heavy, he ordered. The executives in the room texted Gwynne Shotwell what was happening. She rushed from her cubicle, plopped in a chair, and told Musk he could not do that. The Falcon Heavy, with three booster cores, was key to fulfilling its contracts with the military to launch large intelligence satellites. She had the standing to get away with such a challenge. "Once I gave Elon the context, he agreed we couldn't do what he wanted," she says. One problem Musk had was that most people around him were afraid to do that.

Starbase

Boca Chica, at the southernmost tip of Texas, is a scrubby version of paradise. Its sand dunes and beach lack the sparkle of those on Padre Island, a destination resort area just up the coast, but the wildlife preserves that surround it make it a safe place for launching rockets. In 2014, SpaceX built a rudimentary launchpad there as a backup to Cape Canaveral and Vandenberg, but it mainly gathered dust until 2018, when Musk decided to make it a dedicated base for Starship.

Because Starship was so big, it did not make sense to build it in Los Angeles and transport it to Boca Chica. So Musk decided they should build a rocket manufacturing area about two miles from the launchpad amid Boca Chica's sun-parched scrubland and mosquito-infested wetlands. The SpaceX team erected three massive hangar-like tents for the assembly lines and three "high bays" made of corrugated metal that could accommodate the Starships vertically. An old building on the property was retrofitted with office cubicles, a conference room, and a canteen with passable food and excellent coffee. By early 2020, there were five hundred engineers and construction workers, about half of them from the local area, working in shifts around the clock.

"You need to come down to Boca Chica and do whatever you can to make this place great," he told Elissa Butterfield, who was then his assistant. "The future of humanity's progress in space depends on it." The nearest motels were in Brownsville, twenty-three miles inland, so Butterfield created a park of Airstream trailers as living quarters, with palm trees from Home Depot, a tiki bar, and a deck with a fire pit. Sam Patel, the eager young facilities chief, leased drones and crop dusters to try to control the mosquitoes. "Can't get to Mars if the bugs eat us first," Musk said.

Musk focused on the layout and workings of the factory tents, brainstorming how the assembly lines should be arranged. On one visit in late 2019, he became frustrated at the slow pace. The crew had still not made even one dome that would fit perfectly on Starship. Standing in front of one of the tents, he issued a challenge: build a dome by dawn. That was not feasible, he was told, because they didn't have the equipment to calibrate the precise size. "We are going to make a dome by dawn if it fucking kills us," he insisted. Slice off the end of the rocket barrel, he ordered, and use that as your fitting tool. They did so, and he stayed up with the team of four engineers and welders until the dome was finished. "We didn't actually have a dome by dawn," admits one of the team, Jim Vo. "It took us until about nine a.m."

About a mile from the SpaceX facility was a fraying 1960s tract-house development of thirty-one homes, some of them pre-fabs, on two sparse streets. SpaceX had been able to buy most of them, offering up to three times assessed value, although a handful of owners resisted selling, either out of stubbornness or because of the excitement of living next to a launchpad.

Musk picked a two-bedroom for himself. It has an open-space main room, with white walls and lightly stained wood floor, that is a combined living room, dining area, and kitchen. A small wooden table serves as his desk. Underneath is a Wi-Fi box connected to a Starlink dish. The kitchen counters are white Formica, and the only thing that stands out is the industrial-size refrigerator, stocked with caffeine-free Diet Cokes. The art is early dorm room, including posters of *Amazing Stories* magazine covers. On the coffee table is volume three of Winston Churchill's history of World War II, the Onion's *Our Dumb Century*, Isaac Asimov's *Foundation* series, and a photo album prepared by *Saturday Night Live* of his May 2021 appearance. A small adjoining room has a treadmill, which he doesn't use much.

The backyard has scrubby grass and a couple of palm trees that, despite being palm trees, wither in the August heat. The white brick wall in back is covered with squiggly graffiti art painted by Grimes, featuring red hearts and clouds with blue emoji-like bubbles. The solar-tiled roof is connected to two big Tesla Powerwalls. A shed in the backyard is sometimes used by Grimes as a studio or by Maye Musk as a bedroom.

Humble does not begin to describe its status as the primary residence of a billionaire. But Musk found it to be a haven. After long meetings at Starbase or tense inspection tours of the rocket assembly lines, he would drive himself back there and his body would relax as he puttered around the house, whistling like a suburban dad.

54

Autonomy Day

Tesla, April 2019

Night after night, Musk sat upright on the edge of his bed next to Grimes, unable to sleep. Some nights he did not move until dawn. Tesla had survived the surges and storms of 2018, but it needed to raise another round of financing to keep operating, and the short-sellers were still circling like vultures. In March 2019, he reentered crisis-drama mode. "We have to raise money or we're fucked," he said to Grimes one dawn. He needed to come up with a grand idea that would turn the narrative around and convince investors that Tesla would become the world's most valuable car company.

One night he left the light on and just stared into space silently. "Every couple hours I would wake up, and he was just still sitting there, in the thinking man statue pose, just completely silent on the edge of the bed," Grimes says. When she woke up that morning, he said to her, "I solved it." The solution, he explained, was for Tesla to host an Autonomy Day, where investors would get a demonstration of how Tesla was building a car that could drive itself.

Ever since 2016, Musk had been pushing his vision of a completely autonomous car, one that could be summoned and drive itself with nobody behind the steering wheel. In fact, that year he began trying to get rid of the steering wheel altogether. At his insistence, von Holzhausen and his designers had been producing models of a Robotaxi with no brakes or pedals or steering wheel. Musk would go into the design studio on Fridays, pull out his phone, and take pictures of the different mock-ups. "This is where the world is going," he said at one session. "Let's push ourselves there." Every year, he had regularly predicted in public that a fully autonomous car was just a year or so away.

Except that it wasn't. Full autonomy continued to be a receding mirage, always a year or so away.

Nevertheless, Musk concluded that the best way to raise more funding was to hold a dramatic demonstration showing that autonomous vehicles were the way that the company would become phenomenally profitable. He was convinced that his team could put on a demo—even show off a credible prototype—of what the future would be.

He set a marker for four weeks away: on April 22, 2019, they would demonstrate a version of a partially self-driving car for what would be Tesla's first Autonomy Day. "We have to show people this is real," he said, even though it wasn't yet. The result was another of Musk's hallmark surges: an all-hands-on-deck 24/7 frenzy to produce an outcome by a deadline that was artificial and unrealistic.

Musk's Autopilot surge not only drove his team crazy; it drove him crazy as well. "He had to divorce himself from reality in order to get out of a shitty situation when he thought disaster was imminent," says Shivon Zilis, the close friend he had recruited to help with artificial intelligence projects. "He once asked me to tell him if he'd ever gone bananas. This was the only time I've ever walked in the room, looked at him, and said the word 'bananas.' This was the first time he saw me cry."

One evening, his young cousin James Musk, a software coder on the Autopilot team, was having dinner with the team's leader, Milan Kovac, at a fancy San Francisco restaurant when his phone rang. "I saw it was from Elon, and thought, 'Oh, this is bad,'" he remembers. He walked to the parking lot, where he listened to Musk describe in a dark tone how Tesla would go bankrupt if they didn't do something dramatic. For more than an hour, Musk questioned James about who on the Autopilot team was really good. As often happened when he went into crisis mode, he wanted to clean house and fire people, even in the midst of a surge.

He decided he needed to get rid of all the top managers of the Autopilot team, but Omead Afshar intervened to convince him to at least wait until after Autonomy Day. Shivon Zilis, who had the thankless task of trying to serve as a buffer between Musk and the team, also tried to delay the firings, as did Sam Teller. Musk reluctantly agreed to wait until right after Autonomy Day, but he wasn't happy. He moved Zilis out of Tesla to a job at Neuralink. Teller also ended up leaving during the turmoil.

James Musk was given the task of trying to integrate into the Autopilot software the ability to see red and green traffic lights, a pretty basic task that was not yet part of the system. He got it to work pretty well, but it became clear that the team would not be able to meet Musk's challenge of demonstrating a car that would drive on its own through Palo Alto. As Autonomy Day neared, he scaled his demand back to a task that was merely, as he later described it, "insanely difficult": the car would drive around the Tesla headquarters, go onto the highway, do a loop involving seven turns, and then return. "We did not believe we could do what he demanded, but he believed we could," says Anand Swaminathan, a member of the Autopilot team. "In just weeks, we were able to make it do seven difficult turns."

In his Autonomy Day presentation, Musk mixed, as he often did, vision and hype. Even in his own head, he blurred the line between what he believed and what he wanted to believe. Tesla, he said yet again, was within a year of creating a fully autonomous vehicle. At that point the company would deploy a million Robotaxis that people could summon for rides.

In its story, CNBC reported that Musk "presented bold, visionary promises that only his most loyal followers would take at face value." Nor did Musk fully impress major investors. "We asked a lot of tough questions when we had an analysts call with him afterwards," says Joe Fath, the investment manager at T. Rowe Price. "He kept saying, 'You guys just don't get it.' And then he hung up on us."

The skepticism was warranted. A year later—indeed, four years later—there would not be a million Tesla Robotaxis, or even one of them, driving autonomously on city streets. But underneath Musk's hype and willful fantasy was a vision that he remained convinced would, like reusable rockets, someday transform our lives.

55

Giga Texas

Tesla, 2020–2021

Omead Afshar

Austin

What are your favorite cities? It was a game that Musk and others at Tesla started playing in early 2020, often pulling out their phones, firing up their maps app, and calling out names. Chicago and New York? Yeah, but they wouldn't work for this purpose. The Los Angeles or San Francisco area? No, that's what they were trying to escape. California had become too fraught with NIMBYism, clogged with regulations, plagued by meddlesome commissions, and too skittish about COVID. What about Tulsa? No one had thought of Oklahoma, but its local leadership mounted a spirited campaign to be considered. Nashville? It was, Omead Afshar said, a place you'd want to visit but never live. Dallas? Texas was alluring, but Dallas, they agreed, was *too* Texas. How about the university town of Austin, which had better music and took pride in protecting its pockets of weirdness?

The issue was where to build a new Tesla factory, one big enough to merit the label Gigafactory. The Fremont, California, plant was about to become the most productive car-making facility in America, churning out more than eight thousand cars a week, but it was running at capacity, and expanding it would be difficult.

Unlike the way Jeff Bezos conducted a public bakeoff of cities eager for Amazon's HQ2, Musk decided to make the decision as he often did, from the gut, trusting his intuition and those of his executives. He hated the idea of squandering months being subjected to political pitches and the PowerPoint presentations of consultants.

At the end of May 2020, a consensus emerged. As he was sitting in the command center at Cape Canaveral fifteen minutes before SpaceX's first launch of human astronauts, Musk sent Afshar a text. "Would you rather live in Tulsa or Austin?" When Afshar, with all due respect to Tulsa, gave the answer Musk expected, he texted back, "Okay, great. We'll do it in Austin and you should run it."

A similar process led to the choice of Berlin for a European Gigafactory. It and Austin would get built in less than two years and join Fremont and Shanghai as the pillars of Tesla's car production.

By July 2021, a year after construction began, the basic structure of the Austin Gigafactory was complete. Musk and Afshar stood in front of a wall in a temporary construction office and studied photos of the site at various stages. "We're building twice as fast as Shanghai per square foot, despite the regulations we face," Afshar said.

With ten million square feet of factory floor, Giga Texas, as it was dubbed, would have twice as much floor space as Fremont and 50 percent more than the Pentagon. By some measures, Afshar said, it could be the biggest factory in the world by floor area, once some planned mezzanines were added. There was a shopping mall in China with more square feet, and Boeing with its various huge hangar facilities may have more volume. "How much bigger would we need to make this place to be able to say it's the biggest building in the world?" Musk asked. Even with the 500,000-square-foot future expansion that they were contemplating, Afshar answered, "We won't get there." Musk nodded. There was a very long pause. Then he let the idea go.

The builders showed Afshar plans for large windows that went from a few feet above each floor to the ceiling. "Don't we want it to be completely floor to ceiling?" he asked. A proposal came back for specially produced glass panes that were thirty-two feet tall, and Afshar showed Musk photos. Steve Jobs, who was obsessive about glass, would spare no expense to get huge panes for showcase venues like Apple's Fifth Avenue store in New York. Musk was more cautious. He questioned whether the glass needed to be as thick as suggested and asked how it would affect the way the sun heated the building. "We can't do things that are silly from a cost perspective," he said.

As he wandered through the nearly completed factory, Musk stopped at each station along the manufacturing line. At one point he grilled the technician at a station where steel would be cooled. "Can you have the coolant flow at a faster rate?" The guy explained the limits to how fast the cooling process could go. Musk pushed back. Are those limits actually based on the physics of steel? Can steel be like a cookie, baked hard on the outside and gooey in the middle? The technician stood his ground. Musk quit grilling him, but his intuition made him conclude that the process should take less than a minute. He left it to the technician to find a way to meet that goal. "I want to be clear," Musk says. "No more than fifty-nine seconds of cycling time, or I'm going to come here and cut it off personally."

Gigapress

One day in late 2018, Musk was sitting at his desk at Tesla headquarters in Palo Alto playing with a small toy version of the Model S. It looked like a miniaturized copy of the real car, and when he took it apart he saw that it even had a suspension inside. But the entire underbody of the car had been die cast as one piece of metal. At a meeting of his team that day, Musk pulled out the toy and put it on the white conference room table. "Why can't we do that?" he asked.

One of the engineers pointed out the obvious, that an actual car underbody is much bigger. There were no casting machines to handle something that size. That answer didn't satisfy Musk. "Go figure out how to do it," he said. "Ask for a bigger casting machine. It's not as if that would break the laws of physics."

Both he and his executives called the six major casting companies, five of whom dismissed the concept. But a company called Idra Presse in Italy, which specialized in high-pressure die-casting machines, agreed to take on the challenge of building very large machines that would be able to churn out the entire rear and front underbodies for the Model Y. "We did the world's largest casting machine," Afshar says. "It's a six-thousand-ton one for the Model Y, and we will also use a nine-thousand-ton one for Cybertruck."

The machines inject bursts of molten aluminum into a cold casting mold, which can spit out in just eighty seconds an entire chassis that used to contain more than a hundred parts that had to be welded, riveted, or bonded together. The old process produced gaps, rattles, and leaks. "So it went from a horrible nightmare to something that is crazy cheap and easy and fast," Musk says.

The process reinforced Musk's appreciation for the toy industry. "They have to produce things very quickly and cheaply without flaws, and manufacture them all by Christmas, or there will be sad faces." He repeatedly pushed his teams to get ideas from toys, such as robots and Legos. As he walked the floor of the factory, he spoke to a group of machinists about the high-precision molding of Lego pieces. They are accurate and identical to within ten microns, which means any part can easily be replaced by another. Car components needed to be that way. "Precision is not expensive," he says. "It's mostly about caring. Do you care to make it precise? Then you can make it precise."

56

Family Life

2020

With Grimes and Baby X, and with his older children

X Æ A-12

Musk's personal life was transformed in May 2020 by the birth of a son who became known as X. The first of his three children with Grimes, X had an otherworldly sweetness that calmed and beguiled Musk, who craved his presence. He took X everywhere. He would sit on his father's lap through long meetings, ride on his shoulders around the Tesla and SpaceX factories, wander precariously through solar roof installation sites, turn Twitter's lounge areas into his playground, and chatter away in the background during late-night conference calls. He and his father would repeatedly watch rocket launch videos together, and he learned to count down from ten before he could count up from one.

There was also a Musk-like quality to their interactions. They were closely bonded yet also, paradoxically, slightly detached, cherishing each other's presence but respecting each other's space. Musk, like his own parents, was not overprotective or hovering. X was never clingy or dependent. There was a lot of interaction, but not a lot of cuddling.

Musk and Grimes, who conceived the child through in vitro fertilization, had planned to have a girl, but the fertilized egg that got implanted, as they were preparing to go to Burning Man in 2019, turned out to be male. They had already settled on what was (sort of) a girl's name, Exa, as in exaflops, a supercomputer term for the ability to conduct one quintillion operations per second. Up until the day he was born, they were having trouble settling on names for a boy.

They ended up with what seemed like an autogenerated Druid password: X Æ A-12. The X represented, Grimes said, "the unknown variable." Æ, a ligature from Latin and Old English pronounced "ash," was "my elven spelling of Ai (love &/or Artificial intelligence)." The A-12, which had to be spelled A-Xii on the birth certificate because California does not permit numerals in a name, was Musk's contribution, a reference to a great-looking spy plane known as the Archangel. "Fighting with information, not with weapons," Grimes says of the A-12. "The third name is always a battle because Elon wants to delete them because he thinks it's too busy. I'd go to like five names but three's a compromise."

When X was born, Musk took a picture of Grimes having a C-section and sent it around to friends and family, including her father and brothers. Grimes was understandably horrified and scrambled to get it deleted. "It was Elon's Asperger's coming out in full," she says. "He was just clueless about why I'd be upset."

The teenagers

A week later, Musk's older kids came over to see their father and X. Saxon, his autistic son, was especially excited because of his love for babies. Musk had begun collecting the simple, wise observations Saxon made and even sharing them with Justine. "Saxon has a really interesting perception," she says, "because you can see him wrestling with abstract concepts, like time and the meaning of life. He thinks in very literal terms that slip you into a different way of perceiving the universe."

Saxon was a triplet, conceived through IVF, and his two siblings in the set were identical twins: Kai and Damian. At first, they were so alike that Justine says even she had a hard time telling them apart. But they became an interesting study in the role of genetics, environment, and chance. "They lived in the same house and the same room and had the same experiences and did similarly on tests," Musk says. "But Damian thought of himself as smart, and Kai didn't, for some reason. So bizarre."

Their personalities were very different. Damian was an introvert, ate little, and announced at age eight that he was a vegetarian. When I asked Justine why he made that decision, she passed the phone to Damian to answer. "To decrease my carbon footprint," he explained. He became a classical-music prodigy, composing dark sonatas and practicing on the piano hours at a time. Musk would show videos he took on his phone of Damian playing. He also was a wizard in math and physics. "I think Damian is brighter than you," Maye Musk once said to her son, who nodded in agreement.

Kai, taller and strikingly good looking, became more of an extrovert and loved to solve practical problems in a hands-on way. "He's bigger and more athletic than Damian and is very protective of him," Justine says. He is the child most interested in the technical aspects of what his father is doing and was the one most likely to accompany his father to Cape Canaveral for rocket launches. That delighted his father, who says that his greatest moments of sadness are when his kids say they don't want to hang out with him.

Their older brother, Griffin, shared their ethical outlook and sweetness. He also understood his father well. At an event at the Tesla factory in Texas one evening, he was hanging out with some of his friends when his father asked if he would come with him backstage to the holding room. Griffin hesitated and said he wanted to be with his friends, then looked at them, shrugged, and went off to be with his father. Brilliant in science and math, he had a gentleness that his father lacked, and was the most sociable member of the family, at least until X came along.

And then there was Griffin's non-identical twin. Named partly after Musk's favorite character in the Marvel Comics X-Men series, Xavier was strong-willed and developed a deep hatred for capitalism and wealth. There were long and bitter exchanges, in person and by text, in which Xavier repeatedly said, "I hate you and everything you stand for." It was one factor that made Musk decide to sell his houses and live less lavishly, but that had little effect on the relationship. By 2020, the rift had become irreparable. Xavier did not join the other siblings in visiting their new stepbrother.

So Xavier and Elon were already estranged when the sixteen-year-old decided to transition to female around the time X was born. "Hey, I'm transgender, and my name is now Jenna," she texted Christiana, Kimbal's wife. "Don't tell my dad." She also texted Grimes, asking her to keep the secret as well. Eventually, Musk found out from a member of his security detail.

Musk would end up wrestling, often publicly, with transgender issues. A few months after Xavier became Jenna, but before it was known publicly, Musk tweeted out a cartoon of a soldier in pain with the caption "When you put he/him in ur bio." When criticized, he deleted the tweet and tried to explain. "I absolutely support trans, but all these pronouns are an esthetic nightmare." He would become more and more vocal on trans issues and, by 2023, was championing the conservative backlash against allowing medical support for kids under eighteen who wanted to transition.

Christiana insists that Elon is not prejudiced against gay or trans people. The rift with Jenna, she says, was caused more by her radical Marxism than her gender identity. Christiana speaks from some experience. She was at times estranged from her own billionaire father, and before marrying Kimbal she was married to the Black female rock star Deborah Anne Dyer, known as Skin. "When I was still with my ex-wife, Elon tried to convince us to have children," she says. "He has no biases about gay or trans or race."

His disagreements with Jenna, Musk says, "became intense when she went beyond socialism to being a full communist and thinking that anyone rich is evil." He partly blames what he calls the progressive woke indoctrination that pervaded the Los Angeles private school she attended, Crossroads. When his kids were younger, he sent them to a school that he had created for family and friends called Ad Astra. "They went there until they were about fourteen, but then I thought they should be introduced to the real world for high school," he says. "What I should have done is extend Ad Astra through high school."

The rift with Jenna, he says, pained him more than anything in his life since the infant death of his firstborn child Nevada. "I've made many overtures," he says, "but she doesn't want to spend time with me."

Homes

Jenna's anger made Musk sensitive to the backlash against billionaires. He believed that there was nothing wrong with becoming wealthy by building successful companies and keeping the money invested in them. But by 2020, he had come to feel that it was unproductive and unseemly to cash in those riches and lavish them on personal consumption.

Until then, he had lived rather grandly. His primary residence in the Bel Air section of Los Angeles, which he had bought for $17 million in 2012, was a sixteen-thousand-square-foot faux-palace with seven bedrooms and a guest suite, eleven baths, gym, tennis court, pool, two-story library, screening room, and orchard. It was a place that his five kids could feel was their castle. They would stay with him four days a week and had a routine of tennis lessons, martial arts, and other activities at the house.

When the actor Gene Wilder's home across the road went on sale, Musk bought it to preserve it. Then he bought three surrounding houses and toyed with tearing down some to build his own dream house. He also owned a $32 million, thirteen-bedroom, forty-seven-acre Mediterranean-style estate in Silicon Valley.

In early 2020, Musk decided to unload them all. "I am selling almost all physical possessions," he tweeted three days before X was born. "Will own no house." He explained to Joe Rogan the sentiment that led to that decision. "I think possessions kind of weigh you down and they're an attack vector," he said. "In recent years 'billionaire' has become pejorative, like that's a bad thing. They'll say, 'Hey, billionaire, you've got all this stuff.' Well, now I don't have stuff, so what are you going to do?"

Once he finished selling his California homes, Musk moved to Texas, and Grimes soon followed. The small tract home in Boca Chica that he rented from SpaceX became his primary residence. He spent much of his time in Austin, where he borrowed the house of his PayPal friend Ken Howery, who had been ambassador to Sweden and then taken time off to travel the world. The eight-thousand-square-foot home on a lake formed by the Colorado River was part of a gated development where many other Austin billionaires lived. It was a perfect place for him to gather his kids for holidays, until the *Wall Street Journal* reported that he was living there. "I stopped staying at Ken's house after the *Journal* doxed me," he says. "People kept trying to come around, and someone managed to get through the gates and into the house when I wasn't there."

After some half-hearted hunting, he found a house nearby that was big enough and was, in his words, "a cool house though not one that would be in *Architectural Digest*." The sellers were asking $70 million, and he offered $60 million, which is what he had sold his California houses for. But by then the sellers, dealing with the world's richest person in a super-hot real estate market, wanted even more than their original asking price. Musk backed away. Instead, he was content using a condo in Austin owned by a friend or staying at a house that Grimes rented on a secluded cul-de-sac.

Elon and Kimbal reunited

After a trip to Stockholm for Ken Howery's birthday party in November 2020, Musk tested positive for COVID. He called Kimbal, who had been infected around the same time. Their relationship had been strained, especially after the fraught fall of 2018. But they bonded again when Elon flew to Boulder to ride out their mild cases of COVID together.

Kimbal, who was a believer in mind-healing using legal natural hallucinogens, had been planning an Ayahuasca ceremony, which involves drinking hallucinatory teas under the guidance of a shaman. He tried to convince Elon to join him in the experience, which he thought might help tame his demons. "An Ayahuasca ceremony involves an ego death," Kimbal explains. "All of that baggage you have dies. You are a different human after that."

Elon declined. "I've just got emotions buried under so much layers of concrete, I'm just not ready to open that up," he said. Instead, he just wanted to pal around with Kimbal. After watching a SpaceX launch on their computers and goofing around in Boulder, they got bored and took Elon's plane to Austin. There they played Elon's favorite new video-game obsession, *Polytopia*, and binge-watched *Cobra Kai*, a Netflix series based on the *Karate Kid* movie.

In the show, the characters from the original movie were now in their late forties, like Elon and Kimbal, with kids that were the age of the Musk kids. "It hit home to both of us, because it has one super-empathetic person, played by Ralph Macchio, and the other person is the non-empathetic one," Kimbal says. "They're both struggling with their own challenges with their father figure and also with how to be father figures to their own children." The experience was cathartic, even without an Ayahuasca ceremony. "We were like two kids again," Kimbal says. "It was beautiful, the best time ever. We never thought we'd ever get one of those weeks again in our lives."

57

Full Throttle

SpaceX, 2020

With Kiko Dontchev, and at the Cape Canaveral launch tower

Civilians into orbit

Beginning with the retirement of the Space Shuttle in 2011, the United States experienced a lapse in ability, will, and imagination that was astonishing for a nation that, two generations earlier, had made nine missions to the moon. For almost a decade after the last Shuttle mission, the nation had not been able to send humans into space. It was forced to rely on Russian rockets to get its astronauts to the International Space Station. In 2020, SpaceX changed that.

That May, a Falcon 9 rocket topped with a Crew Dragon capsule was ready to carry two NASA astronauts to the International Space Station—the first-ever launch of humans into orbit by a private company. President Trump and Vice President Pence flew down to Cape Canaveral and sat in the viewing stands near Pad 39A for the launch. Musk, wearing headphones and flanked by his son Kai, sat inside the control room. Ten million people watched live on television and various streaming platforms. "I'm not a religious person," Musk later told podcaster Lex Fridman, "but I nonetheless got on my knees and prayed for that mission."

As the rocket lifted, the control room erupted with cheers. Trump and the other politicians came in to offer congratulations. "This is the first big space message in fifty years, think of that," Trump said. "And it is an honor to be delivering it." Musk had little idea what the president was talking about, and he kept his distance. When Trump walked over to Musk and his team and asked, "Are you guys ready to do four more years?" Musk zoned out and turned away.

When NASA had awarded SpaceX the contract to build a rocket that would take astronauts to the Space Station, it had, on the same day in 2014, given a competing contract, with 40 percent more funding, to Boeing. By the time SpaceX succeeded in 2020, Boeing had not even been able to get an unmanned test flight to dock with the station.

To celebrate SpaceX's successful launch, Musk went with Kimbal, Grimes, Luke Nosek, and a few others to a resort in the Everglades two hours south of Cape Canaveral. Nosek recalls that the historic "hugeness of the moment" began to hit them. They danced into the night, Kimbal jumping up at one point and shouting, "My brother has just sent astronauts up into space!"

Kiko Dontchev

After SpaceX's launch of astronauts to the Space Station in May 2020, it had an impressive run of eleven unmanned successful satellite launches in five months. But Musk, as always, feared complacency. Unless he maintained a maniacal sense of urgency, he worried, SpaceX could end up flabby and slow, like Boeing.

Following one of the launches that October, Musk paid a late-night visit to Pad 39A. There were only two people working. Sights like that triggered him. At all of his companies, as the employees at Twitter would discover, he expected everyone to work with an unrelenting intensity. "We have 783 employees working at the Cape," he said in a cold rage to his launch VP there. "Why are there only two of them working now?" Musk gave him forty-eight hours to prepare a briefing on what everyone was supposed to be doing.

When he didn't get the answers he wanted, Musk decided to find out for himself. He went into hardcore, all-in mode. As he did at the Nevada and Fremont Tesla factories, and as he would later do at Twitter, he moved into the building, in this case the hangar at Cape Canaveral, and went to work around the clock. His all-night presence was both performative and real. On his second night, he could not reach the launch VP, who had a wife and family and, in Musk's thinking, had gone AWOL, so he asked to talk to one of the engineers who had been working alongside him at the hangar, Kiko Dontchev.

Dontchev was born in Bulgaria and emigrated to America as a young kid when his father, a mathematician, took a job at the University of Michigan. He got an undergraduate and graduate degree in aerospace engineering, which led to what he thought was his dream opportunity: an internship at Boeing. But he quickly became disenchanted and decided to visit a friend who was working at SpaceX. "I will never forget walking the floor that day," he says. "All the young engineers working their asses off and wearing T-shirts and sporting tattoos and being really badass about getting things done. I thought,

'These are my people.' It was nothing like the buttoned-up deadly vibe at Boeing."

That summer, he made a presentation to a VP at Boeing about how SpaceX was enabling the younger engineers to innovate. "If Boeing doesn't change," he said, "you're going to lose out on the top talent." The VP replied that Boeing was not looking for disrupters. "Maybe we want the people who aren't the best, but who will stick around longer." Dontchev quit.

At a conference in Utah, he went to a party thrown by SpaceX and, after a couple of drinks, worked up the nerve to corner Gwynne Shotwell. He pulled a crumpled résumé out of his pocket and showed her a picture of the satellite hardware he had worked on. "I can make things happen," he told her.

Shotwell was amused. "Anyone who is brave enough to come up to me with a crumpled-up résumé might be a good candidate," she said. She invited him to SpaceX for interviews. He was scheduled to see Musk, who was still interviewing every engineer hired, at 3 p.m. As usual, Musk got backed up, and Dontchev was told he would have to come back another day. Instead, Dontchev sat outside Musk's cubicle for five hours. When he finally got in to see Musk at 8 p.m., Dontchev took the opportunity to unload about how his gung-ho approach wasn't valued at Boeing.

When hiring or promoting, Musk made a point of prioritizing attitude over résumé skills. And his definition of a good attitude was a desire to work maniacally hard. Musk hired Dontchev on the spot.

On that October night during his work binge at the Cape, when Musk asked to speak to Dontchev, the engineer had just gotten home after three straight days of work and cracked open a bottle of wine. At first he ignored the unknown number on his phone, but then one of his colleagues called his wife. Tell Kiko to get back to the hangar right away. Musk wants him. "I'm like super tired, half-drunk, haven't slept in days, so I got in the car, bought a pack of cigarettes to get me going, and made it back to the hangar," he says. "I worried about getting pulled over for drunk driving, but that seemed less of a risk than ignoring Elon."

When Dontchev got there, Musk told him to organize a "skip-level" series of meetings to talk to the engineers one level below the top managers. Out of that came a shake-up. Dontchev was elevated to chief engineer at the Cape, and his mentor Rich Morris, a calm veteran manager, was put in charge of operations. Dontchev then made a smart request. He said he wanted to report to Morris rather than directly to Musk. The result was a smooth-running team led by a manager who knew how to be a Yoda-like mentor and an engineer who was eager to match Musk's intensity.

Defiance

Musk's push to move faster, take more risks, break rules, and question requirements allowed him to accomplish big feats, such as sending humans into orbit, mass-marketing electric vehicles, and getting homeowners off the electric grid. It also meant that he did things—ignoring SEC requirements, defying California COVID restrictions—that got him in trouble.

Hans Koenigsmann was one of the original SpaceX engineers recruited by Musk in 2002. He had been part of the intrepid corps on Kwaj during the failed first three flights and then the successful fourth of the Falcon 1. Musk promoted him to vice president in charge of flight reliability, making sure that flights were safe and followed regulations. It was not an easy job to have under Musk.

In late 2020, SpaceX was preparing to launch an unmanned test of the Super Heavy booster. All flights have to adhere to the requirements imposed by the Federal Aviation Administration, which include weather guidelines. That morning, the FAA inspector monitoring the launch remotely ruled that upper-level winds made it unsafe to proceed. If there was an explosion at launch, nearby houses could be impacted. SpaceX presented its own weather model saying conditions were safe and asked for a waiver, but the FAA refused.

Nobody from the FAA was actually in the control room, and it was slightly (though not very) unclear what the rules were, so the launch director turned to Elon and silently cocked his head as if asking if he should proceed. Musk gave a silent nod. The rocket took off.

"It was all very subtle," says Koenigsmann. "That's typical Elon. A decision to take a risk signaled by a nod of the head."

The rocket launched perfectly, without the weather being a problem, though it did fail when attempting a vertical landing six miles away. The FAA opened an investigation into why its weather ruling was ignored, and it put a two-month hold on SpaceX tests, but it ended up imposing no significant penalties.

As part of his job, Koenigsmann wrote a report on the incident, and he did not whitewash SpaceX's behavior. "The FAA is both incompetent and conservative, which is a bad mixture, but I still needed a sign-off from them before we should have flown, and we did not have that," he told me. "Elon had launched when the FAA said we couldn't. So I wrote a true report that said that." He wanted SpaceX, and Musk, to accept blame.

That was not the attitude that Musk valued. "He didn't see it that way, and got touchy, very touchy," Koenigsmann says.

Koenigsmann had been at SpaceX from the very rough early days, and Musk did not want to fire him on the spot. But he took away his oversight duties and eased him out in a few months. "You did an awesome job over many years, but eventually everybody's time comes to retire," Musk told him in an email. "Yours is now."

58

Bezos vs. Musk, Round 2

SpaceX, 2021

Jeff Bezos right after his trip; Richard Branson right before his

Goading each other

Jeff Bezos and Elon Musk had tangled, beginning in 2013, over who would lease the storied Pad 39A at Cape Canaveral (Musk won), be first to land a rocket that went to the edge of space (Bezos), land a rocket that launched to orbit (Musk), and send humans into orbit (Musk). Space was a personal passion for both men, and their competition—like that of the railway barons a century earlier—would serve to push the field forward. Despite bleats about space becoming a billionaire-boys' hobby, their vision for privatizing launches was what propelled America, which had fallen behind China and even Russia, back into the forefront of space exploration.

The rivalry reignited in April 2021, when SpaceX beat Bezos's Blue Origin for the contract to take NASA astronauts on the final leg of a journey to the moon. Blue Origin unsuccessfully appealed the decision. Its website displayed a graphic criticizing the SpaceX plan, with big letters labeling it "immensely complex" and "high risk." SpaceX responded by pointing out that Blue Origin "has not produced a single rocket or spacecraft capable of reaching orbit." Musk's Twitter fans formed a flash mob ridiculing Blue Origin, and Musk joined in. "Can't get it up (to orbit) lol," he tweeted.

Bezos and Musk were alike in some respects. They both disrupted industries through passion, innovation, and force of will. They were both abrupt with employees, quick to call things stupid, and enraged by doubters and naysayers. And they both focused on envisioning the future rather than pursuing short-term profits. When asked if he even knew how to spell "profit," Bezos answered, "P-r-o-p-h-e-t."

But when it came to drilling down on the engineering, they were different. Bezos was methodical. His motto was *gradatim ferociter*, or "Step by step, ferociously." Musk's instinct was to push and surge and drive people toward insane deadlines, even if it meant taking risks.

Bezos was skeptical, indeed dismissive of Musk's practice of spending hours at engineering meetings making technical suggestions and issuing abrupt orders. Former employees at SpaceX and Tesla told him, he says, that Musk rarely knew as much as he claimed and that his interventions were usually unhelpful or outright problematic.

For his part, Musk felt that Bezos was a dilettante whose lack of focus on the engineering was one reason Blue Origin had made less progress than SpaceX. In an interview in late 2021, he grudgingly praised Bezos for having "reasonably good engineering aptitude," but then added, "But he does not seem to be willing to spend mental energy getting into the details of engineering. The devil's in the details."

Now that Musk had sold all his homes and was living in rented quarters in Texas, he also began to disdain Bezos for his lavish multimansion lifestyle. "In some ways, I'm trying to goad him into spending more time at Blue Origin so they make more progress," Musk says. "He should spend more time at Blue Origin and less time in the hot tub."

Another dispute erupted over their rival satellite communications companies. By the summer of 2021, SpaceX had deployed nearly two thousand Starlinks into orbit. Its space-based internet was available in fourteen countries. Bezos had announced in 2019 plans for Amazon to create a similar constellation and internet service, called Project Kuiper. But so far, no satellites had been launched.

Musk believed that innovation was driven by setting clear metrics, such as cost per ton lifted into orbit or average number of miles driven on Autopilot without human intervention. For Starlink, he surprised Juncosa by asking how many photons were collected by the solar arrays of the satellite versus how many they could usefully shoot down to Earth. It was a huge ratio—perhaps 10,000 to 1—and Juncosa had never considered it. "I certainly never thought of this as a metric," he says. "It forced me to try some creative thinking about how we could improve efficiency."

This led SpaceX to develop a second version of Starlink, and it applied to get approval from the Federal Communications Commission. The application lowered the planned orbital altitude for future Starlinks, which would reduce the network's latency.

That would put them close to the planned orbits of Bezos's competing Kuiper constellation, so Bezos filed an objection. Once again,

Musk attacked him on Twitter, misspelling his name, intentionally, as the Spanish word for "kisses": "Turns out Besos retired to pursue a full-time job filing lawsuits against SpaceX." The FCC ruled that Musk's plans could proceed.

Billionaire jaunts

One of Bezos's dreams was to go into space himself. So in the summer of 2020, amid his tussles with Musk, he announced that he and his brother Mark were going to fly to the edge of space (though not into orbit) on an eleven-minute hop on a Blue Origin rocket. He would be the first billionaire in space.

Sir Richard Branson, the smiley British billionaire who founded Virgin Airlines and Virgin Music, also had that dream. He had created his own space-flight company, Virgin Galactic, with a business model largely dependent on taking wealthy experience-seekers on joyrides. His marketing genius included using himself as the face and spirit of the company. He knew that there was no better way to promote his space-tourism business, and have a boatload of fun himself (which he very much liked to do), than to go up on one of his rockets. So after it was too late for Bezos to change his launch date, Branson announced that he would be going up on July 11, nine days earlier. Ever the showman, he invited Stephen Colbert to host the livecast and the singer Khalid to perform a new song for the occasion.

When Branson woke up just before 1 a.m. the morning of the launch, he went into the kitchen of the house he was using and found Musk standing there with Baby X. "Elon was so sweet to turn up with his new baby to our flight," Branson says. Musk was barefoot and wearing a black T-shirt emblazoned "Five Decades of Apollo" that celebrated the fiftieth anniversary of the moon mission. They sat down and talked for a couple of hours. "He doesn't seem to sleep much," Branson says.

The flight, on a suborbital winged rocket that was lifted to its launch altitude on a cargo jet, went well. Branson and five Virgin Galactic employees reached an altitude of 53.6 miles, setting off a small dispute about whether they had reached "space," which is defined by

NASA as beginning at fifty miles above Earth but by other nations as what is known as the Kármán line, at sixty-two miles up.

Bezos's mission nine days later also succeeded. Musk, of course, did not attend that one. Bezos, his brother, and the crew reached an altitude of sixty-six miles, well above the Kármán line, giving him a dollop of added bragging rights. Their space capsule landed gently by parachute in the Texas desert, where his very anxious mother and calmer father were waiting.

Musk offered a pinch of faint praise to Bezos and Branson. "I thought it was cool that they're spending money on the advancement of space," he told Kara Swisher at a Code Conference in September. But he pointed out that hopping up sixty miles was a minor step. "To put things into perspective, you need about a hundred times more energy to get to orbit versus suborbit," he explained. "And then, to get back from orbit you need to burn off that energy, so you need a heavy-duty heat shield. Orbit is roughly two orders of magnitude more difficult than suborbit."

Musk was cursed with a conspiratorial mindset, which made him believe that much of his negative press was due to the hidden agendas or corrupt interests of the people who own the news organizations. This was particularly pronounced when Bezos bought the *Washington Post*. When the paper contacted Musk about a story it was reporting in 2021, he sent an email that simply said, "Give my regards to your puppet master." In fact, Bezos has always been admirably hands-off when it came to news coverage in the *Post*, and its respected space reporter Christian Davenport regularly published stories that chronicled Musk's successes, including one about his rivalry with Bezos. "For now, Musk is well ahead in virtually every area," Davenport wrote. "SpaceX has dispatched three teams of astronauts to the International Space Station and on Tuesday is scheduled to launch a crew of civilian astronauts on a three-day trip orbiting Earth. Blue Origin has launched a single suborbital mission to space that lasted just over 10 minutes."

59

Starship Surge

SpaceX, July 2021

Andy Krebs (*top*), Lucas Hughes (*bottom*), and a Starship being stacked by the Mechazilla arms

Mechazilla

X, then fifteen months old, toddled on top of the white Starbase conference table in Boca Chica, opening and shutting his outstretched arms. He was mimicking the animation on the screen showing the arms of the Boca Chica launchpad tower. The first three words he had learned to speak were "rocket," "car," and "daddy." Now he was practicing a new one: "chopsticks." His father paid little attention, and the other five engineers in the room that night were practiced in pretending not to be distracted by him.

The story of the chopsticks had begun eight months earlier, at the end of 2020, when the SpaceX team was discussing the landing legs being planned for Starship. Musk's guiding principle was rapid reusability, which he often declared was "the holy grail for making humans a space-faring civilization." In other words, rockets should be like airplanes. They should take off, land, and then take off again as soon as possible.

The Falcon 9 had become the world's only rapidly reusable rocket. During 2020, Falcon boosters had landed safely twenty-three times, coming down upright on landing legs. The video feeds of the fiery yet gentle landings still made Musk leap from his chair. Nevertheless, he was not enamored with the landing legs being planned for Starship's booster. They added weight, thus cutting the size of the payloads the booster could lift.

"Why don't we try to use the tower to catch it?" he asked. He was referring to the tower that holds the rocket on the launchpad. Musk had already come up with the idea of using that tower to stack the rocket; it had a set of arms that could pick up the first-stage booster, place it on the launch mount, then pick up the second-stage spacecraft, and place it atop the booster. Now he was suggesting that these arms could also be used to catch the booster when it returned to Earth.

It was a wild idea, and there was a lot of consternation in the room. "If the booster comes back down to the tower and crashes into it, you can't launch the next rocket for a long time," Bill Riley says. "But we agreed to study different ways to do it."

A few weeks later, just after Christmas 2020, the team gathered to brainstorm. Most engineers argued against trying to use the tower to catch the booster. The stacking arms were already dangerously complex. After more than an hour of argument, a consensus was forming to stick with the old idea of putting landing legs on the booster. But Stephen Harlow, the vehicle engineering director, kept arguing for the more audacious approach. "We have this tower, so why not try to use it?"

After another hour of debate, Musk stepped in. "Harlow, you're on board with this plan," he said. "So why don't you be in charge of it?"

As soon as he made the decision, Musk switched into silly-humor mode. He began laughing about the scene in *The Karate Kid* where the karate master, Mr. Miyagi, uses a pair of chopsticks to catch a fly. The tower arms, Musk said, would be called the chopsticks, and he dubbed the whole tower "Mechazilla." He celebrated with a tweet: "We're going to try to catch the booster with the launch tower arm!" When asked by a follower why he didn't just use landing legs, Musk responded, "Legs would certainly work, but the best part is no part."

On a hot Wednesday afternoon in late July 2021, the final segment of Mechazilla with the movable chopstick arms was put in place at the Boca Chica launch site. When his team showed him an animation of the device, Musk got excited. "Kick ass!" he shouted. "The viewership on this one is going to be huge." He found a two-minute clip from *The Karate Kid* and tweeted it out from his iPhone. "SpaceX will try to catch largest ever flying object with robot chopsticks," he said. "Success is not guaranteed, but excitement is!"

The surge

"We need to stack the ship on the booster," Musk told the impromptu meeting of a hundred workers gathered in a semicircle in one of the three hangar-like tents in Boca Chica. It was a brutally sunny day in July 2021, and he was focused on getting FAA approval for Starship to fly. The best way, he decided, was to stack the booster and the second-stage ship on the launchpad to show that they were ready. "That will force the regulators to get off their butts," he said. "There will be public pressure getting them to move to approval."

It was a somewhat pointless but typical Musk move. Starship, as it turned out, would not be ready to fly until April 2023, another twenty-one months away. But creating a maniacal sense of urgency would, he hoped, light a fire under everyone, including the regulators, the workers, and even himself.

For the next few hours, he lumbered along the assembly lines, his hairless arms swinging, his neck slightly bent, pausing occasionally to stare at something in silence. Increasingly, his face got darker, and his pauses took on an ominous feel. By 9 p.m., a full moon had arisen out of the ocean, and it seemed to be transforming him into a man possessed.

I had seen Musk get into this demon-mode temperament before, so I sensed what it portended. As often happens—at least two or three times a year in a major way—a compulsion was swelling inside him to order up a surge, an all-in burst of round-the-clock activity, like he had done at the Nevada battery factory, the Fremont car-assembly plant, and the autonomous-driving team offices, and would later do in the crazed month after he bought Twitter. The goal was to shake things up and "extrude shit out of the system," as he put it.

The storm clouds building in his head burst when he and a group of his top managers went down the road to the launchpad site and didn't see anybody working. This might not have seemed unusual to most people on a late Friday night, but Musk erupted. His immediate target was a tall, mild-mannered civil engineer named Andy Krebs, who was in charge of building the infrastructure at Starbase. "Why is no one working?" Musk demanded.

Unfortunately for Krebs, it was the first time in three weeks he didn't have a full night shift working on the tower and launchpad. Soft-spoken with a hint of a stutter, he was tentative in his answers, which didn't help. "What is the fucking problem?" Musk demanded. "I want to see activity."

That's when he ordered the surge. Starship's booster and second stage, he said, should be rolled out of the manufacturing bays and stacked on the launchpad within ten days. He wanted five hundred workers from around SpaceX—Cape Canaveral, Los Angeles, Seattle—to be flown immediately to Boca Chica and thrown into the breach. "This is not a volunteer organization," he said. "We are not selling Girl Scout cookies. Get them here now." When he called Gwynne Shotwell, who was in bed in Los Angeles, to figure out what workers and supervisors would come to Boca Chica, she protested that the engineers at the Cape still had Falcon 9 launches to prepare for. Musk ordered them delayed. The surge was his priority.

Shortly after 1 a.m., Musk sent out an email titled "Starship Surge" to all SpaceX employees. "Anyone who is not working on other obviously critical path projects at SpaceX should shift immediately to work on the first Starship orbit," he wrote. "Please fly, drive, or get here by any means possible."

At Cape Canaveral, Kiko Dontchev, who won his spurs when Musk ignited a similar frenzy after seeing almost no one working on Pad 39A one night, began rousing his best workers to fly to Texas. Musk's assistant Jehn Balajadia tried to get hotel rooms in nearby Brownsville, but most were booked for a border-control convention, so she scrambled to make arrangements for workers to sleep on air mattresses. Sam Patel worked through the night figuring out the reporting and supervising structures they would put in place—and also how to get enough food to Boca Chica to feed everyone.

By the time Musk got back from the launchpad to the Starbase main building, the video monitor by the front door had been reprogrammed. It read, "Ship+Rocket Stacked T −196h 44m 23s," and was counting down the seconds. Balajadia explained that Musk does not let them round off into days or even hours. Every second counted. "We need to get to Mars before I die," he said. "There's no forcing function for getting us to Mars other than us, and sometimes that means me."

The surge was successful. In just over ten days, the booster and spacecraft of Starship were stacked on the launchpad. It was also a bit pointless. The rocket was not yet capable of flying, and stacking it did not force the FAA to rush its approval. But the ginned-up crisis pushed the team to remain hardcore, and it provided Musk with a bit of the drama that his headspace craves. "I feel renewed faith in the future of humanity," he said that evening. Another storm had passed.

Raptor costs

A few weeks after the surge, Musk turned his attention to Raptor, the engine that would power Starship. Fueled by supercooled liquid methane and liquid oxygen, it had more than twice the thrust of the Falcon 9's Merlin engine. This meant that Starship would have more thrust than any other rocket in history.

But the Raptor engine would not get humanity to Mars simply by being powerful. It would also have to be manufactured by the hundreds at a reasonable cost. Each Starship would need about forty of them, and Musk envisioned a fleet of scores of Starships. Raptor was too complex to be mass-manufactured. It looked like a spaghetti bush. So in August 2021, Musk fired the person in charge of its design and personally took on the title of vice president for propulsion. His goal was to get the cost of each engine to around $200,000, a tenth of what it then cost.

Gwynne Shotwell and the SpaceX CFO, Bret Johnsen, arranged a small meeting one afternoon with the person in the finance department in charge of overseeing Raptor costs. In walked a studious-looking young financial analyst named Lucas Hughes, whose slightly preppy appearance was mitigated by his hair being scrunched into a ponytail. He had never directly interacted with Musk and wasn't even sure Musk knew his name. So he was nervous.

Musk began with his lecture on collegiality. "I want to be super clear," he began. "You are not the friend of the engineers. You are the judge. If you're popular among the engineers, this is bad. If you don't step on toes, I will fire you. Is that clear?" Hughes stuttered a bit as he assented.

Ever since he flew back from Russia and calculated the costs of building his own rockets, Musk had deployed what he called the "idiot index." That was the ratio of the total cost of a component to the cost of its raw materials. Something with a high idiot index—say, a component that cost $1,000 when the aluminum that composed it cost only $100—was likely to have a design that was too complex or a manufacturing process that was too inefficient. As Musk put it, "If the ratio is high, you're an idiot."

"What are the best parts in Raptor as judged by the idiot index?" Musk asked.

"I'm not sure," Hughes responded. "I will find out." This was not good. Musk's face hardened, and Shotwell shot me a worried glance.

"You better be fucking sure in the future you know these things off the top of your head," Musk said. "If you ever come into a meeting and do not know what are the idiot parts, then your resignation will be accepted immediately." He spoke in a monotone and showed no emotion. "How can you fucking not know what the best and worst parts are?"

"I know the cost chart down to the smallest part," Hughes said quietly. "I just don't know the cost of the raw materials of those parts."

"What are the worst five parts?" Musk demanded. Hughes looked at his computer to see if he could calculate an answer. "NO! Don't look at your screen," Musk said. "Just name one. You should know the problematic parts."

"There's the half nozzle jacket," Hughes offered tentatively. "I think it costs thirteen thousand dollars."

"It's made of a single piece of steel," Musk said, now quizzing him. "How much does that material cost?"

"I think a few thousand dollars?" replied Hughes.

Musk knew the answer. "No. It's just steel. It's about two hundred bucks. You have very badly failed. If you don't improve, your resignation will be accepted. This meeting is over. Done."

When Hughes came into the conference room the next day for a follow-up presentation, Musk showed no sign that he remembered reaming him out. "We are looking at the twenty worst 'idiot index' parts," Hughes began as he pulled up a slide. "There's definitely some themes." Other than wringing a pencil, he was able to hide his nervousness. Musk listened quietly and nodded. "It's mainly the parts that require a lot of high-precision machining, like pumps and fairings," Hughes continued. "We need to cut out as much of the machining as possible." Musk started smiling. This had been one of his themes. He asked a few specific questions about the use of copper and the best way to do stamping and hole-punching. It was no longer a quiz or a confrontation. Musk was interested in figuring out the answers.

"We are looking at some of the techniques that automakers use to keep these costs down," Hughes continued. He also had a slide that showed how they were applying Musk's algorithm to each of the parts. There were columns that showed what requirements had been questioned, what parts had been deleted, and the name of the specific person in charge of each component.

"We should ask each of them to see if they can get the cost of their part down by eighty percent," Musk suggested, "and if they can't, we should consider asking them to step aside if someone else might be able to do so."

By the end of the meeting, they had a roadmap to get the cost of each engine down from $2 million to $200,000 in twelve months.

After these meetings, I pulled Shotwell aside and asked for her assessment of how Musk had treated Hughes. She cares about the human dimension that Musk ignores. She lowered her voice. "I heard that Lucas lost his first child about seven weeks ago," she said. "He and his wife had a baby with birth problems who was never able to leave the hospital." That was why, she felt, Hughes had been flustered and less prepared than usual. Given that Musk had a similar experience when his first baby died, sending him into months of grief, I suggested to Shotwell he should be able to relate. "I still need to tell Elon," she said.

I didn't mention this to Musk when I talked to him later that day, because Shotwell told me it was confidential, but I did ask him whether he thought he was too harsh with Hughes. Musk stared a bit blankly, as if he wasn't sure what I was referring to. After some silence, he answered in the abstract. "I give people hardcore feedback, mostly accurate, and I try not to do it in a way that's ad hominem," he says. "I try to criticize the action, not the person. We all make mistakes. What matters is whether a person has a good feedback loop, can seek criticism from others, and can improve. Physics does not care about hurt feelings. It cares about whether you got the rocket right."

The lesson of Lucas

A year later, I decided to see what had happened to the two people Musk chewed out in the summer of 2021, Lucas Hughes and Andy Krebs.

Hughes remembered every moment vividly. "He kept coming back at me on the costs of the Raptor's half nozzle jacket," he says. "He was correct about what the materials cost, and I couldn't figure out a way in the moment to explain the other costs in a way that was successful." When Musk kept interrupting him, Hughes reached back to his training as a gymnast.

He had grown up in Golden, Colorado, with a passion for gymnastics. Starting when he was eight, he began training thirty hours a week. Gymnastics helped him excel academically. "I was very detail oriented, very Type A, very dedicated and disciplined," he says. At Stanford, he competed in all six of the men's gymnastic routines, which required training year-round, while majoring in engineering and finance. His favorite course was one called Building the Future with Engineering Materials. When he graduated in 2010, he went to work at Goldman Sachs, but yearned to do something that was closer to real engineering. "I was a space nerd as a kid," he says, so he sent in an application when he saw that SpaceX had posted a job for a financial analyst. He went to work there in December 2013.

"When Elon was really chewing me out, I focused hard on trying to keep my composure," he says. "Gymnastics teaches you to stay calm in a high-pressure situation. I was just trying to hold it together and not collapse."

After the second meeting, when he had all of the "idiot index" data at his fingertips, he never had a problem with Musk. When cost questions came up at subsequent Raptor meetings, Musk would often ask Hughes his thoughts, calling on him by name. Did Musk ever acknowledge that he had reamed him out? "That's a good question," Hughes says. "I have no idea. I don't know if he internalizes those meetings or remembers them. All I know is that, afterwards, he at least knew my name."

Was he distracted at the first meeting, I asked, because of the death of his infant daughter? He paused for a while, perhaps surprised that I knew about this, then asked me not to mention it in the book. But a week later he emailed, "After talking with my wife, we are comfortable with you sharing the story." Despite Musk's belief that all feedback should be impersonal, sometimes things are, in fact, personal. Shotwell understands that. "Gwynne definitely cares a lot about people, which I think at the company is an important role for her to fill," Hughes says. "Elon cares a lot about humanity, but humanity in more of a very macro sense."

As someone who spent a dozen years focused on gymnastic training, Hughes appreciated Musk's all-in mindset. "He's willing to just throw his entire being at his mission, and that's what he expects in return," he says. "That has a good and bad side. You definitely realize that you're a tool being used to achieve this larger objective, and that's great. But sometimes, tools get worn down and he feels he can just replace that tool." Indeed, as he showed when he bought Twitter, Musk does feel that way. He thinks that when people want to prioritize their comfort and leisure they should leave.

That's what Hughes did in May 2022. "Working for Elon is one of the most exciting things you can do, but it doesn't allow time for a lot else in your life," he says. "Sometimes that's a great trade. If Raptor becomes the most affordable engine ever created and gets us to Mars, then it may be worth the collateral damage. That's what I believed for more than eight years. But now, especially after the death of our baby, it's time for me to focus on other things in life."

The lesson of Andy

Andy Krebs took the other pill, at least initially. Like Hughes, he is soft-spoken and gentle-natured, with a dimpled chin and big smile, and he's not as comfortable as Mark Juncosa and Kiko Dontchev at being in the target zone of one of Musk's exchanges. At one premeeting when the team was discussing who would present some unpleasant data about methane leaks, Krebs said that he would be away, at which point Juncosa started flapping his elbows and making chicken sounds. But he is popular with Juncosa and others at Starbase, who thought he handled himself well when Musk trained his fire on him at the launchpad incident that precipitated the surge.

Musk often repeats himself in meetings. Partly it's for emphasis, partly it's just a trancelike invocation of a mantra. Krebs learned that one way to reassure him was to parrot back what he said. "He wants to know you've listened," he says. "So I learned to repeat his feedback. If he says the walls should be yellow, I will say, 'I hear you, this is not successful, we're going to paint the walls yellow.'"

The method worked that night on the launchpad. Even though Musk sometimes seems not to notice how people are reacting, he can be good at determining who can handle tough situations. "I actually thought Krebs was quite self-aware when he messed up," Musk says. "His feedback loop was good. I can work with people if they have a good critical feedback loop."

As a result, around midnight on a Friday a few weeks after the surge, Musk called Krebs and gave him additional duties in Boca Chica, including the critical task of getting the propellants into the engines. "He will report to me," Musk emailed the team. "Please give him your full support."

One Sunday a few months later, when Starship was again being stacked on the pad, the winds picked up and some of the workers resisted climbing to the top of the tower, where there was still work to be done scraping off coating and securing the proper connections. So Krebs himself climbed up and began doing the work. "I had to make sure all the workers stayed motivated," he says. Had he done so, I asked, because he was inspired by Musk, who liked being a battlefield general on the front lines, or was it out of fear? "It's like Machiavelli taught," Krebs replied. "You have to have fear and love for the leader. Both."

That attitude would sustain Krebs for another two years. But by Spring 2023, he would become another refugee from Musk's hardcore all-in approach. After getting married and having a child, he decided it was time to move on and find a better work-life balance.

60

Solar Surge

Summer 2021

Inspecting a solar roof installation with Brian Dow on the far right

Musk's surges are sequential. After the Starship stacking surge of the summer of 2021, the next group in his line of fire was the solar roof team.

Musk had helped his cousins, Peter and Lyndon Rive, launch SolarCity in 2006, and he bailed it out ten years later by having Tesla purchase it for $2.6 billion. That provoked a class-action lawsuit from some Tesla shareholders, causing Musk to become obsessed with juicing up the business in order to justify the acquisition in court. He fired his cousins, who had focused on door-to-door sales schemes rather than making a good product. "I fucking hate my cousins," he told Kunal Girotra, one of the four chiefs of Tesla Energy he hired and fired over the subsequent five years. "I don't think I ever will ever speak to them again."

He cycled through leaders by demanding miraculous growth in roof installations, giving them insane deadlines for delivering, and firing them when they didn't. "Everybody was super scared of him," says Girotra, who describes one meeting where Musk got so mad that he started banging on the table while calling him a "fucking failure."

Girotra was replaced by a square-jawed former U.S. Army captain named RJ Johnson, who brought in no-nonsense supervisors to manage the installation crews. At the beginning of 2021, when the number of installations was not rising fast enough, Musk called Johnson in and gave him the usual ultimatum. "You have two weeks to fix this. I fired my cousins and I'll fire you if you don't get installations going ten times faster." Johnson didn't.

Next came Brian Dow, a happy warrior with a can-do enthusiasm who had served at Musk's side during the 2017 Nevada battery factory surge. It started well. Musk, sitting at the little table in his Boca Chica living room, telephoned Dow in California to go over what he wanted. "Don't worry about sales tactics, which is a mistake my cousins made," he said. "Awesome products grow with word of mouth." The main goal was to make a great solar roof that was easy to install.

As always, he invoked to Dow the steps of the algorithm and proceeded to show how they should be applied to the solar roofs. "Question every requirement." Specifically, they should question the requirement that the installers must work around every vent and chimney pipe sticking up from a house. The pipes for dryers and ventilator fans should simply be sheared off and the solar roof tiles placed on top of them, he suggested. The air would still be able to vent under the tiles. "Delete." The roof system had 240 different parts, from screws to clamps to rails. More than half should be deleted. "Simplify." The website should offer just three types of roofs: small, medium, and large. After that, the goal was to "accelerate." Install as many roofs as possible each week.

Musk decided that he needed to find out from the actual installers what could be done to speed things up. So one day in August 2021, he told Dow to come to Boca Chica with a team who could put a roof on one of the thirty-one tract homes in the subdivision next to Starbase, where he lived.

While Dow's workers rushed to see if they could install a roof in one day, Musk spent the afternoon in the Starbase conference room going over the designs for future rockets and engines. As usual, the meetings lasted longer than planned, with Musk raising new ideas and allowing the conversation to wander off on tangents. Dow was hoping that Musk would get to the site before sundown, but it was close to 9 p.m. when he finally got into his Tesla, drove to his house to grab X, then carried him on his shoulders down the block to where the installers were working.

Even at that hour, it was a muggy 94 degrees. Eight sweat-drenched workers were swatting mosquitoes as they tried to keep their balance atop the tract house roof, which was lit by spotlights. As X meandered among the cables and equipment below, Musk clambered up a ladder to the peak of the roof, where he stood precariously. He was not happy. There were too many fasteners, he said. Each had to be nailed down, adding time to the installation process. Half should be deleted, he insisted. "Instead of two nails for each foot, try it with only one," he ordered. "If the house has a hurricane, the whole neighborhood is fucked up, so who cares? One nail is going to be fine." Someone protested that could lead to leaks. "Don't worry about making it as waterproof as a submarine," he said. "My house in California used to leak. Somewhere between sieve and submarine should be okay." For a moment he laughed before returning to his dark intensity.

No detail was too small. The tiles and railings were shipped to the sites packed in cardboard. That was wasteful. It took time to pack things and then unpack them. Get rid of the cardboard, he said, even at the warehouses. They should send him pictures from the factories, warehouses, and sites each week showing that they were no longer using cardboard.

His face got gradually more charged and dark, like the skies heralding a storm moving in from the gulf. "We need to get the engineers who designed this system to come out here and see how hard it is to install," he said angrily. Then he erupted. "I want to see the engineers out here installing it themselves. Not just doing it for five minutes. Up on roofs for days, for fucking days!" He ordered that, in the future, everyone on an installation team, even the engineers and managers, had to spend time drilling and hammering and sweating with the other workers.

When we finally climbed back down to the ground, Brian Dow and his deputy Marcus Mueller gathered the dozen engineers and installers in the side yard to hear Musk's thoughts. They weren't pleasant. Why, he asked, did it take eight times longer to install a roof of solar tiles than one with regular tiles? One of the engineers, named Tony, began showing him all the wires and electronic parts. Musk already knew the workings of each component, and Tony made the mistake of sounding both assured and condescending. "How many roofs have you done?" Musk asked him.

"I've got twenty years of experience in the roof business," Tony answered.

"But how many solar roofs have you installed?"

Tony explained he was an engineer and had not actually been on a roof doing the installation. "Then you don't fucking know what you're fucking talking about," Musk responded. "This is why your roofs are shit and take so long to install."

For more than an hour, Musk's anger ebbed and flowed, but mostly flowed. If they did not figure out ways to install roofs faster, the Tesla Energy division would keep losing money and he would shut it down. That would be a setback not just for Tesla, he said, but for the planet. "If we fail," he said, "we will not get to a sustainable energy future."

Dow, eager to please, agreed heartily with every pronouncement. They had set a record the previous week by installing seventy-four roofs nationwide. "Not enough," Musk replied. "We need to increase that tenfold." Then he strode down the block back to his little house, looking angry. When he reached his front door, he turned and said, "Solar roof meetings are like daggers in my eye."

At high noon the next day, it reached 97 degrees in the shade, of which there was none. Dow and his installers were on top of the house next door to the one they had done the previous day. Two of the installers succumbed to the heat and started vomiting, so Dow sent them home. Some of the rest attached battery fans to their safety vests. Per Musk's instructions, they were using only one nail to hold down each foot of the tiles, but it wasn't working well. The tiles were popping up and rotating. So the team began using two nails again. I asked if Musk would be angry, and I was assured that if they showed him the physical evidence he would change his mind.

They turned out to be right. When Musk arrived at 9 p.m., they showed him why they needed a second nail, and he nodded. It was part of the algorithm: if you don't end up having to restore 10 percent of the parts you deleted, then you didn't delete enough. He was in a better mood this second night, partly because the installation process had been improved and partly just because his moods fluctuate. After a storm there is calm. "Nice work, guys," he said. "You should stopwatch each step. That will make it more fun, like a game."

I asked him about his anger the previous evening. "It's not my favorite way to fix things, but it worked," he says. "The improvement from yesterday to today was gigantic. The big difference is that today the engineers were actually on the roof installing instead of at a keyboard."

Brian Dow's eagerness never waned. "I'm a person who will literally sweep the floors if that's going to help this company," he told Musk. But he had an impossible task. The business of installing solar roofs is labor-intensive and doesn't scale. Musk was a master at designing factories that could bring down the cost of physical products by churning them out in ever-increasing volumes, but the cost of each roof installation is pretty much the same whether you do ten a month or a hundred. Musk did not have the patience for such businesses.

Just three months after tapping him to run Tesla's solar roof business, Musk summoned Dow back down to Boca Chica. It was Dow's birthday, and he had planned to be with his family, but he scrambled to get there. When he missed his connection in Houston, he rented a car and drove the six hours down the Texas coast, arriving at 11 p.m. A crew was redoing the roof at the same house we were on in August, this time with the streamlined new methods and components. When Dow drove up, Musk was standing on top of the roof and things seemed to be going well enough. "The crew was crushing it using our new methods," Dow says. "They were finishing up the install after just one day."

But when Dow climbed up and joined him at the peak, Musk began grilling him about expenses. Dow is a big man, even larger than Musk, and they had trouble keeping their footing on the roof, which was slippery from the sea mist. So they sat on the peak while Dow went over financial data on his iPhone. Musk's jaw clenched when he saw how much money they were losing on each roof they installed. "You've got to cut costs," he said. "You've got to show me a plan by next week to cut costs in half." As before, Dow showed his enthusiasm. "Okay, let's do it," he said. "We'll kick ass and cut costs."

He spent all weekend working on a cost-cutting plan to present to Musk that Monday. But as soon as the meeting began, Musk changed the subject and grilled Dow about how many installations had been completed in the past week and details about personnel redeployments. Dow did not know some of the answers, and he protested that he had been working since his birthday on cost-cutting plans and not the details Musk was now asking about. "Thank you for trying," Musk finally said. "But this isn't cutting it."

It took Dow a while to realize that Musk was firing him. "It was just the most bizarre, weird firing you could imagine," Dow later says. "I had so much history with him, and deep down Elon knows that I have something special. He knows that I can kick ass, because we'd done it together in the past, in the Nevada battery factory. But he thought I was losing my edge, even though I had missed my birthday with my family to be up on that roof with him."

After Dow left, Musk was still not able to make the numbers work. A year later, Tesla Energy was installing only about thirty roofs per week, nowhere close to the one thousand that Musk kept demanding. But his fervor to solve the problem receded in April 2022, when a Delaware court ruled in his favor in the lawsuit over Tesla's purchase of SolarCity. With that threat lifted, he no longer felt quite as desperate to show that the acquisition made financial sense.

61

Nights Out

Summer 2021

With Maye onstage at *Saturday Night Live* and with
Grimes at a party

Saturday Night Live

"To anyone I've offended, I just want to say, I reinvented electric cars and I'm sending people to Mars in a rocket ship. Did you think I was also going to be a chill, normal dude?" Musk grinned sheepishly as he delivered his opening monologue as the guest host of *Saturday Night Live*. Shifting his weight from one leg to the other, he was doing a passable job of making his awkwardness charming.

That was his theme: showing that he could be self-aware about his emotional shortcomings. With the help of producer Lorne Michaels's unerring sense of how to make a guest look good, he used his hosting gig in May 2021 to soften his image. "I'm actually making history tonight as the first person with Asperger's to host *SNL*—or at least the first to admit it," he said. "I won't make a lot of eye contact with the cast tonight, but don't worry, I'm pretty good at running 'human' in emulation mode."

It was Mother's Day, so Maye got a chance to come onstage. At the rehearsal on Friday, she read the cue cards and pronounced, "This isn't funny." She was given permission to improvise on some of her lines, which she did. "We made it more real and funnier," she says. Grimes also appeared, in a sketch based on Super Mario Bros. One idea that they rehearsed, which played off of some of Musk's antiwoke tweets, involved him playing a totally woke James Bond, but it didn't gel and was cut from the show.

The afterparty was held at Ian Schrager's downtown hot spot, the Public Hotel, which had been closed for COVID but reopened just for the event. Chris Rock, Alexander Skarsgård, and Colin Jost were there along with Grimes, Kimbal, Tosca, and Maye. Elon left around 6 a.m. and went with Kimbal and a few others to the house of Tim Urban, the internet writer, where he stayed up a few more hours talking. "He is such a nerdy guy that he didn't really know how to party as a kid," says Maye, "but now he's really made up for it."

Fiftieth birthday

For his birthdays, Musk had often celebrated with well-crafted fantasy parties, most notably the ones that Talulah Riley choreographed. But when he reached the milestone of turning fifty on June 28, 2021, he had just undergone a third neck surgery to ease the pain from the injury that happened when he tried to take down a sumo wrestler at his forty-second birthday party. So he decided to have just a quiet gathering in Boca Chica of close friends.

On the drive down from the Brownsville airport, Kimbal bought out most of the fireworks at a roadside stand, which they shot off with Elon's older sons, Griffin, Kai, Damian, and Saxon. They were real fireworks, not wimpy little bottle rockets, because, as Kimbal explains, "in Texas you can do whatever you want."

In addition to the pain from his neck, Musk was exhausted by work. He had spent the day walking the production tents in Boca Chica, where he became angry about the complexity of the section that connected the Starship booster with the second-stage spaceship. "There are so many openings in the skin that it looks like Swiss cheese!" he railed in an email to Mark Juncosa. "The hole size for antennas should be tiny—just enough to fit a wire through. All loads or other design requirements must have an individual name assigned to them. No design by committee."

For much of his birthday weekend, his friends left him alone so that he could sleep. He eventually woke up and gathered everyone for dinner at Flaps, the employee restaurant that SpaceX had built near the launchpad. Then they all went to his tiny house and gathered in the even tinier backyard studio cottage where Grimes worked. It was furnished only with big floor pillows, and they hung around—Musk lying flat on the floor with a pillow behind his neck—and talked until sunrise.

Burning Man 2021

For Elon and Kimbal, going to Burning Man—the massive late-summer festival of art and self-expression in the Nevada desert—had been, since the late 1990s, a treasured spiritual ritual and a chance to bond, dance, and party in an encampment with Antonio Gracias, Mark Juncosa, and other friends. After the event was canceled in 2020 because of COVID, Kimbal took up the cause of raising money to make sure that it would resume at the end of summer 2021. Elon agreed to chip in $5 million, with the stipulation that Kimbal join the board.

At his first meeting in April 2021, Kimbal was shocked when the rest of the board decided to cancel that summer's event as well. "Are you fucking kidding me?" he kept asking. He and some of the other Burning Man stalwarts organized an unauthorized "Renegade Burn" in the same desert locale. About twenty thousand attendees, rather than the usual eighty thousand, showed up, but that gave the event an intimate rebel magic, like the festival had in its earlier days. Because they had no permit, they could not do the ritual huge bonfire of the wooden effigy that gives the festival its name, so Kimbal worked with a friend to replicate the look of a burning man using lighted drones. "This is a religious experience for a loyal community," Kimbal said. "The Man Must Burn! And it did."

Elon came just for Saturday night and stayed in Kimbal's encampment, which was centered around a lotus-shaped tent that provided room for forty people to dance or hang out. As was often the case, there was a ginned-up crisis—in this case, meetings about supply-chain problems at Tesla—that served as an excuse for him to not take much time off.

Grimes came with Elon, but their relationship was not going well. His romances often involved an unhealthy dose of mutual meanness, and the one with Grimes was no exception. Sometimes he would seem to thrive on the tension, demanding that Grimes do such things as shame him for being fat. When they arrived at Burning Man, they went into their trailer and didn't emerge for hours. "I love you, but I don't love you," he told her. She replied that she felt the same. They were expecting another child via a surrogate at the end of the year, and they agreed that it would be easier to be co-parents if they weren't involved romantically, so they broke up.

Grimes later expressed her feelings in a song she was working on, "Player of Games," a fitting title on many levels for the ultimate strategy gamer:

If I loved him any less
I'd make him stay
But he has to be the best
Player of games. . . .
I'm in love with the greatest gamer
But he'll always love the game
More than he loves me
Sail away
To the cold expanse of space
Even love
Couldn't keep you in your place.

Met Gala, September 2021

The breakup with Grimes did not last, or at least not totally. Instead, their relationship became a roller coaster of companionship, co-parenting, loneliness avoidance, boundary setting, estrangement, blocking, ghosting, and reembracing.

A few weeks after Burning Man, they flew from south Texas to New York for the Met Gala, the costume extravaganza that Grimes relished. They stayed with Maye in her small apartment in Greenwich Village. Musk had just sent his plane to pick up a Shiba Inu dog he had just bought, named Floki, the breed that is the face of the Dogecoin cryptocurrency. He also brought his other dog, Marvin, who did not get along with Floki. Neither were housebroken. Maye's apartment became a two-bedroom circus.

The outfit Grimes assembled for the Gala was an homage to the sci-fi novel and movie *Dune*: a sheer gown, a gray-and-black cape, a silver face mask, and a sword. Musk was ambivalent about going and, not surprisingly, found a work excuse to avoid arriving at the beginning. A Falcon 9 rocket was launching that night, and a bureaucratic snafu caused a delay in getting permission to reenter the spacecraft over Indian air space. It was readily resolved and probably did not require his attention, but he loved throwing himself into work dramas large and small.

After the Gala, he and Grimes hosted a party at the hot club Zero Bond in Manhattan's NoHo neighborhood. Leonardo DiCaprio and Chris Rock were among the celebrities who came. But for much of the party, Musk stayed in a back room, mesmerized by a magician performing tricks. "I went to get him so he would come up front to greet people, but he wanted to stay longer watching the magician," Maye says.

Having reached the pinnacle of celebrity in the summer of 2021, Musk found it exciting but awkward. The next day they went to an art installation Grimes had done as part of a trendy audiovisual exhibition in Brooklyn, featuring an animated video in which she played a war nymph navigating a dystopian future. From there they went directly to Musk's jet and flew to Cape Canaveral for SpaceX's attempt to be the first private company to launch civilians into space. Reality could trump fantasy.

62

Inspiration4

SpaceX, September 2021

Jared Isaacman and Musk with Hans Koenigsmann

The July 2021 flights of Branson and Bezos raised a question: Would Musk follow suit and become the third billionaire to launch himself into space? Although he had a strong appetite for the limelight and for risky adventures, he never considered it. He insisted that his mission was about humanity, not himself, which sounded grandiose but contained a kernel of truth. The idea that rockets were billionaire-boys' toys threatened to give citizen space travel a bad odor.

Instead, for SpaceX's first civilian flight, he chose a low-key tech entrepreneur and jet pilot named Jared Isaacman, who displayed the quiet humility of a square-jawed adventurer who had proven himself in so many fields that he didn't need to be brash. Isaacman dropped out of high school at sixteen to work for a payment-processing company, then started his own company, Shift4 Payments, that handled more than $200 billion in payments each year for restaurants and hotel chains. He became an accomplished pilot, performing in air shows and setting a world record by flying around the world in a light jet in sixty-two hours. He then cofounded a company that owned 150 jets and provided training for the military and defense contractors.

Isaacman bought from SpaceX the right to command a three-day flight—named Inspiration4—that would become history's first private orbital mission. His purpose was to raise money for St. Jude Children's Research Hospital in Memphis, and he invited a twenty-nine-year-old bone-cancer survivor, Hayley Arceneaux, to join the crew, along with two other civilians.

A week before the scheduled launch, Musk held a two-hour prep call with the SpaceX team. As was customary for manned missions, he gave his standard speech about safety. "I want anyone with any worries or any suggestions to send a note to me directly," he said.

But he knew that great ventures involve risks, and he also knew—as did Isaacman—that it was important for adventurers to take them. Early in the call they addressed one that had not been made public. "There is a risk that we wanted to brief you on," one of the flight managers told Musk. "We're planning to fly higher than a typical Space Station mission and most other human space flight experiences." Indeed, the SpaceX Dragon capsule would be orbiting at an altitude of 364 miles (585 kilometers). That was the highest orbit for any human crew since a Space Shuttle mission to service the Hubble Space Telescope in 1999. "The risk is actually a big one involving orbital debris," the manager said.

Orbital debris is the junk floating in space from defunct spacecraft, satellites, and other human-made objects. By the time of the Inspiration4 launch, there were 129 million pieces in space that were too small to track. Several spacecraft had been damaged by them. The mission's super-high altitude made things worse; these flotsam and jetsam persist for longer times in higher altitudes, where there is less drag causing them to burn up or fall to Earth. "We're worried that penetration of the cabin by a piece of debris or damage to the heat shields could compromise the vehicle during reentry," the briefer said.

Hans Koenigsmann, who was being nudged by Musk into retirement, had been replaced as the vice president for flight reliability by Bill Gerstenmaier, a crusty former NASA official known as Gerst. He described to Musk the reliability team's recommendation for reducing the risk: change the way the Dragon capsule was pointed as it orbited the Earth, which would decrease its exposure to debris. Too much of a change would cause the radiators to get too cold, but they had come to a consensus on how to balance these two risks. With the original pointing, the risk of a debris strike would be about 1 in 700. The new pointing would decrease the risk to about 1 in 2,000. But he then showed a slide with a stark warning: "There is *significant* uncertainty in the predicted risk." Musk approved the plan.

Gerstenmaier went on to note that there might be an even safer approach: flying lower. "There are potential orbits in lower altitudes," he said, "including going down to one hundred ninety kilometers." They had already figured out how to do this reduced height and make it to the landing site as planned.

"Why aren't we doing that?" Musk asked.

"The customer wanted to go higher than the International Space Station," Gerstenmaier explained, referring to Isaacman. "He really wanted to go for the highest he could. We briefed him on all this orbital debris stuff. He and his crew understand the risk and accept it."

"Okay, great," replied Musk, who respected people willing to take risks. "I think that's fair, as long he's fully informed."

Later, when I asked why he had not opted for the lower altitude, Isaacman said, "If we're going to go to the moon again, and we're going to go to Mars, we've got to get a little outside our comfort zone."

The last time civilians were launched toward orbit was the 1986 Space Shuttle *Challenger* mission carrying teacher Christa McAuliffe, which exploded a minute after takeoff. Grimes felt that was a psychic wound for America that needed to be healed, and Inspiration4 would do that. So she took on the role of "chief spell master," casting good-luck charms on the rocket before it launched.

As usual during tense moments, Musk diverted his mind by thinking about the future. Sitting in the control room next to Kiko Dontchev, who was trying to focus on the countdown, he asked questions about the Starship system being built in Boca Chica and how to convince engineers to move there from Florida.

Hans Koenigsmann was attending his last launch. After working for twenty years at SpaceX, beginning with the hardy cadre that launched the original Falcon 1 flights on Kwaj, Musk had eased him out after the report he wrote about disobeying FAA weather orders. After the Inspiration4 rocket ascended, he went over and awkwardly hugged Musk to say goodbye. "I worried that I would get a little upset or emotional," Koenigsmann says. "I had been there longer than anyone else." They talked for a few minutes about how important this civilian mission would be to the history of space exploration. As Koenigsmann started to leave, Musk turned to his phone to check his Twitter feed. Grimes nudged him. "It's his last mission," she said.

"I know," Musk replied, then looked up at Koenigsmann and nodded.

"I was not offended by it," Koenigsmann says. "Musk cares a lot, but he's not emotionally nurturing."

"Congratulations to @elonmusk and the @SpaceX team on their successful Inspiration4 launch last night," Bezos tweeted. "Another step towards a future where space is accessible to all of us." Musk replied politely but succinctly, "Thank you."

Isaacman was so thrilled that he offered $500 million for three future flights, which would aim at going to an even higher orbit and doing a spacewalk in a new suit designed by SpaceX. He also asked for the right to be the first private customer on Starship when it was ready.

Other potential customers also tried to reserve flights. One of them, a promoter of mixed martial arts fights, wanted to do a zero-gravity match in space. Musk laughingly considered that possibility one evening over drinks in Boca Chica. "We don't want to do that," Bill Riley said.

"Why not?" asked Musk. "Gwynne said they'd pay a half-billion dollars."

"We will lose that in reputation," replied Sam Patel, the engineer in charge of building Starbase.

"Yeah, it should not be something we do anytime soon." Musk agreed. "Maybe only after it becomes mundane to go into orbit."

The Inspiration4 mission, launched by a private company for private citizens, heralded a new orbital economy, one that would be filled with entrepreneurial endeavors, commercial satellites, and great adventures. "SpaceX and Elon are an amazing success story," NASA Administrator Bill Nelson told me the next morning. "There's synergy between the public sector and the private sector, and it's all to the good of mankind."

As Musk processed the significance of the launch, he became philosophical in his *Hitchhiker's Guide* fashion, ruminating on human endeavor. "Building mass-market electric cars was inevitable," he said. "It would have happened without me. But becoming a space-faring civilization is not inevitable." Fifty years earlier, America had sent men to the moon. But since then, there had been no progress. Just the reverse. The Space Shuttle could only do low-Earth orbit, and after it was retired, America couldn't even do that anymore. "Technology does not automatically progress," Musk said. "This flight was a great example of how progress requires human agency."

63

Raptor Shake-up

SpaceX, 2021

Jake McKenzie atop a high bay; the construction tents and
high bays in Boca Chica

Engineering mode

"My neural net is getting fired up like it's the Fourth of July," Musk exulted. "This is what I like doing most, iterating with kickass engineers!" He was sitting in the Starbase conference room in Boca Chica in early September 2021, sporting a stark fade haircut that looked like it was done by a soon-to-be-executed barber of a North Korean leader. "I cut it myself," he told the engineers. "I had someone else cut the back."

Over the previous weeks, Musk had been cycling through periods of despair and fury about the Starship's Raptor engine. It had become complex, expensive, and difficult to manufacture. "When I see a tube that cost twenty thousand dollars, I want to stab my eye with a fork," he said. Going forward, he announced, he would hold meetings in his SpaceX conference room with the Raptor team at 8 p.m. every evening, including weekends.

Musk took a special interest in the mass of materials being used. The thickness of the engine cylinder was the same as that of its dome, he pointed out, even though they would be exposed to different pressure. "What the fuck is going on?" he asked. "There is a shit ton of metal there that doesn't make any damn sense." Each extra ounce of mass would reduce the amount of payload the rocket could launch.

One major decision—made at a meeting that had been pushed back to midnight because the Inspiration4 astronauts were landing—was to have as much of the engine as possible made out of his favorite material, stainless steel. After being shown a series of slides about ways to minimize the use of expensive alloys, Musk broke in. "Enough said," he declared. "You're getting analysis paralysis. We are moving every part possible to low-cost steel."

At first, the only exceptions he allowed were for parts exposed to hot oxygen-rich gas combustion. Some of the engineers pushed back and suggested that copper, with its better ability to conduct heat, was needed for a face plate. But Musk argued that copper had a worse melt temperature. "I'm convinced you could make a steel faceplate," he said. "Please do it. I think I've been pretty clear: make it out of steel." He admitted there was a reasonable chance that it would not work, but it was better to try and fail rather than analyze the issue for months. "If you make this thing fast, you can find out fast. And then you can fix it fast." He eventually succeeded in converting most of the parts into stainless steel.

Jake McKenzie

As Musk ran the meetings in his conference room each night, he was looking for someone who might be able to oversee Raptor design. "Any leaders emerging?" Shotwell asked him after one of the skip-level sessions.

"My neural net for assessing engineering skill is good, but it's hard to do when they're wearing masks," Musk complained. So he started also having one-on-one sessions, peppering the midlevel engineers with questions.

After a few weeks, a young engineer named Jacob McKenzie began to stand out. The juxtaposition of his cherubic smile with his shoulder-length dreadlocks made him cool in an understated way. There are two types of lieutenants Musk favors: the Red Bulls, such as Mark Juncosa, who are highly caffeinated and voluble as they purge-pulse ideas, and the Spocks, whose measured monotones give them an aura of Vulcan competence. McKenzie was in the latter category.

He had grown up in Jamaica and later moved to Northern California, where he became interested in cars, rockets, and "anything with a lot of heavy engineering." His family was poor, so he worked in a warehouse to make money while in high school. He saved up to go to Santa Rosa Junior College, where he studied engineering, and did well enough that he was able to transfer to Berkeley and then to graduate school at MIT, where he got a PhD in mechanical engineering.

At SpaceX, which he joined in 2015, he managed the team that delivered the valves to the Raptor engine. It's a critical role. When a countdown is stopped, it's often because of a leaky valve. McKenzie had interacted with Musk just a few times, so he was surprised when Musk started talking to him about running the Raptor program. "I didn't think he knew my name," McKenzie says. That indeed may have been the case, but Musk knew his work was succeeding. McKenzie's team had successfully improved Starship's flap actuators, one of the many projects that Musk dove into personally.

Just after midnight one night in September 2021, Musk texted McKenzie, "Are you still up?" Not surprisingly, McKenzie responded, "Yeah, I'm still up, I'll be in the office for at least a few more hours." Musk called and said he was going to promote him. At 4:30 a.m., he sent out the email. "Jake McKenzie is reporting to me directly going forward," he wrote. Among his goals, Musk said, would be to "remove most of the flanges and Inconel parts in favor of weldable steel alloys, as well as delete any part that is even *potentially* unnecessary. If we don't end up adding back some parts later, we haven't deleted enough."

McKenzie set about applying automotive-style solutions, which in some cases resulted in parts that were 90 percent cheaper. He asked Lars Moravy, one of Musk's top Tesla executives, to walk with him through the SpaceX manufacturing line and suggest automotive techniques that would simplify things. At times Moravy was so appalled by the unnecessary complexities on the rocket-engine line that he covered his eyes. "Okay, can you stop putting your face in your palm?" McKenzie asked. "Because it's really, really like hurting my feelings."

The biggest change Musk wrought was to put the design engineers in charge of production, like he had done for a while at Tesla. "I created separate design and production groups a long time ago, and that was a bullshit mistake," he said at one of the first meetings that McKenzie led. "You are responsible for the production process. You can't hand it off to someone else. If the design is expensive to produce, you change the design." McKenzie and his engineering team moved their seventy-five desks to be next to the assembly lines.

The 1337 engine

One method Musk used when a problem got hairy was to turn his attention to designing a future version of the product. That's what he did with Raptor a few weeks after McKenzie took over. He declared that they were going to shift their attention to making a whole new engine. It was going to be different enough that he didn't even want to name it after a breed of falcon, like Merlin or Kestrel. Instead he decided to use a meme from the world of coding and call it 1337, pronounced "LEET." (The numerals kind of look like those letters.) The goal was to get an engine that would cost less than $1,000 per ton of thrust and thus be, he said, "the fundamental breakthrough needed to make life multiplanetary."

The point of leapfrogging to a new engine was to get everyone thinking boldly. "Our goal is the great adventure engine," he said in a pep talk to the team. "Does it have a chance of success above zero? If so, put it in! If we find that there are changes we made that are too adventurous, then we will back up." The guiding principle should be to make an engine that was lean. "There are a lot of ways to skin a cat," he said. "But it's important to know what the post-skinned cat looks like. The answer is muscly and gnarly."

Late that night, he sent out a flurry of texts to emphasize how serious he was about this new push. "We are not shooting for the moon," he wrote. "We are shooting for Mars. A maniacal sense of urgency is our operating principle." In a text sent directly to McKenzie, he added, "The SpaceX 1337 engine is the last major critical breakthrough needed to get humanity to Mars!!! No words are enough to capture how important this is for the future of civilization."

He personally suggested some extreme ideas, such as deleting the whole hot fuel gas manifold and merging the fuel turbo pump with the main chamber injector. "It might result in poor fuel gas distribution, might not. Let's find out." He reinforced his crusade with emails almost every night. "We are on a deletion *rampage*!!" he wrote in one. "Nothing is sacred. Any remotely questionable tubes, sensors, manifolds, etc. will be deleted tonight. Please go ultra-hardcore on deletion and simplification."

Over the course of October 2021, the meetings got pushed back later each night, most of them starting around 11 p.m. Nevertheless, there were usually a dozen people in the conference room and more than fifty joining virtually. Each session usually had a new idea for simplification or deletion. One night, for example, he focused on getting rid of the entire skirt of the booster, which is the unpressurized open part at the very bottom. "It doesn't help contain much of the propellant," he said. "It's like peeing in a swimming pool. Doesn't affect the swimming pool much."

After a month, just as suddenly as he had forced his team to focus on a futurist 1337 engine, Musk turned their attention back to revising the current Raptor engine into a leaner and meaner Raptor 2. "I'm moving the SpaceX propulsion focus back to Raptor," he announced in a 2 a.m. text message. "We need engine production rate to be one per day to keep up a decent launch cadence. It is currently at one every three days." I asked whether that would slow the development of the 1337. "Yes," he replied. "We can't make life multiplanetary with Raptor, as it is way too expensive, but Raptor is needed to tide us over until 1337 is ready."

Was the 1337 surge and retreat a carefully considered strategy by Musk to get his team thinking more boldly, or was it an impulsive act that he later walked back? As usual with him, it was a mix of both. It served a purpose of forcing new ideas, including getting rid of various shrouds and skirts, that would be incorporated into his goals for an improved Raptor. "The exercise helped define what an ideal engine looks like," McKenzie says. "But it was not moving the needle on stuff that was immediately needed to advance the Starship program." Over the next year, McKenzie and his team were able to churn out Raptors almost like they were cars on an assembly line. By Thanksgiving 2022, they were making more than one a day, creating a stockpile for future Starship launches.

64

Optimus Is Born

Tesla, August 2021

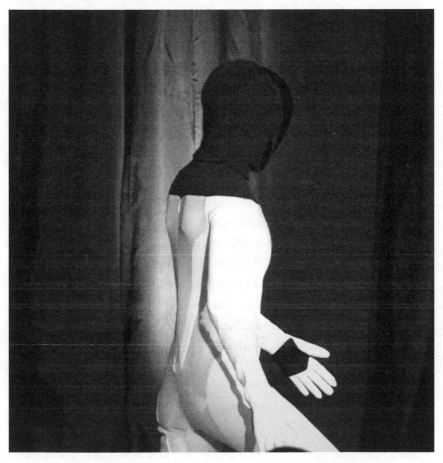

An actress dressed as the proposed Optimus robot

The friendly robot

Musk's interest in creating a humanoid robot stretched back to the fascination and fear he felt about artificial intelligence. The possibility that someone might create, intentionally or inadvertently, AI that could be harmful to humans led him to start OpenAI in 2014. It also led him to push related endeavors, including self-driving cars, a neural network training supercomputer known as Dojo, and Neuralink chips that could be implanted in brains to create a very intimate symbiotic relationship between humans and machines.

An ultimate expression of safe AI, especially for someone who imbibed sci-fi as a kid, would be creating a humanoid robot, one that could process visual inputs and learn to perform tasks without violating Asimov's law that a robot shall not harm humanity or any human. While OpenAI and Google were focusing on creating text-based chatbots, Musk decided to focus on artificial intelligence systems that operated in the physical world, such as robots and cars. "If you can create a self-driving car, which is a robot on wheels, then you can make a robot on legs as well," Musk said.

In early 2021, Musk began mentioning at his executive meetings that Tesla should get serious about building a robot, and at one point he played for them a video of the impressive ones that Boston Dynamics were designing. "Humanoid robots are going to happen, like it or not," he said, "and we should do it so we can guide it in a good direction." The more he talked about it, the more excited he got. "This has the potential to be the far biggest thing we ever do, even bigger than a self-driving car," he told his chief designer, Franz von Holzhausen.

"Once we hear a recurring theme from Elon, we start working on it," von Holzhausen says. They began meeting in the Tesla design studio in Los Angeles, where the Cybertruck and Robotaxi models were on display. Musk gave the specs: the robot should be about five-foot-eight, with an elfish and androgenous look so it "doesn't feel like it could or would want to hurt you." Thus was born Optimus, a humanoid robot to be made by the Tesla teams working on self-driving cars. Musk decided that it should be announced at an event called

"AI Day," which he scheduled for Tesla's Palo Alto headquarters on August 19, 2021.

AI Day

Two days before AI Day, Musk held a prep meeting with the Tesla team virtually from Boca Chica. That day also included a meeting with the Texas Fish and Wildlife Conservation Office to get support for Starship launches, a Tesla finance meeting, a discussion of solar roof finances, a meeting about future launches of civilians, a contentious walk through the tents where Starship was being assembled, an interview for a Netflix documentary, and his second late-night visit to the tract houses where Brian Dow's team was installing solar roofs. After midnight, he got on his plane and headed for Palo Alto.

"It's draining to have to switch between so many issues," he said when he finally relaxed on the plane. "But there are a lot of problems, and I have to solve them." So, why was he now leaping into the world of AI and robots? "Because I'm worried about Larry Page," he said. "I had long conversations with him about AI dangers, but he didn't get it. Now we barely speak."

When we landed at 4 a.m., he went to a friend's house for a few hours of sleep, then to Tesla's Palo Alto headquarters to meet with the team preparing for the robot announcement. The plan was for an actress to dress up as the robot and come onstage. Musk got excited. "She will do acrobatics!" he declared, as if in a Monty Python sketch. "Can we make her do cool stuff that looks impossible? Like tap dancing with a hat and cane?"

He had a serious point: the robot should seem fun rather than frightening. As if on cue, X started dancing on the conference room table. "The kid has a real good power pack," his father said. "He gets his software updates by walking around and looking and listening." That was the goal: a robot that could learn to do tasks by seeing and mimicking humans.

After a few more jokes about hat-and-cane dancing, Musk began drilling down on the final specifications. "Let's make it go five miles per hour, not four, and give it power to lift a bit more weight," he said.

"We overdid making it look gentle." When the engineers said that they were planning to have the batteries swapped out when they ran down, Musk vetoed that idea. "Many a fool has gone down the swappable battery path, and it's usually because they have a lousy battery," he said. "We went down that path with Tesla originally. No swappable pack. Just make the pack bigger so it can operate sixteen hours."

After the meeting, he stayed behind in the conference room. His neck was hurting from his old Sumo wrestling accident, and he lay on the floor with an ice pack behind his head. "If we're able to produce a general-purpose robot that could observe you and learn how to do a task, that would supercharge the economy to a degree that's insane," he said. "Then we may want to institute universal basic income. Working could become a choice." Yes, and some would still be maniacally driven to do it.

Musk was in a foul mood at the next day's practice session for AI Day presentations, which would feature not only the unveiling of Optimus but also the advances Tesla was making in self-driving cars. "This is boring," he kept saying as Milan Kovac, a sensitive Belgian engineer who ran the Autopilot and Optimus software teams, presented very technical slides. "There is too much here that is not cool. This is a recruiting event, and no one will want to join after seeing these fucking slides."

Kovac, who had not yet mastered the art of deflecting Musk's blasts, walked back to his office and quit, throwing plans for that evening's presentation into disarray. Lars Moravy and Pete Bannon, his more seasoned and battle-hardened supervisors, stopped him as he was about to leave the building. "Let's look at your slides and see how we can fix this," Moravy said. Kovac mentioned he could use a whiskey, and Bannon found someone in the Autopilot workshop who had some. They drank two shots, and Kovac calmed down. "I'm going to get through the event," he promised them. "I'm not going to let my team down."

With the help of Moravy and Bannon, Kovac cut in half the number of his slides and rehearsed a new speech. "I sucked up my anger and brought the new slides to Elon," he says. Musk glanced through them and said, "Yep, sure. Okay." Kovac got the impression that Musk did not even remember chewing him out.

The disruption caused the presentation that evening to be delayed by an hour. It was not a very polished event. The sixteen presenters were all male. The only woman was the actress who dressed up as the robot, and she didn't do any fun hat-and-cane dance routines. There were no acrobatics. But in his slightly stuttering monotone, Musk was able to connect Optimus to Tesla's plans for self-driving cars and the Dojo supercomputer. Optimus, he said, would learn to perform tasks without needing line-by-line instructions. Like a human, it would teach itself by observing. That would transform not only our economy, he said, but the way we live.

65

Neuralink

2017–2020

A monkey playing *Pong* using only his brainwaves

Human-computer interfaces

Some of the most important technology leaps in the digital age involved advances in the way that humans and machines communicate with each other, known as "human-computer interfaces." The psychologist and engineer J. C. R. Licklider, who worked on air-defense systems that tracked planes on a monitor, wrote a seminal paper in 1960 titled "Man-Computer Symbiosis," showing how video displays could "get a computer and a person thinking together." He added, "The hope is that, in not too many years, human brains and computing machines will be coupled together very tightly."

MIT hackers used these video displays to create a game called *Spacewar*, which helped spawn commercial games that, in order to be easy enough for a stoned college student to play, had interfaces that were so intuitive they required almost no instructions. ("1. Insert quarter 2. Avoid Klingons" were the only ones on Atari's first *Star Trek* game.) Doug Engelbart combined such displays with a mouse that allowed users to interface with a computer by pointing and clicking, and Alan Kay at Xerox PARC helped develop that into an easy-to-use graphical interface that mimicked a desktop. Steve Jobs adopted that for Apple's Macintosh computer, and at his very last board meeting, as he was dying in 2011, he tested another great leap in human-computer interfaces: an application called Siri that allowed people and computers to interact by voice.

Despite all these advances, the input-output between humans and machines remained crushingly slow. On a trip in 2016, Musk was typing on his iPhone with his thumbs and began complaining about how long it took. Typing allowed information to flow from our brains into our devices at only about a hundred bits per second. "Imagine if you could *think* into the machine," he said, "like a high-speed connection directly between your mind and your machine." He leaned over to Sam Teller, who was riding in the car with him. "Can you get a neuroscientist who can help me understand computer-brain interface?" he asked.

The ultimate human-machine interface, Musk realized, would be a device that connected our computers directly to our brains, such as a chip inside our skull that could send our brain signals to a computer and receive signals back. That could allow information to flow back and forth up to a million times faster. "Then you could have true human-machine symbiosis," he says. In other words, it would assure that humans and machines would work together as partners. To make this happen, he founded, in late 2016, a company that he dubbed Neuralink, which would implant small chips into the brain and allow humans to mind-meld with computers.

Like Optimus, the idea for Neuralink was inspired by science fiction, most notably the *Culture* space-travel novels by Iain Banks, which feature a human-machine interface technology called "neural lace" that is implanted into people and can connect all of their thoughts to a computer. "When I first read Banks," he says, "it struck me that this idea had a chance of protecting us on the artificial intelligence front."

Musk's lofty goals are usually accompanied by practical business models. He had developed Starlink satellites, for example, as a way to fund SpaceX's mission to Mars. Likewise, he planned for Neuralink brain chips to be used to help people with neurological problems, such as ALS, interact with computers. "If we can find good commercial uses to fund Neuralink," he says, "then in a few decades we will get to our ultimate goal of protecting us against evil AI by tightly coupling the human world to our digital machinery."

Among his cofounders were six top neuroscientists and engineers, led by the brain-machine interface researcher Max Hodak. The only member of the founding team who survived the pressure and turmoil of working with Musk was DJ Seo, who had moved from Korea to Louisiana at age four. Because he didn't speak English well as a young boy, he became very frustrated about having thoughts that he could not express. "How can I get this thing that's in my head out as efficiently as possible?" he began asking himself. "It would have to be something tiny put in my head." At Caltech, then at Berkeley, he developed what he called "neural dust," tiny implants that could be put in the brain and send out signals.

Musk also recruited a bright-eyed and sharp-minded technology investor named Shivon Zilis. As a student growing up near Toronto, she starred at hockey, but she also became a tech geek after reading Ray Kurzweil's 1999 book, *The Age of Spiritual Machines: When Computers Exceed Human Intelligence*. After studying at Yale, she worked at a few startup incubators helping new AI ventures, and she became a part-time consultant at OpenAI.

When Musk founded Neuralink, he took her out for coffee and asked her to join. "Neuralink is not just about research," he assured her. "It's about building real devices." She quickly decided that would be more fun and useful than continuing to be a venture investor. "I noticed that I learned more unique lessons from Elon per minute than any other human I've met," she says. "It would be dumb to not spend some of your life with such a person." Initially, she spent her time working on artificial intelligence projects at all three of his companies—Neuralink, Tesla, and SpaceX—but she eventually moved into the role of top manager at Neuralink in addition to being a close personal companion to Musk (about which more later).

The chip

The underlying technology for the Neuralink chip was based on the Utah Array, invented at the University of Utah in 1992, which is a microchip studded with a hundred needles that can be pushed into the brain. Each needle detects the activity of a single neuron and sends the data by wire to a box strapped to someone's skull. Because the brain has roughly 86 billion neurons, this was only a nano-step toward human-computer interfaces.

In August 2019, Musk published a scientific paper describing how Neuralink would improve on the Utah Array to create what he called "an integrated brain-machine interface platform with thousands of channels." Neuralink's chips had more than three thousand electrodes on ninety-six threads. As always, Musk focused not only on the product but also on how it would be manufactured and deployed. Robots working at high speeds would cut a small hole in a human skull, insert the chip, and push the threads into the brain.

He revealed an early version of the device at an August 2020 public presentation at Neuralink featuring a pig named Gertrude with a chip in her brain. A video of her walking on a treadmill showed how the chip could detect the signals in her brain and send it to a computer. Musk held up the chip, which was the size of a quarter. When it was nestled underneath the skull, it could transmit its data wirelessly, assuring that the user did not look like a cyborg from a horror movie. "I could have a Neuralink right now and you wouldn't know," Musk said. "Maybe I do."

A few months later, Musk came by the Neuralink lab in Fremont, near the Tesla factory, where the engineers showed him their latest version. It combined four separate chips, each with about a thousand threads. They would be implanted in different parts of the skull with wires connecting them to a router that was embedded behind the ear. Musk paused silently for almost two minutes, while Zilis and her colleagues watched. Then he delivered his verdict: he hated it. It was too complex, with too many wires and connections.

He was in the process of deleting connections from SpaceX's Raptor engines. Each was a possible failure point. "This has to be a single device," he told the deflated Neuralink engineers. "A single elegant package with no wires, no connections, no router." There was no law of physics—no basic principle—that prevented all of the functionality from being on one device. When the engineers tried to explain the need for the router, Musk's face turned stony. "Delete," he said. "Delete, delete, delete."

After they left the meeting, the engineers went through the usual stages of post-Musk distress disorder: baffled, then angry, then anxious. But within a week they got to the stage of being intrigued, because the new approach, they realized, might actually work.

When Musk returned to the lab a few weeks later, they showed him a single chip that could handle the processing of data from all the threads and transmit it by Bluetooth to a computer. No connections, no router, no wires. "We thought this was impossible," one of the engineers said, "but now we're actually pretty stoked by it."

One problem they faced was caused by the requirement that the chip be very small. That made it a challenge for it to have a long battery life and support many threads. "Why does it have to be so small?" Musk asked. Someone made the mistake of saying that it was one of the requirements they had been given. This flipped on the switch for Musk to intone his algorithm, beginning with questioning every requirement. Then he engaged them on the basic science of the chip size. Our skulls are rounded, so couldn't the chip bulge a bit? And couldn't the diameter be bigger? They came to the conclusion that a human skull could easily accommodate a larger chip.

When they had the new device ready, they implanted it in one of the macaque monkeys, named Pager, housed at the lab. He was taught to play the video game *Pong* by rewarding him with a fruit smoothie when he scored well. The Neuralink device recorded which neurons were firing each time he moved the joystick a certain way. Then the joystick was deactivated, and the signals from the monkey's brain controlled the game. It was a major step toward Musk's goal of creating a direct connection between a brain and a machine. Neuralink uploaded a video of it to YouTube, and within a year it was viewed six million times.

66

Vision Only

Tesla, January 2021

Merge near South Congress and Riverside

Problem:
- Vector Lanes NN incorrectly predicts that the captive rightmost lane can go straight, and we incorrectly lane change into it
- Bollard detection is late (<u>1.2 sec</u> before the intervention, but ego is moving fast).

Solution:
- Feed in **higher resolution map features** into the vector lanes net (in-progress)
- Train on improved **occupancy** (we're improve the panoptic network for thin / small road debris)

A slide showing the progress being made on autonomous cars

Delete radar

The question of whether to use radar in its Autopilot system for self-driving cars—rather than relying solely on visual data from cameras—remained a contentious one at Tesla. It also became a case study of Musk's style of decision-making: oscillating between bold, stubborn, reckless, visionary, guided by the first principles of physics, but at times surprisingly flexible.

He had initially been somewhat open-minded on the issue. When the Tesla Model S was upgraded in 2016, he reluctantly allowed the Autopilot team to use a forward-facing radar in addition to the car's eight cameras. And he authorized his engineers to have a program to build its own radar system, known as Phoenix.

But by the beginning of 2021, the use of radar was causing problems. The microchip shortages arising from COVID meant that Tesla's suppliers could not provide enough of them. Plus, the Phoenix system that Tesla was building in-house was not working well. "We have a choice," Musk declared in a fateful meeting early that January. "We can shut down car production. We can make Phoenix work right away. Or we can remove radar entirely."

There was no doubt which option he preferred. "We should be able to kick ass on this with a pure vision solution," he said. "Not requiring radar and vision to identify the same object is a mega game changer."

Some of his top team, especially automotive president Jerome Guillen, pushed back. Deleting radar, he argued, would be unsafe. Radar could detect objects not easily visible to a camera or the human eye. A meeting was scheduled for the entire team to debate the issue and make a decision. After all the arguments were aired, Musk paused for about forty seconds. "I'm pulling the plug," he finally said. "Delete radar." Guillen continued to push back, and Musk got coldly angry. "If you won't remove it," he said, "I will get someone else who will."

On January 22, 2021, he sent out an email. "Going forward, turn off radar," it said. "It's a terrible crutch. I'm not kidding. And it's clear that camera-only driving is working well." Guillen soon left the company.

Controversy

Musk's decision to delete radar sparked a public debate. A deeply reported *New York Times* investigation by Cade Metz and Neal Boudette revealed that many Tesla engineers had deep misgivings. "Unlike technologists at almost every other company working on self-driving vehicles, Mr. Musk insisted that autonomy could be achieved solely with cameras," they wrote. "But many Tesla engineers questioned whether it was safe enough to rely on cameras without the benefit of other sensing devices—and whether Mr. Musk was promising drivers too much about Autopilot's capabilities."

Edward Niedermeyer, who had written a critical book on Tesla titled *Ludicrous*, unleashed a thread of tweets. "Improvements to common driver assistance systems is moving the industry toward more radar, and even more novel modalities like LiDAR and thermal imaging," he wrote. "Tesla, in a marked contrast, is moving backwards." And Dan O'Dowd, a software security entrepreneur, took out a full-page ad in the *New York Times* calling Tesla's self-driving system "the worst software ever sold by a Fortune 500 company."

Tesla had long been a target of investigations by the National Highway Traffic Safety Administration, and these picked up after the 2021 removal of radar. In a study, it recorded 273 accidents by Tesla drivers using some level of driver-assist systems, five of which resulted in deaths. It also opened an investigation into eleven Tesla crashes with emergency vehicles.

Musk was convinced that bad drivers rather than bad software were the main reason for most of the accidents. At one meeting, he suggested using data collected from the car's cameras—one of which is inside the car and focused on the driver—to prove when there was driver error. One of the women at the table pushed back. "We went back and forth with the privacy team about that," she said. "We cannot associate the selfie streams to a specific vehicle, even when there's a crash, or at least that's the guidance from our lawyers."

Musk was not happy. The concept of "privacy teams" did not warm his heart. "I am the decision-maker at this company, not the privacy team," he said. "I don't even know who they are. They are so private you never know who they are." There were some nervous laughs. "Perhaps we can have a pop-up where we tell people that if they use FSD [Full Self-Driving], we will collect data in the event of a crash," he suggested. "Would that be okay?"

The woman thought about it for a moment, then nodded. "As long as we are communicating it to customers, I think we're okay with that."

Phoenix rises

Although stubborn, Musk can be brought around by evidence. He was adamant about eliminating radar in 2021 because its technical quality at the time did not provide enough resolution to add meaningful information to a vision system. However, he did agree to allow his engineers to continue their Phoenix program to see if they could develop a better radar technology.

Lars Moravy, Musk's head of vehicle engineering, put a Danish-born engineer named Pete Scheutzow in charge. "Elon's not against radar," Moravy says, "he's just against bad radar." Scheutzow's team developed a radar system that focused on cases where a human driver might not be able to see something. "You may be right," Musk said, and he secretly signed off on trying out the new system in the more expensive Model S and Model Y.

"It's a much more sophisticated radar than general automotive radar," Musk says. "It's what you would see in a weapons system. It creates a picture of what's going on rather than just getting a ping back." Did he really plan to put it in Tesla's high-end cars? "It's worth experimenting. I'm always open to evidence from physics experiments."

67

Money

2021–2022

The world's richest person

Tesla's stock price, which had been knocked down to $25 when COVID began to spread in early 2020, rebounded ten-fold by the beginning of 2021. On January 7 it hit $260. That day Musk became the richest person in the world, with $190 billion, vaulting him past Jeff Bezos.

Under the extraordinary compensation bet he had made with his Tesla board in February 2018, amid Tesla's worst production problems, he got no guaranteed salary. Instead, his compensation would depend on hitting very aggressive revenue, profit, and market value targets, which included Tesla's market valuation increasing ten-fold to $650 billion. News articles at the time predicted that most targets would be impossible to achieve. But in October 2021, Tesla became the sixth company in U.S. history to be worth more than $1 trillion. Its market value was greater than its five biggest rivals—Toyota, Volkswagen, Daimler, Ford, and GM—combined. And in April 2022, it reported a profit of $5 billion on revenue of $19 billion, an 81 percent increase from the year before. The result was that Musk's payout from the 2018 compensation deal was around $56 billion and his net worth at the start of 2022 increased to $304 billion.

Musk was angered by the public attacks on him for being a billionaire, a sensitivity exacerbated by the fact that his newly transitioned daughter Jenna, a fervent anticapitalist, would no longer speak to him. He had sold all of his houses because he believed that he should not be criticized if he kept his wealth deployed in his companies rather than spending it on his lifestyle. But he continued to be criticized because, by taking no salary and leaving his money invested in the company, he did not reap any capital gains and paid little tax. In November 2021, he conducted a Twitter poll to see if he should sell some Tesla stock in order to realize some of the capital gains and pay tax on it. There were 3.5 million votes, with 58 percent voting yes. As he already was planning to do, he exercised options that he had been granted in 2012 and were due to expire, which caused him to pay the largest single tax bill in history: $11 billion, enough to fund the entire budget of his antagonists at the Securities and Exchange Commission for five years.

"Let's change the rigged tax code so the Person of the Year will actually pay taxes and stop freeloading off everyone else," Senator Elizabeth Warren tweeted at the end of 2021. Musk shot back, "If you opened your eyes for 2 seconds, you would realize I will pay more taxes than any American in history this year. Don't spend it all at once . . . oh wait you did already."

What money can't buy

If it's true that money cannot buy happiness, one confirming data point was Musk's mood when he became the person with the most of it. He was not happy in the fall of 2021.

When he flew to Cabo San Lucas in Mexico for a birthday party Kimbal had organized for his wife Christiana in October, where Grimes performed as DJ, he shut himself in his room and played *Polytopia* much of the time. "We were underneath this art piece with interactive lights dancing to beautiful music from Claire [Grimes]," Christiana says. "I thought about how our good fortune was thanks to Elon, but he just couldn't let himself enjoy the moment."

As often happened, his mood swings and depression were manifest as stomach pains. He was throwing up and had intense heartburn. "Any great docs you'd recommend?" he texted me when he cut short his visit to Cabo. "They don't need to be famous or have fancy offices." I asked if he was all right. "I'm not super OK, tbh," he responded. "I've been burning the candle at both ends with a flame-thrower for a very long time. It has taken its toll. I was very ill this weekend." A few weeks later, he opened up more. We spoke for more than two hours, much of it about the mental and physical scars he still had in 2021:

> From 2007 onwards, until maybe last year, it's been nonstop pain. There's a gun to your head, make Tesla work, pull a rabbit out of your hat, then pull another rabbit out of the hat. A stream of rabbits flying through the air. If the next rabbit does not come out, you're dead. It takes a toll. You can't be in a constant fight for survival, always in adrenaline mode, and not have it hurt you.
>
> But there's something else I've found this year. It's that fighting to survive keeps you going for quite a while. When you are no longer in a survive-or-die mode, it's not that easy to get motivated every day.

This was an essential insight that Musk had about himself. When things were most dire, he got energized. It was the siege mentality from his South African childhood. But when he was not in survival-or-die mode, he felt unsettled. What should have been the good times were unnerving for him. It prompted him to launch surges, stir up dramas, throw himself into battles he could have bypassed, and bite off new endeavors.

That Thanksgiving, his mother and sister flew to Austin to celebrate with him, his four older sons, X, and Grimes. Two of his cousins and his two half-sisters from his father's second marriage were also there. "We needed to be with him because he gets lonely," Maye says. "He loves to have family around and we have to do that for him, you know, because he's under so much stress."

The following day, Damian cooked pasta for everyone and played classical music on the piano. But Musk decided to focus on the problems of Starship's Raptor engines. After briefly walking through the dining room looking stressed, he spent most of the day on conference calls. Then, abruptly, he announced that he had to fly back to Los

Angeles to deal with the Raptor crisis. It was a crisis that mainly existed in his mind. It was Thanksgiving weekend, and the Raptor was not even expected to be ready for at least another year.

"Last week was a good week," he texted me. "Technically, I did spend all night Friday and Saturday at the rocket factory working on Raptor issues, but still a good week. It is very painful, but we have to just muscle through building Raptor, even though it really needs a complete redesign."

68

Father of the Year

2021

With Shivon, Strider, and Azure; at Tesla with X

Shivon's twins

One thing that may have been distracting Musk on Thanksgiving 2021—or driving him to choose to be distracted by the nozzles and valves of the Raptor engine—was that, a week earlier, he had become the father of two more children, a twin boy and girl. The mother was Shivon Zilis, the bright-eyed AI investor he recruited in 2015 to work at OpenAI and who ended up as the top operations manager of Neuralink. She had become his very close friend, intellectual companion, and occasional gaming partner. "It's been one of the most meaningful friendships of my life, like, by far," she says. "Soon after I met him I said, 'I hope we're friends for life.'"

Zilis had been living in Silicon Valley and working at the Neuralink office in Fremont, but she moved to Austin shortly after Musk did, and she was part of his tight-knit social circle. Grimes considered her a friend and occasionally tried to set her up on dates. At the small 2020 party that Musk and Grimes threw for Halloween, a favorite holiday, Zilis was there along with Musk's energetic SpaceX lieutenant, Mark Juncosa.

Grimes and Zilis connected to opposite facets of Musk's personality. Grimes is feisty in a fun but also fiery way, often getting into fights with Musk and sharing his attraction to tumult. Zilis, on the contrary, says, "In six years, Elon and I have never, never gotten in a fight, never argued." That's a claim that few can make. They talk to each other in a low-key, intellectual way.

Zilis, by her own choice, decided not to get married. But she had "the motherhood bug super hard," she says. Her maternal impulses were further stoked by Musk's evangelizing about how important it was for people to have many children. He feared that declining birthrates were a threat to the long-term survival of human consciousness. "People are going to have to revive the idea of having children as a kind of social duty," he said in a 2014 interview. "Otherwise civilization will just die." His loyal sister, Tosca, who had become a successful producer of romance films and was based in Atlanta, had never married. Elon encouraged her to have children and, when she agreed, helped her find a clinic, pick out an anonymous sperm donor, and pay for the procedure.

"He really wants smart people to have kids, so he encouraged me to," Zilis says. When she decided that she was ready, he suggested that he be the sperm donor so that the kids would be genetically his. The idea appealed to her. "If the choice is between an anonymous sperm donor or doing it with the person you admire most in the world, for me that was a pretty fucking easy decision," she says. "I can't possibly think of genes I would prefer for my children." There was another upside: "It seemed like something that would make him very happy."

Their twins were conceived by in vitro fertilization. Because Neuralink is a privately owned company, it's unclear how the evolving rules surrounding workplace relationships applied. At the time, the issue didn't arise because Zilis did not tell people who the biological father was.

One day that October, she led Musk and other top Neuralink executives on a tour of a new facility the company was building in Austin. It included an office and lab in a strip mall near Tesla's Giga Texas factory and a set of barns nearby to house pigs and sheep used for the chip-implanting experiments. She was visibly pregnant with the twins, though no one there knew that they were also Musk's. Later, I asked if this made her feel awkward. "No," she replied, "I was thrilled to be becoming a mother."

Zilis had a complication at the end of her pregnancy and went into the hospital. The twins were born seven weeks prematurely, but healthy. Musk was listed as the father on the birth certificate, but the children—a boy named Strider Sekhar Sirius and a girl named Azure Astra Alice—were given Zilis's last name. She assumed that he would not be very involved in parenting them. "I thought he would play a role like a godfather," she says, "because the dude's got a lot going on."

Instead, Musk ended up spending a lot of time with the twins and bonding with them, albeit in his own emotionally distracted way. At least once a week, he would stay at Zilis's house, feed the kids, and sit on the floor with them while he did his late-evening virtual meetings on Raptor, Starship, and Tesla Autopilot. He was, given his nature, not quite as cuddly as your average dad. "There's some stuff he just can't do because he's emotionally hardwired a bit differently," Zilis says. "But when he comes in, they light up and have eyes only for him, which lights him up as well."

Baby Y

Even though they were in a rough patch in their relationship, Grimes and Musk were having such a great time being co-parents of X that they had decided to have another baby. "I really wanted him to have a daughter so bad," she says. Because she had had a rough first pregnancy and her very slender body made her prone to complications, they decided to use a surrogate.

That led to an improbably weird and potentially awkward situation worthy of a new-age French farce. When Zilis was in the Austin hospital with complications from her pregnancy, so too was the surrogate mother carrying the baby girl that Musk and Grimes had secretly conceived in vitro. Because the surrogate mother was having a troubled pregnancy, Grimes was staying with her. She was unaware that Zilis was in a nearby room, or that she was pregnant by Musk. Perhaps it is no surprise that Musk decided to fly west that Thanksgiving weekend to deal with the simpler issues of rocket engineering.

When their daughter was born in December, just a few weeks after her twin half-siblings, Musk and Grimes began their drawn-out process of settling on names. At first they called her Sailor Mars, after one of the heroines in the *Sailor Moon* manga, which features female warriors who protect the solar system from evil. It seemed a fitting though not exactly conventional name for a child who might be destined to go to Mars. By April, they decided they needed to give her a less serious name (yes), because "she's all sparkly and a lot goofier troll," Grimes said. They settled on Exa Dark Sideræl, but then in early 2023 toyed with changing her name to Andromeda Synthesis Story Musk. For simplicity's sake, they mainly just called her Y, or sometimes Why?, with a question mark as part of her name. "Elon always says we need to figure out what the question is before we can know the answers to the universe," Grimes explains, referring to what he learned from *The Hitchhiker's Guide to the Galaxy*.

When Musk and Grimes brought Y home from the hospital, they introduced her to X. Christiana Musk and other relatives were there, and everybody played on the floor as if they were a conventional family. Musk never said anything about just having twins with Shivon. After an hour of playing and a quick dinner, he scooped up X and took him on his jet to New York, where the toddler sat on his lap at the *Time* magazine ceremony anointing him Person of the Year.

The magazine's accolade marked a peak in his popularity. In 2021, he became the richest person in the world, SpaceX became the first private company to send a civilian crew into orbit, and Tesla reached a trillion-dollar market value by leading the world's auto industry in a historic shift into the era of electric vehicles. "Few individuals have had more influence than Musk on life on Earth, and potentially life off Earth too," *Time*'s editor Ed Felsenthal wrote. The *Financial Times* also named him Person of the Year, stating, "Musk is staking a claim to be the most genuinely innovative entrepreneur of his generation." In his interview with the paper, Musk stressed the missions that drove his companies. "I'm just trying to get people to Mars, and enable freedom of information with Starlink, accelerate sustainable technology with Tesla, and free people from the drudgery of driving," he said. "It's certainly possible that the road to hell to some degree is paved with good intentions—but the road to hell is mostly paved with bad intentions."

69

Politics

2020–2022

"Take the red pill"

"The coronavirus panic is dumb," Musk tweeted. It was March 6, 2020, and COVID had just shut down his new factory in Shanghai and begun to spread in the U.S. That was decimating Tesla's stock price, but it was not just the financial hit that upset Musk. The government-imposed mandates, in China and then California, inflamed his anti-authority streak.

When California issued a stay-at-home order later in March, just when the Fremont factory was starting to produce the Model Y, he became defiant. The factory would remain open. He wrote in a company-wide email, "I'd like to be super clear that if you feel the slightest bit ill or even uncomfortable, please do not feel obligated to come to work," but then he added, "I will personally be at work. My frank opinion remains that the harm from the coronavirus panic far exceeds that of the virus itself."

After county officials threatened to force the plant to shut down, Musk filed suit against the orders. "If somebody wants to stay in their house, that's great," Musk said. "But to say that they cannot leave their house, and they will be arrested if they do, this is fascist. This is not democratic. This is not freedom. Give people back their goddamn freedom." He kept the plant open and challenged the county sheriff to make arrests. "I will be on the line with everyone else," he tweeted. "If anyone is arrested, I ask that it only be me."

Musk prevailed. The local authorities reached an agreement with Tesla to let the Fremont factory stay open so long as certain mask-wearing and other safety protocols were followed. These were honored mainly in the breach, but the dispute died down, the assembly line churned out cars, and the factory experienced no serious COVID outbreak.

The controversy became a factor in his political evolution. He went from being a fanboy and fundraiser for Barack Obama to railing against progressive Democrats. One Sunday afternoon in May, in the middle of the controversy, he unleashed a cryptic four-word tweet: "Take the red pill." It was a reference to the 1999 movie *The Matrix,* in which a hacker discovers that he has been living in a computer simulation (a concept that has always intrigued Musk) and is given a choice of taking a blue pill, which will allow him to forget everything and return pleasantly to his life, or a red pill, which will expose him to the real truth of the Matrix. The phrase "Take the red pill" was adopted by many, including some men's-rights activists and conspiracy theorists, as a rallying cry that signaled willingness to face the truth about secretive elites. Ivanka Trump caught the reference. She retweeted him with the comment "Taken!"

The woke-mind virus

"traceroute woke_mind_virus"

It was a rather obscure tweet by Musk in December 2021, but it reflected the shift that was underway in his politics. "Traceroute" is a networking command to determine the path to the source server of some information. Musk had taken up the cause of battling what he considered to be the excesses of political correctness and the woke culture of progressive social-justice activists. When I asked him why, he responded, "Unless the woke-mind virus, which is fundamentally antiscience, antimerit, and antihuman in general, is stopped, civilization will never become multiplanetary."

Musk's reaction was partly triggered by his daughter Jenna's transition, her embrace of radical socialist politics, and her decision to break off relations with him. "He feels he lost a son who changed first and last names and won't speak to him anymore because of this woke-mind virus," says Jared Birchall, the manager of his personal office. "He is a firsthand witness on a very personal level of the damaging effect of being indoctrinated by this woke-mind religion."

On a more mundane level, he had become convinced that woke-ness was destroying humor. His own jokes tended to be filled with smirking references to 69, other sex acts, body fluids, pooping, farts, dope smoking, and topics that would crack up a dorm room of stoned freshmen. Once a fan of the satirical news site *The Onion*, he switched his loyalty to the *Babylon Bee*, a Christian conservative site, and gave them an interview at the end of 2021. "Wokeness wants to make comedy illegal, which is not cool," he contended. "Trying to shut down David Chappelle, come on, man, that's crazy. Do we want a humorless society that is simply rife with condemnation and hate and no forgiveness? At its heart wokeness is divisive, exclusionary, and hateful. It gives mean people a shield to be mean and cruel, armed with false virtue."

In May 2022, Musk got a call from *Business Insider*, which was about to run a story saying that he exposed himself to a flight attendant on his private jet and asked for a hand job. In return, the story went, he would buy her a pony, because she loved horses. Musk denied the claims—and noted that he had no flight attendants on his jet—but documents showed that Tesla had paid the woman $250,000 in severance in 2018. When the story appeared, the company's stock fell 10 percent and Musk's political resentments were further inflamed. He believed that the story was leaked by a friend of the woman who was, in his words, "an activist, woke, far-left Democrat."

As soon as he heard the story was about to run, Musk tried to in-oculate himself with a tweet casting it in political terms. "In the past I voted Democrat, because they were (mostly) the kindness party," he wrote. "But they have become the party of division & hate, so I can no longer support them and will vote Republican. Now, watch their dirty tricks campaign against me unfold." He was on his way to Brazil to meet with the right-wing populist president Jair Bol-sonaro, another example of his own political shift, and as his plane took off he sent another tweet: "The attacks against me should be viewed through a political lens—this is their standard (despicable) playbook—but nothing will deter me from fighting for a good future and your right to free speech."

By the following day, when the story ended up not being as explosive as he feared, Musk snapped back into sunnier mode. "Finally, we get to use Elongate as scandal name. It's kinda perfect," he tweeted. And when Chad Hurley, the cofounder of YouTube, made a joke about him horsing around, Musk replied, "Hi Chad . . . Fine, if you touch my wiener, you can have a horse."

Biden

As he became more concerned about wokeness, Musk's party loyalties shifted. "This woke-mind virus resides primarily in the Democratic Party, even though most Dems don't agree with it," he said. His evolution was also a reaction to attacks on him by some Democrats. "Elizabeth Warren actually called me a freeloading grifter who doesn't pay taxes, when I'm literally paying the most tax of any individual in history," he says. He was especially infuriated by an attack from a progressive California assemblywoman, Lorena Gonzalez. "F*ck Elon Musk," she tweeted. That added to his frustrations with California. "I came there when it was the land of opportunity," he says. "Now it's the land of litigation, regulation, and taxation."

He had developed a deep disdain for Donald Trump, whom he considered a con man, but he wasn't impressed by Joe Biden. "When he was vice president, I went to a lunch with him in San Francisco where he droned on for an hour and was boring as hell, like one of those dolls where you pull the string and it just says the same mindless phrases over and over." Nevertheless, he says he would have voted for Biden in 2020, but he decided that going to the polls in California, where he was then registered, was a waste of time because it was not a contested state.

His disdain for Biden grew in August 2021 when the president held an event at the White House to celebrate electric vehicles. The heads of GM, Ford, and Chrysler, along with the leader of the United Auto Workers union, were invited, but not Musk, even though Tesla sold far more electric cars in the U.S. than all other companies combined. Biden's press secretary Jen Psaki was forthright about the reason. "Well, these are the three largest employers of the United Auto Workers," she said, "so I'll let you draw your own conclusions." The UAW had failed to unionize Tesla's Fremont plant, partly because of what the National Labor Relations Board deemed to be illegal anti-union actions by the company and partly because its workers (as at the other new electric-vehicle companies, Lucid and Rivian) got stock options, not usually part of union contracts.

Biden went even further that November when he visited a GM factory in Detroit with CEO Mary Barra and members of the UAW leadership. "Detroit's leading the world in electric vehicles," Biden said. "Mary, I can remember talking to you way back in January about the need for America to lead in electric vehicles. You changed the whole story, Mary. You electrified the entire automobile industry. I'm serious. You led, and it matters."

In fact, GM had started to lead the way to electric vehicles in the 1990s, but it had pulled the plug on the effort. When Biden made this statement, GM had only one electric vehicle, the Chevy Bolt, which had been recalled and was not being produced at the time. In the last quarter of 2021, GM sold a grand total of 26 electric vehicles in the U.S. That year Tesla sold about 300,000 electric vehicles in the U.S. "Biden is a damp sock puppet in human form," Musk responded. Dana Hull, a reporter from *Bloomberg* who was often critical of Musk (he blocked her on Twitter), wrote, "Biden would do best to stick to the facts and acknowledge—as the market has—Tesla's role as the leader in the EV revolution."

Biden's staffers, many of whom drove Teslas, became concerned about the growing rift, and in early February 2022 his chief of staff Ron Klain and top economic advisor Brian Deese called Musk. He found the pair refreshingly reasonable. Eager to defuse Musk's anger, they promised that the president would praise Tesla publicly, and they inserted a phrase into a speech he was giving the next day: "Companies have announced investments totaling more than $200 billion in domestic manufacturing here in America—from iconic companies like GM and Ford building out new electric vehicle production to

Tesla, our nation's largest electric vehicle manufacturer." It was not the most fulsome endorsement, but it mollified Musk, at least for a while.

The détente with the Biden administration was not destined to last. Musk sent an email to his top executives at Tesla expressing his "super bad feeling" about the economy and asking them to make plans for a recession. When the email leaked, Biden was asked about it. He blurted out a sarcastic barb: "So, you know, lots of luck on his trip to the moon." It was as if he thought Musk was some oddball trying to fly to the moon. In fact, SpaceX's moon lander was being built for the U.S. under a contract from NASA. A few minutes after Biden's remark, Musk poked fun at his cluelessness by tweeting, "Thanks Mr. President!" and included a link to the NASA press release saying that SpaceX had won a contract to land American astronauts on the moon.

On a phone call in April, Biden's advisors described the incentives for electric cars that were in the pending inflation-reduction act. Musk was pleasantly surprised at how well conceived they were. But he pushed back on plans for the government to spend $5 billion over three years to create a network of electric vehicle charging stations. Even though that could help Tesla, Musk felt that the government should not be in the business of building charging stations, just as it shouldn't be building gas stations. This was better done by the private sector, including both big companies and mom-and-pop small businesses. Businesses would come up with ways to attract customers by building charging stations at restaurants, roadside attractions, convenience stores, and other locales. But if the government built stations, it would quash those entrepreneurial impulses. He promised that Tesla's chargers would be open to other cars. "I want you to know that our charging mechanisms both in the car and our stations are going to be interoperable," he pledged on the call.

That was a bit more complicated than it sounded. Tesla's superchargers would need adapters for the connectors used in other electric vehicles, and the financial arrangements had to be negotiated. Mitch Landrieu, the White House infrastructure czar, went to Tesla's Nevada battery factory and was given a briefing on the technological details. Then he and John Podesta, Biden's advisor for clean energy innovation, had a small meeting with Musk in Washington to agree on details. It led to a rare exchange of supportive tweets. "Elon Musk will open a big part of Tesla's network up to all drivers," read a tweet that the advisors wrote for Biden to post. "That's a big deal, and it'll make a big difference." Replied Musk, "Thank you. Tesla is happy to support other EVs via our Supercharger network."

A libertarian circle

One day early in 2022, Musk decided to throw an impromptu party at Tesla's almost finished Giga Texas factory. His deputy Omead Afshar commandeered a prototype of the Cybertruck and had it lifted to one of the open spaces on the factory's second floor. He set up a bar, used seats from unfinished cars to make a lounge space, and had a few assembly-line robots around for fun.

Musk invited his friend Luke Nosek, the PayPal cofounder and SpaceX investor, who suggested adding Joe Rogan, the proudly politically incorrect podcaster based in Austin, on whose show Musk had taken a toke during the turmoil of 2018. Nosek also invited Jordan Peterson, the Canadian psychologist and occasional anti-woke provocateur, who was visiting. Peterson arrived in a gray velvet collared jacket with a matching gray velvet–trimmed vest. After the party, a small group that included Musk, Rogan, Peterson, and Grimes went to Nosek's house, where they talked until close to 3 a.m.

Nosek, who was born in Poland, had been a dedicated libertarian since his days at the University of Illinois, where he had had long discussions with Max Levchin. They would become cofounders, with Musk, of PayPal, along with the even more ardent libertarian Peter Thiel. Nosek had been one of a handful of people celebrating at Thiel's house the victory of Trump in 2016.

Musk's set of Austin friends also included PayPal cofounder Ken Howery, who was Trump's ambassador to Sweden, and the young tech entrepreneur Joe Lonsdale, another protégé of Thiel. Another friend from PayPal days was the San Francisco entrepreneur and venture capitalist David Sacks. His politics were not rigidly partisan;

he had supported both Mitt Romney and Hillary Clinton. But he had been concerned since his student days with what was then called political correctness, and in 1995 he coauthored with Thiel a book called *The Diversity Myth: Multiculturalism and Political Intolerance on Campus*, which decried, using their alma mater Stanford as an example, "the debilitating impact that politically-correct 'multiculturalism' has had upon higher education and academic freedom."

None of these people determined Musk's political views, and it would be wrong to cast them as shadowy backstage influencers. Musk was willfully opinionated by his own nature and instinct. But they tended to reinforce his anti-woke sentiments.

Musk's hopscotch path to the right in 2022 disconcerted his progressive friends, including his first wife Justine and current girlfriend Grimes. "The so-called war against wokeism is one of the dumbest things ever," Justine tweeted that year. When he began texting right-wing memes and conspiracy theories to Grimes, she replied, "Is this from 4chan or something? You're actually starting to sound like someone from the far right."

There was an oddness to his newfound anti-woke fervor and occasional endorsements of alt-right conspiracy theories. It came in waves, like his demon-mode personality; it was not his default setting. Much of the time, he claimed to be a centrist moderate, albeit one with a libertarian streak born of his natural resistance to regulations and rules. He had contributed to Obama's campaigns and once stood in line for six hours to shake his hand at an event. "I'm thinking of creating a 'Super Moderate Super PAC' that supports candidates with centrist views from all parties," he tweeted at one point in 2022. And when he flew out later that summer to appear at a fundraiser for the PAC of Republican House leader Kevin McCarthy, he inoculated himself with a tweet that tried to reassure those who felt he might be going full MAGA: "To be clear, I support the left half of the Republican Party and the right half of the Democratic Party!"

But his politics, like his moods, were mercurial. Throughout 2022, he would cycle from sunny praise for moderation to angry brooding about how wokeness and censorship perpetrated by media elites were an existential threat to humanity.

Polytopia

One key to understanding Musk—his intensity, focus, competitiveness, die-hard attitudes, and love of strategy—is through his passion for video games. Hours of immersion became the way he let off (or built up) steam and honed his tactical skills and strategic thinking for business.

At age thirteen in South Africa, after teaching himself how to code, he wrote a video game called *Blastar*. He learned to hack ways to play arcade games for free, considered starting his own arcade, and interned at a game-making company. As an undergraduate, he began to focus on the genre known as strategy games—beginning with *Civilization* and *Warcraft: Orcs and Humans*—in which players take turns making moves as they compete to win a military or economic campaign using clever strategy, resource management, and decision-tree tactical thinking.

In 2021, he became obsessed with a new multiplayer strategy game on his iPhone, *Polytopia*. In it, players choose to be one of sixteen characters, known as tribes, and compete to develop technologies, corner resources, and wage battles in order to build an empire. He became so good he was able to beat the game's Swedish developer, Felix Ekenstam. What did his passion for the game say about him? "I am just wired for war, basically," he answers.

Shivon Zilis downloaded it onto her phone so they could play together. "I just fell down a fucking rabbit hole, and there's so many life lessons you learn, so many weird things about yourself and your opponents," she says. One day in Boca Chica, after a tense argument with some engineers over the need for the safety chains being used when moving the Starship booster, Musk retreated to sit on a piece of equipment on the edge of the parking lot and played two intense games of *Polytopia* on his phone against Zilis, who was in Austin. "He just absolutely crushed me both games," she says.

He also convinced Grimes to download the game. "He doesn't have hobbies or ways to relax other than video games," she says, "but he takes those so seriously that it gets very intense." During one game when they had agreed to be a united front against other tribes, she surprise-attacked him with a flame ball. "It was one of our biggest fights ever," she remembers. "He took it as this deep betrayal moment." Grimes protested it was only a video game and not a big deal. "It's a huge fucking deal," he told her. He did not speak to her for the rest of the day.

On a visit to Tesla's Berlin factory, he got so wrapped up in *Polytopia* that he delayed meetings with the local managers. His mother, who was on the trip, scolded him. "Yeah, I was wrong," he conceded. "But it's the best game ever." During the ride home on his plane, he played it all night.

A couple of months later, in Cabo San Lucas for Christiana Musk's birthday party, he spent hours by himself in his room or in the corner playing the game. "Come on, you got to come hang out," she pleaded, but he refused. Kimbal had learned the game in order to bond closer with his brother. "He said it would teach me how to be a CEO like he was," Kimbal says. "We called them *Polytopia* Life Lessons." Among them:

Empathy is not an asset. "He knows that I have an empathy gene, unlike him, and it has hurt me in business," Kimbal says. "*Polytopia* taught me how he thinks when you remove empathy. When you're playing a video game, there is no empathy, right?"

Play life like a game. "I have this feeling," Zilis once told Musk, "that as a kid you were playing one of these strategy games and your mom unplugged it, and you just didn't notice, and you kept playing life as if it were that game."

Do not fear losing. "You will lose," Musk says. "It will hurt the first fifty times. When you get used to losing, you will play each game with less emotion." You will be more fearless, take more risks.

Be proactive. "I'm a little bit Canadian pacifist and reactive," Zilis says. "My gameplay was a hundred percent reactive to what everyone else was doing, as opposed to thinking through my best strategy." She realized that, like many women, this mirrored the way she behaved at work. Both Musk and Mark Juncosa told her that she could never win unless she took charge of setting the strategy.

Optimize every turn. In *Polytopia*, you get only thirty turns, so you need to optimize each one. "Like in *Polytopia*, you only get a set number of turns in life," Musk says. "If we let a few of them slide, we will never get to Mars."

Double down. "Elon plays the game by always pushing the edge of what's possible," Zilis says. "And he's always doubling down and putting everything back in the game to grow and grow. And it's just like he's just done his whole life."

Pick your battles. In *Polytopia*, you might find yourself surrounded by six or more tribes, all taking swipes at you. If you swipe back at all of them, you're going to lose. Musk never fully mastered that lesson, and Zilis found herself coaching him on it. "Dude, like, everyone's swiping at you right now, but if you swipe back at too many, you'll run out of resources," she told him. She called that approach "front minimization." It was a lesson she also tried and failed to teach him about his behavior on Twitter.

Unplug at times. "I had to stop playing because it was destroying my marriage," Kimbal says. Shivon Zilis also deleted *Polytopia* from her phone. So did Grimes. And, for a while, Musk did so as well. "I had to take *Polytopia* off my phone because it was taking up too many brain cycles," he says. "I started dreaming about *Polytopia*." But the lesson about unplugging was another one that Musk never mastered. After a few months, he put the game back onto his phone and was playing again.

70

Ukraine

2022

Starlink to the rescue

An hour before Russia launched its invasion of Ukraine on February 24, 2022, it used a massive malware attack to disable the routers of the American satellite company Viasat that provided communications and internet to the country. The command system of the Ukrainian military was crippled, making it almost impossible to mount a defense. Top Ukrainian officials frantically appealed to Musk for help, and the vice prime minister, Mykhailo Fedorov, used Twitter to urge him to provide connectivity. "We ask you to provide Ukraine with Starlink stations," he pleaded.

Musk agreed. Two days later, five hundred terminals arrived in Ukraine. "We have the US military looking to help us with transport, State has offered humanitarian flights and some compensation," Gwynne Shotwell emailed Musk. "Folks are rallying for sure!"

"Cool," Musk responded. "Sounds good." He got on a Zoom call with President Volodymyr Zelenskyy, discussed the logistics of a larger rollout, and promised to visit Ukraine when the war was over.

Lauren Dreyer, SpaceX's director of Starlink business operations, began sending Musk updates twice a day. "Russia took offline a bunch of Ukraine communications infrastructure today, and a number of Starlink kits are already allowing Ukraine Armed Forces to continue operating theater command centers," she wrote on March 1. "These kits can be life or death, as the opponent is now focusing heavily on comms infrastructure. They are asking for more."

The next day SpaceX sent two thousand more terminals via Poland. But Dreyer said that the electricity was off in some areas, so many of them wouldn't work. "Let's offer to ship some field solar+battery kits," Musk replied. "They can have some Tesla Powerwalls or Megapacks too." The batteries and solar panels were soon on their way.

Every day that week, Musk held regular meetings with the Starlink engineers. Unlike every other company and even parts of the U.S. military, they were able to find ways to defeat Russian jamming. By Sunday, the company was providing voice connections for a Ukrainian special operations brigade. Starlink kits were also used to connect the Ukrainian military to the U.S. Joint Special Operations Command and to get Ukrainian television broadcasts back up. Within days, six thousand more terminals and dishes were shipped, and by July there were fifteen thousand Starlink terminals operating in Ukraine.

Starlink was soon garnering lavish press coverage. "The conflict in Ukraine has provided Musk and SpaceX's fledgling satellite network with a trial-by-fire that has whetted the appetite of many Western militaries," *Politico* reporters wrote after profiling Ukrainian soldiers on the front lines using the service. "Commanders have been impressed by the company's ability, within days, to deliver thousands of backpack-sized satellite stations to the war-torn country and to keep them online despite increasingly sophisticated attacks from Russian hackers." The *Wall Street Journal* also did a feature. "Without Starlink, we would have been losing the war," one Ukrainian platoon commander told the paper.

Starlink contributed about half of the cost of the dishes and services it provided. "How many have we donated so far?" Musk wrote Dreyer on March 12. She replied, "2000 free Starlinks and monthly service. Also, 300 heavily discounted to Lviv IT association and we waived the monthly service for ~5500." The company soon donated sixteen hundred additional terminals, and Musk estimated its total contribution to be around $80 million.

Other funding came from government agencies, including those in the U.S., Britain, Poland, and the Czech Republic. There were also contributions from private individuals. The historian Niall Ferguson sent out an email to friends seeking to raise $5 million for the purchase and transport of five thousand more Starlink kits. "If you would like to contribute, please let me know as soon as you can," he wrote. "I cannot overstate the importance of the role Starlink has played in keeping the communications of the Ukrainian government from being taken out by the Russians." Three hours later, he got a reply from Marc Benioff, the billionaire cofounder of Salesforce. "I'm in for $1M," he wrote. "Elon rocks."

No good deed . . .

"This could be a giant disaster," Musk texted me. It was a Friday evening in September 2022, and Musk had gone into crisis-drama mode, this time with reason. A dangerous and knotty issue had arisen, and he believed that there was "a non-trivial possibility," as he put it, that it could lead to a nuclear war, with Starlink partly responsible. The Ukrainian military was attempting a sneak attack on the Russian naval fleet based at Sevastopol in Crimea by sending six small drone submarines packed with explosives, and they were using Starlink to guide them to the target.

Although he had readily supported Ukraine, his foreign policy instincts were those of a realist and student of European military history. He believed that it was reckless for Ukraine to launch an attack on Crimea, which Russia had annexed in 2014. The Russian ambassador had warned him, in a conversation a few weeks earlier, that attacking Crimea would be a red line and could lead to a nuclear response. Musk explained to me the details of Russian law and doctrine that decreed such a response.

Throughout the evening and into the night, he personally took charge of the situation. Allowing the use of Starlink for the attack, he concluded, could be a disaster for the world. So he reaffirmed a secret policy that he had implemented, which the Ukrainians did not know about, to disable coverage within a hundred kilometers of the Crimean coast. As a result, when the Ukrainian drone subs got near the Russian fleet in Sevastopol, they lost connectivity and washed ashore harmlessly.

When the Ukrainian military noticed, in the midst of the mission, that Starlink was disabled in and around Crimea, Musk got frantic calls and texts asking him to turn the coverage back on. Mykhailo Fedorov, the vice prime minister who had originally enlisted his help, secretly shared with him the details of how the drone subs were crucial to their fight for freedom. "We made the sea drones ourselves, they can destroy any cruiser or submarine," he texted using an encrypted app. "I did not share this information with anyone. I just want you—the person who is changing the world through technology—to know this."

Musk replied that the design of the drones was impressive, but he refused to turn the coverage for Crimea back on, arguing that Ukraine "is now going too far and inviting strategic defeat." He discussed the situation with Biden's national security advisor, Jake Sullivan, and chairman of the joint chiefs, General Mark Milley, explaining to them that SpaceX did not wish Starlink to be used for offensive military purposes. He also called the Russian ambassador to assure him that Starlink was being used for defensive purposes only. "I think if the Ukrainian attacks had succeeded in sinking the Russian fleet, it would have been like a mini Pearl Harbor and led to a major escalation," Musk says. "We did not want to be a part of that."

Musk's siege mentality was often apocalyptic. In business and in politics, he had a tendency to perceive—and be energized by—dire threats. In 2022, he became alarmed by what he saw as multiple catastrophic dangers looming in world affairs. There was a strong likelihood, he came to believe, that there would be a major confrontation with China over Taiwan within a year, which could decimate the world economy. He also became convinced that if the war in Ukraine dragged on, it could lead to military and economic disasters.

He took it upon himself to help find an end to the Ukrainian war, proposing a peace plan that included new referenda in the Donbas and other Russian-controlled regions, accepting that Crimea was a part of Russia, and assuring that Ukraine remained a "neutral" nation rather than becoming part of NATO. It provoked an uproar. "Fuck off is my very diplomatic reply to you," tweeted Ukraine's ambassador to Germany. President Zelenskyy was a bit more cautious. He posted a poll on Twitter asking, "Which Elon Musk do you like more?: One who supports Ukraine, or One who supports Russia."

Musk backed down a bit in subsequent tweets. "SpaceX's out of pocket cost to enable and support Starlink in Ukraine is ~$80M so far," he wrote in response to Zelenskyy's question. "Our support for Russia is $0. Obviously, we are pro Ukraine." But then he added, "Trying to retake Crimea will cause massive death, probably fail and risk nuclear war. This would be terrible for Ukraine and Earth."

In early October, Musk extended his restrictions on the use of Starlink for offensive operations by disabling some of its coverage in the Russian-controlled regions of southern and eastern Ukraine. This resulted in another flurry of calls and highlighted the outsized role that Starlink was playing. Neither Ukraine nor the U.S. had been able to find any other satellite providers or communication systems that could match Starlink or fend off attacks from Russian hackers. Feeling unappreciated, he suggested that SpaceX was no longer willing to bear some of the financial burden.

Shotwell also felt strongly that SpaceX should stop subsidizing the Ukrainian military operation. Providing humanitarian help was fine, but private companies should not be financing a foreign country's war. That should be left to the government, which is why the U.S. has a Foreign Military Sales program that puts a layer of protection between private companies and foreign governments. Other companies, including big and profitable defense contractors, were charging billions to supply weapons to Ukraine, so it seemed unfair that Starlink, which was not yet profitable, should do it for free. "We initially gave the Ukrainians free service for humanitarian and defense purposes, such as keeping up their hospitals and banking systems," she says. "But then they started putting them on fucking drones trying to blow up Russian ships. I'm happy to donate services for ambulances and hospitals and mothers. That's what companies and people should do. But it's wrong to pay for military drone strikes."

Shotwell began negotiating a contract with the Pentagon. SpaceX would continue to provide another six months of free service to the terminals that were being used for humanitarian purposes, but it would no longer provide free service to ones used by the military; the Pentagon should pay for that. An agreement was struck that the Pentagon would pay SpaceX $145 million to cover the service.

But then the story leaked, igniting a backlash against Musk in the press and Twitterverse. He decided to withdraw his request for funding. SpaceX would provide free service indefinitely for the terminals that were already in Ukraine. "The hell with it," he tweeted. "Even though Starlink is still losing money & other companies are getting billions of taxpayer $, we'll just keep funding Ukraine govt for free."

Shotwell thought that was ridiculous. "The Pentagon had a $145 million check ready to hand to me, literally. Then Elon succumbed to the bullshit on Twitter and to the haters at the Pentagon who leaked the story."

"No good deed goes unpunished," his friend David Sacks tweeted.

"Even so, we should still do good deeds," Musk replied.

Vice Prime Minister Fedorov tried to smooth things over by sending Musk encrypted text messages lavishing him with thanks. "Not everyone understands your contribution to Ukraine. I am confident that without Starlinks, we would be unable to function successfully. Thanks again."

Fedorov said that he understood Musk's position of not allowing Starlink service to be used for attacks in Crimea. But he pushed Musk to allow Ukraine to use the service to fight in the Russian-controlled regions in the south and east. That led to an amazingly candid secret encrypted exchange:

Fedorov: The exclusion of these territories is absolutely unfair. I come from Vasylivka village in Zaporizhzhia region, my parents and friends live there. Now this village is occupied by Russian troops, and there is complete lawlessness and outrage—the residents are impatiently waiting for liberation. . . . At the end of September, we noticed that Starlink does not work in the liberated villages, which makes it impossible to restore the critical infrastructure of these territories. For us it is a matter of life and death.

Musk: Once Russia is fully mobilized, they will destroy all infrastructure throughout Ukraine and push far past the current territories. NATO will have to intervene to prevent all of Ukraine falling to Russia. At that point, risk of WW3 becomes very high.

Fedorov: Mobilization does not affect the course of the war as much as technology—this is a technology war. . . . Mobilization in Russia can lead to the overthrow of Putin. This is not a war of Russian people and they don't want to go to Ukraine.

Musk: Russia will stop at nothing, nothing, to hold Crimea. This poses catastrophic risk to the world. . . . Seek peace while you have the upper hand. . . . Let's discuss this. [Musk included his new private cell phone number.] I will support any pragmatic path to peace that serves the greater good for all of humanity.

Fedorov: I understand. We look through the eyes of Ukrainians, and you from the position of a person who wants to save humanity. And not just wants, but does more than anybody else for this.

After his exchange with Fedorov, Musk felt frustrated. "How am I in this war?" he asked me during a late-night phone conversation. "Starlink was not meant to be involved in wars. It was so people can watch Netflix and chill and get online for school and do good peaceful things, not drone strikes."

In the end, with Shotwell's help, SpaceX made arrangements with various government agencies to pay for increased Starlink service in Ukraine, with the military working out the terms of service. More than 100,000 new dishes were sent to Ukraine at the beginning of 2023. In addition, Starlink launched a companion service called Starshield, which was specifically designed for military use. SpaceX sold or licensed Starshield satellites and services to the U.S. military and other agencies, allowing the government to determine how they could and should be used in Ukraine and elsewhere.

71

Bill Gates

2022

With Gates at the Boao Forum for Asia in Qionghai, China, 2015

The visit

"Hey, I'd love to come see you and talk about philanthropy and climate," Bill Gates said to Musk when they happened to be at the same meeting in early 2022. Musk's stock sales had led him, for tax reasons, to put $5.7 billion into a charitable fund he had established. Gates, who was then spending most of his time on philanthropy, had many suggestions he wanted to make.

They'd had friendly interactions a few times in the past, including when Gates brought his son Rory to SpaceX. Musk, who had always liked the Microsoft operating system more than most other techies did, could relate to a guy who had built a company by being hardcore and relentless. They agreed to set up a visit, and Gates, who has a team of schedulers and assistants, said he would have his office call Musk's scheduler.

"I don't have a scheduler," Musk replied. He had decided to get rid of his personal assistant and scheduler because he wanted complete control of his calendar. "Just have your secretary call me directly." Gates, who thought it was "bizarre" that Musk had no scheduler, felt weird having one of his assistants call Musk, so he did so directly and arranged a time they could meet in Austin.

"Just landed," Gates texted on the afternoon of March 9, 2022.

"Cool," replied Musk, who sent Omead Afshar down to the Gigafactory entrance to meet him.

In the rarefied fraternity of people who have held the title of richest person on Earth, Musk and Gates have some similarities. Both have analytic minds, an ability to laser-focus, and an intellectual surety that edges into arrogance. Neither suffers fools. All of these traits made it likely they would eventually clash, which is what happened when Musk began giving Gates a tour of the factory.

Gates argued that batteries would never be able to power large semitrucks and that solar energy would not be a major part of solving the climate problem. "I showed him the numbers," Gates says. "It's an area where I clearly knew something that he didn't." He also gave Musk a hard time on Mars. "I'm not a Mars person," Gates later told me. "He's overboard on Mars. I let him explain his Mars thinking to me, which is kind of bizarre thinking. It's this crazy thing where maybe there's a nuclear war on Earth and so the people on Mars are there and they'll come back down and, you know, be alive after we all kill each other."

Nevertheless, Gates found himself impressed by the factory Musk had built and his detailed knowledge of every machine and process. He also admired SpaceX for deploying a large constellation of Starlink satellites to provide internet from space. "Starlink is the realization of what I tried to do with Teledesic twenty years ago," he says.

At the end of the tour, the conversation turned to philanthropy. Musk expressed his view that most of it was "bullshit." There was only a twenty-cent impact for every dollar put in, he estimated. He could do more good for climate change by investing in Tesla.

"Hey, I'm going to show you five projects of a hundred million each," Gates responded. He listed money for refugees, American schools, an AIDS cure, eradicating some mosquito types through gene drives, and genetically modified seeds that will resist the effects of climate change. Gates is very diligent about philanthropy, and he promised to write for Musk a "super-long description of the ideas."

There was one contentious issue that they had to address. Gates had shorted Tesla stock, placing a big bet that it would go down in value. He turned out to be wrong. By the time he arrived in Austin, he had lost $1.5 billion. Musk had heard about it and was seething. Short-sellers occupied his innermost circle of hell. Gates said he was sorry, but that did not placate Musk. "I apologized to him," Gates says. "Once he heard I'd shorted the stock, he was super mean to me, but he's super mean to so many people, so you can't take it too personally."

The dispute reflected different mindsets. When I asked Gates why he had shorted Tesla, he explained that he had calculated that the supply of electric cars would get ahead of demand, causing prices to fall. I nodded but still had the same question: Why had he shorted the stock? Gates looked at me as if I had not understood what he just explained and then replied as if the answer was obvious: he thought that by shorting Tesla he could make money.

That way of thinking was alien to Musk. He believed in the mission of moving the world to electric vehicles, and he put all of his available money toward that goal, even when it did not seem like a safe investment. "How can someone say they are passionate about fighting climate change and then do something that reduced the overall investment in the company doing the most?" he asked me a few days after Gates's visit. "It's pure hypocrisy. Why make money on the failure of a sustainable energy car company?"

Grimes added her own interpretation: "I imagine it's a little bit of a dick-measuring contest."

Gates followed up in mid-April, sending Musk the promised paper on philanthropy options that he had personally written. Musk responded by text with a simple question: "Do you still have a half billion dollar short position against Tesla?"

Gates was sitting in the dining room of the Four Seasons hotel in Washington, DC, with his son Rory, who was just starting graduate school. He laughed, showed Rory the text, and asked for his advice on how to answer.

"Just say yes, and then change the subject quickly," Rory suggested.

Gates tried that. "Sorry to say I haven't closed it out," he texted back. "I would like to discuss philanthropy possibilities."

It didn't work. "Sorry," Musk shot back instantly. "I cannot take your philanthropy on climate seriously when you have a massive short position against Tesla, the company doing the most to solve climate change."

When angry, Musk can get mean, especially on Twitter. He tweeted a picture of Gates in a golf shirt with a bulging belly that made him look almost pregnant. "In case u need to lose a boner fast," Musk's comment read.

Gates was truly puzzled about why Musk was upset that he shorted the stock. And Musk was just as puzzled that Gates could find it puzzling. "At this point, I am convinced that he is categorically insane (and an asshole to the core)," Musk texted me right after his exchange with Gates. "I did actually want to like him (sigh)."

For his part, Gates was far more gracious. Later that year, he was at a dinner in Washington, DC, where people were criticizing Musk. "You can feel whatever you want about Elon's behavior," Gates said, "but there is no one in our time who has done more to push the bounds of science and innovation than he has."

Philanthropy

Musk had shown little interest in philanthropy over the years. He felt that the good he could do for humanity was best accomplished by keeping his money deployed in his companies that pursued energy sustainability, space exploration, and artificial intelligence safety.

A few days after Bill Gates visited him with philanthropy suggestions, Musk sat down at an open table on the mezzanine overlooking the assembly lines at Tesla's new Giga Texas with Birchall and four estate-planning advisors. Even though he had not been persuaded by Gates to dive into philanthropy, he wanted ideas for funding something that would be more operational than a traditional foundation.

The option Birchall proposed was creating a nonprofit holding company, which is like a business that guides and funds multiple nonprofit companies under its protection. As Birchall explained, the structure would be similar to that of the Howard Hughes Medical Institute. "We're going to do it like in baby steps," Birchall told me, "but ultimately it can become a pretty big thing, maybe a full-fledged institute of higher learning."

Although the concept appealed to Musk, he was not ready to commit. "I've got too much else to think about now," he said as he left the table.

Yes, he did. That day—April 6, 2022—he was preparing for the opening of Giga Texas, and he had spent the morning doing an intense inspection walk on the Model Y assembly line and approving the details of the Giga Rodeo party being planned. It was also the day of his conference call with White House officials on trade, China, and battery subsidies. And then there was the issue that was taking up most of his mind-space that day: an offer he had just accepted, but was having second thoughts about, to join the board of a company whose stock he had been secretly accumulating since January.

72

Active Investor

Twitter, January–April 2022

Parag Agrawal and Jack Dorsey

Before the storm

In April 2022, things were going surprisingly well for Musk. Tesla sales had grown 71 percent in the past twelve months, without spending a penny on advertising. Its stock had gone up fifteen-fold in five years, and it was now worth more than the next nine auto companies combined. Musk's fierce browbeating of microchip suppliers meant that Tesla, unlike other manufacturers, had survived the supply-chain dislocations caused by the pandemic, allowing it to achieve record deliveries in the first quarter of 2022.

As for SpaceX, in the first quarter of 2022 it launched twice as much mass into orbit as all other companies and countries combined. In April it sent up its fourth manned mission to the International Space Station, carrying three astronauts for NASA (which still didn't have its own launch capability) and one for the European Space Agency. It also that month sent into orbit another batch of Starlink communications satellites, bringing to twenty-one hundred the number in the SpaceX constellation that was by then providing internet connectivity to 500,000 subscribers in forty countries, including Ukraine. No other company or country had been able to land orbital rockets safely and reuse them. "The super-weird thing is that Falcon 9 is still the only orbital booster to land or re-fly after all these years!" Musk tweeted.

The upshot was that the value of the four companies he had initially funded and built were:

Tesla: $1 trillion

SpaceX: $100 billion

The Boring Company: $5.6 billion

Neuralink: $1 billion

It promised to be a glorious year, if only he could leave well enough alone. But it was not in Musk's nature to leave well enough alone.

Shivon Zilis noticed that by early April he had the itchiness of a video-game addict who has triumphed but couldn't unplug. "You don't have to be in a state of war at all times," she told him that month. "Or, is it that you find greater comfort when you're in periods of war?"

"It's part of my default settings," he replied.

"It was like he was winning the simulation and now felt at a loss for what to do," she says. "Extended periods of calm are unnerving for him."

During a conversation that month about the milestones his companies had reached, he explained to me why he thought Tesla was on a trajectory to be the most valuable company in the world, one that made $1 trillion in profits every year. Yet there were no notes of celebration or even satisfaction in his voice. "I guess I've always wanted to push my chips back on the table or play the next level of the game," he said. "I'm not good at sitting back."

Usually at such moments of unnerving success, Musk manufactures a drama. He launches a surge, scrambles the jets, announces an unrealistic and unnecessary deadline. Autonomy Day, Starship stacking, solar roof installations, car production hell—he yanks the alarm chain and forces a fire drill. "Normally, he would go into one of his companies and find something to turn into a crisis," Kimbal says. But this time, Musk didn't do that. Instead, without fully thinking it through, he decided to buy Twitter.

Flamethrower for the thumbs

Musk's period of unnerving calm in early 2022 coincided, fatefully, with a moment when he suddenly had a lot of cash in his pocket. His stock sales had left him with about $10 billion. "I didn't want to just leave it in the bank," he says, "so I asked myself what product I liked, and that was an easy question. It was Twitter." In January, he confidentially told his personal manager Jared Birchall to start buying shares.

Twitter is an ideal—almost too ideal—playground for Musk. It rewards players who are impulsive, irreverent, and unfiltered, like a flamethrower for the thumbs. It has many of the attributes of a school yard, including taunting and bullying. But in the case of Twitter, the clever kids win followers rather than get pushed down the concrete steps. And if you're the richest and cleverest of all, you can even decide, unlike back when you were a kid, to become king of the school yard.

Musk first used Twitter soon after it was launched in 2006, but dropped his account after being "bored by tweets about what kind of latte somebody had at Starbucks." His friend Bill Lee urged him to reengage so that he could have an unfiltered method of communicating with the public, and he turned on the spigot in December 2011. His early tweets included a picture of him at a Christmas party wearing a fright wig and pretending to be Art Garfunkel and another that became the beginning of a fraught friendship. "Got called randomly by Kanye West today and received a download of his thoughts, ranging from shoes to Moses," Musk wrote. "He was polite, but opaque."

Over the next decade, Musk composed nineteen thousand tweets. "My tweets are like Niagara Falls sometimes and they come too fast," he says. "Just dip a cup in there and try to avoid the random turds." His 2018 "pedo guy" and "funding secured" tweets showed that Twitter could be dangerous in his twitchy fingers, especially late on some agitated nights fueled by Red Bull and Ambien. When asked why he doesn't restrain himself, he merrily admits that he too often "shoots himself in the foot" or "digs his own grave." But life needs to be interesting and edgy, he says, then quotes his favorite line from the 2000 movie *Gladiator*: "Are you not entertained? Is that not why you are here?"

By early 2022, a new ingredient had been added to this combustible cauldron: Musk's swelling concern with the dangers of the "woke-mind virus" that he believed was infecting America. He disdained Donald Trump, but he felt it was absurd to ban permanently a former president, and he became increasingly riled up by complaints from those on the Right who were being suppressed on Twitter. "He saw the direction Twitter was heading, which was that if you were on the wrong end of the spectrum you were censored," says Birchall.

His libertarian tech friends cheered him on. When Musk suggested in March that Twitter should make public the algorithms it used to boost or downplay content, his young friend Joe Lonsdale expressed support. "Our public square needs to not have arbitrary sketchy censorship," he texted. "I'm actually speaking to over 100 members of congress tomorrow at GOP policy retreat and this is one of the ideas I'm pushing."

"Absolutely," Musk responded. "What we have now is hidden corruption!"

Their Austin friend Joe Rogan also weighed in. "Are you going to liberate Twitter from the censorship happy mob?" he texted Musk.

"I will provide advice, which they may or may not choose to follow," Musk answered.

His view of free speech was that the more there was, the better it would be for democracy. At one point in March he conducted a poll on Twitter: "Free speech is essential to a functioning democracy. Do you believe Twitter rigorously adheres to this principle?" When more than 70 percent answered no, Musk posed another question: "Is a new platform needed?"

Twitter's cofounder Jack Dorsey, then still on the company's board, privately texted an answer to Musk: "Yes."

Replied Musk, "I'd like to help if I'm able to."

Board seat

At that point, Musk was considering whether to start a new platform. But in late March, he had some private conversations with a few members of the Twitter board who urged him to become more involved with the company. One night, right after he finished his 9 o'clock meeting with the Tesla Autopilot team, he called Parag Agrawal, the software engineer who had taken over from Dorsey as Twitter CEO. The two of them decided to meet secretly for dinner on March 31, along with Twitter's board chair Bret Taylor.

The Twitter staff arranged for them to use an Airbnb farmhouse near the San Jose airport. When Taylor arrived first, he texted Musk to warn him. "This wins for the weirdest place I've had a meeting recently," he wrote. "There are tractors and donkeys."

Musk replied, "Maybe Airbnb's algorithm thinks you love tractors and donkeys (who doesn't)."

At the meeting, Musk found Agrawal to be likable. "He's a really nice guy," he says. But that was the problem. If you ask Musk what are the traits needed in a CEO, he would not include "being a really nice guy." One of his maxims is that managers should not aim to be liked. "What Twitter needs is a fire-breathing dragon," he said after that meeting, "and Parag is not that."

Fire-breathing dragon. That's a pithy description of Musk. But he hadn't yet thought about taking over Twitter himself. At their meeting, Agrawal told him that Dorsey had proposed a while back that Musk join the board. Agrawal urged him to do so.

Musk was traveling in Germany two days later when the Twitter board sent over its official offer for him to join. But to Musk's surprise, it was not a friendly agreement. It was based on what Twitter had used two years earlier when it agreed to put two hostile activist investors on the board. It was seven pages long and included provisions that would bar him from making public statements (and presumably tweets) critical of the company. From the Twitter board's perspective, that was understandable. History showed, as would the future, the damage Musk could do when not compelled to holster his flamethrowers. His battle with the SEC also showed how hard it was to force such restrictions on him.

Musk told Birchall to reject the agreement. It was "the ultimate irony," he said, for a company that was supposed to be "the public square" to try to restrict his freedom of speech. Within a few hours, the Twitter board backed down. They sent back a very friendly revised agreement that was only three paragraphs long. Its only major restriction was that he could not purchase more than 14.9 percent of Twitter stock. "Well, if they're going to roll out the red carpet, I'll do it," he told Birchall.

After Musk belatedly disclosed to the SEC that he owned about 9 percent of Twitter's stock, he and Agrawal exchanged celebratory tweets. "I'm excited to share that we're appointing @elonmusk to our board!" Agrawal posted early on the morning of April 5. "He's both a passionate believer and intense critic of the service, which is exactly what we need."

Musk responded seven minutes later with a carefully scripted tweet. "Looking forward to working with Parag & Twitter board to make significant improvements to Twitter in coming months!"

For a brief couple of days, it looked as if there would be peace in the valley. Musk liked the fact that Agrawal was an engineer, not a typical CEO. "I interface way better with engineers who are able to do hardcore programming than with program manager/MBA types of people," he texted. "I love our conversations!"

"In our next convo, treat me like an engineer instead of CEO and let's see where we get to," Agrawal replied.

Brainstorming

Luke Nosek and Ken Howery, Musk's close friends and fellow PayPal cofounders, paced around the mezzanine workspace of Giga Texas on the afternoon of April 6, waiting for him to finish his discussion on philanthropy with Birchall and then his call with Biden administration officials about China tariffs. He had been living at Howery's house and also sometimes stayed at Nosek's. "My two landlords!" he declared when he finally broke free and wandered over.

It was the day after the announcement that he was joining the Twitter board, and Nosek and Howery were skeptical about the decision. "It's probably a recipe for trouble," Musk merrily conceded as he sat down at a conference table overlooking the Tesla assembly lines. "I had a bunch of cash sitting around!" Howery and Nosek chuckled, then waited for more. "I think it's important to have a forum that is trusted, or at least not too distrusted," Musk added. The Twitter board, he complained, had little personal investment in the service, either as stockholders or users. "Parag is a technologist and has a medium idea of what's going on, but it's very clear that the inmates are running the asylum."

He repeated his simple view that it would be good for democracy if Twitter stopped trying to restrict what users could say. "Twitter has to move more in the direction of free speech, at least as defined by the law," he said. "Right now, Twitter's suppression of speech is far in excess of the law."

Despite sharing Musk's libertarian views on free speech, Howery pushed back gently with some sophisticated thoughts, posed as gentle questions. "Should it be like a telephone system, where the words that go in one end come out exactly the same on the other end?" he asked. "Or do you think this is more like a system that is governing the discourse of the world, and maybe there should be some intelligence put into the algorithm that prioritizes and deprioritizes things?"

"Yeah, it's a thorny question," Musk answered. "There's an ability to say something, and then there is also the issue of to what degree it's promoted or demoted or amplified." Perhaps the formula for promoting tweets should be more open. "It could be an open-source algorithm placed on GitHub so people can sift through it." This was an idea that appealed to conservatives who felt that there were liberal biases secretly baked into the algorithm, but it didn't really address the issue of whether Twitter should try to prevent the spread of dangerous, false, or harmful content.

Musk then threw out a few other ideas. "What if we charged people a small amount, like two dollars a month, to be verified?" he asked. This would become one of Musk's core ideas for Twitter: making people subscribe using their credit card and cell phone number would be a way to verify and authenticate their identity. The algorithm could favor those users, who would probably be less likely to engage in scams, bullying, and spreading what they knew to be lies. It might reduce how quickly any discussion degenerated into comparing people to Nazis.

Getting a user's credit card, he said, would have an additional advantage: it could facilitate turning Twitter into a payments platform where people could send money, hand out tips, and pay for stories, music, and videos. Because Howery and Nosek had been with Musk at PayPal, they liked the idea. "It could fulfill my original vision for X.com and PayPal," Musk said with a gleeful laugh. From the very beginning, he saw the potential that Twitter could become what he had envisioned for X.com, a social network that supported financial transactions.

The conversation continued over a late dinner at the Pershing, an elegant but unpretentious club in Austin, where Nosek had reserved an upstairs room. Also there were Griffin and Saxon; Chris Anderson of TED, who was in town to record an interview for his upcoming conference; Maye, who had just arrived from Prague, where she was doing appearances for *Vogue*; and later Grimes.

Griffin and Saxon allowed that they rarely used Twitter, but Maye said she did so often, which perhaps should have been a warning sign about the demographics of the service's users. "I probably spend too much time on Twitter," Elon said. "It's a good place to dig your own grave. You get your shoulder into it, and you keep on digging."

Giga Rodeo

The grand opening of the Giga Texas factory was set for the next night, April 7. Omead Afshar had planned what he dubbed a Giga Rodeo, with fifteen thousand guests. Instead of overseeing the preparations and rehearsing his show, Musk flew to Colorado Springs for a three-hour visit to the U.S. Air Force Academy, where he had agreed to give a lecture. It was a welcome break. He could process his thoughts about Twitter in the background while he engaged in something else.

He pushed the cadets not to fall prey to the cautious bureaucratic mindset that he believed stymied government programs. "If we're not blowing up engines, we're not trying hard enough," he told them. He seemed unhurried, despite all that was going on. After his talk, he met with a small group of students to discuss their research on artificial intelligence and the development of autonomous drones.

When he returned in the late afternoon, Giga Texas had been transformed. The parking area was festooned with art installations like those at Burning Man, arcade games, bandstands, a mechanical bull, a giant rubber duck, and two towering Tesla coils. Inside, parts of the factory were staged to look like a nightclub. Kimbal helped put together a drone show that featured likenesses of Nikola Tesla, the Dogecoin dog mascot, and a Cybertruck in the night sky. Celebrities included Harrison Ford, Spike Lee, and the artist Beeple, who had created an installation.

Musk came onstage to a blaring Dr. Dre song driving the black Tesla Roadster that was the first car the company had ever made. He gave many statistics about the enormity of the 10-million-square-foot factory, then he put it in perspective by saying it could fit 194 billion hamsters. After listing the many milestones that Tesla had achieved, he emphasized what he said would be the ultimate one. "Full Self-Driving," he promised, "is going to revolutionize the world."

The opening of Giga Texas should have been a moment of triumph. Musk had led the way into the era of electric vehicles, and now he was showing that manufacturing could thrive in America. But the buzz at the opening celebration and the afterparty was not about miracles of manufacturing. Especially among Musk's close friends and family—Kimbal, Antonio, Luke, and even Maye—the conversation was about Twitter. Why was he throwing himself into that snake-infested swamp? Would this be his Wilderness Campaign? Should we try to talk him out of it?

73

"I made an offer"

Twitter, April 2022

Pause

The day after the Giga Rodeo—Friday, April 8, 2022—Musk met Kimbal for brunch. He was frustrated by his talks with members of the Twitter board. "They're nice, but none of them use Twitter," he said. "I don't feel like anything will happen."

Kimbal was not encouraging. "Dude, you've never been on a board, so you don't know how much this is going to suck for you," he said. "You tell people what you think, and then they smile and nod and ignore you."

Kimbal thought that it would be better for his brother to start his own social media platform based on the blockchain. Perhaps it could include a payment system using Dogecoin, Elon mused. After brunch, he sent Kimbal a few texts fleshing out the idea for "a block-chain social media system that does both payments and short text messages like Twitter." Because there would be no central server, "there'd be no throat to choke, so free speech is guaranteed."

The other option, Elon said, was not merely to join the board of Twitter but to buy it. "I began to believe that Twitter was heading off a cliff and that I couldn't save it by just being a board member," he says. "So I thought, maybe I should just buy it, take it private, and fix it."

He had already accepted, by text message and public tweet, the friendly agreement to join Twitter's board. But after his brunch with

Kimbal, he phoned Birchall and told him not to finalize anything. He still had some thinking to do.

Hawaii

That evening, Musk flew to Larry Ellison's Hawaiian island, Lanai. The Oracle founder had built himself a serene compound on a hill in the center of the island, and he let Musk use his older house down by the beach. Musk had planned the trip as a quiet rendezvous with one of the women he was occasionally dating, the Australian actress Natasha Bassett. But instead of being a relaxed mini-vacation, Musk spent most of his four days there figuring out what to do about Twitter.

He stayed awake most of his first night stewing about the problems Twitter faced. When he looked at a list of the people with the most followers—such as Barack Obama, Justin Bieber, and Katy Perry—he realized that they were no longer very active. So at 3:32 a.m. Hawaii time, he posted a tweet: "Most of these 'top' accounts tweet rarely and post very little content. Is Twitter dying?"

In San Francisco, where Twitter CEO Agrawal was, it was 6:30 a.m. About ninety minutes later, he sent Musk a text message: "You are free to tweet 'Is twitter dying?' or anything else about Twitter, but it's my responsibility to tell you that it's not helping me make Twitter better in the current context." It was a restrained text, carefully worded to avoid implying that Musk no longer had the right to disparage the company. He added that they should talk soon about how to avoid the "distractions" that were "hurting our ability to do work."

When Musk got the text, it was just after 5 a.m. in Hawaii, but he was still going strong, perhaps a bit too strong for that hour and situation. One minute later, he shot back a scathing reply: "What did you get done this week?" It was the ultimate Musk put-down.

Then he unleashed a fateful three-shot volley: "I'm not joining the board. This is a waste of time. Will make an offer to take Twitter private."

Agrawal was shocked. They had already announced he was joining the board. There had been no warning that he would instead attempt a hostile takeover. "Can we talk?" he asked plaintively.

Within three minutes, Bret Taylor, the Twitter board chair, texted Musk with a similar plea to talk. Their Saturday morning was not starting well.

Just at that moment, in the midst of his dialogue with Taylor and Agrawal, Elon got a reply from Kimbal to his texts from earlier that morning about the possibility of creating a new social network based on the blockchain. "I'd love to learn more," Kimbal said. "I've dug deep on Web3 (not crypto as much) and the voting powers are amazing and verified. Blockchain prevents people from deleting tweets. Pros and cons, but let the games begin!"

"I think a new social media company is needed that is based on the blockchain and includes payments," Elon replied.

Yet even while he was musing with Kimbal about creating a new social network, he reiterated to Agrawal and Taylor that he wanted to take over Twitter. "Please expect a take private offer," he texted them.

"Do you have five minutes so I can understand the context?" Taylor asked him.

"Fixing Twitter by chatting with Parag won't work," Musk answered. "Drastic action is needed."

"It has been 24 hours since you joined the board," Taylor replied. "I get your point, but just want to understand the sudden pivot."

Musk waited almost two hours to reply. When he did, it was after 7 a.m. in Hawaii, and he still had not gone to bed. "I'm about to take off, but can talk tomorrow," he wrote.

Musk says that it became clear to him when he got to Hawaii that he would not be able to fix Twitter by going on the board. "I was basically being rope-a-doped," he says. "They would listen, nod, and then not do anything. I decided I didn't want to be co-opted and be some sort of quisling on the board." In retrospect, this sounds like a well-considered reason. But at the time there was one other factor. Musk was in a manic mood, and as often happens, he was acting impetuously.

That afternoon—Saturday, April 9—he texted Birchall to say that he had decided he wanted to acquire Twitter. "This is real," he assured him. "There is no way to fix the company as a 9% shareholder, and the public markets have trouble thinking past the next quarter. Twitter needs to scrub out the bots and scammers, which will seem like a massive drop in daily users."

Birchall texted a banker at Morgan Stanley, "Call me when you have a minute." That night, they started work on figuring out a reasonable price for Twitter and how Musk could finance it.

In the meantime, Musk continued taking potshots at Twitter. He posted a poll about the company's San Francisco offices. "Convert Twitter SF HQ to homeless shelter since no one shows up anyway?" he tweeted. Within a day there were 1.5 million votes, more than 91 percent in favor.

"Hey—can you speak this evening?" Taylor texted him. "I've seen your tweets and feel more urgency about understanding your position." Musk didn't answer.

On Sunday, Taylor gave up. He told Musk that Twitter would announce that he had changed his mind and would not join the board. "Sounds good," Musk replied. "It is better, in my opinion, to take Twitter private, restructure and return to the public markets once that is done."

Agrawal made it official in a tweet late that night: "Elon's appointment to the board was to become officially effective 4/9, but Elon shared that same morning that he will no longer be joining the board. I believe this is for the best. We have and will always value input from our shareholders whether they are on our board or not."

Musk had a conference call with Birchall and the Morgan Stanley bankers on Monday afternoon Hawaii time. They had come up with a proposed share price to offer: $54.20. Musk and Birchall laughed, because it again played into the internet slang for marijuana, just like the "take private" price of $420 for Tesla. "This may be the most overplayed joke," Musk said. Excited about the prospect of buying Twitter, he started referring to the idea for a blockchain-based alternative as "Plan B."

Vancouver

Grimes had been pushing Musk to go with her to her hometown of Vancouver, so that she could introduce X to her parents and aging grandparents. "My grandpa is an engineer, and he's just been wanting a great-grandchild for so long," Grimes says, "and my grandma's super old and is just barely holding on."

They decided a good date would be Thursday, April 14, when Chris Anderson was hosting his annual TED Conference there. Anderson had taped an interview with Musk a week earlier at Giga Texas, but he was eager, especially given the fast-changing Twitter saga, to interview him live at the conference as well.

They arrived in Vancouver that Wednesday, April 13, Grimes from Austin and Musk from Hawaii. Musk went to a Nordstrom store to buy a black suit, since he had not brought one to Hawaii. That afternoon, Grimes took X on the seventy-five-mile trip to the town of Agassiz, where her grandparents lived, leaving Musk back at the hotel. "I could tell that he was in stress mode and all the Twitter stuff was happening," she says.

Indeed it was. Late that afternoon, from his Vancouver hotel room, Musk texted Bret Taylor his official decision. "After several days of deliberation—this is obviously a matter of serious gravity—I have decided to move forward with taking Twitter private," he said. "I will send you an offer letter tonight." The letter read:

> I invested in Twitter as I believe in its potential to be the platform for free speech around the globe, and I believe free speech is a societal imperative for a functioning democracy.
>
> However, since making my investment I now realize the company will neither thrive nor serve this societal imperative in its current form. Twitter needs to be transformed as a private company.
>
> As a result, I am offering to buy 100% of Twitter for $54.20 per share in cash, a 54% premium over the day before I began investing in Twitter and a 38% premium over the day before my investment was publicly announced. My offer is my best and final

offer and if it is not accepted, I would need to reconsider my position as a shareholder.

Twitter has extraordinary potential. I will unlock it.

That night, Musk attended a small dinner for TED speakers at a local restaurant. Instead of talking about Twitter, he asked the other guests about their views on the meaning of life. Then he and Grimes went back to their hotel, where he unwound by immersing himself in a new video game, *Elden Ring*, which he had downloaded onto his laptop.

The game involves navigating through a fantasy world filled with bizarre beasts that want to destroy you. Elaborately rendered with cryptic clues and strange plot twists, it requires intense focus and a lot of attention to detail, especially when it comes to calculating when to attack. "I played a couple of hours, then answered some texts and emails, then played some more," he says. He spent a lot of time in the game's most dangerous regions, a fiery-red demon hellscape known as Caelid. "Instead of sleeping," Grimes said, "he played until five-thirty in the morning."

Moments after he finished, he sent out a tweet: "I made an offer."

Not since he crashed his McLaren by flooring it at Peter Thiel's behest had there been such an expensive display of his impulsiveness.

Navaid visits

When Musk arrived back in Austin, he was visited by his friend from Queen's University, Navaid Farooq, now living in London. More than thirty years after they had bonded as socially awkward geeks playing strategy games and reading science fiction, Farooq was one of Musk's true friends, among the few who could ask him personal questions, discuss his father and family, and talk about occasional bouts of loneliness. On Saturday, when they flew down to Boca Chica to see Starbase, Farooq asked the question that many of Musk's friends had about Twitter: "Why are you doing this?"

Musk had moved beyond thinking just about free speech issues. He answered Farooq by describing how he hoped to make Twitter a great platform for user-generated content, including music and videos and stories. Celebrities, professional journalists, and ordinary people could post their creations, like they did on Substack or We-Chat, and get paid if they chose.

When they got to Starbase, Musk did his walk through the Starship assembly tents. As often happened, he got upset by how long some things were taking. That gave Farooq an opening, when they arrived back in Austin on Easter Sunday, to raise another of the questions that were bothering his friends. "What about your time and sanity?" he asked. "Tesla and SpaceX still need your help. How long would it take to turn Twitter around?"

"At least five years," Musk answered. "I would have to get rid of much of the staff. They don't work hard or even show up."

"Do you want to go through all that pain?" Farooq asked. "You slept on the factory floor for Tesla, doubled down for SpaceX. Do you really want to take all this on again?"

Musk did one of his very long pauses. "Yes, I actually would," he finally said. "I wouldn't mind."

A vision

Musk had already formulated the business case for why he was seeking to buy Twitter. He believed that he could quintuple Twitter's revenue to $26 billion by 2028, even as he reduced its reliance on advertising from 90 percent of the revenue to 45 percent. The new revenue would come from user subscriptions and data licensing. He also projected revenue from enabling users to make payments, including small ones for newspaper articles and other content through Twitter, like they could on WeChat.

"We have to match the functionality of WeChat," he told me after a call with bankers in April. "One of the most important things will be enabling people who create content to get paid on Twitter." An online payment system would have the added benefit of authenticating users. Twitter would be able to verify which users were real humans by requiring them to pay a small monthly fee and having their credit card information. If it worked, it could have a real impact on the internet at large. Twitter could serve as the platform that verified people's identity, and it could offer content creators, ranging from big media companies to individuals, new ways to make money for what they produced.

He also explained why he wanted to "open the aperture" of what speech was permissible on Twitter and avoid permanent bans of people, even those with fringe ideas. On talk radio and cable TV, there were separate information sources for progressives and conservatives. By pushing away right-wingers, the content moderators at Twitter, more than 90 percent of whom, he believed, were progressive Democrats, might be creating a similar Balkanization of social media. "We want to prevent a world in which people split off into their own echo chambers on social media, like going to Parler or Truth Social," he said. "We want to have one place where people with different viewpoints can interact. That would be a good thing for civilization." It was a noble sentiment, but he would end up undermining that important mission with statements and tweets that ended up chasing off progressives and mainstream media types to other social networks.

Then I pressed him on the question that Farooq and other friends had asked: Wouldn't all this be extremely difficult, time-consuming, and controversial, thus harming his missions at Tesla and SpaceX? "I don't think from a cognitive standpoint it's nearly as hard as SpaceX or Tesla," he said. "It's not like getting to Mars. It's not as hard as changing the entire industrial base of Earth to sustainable energy."

Yes, but why?

Musk had founded SpaceX, he liked to say, to increase the chances for the survival of human consciousness by making us a multiplanetary species. The grand rationale for Tesla and SolarCity was to lead the way to a sustainable energy future. Optimus and Neuralink were launched to create human-machine interfaces that would protect us from evil artificial intelligence.

And Twitter? "At first I thought it didn't fit into my primary large missions," he told me in April. "But I've come to believe it can be part of the mission of preserving civilization, buying our society more time to become multiplanetary." How so? Partly it involved free speech.

"There seems to be more and more group-think in the media, toeing the line, so if you weren't in step, you're just going to be ostracized or your voice will be shut off." For democracy to survive, it was important, he felt, to purge Twitter's woke culture and root out its biases, so people had the perception that it was an open space for all opinions.

But there were two other reasons, I think, that Musk wanted to own Twitter. The first was a simple one. It was fun, like an amusement park. It offered political smackdowns, intellectual gladiator matches, dopey memes, important public announcements, valuable marketing, bad puns, and unfiltered opinions. *Are you not entertained?*

And second, I believe there was a psychological, personal yearning. Twitter was the ultimate playground. As a kid, he was beaten and bullied on the playground, never having been endowed with the emotional dexterity needed to thrive on that rugged terrain. It instilled a deep pain and sometimes caused him to react to slights far too emotionally, but it also is what girded him to be able to face the world and fight every battle fiercely. When he felt dinged up, cornered, bullied, either online or in person, it took him back to a place that was super painful, where he was dissed by his father and bullied by his classmates. But now he could own the playground.

74

Hot and Cold

Twitter, April–June 2022

The deal

The Twitter board and Musk's lawyers finished work on the details of a purchase plan on Sunday, April 24. When Musk texted me at 10 a.m., he mentioned that he had stayed up all night. I asked if that was because he was working on the final deal points or was worried about buying Twitter. "No," he replied, "it was because I went to a party with friends and drank too much Red Bull."

Perhaps he should cut back on the Red Bull?

"But it gives me wings?" he replied.

He spent that day trying to find outside investors who would help him finance the purchase. He asked Kimbal, who declined. He was more successful with Larry Ellison. "Yes, of course," Ellison had answered when Musk asked earlier in the week if he was interested in investing in the deal.

"Roughly what dollar size?" Musk asked. "Not holding you to anything, but the deal is oversubscribed, so I have to reduce or kick out some participants."

"A billion," said Ellison, "or whatever you recommend."

Ellison had not tweeted in a decade. In fact, he could not remember his Twitter password, so Musk had to personally get it reset for him. But he believed that Twitter was important. "It's a real-time news service, and there's nothing really like it," he told me. "If you agree it's important for a democracy, then I thought it was worth making an investment in it."

One person who was eager to be in the deal was Sam Bankman-Fried, the soon-to-be-disgraced founder of the cryptocurrency exchange FTX, who believed that Twitter could be rebuilt on the blockchain. He claimed to be a supporter of effective altruism, and the founder of that movement, William MacAskill, texted Musk to try to arrange a meeting. So did Michael Grimes, Musk's primary banker at Morgan Stanley, who was working to put together the financing. "I'm backlogged with a mountain of critical work matters," Musk texted Grimes. "Is this urgent?"

Grimes replied that Bankman-Fried "would do the engineering for social media blockchain integration" and put $5 billion in the deal. He was available to fly to Austin the next day, if Musk was willing to meet with him.

Musk had discussed with Kimbal and others the possibility of using the blockchain as a backbone for Twitter. But despite the fun he had with Dogecoin and other cryptocurrencies, he was not a blockchain acolyte, and he felt it would be too sluggish to support fast-paced Twitter postings. So he had no desire to meet with Bankman-Fried. When Michael Grimes persisted by texting that Bankman-Fried "could do $5bn if everything vision lock," Musk responded with a "dislike" button. "Blockchain Twitter isn't possible, as the bandwidth and latency requirements cannot be supported by a peer to peer network." He said he might at some point meet with Bankman-Fried, "so long as I don't have to have a laborious blockchain debate."

Bankman-Fried then texted Musk directly to say he was "really excited about what you'll do with TWTR." He said he had $100 million of Twitter stock that he'd like to "roll," meaning that his Twitter stock would be converted into a stake in the new company once Musk took it private. "Sorry, who is sending this message?" Musk texted back. When Bankman-Fried apologized and introduced himself, Musk replied curtly, "You're welcome to roll."

That led Bankman-Fried to call Musk in May. "My bullshit detector went off like red alert on a Geiger counter," Musk says. Bankman-

Fried began talking rapidly, all about himself. "He was talking like he was on speed or Adderall, a mile a minute," Musk says. "I thought he was supposed to be asking me questions about the deal, but he kept telling me the things he was doing. And I was thinking, 'Dude, calm down.'" The feeling was mutual; Bankman-Fried thought Musk seemed nuts. The call lasted a half-hour, and Bankman-Fried ended up neither investing nor rolling over his Twitter stock.

The top investors Musk lined up included Ellison, Mike Moritz's Sequoia Capital, the cryptocurrency exchange Binance, Andreessen Horowitz, a Dubai-based fund, and a Qatar-based fund. (Part of the deal for the Qatar investment was promising to go there for the final of the World Cup.) Prince Alwaleed bin Talal of Saudi Arabia agreed to roll over the investment he already had in Twitter.

On Monday afternoon, April 25, the Twitter board accepted the plan. Assuming the stockholders approved it, the deal would close in the fall. "This is the right path," the company's cofounder Jack Dorsey texted Musk. "I'll continue to do whatever it takes to make it work."

Instead of celebrating, Musk flew from Austin down to Starbase in south Texas. There he called in to the regular nightly meeting on redesigning the Raptor engine and, for more than an hour, wrestled with how to deal with unexplained methane leaks they were experiencing. The Twitter news was the burning topic online and around the world, but not at the Raptor meeting. The engineers knew he liked to stay focused on the task at hand, and no one mentioned Twitter. Then he met Kimbal at a roadside café in Brownsville that featured local musicians. They stayed there until 2 a.m., sitting at a table right in front of the bandstand, just listening to the music.

Warning flags

On the Friday after the Twitter board accepted his offer, Musk flew to Los Angeles to have dinner with his four older boys at the rooftop restaurant of the Soho Club in West Hollywood. They did not use Twitter very much and were puzzled. Why was he buying it? Just from their questioning, it was clear that they didn't think it was a great idea.

"I think it's important to have a digital public square that's inclusive and trusted," he replied. Then, after a pause, he asked, "How else are we going to get Trump elected in 2024?"

It was a joke. But with Musk, it was sometimes hard to tell, even for his kids. Maybe even for himself. They were aghast. He reassured them that he was just kidding.

By the end of the dinner, they accepted most of his reasons for buying Twitter but were still uncomfortable. "They thought that I was asking for trouble," he says. They were, of course, right. They also knew that their father actually liked asking for trouble.

That trouble began a week later, on May 6, when he strode into Twitter headquarters in San Francisco to meet with its management. Despite his tweets disparaging remote work, the lavish Art Deco headquarters was still almost empty when he got there. Even Agrawal wasn't there. Having tested positive for COVID, he joined the meeting remotely.

The meeting was led by Twitter CFO Ned Segal, who rubbed Musk the wrong way. In its public disclosures, Twitter estimated that bots and fake accounts made up about 5 percent of its users. Musk's own experience convinced him that was wildly understating the problem. Twitter allowed—indeed encouraged—users to create new accounts under different names and aliases. Some troll farms burned through hundreds of identities. Not only did these fake accounts pollute the service; they were not monetizable.

He asked Segal to explain the process the company used to determine the number of fake accounts. The Twitter executives suspected that Musk was laying the ground for revising or backing out of his purchase offer, so they were cautious about answering. "They said they didn't know the precise answer," Musk said right afterward. "I was like, 'What do you mean? You don't know?' The whole exchange was so preposterous that if it was in that *Silicon Valley* sitcom, you'd think this is just too ridiculous. My jaw was really aching from hitting the floor so many times."

When annoyed, Musk often challenges people with very specific questions. With the Twitter execs, he unleashed a barrage. How many lines on average each day did their software coders write? His Auto-pilot team at Tesla had two hundred software engineers, so why did Twitter have twenty-five hundred? Twitter spent $1 billion a year on servers. What are the functions taking up most of that computing time and storage, and how were they ranked? He found it hard to get straight answers. At Tesla, he fired people for not knowing such details. "It was the worst diligence meeting I have ever witnessed in my life," he said. "I did not make the deal contingent on full due diligence, but I did believe they could justify their own public disclosures. Otherwise it was fraud."

Second thoughts

Musk's pointed questions and angry challenges reflected the fact that he was not sure he wanted to go through with the deal. On most days he did. Sort of. But his appetite fluctuated and his emotions were conflicted.

He felt strongly that he had overpaid, which was true. Advertising spending was down in the summer of 2022 because of uncertainty about the economy, and the stock price of social media companies was plummeting. Facebook had fallen 40 percent so far that year, and Snap 70 percent. Twitter was now trading at 30 percent below the $54.20 that Musk had offered, a sign that Wall Street was not certain the deal would actually close. As his father had taught him when they visited amusement parks in Florida, a Coke that costs too much does not taste as good. So in the back of his mind when he went to his meeting at Twitter was a desire to lay the ground for either getting out of the deal or repricing it.

"There's no way to move forward after what they said," he told me right after his meeting at Twitter headquarters. "The forty-four-billion-dollar price requires taking on a lot of debt, both the company and me personally. I think Twitter may be headed off the rails. It might work out, at a much lower price, I mean literally half or something."

He also was having broader doubts about taking on such a messy challenge. "I've got a bad habit of biting off more than I can chew," he admitted. "I think I just need to think about Twitter less. Even this conversation right now is not time well spent."

The following week, at around 4 a.m. Central Time on May 13, he unleashed a tweet: "Twitter deal temporarily on hold pending details supporting calculation that spam/fake accounts do indeed represent less than 5% of users." Twitter shares fell 20 percent in pre-market trading. Jared Birchall, his business manager, and Alex Spiro, his lawyer, desperately urged him to walk back the declaration. It might be possible to wriggle out of the deal, they told him, but it was legally perilous for him to be announcing his desire to do so. Two hours later, Musk posted a four-word addendum: "Still committed to acquisition."

It was one of the few times I witnessed Musk being unsure of himself. Over the next five months, through the close of the deal in October, he would at times express great excitement about the chance to turn Twitter into an "everything app," featuring financial services and great content, while helping to save democracy in the process. At other times, he would get coldly angry, threaten to sue the Twitter board and management, and insist that he wanted to call the whole deal off.

Town hall

Without consulting his lawyers, Musk agreed to attend a virtual town hall meeting with Twitter employees on June 16. "It was one of those examples of Elon just being Elon and accepting an invitation without talking to any of us or getting prepped," Birchall says. He did it sitting in his Austin living room and initially had trouble getting into the virtual conference because it was held on Google Meet, and he didn't have a Google account on his laptop. He finally got in on his iPhone. While we were waiting, one of the meeting organizers asked, "Does anyone know who Jared Birchall is?" He was denied entry.

I wondered whether Musk had some scheme in mind. Perhaps he was going to throw a little bomb into the works by provoking a revolt of the Twitter staff. Maybe he would tell them, either out of calculation or his compulsion to be brutally honest, what he really thought: that they were wrong to kick off Trump, that their content moderation policies crossed the line into unjustifiable censorship, that the staff had been infected by the woke-mind virus, that people should show up to work in person, and that the company was way over-staffed. The ensuing explosion might not scuttle the deal, but it could shake up the chessboard.

Musk didn't do that. Instead, he was rather conciliatory on these hot-button issues. Leslie Berland, the chief marketing officer of Twitter, began with the issue of content moderation. Instead of sim-ply invoking his mantra about the goodness of free speech, Musk went deeper and made a distinction between what people should be allowed to post and what Twitter should cause to be amplified and spread. "I think there's a distinction between freedom of speech and freedom of reach," he said. "Anyone can just go into the middle of Times Square and say anything, even deny the Holocaust. But that doesn't mean that needs to be promoted to millions of people."

He also explained why some limits on hate speech were impor-tant. "You want as many people as possible on Twitter," he said. "For that to happen, people must enjoy being on Twitter. If they're being harassed or made uncomfortable, they're not going to use Twitter. We have to strike this balance of allowing people to say what they want to say, but also making people comfortable."

When asked about diversity, equity, and inclusion, Musk pushed back a bit. "I believe in a strict meritocracy," he said. "Whoever is doing great work, they get more responsibility. And that's that." But he also insisted he had not become an ideological conservative. "My political views, I think, are moderate, close to the center." He did not please most people on the call, but he did avoid causing any explosions.

75

Father's Day

June 2022

Feeding Tau *(top left)*; X watching a rocket launch video
on Musk's plane *(top right)*; with Lord Norman Foster
in Austin, dreaming of a house *(bottom)*

All my kids

"Happy Father's Day. I love all my kids so much."

On its surface, Musk's tweet at 2 a.m. on Father's Day—June 19, 2022—seemed innocuous, even sweet. But lurking beneath the word *all* was a drama. His trans daughter Jenna had just turned eighteen and gone to court in Los Angeles, where she lived with her mother, to change her name officially from Xavier Musk to Vivian Jenna Wilson. She called herself "Jenna," which was similar to the name that her mother Justine used, Jennifer Wilson, before she met and married Musk. "I no longer live with or wish to be related to my biological father in any way, shape or form," she declared to the court.

Musk had made peace with Jenna's transitioning, even though he had not embraced the protocols about listing one's pronouns. He believed that she was rejecting him because of her political ideology. "It's full-on communism, and a general sentiment that if you're rich, you're evil," he said.

It was all very jangling for Musk. "We are simultaneously being told that gender differences do not exist and that genders are so profoundly different that irreversible surgery is the only option," he tweeted that week. "Perhaps someone wiser than me can explain this dichotomy." Then, almost as a memo to himself as well as a pronouncement, he added, "It is a better world if we are all less judgy."

Jenna's rejection made for a painful Father's Day. "He loves Jenna so much and truly accepts her," says Grimes, who stayed friendly with her. "I've never seen him as heartbroken about anything. I know he'd do anything to be able to see her or have her, like, accept him again."

Adding to the turmoil was that the secret of the twin children he had with Shivon Zilis was made public. When they were born, they had been given her last name. But Musk's estrangement from his daughter caused him to want to change that. "When Jenna deleted 'Musk' from her name, he was just really sad," Zilis says. "And he asked me, 'Hey, would you be open to our twins taking my name?'" The court filing they made soon leaked.

That's when Grimes discovered that Zilis, whom she considered a friend, had given birth to twins with Musk. When she confronted Musk, he simply said Zilis had the right to do what she wanted. Grimes was outraged. By Father's Day, they were all involved in contentious discussions over such issues as whether Zilis and her twins could spend time with Grimes's children X and Y. It was a mess.

Musk and Zilis continued to attend weekly Neuralink meetings together without commenting on their parenting status. The way to defuse an awkward situation, he felt, was to joke about it on Twitter. "Doing my best to help the underpopulation crisis," he tweeted. "A collapsing birth rate is the biggest danger civilization faces by far."

Techno Mechanicus Musk

As if Father's Day 2022 was a multiplayer game, it had yet one other subplot. Secretly, Musk and Grimes had a third child that week, a son named Techno Mechanicus Musk. The boy, who was birthed by a surrogate mother, was nicknamed Tau, after the Greek letter representing the irrational number that is equal to two times pi. Its approximation, 6.28, reflected Musk's own birthday, June 28.

They kept the existence of this third child private. But Musk was soon bonding with him. On a visit to Grimes's home when Tau was two months old, he sat on the floor feeding baby food to Tau, who kept reaching up to play with the stubble on his father's chin. "Tau is so amazing," Grimes says. "He came out with eyes that could just see so deeply into your soul, with so much knowledge. He looks like a little Spock. He's definitely a Vulcan."

A few weeks later, Musk was sitting quietly between meetings at Giga Texas, scrolling through the news on his iPhone, when he saw Lucid Motors' report of its lame quarterly sales numbers. He laughed for a few minutes, then dashed off a tweet. "I had more kids in Q2 than they made cars!" he wrote. Then he kept laughing loudly to himself. "I mean, I love my own humor, even if others don't," he said. "I kill me."

Around that time, the *Wall Street Journal* started working on a story about an alleged one-night stand that Musk had with the estranged wife of Google cofounder Sergey Brin a few months earlier. The rationale for the story was that it had harmed relations between the two men. Right after the story broke, they were at a party together, and Musk maneuvered himself into a position where he could take a selfie with Brin, which Brin tried to avoid. Musk sent the picture to the *New York Post* to rebut the allegation that they'd had a falling-out. "The amount of attention on me has gone supernova, which super sucks," he tweeted. "Unfortunately, even trivial articles about me generate a lot of clicks :(Will try my best to be heads down focused on doing useful things for civilization."

Keeping his head down, however, did not come naturally.

Sins of the father

Level five of Father's Day 2022 may have been the spookiest of them all. It involved, alas, his own estranged father, Errol Musk.

In an email to Elon dated "Father's Day," Errol wrote, "I'm sitting here freezing cold in a hanger wrapped in blankets and newspapers. There is no electricity. If I'm bothered to write to you like this, you can bother to read it." That was followed by a rambling screed in which he called Biden a "freak, criminal, pedophile president" who was out to destroy everything that the U.S. stood for, "including you." Black leaders in South Africa, he said, were engaged in anti-white racism. "With no Whites here, the Blacks will go back to the trees." Vladimir Putin was "the only world leader talking." He followed up with a subsequent email showing a picture of a stadium scoreboard saying, "TRUMP WON—F**K Joe Biden," adding the comment, "This is irrefutable."

Errol's letter was startling on so many levels, most notably his racism. But one other aspect would have an unsettling resonance later that year: how conspiratorial he had become. He had gone down the alt-right rabbit holes of labeling Biden a pedophile and praising Putin. And in other posts and emails, he denounced COVID as "a lie," attacked COVID expert Anthony Fauci, and claimed that the vaccines were deadly, positions Elon would later echo.

His description of his cold and impoverished circumstances was meant as a rebuke to his son for no longer supporting him financially. Up until recently, Elon had been sending, off and on, varying amounts of monthly stipends. This began back in 2010, with payments of $2,000 a month to help Errol support his younger children after his second divorce. Over the years, Elon would occasionally provide more funding, then cut back whenever Errol gave interviews aggrandizing his own role in his son's success. When Errol had heart surgery in 2015, Elon's support was temporarily increased to $5,000 a month. But he cut off the funds after learning that Errol had impregnated Jana, the stepdaughter he had raised from age four, whom Elon and Kimbal considered a half-sister.

At the end of March 2022, Errol wrote asking that his stipends be restored. "At 76, I cannot generate income easily," he wrote. "The alternative for me is starvation and unbearable humiliation or death by suicide. Death by suicide does not worry me, but it should worry you. The truth is too well known. You will be ruined, make no mistake, and people will know who you really are, or have become." He blamed Elon's attitude on the "National Socialist, cruel, self-serving and cowardly maternal family background," adding, "Has the wickedness that was the Haldeman's prevailed?"

Around the time of Father's Day, Elon resumed the $2,000 monthly payments. But his financial manager Jared Birchall asked Errol to stop making a series of YouTube videos, titled *Dad of a Genius*, that he had produced with a clinical psychologist. Errol reacted angrily. "My silence to enable the devilish sh,t to continue brewing is not worth $2,000," he shot back. "It's also wrong to silence me. I have much to teach people."

As if following a perverse script, Father's Day 2022 brought one more complication to this situation. Errol revealed that he had fathered a second child with Jana, a daughter. "The only thing we are on Earth for is to reproduce," he said. "If I could have another child I would. I can't see any reason not to."

Bonding attempts

Through all of the tumult in his personal life, Musk had one lovely steadying influence: Talulah Riley, the English actress who married him in 2010 and, after a divorce and remarriage, finally left him to return to village England tranquility in 2015. She continued to feel warmly toward him, and Musk felt the same about her, though he was afflicted by preferring extreme heat and cold rather than warmth in relationships.

When a close friend of hers died in 2021, Musk flew to England and spent a day at her house. "We just watched stupid TV and laughed and hung out and he just made me laugh instead of cry," she says. And amid his personal and Twitter-deal tumults in the early summer of 2022, she flew to Los Angeles and met him for dinner at the Beverly Hills Hotel.

She traveled with her new boyfriend, the young actor Thomas Brodie-Sangster, to publicize a movie they had costarred in, *Pistol*, about the pioneering punk rock band The Sex Pistols. But Brodie-Sangster did not come to the dinner. Instead, Musk and Riley were joined by his four older boys, who had bonded with her over the years. "I can't get over how completely gorgeous they all are," she texted me. "Griffin is handsome, hilarious and still an utter charmer, Damian has blossomed into an incredibly sophisticated and beautiful soul, Kai is still a thoroughly decent chap and now so gorgeously geeky, and Saxon's language development is more than I could have possibly hoped for—we had full and detailed conversations. Except at one point he said, 'The interesting thing about you and Elon is you have a significant age gap . . . But you look the same.' 😂😂."

The reunion was very emotional. There was a part of her that still loved Musk. When she got back to her hotel room that night, Brodie-Sangster had to cope with her bursting into tears.

Musk reacted to his family turmoil in the summer of 2022 by launching another surge, this one fatherly. He took his four older boys along with Grimes and X to Spain to vacation with James and Elisabeth Murdoch and their children. James, a member of the Tesla board, is the liberal member of the Rupert Murdoch family, and Elisabeth is more so. They provided Musk with a calming personal influence and political counterbalance.

A few weeks later, he and the boys went to Rome, where they were granted an audience with Pope Francis. Musk tweeted out a photo of the meeting, which showed him in an ill-fitting suit, Saxon twisted nervously, and the other boys dressed in black shirts and looking somber. "My suit is tragic," Musk admitted. When the boys woke up the next day, they were upset that their father had tweeted out the picture. One of them even cried. On a group chat they do with their father, even when traveling together, one asked him to not tweet out pictures of them without their permission. Musk got depressed, dropped off the group chat, and a few minutes later sent word that they were returning to the U.S.

A house, not a home

Musk realized that it was difficult to have a stable family life if he didn't have a family home. So amid the domestic drama in the summer of 2022, he started dreaming about a home of his own in Austin. He considered a few houses for sale, but deemed them too expensive. Instead, he decided to build one on a sprawling horse farm, with a tranquil lake, that he had bought right across the Colorado River from Giga Texas. He thought he might use other parts of the property for Neuralink and his other companies.

He walked the property one Saturday night with Grimes and Omead Afshar, who was in charge of building Giga Texas, and they came up with a variety of ideas, including that The Boring Company could dig a tunnel under the river to connect the house and the factory. He also walked the property a few days later with Shivon Zilis. "One thing I've been harassing him about, lovingly, is finding a place he can call home," she says. "He needs a place where his soul resides, and that's what the horse farm will be for him."

One hot afternoon in the summer of 2022, Musk sat under a pop-up canopy on the property with Lord Norman Foster, the architect who designed, among other things, the space-age circular headquarters of Apple for Steve Jobs. Foster had flown from London, carrying his sketch pad, to brainstorm with Musk. Sitting at a card table, Musk looked through some of Foster's sketches, then began free-associating ideas. "It should be like something fell out of space, like a structure from another galaxy landed in the lake," Musk said.

Birchall, who was with them, Googled images of futuristic buildings, while Foster made more sketches in his notebook. Maybe, Musk suggested, a shard of glass coming out of the lake? The bottom floor could be partly submerged in the water, accessible by a tunnel from another structure on the shore.

I later commented that it did not actually seem like a family home. Musk agreed. "It's more an art project than a house," he explained. He put off building it.

76

Starbase Shake-up

SpaceX, 2022

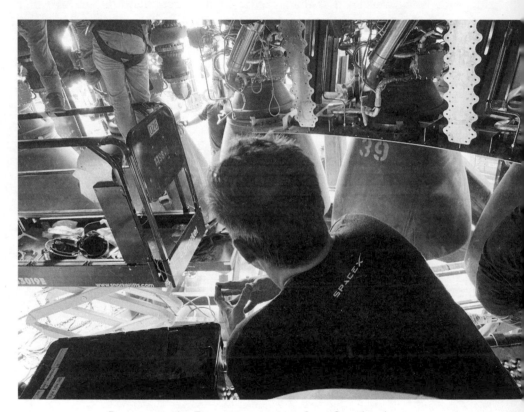

Inspecting the Raptor engines under a Starship booster

Showing off Starship

Always vigilant against complacency, Musk decided in early 2022 that it was time for another surge in Boca Chica. It had been six months since he had pushed Andy Krebs and the team in south Texas to stack Starship on the launchpad. Now he wanted to have a public presentation of the rocket. This time the two stages would be stacked by Mechazilla's chopstick arms.

Bill Riley warned that it would be hard to get this done before the end of February, so Musk used Twitter as a forcing mechanism. He tweeted out that there would be a public showing of Starship at 8 p.m. on Thursday, February 10, 2022.

The night of the presentation, he had dinner at Flaps, the funky-casual restaurant for SpaceX employees. Joining him were three of NASA's top directors, all women: Janet Petro of the Kennedy Space Center at Cape Canaveral, Lisa Watson-Morgan of the Human Landing System Program, and Vanessa Wyche of Johnson Space Center in Houston.

X toddled up to the table and started eating blue cheese dip with a fork. Musk joked that X served as his "cuteness prop." Petro whispered to me, "I'm suppressing my maternal instincts," but she finally succumbed and took the fork away from him, handing him a spoon instead.

"He's fearless," Musk says. "He could probably use more fear instincts. It's genetic." Yes, but it was also the result of the free-range way Musk has brought him up. It's not in Musk's nature to be doting.

"Falcon nine," said X, pointing in the distance.

"No," his father corrected him. "Starship."

"Ten, nine, eight," X said.

"People say he's so smart to be able to count backwards," Musk said. "But I'm not sure he can count forward."

Musk asked the NASA guests whether they had children, and their responses prompted him to give his thoughts once again on how declining birthrates are a threat to the future of human consciousness. "Among my friends, the average number of kids is one," he said.

"Some have zero. I try to set a good example." He didn't mention that he'd just had three more children.

The conversation turned to China, which was the only entity that was launching as many orbital missions as SpaceX. NASA itself was not even in the game. "If China gets to the moon before we do again, it will be a Sputnik moment," he told the NASA directors. "It's going to be a shock when we wake up and realize they got to the moon while we were suing each other." He said that when he visits China, he is often asked how that country can be more innovative. "The answer I give is to challenge authority."

Later that night, a crowd of a few hundred workers, reporters, government officials, and locals gathered in front of the stacked Starship, lit by spotlights. "There have to be things that inspire you, that move your heart," Musk said in his speech. "Being a space-faring civilization, making science fiction not fiction, is one of those." During the presentation, I sat on the side with Krebs, who had not yet decided to leave SpaceX, and we talked about how he had survived being in the line of Musk's fire at this spot seven months earlier. When I asked whether it was worth it, he nodded up at Mechazilla. "Every time I see the tower my heart soars," he said.

After the presentation, Musk wandered over to a group gathered at the tiki bar behind the main Starbase building. After a few minutes, the Inspiration4 astronaut Jared Isaacman, who had flown his own high-performance jet in for the presentation, joined the group.

Isaacman has a quietly confident humility that relaxes Musk. It was good, he remarked, that Musk decided not to go to space himself after Branson and Bezos did. "That would have been strike three," he said. It would have looked like billionaire-boys' narcissism. "We were one strike away from Americans saying 'Screw space.'"

"Yes," Musk said with a rueful laugh, "it was better to send up four people out of central casting."

Jolting the team

The Starlink satellites being built in Seattle were beginning to pile up in July 2022. Falcon 9 rockets were launching from Cape Canaveral at least once a week, each flight carrying about fifty Starlinks into orbit. But Musk had been counting on the mammoth Starship to be regularly launching by then from the pad in Boca Chica. As usual, he had been unrealistic about schedules.

"Do you want me to send a few people down to Boca?" asked Mark Juncosa, who had moved to Seattle to oversee Starlink production.

"Yes," Musk replied. "You should go there as well." It was time for a management shake-up. By the beginning of August, Juncosa was sweeping around the assembly-line tents in Boca Chica like a whirlwind, kicking up dust.

Juncosa is blessed with a lot of Musk's craziness. With his wild hair and even wilder eyes, he jumps around and spins his phone in a way that creates a high-energy field around him. "He is quite charismatic in a goofy, hard-ass way," Musk says. "He can tell people they are fucking up and their idea sucks, but do it in a way that doesn't make them mad. He's my Mark Antony."

Musk and Juncosa liked the team in Boca Chica, especially Riley and Patel, but felt they were not tough enough. "Bill is a great person, but he has a hard time giving anyone negative feedback and just can't fire anyone," Musk told me. SpaceX president Gwynne Shotwell felt the same about Patel, who had overseen the building of the facilities. "Sam works his ass off," she said, "but he doesn't know how to give Elon bad news. Sam and Bill are chickens."

Musk held a video call with the Starship team on August 4 from a conference room at Giga Texas, where he was preparing for the annual Tesla shareholder meeting that afternoon. As they walked him through slides, he got increasingly angry. "These timelines are bullshit, a mega fail," he explained. "Like, no fucking way these should take so long." He decreed that they would start having meetings on Starship every night, seven days a week. "We are going to go through the first-principles algorithm every night, questioning requirements and deleting," he said. "That's what we did to unfuck the bullshit that was Raptor."

How soon, he asked, would it take to get a booster onto the launchpad to test the engines? Ten days, he was told. "That's too long," he replied. "This is critical for all of human destiny. It's hard to change destiny. You can't just do it from nine to five."

Then he abruptly ended the meeting. "See you guys tonight," he said to the Boca Chica team. "I've got a Tesla shareholder meeting this afternoon, and I haven't even seen the slides yet."

The tiki bar break-in

When Musk arrived in Boca Chica from Austin late that night, after conducting a Tesla shareholder meeting that resembled a fan club convention, he went right to the Starbase conference room, where the team had regathered. It looked like a scene out of *Star Wars*. Musk brought along X, who despite the late hour was fully charged and ran around the table shouting, "Rockets!" Also there was Grimes, who had dyed her hair pink and green. Juncosa had grown an even wilder beard. Shotwell had flown in from Los Angeles to help manage the personnel shake-up; a no-nonsense morning person, she commented that it was past her bedtime. The only other woman among the dozen or so at the table was Shana Diez, an MIT aeronautics engineer who had worked at SpaceX for fourteen years and, having impressed Musk with her plainspoken competence, was now director of Starship engineering. Filling out the table were the other members of the team—Bill Riley, Joe Petrzelka, Andy Krebs, Jake McKenzie—all wearing the standard uniform of jeans and a black T-shirt.

Musk again pushed them to get a booster on the launchpad to test the engines as soon as possible. Ten days would be too long. He was particularly interested in determining how important the heat shields around the engines were. He was always looking for ways to delete parts, especially those that added mass to the booster. "It doesn't seem like we need shields in all those places," he said. "I went out there with a flashlight, and the heat shields are blocking things so you can't see jack shit."

The meeting meandered, as his tend to do, and before they could agree on a timetable for the tests, they had lapsed into discussing the Quentin Tarantino movie *True Romance*. After more than an hour,

Shotwell tried to bring it to a conclusion. "What have we decided?" she asked.

The answer was not exactly clear. Musk was staring off into the distance, thinking. Everyone had seen this trance before. At some point, after processing the information on his own, he would issue a pronouncement. But it was now after 1 a.m., and the engineers gradually drifted away, leaving Musk to think alone.

As the participants wandered out of the conference room and into the parking lot, they gravitated around Juncosa, who was spinning his phone, holding court, and clearly not ready to retire to his Airstream trailer for the night. In addition to being pumped up, he knew that the troops were unnerved by the personnel shake-up that was brewing and could use some rallying. Like a high-school team captain who knew just what level of naughtiness was appropriate, he proposed that they break into the nearby employee tiki bar and throw a party. Using a credit card to jimmy the lock, he led a dozen followers into the bar and designated one of them to start pouring beer, Macallan Scotch, and Elijah Craig Small Batch Bourbon. "If we get in trouble, we can blame it all on you, Jake," he said, pointing at McKenzie, the youngest, shyest, and least likely of them to break into a bar.

Without Musk around, Juncosa was able to loosen everyone up but also impart a few lessons. He made fun of one of them for being hesitant to tell Musk that a testing facility wasn't going to be ready in time and then danced around him flapping his elbows and making chicken sounds. When a young engineer tried to impress him by describing his adventures as an extreme skier, Juncosa whipped out his phone and showed a video of himself skiing wildly in Alaska as he outran an avalanche.

"Is that really you?" the awed engineer asked.

"Yes," Juncosa replied. "You got to take risks. You got to *love* taking risks."

Around that time—3:24 a.m., to be precise—my phone buzzed with a text message from Musk, who was still awake in his little house a mile away. "The prior schedule for the booster was ten days to pad," it read. "However, I'm 90% sure that we will discover our next showstopper development issue without needing B7 to be complete."

I showed it to McKenzie to decipher, and he showed it to Juncosa. They became silent for a moment. What it meant was that Musk had processed what he heard in the meeting and decided that they would not wait ten days to move the booster, known as B7, to the launch-pad for testing. They would do it before they installed all thirty-three engines. Musk followed up moments later with further details: "One way or another, we are going to put B7 back on the launch mount by midnight tonight or sooner." In other words, they would do it in one day, not ten days. He had ordered yet another surge.

High bay

That morning, after a few hours of sleep, Musk went to one of the high bay assembly buildings, wearing his "Occupy Mars" black T-shirt, to watch as Booster 7 was outfitted with Raptor engines. Climbing a steep industrial ladder, he clambered onto a platform be-neath the booster. It was crammed with cables, engine parts, tools, swinging chains, and at least forty people working shoulder-to-shoulder as they attached engines and welded shrouds. Musk was the only one not wearing a helmet.

"Why is that part needed?" he asked one of the veteran engineers, Kale Odhner, who took Musk's presence in stride, giving matter-of-fact answers while continuing his work. Musk's inspection visits to the assembly areas are so frequent that the workers barely pay atten-tion to him unless he gives them orders or asks a question. "Why can't that be done faster?" is one of his favorites. Sometimes he just stands and stares in silence for four or five minutes.

After more than an hour, he climbed down from the platform and then ran, lumbering, the two hundred yards across a parking lot to the canteen. "I think he does that so everyone can see how much he's hustling," Andy Krebs said. I later asked Musk if that was his reason. "No," he laughed. "I did it because I forgot to put on sunscreen and didn't want to get burned." But then he added, "It's true that if they see the general out on the battlefield, the troops are going to be motivated. Wherever Napoleon was, that's where his armies would do best. Even if I don't do anything but show up, they'll look at me and say that at least I wasn't spending all night partying." Apparently, he had found out about the tiki bar escapade.

Shortly after midnight, the deadline Musk had set, a truck with the upright booster started moving the half-mile down the road in Boca Chica from the assembly high bay to the launch site. Grimes drove over from their little house to witness the spectacle with X, who danced around the slowly moving rocket. When the booster got to the launch area and was placed upright on the pad, it made a dramatic scene glistening under an almost-full moon.

All was going well until a line broke loose and hydraulic fluid, a mix of oil and water, started spraying over the area. Everyone got doused, including Grimes and X. She was initially freaked out that it was some toxic chemical, but Musk told her not to worry. "I love the smell of hydraulic fluid in the morning," he said, echoing a line from *Apocalypse Now*. X likewise was unfazed, even when Grimes rushed him back to the house to bathe. "I feel like he's developing a higher than average tolerance for danger," Musk said. Showing only the tiniest bit of self-awareness, he added, "His tolerance for danger is almost problematic, honestly."

77

Optimus Prime

Tesla, 2021–2022

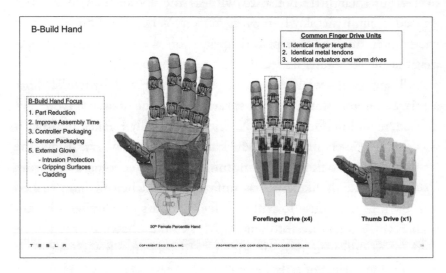

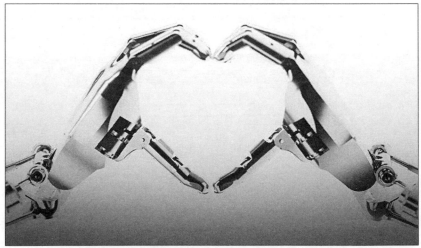

A slide showing components of Optimus's hand *(top)*;
the robot making a heart, the logo for AI Day 2 *(bottom)*

Human touch

When Musk announced his plans to build Optimus in August 2021, an actress dressed in a white body suit tottered around the stage emulating a robot. A few days later, Tesla's design chief, Franz von Holzhausen, convened a group to begin building the real thing: a robot that could emulate a human.

Musk gave one directive: it was to be a *humanoid* robot. In other words, it was supposed to look like a person rather than a mechanical contraption with wheels or four legs like Boston Dynamics and others were making. Most workspaces and tools are designed to accommodate the way humans do things, so Musk believed that a robot should approximate human forms in order to operate naturally. "We want to make it as human as possible," von Holzhausen told the ten engineers and designers seated around his conference table. "But we can also add improvements to what humans can do."

They started with the hand. Von Holzhausen picked up a power drill, and they studied how the fingers and heel of the palm interacted with it. At first it seemed sensible to consider making a hand with four fingers, since the pinky didn't seem necessary. But in addition to looking creepy, that turned out not to be quite as functional. Instead, they decided to elongate the pinky, so that it was more useful. But they also did one simplification: they could make each finger with two joints, not three.

Another improvement was to make the bottom of the palm longer so that it could wrap around a power tool, relieving the thumb from bearing as much of the load. That would make Optimus's hand more powerful than a human's. They also considered even more innovative bionic tactics, such as having strong magnets in the tip of each finger. That idea was rejected; too many devices could get messed up by magnets.

Perhaps the fingers could flap away from the palm, not just toward it? Maybe the wrist should be able to hinge farther back, as well as forward? Everyone at the table started flapping their hands and wrists to see what that would mean. "That would be useful if the robot needed to push against a wall," said von Holzhausen. "It could do it without putting pressure on the fingers." Someone suggested that the hand could be made to go so far back that the fingers touched the arm. That would allow the arm to apply pressure to something without the hand even being involved. "Wow," said von Holzhausen, "but people would get a bit freaked out. Let's not go that far."

"Now the challenging part," von Holzhausen said near the end of the two-hour meeting. "How do we make this sausage look good?" He doled out assignments for what they would show Musk at the weekly review meetings. "Start with figuring out what the fingers will look like and how they will taper, especially since we're going to elongate the pinky. Elon wants feminine tapers for the fingers."

Young Frankenstein

Human bodies, Musk and his engineers discovered, are amazing. For example, at one of the weekly meetings, they discussed how our fingers not only apply pressure to things; they also could feel pressure. How could they best make Optimus's fingers assess pressure? "We could look at the current in the actuator of the finger joint, which will correlate to the pressure being applied to the tip," one engineer suggested. Another thought of putting capacitors in the fingertips, like in a touch screen, or perhaps a barometric pressure sensor or chip embedded in rubber, or even a tiny camera inside a gel fingertip. "What are the differences in cost?" von Holzhausen asked. They decided that measuring the pressure using current flow in the actuator of the joint would be most effective because it wouldn't add parts.

No matter how hectic his schedule, Musk tried to make the weekly Optimus design sessions. For one of them in February, he was at the VIP room in the Miami Marlins' stadium attending a listening party hosted by Kanye West, known as Ye, for his new album, *Donda 2*. He was standing with rappers French Montana and Rick Ross, eating tacos and talking about cryptocurrency, when he got a text from Omead Afshar reminding him about the 9 p.m. Optimus meeting. Musk dialed in, leaving his phone camera on, unintentionally allowing the Optimus team to witness the party in the background. Members of Ye's VIP posse gave Musk curious glances as he paced around the room wiggling his fingers and discussing the number of actuators that would be needed to give Optimus's hands enough dexterity. "It needs to be able to pick up a pencil from any angle," Musk said. One rapper in the background nodded and started wiggling his fingers.

Sometimes the Optimus meetings rambled on for more than two hours as Musk considered ideas large and small. "Maybe the robots could swap their arms with different tools," someone suggested. Musk rejected that. At another meeting, he asked whether there should be a screen where the face would be. "It can be display only," he said. "It doesn't need to be a touch screen. But you should be able to know what it's doing from afar." They decided it was a good idea, but not necessary for the first iteration of Optimus.

The discussions often elicited Musk's futuristic fantasies. The team prepared a video simulation of Optimus working in a colony on Mars, which led to a lengthy discussion about whether the robots on Mars would be working on their own or under the direction of human supervisors. Von Holzhausen tried to bring things back to Earth. "I think the Mars simulation is fun," he finally interjected, "but we should do one that shows the robots working in one of our factories, maybe performing the repetitive tasks that no one wants to do." At another meeting they discussed whether they could put an Optimus in the driver's seat of a Robotaxi to meet the legal requirements of a car needing a driver. "Do you remember the original *Blade Runner* movie did something like that," Musk said. "Also the most recent *Cyberpunk* game." He liked taking the fiction out of science fiction.

Other ideas seemed more influenced by the silly side of Musk's limbic system. "Maybe we should have the charger cord plug into the butt," he joked at one point. After a few loud laughs, he rejected the idea. "The giggle factor would be too high," he said. "For humans, orifices are a big deal."

"This is reminding me of *Young Frankenstein*," he said at one point, referring to the Mel Brooks movie parody. "It's epic." But that triggered a more serious discussion of how to make sure that the robots did not turn into monsters, which was the original impulse that led Musk into the field of artificial intelligence and robotics. At one meeting he went over the "stop command path," which would give a human the ultimate power to override a robot. "There can't be a scenario where somebody could gain access to the mothership and take control of the robots in a way that's malicious," he said, ruling out the use of any electronic signals that could be hacked. Citing Asimov's rules of robotics, he game-planned strategies that would allow humans to prevail over "deadly robot armies."

Even as he envisioned futuristic scenarios, Musk focused on making Optimus a business. By June 2022, the team had completed a simulation of robots carrying boxes around a factory. He liked the fact that, as he put it, "our robots are going to work harder than humans work." He came to believe that Optimus would become a main driver of Tesla profits. "The Optimus humanoid robot," he told analysts, "has the potential to be more significant than the vehicle business."

With these profits in mind, Musk pushed the Optimus team to create a detailed chart of any functionality they wanted and the cost of manufacturing it at scale. For example, one spreadsheet looked at the three ways a human wrist can move: it can wave the hand up and down, move it to the left or right, or rotate. Achieving two of these "degrees of freedom," the engineers calculated, would mean that each wrist would cost $712. Adding extra actuators to achieve three degrees of freedom would bring the cost to $1,103. Musk marveled as he studied the ways his wrist could move and which muscles were involved. He then said the robot should have the same capability as a human. "The answer is we want the three degrees of freedom, so we have to figure out how we get there more efficiently," he said. "This is a shitty design. I eyeball it and it looks terrible. Use the damn lift gate actuators from our cars, which we know how to make cheaply."

Every week he went over the most recent timetables and expressed, often rather strongly, his dissatisfaction. "Pretend we are a startup about to run out of money," he said at one of these sessions. "Faster. Faster! Please mark anytime a date has slipped. All bad news should be given loudly and often. Good news can be said quietly and once."

Walking

One of the most difficult challenges was getting Optimus to walk. X was then almost two and learning to do the same, and Musk kept comparing how humans and machines learn. "At first kids walk flat-footed, then they begin walking on their toes, but they still walk like a monkey," he said. "It takes them quite a while before they walk like an adult. The gait is rather complicated."

In March the team opened their weekly meeting with a video celebrating a milestone: "First steps on the ground!" By April they had conquered the next level: getting Optimus to walk while carrying a box. "But we have not been able to coordinate the arms and legs to keep it in balance," an engineer said. One problem was that the head had to swivel for the robot to see its surroundings. "If we put in several cameras," Musk suggested, "we won't need to swivel the head."

Musk brought some toys, including a robot that could follow a person with its eyes and another that could break-dance, to one of the design reviews in mid-July. He believed that toys could offer lessons; a little model car had inspired him to make real cars using big casting presses, for example, and Legos helped him understand the importance of precision manufacturing. Optimus was standing in the middle of the workshop supported by a gantry. It slowly walked around him and deposited a box it was carrying. Musk then took the joystick controller and guided Optimus to pick up the box and hand it to von Holzhausen. After Optimus finished, Musk gave a gentle push to its chest to see if it would fall over. The stabilizers worked; it stayed upright. Musk nodded appreciatively and shot some video of Optimus. "Whenever Elon pulls out his phone to take a video, you know that you've impressed him," Lars Moravy says.

Afterward, Musk announced that they would hold a public demonstration that would feature Optimus, Full Self-Driving, and Dojo. "In all of these," he said, "we're tackling the huge task of creating artificial general intelligence." The event would be at Tesla's Palo Alto headquarters on September 30, 2022, and be called AI Day 2. His design team created a logo that showed Optimus touching together its beautifully tapered fingers to form the shape of a heart.

78

Uncertainty

Twitter, July–September 2022

Ari Emanuel hosing Musk down in
Mykonos; Alex Spiro

The terminator

Unsure what he wanted to do about Twitter, Musk asked for three options in June 2022. Plan A was to proceed as agreed with a $44 billion purchase. Plans B and C involved trying to reprice the deal or to get out of it entirely, somehow. To help do the financial modeling for those options, he brought in Bob Swan, a former CEO of eBay and Intel and a partner at the venture capital firm Andreessen Horowitz, which was investing in Musk's offer.

The problem was that Swan, a straight shooter, was committed to Plan A. He felt there was no real justification for getting out of the deal. He accepted most of the numbers in Twitter's proxy statement, applied a bit of a discount, and presented a somewhat rosy financial model. Musk, convinced that the world was entering a recession and that Twitter was misstating its bot problem, challenged Swan angrily. "If you can present this to me with a straight face, then you're probably not the guy for the job," he said.

Swan had been too successful to be treated that way. "Since I presented this to you with a straight face, you're right," he responded. "I'm probably not the right guy for the job." And he quit.

Once again, Musk put in a call to his close friend and early Tesla investor Antonio Gracias, whose SWAT team had uncovered the problems at Tesla in 2007. Gracias was vacationing in Europe with some of his kids when the call came. "You said when you left the Tesla board that I should call you if I need help," Musk reminded him. Gracias agreed to put together a team to do a deep dive on Twitter's finances.

Gracias felt he needed to enlist an independent investment bank to help sort through the proper valuation and capital structure. He talked to his friend Robert Steel of Perella Weinberg Partners, who in his straightforward way asked Musk directly what his goal was: to get out of buying Twitter or to buy Twitter at a lower price? Musk said he wanted the latter option. That was true, at least most of the time, but he was constrained, both legally and psychologically, from saying something even truer, namely that there were some mornings, and some nights, when he felt that he may have stumbled onto a fool's errand and would be happy if the whole thing went away. Steel had an interesting insight about Musk. When most clients are given three or four options, they will ask which one the banker recommends. Musk, instead, asked detailed questions about each option but did not solicit a recommendation. He liked to make his own decision.

When Musk demanded the raw data and methodology for determining how many real users it had, Twitter provided floods of data in formats that his team deemed almost unusable. Musk used this as a pretext for trying to withdraw from the deal. "For nearly two months, Mr. Musk has sought the data and information necessary to make an independent assessment of the prevalence of fake or spam accounts," his lawyers wrote. Twitter's resistance meant that Musk was exercising his "right to terminate the Merger Agreement."

Twitter's management responded by suing Musk in Delaware's chancery court, charging that he "refuses to honor his obligations to Twitter and its stockholders because the deal he signed no longer serves his personal interests." Chancellor Kathaleen McCormick set a trial for October.

Musk's business manager Jared Birchall and lawyer Alex Spiro tried to restrain him from sending texts and tweets that would undermine his case by suggesting that the reason he wanted out of the deal was because advertising was collapsing and the economy declining. "I'm calling him right now to tell him no more tweeting," Spiro told Birchall one day. But Spiro was an overmatched lion tamer. Within ten minutes, Musk sent a barrage of tweets that almost seemed designed to spite his legal team. "So much for the conversation about tweeting," Birchall told Spiro.

Even Musk's wacky unrelated tweets became a problem. "I'm buying Manchester United ur welcome," he posted in August. Birchall called Spiro to ask if the SEC might see that as an improper disclosure. "Is he really going to?" Spiro asked. It turned out that Musk was just riffing on a meme about how Manchester United fans were always begging people to buy the team. Spiro made him send a follow-up tweet: "No, this is a long-running joke on Twitter. I'm not buying any sports teams."

Ari Emanuel wades in

Ari Emanuel is often referred to as a Hollywood superagent, but by 2022 he had become more than that. He was the CEO of Endeavor, a sprawling entertainment enterprise, and he was so plugged in that he never ran out of energy. With his high-pitched and fast-paced ability to connect people and drop f-bombs, talents he shared with his brothers Rahm and Zeke, he exulted in dipping his fingers in every interesting pie.

After the terrorist attacks of September 11, 2001, he decided he didn't want to be giving the Saudis more oil money, so he traded in his Ferrari for a Prius. But he hated the car. It was too wimpy. He was looking for someone who would actually make a great electric vehicle, and that's when he read about Musk. "I do what I normally do, which is create serendipity," Emanuel says. "I called him up and said, 'I want to meet you.' We were just two young pishers trying to fucking figure it out, and we became friends." Emanuel put in an order for a Tesla Roadster, "because I wanted to fucking get out of that goddamn Prius," and ended up in 2008 taking delivery of the eleventh one. He still has it.

In May 2022, Musk flew to Saint-Tropez, France, for the celebrity-packed (Sean "Diddy" Combs, Emily Ratajkowski, Tyler Perry) wedding of Emanuel and fashion designer Sarah Staudinger. The Cannes Film Festival made it a hot time to be on the Riviera. Musk met for lunch with Natasha Bassett, the Australian actress who was with him in Hawaii a month earlier when he decided to go hostile on Twitter.

Curb Your Enthusiasm comedian Larry David, who was officiating at the wedding, was at Musk's table, and when they sat down, David seemed to be fuming. "Do you just want to murder kids in schools?" he asked Musk.

"No, no," Musk stuttered, both baffled and annoyed. "I'm anti–kid murder."

"Then how could you vote Republican?" David asked.

David confirms that he confronted Musk. "His tweets about voting Republican because Democrats were the party of division and hate were sticking in my craw," he says. "Even if Uvalde never happened, I probably would have brought it up, because I was angry and offended."

MSNBC's Joe Scarborough was also at the table, and David described the encounter to him. Scarborough found it all pretty amusing. "I had told Ari I was not a big fan of Elon, so he seated me with him," he laughs. "Elon stayed pretty quiet." For his part, Emanuel says he wasn't trying to stir up trouble. "I actually thought that would be a great table." It ended up being a microcosm of Twitter.

There was another issue at the wedding. Among the guests was Egon Durban, a venture capitalist who was a big Twitter shareholder and on its board. Musk was angry because, he said, Durban had badmouthed him to Morgan Stanley's CEO, James Gorman. Emanuel tried to repair the damage at the wedding. "You're being a fucking fool," he told Durban. "Go over and talk to him." They had a twenty-minute conversation, during which, according to Musk, "he tried to kiss my ring," but their tension did not get resolved.

A dealmaker by nature, Emanuel offered to facilitate back-channel negotiations between Musk and Twitter's board. He asked Musk how much he would be willing to pay for Twitter. Perhaps there was a discount to be negotiated, below the $44 billion that the board had accepted. Musk suggested perhaps half that price. Neither Durban nor the rest of the Twitter board thought that even merited a response.

Emanuel tried to jump-start the negotiations again in July, when he invited Musk to come to a vacation house he had in Mykonos, Greece. Musk flew from Austin and spent two days, which were made memorable when he was photographed on a yacht looking pale and blubbery alongside Emanuel, who looked preternaturally trim and tanned.

Musk told Emanuel that he might be willing to strike a deal with Twitter rather than proceed with the October trial in Delaware. Emanuel again called Durban, who was not in favor of trying to negotiate a lower price. But some other board members were eager to see if there was a way to avoid the bloody battle, and so they let informal settlement talks begin.

Going for it

Musk's negotiations with Twitter to lower the price of the deal did not get far. The company made some proposals that could have reduced the $44 billion price by about 4 percent, but Musk insisted that the reduction had to be more than 10 percent before he would consider it. At certain moments, it seemed there might be ways to get the two sides closer, but there was an additional problem. If the deal was restructured or repriced, it would allow the banks that had committed to provide loans to renegotiate the terms. The commitments had been made when interest rates were low, so the new interest rates they would charge might wipe out any savings.

There was also a more emotional obstacle. Twitter's executives and board members insisted that any renegotiated deal must protect them from future lawsuits from Musk. "We are never going to give them a legal release," Musk said. "We will hunt every single one of them till the day they die."

Throughout September, Musk was on the phone with his lawyers Alex Spiro and Mike Ringler three or four times a day. Some days he was in an aggressive mood and insisted that they could fight and win the case in Delaware. Revelations from a whistle-blower and others had inflamed his conviction that Twitter had been lying about the number of bots. "They are shitting bricks about the dumpster fire they're in," he said of the Twitter board. "I cannot believe that the judge will railroad the deal through. It would not pass muster with the public." At other times, he thought they should go through with the deal and then sue the Twitter board and management for fraud. Perhaps he would even be able to claw back some of his purchase price from them later. "The problem," he said angrily, "is that the board members own so little of the stock that recovering from them would be difficult."

His lawyers finally convinced him at the end of September that he would lose the case if they took it to trial. It was best just to close the deal on the original terms, $54.20 a share, $44 billion in total. By that point Musk had even regained some of his enthusiasm about taking over the company. "Arguably, I should just pay full price, because these people running Twitter are such blockheads and idiots," he told me in late September. "Its stock was seventy last year with such a ship of fools. The potential is so great. There are so many things I could fix." He agreed to an official closing of the deal in October.

Once it was clear that the deal was going through, Ari Emanuel came back to Musk, in a three-paragraph message sent on the encrypted text service Signal, with a proposal: let him and his agency Endeavor run Twitter. For a fee of $100 million, he said, he would take charge of cutting costs, creating a better culture, and managing relations with advertisers and marketers. "We'd operate it, but he would tell us what he wanted and be in charge of all the engineering and technical stuff," Emanuel says. "We do a ton of business with advertisers, and it's not like we haven't done this before, you know?"

Birchall called it "the most insulting, demeaning, insane message." Musk was more sanguine and polite. He valued his friendship with Emanuel. "Look, I appreciate the offer," he said. "But Twitter is a tech company, a programming company." Emanuel countered that they could just hire the tech people, but Musk gave him a firm no. He had a core belief that you could not separate engineering from product design. In fact, product design should be driven by engineers. The company, like Tesla and SpaceX, should be engineering-led at all levels.

There was another thing that Emanuel did not understand. Musk wanted to run Twitter himself, just as he was doing with Tesla, SpaceX, The Boring Company, and Neuralink.

79

Optimus Unveiled

Tesla, September 2022

X shakes hands with Optimus as Milan Kovac and
Anand Swaminathan watch

Hair on fire

"My psychic health goes in waves," Musk said as he flew from Austin to Silicon Valley on Tuesday, September 27, to get ready for AI Day 2, the big public presentation he had promised of Tesla's artificial intelligence work, self-driving cars, and the launch of Optimus the robot. "It's bad when there is extreme pressure. But if a lot of things start going right, it's also not great for my psychic health."

A lot was hitting him that week. He was scheduled to give depositions in the Delaware court case seeking to force him to close the Twitter deal, an SEC investigation, and a lawsuit challenging his Tesla compensation. He was also worried about controversies over the use of Starlink satellites in Ukraine, difficulties in reducing Tesla's supply-chain dependence on China, a Falcon 9 launch of four astronauts (including one Russian woman cosmonaut) to the International Space Station, a West Coast launch the same day of a Falcon 9 carrying fifty-two Starlink satellites, and sundry personal issues regarding children, girlfriends, and former wives.

Musk sublimates stress in a variety of ways, goofiness being one. On the flight west, he became excited by his latest idea for swag they could sell: a perfume with the scent of singed human hair. When he landed, he called Steve Davis, his CEO at The Boring Company, who had previously executed Musk's idea to sell a toy flamethrower. "Burnt hair perfume!" Musk said, imagining the marketing pitch. "Do you like that smell you experienced after the flamethrower? We have that scent for you!" Davis was always eager to indulge Musk. He sent out a request to scent labs saying the first to match the smell would get the contract. When The Boring Company offered it on its website, Musk tweeted, "Please buy my perfume, so I can buy Twitter." Within a week, it sold out thirty thousand orders for $100 apiece.

When he got to Tesla headquarters, he went to a makeshift stage in a cavernous showroom that was being readied for that Friday's AI Day 2. An almost finished version of Optimus was dangling from a gantry, ready to practice. When an engineer shouted "Activate," another pushed a red button that started Optimus walking. It shuffled to the front of the stage, paused, and waved its hand like a serene monarch. For the next hour, the team put Optimus through its paces twenty more times. The sight of it getting to the edge of the stage, stopping, looking around, and then waving became mesmerizing. After its last circuit for the day, X walked up to Optimus and touched its fingers.

The engineer directing the practice sessions was Milan Kovac. "I think I have PTSD," he said. "After last time, it's really hard to stay composed." I realized that he was the engineer who was the target of Musk's fury a year earlier, during the rehearsals for AI Day 1, because his slides were deemed to be too boring. After that incident, he brooded for weeks about quitting. "But I decided that the mission was too important," he says.

As AI Day 2 approached in September 2022, Kovac worked up the courage to raise with Musk the topic of the run-in they had a year earlier. Musk looked at him blankly. "You remember how you hated my planned presentation and kept telling me how horrible it was?" Kovac asked. "And everyone was worried I had quit?" Musk continued to stare blankly. He didn't remember.

The AI Day rehearsal

After he had been photographed looking blubbery during his two-day Greek vacation with Ari Emanuel, Musk decided to go on the diet drug Ozempic and follow an intermittent fasting diet, eating only one meal per day. That meal, in his case, was a late breakfast, and his version of the diet allowed him to gorge as he pleased for that. At 11 a.m. on Wednesday, he went to the Palo Alto Creamery, a retro-hip diner, and ordered a bacon-cheese barbecue burger with sweet potato fries and an Oreo and a cookie-dough ice-cream milkshake. X helped by eating some of the fries.

Then he visited Neuralink's lab in a strip mall in Fremont, where he focused on the mechanics and signals involved in walking. Donning lab coats and shoe covers, Shivon Zilis, DJ Seo, and Jeremy Barenholtz brought him into a windowless room where a pig named Mint was walking on a treadmill and being rewarded by apple slices dipped in honey. Every few moments, he was given a jolt to make his muscles twitch. They were trying to decode what actuators were involved in the act of walking.

When Musk arrived at Tesla headquarters, the engineers there were also focused on walking. In preparation for the unveiling of Optimus scheduled for the following night, they had programmed the robot to take slightly shorter strides because the presentation stage was smoother than the concrete floor of their workshop. But Musk liked the longer stride and started mimicking John Cleese high-stepping in the Monty Python sketch "The Ministry of Silly Walks." "It looked cooler with the groovy walk," Musk said. The engineers started making tweaks.

Afterward, thirty of the engineers gathered around Musk for a pep talk. "Humanoid robots will uncork the economy to quasi-infinite levels," he said.

"Robot workers would solve the problem of lack of population growth," Drew Baglino added.

"Yes, but people should still have kids," Musk replied. "We want human consciousness to survive."

Later that night, we went on a little nostalgia tour to the three-story building on the edge of downtown Palo Alto that once housed the tiny office of Zip2, the startup that he and Kimbal founded twenty-seven years earlier. Whistling as if in a reverie, he walked around the building trying to get in. But all the doors were locked, and a "For Lease" sign was in the window. Then he headed the two blocks to Jack in the Box, where he and Kimbal ate every day. "I'm supposed to be fasting now, but I just have to get something here," he said. At the drive-through speaker, he asked, "Do you still have the teriyaki bowl?" They did. He ordered one for himself and a hamburger for X. "I wonder if it will still be here twenty-five years from now so X can bring his kids here?" he mused.

AI Day 2

When Musk arrived the following afternoon for the grand unveiling of Optimus at AI Day 2, dozens of engineers were scurrying through the halls with worried looks. A connection had come loose in the chest of Optimus, and it was no longer working. "I can't believe this is happening," said Kovac, who was having flashbacks to his trauma at AI Day 1 a year earlier. Eventually, some of the engineers were able to jam the connection back together, and they hoped it would stay in place. They decided to take that risk. With Musk hovering, they had no other choice.

The twenty engineers who were scheduled to be part of the presentation huddled in a backstage area telling war stories. Phil Duan, a young machine-learning expert on the Autopilot team, studied optic information science in his hometown of Wuhan, China, then got a PhD at Ohio University. He joined Tesla in 2017, just in time for the crazed surges that culminated with Musk's push to unveil a self-driving car on Autonomy Day in 2019. "I worked for months without a day off and got so tired that I quit Tesla right after Autonomy Day," he said. "I was burned out. But after nine months, I was bored, so I called my boss and begged him to let me come back. I decided I'd rather be burned out than bored."

Tim Zaman, who led the artificial intelligence infrastructure team, had a similar story. From northern Holland, he joined Tesla in 2019. "When you're at Tesla, you're afraid to go anywhere else, because you will become so bored." He just had his first child, a daughter, and knows that Tesla is not conducive to a work-life balance. Nevertheless, he plans to stay. "I'm going to spend the next few days off with my wife and daughter," he says, "but if I take a whole week off, my brain gets fried."

At the previous AI Day, none of the twenty presenters were women. This time, one of the cohosts was a charismatic mechanical design engineer named Lizzie Miskovetz. As the blaring music subsided and Optimus was about to make its entrance, she revved up the audience by announcing, "This is the first time we are going to try this robot without any backup support, cranes, mechanisms—no cables, nothing!"

The curtains, emblazoned with the logo of Optimus's hands forming a heart, parted. Optimus, untethered, stood confidently and started to raise its arms. "It moved, it's working," Duan said backstage. Then it wiggled its hands, rotated its forearms, and flexed its wrists. The engineers held their breath as it started to move its right leg forward. Marching stiffly but confidently to the front of the stage, it executed its regal wave. Victorious, it pumped its right fist into the air, did a little dance, then turned around and walked back behind the curtain.

Even Musk looked relieved. "Our goal is to make a useful humanoid robot as quickly as possible," he told the audience. Eventually, he promised, there would be millions of them. "This means a future of abundance, a future where there is no poverty. We can afford to have a universal basic income we give people. It really is a fundamental transformation of civilization."

Milan Kovac

80

Robotaxi

Tesla, 2022

Omead Afshar, Musk, Franz von Holzhausen, Drew Baglino,
Lars Moravy, and Zach Kirkhorn; a Robotaxi concept

We are all in on autonomy

Self-driving cars, Musk believed, would do more than merely free folks from the drudgery of driving. They would, to a large extent, eliminate the need for people to own cars. The future would belong to the Robotaxi: a driverless vehicle that would appear when you summoned it, take you to your destination, then ride off to the next passenger. Some might be owned by individuals, but most would be owned by fleet companies or Tesla itself.

That November, Musk gathered his top five lieutenants in Austin to brainstorm this future over an informal dinner at the half-furnished house of Omead Afshar, who hired a private chef to cook super-thick aged ribeye steaks. Present were Franz von Holzhausen, Drew Baglino, Lars Moravy, and Zach Kirkhorn. They decided that the Robotaxi would be a smaller, less expensive, less speedy car than the Model 3. "Our main focus has to be volume," Musk said. "There is no amount that we could possibly build that will be enough. Someday we want to be at twenty million a year."

A central challenge was figuring out how to design a car with no steering wheel or pedals that could meet government safety standards and handle special situations. Week after week, Musk weighed in on every detail. "What if someone forgets to shut the door of the Robotaxi when they get out?" he asked. "We have to make sure it can shut its own doors." How would a Robotaxi get into a gated community or parking garage? "Maybe it needs an arm that can punch a button or take a ticket," he said. But that seemed like a nightmare. "Perhaps we just exclude it from places that you can't easily drive into," he decided. At times the conversations were so earnest and detailed they belied how wild the entire concept was.

By the end of the summer of 2022, Musk and his team realized they had to make a final decision on the issue they had wrestled with for a year. Should they play it safe and build in a steering wheel, pedals, side mirrors, and other things that were currently required by regulation? Or should they build it to be truly autonomous?

Most of his engineers were still pushing for the safer alternative. They had a more realistic outlook on how long it would take for Full

Self-Driving (FSD) to be ready. At a fateful and dramatic meeting on August 18, they gathered to hash the issue out.

"We want to make sure we are assessing the risk with you," von Holzhausen told Musk. "If we go down a path of having no steering wheel, and FSD is not ready, we won't be able to put them on the road." He suggested that they make a car that had a steering wheel and pedals that could be easily removed. "Basically our proposal is to bake them in right now but remove them when we are allowed to."

Musk just shook his head. The future would not get here fast enough unless they forced it.

"Small ones," von Holzhausen persisted, "which we can remove pretty easily and design around."

"No," Musk said. "No. NO." There was a long pause. "No mirrors, no pedals, no steering wheel. This is me taking responsibility for this decision."

The executives sitting around the table hesitated. "Uh, we will come back to you on that," one said.

Musk got into one of his very cold moods. "Let me be clear," he said slowly. "This vehicle must be designed as a clean Robotaxi. We're going to take that risk. It's my fault if it fucks up. But we are not going to design some sort of amphibian frog that's a halfway car. We are all in on autonomy."

A few weeks later, he was still jazzed about the decision. On his plane flying from dropping Griffin off at college, he joined the weekly Robotaxi meeting by phone. As always, he tried to instill a sense of urgency. "This will be a historically mega-revolutionary product," he said. "It will transform everything. This is the product that makes Tesla a ten-trillion company. People will be talking about this moment in a hundred years."

The $25,000 car

As the Robotaxi discussions showed, Musk could be fiercely stubborn. He had a reality-distorting willfulness and a readiness to run roughshod over naysayers. This steeliness may have been one of the superpowers that produced his successes, along with his flameouts.

But here's a lesser-known trait: he could change his mind. He could take in arguments that he seemed to be rejecting and recalibrate his risk calculations. And that is what happened with the steering wheels.

At the end of the summer of 2022, after Musk made his pronouncements about being "all in" on a Robotaxi with no steering wheel, von Holzhausen and Moravy set about persuading him to cover his bet. They knew how to do it in a nonchallenging way. "We brought him new information that maybe he wasn't fully digesting in the summer," Moravy says. Even if self-driving vehicles were approved by regulators in the U.S., he argued, it would be years before they were approved internationally. So it made sense to build a version of the car with a steering wheel and pedals.

For years they had talked about what should be Tesla's next-generation offering: a small, inexpensive, mass-market car selling for around $25,000. Musk himself had teased the possibility in 2020, but then he put a hold on those plans, and over the next two years he repeatedly vetoed the idea, saying that the Robotaxi would make the other car unnecessary. Nevertheless, von Holzhausen had quietly kept it alive as a shadow project in his design studio.

Late on a Wednesday evening during his September 2022 trip to launch Optimus, Musk ensconced himself in his longtime haunt, the windowless Jupiter conference room of the Fremont factory. Moravy and von Holzhausen led a few top members of the Tesla team in for a secretive meeting. They presented data showing that in order for Tesla to grow at 50 percent a year, it needed to have an inexpensive small car. The global market for such a car was huge. By 2030, there might be up to 700 million of them, almost twice as many as for the Model 3/Y category. Then they showed that the same vehicle platform and the same assembly lines could be used to make both the $25,000 car and the Robotaxi. "We convinced him that if we build these factories and we have this platform, we could churn out both Robotaxis and a $25,000 car, all on the same vehicle architecture," von Holzhausen says.

After the meeting, Musk and I sat alone in the conference room, and it was clear that he was unenthusiastic about the $25,000 car.

"It's really not that exciting of a product," he said. His heart was in transforming transportation through Robotaxis. But over the next few months, he got increasingly more enthusiastic. At a design review session one afternoon in February 2023, von Holzhausen put models of the Robotaxi and the $25,000 car next to each other in the studio. Both had a Cybertruck futuristic feel. Musk loved the designs. "When one of these comes around a corner," he said, "people will think they are seeing something from the future."

The new mass-market vehicle, both with a steering wheel and as a Robotaxi, became known as "the next generation platform." Musk initially decided that Tesla would build a new factory in northern Mexico, four hundred miles south of Austin, designed from the ground up to build such cars. It would use a completely new manufacturing method that was highly automated.

But a problem soon arose in his mind: He had always believed that Tesla's design engineers needed to be located right next to the assembly line, rather than allowing manufacturing to be done at a remote location. That way, engineers could get instant feedback on how to design innovations that would both improve the car and make it easier to manufacture. This was particularly true for a completely new car and manufacturing process. But he realized he would have trouble getting his top engineers to relocate to the new factory. "Tesla engineering will need to be on the line to make it successful, and getting everyone to move to Mexico is never going to happen," he told me.

So in May 2023, he decided to change the initial build location for the next-generation cars and Robotaxis to Austin, where his own workspace and that of his top engineers would be right next to the new high-speed ultra-automated assembly line. Throughout the summer of 2023, he spent hours each week working with his team to design each station on the line, finding ways to shave milliseconds off each step and process.

81

"Let that sink in"

Twitter, October 26–27, 2022

Entering Twitter headquarters and visiting the
coffee bar on the tenth floor

Clash of cultures

In the days leading up to his takeover of Twitter at the end of October 2022, Musk's moods fluctuated wildly. "I am very excited about finally implementing X.com as it should have been done, using Twitter as an accelerant!" he texted me out of the blue at 3:30 one morning. "And, hopefully, helping democracy and civil discourse while doing so." It could become the combination of financial platform and social network he had envisioned twenty-four years earlier for X.com, and he decided to rebrand it with that name, which he loved. A few days later, he was more somber. "I will need to live at Twitter HQ. This is a super tough situation. Really bumming me out :(Sleep is difficult."

He scheduled a visit to Twitter headquarters in San Francisco for Wednesday, October 26, to poke around and prepare for the official closing of the deal later that week. Parag Agrawal, Twitter's mild-mannered CEO, stood in the conference-floor lobby on the second floor, preparing to greet him. "I have a lot of optimism," he said as he awaited Musk's entrance. "Elon can inspire people to do things bigger than themselves." He was being guarded, but I think he believed it. The CFO, Ned Segal, whose tense meeting with Musk in May had gone badly, stood next to him looking more skeptical.

Then Musk burst in carrying a sink and laughing. It was one of those visual puns that amuses him. "Let that sink in!" he exclaimed. "Let's party on!" Agrawal and Segal smiled.

Musk seemed amazed as he wandered around Twitter's headquarters, which was in a ten-story Art Deco former merchandise mart built in 1937. It had been renovated in a tech-hip style with coffee bars, yoga studio, fitness room, and game arcades. The cavernous ninth-floor café, with a patio overlooking San Francisco's City Hall, served free meals ranging from artisanal hamburgers to vegan salads. The signs on the restrooms said, "Gender diversity is welcome here," and as Musk poked through cabinets filled with stashes of Twitter-branded merchandise, he found T-shirts emblazoned with the words "Stay woke," which he waved around as an example of the mindset that he believed had infected the company. In the second-floor conference facilities, which Musk commandeered as his base camp, there were long wooden tables filled with earthy snacks and five types of water, including bottles from Norway and cans of Liquid Death. "I drink tap water," Musk said when offered one.

It was an ominous opening scene. One could smell a culture clash brewing, as if a hardscrabble cowboy had walked into a Starbucks.

The issue was not merely the facilities. Between Twitterland and the Muskverse was a radical divergence in outlook that reflected two different mindsets about the American workplace. Twitter prided itself on being a friendly place where coddling was considered a virtue. "We were definitely very high-empathy, very caring about inclusion and diversity; everyone needs to feel safe here," says Leslie Berland, who was chief marketing and people officer until she was fired by Musk. The company had instituted a permanent work-from-home option and allowed a mental "day of rest" each month. One of the commonly used buzzwords at the company was "psychological safety." Care was taken not to discomfort.

Musk let loose a bitter laugh when he heard the phrase "psychological safety." It made him recoil. He considered it to be the enemy of urgency, progress, orbital velocity. His preferred buzzword was "hardcore." Discomfort, he believed, was a good thing. It was a weapon against the scourge of complacency. Vacations, flower-smelling, work-life balance, and days of "mental rest" were not his thing. Let that sink in.

Very hot coffee

That Wednesday afternoon, even though he had not yet closed on his purchase, Musk held product-review meetings. Tony Haile, a British director of product who had been a cofounder of a startup that tried to sell subscriptions to an online news bundle, asked about getting users to pay for journalism. Musk said he liked the idea of having easy small payments a user could make to watch video or read a story. "We want to build a way to have media makers get paid for their work," he said. He had privately come to the conclusion that Twitter's biggest competitor was going to be Substack, the on-

line platform that journalists and others were using to publish content and get paid by users.

During a break in the sessions, Musk decided to wander through
the building to meet employees. His Twitter sherpa looked nervous
and told him that not many people were around because employees
liked to work from home. It was a Wednesday mid-afternoon, but
the workspaces were almost deserted. Finally, when he got to the
tenth-floor espresso bar, he found a couple dozen employees looking
hesitant and keeping their distance. With some encouragement from
the sherpa, they eventually gathered around.

"Could you put it in the microwave and heat it up to super-hot?" he
asked when he got his coffee. "If it's not super-hot, I chug it too fast."

Esther Crawford, who led development of early-stage products,
was eager to describe her ideas for a wallet on Twitter that could be
used for making small payments. Musk suggested that the money in
it could be in a high-yield account. "We need to make Twitter the
number-one payment system in the world, like I wanted to do at
X.com," he said. "If you have a wallet connected to a money-market
account, that's the key piece that makes the crystal glow."

Also speaking up, though somewhat reticently, was a young midlevel engineer, born in France, named Ben San Souci. "Can I give you
an idea in nineteen seconds?" he asked. It was about ways to crowd-
source moderation of hate speech. Musk interjected with his idea for
giving each user a slider they could manipulate to determine the intensity of tweets they were shown. "Some will want teddy bears and
puppies, others will love combat and say 'Bring it all on.'" It wasn't
quite the point San Souci was making, but when he started to follow
up, a woman tried to say something and he did a surprising thing for
a tech bro: he deferred to her. She asked the question that was hovering in the air: "Are you going to fire seventy-five percent of us?" Musk
laughed and paused. "No, that number didn't come from me," he answered. "This unnamed sources bullshit has to stop. But we do face a
challenge. We are headed to recession, and revenue is below cost, so
we have to find ways to bring in more money or reduce costs."

It wasn't exactly a denial. Within three weeks, that 75 percent estimate would turn out to be accurate.

When Musk got back down to the second floor from the coffee bar, three of its conference rooms were filling up with a mercenary force of loyal engineers from Tesla and SpaceX who, at Musk's direction, were combing through Twitter's code and sketching org charts on the whiteboards to determine which employees were worth keeping. Another two rooms were occupied by his platoon of bankers and lawyers. They seemed girding for battle.

"Have you spoken to Jack?" Gracias asked Musk. Twitter's cofounder and former CEO Jack Dorsey had been initially supportive of Musk buying the company, but in the past few weeks had become unnerved by the controversy and drama. Musk, he worried, was going to gut his baby. He wasn't sure he wanted to condone that. More significantly, he was balking at allowing his stock in Twitter to be rolled over into equity in the new Musk-controlled private company. If he didn't roll over his stock, it could be bad for Musk's financing plans. Musk had called him almost daily over the past week, reassuring Dorsey that he truly loved Twitter and wouldn't harm it. Finally, he made a deal with Dorsey: if he rolled over his stock, Musk would pledge to pay him full price in the future if he ever needed the money. "He's agreed to fully roll," Musk said. "We are still friends. He worries about liquidity in the future, so I gave him my word at $54.20."

Late in the afternoon, Agrawal quietly walked into the second-floor lounge area and found Musk. They would be maneuvering like gladiators the next night, but at this moment both feigned casual collegiality.

"Hi," Agrawal said gently. "How was your day?"

"My brain is full," Musk answered. "It will take a night of sleep to turn the data into something."

82

The Takeover

Twitter, Thursday, October 27, 2022

Antonio Gracias, Kyle Corcoran, Kate Claassen, and Musk with Pappy
Van Winkle bourbon; David Sacks and Gracias standing in the war room

The closing bell

The closing of the Twitter deal had been scheduled for Friday, October 28. That's what Twitter's management thought, and that's what the public and Wall Street thought. An orderly transition had been carefully scripted for the opening of the stock market that morning. The money would transfer, the documents would be signed, the stock would be delisted, and Musk would be in control. That would provide a dual trigger—delisting of the stock and change of control—permitting Parag Agrawal and his top Twitter deputies to collect severance and have their stock options vest.

But Musk did not want that, and he secretly hatched a plan with his team that would disrupt things. Throughout Thursday afternoon, he wandered in and out of a cramped conference room where Antonio Gracias, Alex Spiro, Jared Birchall, and a few others methodically planned a jiu-jitsu maneuver: they would force a fast close on Thursday night. If they timed everything right, Musk could fire Agrawal and other top Twitter executives "for cause" before their stock options could vest.

It was somewhat audacious, even ruthless. But it was justified in Musk's mind because of the price he was paying and his conviction that Twitter's management had misled him. "There's two-hundred-million differential in the cookie jar between closing tonight and doing it tomorrow morning," he told me late Thursday afternoon in the war room as the plan unfolded.

In addition to extracting vengeance and saving some money, there was a gamesmanship that was driving Musk. The surprise finale would be dramatic, like a well-timed strike in *Polytopia*.

The field marshal for the Thursday-night surprise closing was Musk's longtime lawyer, Alex Spiro. An edgy and funny legal gunslinger, he was always eager for battle. He had become Musk's trusted advisor during the storms of 2018, when he helped him fend off the legal blowback from his "pedo guy" and "take private" tweets. Musk made it a rule to be wary of anyone whose confidence was greater than their competence. Spiro was extremely high in both categories, which made Musk value him, albeit sometimes watchfully.

"We can't fire Parag until he signs the certificate, right?" Musk asked at one point.

"I would rather fire them before the thing is consummated," Spiro replied. He checked with his colleagues and worked out options as they waited for the Federal Reserve reference numbers showing that funds had been transferred.

At 4:12 p.m. Pacific Time, once they had confirmation that the money had transferred and the necessary documents had in fact been signed, Musk and his team pulled the trigger to close the deal. Jehn Balajadia, a longtime Musk assistant who had been reenlisted to help with the Twitter takeover, delivered at precisely that moment letters of dismissal to Agrawal, Ned Segal, Vijaya Gadde, and general counsel Sean Edgett. Six minutes later, Musk's top security officer came in to say that all had been "exited" from the building and their access to email cut off.

The instant email cutoff was part of the plan. Agrawal had his letter of resignation, citing the change of control, ready to send. But when his Twitter email was cut off, it took him a few minutes to get the document into a Gmail message. By that point, he had already been fired by Musk.

"He tried to resign," Musk said.

"But we beat him," Spiro replied.

In an adjoining part of Twitter headquarters, the company was throwing a Halloween party, filled with farewell hugs, called "Trick or Tweet." Birchall joked to the others in the war room, "Ned Segal came costumed as a CFO." In the nearby conference rooms, some of the SpaceX engineers were glued to a video stream on their computers. Just after 6 p.m., a Falcon 9 rocket lifted off from Vandenberg carrying fifty-two Starlink satellites.

Michael Grimes, the lead banker at Morgan Stanley, flew up from Los Angeles and arrived in the war room bearing gifts. The first was a montage showing historical defenses of free speech, beginning with John Milton in 1644 and culminating with Musk walking into Twitter headquarters and saying, "Let that sink in!" He also brought a bottle of Pappy Van Winkle, the world's best bourbon, which his wife had received on her birthday. Small tastes were passed around, and then Musk signed the half-empty bottle for her.

A few minutes later, he made his first product tweak. Until then, when people went to the Twitter.com site on the web, the first screen they saw was one instructing them to log in. Musk felt they should instead land on the "Explore" page, which showed what was hot and trending at that moment. A message was sent to the person in charge of the Explore page, a young engineer named Tejas Dharamsi, who happened to be flying back from a family visit to India. He sent back a message saying he would make the fix when he got to the office on Monday. Do it right now, he was told. So using the Wi-Fi on the United flight, he got the change made that night. "We had worked on many possible new features for years, but no one ever made decisions about them," he said later. "Suddenly, we had this guy making rapid decisions."

Musk was staying at the home of David Sacks. When he got back around 9 p.m., Ro Khanna, the local Democratic congressman, was there. Khanna is a techno-savvy advocate of free speech, but the conversation was not about Twitter. Instead, they discussed Tesla's role in bringing manufacturing back to America and the danger of not finding a diplomatic resolution to the war in Ukraine. It was an animated conversation lasting almost two hours. "He had just come from closing the Twitter deal, and I was surprised that we didn't talk about it," Khanna says. "He seemed to want to talk about other things."

83

The Three Musketeers

Twitter, October 26–30, 2022

With James Musk, Dhaval Shroff and Andrew Musk judging code *(top)*;
Ross Nordeen studying Twitter's software architecture *(bottom left)*;
James and Andrew Musk *(bottom right)*

James, Andrew, and Ross

Mustering the young tech troops in the second-floor conference rooms that Thursday was a twenty-nine-year-old who looked eerily like Musk. James Musk, son of Errol's younger brother, had the same hair, toothy grin, hand-on-the-neck mannerisms, and flat South African accent as his first cousin. There was a sharpness to his mind and eyes, but it was leavened by a big smile, emotional alertness, and eagerness to please that were not part of Elon's repertoire. A hard-working software engineer on the Autopilot team at Tesla, James became the nucleus of a small band of loyalist musketeers coordinating the three dozen Tesla and SpaceX engineers who descended like an expeditionary force on Twitter headquarters that week.

Ever since he was twelve, James had been avidly following Elon's adventures, and he regularly wrote him letters. Like Elon, he left South Africa on his own when he was just turning eighteen, and he spent a year bumming around the Riviera, working on yachts and staying in youth hostels. Afterward, he went to Berkeley and then joined Tesla just in time to be enlisted by Elon into the crazed 2017 surge at the Nevada battery factory. He then became part of the Autopilot team developing the neural network planning path that analyzes video data from human drivers to learn how a self-driving car should behave.

When Elon called in late October and "voluntold" him to come help with the impending Twitter takeover, James was momentarily reluctant. His girlfriend's birthday was that weekend, and they were traveling to be part of her best friend's wedding. But she understood that he needed to help his cousin. "You've got to be there," she told him.

Joining him on the mission was his red-haired, shyer younger brother Andrew, a software engineer at Neuralink. As kids in South Africa, they were national-level cricket players as well as star engineering students. A half-generation younger than Elon and Kimbal, they were not part of the youth gang that included the Rive brothers, Elon's cousins from his mother's side. Elon took Andrew and James under his wing when they left South Africa, paying for their college tuition and living expenses. Andrew went to UCLA, where he researched blockchain technology with the pioneer of internet packet-switching theory, Len Kleinrock. As if it were a genetic family trait (which it might have been), James and Andrew became addicted to the strategy game *Polytopia*. "My ex-girlfriend hated me for it," Andrew says. "Maybe that's why she's my ex-girlfriend."

While on the Riviera, James was staying at a youth hostel in Genoa when another kid spied him eating peanut butter from a jar using two fingers. "Dude, that's disgusting," the kid said, laughing. That was how James met Ross Nordeen, a skinny, floppy-haired computer wiz and wanderer from Wisconsin. After graduating from Michigan Tech, Ross became an itinerant code jockey, working remotely and indulging his wanderlust. "I would meet people and say, 'Where should I go next?,' which is how I ended up in Genoa."

In an example of the serendipity that happens to people who travel around, especially in rarefied places, Ross said he was applying for a job at SpaceX. "Oh, that's my cousin's company," James replied. Ross had run out of cash, so James invited him to stay at a house he and a friend had rented near Antibes. Ross slept on a pad outside.

One evening they went to a nightclub in the fashionable village of Juan-les-Pins. James was chatting with a young woman when a man came up and said she was his girlfriend. They went outside, a fight ensued, and James, Ross, and their friend ran away. But they had left their jackets behind, so Ross was delegated to retrieve them. "They sent me back because I was the smallest and meekest-looking one," he says. On their way home, they were ambushed, threatened with a broken bottle, and chased until they jumped over a fence and hid in some bushes.

This and other escapades bonded Ross and James. At a conference a year later, Ross met an executive who gave him a job at Palantir, the somewhat secretive data analytics and intelligence company cofounded by Peter Thiel, and Ross helped get James an internship there. Ross eventually ended up working on the Autopilot team at Tesla with James.

James, Andrew, and Ross became the three musketeers of Musk's takeover of Twitter, the kernel of a corps that included three dozen engineers from Tesla and SpaceX who gathered that week in the company's second-floor conference spaces to execute the transformation. The musketeers' first mission, which was both audacious and somewhat awkward because they were still in their twenties, was to form an analysis unit that would assess the code-writing skills, productivity, and even the attitudes of more than two thousand Twitter engineers and decide which of them, if any, should survive.

Code graders

James and Andrew sat with their laptops at a small round table in the open space near the second-floor conference room that Musk had commandeered as his battlefield camp. X was nearby on the floor playing with four large Rubik's cubes. (No, he could not actually solve the puzzle yet. He was only two and a half.) It was Thursday, October 27, the day Musk was rushing toward the surprise flash-close of his takeover, but he found an hour to break away from his meetings to discuss with his cousins how to cull Twitter's engineering ranks. Joining them was another young engineer from the Autopilot team, Dhaval Shroff, who had been one of the presenters on AI Day 2.

James, Andrew, and Dhaval had access on their laptops to the entire trove of code that had been written at Twitter over the past year. "Do a search to see who's done a hundred lines of code or more in the last month," Musk told them. "I want you to go through the directory and see who's committing code."

His plan was to lay off most of the engineers while retaining the really good ones. "Let's figure out who did a nontrivial amount of coding, then within that group who did the best coding," he said. It was a mammoth task, made more difficult because they did not have the code in a format that made it easy to determine who made each insertion or deletion.

James had an idea. He and Dhaval had met a young Twitter software engineer at a conference in San Francisco a few days earlier. His name was Ben. James called his number, put him on speakerphone, and started peppering him with questions.

"I have the list of everyone's insertions and deletions," Ben said.

"Can you send it?" James asked. They spent time figuring out how to use a Python script and pruning techniques to get it to transfer faster.

Then Musk broke in. "Thanks for helping, man," he said.

There was a long pause. "Elon?" Ben asked. He seemed a little awed that his incoming boss was spending time digging through the source code on the day they were rushing to close the deal.

Hearing his French accent, I realized he was the same Ben—Ben San Souci—who had asked Musk about content moderation at the coffee-bar visit. An engineer by demeanor, he wasn't a natural net-worker, but he was suddenly being swept into the inner circle. It was a testament to the value of serendipity—and of showing up in person.

The following morning, with Twitter now officially in Musk's hands, the musketeers went to the ninth floor, where the café was serving free breakfast. Ben was there and, along with a couple of other Tesla engineers, they went onto the sunny patio overlooking City Hall. There were a dozen tables surrounded by playful furnishings, but no one else from Twitter was around.

When James, Andrew, and Ross described how their layoff lists were progressing, Ben was not afraid to speak his mind. "In my expe-rience, individuals are important, but the teams are also important," he said. "Instead of just singling out good coders, I think it would be useful to find the teams that work really well together."

Dhaval processed this information and agreed. "Me and James and the people on our Autopilot team are always sitting together, and the ideas flow real fast, and what we do as a team is better than what any one of us could do," he said. Andrew noted that was why Musk favored in-person rather than remote work.

Again, Ben was willing to disagree. "I believe in coming in, and I do," he said. "But I'm a programmer and can't be good if I get inter-rupted every hour. So sometimes I don't come in. Perhaps hybrid is best."

In charge

In the halls of Twitter, as well as at Tesla and SpaceX and on Wall Street, there was talk about whether Musk would tap someone to help him run the company. That first day as owner, he secretly met with one possibility, Kayvon Beykpour, the cofounder of the video-streaming app Periscope, which was acquired and then killed by Twitter. Beykpour had become president of product development at Twitter but was fired by Agrawal earlier in 2022 without explanation.

Their conversation in Musk's conference room, which also included tech-investor Scott Belsky, showed a real mind-meld. "I have an idea on the ads," Beykpour suggested. "Ask people who subscribe what their interests are and offer to personalize their experience. You could make it a benefit of subscribing."

"Yeah, and advertisers would love that," Musk said.

"Also a down-vote button for tweets," Beykpour said. "You need some negative user signal that can feed into rankings."

"Only paid and verified users should be allowed to do a down-vote," Musk said, "because otherwise you could be subject to a bot attack."

At the end of the conversation, Musk made Beykpour a casual offer. "Why don't you come back to work here?" he asked. "It seems like you love it." He then laid out his whole vision of making Twitter a financial and content platform, with all the elements he had envisioned for X.com.

"Well, I'm conflicted," Beykpour responded. "I look up to you. I've purchased every product you ever created. Let me get back to you."

It was clear, however, that Musk was not going to cede much control, just as he hadn't at his other companies. A month later, I asked Beykpour what he concluded. "I just don't see a role for me," he said. "Elon is passionate about directly driving engineering and product himself."

Musk was in no hurry to bring in anyone else to run Twitter right away, even after he conducted an online poll that said he should. He even dispensed with having a chief financial officer. He wanted it to be his playground. At SpaceX he had at least fifteen direct reports, and at Tesla there were about twenty. At Twitter, he told his team, he was willing to have more than twenty. And he decreed that they and the most dedicated engineers should all work in a huge open workspace on the tenth floor, where he would deal with them directly each day and night.

Round one

Musk had tasked his young musketeers to develop a strategy for making deep cuts in the bloated engineering ranks, and they had been scouring the code base to assess who was excellent and all in. At 6 p.m. on Friday, October 28, twenty-four hours after the closing, Musk gathered them and three dozen other trusted mercenaries from Tesla and SpaceX to begin implementing the plan.

"Twitter now has twenty-five hundred software engineers," Musk told them. "If each wrote only three lines of code per day, a ridiculously low bar, that should make three million lines a year, which is enough for a whole operating system. This is not happening. Something is deeply amiss. I feel like I'm in a comedy show here."

"Product managers who don't know anything about coding keep ordering up features they don't know how to create," James said. "Like cavalry generals who don't know how to ride a horse." It was a line Musk himself often used.

"I'm going to set a rule," Musk decreed. "We have one hundred fifty engineers doing Autopilot. I want to get down to that number at Twitter."

Even granting Musk's view of the low productivity at Twitter, a layoff of more than 90 percent of the engineers made most at the table flinch. Milan Kovac, now less intimidated by Musk than he was in the early Optimus days, explained why more were necessary. Alex Spiro, the lawyer, also urged caution. He felt that some jobs at Twitter did not require genius computer skills. "I don't understand why every single person that works at a social media company has to have one-sixty IQ and work twenty hours a day," he argued. Some people need to be good at selling, others need the emotional skills of good managers, and some are merely uploading user videos and don't have to be superstars. Plus, cutting to the bone risked having the system fail if anyone got sick or fed up.

Musk did not agree. He wanted deep cuts not only for financial reasons but also because he wanted a hardcore, fanatic work culture. He was willing, indeed eager to take risks and fly without a net.

James, Andrew, Ross, and Dhaval began meeting with Twitter's managers and asking them to meet Musk's targets of getting rid of up to 90 percent of their employees. "They were pretty unhappy," Dhaval says. "They argued that the company would just crash." He and the other musketeers had a standard response: "Elon has asked for this, and this is how he operates, so we have to come up with a plan."

On Sunday night, October 30, James sent Musk the official list that he and the other musketeers had made of the best engineers who should be retained. The others could be let go. Musk was ready to pull the trigger immediately. If the layoffs were executed before November 1, the company would not have to pay the bonuses and option grants that were due then. But Twitter's human resources managers pushed back. They wanted to vet the list for diversity. Musk dismissed that suggestion. But he was given pause by another of their warnings. The firings, if done summarily, would trigger fines for breach of contract and violations of California's employment laws. That would cost millions of dollars more than waiting until after the contracted bonuses.

Musk reluctantly agreed to delay the mass firings until November 3. They were announced that night in an unsigned email: "In an effort to place Twitter on a healthy path, we will go through the difficult process of reducing our global work force." About half of the company's employees worldwide, and close to 90 percent of some infrastructure teams, were let go, their access to company computers and email immediately switched off. He also fired most of the human resources managers.

And that was just round one in what would be a three-round bloodbath.

Content Moderation

Twitter, October 27–30, 2022

Clockwise, from top left: With Kanye West at SpaceX; Yoel Roth; Jason Calacanis; David Sacks

Council of one

The musician and fashion designer Ye, formerly known as Kanye West, was a friend of Musk, sort of, in that odd way that the word is sometimes applied to celebrity party-pals who share energy and limelight but little intimacy. Musk gave Ye a tour of the SpaceX factory in Los Angeles in 2011. A decade later, Ye paid a visit to Starbase in south Texas and Musk went to his *Donda 2* party in Miami. They had certain traits in common, including being unfiltered, and they were both thought to be half-crazy, though in Ye's case that description would eventually seem to be only half-right. "Kanye's belief in himself and his incredible tenacity got him to where he is today," Musk said in *Time* in 2015. "He fought for his place in the cultural pantheon with a purpose. He's not afraid of being judged or ridiculed in the process." Musk could have been describing himself.

Early in October, a few weeks before Musk closed the Twitter deal, Ye and his models wore "White Lives Matter" T-shirts at a fashion show, which spun into a social media firestorm culminating with a tweet from Ye proclaiming, "When I wake up I'm going death con 3 On JEWISH PEOPLE." Twitter then banned him. A couple of days later, Musk tweeted, "Talked to Ye today & expressed my concerns about his recent tweet, which I think he took to heart." But the musician remained banned.

Ye's Twitter saga would end up teaching Musk a series of lessons about the complexity of free speech and the downsides of impulsive policymaking. Alongside the layoff decisions, the issue of content moderation dominated Musk's first week at Twitter.

He had been waving the banner of free speech, but he was learning that his views were too simplistic. On social media, a lie can travel halfway around the world while the truth is still putting on its shoes. Disinformation was a problem, as were crypto scams, fraud, and hate speech. There was also a financial problem: jittery advertisers did not want their brands to be in a toxic-speech cesspool.

In early October, a few weeks before he was due to take over Twitter, Musk had raised in one of our conversations the idea of creating a content moderation council that would decide these issues.

He wanted diverse voices on it from around the world, and he described the type of members he had in mind. "I won't make any decisions about who to reinstate until the council is up and running," he told me.

He made that pledge publicly on Friday, October 28, the day after his Twitter purchase closed. "No major content decisions or account reinstatements will happen before that council convenes," he tweeted. But it was not in his nature to cede control. He had already begun diluting the idea. The council's opinions would be purely "advisory," he told me. "I have to make the ultimate calls." As he wandered among the meeting rooms that afternoon, discussing layoffs and product features, it was clear that he was losing interest in creating the council. When I asked him if he had decided who might be on it, he said, "No, it's not really a priority now."

Yoel Roth

When Musk fired Twitter's chief legal officer Vijaya Gadde, the task of dealing with content moderation, and the equally difficult task of dealing with Musk, fell to a somewhat academic but cheerful, fresh-faced thirty-five-year-old named Yoel Roth. It was an awkward fit. Roth was a left-leaning Democrat who had left a trail of anti-Republican tweets. "I've never donated to a presidential campaign before, but I just gave $100 to Hillary for America," he posted in 2016, the year after he joined the company's trust and safety team. "We can't f—k around anymore." On election day 2016, he mocked Trump supporters by tweeting, "I'm just saying, we fly over those states that voted for a racist tangerine for a reason." After Trump became president, he tweeted, "ACTUAL NAZIS IN THE WHITE HOUSE," and he called Mitch McConnell a "personality-free bag of farts."

Nevertheless, Roth had a combination of optimism and eagerness that caused him to hope that he could work with Musk. They first met on the crazed Thursday afternoon when Musk was pulling off the flash-closing of his Twitter deal. At 5 p.m., Roth's phone rang. "Hi, this is Yoni," the caller said. "Can you please come over to the second floor? We need to talk." Roth did not know who Yoni was, but he headed through the forlorn Halloween party that was under-way and arrived at the big open space of the conference areas where Musk, his bankers, and the musketeers were bustling about.

There he was greeted by Yoni Ramon, a short, energetic, long-haired Tesla information security engineer, originally from Israel. "I'm Israeli myself, so I could tell he was Israeli," Roth says. "But otherwise I had no idea who he was."

Musk had given Ramon the task of preventing any disgruntled Twitter employees from sabotaging the service. "Elon is absolutely paranoid, and with reason, that some angry employee is going to dis-rupt things," he told me just before Roth arrived. "He's made it my job to stop it."

When they sat at a table in the open area, near the buffet of bot-tled waters, Ramon began by asking Roth, with no explanation, "How do I get access to Twitter's tools?"

It was still unclear to Roth who this guy was. "There's a lot of re-strictions on who gets access to Twitter tools," he replied. "There's a lot of privacy considerations."

"Well there's been a corporate transition," Ramon said. "I work for Elon and we need to secure things. At least show me what the tools look like."

Roth thought that was reasonable. He pulled out his laptop and showed Ramon the content moderation tools that Twitter used and recommended some measures they could take to guard against an in-sider threat.

"Can you be trusted?" Ramon suddenly said, looking Roth in the eye. Roth, taken aback by the earnestness, said yes.

"Okay, I'm going to go and get Elon," Ramon said.

A minute later, Musk emerged from the war room where the deal had just closed, sat at one of the round tables in the lounge, and asked for a demonstration of the security tools. Roth pulled up Musk's own account and showed what Twitter's tools could do with it.

"Access to those tools should be restricted to just one person for now," Musk said.

"I did that yesterday," Roth replied. "The one person is me." Musk nodded silently. He seemed to like how Roth was handling things.

He then asked Roth for the names of ten people "you would trust with your life" who should be given access to the highest-level tools. Roth said he would make a list. Musk stared him in the eye. "I mean, trust with your life," he said. "Because if they do something wrong, they're fired and you're fired and your entire team is fired." Roth thought to himself that he was familiar with how to deal with that type of boss. He nodded and headed back to his office.

The Bee *in his bonnet*

The first sign of trouble for Yoel Roth came the next morning, Friday, when he got a text from Yoni Ramon saying that Musk wanted to reinstate the *Babylon Bee*, a conservative humor site that Musk liked. The site had been banned under Twitter's "misgendering" policy for satirically anointing Rachel Levine, a transgender woman in the Biden administration, "Man of the Year."

Roth was familiar with Musk's mercurial reputation, so he expected him to pop some impulsive decision at some point. He thought it would be about Trump, but his request to reinstate the *Babylon Bee* raised the same issue. Roth's goal was to prevent Musk from doing reinstatements unilaterally in an arbitrary manner. In other words, he was hoping to prevent Musk from being Musk.

Roth had met that morning with Musk's lawyer, Alex Spiro, who was now managing policy issues. "If you ever need something or anything crazy comes up, call me directly," Spiro told him. So Roth did.

After explaining Twitter's misgendering policy, and saying that the *Babylon Bee* refused to delete the offending tweet, Roth said there were three options: keep the *Bee* banned, get rid of the rule against misgendering, or simply reinstate the *Bee* arbitrarily without wringing hands about policies and precedents. Spiro, who knew how Musk operated, chose option three. "Why can't he just do that?" he asked.

"Well, he can," Roth conceded. "He bought the company, and he can make whatever decisions he wants." But that could cause problems. "What do we do when another user does the same thing and our rules are enforced? You have a consistency problem."

"Okay, then, should we change the policy?" Spiro asked.

"You can do that," Roth answered. "But you should know this is a major culture war issue." There was a lot of advertiser concern about how Musk was going to handle content moderation. "If the very first thing that he does is remove Twitter's hateful conduct policy related to misgendering, I don't believe it will go well."

Spiro thought about it, then said, "We need to talk to Elon about this." As they were leaving the room, Roth got another message. "Elon wants to reinstate Jordan Peterson." Peterson, a Canadian psychologist and author, had been suspended from Twitter earlier in the year for insisting on referring to a transgender male celebrity as a woman.

Musk stepped out of one of the conference rooms an hour later to meet with Roth and Spiro. They stood in the public snack-bar area with people milling around, which made Roth uncomfortable, but he launched into the issue of random reinstatements. "Well, what about the concept of a presidential pardon?" Musk asked. "That's in the Constitution, right?"

Roth, who could not tell if he was joking, conceded that Musk had the right to issue random pardons, but asked, "What if somebody else does the same thing?"

"We're not changing the rules, we're granting them a pardon," Musk replied.

"But on social media, it doesn't exactly work that way," said Roth. "People test the rules, especially on this issue, and they're going to want to know if Twitter's policy has changed."

Musk paused for a while and decided to back off a bit. He was familiar with the issue. His own child had transitioned. "Look, I want to be clear, I don't think misgendering people is cool. But it's not sticks and stones, like if you threaten to kill somebody."

Roth was again pleasantly surprised. "I actually agreed with him," he says. "Even though I had a reputation of being the censorship brigade, it was actually my long-standing view that Twitter removed too much speech when there were other, less invasive options available." Roth put his laptop on a counter to show some ideas he was developing to put warning messages on tweets rather than deleting them or banning users.

Musk nodded enthusiastically. "That sounds like exactly what we should do," he said. "These problem tweets shouldn't show up in search. They shouldn't show up in your timeline, but like, if you navigate to somebody's profile, maybe you see them."

For more than a year, Roth had been working on such a plan for downplaying the reach of certain tweets and users. He saw it as a way to avoid banning controversial users outright. "One of the biggest areas I'd love research on is non-removal policy interventions like disabling engagements and de-amplification/visibility filtering," he wrote in a Slack message to his Twitter team in early 2021. Ironically, when that message emerged as part of Musk's transparency data dump known as "the Twitter Files" in December 2022, it was seen as a smoking-gun confirmation that conservatives had been subjected to "shadow banning" by liberals at Twitter.

Musk approved Roth's idea of using "visibility filtering" to de-amplify problematic tweets and users as an alternative to permanent bans. He also agreed to hold off on reinstating the *Babylon Bee* or Jordan Peterson. "Instead," Roth suggested, "why don't we take a couple of days to build a version of what this de-amplification system could be." Musk nodded. "I can do this for you by Monday," Roth promised.

"Sounds good," Musk said.

Sacks and Calacanis

Yoel Roth was having lunch with his husband the next day, a Saturday, when he got a call telling him to come to the office. David Sacks and Jason Calacanis wanted to ask him some questions. "You should do it," a friend at Twitter advised, knowing the importance of those two. So he drove from Berkeley, where he lived, across the Bay to Twitter headquarters.

Musk was staying that week at Sacks's five-story house in San Francisco's Pacific Heights. They had known each other since their days at PayPal. Even back then, Sacks was an outspoken libertarian and free speech advocate. His disdain for wokeness pushed him toward the right, though with a populist-nationalist edge that made him a skeptic of American interventionism.

At a fiftieth birthday dinner for internet entrepreneur and fellow libertarian Sky Dayton in Tuscany in 2021, Sacks and Musk discussed how big tech companies were colluding to restrict free speech online. Sacks had a populist take, arguing that a "speech cartel" of corporate elites was weaponizing censorship to keep down outsiders. Grimes pushed back, but Musk generally sided with Sacks. He had not focused much on speech and censorship until then, but the issue resonated with his growing anti-woke sentiments. When Musk took over Twitter, Sacks became a fixture there, helping to coordinate meetings and offering advice.

His friend and poker buddy Jason Calacanis, with whom he did a weekly podcast, was a Brooklyn-born internet startup jockey and eager-beaver Musk sidekick. He had a boyish enthusiasm that contrasted with Sacks's dour reticence, and he was more politically moderate. When Musk made his first moves on Twitter in April, Calacanis texted his excitement about helping. "Board member, advisor, whatever . . . you have my sword," he wrote. "Put me in the game coach! Twitter CEO is my dream job." His eagerness occasionally drew a brushback from Musk, such as when he created a financial special purpose vehicle to line up investments in Musk's Twitter bid. "What is going on with you marketing an SPV to randos?" Musk texted. "This is not ok." Calacanis apologized and backed off. "This deal has just captured the world's imagination in an unimaginable way. It's bonkers. . . . I'm ride or die brother—I'd jump on a grenade for you."

When Roth arrived at headquarters to see Sacks and Calacanis, a crisis was unfolding. Twitter was being inundated with racist and anti-Semitic posts. Musk had declared his opposition to censorship, and now swarms of trolls and provocateurs were testing the limits. Use of the N-word went up 500 percent in the twelve hours after Musk took control. Unfettered free speech, the new team quickly discovered, had a downside.

Roth knew that Sacks had read the stories about his leftward leanings, so he was surprised at how polite and solicitous he was. They discussed the data about the hateful onslaught and what tools they had to deal with it. Roth explained that most were not from individual users expressing personal opinions; instead, most were the result of organized troll and bot assaults. "It was clearly a coordinated thing," Roth says, "not just actual people being more racist."

After about an hour, Musk wandered into the conference room. "So what's going on with this racist stuff?" he asked.

"It's a troll campaign," Roth said.

"Burn that stuff down right away," Musk said. "Nuke it." Roth was thrilled. He thought Musk would oppose any attempts at moderation. "Hate speech has no place on Twitter," Musk continued, as if making a pronouncement for the record. "Can't do it."

Calacanis told Roth that he was very good at explaining the situation. "Why don't you post some tweets about it?" he asked. So Roth posted a thread. "We've been focused on addressing the surge in hateful conduct on Twitter," he wrote. "More than 50,000 tweets repeatedly using a particular slur came from just 300 accounts. Nearly all of these accounts are inauthentic. We've taken action to ban the users involved in this trolling campaign."

Musk retweeted Roth's posts and added his own that was intended to reassure advertisers who were starting to flee Twitter. "To be super clear," he tweeted, "we have not yet made any changes to Twitter's content moderation policies."

As he does with people he considers his inner circle, Musk began texting Roth regularly with questions and suggestions. Even when a spate of new stories appeared rehashing Roth's leftist tweets from five years earlier, Musk supported him, both privately and publicly. "He told me that he thought some of my old tweets were funny, and he was genuinely supportive even though a lot of conservatives were calling for my head," Roth says. Musk even responded to one conservative on Twitter with a defense of Roth. "We've all made some questionable tweets, me more than most, but I want to be clear that I support Yoel," he wrote. "My sense is that he has high integrity, and we are all entitled to our political beliefs."

Even though Musk had not quite figured out how to pronounce his name (Yo-El), it seemed like this might be the beginning of a beautiful friendship.

85

Halloween

Twitter, October 2022

Maye dressed for Halloween 2022 and watching
one of her son's presentations

New York visit

Just as Yoel Roth's relationship with Musk seemed to be going surprisingly well, his husband turned to him in the late morning on Sunday, October 30, and asked, "What the fuck is this?" The question reminded Roth of the Trump days, when each morning he'd wake up and brace himself for what was tweeted. In this case it was a tweet by Musk about an attack by a hammer-wielding intruder on Paul Pelosi, the eighty-two-year-old husband of the Speaker of the House. Hillary Clinton had posted a tweet that blamed people who "spread hate and deranged conspiracy theories" for such violence. Musk responded by linking to a right-wing conspiracy site that falsely suggested, without offering any evidence, that Pelosi might have been hurt "in a dispute with a male prostitute." Musk commented, "There is a tiny possibility there might be more to this story than meets the eye."

Musk's tweet showed his growing tendency (like his father) to read wacky fake-news sites purveying conspiracy theories, a problem that Twitter had writ large. He quickly deleted the tweet, apologized, and later said privately that it was one of his dumbest mistakes. It was also a costly one. "It's definitely going to be a problem with advertisers," Roth texted Alex Spiro.

Musk had begun to realize that creating a good venue for advertisers conflicted with his plans to open the aperture to more raucous free speech. A few days earlier, he wrote a "Dear Twitter advertisers" letter promising, "Twitter obviously cannot become a free-for-all hellscape, where anything can be said with no consequences!" But his Paul Pelosi tweet undermined that pledge by exemplifying what advertisers disliked about Twitter: it could be a cesspool of falsehoods and weaponized disinformation that people (including Musk) spread in impulsive and reckless ways. Advertising accounted for 90 percent of Twitter's revenue. It was already declining due to an ad recession, but after Musk took over it began to fall much faster. It would tumble by more than half in the next six months.

Late that Sunday night, Musk flew to New York City to meet with Twitter's ad sales team and try to reassure advertisers and their agencies. He brought X with him, and they arrived around 3 a.m. at Maye's Greenwich Village apartment. He did not like hotels or being alone. Later that morning, both Maye and X went with him to Twitter's Manhattan headquarters, serving as shields and emotional support companions for what were destined to be tense meetings.

Musk has an intuitive feel for engineering issues, but his neural nets have trouble when dealing with human feelings, which is what made his Twitter purchase such a problem. He thought of it as a technology company, when in fact it was an advertising medium based on human emotions and relationships. He knew he had to be solicitous on his New York trip, but he was angry. "There's been an aggressive campaign against me ever since the deal was announced in April," he told me. "Activist groups have been pushing to stop advertisers from signing deals."

The meetings that Monday did little to reassure advertisers. As his mother watched and X played, Musk spoke in a dull monotone, first to his sales staff and then on calls with the advertising community. "I want Twitter to be interesting to a broad number of people, maybe someday a billion," he said in one of these conversations. "That goes hand-in-hand with safety. If you are hit with a barrage of hate speech or get attacked, you're going to leave." At each meeting, he was asked about his Paul Pelosi tweet. "I am who I am," he said at one point, which was not actually reassuring to any of his listeners, who somehow hoped otherwise. "My Twitter account is an extension of me personally, and, like, I'm going to tweet some things that are going to be stupid, and I'm going to make mistakes." He said it not with an aw-shucks humility but instead with a cold diffidence. On one of the Zoom calls, some of the advertisers could be seen folding their arms or signing off. "What the fuck?" one of them muttered. Twitter was supposed to be a billion-dollar business, not an extension of Elon Musk's flaws and quirks.

The next day, many of Twitter's top executives who were trusted by the advertising community quit or were fired, most notably Leslie Berland, Jean-Philippe Maheu, and Sarah Personette. More major brands and advertising agencies announced their intention to pause Twitter advertising or just did so quietly. Sales fell 80 percent for the month. Musk's messages moved from reassuring to cajoling to threatening. "Twitter has had a massive drop in revenue, due to activist groups pressuring advertisers, even though nothing has changed with content moderation and we did everything we could to appease the activists," he tweeted after the meetings. "They're trying to destroy free speech in America."

Space commanders

Halloween is one of Musk's favorite holidays, a chance for serious role-playing games. Another reason he had flown to New York, in addition to appeasing advertisers, was that he had promised to accompany his mother to the model Heidi Klum's annual Halloween party, which featured over-the-top costumes paraded on a red carpet to delight paparazzi.

Musk did not get back to Maye's apartment from his advertising meetings until 9 p.m., at which point she and a friend helped strap him into a red-and-black leather body armor "devil's champion" costume that she had procured. Even though they were ushered into a VIP area, they hated the party. Maye found it too loud, and Elon was annoyed that everyone was trying to take selfies with him. So they left after ten minutes. But Musk did change his Twitter profile picture to one of him in the devil's champion body armor. He figured it suited his current situation.

The next morning, he got up early so that he could watch with his mother and son the livestream of a Falcon Heavy liftoff, the first time in three years that SpaceX's twenty-seven-engine rocket had been launched. Then he flew to Washington for a ceremony marking a change of top generals at the U.S. Space Command. Despite the tensions he had with the Biden administration, Musk was still warmly embraced by the Pentagon, especially because SpaceX was the only American entity capable of sending major military satellites and crews into orbit. During the ceremony, he was singled out by General Mark Milley, the Chairman of the Joint Chiefs of Staff. "What he symbolizes," Milley said, "is the combination of the civil and military cooperation and teamwork that makes the United States the most powerful country in space."

86

Blue Checks

Twitter, November 2–10, 2022

A presentation in the conference room; James Musk,
Dhaval Shroff, and Andrew Musk assessing engineers

Thermonuclear

Yoel Roth and most of the content moderation team had survived round one of the layoffs and firings. Given the battle against racist trolling and the revolt among advertisers, it seemed prudent not to decimate that team right away. "I cut a very small number of roles that I thought were nonessential, but nobody pressured me to fire people," Roth says. That day he tweeted a reassurance to advertisers that the company's "core moderation capabilities remain in place."

He finished crafting the new misgendering policy he had promised Musk. The plan was to put a warning on any offending tweet, lower its visibility, and not let it be retweeted. Musk approved.

Musk then suggested an additional idea for content moderation. Twitter had a little-known feature called "Bird Watch." It allowed users to put corrections or contextual statements on tweets they found false. Musk loved the idea but hated the name. "From now on we're calling it Community Notes," he said. It appealed to him as a way to avoid censoring things and instead, as he put it, "let collective humanity start a conversation and negotiate whether it was true or false."

Advertisers had been pulling away for a week, but by Friday, November 4, the exodus was flowing faster. Part of the reason was a boycott led by online activists who were urging companies, such as Oreo cookies, to remove their ads. Musk threatened to go after advertisers who succumbed to pressure. "A thermonuclear name & shame is exactly what will happen if this continues," he tweeted.

That evening, Musk went into demon mode. Most people at Twitter, including Roth, had seen him be arbitrary and insensitive at times, but they had not been exposed to the cold fury of his trance-like darkest persona nor learned how to ride out the storm. He called Roth and ordered him to stop users from urging advertisers to boycott Twitter. This did not, of course, align with his professed fealty to free speech, but Musk's anger takes on a moral righteousness that can brush away inconsistencies. "Twitter is a good thing," he told Roth. "It is morally right for it to exist. These people are doing something immoral." The users who were pressuring advertisers to boycott Twitter were engaged in blackmail, he said, and should be banned.

Roth was appalled. There was no rule on Twitter against advocating boycotts. It was done all the time. Indeed, it was the type of advocacy, Roth felt, that made Twitter important. Plus, there was the Barbra Streisand effect, named after the singer sued a photographer for posting a photo of her home, thus causing the photo to get a thousand times more attention. Banning tweets that called for an advertising boycott would increase awareness of the boycott. "I think tonight is the night I'm going to have to quit," Roth told his husband.

After exchanging a few text messages, Musk called Roth on the phone. "It's unfair," he said. "It's blackmail."

"These tweets are not a violation of our rules," Roth replied. "If you remove them, it's going to backfire." The conversation lasted for fifteen minutes and did not go well. After Roth made his case, Musk started talking quickly, and it was clear he wanted no pushback. He didn't raise his voice, which made his anger feel even more menacing. Musk's authoritarian side unnerved Roth.

"I'm changing Twitter policy right now," he declared. "Blackmail is prohibited as of right now. Ban it. Ban them."

"Let me see what I can find out," Roth said. He was trying to buy time. "I was like, I need to get the fuck off the phone," Roth recalls.

Roth called Robin Wheeler, who had quit as Twitter's head of advertising sales but been lured back by Musk and Jared Birchall. "You know how this shit works," Roth told her. "If we ban an activist campaign, that is a great way to make it take off even more."

Wheeler agreed. "Don't do anything," she told Roth. "I'll text Elon too and then he'll hear it from multiple people."

The next thing that Roth heard from Musk was a question about a totally different subject: What was happening with the elections in Brazil? "He and I suddenly went back to having normal interactions, where he's asking questions and I'm giving him answers," Roth says. Musk had moved on from demon mode. His mind had switched to other things, and he never mentioned the advertising boycott again or followed up on his orders.

Henry Kissinger once quoted an aide saying that the Watergate scandal had happened "because some damn fool went into the Oval Office and did what Nixon told him to do." Those around Musk knew how to ride out his periods of demon mode. Roth later described the encounter in a conversation with Birchall. "Yeah, yeah, yeah," Birchall told him. "That happens with Elon. You need to just ignore it and don't do what he says. Then later on, go back to him after he has processed the inputs."

Twitter Blue check marks

Subscriptions were a key part of Musk's plans for Twitter. He called it Twitter Blue. Already, blue check marks were available to celebrities and officials who went through a process (or pulled strings) to get Twitter to deem them notable enough. Musk's idea was to create a new authentication badge for anyone willing to pay a monthly fee. Jason Calacanis and others suggested that it would be elitist to have different marks for those who had been knighted as "notables" and those who paid, so Musk decided that both categories would get the same blue check mark.

Twitter Blue would serve many purposes. First, it would cut back on troll farms and bot armies, because only one verified account would be permitted on any one credit card and phone. Second, it would be a new revenue stream. It would also get a user's credit card information into the system, enabling Twitter someday to become the broader financial-services and payments platform that Musk envisioned. And it could help solve the hate-speech and scam issues.

He asked to have it ready by Monday, November 7. They succeeded in getting the engineering done, but even before the launch they realized they had a human problem: thousands of pranksters, scam artists, and provocateurs would be looking for ways to game the verification system, get a blue check, and then change their profiles to impersonate someone else. Roth presented a seven-page memo describing the dangers. He pushed to delay the new feature at least until after the November 8 midterm elections in the U.S.

Musk understood the issue and agreed to a two-day delay. He

gathered product manager Esther Crawford and twenty engineers around his conference table at midday on November 7 to emphasize the importance of preventing people from messing with Twitter Blue. "There will be a massive attack," he warned. "There's going to be a swarm of bad actors who will test the defenses. They will try to impersonate me and others and then go to the press, which will want to destroy us. It will be World War Three over the blue check marks. So we have to do everything possible to not have this be a total exploding-egg-on-face situation." When one of the engineers tried to raise another issue, Musk shut him down. "Don't even think about it right now," he said. "There is only one priority: stopping the massive impersonation onslaught that's going to happen."

One problem was that this required humans as well as lines of code. Musk had laid off 50 percent of the staff and 80 percent of the outside contractors who worked on vetting users. Antonio Gracias, who was helping to enforce tighter budgets, had ordered Roth to drastically reduce spending on moderators.

When Twitter Blue began rolling out on the morning of Wednesday, November 9, the impersonation problem was as bad as Musk and Roth had feared. There was a tsunami of fake accounts with blue checks pretending to be famous politicians and, worse yet, big advertisers. One purporting to be the drugmaker Eli Lilly tweeted, "We are excited to announce insulin is free now." The company's stock price fell more than 4 percent in an hour. A Coca-Cola impersonator said, "If this gets 1000 retweets we will put cocaine back in Coca-Cola." (It did, but Coke didn't.) A Nintendo impostor showed Mario flipping the bird. Nor was Tesla spared. "Our cars do not respect school zone speed limits. Fuck them kids," read one tweet from a blue-checked account purporting to be Tesla. Another tweeted, "BREAKING: A second Tesla has hit the World Trade Center."

For a few hours Musk kept pushing forward, issuing new rules and making threats about impersonators. But the following day, he decided to suspend the entire Twitter Blue experiment for a few weeks.

Return to work

While the Twitter Blue rollout was turning into a *Hindenburg*-level flameout, Musk went into crisis mode. Sometimes crises energize him. They make him happy and excited. Not this time. That Wednesday and Thursday he became dark, angry, resentful, and churlish.

Part of it was Twitter's increasingly dire financial situation. When he made his buyout offer in April, Twitter was basically cash-neutral. But now, in addition to the drop in advertising revenue, it had to service the interest on more than $12 billion in debt. "This is one of the most terrifying financial pictures I have ever seen," he said. "I think we may see in excess of a $2 billion shortfall of cash next year." To be able to tide Twitter over, he sold another $4 billion of his Tesla stock.

That Wednesday night, he sent an email to Twitter staff. "There is no way to sugarcoat the message," he began. "Frankly, the economic picture ahead is dire." As he had done before at Tesla and SpaceX and even Neuralink, he threatened to shut down the business, even declare bankruptcy, if they didn't turn things around. Success would require a complete change in the company's mellow, easygoing, and nurturing culture. "The road ahead is arduous and will require intense work."

Most notably, this meant reversing Twitter's policy, announced by Jack Dorsey early in the pandemic and reaffirmed by Parag Agrawal in 2022, that employees could work at home forever. "Remote work is no longer allowed," Musk declared. "Starting tomorrow, everyone is required to be in the office for a minimum of 40 hours per week."

His new policy was partly motivated by his belief that being together in an office facilitated the flow of ideas and energy. "People are way more productive when they're in person because the communication is much better," he told a hastily gathered employee meeting in the ninth-floor café. But the policy also arose from his personal work ethic. When one of the employees at the meeting asked why it was necessary to come into the office if most of the people they dealt with were based elsewhere, Musk got angry. "Let me be crystal clear," he began, slowly and coldly. "If people do not return to the office when they are able to return to the office, they cannot remain at the company. End of story. If you can show up in an office and you do not show up at the office: resignation accepted. End of story."

The Apple issue

In addition to the problems with impersonations, Yoel Roth realized there was another problem for Twitter Blue: Apple. Musk's plan was that users would sign up on their iPhones using the Twitter app. Twitter would get the $8, and it would also get data from Apple verifying the user's name and other information, including, Musk assumed, their credit card number. "The problem was that nobody bothered to fucking check if Apple would share this information," Roth says.

Apple had a firm policy regarding apps. It took a 30 percent cut of any payments made for an app or for purchases inside an app. What was even more onerous, Apple would not share user data. Any service that tried to violate these rules would be yanked from Apple's App Store. It justified the policy on privacy and safety grounds. If you were on your iPhone and made a purchase, Apple would keep private your data and credit card information.

"This is not going to work," Roth said when he got Elon on the phone. "The fundamental premise of Twitter Blue is flawed when it comes to the iPhone."

Musk was annoyed. Though he understood Apple's policies, he assumed that Twitter could work around them. "Have you called somebody at Apple?" he asked. "Just call Apple and tell them to give you the data you need."

Roth was taken aback. If a midlevel employee like himself called Apple and asked them to change their policies on information privacy, they would, as he put it, "tell me to go fuck myself."

Musk insisted the problem was fixable. "If I need to call Apple, I'll call Apple," he said. "I'll call Tim Cook, if I have to."

Yoel Roth resigns

That conversation was the final straw for Roth. The business model for Twitter Blue was imperiled given the constraints imposed by

Apple. The issue of blue-checked impersonators was impossible to control immediately because Musk had laid off most of the human moderators. Musk's authoritarian outbursts continued to be unnerving. And he was demanding a list of more people to be laid off.

Roth had told himself he would stay through the November 8 midterms, which had now passed peacefully. At the end of his phone call with Musk, he decided it was time to leave. So while Musk was holding an employee town hall in the ninth-floor café, Roth was on the tenth floor drafting his resignation letter.

He had a brief conference call informing some of his team, hit the Send button, and left the office immediately because he didn't want to get walked out by security. When Musk was given the news, he was genuinely disappointed. "Wow," he said, "I thought he was going to be doing this with us."

As he was crossing the Bay Bridge to Berkeley, Roth's phone started vibrating. The news had leaked out. "I didn't answer the calls while I was driving, because I'm a very nervous driver at the best of times," he says. When he got home and looked at his phone, there was a text from Yoni Ramon asking, "Can we talk?" Similar ones came from Alex Spiro and Jared Birchall.

He called Birchall, who told him that Musk was disappointed and hoped he would reconsider. "Is there anything we can do to persuade you to come back?" Birchall asked. They spoke for a half-hour, with Birchall explaining how to ride out Musk's moments of demon mode. Roth said he had made up his mind, but he would be willing to talk to Musk as a friendly exit interview. He ate a late lunch, made an outline of what he wanted to say, and at 5:30 texted Musk saying, "I'm available to talk."

Musk phoned right away. Most of the conversation consisted of Roth going through his outline of what he thought were the most pressing challenges for Twitter. Musk then asked directly, "Would you consider coming back?"

"No, that's not the right decision for me," Roth replied.

Roth's feelings toward Musk were complex. Most of their interactions had been good. "He was reasonable, funny, engaging, and would talk about his vision in a way that was a bit bullshit but mainly something you could totally be inspired by," Roth says. But then there were the times when Musk showed an authoritarian, mean, dark streak. "He was the bad Elon, and that's the one I couldn't take."

"People want me to say I hate him, but it's much more complicated, which, I suppose, is what makes him interesting. He's a bit of an idealist, right? He has a set of grand visions, whether it's multiplanetary humanity or renewable energy and even free speech. And he has constructed for himself a moral and ethical universe that is focused on the delivery of those big goals. I think that makes it hard to villainize him."

Roth didn't ask for a severance package. "I just wanted to walk away while my reputation was still intact and I could still be employable," he says, wistfully. He also wanted his safety. He had been hit by frightening anti-Semitic and anti-gay death threats when the *New York Post* and other outlets wrote about his earlier tweets supporting Democrats and denouncing Trump. "I was very worried that if Elon and I parted on bad terms, he would tweet bad things about me and call me a libtard, and then his hundred million followers, some of whom may be violent, would come after me and my family." Roth turned plaintive as he talked about his worries. "What Elon doesn't understand," he said at the end of our conversation, "is that the rest of us do not have security people the way he does."

Despair

Following Roth's resignation and the flameout of Twitter Blue, Musk held a late-night video conference with Franz von Holzhausen and the rest of Tesla's Robotaxi design team. Before they could start showing him the latest renderings of the car, he vented his frustrations about Twitter. "I don't know why I did it," he said, looking tired and dejected. "The judge basically said that I have to buy Twitter or else, and now I'm like, okay, shit."

It was exactly two weeks after Musk had closed the Twitter deal. Since then he had been working around the clock at Twitter headquarters while juggling his work at Tesla, SpaceX, and Neuralink. His reputation was being shredded, and the exhilaration of the Twitter drama had given way to pain. "I'm hoping to be out of Twitter hell at some point," he said, promising to try to get back down to Los Angeles to do a Robotaxi meeting in person.

Von Holzhausen tried to change the subject back to the very futuristic Robotaxi design they had developed, but Musk returned to the Twitter situation. "However bad you may think the Twitter culture is, multiply that by ten," he said. "The laziness and entitlement here is insane."

Afterward, he was interviewed by video for a business summit in Indonesia. The moderator asked what advice he would give to someone who wanted to be the next Elon Musk. "I'd be careful what you wish for," he replied. "I'm not sure how many people would actually like to be me. The amount that I torture myself is next level, frankly."

87

All In

Twitter, November 10–18, 2022

Christopher Stanley, far right, taking a selfie with Musk and engineers after a hackathon *(top)*; Ross Nordeen and James Musk *(bottom)*

Moving in

The Twitter Blue rollout, which Musk thought would be the elixir to save the company, was now on hold, and the collapse of ad sales showed no signs of abating. New rounds of layoffs that would cut staff again were being planned. Those who remained would have to be as maniacally driven as the engineers at Tesla and SpaceX. "I'm a big believer that a small number of exceptional people who are highly motivated can do better than a large number of people who are pretty good and moderately motivated," he told me at the end of that painful second week at Twitter.

If he wanted the survivors at Twitter to be hardcore, he was going to have to show them how hardcore he could be. He had slept on the floor of his first office at Zip2 in 1995. He had slept on the roof of Tesla's Nevada battery factory in 2017. He had slept under his desk at the Fremont assembly plant in 2018. It wasn't because it was truly necessary. He did it because it was in his nature to love the drama, the urgency, and the sense that he was a wartime general who could rally his troops into battle mode. Now it was time for him to sleep at Twitter headquarters.

When he arrived back from a weekend trip to Austin late on the night of Sunday, November 13, he went straight to the Twitter office and commandeered a couch in a seventh-floor library. Steve Davis, his fix-it chief, had come to Twitter to oversee cost-cutting. Along with his wife Nicole Hollander and two-month-old baby, Davis moved into a conference room nearby. Twitter's cushy headquarters had showers, a kitchen, and a game room. They joked that it was all quite luxurious.

The second round

As he was flying into San Francisco that Sunday night, Musk called his cousin James and told him that he and his brother Andrew needed to report to duty and meet him at Twitter when he arrived. It was Andrew's birthday, and they were out to dinner with friends. But they both came in. "People at the company were shit-posting things about Elon, and he said he needed a few of us there he could trust," James says.

Ross Nordeen, the third musketeer, was already there. He had been in the office all weekend, reviewing the code of Twitter engineers to see who was good and bad. After subsisting mainly on crackers for two weeks, his skinny frame now looked skeletal. That Sunday, he fell asleep in the company's fifth-floor game room. When he woke up Monday morning and heard that Musk was intent on making more deep cuts, his stomach churned. "I just felt like shit that we were going to fire another eighty percent of the company." He went to the bathroom and vomited. "I just woke up and puked," he says. "I had never done that before."

He walked to his apartment to shower and think things over. "I went out and felt I didn't want to be here now," he says. But by noon he decided he would not abandon the team, so he returned. "I didn't want to let down James."

The musketeers, joined by Dhaval Shroff and other young loyalists, set up a war room, known as "the hot box," in a stifling tenth-floor windowless room near the big conference room that Musk was now using. They could feel the resentment from many of the Twitter employees, who had dubbed them "the goon squad." But a handful of dedicated Twitter engineers, such as Ben San Souci, wanted to be part of the new order of battle, and they joined the musketeer team in the floor's open workspace.

Musk met with the musketeers early that afternoon. "We got a shit-show here," he told them. "I'd be surprised if there were three hundred excellent engineers in this company." They needed to cut down to that muscle, which meant firing close to another 80 percent.

There was some pushback. The World Cup was coming up, along with Thanksgiving and its big shopping days. "We can't afford to go down then," Yoni Ramon said. James agreed. "I got the sense this could be bad," he says. Musk got angry. He was adamant that deep cuts were still needed.

The engineers who stayed, he said, had to meet three criteria. They had to be excellent, trustworthy, and driven. The first round of cuts, made the week before, had been designed to weed out those who were not excellent. They agreed that the next priority would be identifying and firing those who were not trustworthy, or more specifically, those who did not seem to be completely loyal to Musk.

The team began going over the Slack messages and social media postings of Twitter employees, focusing on those who had high levels of access to the software stack. "He told us to find the people who might be disgruntled or a threat," Dhaval says. They searched for keywords, including "Elon," on the public Slack channel. Musk hung out with them in the hot box, joking about the things they were seeing.

There were occasional moments of amusement. They stumbled across the list of words that were automatically prevented from being trending topics on Twitter. When they got to the word "turdburger," Musk started laughing so hard that he fell to the floor wheezing. But some of the messages they found, including threats of revenge, inflamed his paranoia. "One guy literally wrote a command that could take down a whole data center and said, 'I wonder what happens if you run this,'" James says. "He posted it." They immediately cut off his access and fired him.

The messages they read were mainly those in the public portions of Slack, but that still discomforted Ross, who was recovering from his morning nausea. "It seems like we were violating privacy and free speech and all that stuff," he said later. "They had a culture of shitting on their bosses." Andrew, who like James was very sensitive to the privacy concerns, said they did not look at private messages. "It's striking a balance in a company," he says. "To what extent do you allow dissent?"

Musk did not share these qualms. Unfettered free speech did not extend to the workplace. He told them to root out people who were making very snarky comments. He wanted to rid the workforce of negativity. The team worked past midnight and delivered a list of three dozen malcontents. "Do you want to speak to this person and show them what they've said?" James asked. Musk said no. They should be fired. And they were.

Yes or no?

The next trait Musk wanted to filter for—after excellence and trustworthiness—was drive. For his entire life, he had been hardcore and all in. It was a badge of honor to him. He scorned successful people who liked to take vacations.

James and Ross spent Tuesday thinking of ways to determine which employees were truly driven. Then they saw a post someone had made on Slack. "Please let me go with severance and I will leave," it said. It dawned on them that they could rely on self-selection. Some people might be happy to work late nights and weekends. But others, understandably, didn't relish that prospect and were not embarrassed to say so.

James and Ross realized that people were willing, indeed proud to declare what camp they were in. So they suggested to Musk that he give employees the chance to opt out of the new hardcore Twitter. He liked the idea, and Ross engineered a simple form with a button that employees could click to say they wanted to leave on good terms and get three months' severance. "We were so excited," James said. "We won't have to do all this additional firing."

A couple of hours later, Musk emerged from a meeting and came into the hot box smiling. "I have a great idea," he said. "We're flipping it. Don't make the choice opt-out. Instead, make it opt-in. We want to make it sound like the Shackleton expedition. We want people who declare they are hardcore."

Musk flew to Delaware late that night to testify in a shareholder lawsuit that challenged his Tesla compensation package. Shortly before 4 a.m. Eastern Time, he tested the opt-in link from the airplane, becoming the first person to say yes to the new Twitter expectations. Then he sent an email to all employees:

From: Elon Musk
Subj: A Fork in the Road
Date: Nov. 16, 2022

Going forward, to build a breakthrough Twitter 2.0 and
succeed in an increasingly competitive world, we will need to be

extremely hardcore. This will mean working long hours at high intensity. . . .

If you are sure that you want to be part of the new Twitter, please click yes on the link below. Anyone who has not done so by 5pm ET tomorrow (Thursday) will receive three months of severance.

James and Ross stayed up all night watching the results come in. They put down bets. How many would say yes? James thought it would be 2,000 out of the approximately 3,600 remaining employees. Ross wagered it would be 2,150. Musk chimed in with a low prediction: 1,800 would choose to stay. In the end, 2,492 said yes, a surprisingly high 69 percent of the workforce. Musk's assistant Jehn Balajadia handed out vodka-spiked Red Bulls to celebrate.

Code reviews

That Thursday night, a somewhat alarming message went out to Twitter employees. The following day—Friday, November 18—Twitter's offices would be closed and badge access would be suspended until Monday. The edict came about because of security concerns that the people who had just been fired or had chosen to leave might try to sabotage things. But Musk ignored the email. After working until 1 a.m. Friday morning, he sent out a contradictory message: "Anyone who actually writes software, please report to the 10th floor at 2pm today." A little later he added, "Please be prepared to do brief code reviews as I'm walking around the office."

It was confusing. One engineer based in Boston was the only person left on the team in charge of caching important data. He was afraid that if he boarded a plane, the system might go down while he was flying across the country and he'd be unable to fix it. He was also afraid that if he didn't come in, he would be fired. He flew to San Francisco.

By 2 p.m., almost three hundred engineers had made it to the office, some carrying their suitcases, despite not knowing if their travel was going to be reimbursed. But Musk stayed in meetings all afternoon, ignoring them. There was no food, and by 6 p.m., the engineers were not only irritated but hungry, so Andrew and security engineering director Christopher Stanley went out and got boxes of pizzas. "The mood had gotten edgy by then, and I think Elon was keeping them waiting on purpose," says Andrew. "The pizza calmed things."

When Musk finally emerged at 8 p.m., he began what he called "desk-siding," standing next to the workstations of the young engineers and going over their code. His suggestions, they later said, were sometimes good and at other times shallow. They often involved ways to simplify a process. He also stood with them at whiteboards, where they drew the architecture of the Twitter system. Musk peppered the clusters of engineers with questions. Why does search suck? Why are the ads so irrelevant to user interests? It was well after 1 a.m. when he scooped up X and left.

88

Hardcore

Twitter, November 18–30, 2022

James Musk and Ben San Souci

Reinstatements

"Kathy Griffin, Jordan Peterson & Babylon Bee have been reinstated," Musk tweeted that Friday afternoon, November 18. "Trump decision has not yet been made." With Yoel Roth and other minders gone, he unilaterally decided to lift the bans not only on the *Bee* and Peterson but also on the progressive comedian Kathy Griffin, who had created an account impersonating Musk and tweeted out parody pronouncements from him.

In making the reinstatements, he announced the "visibility-filtering" policy that he and Roth had devised. "New Twitter policy is freedom of speech, but not freedom of reach," he wrote. "Negative/hate tweets will be max deboosted & demonetized, so no ads or other revenue to Twitter. You won't find the tweet unless you specifically seek it out."

He drew the line at Alex Jones, the conspiracy theorist who claimed that the 2012 Sandy Hook Elementary School shooting was "a giant hoax." Musk said Jones would stay banned. "My firstborn child died in my arms," Musk tweeted. "I felt his last heartbeat. I have no mercy for anyone who would use the deaths of children for gain, politics or fame."

As for Ye, once known as Kanye West, he was still teaching Musk lessons about the complexities of free speech. He appeared on Alex Jones's podcast and declared, "I love Hitler." He then posted on Twitter a picture of Musk in a bathing suit being sprayed with a hose by Ari Emanuel, which oozed controlled-by-Jews, anti-Semitic undertones. "Let's always remember this as my final tweet," Ye wrote, then posted a swastika inside a Star of David.

"I tried my best," Musk announced. "Despite that, Ye again violated our rule against incitement to violence. Account will be suspended."

Then there was the question of whether Donald Trump should be reinstated. "I want to avoid the bullshit disputes about Trump," Musk had told me a few weeks earlier, emphasizing that his principle had always been to allow free speech only if it was within the bounds of the law. "If he's engaged in criminal activity—it seems increasingly that he has—that's not okay," Musk said. "It's not free speech to subvert democracy."

But by November 18—the Friday that he summoned engineers in for code reviews—he was in a feisty mood and ready to reverse himself. James and his musketeers were desperately trying to keep Twitter up and running despite the sudden departure of hundreds of engineers and the strain caused by World Cup videos. The last thing they wanted was another wrench thrown into the system. That is when Musk emerged from a meeting in his glass-walled conference room with Robin Wheeler, who had been hanging on as Twitter's ad sales chief, and showed James and Ross his iPhone. "Look what I just tweeted," he said with a mischievous grin.

It was a poll question: "Reinstate former President Trump? Yes. No." Leaving aside the propriety of lifting the ban on Trump and of letting a free-for-all online poll make the decision, there was the engineering issue. Conducting a poll, where millions of votes would have to be tabulated instantly and populated in real time on user feeds, could push Twitter's undermanned servers into a meltdown. But Musk relished risk. He wanted to see how fast a car could drive, what happened when you floored it, how close to the sun you could fly. James and Ross were "shitting bricks," they said, but Musk seemed gleeful.

When the poll closed the next day, more than 15 million users had voted. The tally was close: 51.8 percent to 48.2 percent in favor of reinstating Trump. "The people have spoken," Musk declared. "Trump will be reinstated. Vox Populi, Vox Dei."

I asked him right afterward whether he had a sense in advance of how the poll would turn out. No, he said. And if it had gone the other way, would he have kept Trump banned? Yes. "I'm not Trump's fan. He's disruptive. He's the world's champion of bullshit."

Round three

In her meeting with Musk that Friday afternoon, ad sales chief Robin Wheeler told him she was resigning. She had tried to do so a week earlier, at the same time as Yoel Roth, but Musk and Jared Birchall had persuaded her to stay.

Most people, including Ross and James, assumed her resignation was in reaction to Musk's decision to make unilateral reinstatements and launch a poll about unbanning Trump. But what actually bothered Wheeler more was that Musk was hell-bent on another round of firings, and he demanded that she make a list of who she would let go. Earlier that week, she had stood in front of her sales organization and told them why they should opt in with the "yes" button to be part of the new, demanding Twitter. Now she would have to look some of those same people in the eye, the ones who had said yes, and tell them they were fired.

Musk's firing and layoff targets kept changing, depending on his mood. At one point he told the musketeers that he wanted to bring the software-writing team down to fifty. At other times that week, he said they should not worry about absolute numbers. "Just make a list of who the really good engineers are and weed out the rest," he told them.

To facilitate the process, Musk ordered all of Twitter's software engineers to send him samples of code they had recently written. Over the weekend, Ross worked to get the replies transferred from Musk's mailbox to his own so that he and James and Dhaval could assess the work. "I have five hundred email submissions in my inbox," he said wearily on Sunday night. "We've somehow got to go through them all tonight to see what engineers should stay."

Why was Musk doing this? "He believes that a small group of really great generalist engineers can outperform a regular group a hundred times larger," Ross said. "Like a small battalion of marines that is really tight can do amazing things. And I think he wants to rip the Band-Aid off. He doesn't want to drag this out."

Ross, James, and Andrew met with Musk on Monday morning and presented the criteria they had used to assess the submissions. Musk approved the plan and then headed down the stairs with Alex Spiro to the café, where he had hastily called another all-hands employee meeting. As they walked, he asked what he should say if he was questioned about possible additional layoffs. Spiro suggested he deflect the topic, but Musk decided he wanted to say there would be "no more layoffs." His rationale was that the impending round of exits would be firing people "for cause" because their work was allegedly not good enough, rather than reduction-in-force layoffs, for which people would be due a generous severance. He was making a distinction that most people missed. "There are no more RIFs planned," he declared at the outset of the meeting, to great applause.

Afterward, he met with a dozen young coders who had been chosen by Ross and James for their excellence. It relaxed him to be talking about engineering, and he drilled down with them on issues such as ways to make video uploads easier. In the future, he told them, the teams at Twitter would be led by engineers like themselves rather than designers and product managers. It was a subtle shift. It reflected his belief that Twitter should be, at its core, a software engineering company, led by people with a feel for coding, rather than a media and consumer-product company, led by people with a feel for human relationships and desires.

Why so demanding?

The final round of firing notices went out the day before Thanksgiving. "Hi, As a result of the recent code review exercise, it has been determined that your code is not satisfactory, and we regret to inform you that your employment with Twitter will be terminated effective immediately." Fifty engineers were let go, their passwords and access immediately cut off.

The three rounds of layoffs and firings were so scattershot that it was initially hard to tally up the toll. When the dust settled, about 75 percent of the Twitter workforce had been cut. There were just under eight thousand employees when Musk took over on October 27. By mid-December, there were just over two thousand.

Musk had wrought one of the greatest shifts in corporate culture ever. Twitter had gone from being among the most nurturing workplaces, replete with free artisanal meals and yoga studios and paid rest days and concern for "psychological safety," to the other extreme. He did it not only for cost reasons. He preferred a scrappy, hard-driven environment where rabid warriors felt psychological danger rather than comfort.

Sometimes that meant he broke things, and it looked like it was possible he would do so with Twitter. A hashtag #twitterdeathwatch began trending. Tech and media pundits wrote their farewells to the service, assuming it would disappear any hour. Even Musk laughingly admitted that he thought it might collapse. He showed me a gif of a flaming dumpster rolling down a road and admitted, "Some days I wake up and look at Twitter to see if it's still working." But every morning when he checked, it was running. It made it through record traffic during the World Cup. More than that, with its kernel of driven engineers, it began to innovate and add features faster than it ever had before.

Zoë Schiffer, Casey Newton, and Alex Heath at *The Verge* and *New York Magazine* had produced some well-reported, hair-raising insider stories about the turmoil at Twitter. They showed how Musk had broken "the company culture that built Twitter into one of the world's most influential social networks." But they also noted that the dire predictions many of their colleagues had made did not come to pass. "In some ways, Musk was vindicated," they wrote. "Twitter was less stable now, but the platform survived and mostly functioned even with the majority of employees gone. He had promised to right-size a bloated company, and now it operated on minimal head count."

It was not always a pretty sight. Musk's method, as it had been since the Falcon 1 rocket, was to iterate fast, take risks, be brutal, accept some flameouts, then try again. "We were changing the engines while the plane was spiraling out of control," he says of Twitter. "It's a miracle we survived."

Apple visit

"Apple has mostly stopped advertising on Twitter," Musk tweeted at the end of November. "Do they hate free speech in America?"

That evening, Musk had one of his regular long phone conversations with his mentor and investor Larry Ellison, who was then living mainly on Lanai, the island he owned in Hawaii. Ellison, who had been a mentor of Steve Jobs, gave Musk a piece of advice: he should not get into a fight with Apple. It was the one company that Twitter could not afford to alienate. Apple was a major advertiser. More importantly, Twitter could not survive unless it continued to be available in the iPhone's App Store.

In some ways, Musk was like Steve Jobs, a brilliant but abrasive taskmaster with a reality-distortion field who could drive his employees crazy but also drive them to do things they thought were impossible. He could be confrontational, with both colleagues and competitors. Tim Cook, who took over Apple in 2011, was different. He was calm, coolly disciplined, and disarmingly polite. Although he could be steely when warranted, he avoided unnecessary confrontations. Whereas Jobs and Musk seemed drawn to drama, Cook had an instinct for defusing it. He had a steady moral compass.

"Tim doesn't want any animosity," a mutual friend told Musk. That was not the type of information that would usually have moved Musk out of warrior mode, but he realized that being at war with Apple was not a great idea. "I thought, well, I don't want any animosity either," Musk says. "So I'm like, cool, I will go visit him at the Apple headquarters."

There was another incentive. "I was looking for an excuse to visit the Apple headquarters, because I heard it was incredible," he says. The huge circular building of bespoke curved glass surrounding a serene pond had been designed, under Jobs's close supervision, by the British architect Norman Foster, who had met with Musk in Austin to discuss building him a home.

Musk emailed Cook directly, and they agreed to meet that Wednesday. When Musk arrived at Apple headquarters in Cupertino, the Apple staff's first impression was that he looked like someone who hadn't slept well for weeks. They went into Cook's conference room for a one-on-one session that lasted just over an hour. It began with them swapping supply-chain horror stories. Ever since the debacle of the Roadster production process, Musk had a deep appreciation for the difficulty of supply-chain management, and he considered, rightly, that Cook was the master. "I don't think very many people could have done a better job than Tim has," Musk says.

On advertising issues, they reached a détente. Cook explained that protecting the trust surrounding the Apple brand was his highest priority. The company did not want its ads to be in a toxic swamp filled with hate, misinformation, and unsafe content. But he promised that Apple was not ending its ads on Twitter, nor did it have any plans to pull Twitter off the App Store. When Musk raised the 30 percent cut that Apple extracted from any App Store sale, Cook explained how that went down to 15 percent over time.

Musk was partly mollified, at least for the moment, but there was still the issue that Yoel Roth had warned him about: Apple's unwillingness to share data about purchases or customer information. That would make it far harder for Musk to pursue his vision of adding X.com financial services to Twitter. It was an issue that was being fought in the American courts as well as by regulators in Europe, and Musk decided not to force the question at his meeting with Cook. "That's a future battle that we will have to fight," he says, "or at least a conversation that Tim and I will need to have."

When the meeting was over, Cook walked Musk to the apricot trees and serenity pond in the middle of the circular campus that Jobs had envisioned. Musk pulled out his iPhone to take a video. "Thanks @tim_cook for taking me around Apple's beautiful HQ ," he tweeted as soon as he got back into his car. "We resolved the misunderstanding about Twitter potentially being removed from the App Store. Tim was clear that Apple never considered doing so."

89

Miracles

Neuralink, November 2022

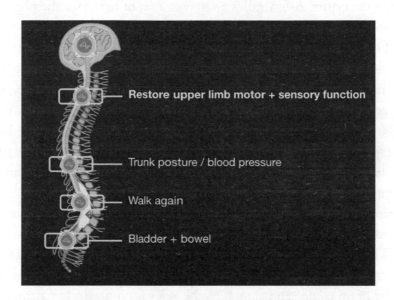

A slide showing the goal and Jeremy Barenholtz

Cures

When Musk moved to Texas, followed by Shivon Zilis, he decided to open a Neuralink facility in Austin in addition to the one in Fremont, California. The Austin office and lab were in a strip-mall building with a sign saying "Hatchet Alley" on the door. It had been an axe-throwing venue and bowling alley. Zilis retrofitted it to include open workspaces, labs, a glass-enclosed conference room, and a long coffee bar in the center. A few miles away was a set of barns for the pigs and sheep that were used in experiments.

During a visit to the pig barns in late 2021, Musk became impatient with the pace of work at Neuralink. It had implanted a chip into the brain of a monkey and taught it to play *Pong* telepathically, but so far that had mainly served to get Neuralink a lot of views on YouTube rather than transforming humanity. "Guys, this is a little hard to explain to people in a way that really grabs them," he said as they walked around. "A paralyzed person might someday use their mind to move a cursor on a computer, and that's kind of cool, especially for someone like a Stephen Hawking. But it's not enough. It's hard to get most people excited by that."

That's when Musk started pushing the idea of using Neuralink to enable paralyzed people to actually use their limbs again. A chip in the brain could send signals to the relevant muscles, bypassing any spinal-cord blockage or neurological malfunction. As soon as he got back to Hatchet Alley from the pig barn, he gathered his top Austin team, with their colleagues in Fremont dialing in, to announce this new additional mission. "Getting someone in a wheelchair to walk again, people will get it right away," he said. "It's a gut-punch idea, a fucking bold thing. And a good thing."

Musk made weekly visits to the Neuralink labs for review meetings. During one of them, in August 2022, lead engineer Jeremy Barenholtz waited at the coffee bar for the meeting to begin. He had graduated from Stanford with a master's in computer science systems a year earlier, but with his rusty-red cowlick and wispy facial hair, he could still pass for a middle-school science-fair contestant. "Elon felt that controlling a computer with your mind is nice, but it doesn't have the same limbic resonance as making paralyzed people walk again," he said. "So we've been focused on a plan for that." He walked me through the different muscle-stimulation methods and ventured into a discussion of why he believes that signals in the brain are propagated by the chemical diffusion of charged molecules rather than electromagnetic waves, as conventional theory has it.

When Musk finished sending emails and tweets on his phone, a dozen young engineers gathered in the conference room, all of them, including Zilis, wearing black T-shirts, as he always did. Barenholtz passed around a sample of hydrogel that resembled the soft tissues of a brain cortex and showed a video of two experimental pigs, named Captain and Tennille, moving their legs in response to electrical signals. "We have to be able to distinguish between pain reactions and muscle actuation, otherwise it's simply, 'You can walk again but in agony,'" Musk said. "But it does show we're not breaking the laws of physics in trying to enable people to walk again, which would be just insanely mind blowing, Jesus-level stuff."

When he asked what other miracles they might aim for, Barenholtz suggested audio and visual stimulation—in other words, enabling the deaf to hear and the blind to see. "The easiest would be fixing deafness through cochlear stimulation," he said. "Vision is super interesting. To get really high-fidelity vision, you need a lot of channels."

"We can give people crazy vision, you know?" Musk added. "Want to see infrared? Ultraviolet? How about radio waves or radar? Yeah, that one's cool for augmentation."

Then he broke into his laugh. "I was rewatching *Life of Brian*," he said, referring to the Monty Python movie. He recounted the scene where a beggar complains that Jesus cured him of leprosy, making it harder for him to make a living begging: "I was hopping along, minding my own business, all of a sudden, up he comes, cures me! One minute I'm a leper with a trade, next minute my livelihood's gone. Not so much as a by-your-leave! 'You're cured, mate.' Bloody do-gooder."

The presentation

By the end of September, Musk was impatient again. He had been pushing Zilis and Barenholtz to hold a public event to show off their progress, but they said they weren't ready. At one of his weekly review sessions, his face went dark. "If we don't accelerate, we're not going to achieve much in our lifetimes," he warned. Then he decreed a date for the presentation: Wednesday, November 30. As it turned out, that was the same day he visited Tim Cook at Apple.

When Musk arrived that night, there were two hundred chairs set up in Neuralink's Fremont facility. One of Musk's favorite podcasters, Lex Fridman, had come in for the event, as had Justin Roiland of the animated TV show *Rick and Morty*. The three musketeers—James, Andrew, and Ross—had not been invited, but they were able to get in through a back door.

Musk wanted the presentation to show off both his ultimate ambitions and his more immediate goals. "My prime motivation with Neuralink," he told the audience, "is to create a generalized input-output device that could interface with every aspect of your brain." In other words, it would be the ultimate mind-meld of humans and machine, thus guarding against artificial intelligence machines running amok. "Even if AI is benevolent, how do we make sure that we get to go along with the ride?"

Then he unveiled the new shorter-term missions that he had set for Neuralink. "The first is restoring vision," he said. "Even if someone was born blind, we believe we can allow them to see." Next, he talked about paralysis. "As miraculous as it may sound, we're confident that it is possible to restore full-body functionality to someone who has a severed spinal cord." The presentation lasted three hours. He stuck around until 1 a.m., partying with his engineers. It was, he later said, a welcome break from the "dumpster fire" at Twitter.

90

The Twitter Files

Twitter, December 2022

Matt Taibbi and Bari Weiss

"You want me to whistle-blow on your own company?" the journalist Matt Taibbi asked Musk somewhat incredulously.

"Go to town," Musk replied. "This is not a North Korean guided tour. You can go wherever you want."

Over the years, Twitter's content moderators had become increasingly active in banning what they considered harmful speech. Depending on your outlook, there were three ways to view this: (1) as a laudable effort to prevent the spread of false information that was medically dangerous, undermined democracy, provoked violence, stirred up hate, or perpetrated scams; (2) as an effort that was originally well-intentioned but had now gone too far in repressing opinions that dissented from the medical and political orthodoxy or offended the hair-trigger sensitivities of Twitter's progressive and woke staff; or (3) as a dark collusion between Deep State actors conspiring with Big Tech and legacy media to preserve their power.

Musk was generally in the middle category, but he came to harbor darker suspicions that pushed him toward the third category. "There seems to be a lot of stuff swept under the rug," he said one day to his fellow anti-woke warrior David Sacks. "A lot of shady stuff."

Sacks suggested that he talk to Taibbi, a former writer for *Rolling Stone* and other publications, who was difficult to pigeonhole ideologically. He had a willingness, indeed eagerness to challenge entrenched elites. Musk, who didn't know him, asked him to Twitter headquarters in late November. "He seemed like someone who isn't afraid of offending people," Musk says, which for him is a more unalloyed compliment than it would be for most people. He invited Taibbi to spend time at Twitter headquarters rummaging through the old files, emails, and Slack messages of the company's employees who had wrestled with content-moderating issues.

Thus was launched what became known as "the Twitter Files," which could and should have been a healthy linen-airing and transparency exercise, suitable for judicious reflection about media bias and the complexities of content moderation, except that it got caught in the vortex that these days sends people scurrying into their tribal bunkers on talk shows and social media. Musk helped stoke the reaction with excited arm-waving as he heralded the forthcoming Twitter threads with popcorn and fireworks emojis. "This is a battle for the future of civilization," he tweeted. "If free speech is lost even in America, tyranny is all that lies ahead."

Just when Taibbi was ready to unleash his first report, on December 2, Musk made a quick trip to New Orleans for a secret meeting with French president Emmanuel Macron to discuss, ironically, the need for Twitter to honor Europe's hate-speech regulations. When last-minute legal issues came up regarding what Taibbi planned to publish, the release had to be delayed until Musk finished his Macron meeting and could push back on the lawyers.

Taibbi's initial thirty-seven-tweet thread showed how Twitter had set up special systems for politicians, the FBI, and intelligence agencies to provide input on what tweets should be considered for deletion. Most notably, Taibbi included messages from 2020, when Yoel Roth and others at Twitter debated whether to block links to a *New York Post* story about what was purported to be (correctly, as it turned out) a laptop abandoned by Joe Biden's son Hunter. The messages showed many of them scrambling to find rationales for banning mention of the story, such as claiming that it violated policies against using hacked material or might be part of a Russian disinformation plot. Those were flimsy covers for censoring a story, and both Roth and Jack Dorsey would later concede that doing so was a mistake.

These and subsequent revelations by Taibbi were covered by some big press organizations, such as Fox News, but much of the traditional media labeled it, as one Twitter hashtag put it, a "#nothingburger." Joe Biden was not a government official at the time the laptop story broke, so the requests did not reveal direct government censorship nor a flagrant violation of the First Amendment. Many of the requests that Biden's team made, done through the established Twitter channels, were understandable, such as removal of a post that James Woods, a former actor, had made of a salacious selfie that was on Hunter Biden's laptop. "No, You Do Not Have a Constitutional Right to Post Hunter Biden's Dick Pic on Twitter," read the headline in *The Bulwark*.

But there was a more significant finding exposed in Taibbi's threads: Twitter had become a de facto collaborator with the FBI and other government agencies, giving them the power to flag large amounts of content for suggested removal. "A long list of government enforcement agencies essentially got to operate Twitter as an involuntary contractor," Taibbi wrote.

Actually, I think it was slightly different: often Twitter acted as a *voluntary* contractor. Instead of blowing the whistle when they felt too much government pressure, Twitter's managers seemed eager to be accommodating. Taibbi's revelations illustrated the problematic but unsurprising fact that the moderators at Twitter were biased in favor of suppressing stories that would help Trump. More than 98 percent of the donations made by people at the company went to Democrats. One case involved the allegations that the FBI had spied on the Trump campaign. The mainstream press wrote that these allegations had been whipped up by Russian bots and troll farms. Yoel Roth was, behind the scenes, a voice of honesty at Twitter. "I just reviewed the accounts," he wrote in an internal memo. "None of them show any signs of affiliation to Russia." Nevertheless, Twitter executives refrained from challenging the accepted "Russiagate" narrative.

One side note on how social media can be polarizing: Taibbi is a politically independent iconoclast, but when I followed him on Twitter I noticed how its algorithms can reinforce the ideological pigeonholing that sends people into far-left or far-right echo chambers. My Twitter's "You might like" section immediately suggested that I follow Roger Stone, James Woods, and Lauren Boebert.

Bari Weiss

On the evening of December 2, Bari Weiss was at home in Los Angeles with her wife, Nellie Bowles, reading the Twitter Files that were being unleashed by Taibbi. She felt jealous. "This is a perfect story for us to be doing," she remembers thinking. That is when she got an unexpected text from Musk asking if she would fly up to San Francisco that night.

Like Taibbi, Weiss was an independent journalist who was not easy to categorize ideologically. They had both embraced, as had Musk, the banner of free speech in opposition to what they saw as a progressive wokeness that produced a censorious cancel culture, especially in the establishment media and elite educational institutions. Weiss called herself "a reasonable liberal concerned that far-left critiques stifled free speech." After working on the editorial pages of the *Wall Street Journal* and *New York Times*, she gathered a group of independent journalists to create *The Free Press*, a subscription-based newsletter on Substack.

Musk had met her briefly after he was interviewed by Sam Altman, his cofounder of OpenAI, at the Allen & Company conference in Sun Valley a few months earlier. She went backstage to say how glad she was that he was trying to buy Twitter, and they chatted for a couple of minutes. When Taibbi was preparing to publish his Twitter Files in early December, Musk realized there was too much material for one journalist to digest. His investor and fellow free speech tech bro Marc Andreessen suggested he call in Weiss, so on the plane flying back from his quick trip to New Orleans to talk to President Macron, he sent the unexpected text that she got on the evening of December 2.

She and Bowles, along with their three-month-old baby, rushed to get on a flight to San Francisco two hours later. When they arrived on the tenth floor of Twitter headquarters that Friday night at 11, Musk was standing by the coffee machine wearing a blue Starship jacket. In one of his giddy moods, he took them running around the building showing off the stashes of "Stay Woke" T-shirts and other vestiges of the old regime. "The barbarians have crashed through the gates and are pillaging the merch!" he proclaimed. Weiss marveled that he was like a kid who had just bought a candy store and still couldn't believe he owned it. The musketeers Ross Nordeen and James Musk showed Weiss and Bowles some of the computer tools for delving into the company's Slack archives. They were there until 2 a.m., then James drove them to where they were staying.

When Weiss and Bowles came in the next morning, a Saturday, they found Musk, who was still spending nights on a couch in Twitter's library, again by the coffee machine, eating cereal out of a paper cup. For two hours they sat in his conference room and discussed his vision for Twitter. Why was he doing this? they asked. At first he answered that he had been forced into buying the company after having second thoughts about his April offer. "Really, I wasn't sure I still wanted to do it, but the lawyers told me I had to chew down this hairball, so I am," he said.

But then Musk began talking earnestly about his desire to create a public forum dedicated to free speech. At stake was "the future of civilization," he said. "Birth rates are plummeting, the thought police are gaining power." Twitter was distrusted by half the country, he believed, because it had suppressed certain viewpoints. To reverse that would require radical transparency. "We have a goal here, which is to clear the decks of any prior wrongdoing and move forward with a clean slate. I'm sleeping at Twitter HQ for a reason. This is a code-red situation."

"You almost believe him," Weiss told me afterward. It was an earnest rather than caustic comment.

But even though she was impressed, she retained some of the skepticism that made her an independent journalist. At one point during their two-hour conversation, she asked how Tesla's business interests in China might affect the way he managed Twitter. Musk got annoyed. That was not what the conversation was supposed to be about. Weiss persisted. Musk said that Twitter would indeed have to be careful about the words it used regarding China, because Tesla's business could be threatened. China's repression of the Uyghurs, he said, had two sides. Weiss was disturbed. Finally, Bowles stepped in to defuse the issue with a few jokes. They moved on to other topics.

Adding to the irony, or at least complexity, was that Musk had to end the conversation so that he could fly to Washington. He had a meeting scheduled with top government officials there on a highly classified topic involving SpaceX satellite launches.

Weiss and Bowles had rushed up on Friday night to work on the Twitter Files, but they became frustrated over the weekend because they still did not have the tools to get into Twitter's archive of Slack messages and emails. The legal department, worried about privacy issues, was blocking them from getting direct access. Nordeen, the ubiquitous musketeer, used his own laptop on Saturday to help them. But by the next day, he was exhausted and hungry, needed to do his laundry, and decided not to come in. It was, after all, a Sunday. So he invited Weiss and Bowles to his apartment overlooking the Castro district of San Francisco, where they used his laptop to look through messages in Twitter's public Slack channel.

As Weiss pushed the legal department to process more searches for her, she got a call from the company's deputy general counsel, who said his name was Jim. When she asked his last name, he said "Baker." Recalls Weiss, "My jaw dropped." Jim Baker had been the general counsel of the FBI, and he was distrusted in some conservative circles for being on the periphery of various controversies. "What the fuck?" she texted Musk. "You're like asking the guy to do searches on himself? This makes no fucking sense."

Musk flipped out. "It's like asking Al Capone to, like, look into his own taxes," he said. He summoned Baker to a meeting, and they got into a clash over what privacy guarantees were mandated by a consent decree between Twitter and the Federal Trade Commission. "Can you tell me what the main principles are in the consent decree?" Musk challenged him. "Because I have it in front of me. Can you name anything that's in it?" It was not a discussion destined to have a happy conclusion. Baker was well versed in the matter, but there was no way his answers were going to satisfy Musk, who promptly fired him.

Visibility filtering

Taibbi and Weiss enlisted a few colleagues to help, and they set up shop in the windowless hot box room, always redolent with the smells of unshowered musketeers and takeout Thai food. James and Ross, who were helping them use the digital search tools, had been working twenty hours a day, and they looked like their eyeballs were falling out. On some nights Musk would walk in, eat some leftover food, and launch into long discourses.

While rummaging through Twitter employees' old emails and Slack comments, Weiss wondered what she would think if people read her old private communications. It made her feel dirty. Ross was likewise squeamish. "To be honest, I wanted to be as far away from what they were doing as possible," he says. "I was sort of trying to help, but I didn't want to be too involved. I'm not a very political person, and it seemed like it had all kinds of crap written all over it."

One story Weiss and her team wrote based on the Twitter Files described what was known as "visibility filtering," the practice of downplaying certain tweets or users by making sure they did not show up high in searches or were touted as trending. At the extreme was a practice known as "shadow banning," in which users could post tweets and see them, but they were never told that those tweets were invisible to every other user.

Twitter did not engage in outright shadow banning in a technical sense, but it did use visibility filtering. In discussions with Yoel Roth, Musk himself had embraced the idea as an alternative to outright user bans, and he had publicly touted the policy a few weeks earlier. "Negative/hate tweets will be max deboosted & demonetized, so no ads or other revenue to Twitter," he had tweeted. "You won't find the tweet unless you specifically seek it out."

The problem came when the visibility filtering was done with a political bias. Weiss concluded that Twitter moderators were more aggressive at suppressing right-wing tweets. "It operated a secret blacklist, with teams of employees tasked with suppressing the visibility of accounts or subjects deemed undesirable," Weiss and her team wrote. In addition, Twitter, like many media and educational institutions, narrowed the definition of what was acceptable discourse. "The people in charge of these institutions enforced the new parameters by expanding the definitions of words like 'violence,' 'harm,' and 'safety.' "

COVID was an interesting case. At one extreme was clearly harmful medical misinformation, such as touting quack cures and practices that could kill people. But Weiss found that Twitter was too willing to suppress posts that did not comport with official pronouncements, including ones on legitimate topics for debate, such as whether mRNA vaccines caused heart problems, whether mask mandates worked, and whether the virus emerged from a lab leak in China.

For example, Twitter put Stanford professor Jay Bhattacharya on the Trends blacklist, which meant that the visibility of his tweets was curtailed. He had organized a declaration by some scientists arguing that lockdowns and school closures would be more harmful than helpful, a controversial view that turned out to have some validity. When Weiss uncovered how Bhattacharya had been suppressed, Musk texted him, "Hi. Can you come this weekend to Twitter headquarters so we can show you what Twitter 1.0 did?" Musk, who had espoused similar views on COVID lockdowns, and Bhattacharya spoke for almost an hour.

The Twitter Files highlighted an evolution of mainstream journalism over the past fifty years. During Watergate and Vietnam, journalists generally regarded the CIA, military, and government officials with suspicion, or at least a healthy skepticism. Many of them had gotten into the craft inspired by the Vietnam reporting of David Halberstam and Neil Sheehan and the Watergate reporting of Bob Woodward and Carl Bernstein.

But beginning in the 1990s and accelerating after 9/11, established journalists felt increasingly comfortable sharing information and cooperating with top people in the government and intelligence communities. That mindset was replicated at social media companies, as shown by all the briefings Twitter and other tech companies received. "These companies seem not to have had much choice in being made key parts of a global surveillance and information control apparatus," Taibbi wrote, "although evidence suggests their Quislingian executives were mostly all thrilled to be absorbed." I think the second half of his sentence is more true than the first.

The Twitter Files brought some transparency to how Twitter had handled content moderation, but they also showed how difficult the task can be. The FBI, for example, flagged Twitter that some accounts tweeting negatively about vaccines and Ukraine were being secretly run by Russia's intelligence directorate. If that was indeed the case, was it valid for Twitter to suppress these accounts? As Taibbi himself wrote, "This is a difficult speech dilemma."

91

Rabbit Holes

Twitter, December 2022

@elonjet

Nothing would more surely make Musk go ballistic than a threat to his two-year-old son X, his constant companion and cheerful energizer. One Tuesday night in December, as the Twitter Files were unspooling, Musk perceived that such a threat had occurred, and the reverberations rattled the foundations of his proclaimed battle for free speech.

A longtime stalker of Grimes had been lurking for a day on the road around the house where she and Musk were staying in the Los Angeles area, and at one point, they say, he followed a car driven by one of Musk's security detail that was taking X and his nanny to a nearby hotel. The security person pulled into a gas station and confronted the driver, taking a video of him dressed like a ninja with gloves and mask. The guy either jumped on the car hood or tried to climb over it when the car cornered him—the details were disputed—and when the police arrived they made no arrests. Using the video that Musk posted, the *Washington Post* tracked down the guy, who told the paper that he believed Grimes was sending him coded messages through her Instagram posts. Musk tweeted, "Last night, car carrying lil X in LA was followed by crazy stalker (thinking it was me), who later blocked car from moving & climbed onto hood."

Musk believed that the stalker had been able to find where he and Grimes were staying because of a Twitter account called @elonjet, run by a student named Jack Sweeney, that posted the real-time take-offs and landings of Musk's jet based on public flight information. The connection was murky: Musk had landed in Los Angeles a day before, but Grimes said that is when she started noticing the stalker's car lurking outside.

Musk had long been infuriated by the @elonjet account, which he thought was doxing and endangering him. In April, when he was first thinking of buying Twitter, he discussed it at a dinner of friends and family in Austin, and both Grimes and his mother argued strongly that he should ban it. He agreed, but once he took over Twitter he decided not to. "My commitment to free speech extends even to not banning the account following my plane, even though that is a direct personal safety risk," he tweeted in early November.

That impressed Bari Weiss, but when she was putting together her first Twitter File thread, she discovered that Musk had done to @elonjet what the previous Twitter regime had done to some on the far right: @elonjet was being severely "visibility filtered" so that it did not show up in searches. She was disappointed; it seemed hypocritical. Then, after the incident involving X, Musk made the unilateral decision to suspend @elonjet altogether. He justified it by saying that Twitter now had a policy against doxing people's location.

Worse yet, especially from the vantage of making the site a haven for free speech, Musk arbitrarily suspended a handful of journalists who wrote about what he had done to @elonjet. His ostensible reason was that their stories had linked to the @elonjet account and were thus also doxing him, but in fact @elonjet was no longer available and the links simply led to a page that said "Account suspended." It thus seemed that Musk had acted partly out of pique, retaliating against journalists whose stories had been critical of him. These included Ryan Mac of the *New York Times*, Drew Harwell and Taylor Lorenz of the *Washington Post*, and at least eight others.

Weiss, who was still toiling in the hot box to produce more installments of the Twitter Files, found herself in a difficult situation. "He was doing the very things that he claimed to disdain about the previous overlords at Twitter," she says. "Some of the people he was kicking off were my biggest bullies on Twitter. I don't like some of these people at all. But I felt like he was betraying the things he was claiming to want Twitter to be about—a public square that wasn't rigged in favor of one side or the other. And just from a purely strategic perspective, he was martyring a lot of assholes."

Weiss wrote Musk a private message on Signal, an encrypted messaging service: "Hey, what's going on here?"

"They doxed my plane," he answered. "They attacked my son."

Weiss discussed the matter with some of the other journalists in the hot box, but ultimately she was the only one willing to speak up. "You can't be a journalist and watch journalists get kicked off Twitter and say nothing," she says. "Principles still matter to me." She knew it might mean that she would lose her access to report on the Twitter Files. And, as she joked to Nellie Bowles, "I guess Elon won't ever be our sperm donor now."

"The old regime at Twitter governed by its own whims and biases, and it sure looks like the new regime has the same problem," Weiss tweeted on the morning of December 16, the day after the journalists had been kicked off. "I oppose it in both cases."

"Rather than rigorously pursuing truth," Musk responded on Twitter, "you are virtue-signaling to show that you are 'good' in the eyes of media elite to keep one foot in both worlds." He then restricted her access to the Twitter Files.

Twitter Spaces

"This is crazy," Jason Calacanis texted David Sacks about Musk's decision to suspend journalists. "This is going to ruin attention to the Twitter Files. We've got to reverse it." So they jointly texted Musk, "You got to let these people come back." Musk was noncommittal.

In the middle of their text exchanges, Calacanis noticed that on Twitter Spaces, where users can organize audio discussions, a large group was chatting about the issue. Two of the suspended journalists, Drew Harwell of the *Post* and Matt Binder of *Mashable*, were participating. Although they were banned from posting, Twitter's software had not blocked them from the audio conversations. Calacanis told Musk, who surprised the participants by going to Spaces and—

sounding very defensive and bristly—joining in the conversation. Word quickly spread, and within minutes thirty thousand users were listening.

When the organizer, *BuzzFeed News* reporter Katie Notopoulos, asked Musk to explain the suspensions, he said it was because they had linked to places that were doxing him. "You're suggesting that we're sharing your address, which is not true," Harwell said. "I never posted your address."

"You posted a link to the address," Musk retorted.

"We posted links to elonjet, which is now not online," Harwell replied. He accused Musk of "using the same exact link-blocking technique that you have criticized as part of the Hunter Biden *New York Post* story."

Musk got angry and then disappeared from the session. A few minutes later, Twitter abruptly shut it down. In fact, it shut down all of Spaces for a day in order to make it impossible for suspended users to join conversations. "We're fixing a legacy bug," Musk tweeted about the shutdown of Spaces. "Should be working tomorrow."

Musk soon realized he had gone too far and looked for some way to reverse himself. He posted a poll asking users whether the barred journalists should have their accounts restored. More than 58 percent of the 3.6 million voters said yes. The accounts were restored.

Prosecute/Fauci

As the controversy swirled, Musk alternated between being angry and jokey. Sitting in the hot box conference room one evening with Weiss, some of her colleagues, and James, he started poking fun at the practice of people posting their preferred pronouns. Someone made a joke that Musk's should be "prosecute/Fauci." There were a few nervous laughs—Weiss admits not wanting to challenge Musk at that moment—and Musk started cackling. He repeated the joke three times. Then, at around 3 a.m., he impulsively tweeted it out: "My pronouns are Prosecute/Fauci." It made little sense, wasn't funny, and managed, in just five words, to mock transgender people, conjure up conspiracies about the eighty-one-year-old public health official

Anthony Fauci, scare off more advertisers, and create a new handful of enemies who would now never buy Teslas.

His brother was among those who were outraged. "What the heck, man, this is an old guy who was just trying to figure things out during COVID," Kimbal told him. "This is not okay." Even Jay Bhattacharya, the Stanford professor whose criticism of Fauci's policies caused him to be filtered on Twitter, criticized the tweet. "I think that Fauci made tremendous mistakes," he said. "But I think the right redress is not to prosecute him, but for history to remember him having made those mistakes."

The Fauci tweet was not merely an example of Musk expressing anti-woke or right-wing sentiments. He was skittering at times on the edges of the rabbit holes of conspiracy theories about sinister global elite forces. It was a flip side to his impish speculations that we might actually live in a simulation. In his darker moods, he brooded that behind our reality were dark conspiratorial forces, like in *The Matrix*. For example, he retweeted comments by Robert Kennedy Jr., a fervent antivaxxer who alleged that the CIA had killed his uncle the president. After Musk's Fauci tweet, Kennedy posted, "Fauci purchased omertà among virologists globally with a total of $37 billion in annual payoffs in research grants. With the paymaster gone, the orthodoxies will unravel."

"Precisely," Musk replied. He would later host a Twitter Spaces with Kennedy when he decided to run for president against Biden.

As often, there were unnerving echoes of his father. Errol had been spouting conspiracy theories about COVID for more than two years. "This man should be fired!" he said of Fauci on Facebook in April 2020. Later that year, he alleged that Bill Gates knew about COVID six months before it spread and had negotiated a $100 billion contract to trace it. By 2021, he was a full-throated denier of COVID vaccines, Trump's election loss, and the 9/11 terrorist attacks. "From all the info coming out, it appears the 9/11 attacks were a setup and the evidence is overwhelming," he said. And just a few weeks before Elon launched the Twitter Files, Errol posted a rant on Facebook about how COVID was "a lie." He said of the vaccines, "If you were stupid enough to have the injection, and especially 'boosters,' you are going to die soon."

After the Twitter Files were published, Errol sent his son another unsolicited message. "The Left (or gangsters) have got to be stopped," he wrote. "Civilization is at stake." The election had been stolen from Trump, and it was "essential" to let him back on Twitter. "He is our only ray of light." He then advised his son to remember the lesson he learned as a child on the playgrounds of South Africa: "Trying to placate the gangsters is futile. The more you try, the less they fear or respect you. Hit them hard, or hit anyone hard, and they will respect you."

Elon never saw these messages. In an attempt to purge his father's demons, he had changed his email address and not given Errol the new one.

Fallout

When Yoel Roth resigned from Twitter in November, his major worry was that Musk would unleash a Twitter mob on him that would threaten his safety. At first, it seemed he had been spared. But then, when his emails and Slack messages were released in the Twitter Files in December, Musk trained his flamethrower on him.

The Twitter Files showed Roth discussing how to handle such issues as the Hunter Biden laptop story. Most of his comments were thoughtful, but they still elicited angry reactions on Twitter. At one point a user posted a tweet saying, "I think I may have found the problem." It pointed to a post Roth had made in 2010 that linked, without comment, to a journal article asking whether it was wrong for a teacher to have sex with an eighteen-year-old student. "That explains a lot," Musk replied. Musk then took up the bludgeon on his own. He tweeted out a screenshot of a paragraph of Roth's University of Pennsylvania doctoral dissertation, titled "Gay Data," which noted discussed ways that gay hookup sites such as Grindr could deal with users under the age of eighteen. Musk commented, "Looks like Yoel is arguing in favor of children being able to access adult Internet services."

Roth had nothing to do with pedophilia, but Musk's insinuations stirred up Pizzagate-style conspiracists lurking in the dark recesses of Twitter who unleashed a barrage of homophobic and anti-Semitic attacks. A tabloid then published Roth's address, forcing him to go into hiding. "Musk made the decision to share a defamatory allegation that I support or condone pedophilia," Roth later said. "I had to leave my home and sell it. Those are the consequences for this type of online harassment and speech."

On the Sunday that he stirred up outrage with his Fauci tweet, Musk dropped in on the hot box at Twitter and offered the musketeers and others tickets for a Dave Chappelle comedy event that evening. Even at a show by the famously anti-woke comedian, it became evident that Musk's tweets had added a new layer of damage to his reputation. "Ladies and gentlemen, make some noise for the richest man in the world," Chappelle proclaimed as he invited Musk onstage. There was some applause, but also a long chorus of boos. "It sounds like some of those people you fired are in the audience," Chappelle said. He jokingly reassured Musk that the booing was mainly from people in the "terrible seats."

Musk's erratic tweets further hurt Twitter with advertisers. He asked for a call with David Zaslav, the CEO of Warner Bros. Discovery, and they spoke for more than an hour. Zaslav told him that he was doing self-destructive things that made it harder to attract brands that were aspirational. He should focus on improving the product by adding longer video offerings and making ads more effective.

The damage even spilled over to Tesla. Its stock had dropped to $156 a share, down from $340 when he first announced his interest in Twitter. At its meeting in Austin on December 14, the Tesla board, usually very compliant, told Musk that the Twitter controversies were hurting the Tesla brand. Musk pushed back, saying that sales numbers were bad around the world, even where people were not paying attention to the controversies, and it was due mainly to macroeconomic factors. But both Kimbal and board chair Robyn Denholm kept pressing him, saying that his behavior was a factor. "The giant elephant in the room was that he was acting like a fucking idiot," Kimbal says.

92

Christmas Capers

December 2022

The Musketeers with the movers in Sacramento;
James pushing a server rack

Head-explosion emoji

"Does this timeframe seem like something that I would find remotely acceptable?" Musk asked. "Obviously not. If a timeline is long, it's wrong."

It was late at night on December 22, and the meeting in Musk's tenth-floor Twitter conference room had become tense. He was talking to two Twitter infrastructure managers who had not dealt with him much before, and certainly not when he was in a foul mood.

One of them tried to explain the problem. The data-services company that housed one of Twitter's server farms, located in Sacramento, had agreed to allow them some short-term extensions on their lease so they could begin to move out during 2023 in an orderly fashion. "But this morning," the nervous manager told Musk, "they came back to us and said that plan was no longer on the table because, and these are their words, they don't think that we will be financially viable."

The facility was costing Twitter more than $100 million a year. Musk wanted to save that money by moving the servers to one of Twitter's other facilities, in Portland, Oregon. Another manager at the meeting said that couldn't be done right away. "We can't get out safely before six to nine months," she said in a matter-of-fact tone. "Sacramento still needs to be around to serve traffic."

Over the years, Musk had been faced many times with a choice between what he thought was necessary and what others told him was possible. The result was almost always the same. He paused in silence for a few moments, then announced, "You have ninety days to do it. If you can't make that work, your resignation is accepted."

The manager began to explain in detail some of the obstacles to relocating the servers to Portland. "It has different rack densities, different power densities," she said. "So the rooms need to be upgraded." She started to give a lot more details, but after a minute, Musk interrupted.

"This is making my brain hurt," he said.

"I'm sorry, that was not my intention," she replied in a measured monotone.

"Do you know the head-explosion emoji?" he asked her. "That's what my head feels like right now. What a pile of fucking bullshit. Jesus H fucking Christ. Portland obviously has tons of room. It's trivial to move servers one place to another."

The Twitter managers again tried to explain the constraints. Musk interrupted. "Can you have someone go to our server centers and send me videos of the insides?" he asked. It was three days before Christmas, and the manager promised the video in a week. "No, tomorrow," Musk ordered. "I've built server centers myself, and I can tell if you could put more servers there or not. That's why I asked if you had actually visited these facilities. If you've not been there, you're just talking bullshit."

SpaceX and Tesla were successful because Musk relentlessly pushed his teams to be scrappier, more nimble, and to launch fire-drill surges that extruded all obstacles. That's how they had cobbled together a car production line in a tent in Fremont and a test facility in the Texas desert and a launch site at Cape Canaveral made of used parts. "All you need to do is just move the fucking servers to Portland," he said. "If it takes longer than thirty days, that would blow my mind." He paused and recalculated. "Just get a moving company, and it will take a week to move the computers and another week to plug them in. Two weeks. That's what should happen." Everyone was silent. But Musk was still warming up. "If you got a goddamn U-Haul, you could probably do it by yourself." The two Twitter managers looked to see if he was serious. Steve Davis and Omead Afshar were also at the table. They had seen him like this many times before, and they knew that he might be.

The Sacramento raid

"Why don't we do it right now?" James Musk asked.

He and his brother Andrew were flying with Elon from San Francisco to Austin on Friday evening, December 23, the day after the frustrating infrastructure meeting about how long it would take to move the servers out of the Sacramento facility. Avid skiers, they had planned to go by themselves to Tahoe for Christmas, but Elon that day invited them to come to Austin instead. James was reluctant. He was mentally exhausted and didn't need more intensity, but Andrew convinced him that they should go. So that's how they ended up on the plane—with Musk, Grimes, and X, along with Steve Davis and Nicole Hollander and their baby—listening to Elon complain about the servers.

They were somewhere over Las Vegas when James made his suggestion that they could move them now. It was the type of impulsive, impractical, surge-into-the-breach idea that Musk loved. It was already late evening, but he told his pilot to divert, and they made a loop back up to Sacramento.

The only rental car they could find when they landed was a Toyota Corolla. Musk's chief security guard drove, Grimes sat on Elon's lap in the passenger seat, and others crammed into the back. They were not sure how they would even get inside the data center at night, but one very surprised Twitter staffer, a guy named Alex from Uzbekistan, was still there. He merrily let them in and showed them around.

The facility, which housed rooms of servers for many other companies as well, was very secure, with a retinal scan required for entry into each of the vaults. Alex the Uzbek was able to get them into the Twitter vault, which contained about fifty-two hundred refrigerator-size racks of thirty computers each. "These things do not look that hard to move," Elon announced. It was a reality-distorting assertion, since each rack weighed about twenty-five hundred pounds and was eight feet tall.

"You'll have to hire a contractor to lift the floor panels," Alex said. "They need to be lifted with suction cups." Another set of contractors, he said, would then have to go underneath the floor panels and disconnect the electric cables and seismic rods.

Musk turned to his security guard and asked to borrow his pocket knife. Using it, he was able to lift one of the air vents in the floor, which allowed him to pry open the floor panels. He then crawled under the server floor himself, used the knife to jimmy open an electrical cabinet, pulled the server plugs, and waited to see what happened. Nothing exploded. The server was ready to be moved. "Well that doesn't seem super hard," he said as Alex the Uzbek and the rest of the gang stared. Musk was totally jazzed by this point. It was, he said with a loud laugh, like a remake of *Mission: Impossible*, Sacramento edition.

The next day—Christmas Eve—Musk called in reinforcements. Ross Nordeen drove from San Francisco. He stopped at the Apple Store in Union Square and spent $2,000 to buy out the entire stock of AirTags so the servers could be tracked on their journey, and then stopped at Home Depot, where he spent $2,500 on wrenches, bolt-cutters, headlamps, and the tools needed to unscrew the seismic bolts. Steve Davis got someone from The Boring Company to procure a semi truck and line up moving vans. Other enlistees arrived from SpaceX.

The server racks were on wheels, so the team was able to disconnect four of them and roll them to the waiting truck. This showed that all fifty-two hundred or so could probably be moved within days. "The guys are kicking ass!" Musk exulted.

Other workers at the facility watched with a mix of amazement and horror. Musk and his renegade team were rolling servers out without putting them in crates or swaddling them in protective material, then using store-bought straps to secure them in the truck. "I've never loaded a semi before," James admitted. Ross called it "terrifying." It was like cleaning out a closet, "but the stuff in it is totally critical."

At 3 p.m., after they had gotten four servers onto the truck, word of the caper reached the top executives at NTT, the company that owned and managed the data center. They issued orders that Musk's team halt. Musk had the mix of glee and anger that often accompanied one of his manic surges. He called the CEO of the storage division, who told him it was impossible to move server racks without a bevy of experts. "Bullshit," Musk explained. "We have already loaded four onto the semi." The CEO then told him that some of the floors could not handle more than five hundred pounds of pressure, so rolling a two-thousand-pound server would cause damage. Musk replied that the servers had four wheels, so the pressure at any one point was only five hundred pounds. "The dude is not very good at math," Musk told the musketeers.

Having ruined the Christmas Eve of the NTT managers, as well as hitting them with a potential loss of more than $100 million in revenue for the coming year, Musk showed pity and said he would suspend moving the servers for two days. But they would resume, he warned, the day after Christmas.

Family Christmas

Late Christmas Eve, with the temporary ceasefire in place at the Sacramento data center, Musk invited James and Andrew, their ski plans foiled, to come to Boulder to spend Christmas with Kimbal and his family. Christiana scrambled to buy gifts and stuff stockings for the two unexpected guests. Kimbal cooked roast beef and a foot-high Yorkshire pudding. Elon's son Damian, also an avid chef, made a yam dish. X played with an air-pump rocket, chanting the countdown, then stomping on the release button to make it launch. James and Andrew soaked in the hot tub, decompressing.

The visit was a chance for Kimbal to have a serious conversation with his brother about how, since the Twitter deal, he had been spinning out of control. A year earlier, he had been Person of the Year and the world's richest, and now he was neither. It was like what happened in 2018, and it was time for another open-loop warning. You're making enemies at a dangerous pace, and at dangerous levels, Kimbal told him. "It's like the days of high school, when you kept getting beaten up."

Kimbal even broached the topic of whether Elon wanted to remain as CEO of Tesla. It was in deep trouble, and he wasn't focused on it. "Why don't you just not be CEO?" Kimbal asked. Elon was not ready to answer that.

There was also the issue of his late-night tweeting. Kimbal had stopped following Elon on Twitter because it was too nervewracking. Elon admitted that the tweet about Paul Pelosi was a mistake. He had not realized that the story he saw online about a male prostitute was from an unreliable site. "You're an idiot," Kimbal said.

"Stop falling for weird shit." The same was true for his Fauci tweet. "It's not okay. It's not funny. You can't do that shit." Kimbal also lectured James and Andrew for abetting him. "This is not okay, guys. This is not okay."

One topic they did not discuss was Twitter the company. When Elon brought it up, Kimbal refused to talk about it. "I really don't give a shit about Twitter," he said. "It's just a pimple on the ass of what should be your impact on the world." Elon disagreed, but they didn't argue about it.

One Christmas tradition that Kimbal and Christiana had was to ask everyone to reflect on a question. This year it was "What regrets do you have?" "My main regret," Elon answered, "is how often I stab myself in the thigh with a fork, how often I shoot my own feet and stab myself in the eye."

Christmas gave Musk the opportunity to reconnect with his sons Griffin, Damian, and Kai, who had become distanced from him during the turmoil stirred up by Twitter and his tweets. Like James and Andrew, they were bestowed with outsized capabilities in math and science, but without the demons and harshness of their father and grandfather. Being the sons of Elon Musk was difficult, but they were "stoics," as Musk called them.

He discussed with Kai, then sixteen, the possibility of leaving high school and coming to work at Twitter. "He's an outstanding programmer, so he could write software and do high school online, which is what Damian has done," Musk says. "I'm not pushing hard, because I know there's a social element to school, but he's way too smart for high school. It's kind of ridiculous." Kai said he would think about it.

Damian, Kai's identical twin, had the same brilliance but different interests. For more than a year, he had been working on quantum computation and cryptography in the academic lab of a particle physicist. After doing high school online, he was accepted at one of the nation's top research universities, but Musk thought it might not be intellectually challenging enough for him to enroll there as an undergraduate. "He's already at the graduate-school level in math and physics."

Griffin was the most easygoing extrovert of the Musk family. As a freshman at an Ivy League college, he was dealing with the animosity directed at his father. In talking about himself, he is very deferential and humble, but he did say, almost apologetically, "I'm sorry this may sound a bit boastful, but I was number one in my class of four hundred fifty in computer science." He spent a lot of his time, like his father did as a teenager, programming video games. His favorite to play was *Elden Ring*.

Jenna, who was once known as Xavier, wasn't there, of course. But Christiana sent her a text message saying the whole family missed her and that she was sending along the Christmas stocking she had made for her. "Thank you," Jenna responded. "This means so much to me."

As for Saxon, who is autistic, he again showed his wisdom. At one point the family was discussing how they needed to use pseudonyms when they went to a restaurant. "Oh, yes," he said. "If anyone finds out I'm Elon Musk's son, they are going to be mad at me because he's ruining Twitter."

The heist continued

After Christmas, Andrew and James headed back to Sacramento to see how many more servers they could move. They hadn't brought enough clothes, so they went to Walmart and bought jeans and T-shirts.

The NTT supervisors who ran the facility continued to throw up obstacles, some quite understandable. Instead of letting them prop open the door to the vault, for example, they required the musketeers and their crew to go through a retinal security scan each time they went in. One of the supervisors watched them at all times. "She was the most insufferable person I've ever worked with," James says. "But to be fair, I could understand where she was coming from, because we were ruining her holidays, right?"

The moving contractors that NTT wanted them to use charged $200 an hour. So James went on Yelp and found a company named Extra Care Movers that would do the work at one-tenth the cost. The motley company pushed the ideal of scrappiness to its outer limits. The owner had lived on the streets for a while, then had a kid, and he was trying to turn his life around. He didn't have a bank account, so James ended up using PayPal to pay him. The second day, the crew wanted cash, so James went to a bank and withdrew $13,000 from his personal account. Two of the crew members had no identification, which made it hard for them to sign into the facility. But they made up for it in hustle. "You get a dollar tip for every additional server we move," James announced at one point. From then on, when they got a new one on a truck, the workers would ask how many they were up to.

The servers had user data on them, and James did not initially realize that, for privacy reasons, they were supposed to be wiped clean before being moved. "By the time we learned this, the servers had already been unplugged and rolled out, so there was no way we would roll them back, plug them in, and then wipe them," he says. Plus, the wiping software wasn't working. "Fuck, what do we do?" he asked. Elon recommended that they lock the trucks and track them. So James sent someone to Home Depot to buy big padlocks, and they sent the combination codes on a spreadsheet to Portland so the trucks could be opened there. "I can't believe it worked," James says. "They all made it to Portland safely."

By the end of the week they had used all of the available trucks in Sacramento. Despite the area being pummeled by rain, they moved more than seven hundred of the racks in three days. The previous record at that facility had been moving thirty in a month. That still left a lot of servers in the facility, but the musketeers had proven that they could be moved quickly. The rest were handled by the Twitter infrastructure team in January.

Elon had promised James a big bonus, up to $1 million, if he got the servers moved by the end of the year. Nothing was put in writing, but James trusted his cousin. After the move, he heard from Jared Birchall that the deal applied only to the number of servers that got up and running in Portland. Because they needed new electrical connections, that was zero. James texted Elon, who came back with the proposal that he would get $1,000 for every server that arrived safely in Portland, whether or not it was plugged in. That amounted to just over $700,000. Elon also offered him a stock option package to join Twitter. James accepted both.

James loved his family in South Africa. Having missed the chance to spend Christmas with them, he planned to use part of the bonus to buy them tickets to visit the U.S. in the spring. He also was saving up to buy his parents a home in California. "My father loves woodworking, but he just sliced off part of his finger and is going through a rough time now," James says. "I'm very close to my dad."

All very exciting and inspiring, right? An example of Musk's bold and scrappy approach! But as with all things Musk, it was, alas, not that simple. It was also an example of his recklessness, his impatience with pushback, and the way he intimidated people. Twitter's infrastructure engineers had tried to explain to him, in that head-explosion-emoji meeting a week earlier, why a quick shutdown of the Sacramento center would be a problem, but he shot them down. He had a good track record of knowing when to ignore naysayers. But not a perfect one. For the next two months, Twitter was destabilized. The lack of servers caused meltdowns, including when Musk hosted a Twitter Spaces for presidential candidate Ron DeSantis. "In retrospect, the whole Sacramento shutdown was a mistake," Musk would admit in March 2023. "I was told we had redundancy across our data centers. What I wasn't told was that we had seventy thousand hard-coded references to Sacramento. And there's still shit that's broken because of it."

His most valuable lieutenants at Tesla and SpaceX had learned ways to deflect his bad ideas and drip-feed him unwelcome information, but the legacy employees at Twitter didn't know how to handle him. That said, Twitter survived. And the Sacramento caper showed Twitter employees that he was serious when he spoke about the need for a maniacal sense of urgency.

New Year's Eve

Musk badly needed to decompress. He was not good at vacations, but a few times each year he would get away for two or three days to

Lanai, Hawaii, to stay at one of the homes of his mentor, Larry Ellison, as he had done in April when he decided to buy Twitter. At the end of December, he went there with Grimes and X.

Ellison had recently built a domed astronomical observatory on the island with a one-meter mirror telescope weighing three thousand pounds. Musk asked to have it pointed toward Mars. After looking through the eyepiece for a while in silence, he called X over and lifted him up to see. "Look at this," he said. "This is where you are going to live someday."

Then he and Grimes and X flew to Cabo San Lucas, Mexico, to celebrate the welcome end to a tumultuous 2022 with Kimbal and his family. His four older sons were there. So were all of Kimbal's. "It was good for our nervous system to be together," Kimbal says. "We are a very complex family, and it's really unusual for everyone to be happy at the same time."

Ever since the Twitter purchase, Musk had been in war mode, feeling the siege mentality that had suffused his childhood and bred inside him easily triggered resentments. His feet were heavy, his body language fierce, and his posture tense for battle. But the family gatherings produced a few periods of intermittent calm. On his first evening in Cabo, he went to dinner with just Kimbal, Kai, and Antonio Gracias at a very quiet restaurant. The next day they played board games and watched movies. The one that Musk picked was the 1993 action drama *Demolition Man,* in which Sylvester Stallone plays a risk-loving policeman who pursues his work with such intensity that he wreaks great collateral damage. He found it funny.

There was a community party to celebrate New Year's Eve, which culminated with the traditional midnight countdown. After the hugging and fireworks were over, Musk took on his vacant look and started staring into the distance. His friends knew not to interrupt when he was in such a trance, but finally Christiana put her hand on his back and asked if everything was okay. He stayed silent for another minute. "Got to get Starship into orbit," he finally said. "We've got to get Starship into orbit."

93

AI for Cars

Tesla, 2022–2023

Dhaval Shroff and his Tesla desk

Cars that learn from humans

"It's like ChatGPT, but for cars," Dhaval Shroff told Musk. He was comparing his project at Tesla to the artificial intelligence chatbot that had just been released by OpenAI, the lab that Musk had cofounded with Sam Altman in 2015. For almost a decade, Musk had been working on various forms of artificial intelligence, including self-driving cars, Optimus the robot, and the Neuralink brain-machine interface. Shroff's project involved the latest machine-learning frontier: devising a self-driving car system that would learn from human behavior. "We process an enormous amount of data on how real humans acted in a complex driving situation, and then we train a computer's neural network to mimic that."

Musk had asked to meet with Shroff—who had occasionally served as a fourth musketeer with James, Andrew, and Ross—because he was thinking about persuading him to leave Tesla's Autopilot team and come work at Twitter. Shroff was hoping to avoid that by convincing Musk of the crucial importance, to Tesla and to the world, of the project he was working on, a "learn-from-humans" component to Tesla's self-driving software that they were calling "the neural network path planner."

Their meeting was scheduled for a day that turned out to be so wildly crammed with plot lines that it would seem too contrived if it were part of a screenplay: Friday, December 2, 2022, which was when the first set of Twitter Files was due to be posted by Matt Taibbi. Shroff arrived at Twitter headquarters that morning, as requested, but Musk, who had just come back from unveiling the Cybertruck in Nevada, apologized. He had forgotten that he was due to fly to New Orleans to meet with President Macron to talk about European content moderation regulations. He asked Shroff to come back that evening. As he was waiting for Macron, Musk sent Shroff texts pushing their meeting later. "I'm going to be delayed by four hours," Musk texted at one point. "Do you mind waiting?" That's also when he texted Bari Weiss and Nellie Bowles out of the blue asking them to fly up to San Francisco and meet him that night to help with the Twitter Files.

When Musk arrived back in San Francisco late that night, he finally got a chance to sit down with Shroff, who explained the details of the neural network planner project he was working on. "I think it's super important that I continue doing what I'm doing," Shroff said. Listening to him, Musk got excited again about the project and agreed. In the future, he realized, Tesla was going to be not just a car company and not just a clean-energy company. With Full Self-Driving and the Optimus robot and the Dojo machine-learning supercomputer, it was going to be an artificial intelligence company—one that operated not only in the virtual world of chatbots but also in the physical real world of factories and roads. He was already thinking about hiring a group of AI experts to compete with OpenAI, and Tesla's neural network planning team would complement their work.

For years, Tesla's Autopilot system relied on a rules-based approach. It took visual data from a car's cameras and identified such things as lane markings, pedestrians, vehicles, traffic signals, and anything else in range of the eight cameras. Then the software applied a set of rules, such as *Stop when the light is red*; *Go when it's green*; *Stay in the middle of the lane markers*; *Don't cross double-yellow lines into incoming traffic*; *Proceed through an intersection only when there are no cars coming fast enough to hit you*; and so on. Tesla's engineers manually wrote and updated hundreds of thousands of lines of C++ code to apply these rules to complex situations.

The neural network planner project that Shroff was working on would add a new layer. "Instead of determining the proper path of the car based only on rules," Shroff says, "we determine the car's proper path by also relying on a neural network that learns from millions of examples of what humans have done." In other words, it's human imitation. Faced with a situation, the neural network chooses a path based on what humans have done in thousands of similar situations. It's like the way humans learn to speak and drive and play chess and eat spaghetti and do almost everything else; we might be given a set of rules to follow, but mainly we pick up the skills by observing how other people do them. It was the approach to machine learning envisioned by Alan Turing in his 1950 paper, "Computing Machinery and Intelligence."

Tesla had one of the world's largest supercomputers to train neural networks. It was powered by graphics processing units (GPUs) made by the chipmaker Nvidia. Musk's goal for 2023 was to transition to using Dojo, the supercomputer that Tesla was building from the ground up, to use video data to train the AI system. With chips and infrastructure designed in-house by Tesla's AI team, it has nearly eight exaflops (10^{18} operations per second) of processing power, making it the world's most powerful computer for that purpose. It would be used for both self-driving software and for Optimus the robot. "It's interesting to work on them together," Musk says. "They are both trying to navigate the world."

By early 2023, the neural network planner project had analyzed 10 million frames of video collected from the cars of Tesla customers. Does that mean it would merely be as good as the average of human drivers? "No, because we only use data from humans when they handled a situation well," Shroff explains. Human labelers, many of them based in Buffalo, New York, assessed the videos and gave them grades. Musk told them to look for things "a five-star Uber driver would do," and those were the videos used to train the computer.

Musk regularly walked through Tesla's Palo Alto building, where the Autopilot engineers sat in an open workspace, and he would kneel down next to them for impromptu discussions. One day Shroff showed him the progress they were making. Musk was impressed, but he had a question: Was this whole new approach truly needed? Might it be a bit of overkill? One of his maxims was that you should never use a cruise missile to kill a fly; just use a flyswatter. Was using a neural network to plan paths an unnecessarily complicated way to deal with a few very unlikely edge cases?

Shroff showed Musk instances where a neural network planner would work better than a rules-based approach. The demo had a road littered with trash cans, fallen traffic cones, and random debris. A car guided by the neural network planner was able to skitter around the obstacles, crossing the lane lines and breaking some rules as necessary. "Here's what happens when we move from rules-based to network-path-based," Shroff told him. "The car will never get into a collision if you turn this thing on, even in unstructured environments." It was the type of leap into the future that excited Musk. "We should do a James Bond–style demonstration," he said, "where there are bombs exploding on all sides and a UFO is falling from the sky while the car speeds through without hitting anything."

Machine-learning systems generally need a goal or metric that guides them as they train themselves. Musk, who liked to manage by decreeing what metrics should be paramount, gave them their lodestar: the number of miles that cars with Tesla Full Self-Driving were able to travel without a human intervening. "I want the latest data on miles per intervention to be the starting slide at each of our meetings," he decreed. "If we're training AI, what do we optimize? The answer is higher miles between interventions." He told them to make it like a video game where they could see their score every day. "Video games without a score are boring, so it will be motivating to watch each day as the miles per intervention increases."

Members of the team installed massive eighty-five-inch television monitors in their workspace that displayed in real time how many miles the FSD cars were driving on average without interventions. Whenever they would see a type of intervention recurring—such as drivers grabbing the wheel during a lane change or a merge or a turn into a complex intersection—they would work with both the rules and the neural network planner to make a fix. They put a gong near their desks, and whenever they successfully solved a problem causing an intervention, they got to bang the gong.

An AI test drive

By mid-April 2023, it was time for Musk to put this new neural network planner to the test. He took it for a drive through Palo Alto. Shroff and the Autopilot team had configured a car to rely on software that had been trained by the neural network to imitate human drivers. The software had only a bare minimum of traditional rules-based code.

Musk sat in the driver's seat next to Ashok Elluswamy, Tesla's director of Autopilot software. Shroff got in the back with the two other members of his team, Matt Bauch and Chris Payne. The trio had been working at adjoining desks at Tesla for eight years, and they all lived within blocks of each other in San Francisco. On their desks, where most people have a picture of their family, they each had identical pictures of the three of them posing together at a Halloween party. James Musk had been the fourth member of their team, until his uncle took over Twitter and redeployed him there, the fate Shroff had avoided.

As they prepared to leave the parking lot at Tesla's Palo Alto office complex, Musk selected a location on the map for the car to go, clicked on Full Self-Driving, and took his hands off the wheel. When the car turned onto the main road, the first scary challenge arose: a bicyclist was heading their way. "We were all holding our breath, because cyclists can be unpredictable," Shroff says. But Musk was unconcerned and didn't try to grab the wheel. On its own, the car yielded. "It felt exactly like what a human driver would do," says Shroff.

Shroff and his two teammates explained in detail how the FSD software they were using had been trained on millions of video clips collected from the cameras on customers' cars. The result was a software stack that was much simpler than the traditional one based on thousands of rules coded by humans. "It runs ten times faster and it could eventually allow for the deletion of 300,000 lines of code," Shroff said. Bauch said it was like an AI bot playing a really boring video game. Musk let out his laughing snort. Then, as the car wove on its own through traffic, he pulled out his phone and started tweeting.

For twenty-five minutes, the car drove on fast roads and neighborhood streets, handling complex turns and avoiding cyclists, pedestrians, and pets. Musk never touched the wheel. Only a couple of times did he intervene by tapping the accelerator when he thought the car was being overly cautious, such as when it was too deferential at a four-way stop sign. At one point the car conducted a maneuver that he thought was better than he would have done. "Oh wow," he said, "even my human neural network failed here, but the car did the right thing." He was so pleased that he started whistling Mozart's "A Little Night Music" serenade in G major.

"Amazing work guys," Musk said at the end. "This is really impressive." They all then went to the weekly meeting of the Autopilot team, where twenty guys, almost all in black T-shirts, sat around a conference table to hear the verdict. Many had not believed that the neural network project would work. Musk declared that he was now a believer and they should move a lot of resources to push it forward.

During the discussion, Musk latched on to a key fact the team had discovered: the neural network did not work well until it had been trained on at least a million video clips, and it started getting really good after one-and-a-half million clips. This gave Tesla a huge advantage over other car and AI companies. It had a fleet of almost two million Teslas around the world collecting billions of video frames per day. "We are uniquely positioned to do this," Elluswamy said at the meeting.

The ability to collect and analyze vast flows of real-time data would be crucial to all forms of AI, from self-driving cars to Optimus robots to ChatGPT–like bots. And Musk now had two powerful gushers of real-time data, the video from self-driving cars and the billions of postings each week on Twitter. He told the Autopilot meeting that he had just made a major purchase of 10,000 more GPU data-processing chips for use at Twitter, and he announced that he would hold more frequent meetings on the potentially more powerful Dojo chips being designed at Tesla. He also ruefully admitted that his impulsive Christmastime caper of gutting Twitter's Sacramento data center was a mistake.

Listening in on the meeting was a superstar AI engineer. Musk had just that week hired him for a secret new project he was about to launch.

94

AI for Humans

X.AI, 2023

In Austin with Shivon Zilis and their twins, Strider and Azure

The great race

Technology revolutions usually start with little fanfare. No one woke up one morning in 1760 and shouted, "OMG, the Industrial Revolution has just begun!" Even the Digital Revolution chugged away for many years in the background, with hobbyists cobbling together personal computers to show off at geeky gatherings such as the Homebrew Computer Club, before people noticed that the world was being fundamentally transformed. But the Artificial Intelligence Revolution was different. Within a few weeks in the spring of 2023, millions of tech-aware and then ordinary folks noticed that a transformation was happening with head-snapping speed that would change the nature of work, learning, creativity, and the tasks of daily life.

For a decade, Musk had been worried about the danger that artificial intelligence could someday run amok—develop a mind of its own, so to speak—and threaten humanity. When Google cofounder Larry Page dismissed his concerns, calling him a "specist" for favoring the human species over other forms of intelligence, it destroyed their friendship. Musk tried to prevent Page and Google from purchasing DeepMind, the company formed by AI pioneer Demis Hassabis. When that failed, he formed a competing lab, a nonprofit called OpenAI, with Sam Altman in 2015.

Humans can be pricklier than machines, and Musk eventually split with Altman, left the board of OpenAI, and lured away its high-profile engineer Andrej Karpathy to lead the Autopilot team at Tesla. Altman then formed a for-profit arm of OpenAI, got a $13 billion investment from Microsoft, and recruited Karpathy back.

Among the products that OpenAI developed was a bot called ChatGPT that was trained on large internet data sets to answer questions posed by users. When Altman and his team showed an early version of it to Bill Gates in June 2022, he said he would not be interested until it could do something like pass an advance-placement biology exam. "I thought that would make them go away for two or three years," he says. Instead, they were back in three months. Altman, Microsoft CEO Satya Nadella, and others came to dinner at his house to show him a new version, called GPT-4, and Gates bombarded it with biology questions. "It was mind-blowing," Gates says. He then asked what it would say to a father with a sick child. "It gave this very careful excellent answer that was perhaps better than any of us in the room might have given."

In March 2023, OpenAI released GPT-4 to the public. Google then released a rival chatbot named Bard. The stage was thus set for a competition between OpenAI-Microsoft and DeepMind-Google to create products that could chat with humans in a natural way and perform an endless array of text-based intellectual tasks.

Musk worried that these chatbots and AI systems, especially in the hands of Microsoft and Google, could become politically indoctrinated, perhaps even infected by what he called the woke-mind virus. He also feared that self-learning AI systems might turn hostile to the human species. And on a more immediate level, he worried that chatbots could be trained to flood Twitter with disinformation, biased reporting, and financial scams. All of those things were already being done by humans, of course. But the ability to deploy thousands of weaponized chatbots would make the problem two or three orders of magnitude worse.

His compulsion to ride to the rescue kicked in. The two-way competition between OpenAI and Google needed, he thought, a third gladiator, one that would focus on AI safety and preserving humanity. He was resentful that he had founded and funded OpenAI but was now left out of the fray. AI was the biggest storm brewing. And there was no one more attracted to a storm than Musk.

In February 2023, he invited—perhaps a better word is "summoned"—Sam Altman to meet with him at Twitter and asked him to bring the founding documents for OpenAI. Musk challenged him to justify how he could legally transform a nonprofit funded by donations into a for-profit that could make millions. Altman tried to show that it was all legitimate, and he insisted that he personally was not a shareholder or cashing in. He also offered Musk shares in the new company, which Musk declined.

Instead, Musk unleashed a barrage of attacks on OpenAI and Altman. "OpenAI was created as an open-source (which is why I named it 'Open' AI), non-profit company to serve as a counterweight to Google, but now it has become a closed source, maximum-profit company effectively controlled by Microsoft," he said. "I'm still confused as to how a non-profit to which I donated $100M somehow became a $30B market cap for-profit. If this is legal, why doesn't everyone do it?" He called AI "the most powerful tool that mankind has ever created," and then lamented that it was "now in the hands of a ruthless corporate monopoly."

Altman was pained. Unlike Musk, he is sensitive and nonconfrontational. He was not making any money off of OpenAI, and he felt that Musk had not drilled down enough into the complexity of the issue of AI safety. However, he did feel that Musk's criticisms came from a sincere concern. "He's a jerk," Altman told Kara Swisher. "He has a style that is not a style that I'd want to have for myself. But I think he does really care, and he is feeling very stressed about what the future's going to look like for humanity."

Musk's data streams

The fuel for AI is data. The new chatbots were being trained on massive amounts of information, such as billions of pages on the internet and other documents. Google and Microsoft, with their search engines and cloud services and access to emails, had huge gushers of data to help train these systems.

What could Musk bring to the party? One asset was the Twitter feed, which included more than a trillion tweets posted over the years, five hundred million added each day. It was humanity's hive mind, the world's most timely data set of real-life human conversations, news, interests, trends, arguments, and lingo. Plus it was a great training ground for a chatbot to test how real humans react to its responses. The value of this data feed was not something Musk considered when buying Twitter. "It was a side benefit, actually, that I realized only after the purchase," he says.

Twitter had rather loosely permitted other companies to make use of this data stream. In January, Musk convened a series of late-night meetings in his Twitter conference room to work out ways to charge for it. "It's a monetization opportunity," he told the engineers. It was also a way to restrict Google and Microsoft from using this data to improve their AI chatbots.

There was another data trove that Musk had: the 160 billion frames *per day* of video that Tesla received and processed from the cameras on its cars. This data was different from the text-based documents that informed chatbots. It was video data of humans navigating in real-world situations. It could help create AI for physical robots, not just text-generating chatbots.

The holy grail of artificial general intelligence was building machines that could operate like humans in physical spaces, such as factories and offices and on the surface of Mars, not just wow us with disembodied chatting. Tesla and Twitter together could provide the data sets and the processing capability for both approaches: teaching machines to navigate in physical space and to answer questions in natural language.

The Ides of March

"What can be done to make AI safe?" Musk asked. "I keep wrestling with that. What actions can we take to minimize AI danger and assure that human consciousness survives?"

He was sitting cross-legged and barefoot on the poolside patio of the Austin house of Shivon Zilis, the Neuralink executive who was the mother of two of his children and who had been his intellectual companion on artificial intelligence since the founding of OpenAI eight years earlier. Their twins, Strider and Azure, now sixteen months old, were sitting on their laps. Musk was still on his intermittent-fasting diet; for his late brunch, he had doughnuts, which he had begun eating regularly. Zilis made coffee and then put his in the microwave to get it superhot so he wouldn't chug it too fast.

A week earlier, Musk had texted me, "There are a few important things I would like to talk to you about. Can only be done in person." When I asked where and when he wanted to meet, he answered, "The Ides of March in Austin."

I was baffled and, admittedly, a bit worried. Should I beware? It turned out that he wanted to talk about issues he was facing in the future, and the first on his mind was AI. We had to leave our phones in the house while we sat outside, because, he said, someone could use them to monitor our conversation. But he later agreed that I could use what he said about AI in the book.

He spoke in a low monotone punctuated by bouts of almost manic laughter. The amount of human intelligence, he noted, was leveling off, because people were not having enough children. Meanwhile, the amount of computer intelligence was going up exponentially, like Moore's Law on steroids. At some point, biological brainpower would be dwarfed by digital brainpower.

In addition, new AI machine-learning systems could ingest information on their own and teach themselves how to generate outputs, even upgrade their own code and capabilities. The term "singularity" was used by the mathematician John von Neumann and the sci-fi writer Vernor Vinge to describe the moment when artificial intelligence could forge ahead on its own at an uncontrollable pace and leave us mere humans behind. "That could happen sooner than we expected," Musk said in an ominous, flat tone.

For a moment I was struck by the oddness of the scene. We were sitting on a suburban patio by a tranquil backyard swimming pool on a sunny spring day, with two bright-eyed twins learning to toddle, as Musk somberly speculated about the window of opportunity for building a sustainable human colony on Mars before an AI apocalypse destroyed Earthly civilization. It made me recall the words of Sam Teller on his second day working for Musk, when he attended a SpaceX board meeting: "They're sitting around seriously discussing plans to build a city on Mars and what people will wear there, and everyone's just acting like this is a totally normal conversation."

Musk lapsed into one of his long silences. He was, as Shivon called it, "batch processing," referring to the way an old-fashioned computer would cue up a number of tasks and run them sequentially when it had enough processing power available. "I can't just sit around and do nothing," he finally said softly. "With AI coming, I'm sort of wondering whether it's worth spending that much time thinking about Twitter. Sure, I could probably make it the biggest financial institution in the world. But I have only so many brain cycles and hours in the day. I mean, it's not like I need to be richer or something."

I started to speak, but he knew what I was going to ask. "So what should my time be spent on?" he said. "Getting Starship launched. Getting to Mars is now far more pressing." He paused again, then added, "Also, I need to focus on making AI safe. That's why I'm starting an AI company."

X.AI

Musk dubbed his new company X.AI and personally recruited Igor Babuschkin, a leading AI researcher at Google's DeepMind unit, to be the chief engineer. X.AI would initially house some of its new employees at Twitter. But it would be necessary, said Musk, to turn it into an independent startup, like Neuralink. He was having some trouble recruiting AI scientists because the new frenzy about the field meant that anyone with experience could command starting bonuses of a million dollars or more. "It will be easier to get them if they can become founders of a new company and get equity in it," he explained.

I calculated that would mean he would be running six companies: Tesla, SpaceX and its Starlink unit, Twitter, The Boring Company, Neuralink, and X.AI. That was three times as many as Steve Jobs (Apple, Pixar) at his peak.

He admitted that he was starting off way behind OpenAI in creating a chatbot that could give natural-language responses to questions. But Tesla's work on self-driving cars and Optimus the robot put it way ahead in creating the type of AI needed to navigate in the physical world. This meant that his engineers were actually ahead of OpenAI in creating full-fledged artificial general intelligence, which requires both abilities. "Tesla's real-world AI is underrated," he said. "Imagine if Tesla and OpenAI had to swap tasks. They would have to make Self-Driving, and we would have to make large language-model chatbots. Who wins? We do."

In April, Musk assigned Babuschkin and his team three major goals. The first was to make an AI bot that could write computer code. A programmer could begin typing in any coding language, and the X.AI bot would auto-complete the task for the most likely action they were trying to take. The second product would be a chatbot competitor to OpenAI's GPT series, one that used algorithms and trained on data sets that would assure its political neutrality.

The third goal that Musk gave the team was even grander. His overriding mission had always been to assure that AI developed in a way that helped guarantee that human consciousness endured. That was best achieved, he thought, by creating a form of artificial general intelligence that could "reason" and "think" and pursue "truth" as its guiding principle. You should be able to give it big tasks, such as "Build a better rocket engine."

Someday, Musk hoped, it would be able to take on even grander and more existential questions. It would be "a maximum truth-seeking AI. It would care about understanding the universe, and that would probably lead it to want to preserve humanity, because we are an interesting part of the universe." That sounded vaguely familiar, and then I realized why. He was embarking on a mission similar to the one chronicled in the formative (perhaps too formative?) bible of his childhood years, the one that pulled him out of his adolescent existential depression, *The Hitchhiker's Guide to the Galaxy*, which featured a supercomputer designed to figure out the "Answer to The Ultimate Question of Life, the Universe, and Everything."

95

The Starship Launch

SpaceX, April 2023

Musk, Juncosa, and McKenzie atop a high bay in Boca Chica *(top left)*; watching the Starship launch from the control room *(top right)*; with Griffin and X in the control room *(bottom left)*; with Grimes and Tau outside the control room *(bottom right)*

Risky business

"My stomach is twisted in knots," Musk told Mark Juncosa as they stood on the balcony atop the 265-foot-tall high-bay assembly building at Starbase. "It always happens before a big launch. I have PTSD from the failures on Kwaj."

It was April 2023, time for the experimental launch of Starship. When he arrived in south Texas, Musk did what he often did before a major rocket launch, including his first one seventeen years earlier: he retreated into the future. He peppered Juncosa with ideas and edicts for replacing Starbase's four football-field-size assembly tents with a mammoth factory building that could make rockets at a rate of more than one a month. They should start constructing the factory right away, along with a new village of solar-roofed homes for workers. Creating a rocket like Starship was hard, but he knew that the more important step was being able to churn it out at scale. It would eventually take a fleet of a thousand to sustain a human colony on Mars. "My biggest concern is our trajectory. Are we on a trajectory to get to Mars before civilization crumbles?"

When the other engineers joined them for a three-hour pre-launch review in the conference room atop the high bay, Musk gave them a pep talk. "It's worth keeping in mind as you go through all the tribulations that the thing you're working on is the coolest fucking thing on Earth. By a lot. What's the second coolest? This is far cooler than whatever is the second coolest."

The talk then turned to the topic of risk. The dozen or so regulatory agencies that had to approve the flight test did not share Musk's love of it. The engineers briefed him on all the safety reviews and requirements they had endured. "Getting the license was existentially soul-sucking," Juncosa said. Shana Diez and Jake McKenzie provided details. "My fucking brain is hurting," Musk said, holding his head. "I'm trying to figure out how we get humanity to Mars with all this bullshit."

He processed in silence for two minutes, and when he emerged from his trance, he was philosophical. "This is how civilizations decline. They quit taking risks. And when they quit taking risks, their arteries harden. Every year there are more referees and fewer doers." That's why America could no longer build things like high-speed rail or rockets that go to the moon. "When you've had success for too long, you lose the desire to take risks."

"An awesome day"

The countdown that Monday was aborted with forty seconds left because of a valve problem, and the launch was rescheduled for three days later, April 20. Was the 4/20 date intentional, yet another reference to the 420 dope-smoking meme, along the lines of his $420 offer to take Tesla private and $54.20 offer to buy Twitter? In fact, it was mainly guided by weather predictions and readiness, but it amused Musk, who had been saying for weeks that the 4/20 date was "fated." The filmmaker Jonah Nolan, who was documenting the mission, had a maxim that the most ironic outcome is the most likely. Musk added his corollary: "The most entertaining outcome is the most likely."

Musk had flown to Miami after the aborted first countdown to speak to an advertising conference and reassure them about his plans for Twitter. He arrived back in Boca Chica just after midnight on April 20, slept for three hours, then had some Red Bull and got to the launch control room at 4:30 a.m., four hours before the scheduled liftoff. Forty engineers and flight operations officers, many wearing "Occupy Mars!" T-shirts, sat in rows of consoles in a heat-shielded building with a view across the wetlands to the launchpad six miles away. At dawn, Grimes arrived with X, Y, and their new baby boy, Techno Mechanicus, known as Tau.

A half-hour before the scheduled launch, Juncosa came out to the deck and briefed Musk on an issue that had been detected by one of the sensors. Musk processed it for a few seconds and then declared, "I don't think that would be an actual risk." Juncosa did a quick jig, said "Perfect!," and darted back into the control room. Musk soon followed and took his seat at a front-row console, whistling Beethoven's "Ode to Joy."

After a brief pause at T-minus-forty-seconds to make final assessments, Musk gave a nod and the countdown proceeded. At ignition, the flames from the booster's thirty-three Raptors could be seen out of the control room window and on a dozen monitors. The rocket lifted very slowly. "Holy shit, it's going up!" Musk shouted, then leaped from his chair and ran outside onto the deck in time to hear the deep-rumbling boom from the blastoff. For more than three minutes, the rocket lifted into the air and rose out of sight.

But when Musk went back inside, it was clear on the monitors that the rocket was wobbling. Two of the engines had started up poorly in the seconds before launch, and a command had been sent to shut them down. That left thirty-one engines on the booster, which would have been enough to complete the mission. But thirty seconds into the flight, two more engines on the rim of the booster blew out due to fuel bleeding from an open valve, and the fire started to spread to adjacent engine bays. The rocket kept climbing, but it was clear by then that it was not going to get into orbit. Protocols required that they intentionally blow it up over water, where it would not be a danger. Musk nodded to the launch director, who sent a "destruct signal" to the rocket three minutes and ten seconds into the flight. Forty-eight seconds later, the video feed from the rocket went black, just as had happened on the first three launches from Kwaj. Once again, the team got to use the slightly ironic phrase "rapid unscheduled disassembly" to describe what had happened.

As they rewatched the videos of the launch, it was clear that the blasts of the Raptor engines had shattered the base of the launchpad, sending huge chunks of concrete into the air. Some of the engines may have been struck by the debris.

Musk, as usual, had been willing to take some risks. When building the pad in 2020, he had decided not to dig a flame trench beneath the launch mount, like most pads have, that would divert the blast from the engines. "This could turn out to be a mistake," he had said at the time. In addition, in early 2023 the launchpad team had started building a big steel plate that would go on top of the launch mount's foundation and be cooled by gushers of water. But it turned out not to be ready by the time of the launch, and Musk had calculated, based on data from static-fire tests, that the high-density concrete would survive.

Like the decision to forgo slosh baffles on the early version of the Falcon 1, taking these risks turned out to be a mistake. It's unlikely that NASA or Boeing, with their stay-safe approach, would have made those decisions. But Musk believed in a fail-fast approach to building rockets. Take risks. Learn by blowing things up. Revise. Repeat. "We don't want to design to eliminate every risk," he said. "Otherwise, we will never get anywhere."

He had declared beforehand that he would consider the experimental launch a success if the rocket cleared the pad, rose high enough to blow up out of sight, and provided a lot of useful new information and data. It accomplished those goals. Nevertheless, it had exploded. Most of the public would consider it a flaming failure. And for a moment, as he stared at the monitor, Musk seemed subdued.

But the rest of the control room began applauding. They were jubilant at what they had achieved and what they had learned. Musk finally stood up, put his hands above his head, and turned to the room. "Nicely done guys," he said. "Success. Our goal was to get clear of the pad and explode out of sight, and we did. There's too much that can go wrong to get to orbit the first time. This is an awesome day."

That evening, a hundred or so SpaceX employees and friends gathered at the Tiki Bar at Starbase for a semi-celebratory party featuring slow-roasted suckling pig and dancing. Behind the bandstand were some older Starships, their stainless steel reflecting the lights from the party, with Mars, bright and red, rising as if on cue in the night sky just above them.

On one side of the lawn, Gwynne Shotwell talked to Hans Koenigsmann, the fourth employee of SpaceX, who had brought her to meet Musk twenty-one years earlier. Koenigsmann, a veteran of the Kwaj launches, had flown to south Texas on his own to watch this one as a spectator. He had not seen Musk since the Inspiration4 launch in 2021, when he was being eased out of the company. He thought about going over to say hello but decided against it. "Elon is not one for looking back and being sentimental," he said. "He's not good at that type of empathy."

Musk and Grimes sat at one of the picnic tables with his mother,

Maye, who had arrived late the night before after celebrating her seventy-fifth birthday in New York. She reminisced about how her parents had flown the family to explore South Africa's Kalahari Desert every year when she was a child. Elon took after them, she said, one generation of risk-seekers passing along the trait to the next.

X wandered over to one of the fire pits, and when Musk gently tried to pull him away, he squirmed and squealed, not happy to be restrained. So Musk let him go. "One day when I was young, my parents warned me against playing with fire," he recalled. "So I took a box of matches behind a tree and started lighting them."

"Molded out of faults"

The explosion of Starship was emblematic of Musk, a fitting metaphor for his compulsion to aim high, act impulsively, take wild risks, and accomplish amazing things—but also to blow things up and leave smoldering debris in his wake while cackling maniacally. His life had long been an admixture of historically transforming achievements along with wild flameouts, broken promises, and arrogant impulses. Both his accomplishments and his failures were epic. That made him revered by fanboys and reviled by critics, each side exhibiting the feverish fervor of the hyperpolarized Age of Twitter.

Driven since childhood by demons and heroic compulsions, he stoked the controversies by making inflammatory political pronouncements and picking unnecessary fights. Completely possessed at times, he regularly propelled himself to the Kármán line of craziness, the blurry border that separates vision from hallucination. His life had too few flame diverters.

In these regards, the launch had been part of a typical week, one filled with a willingness to embrace the type of risks seldom taken in mature industries or by mature CEOs.

- On a Tesla earnings call that week, he doubled down on his strategy of cutting prices in order to increase sales volume, , and once again he predicted, as he had every year since 2016, that Full Self-Driving would be ready within a year.

- At the ad sales conference he attended in Miami that week, the person who interviewed him onstage, NBC Universal's advertising chief Linda Yaccarino, made a surprising private suggestion: she could be the person he was seeking to run Twitter. They had never met before, but ever since he bought Twitter, she had been pursuing him by text and phone to convince him to come to the conference. "We had a similar vision of what Twitter could become, and I wanted to help him, which led to me stalking him to let me interview him in Miami," she says. She arranged a dinner for him that night with a dozen top advertisers, and he stayed for four hours. He realized that she might be a perfect fit; she was wickedly smart, eager for the job, understood advertising and subscription revenues, and had the right down-to-earth spunkiness to smooth relationships, like Gwynne Shotwell did at SpaceX. But he didn't want to cede too much control. "I would still have to work at Twitter," he told her, which was a polite way of saying that he would still be in charge. She told him to think about it as a relay race. "You build the product, you pass the baton to me, and I execute and sell it." He would end up offering her the title of Twitter CEO, with him remaining executive chairman and chief technology officer.

- On the morning of the launch, he barreled ahead at Twitter with his plan to remove the identity-verification blue check marks that had been bestowed on celebrities, journalists, and other notables. Only those who had signed up to pay a subscription fee, which few had, would be able to keep them. He acted out of an overly righteous sense of moral fairness rather than considering what would make the service best for users, and it detonated paroxysms of knicker-twisting indignation among the Twitterati about who did or did not desire or deserve check marks.

- Over at Neuralink that week, a final round of animal studies was completed and the company started working with the Food and Drug Administration to allow chips to be implanted into the brains of human test subjects. The approval would come four weeks later. Musk urged them to hold public demonstrations of their progress. "We want to bring the public in on everything we're doing," he told the team. "Then they will support us. That's why we live-streamed the Starship launch, even knowing it was likely to explode at some point."

- After another test drive at Tesla, he declared that he was now convinced they should go all in on AI by using the neural network path planner being developed by Dhaval Shroff and his teammates, which learns from video clips how to imitate a good human driver. He told them to create one integrated neural network for Full Self-Driving. Just like ChatGPT can predict the next words in a conversation, FSD's AI system should take in images from a car's cameras and predict the next actions for the steering wheel and pedals.

- A SpaceX Dragon capsule departed the International Space Station and splashed down safely off the Florida coast. It was still the only American craft that could go up to the Space Station and return, as it had done a month earlier with four astronauts, including one from Russia and one from Japan, as it would do again four weeks later.

Do the audaciousness and hubris that drive him to attempt epic feats excuse his bad behavior, his callousness, his recklessness? The times he's an asshole? The answer is no, of course not. One can admire a person's good traits and decry the bad ones. But it's also important to understand how the strands are woven together, sometimes tightly. It can be hard to remove the dark ones without unraveling the whole cloth. As Shakespeare teaches us, all heroes have flaws, some tragic, some conquered, and those we cast as villains can be complex. Even the best people, he wrote, are "molded out of faults."

During launch week, Antonio Gracias and some other friends talked to Musk about the need to restrain his impetuous and destructive instincts. If he was going to lead a new era of space exploration, they said, he needed to be more elevated, to be above the fray politically. They recalled the time Gracias made him put his phone in a hotel safe overnight, with Gracias punching in the code so Musk couldn't get it out to tweet during the wee hours; Musk woke up at 3 a.m. and summoned hotel security to open the safe. After the launch, he displayed a touch of self-awareness. "I've shot myself in the foot so often I ought to buy some Kevlar boots," he joked. Perhaps, he ruminated, Twitter should have an impulse-control delay button.

It was a pleasing concept: an impulse-control button that could defuse Musk's tweets as well as all of his dark impulsive actions and demon-mode eruptions that leave rubble in his wake. But would a restrained Musk accomplish as much as a Musk unbound? Is being unfiltered and untethered integral to who he is? Could you get the rockets to orbit or the transition to electric vehicles without accepting all aspects of him, hinged and unhinged? Sometimes great innovators are risk-seeking man-children who resist potty training. They can be reckless, cringeworthy, sometimes even toxic. They can also be crazy. Crazy enough to think they can change the world.

With Grimes and Maye after the launch

Acknowledgments

Elon Musk allowed me to shadow him for two years, invited me to sit in on his meetings, indulged scores of interviews and late-night conversations, provided emails and texts, and encouraged his friends, colleagues, family members, adversaries, and ex-wives to talk to me. He did not ask to, nor did he, read this book before it was published, and he exercised no control over it.

I am grateful to all of the people listed in the sources who gave me interviews. I would like to single out a few who provided special help, photographs, and guidance: Maye Musk, Errol Musk, Kimbal Musk, Justine Musk, Claire Boucher (Grimes), Talulah Riley, Shivon Zilis, Sam Teller, Omead Afshar, James Musk, Andrew Musk, Ross Nordeen, Dhaval Shroff, Bill Riley, Mark Juncosa, Kiko Dontchev, Jehn Balajadia, Lars Moravy, Franz von Holzhausen, Jared Birchall, and Antonio Gracias.

Crary Pullen was the intrepid photo editor, as she was on many of my previous books. All of them were published by Simon & Schuster, which will forever have my loyalty because of its values and the great team it has, in this case: Priscilla Painton, Jonathan Karp, Hana Park, Stephen Bedford, Julia Prosser, Marie Florio, Jackie Seow, Lisa Rivlin, Kris Doyle, Jonathan Evans, Amanda Mulholland, Irene Kheradi, Paul Dippolito, Beth Maglione, and the ever-present spirit of the late Alice Mayhew. Judith Hoover came out of retirement at my request to be the copyeditor again. I also want to thank my agent, Amanda Urban, along with her international colleagues Helen Manders and Peppa Mignone, and my assistant at Tulane, Lindsey Billips.

And, as always, Cathy and Betsy.

Sources

Interviews

Omead Afshar. Deputy to Musk.
Parag Agrawal. Former CEO of Twitter.
Deepak Ahuja. Former CFO of Tesla.
Sam Altman. Cofounder of OpenAI with Musk.
Drew Baglino. Senior vice president, Tesla.
Jehn Balajadia. Assistant to Musk.
Jeremy Barenholtz. Head of brain interfaces software, Neuralink.
Melissa Barnes. Former VP of Twitter for Latin America and Canada.
Leslie Berland. Former chief marketing officer of Twitter.
Kayvon Beykpour. Former head of product of Twitter.
Jeff Bezos. Founder of Amazon.
Jared Birchall. Musk's personal business manager.
Roelof Botha. Former CFO of PayPal, partner at Sequoia Capital.
Claire Boucher (Grimes). Performance artist, mother of three of Musk's children.
Nellie Bowles. Journalist at *Common Sense*, wife of Bari Weiss.
Richard Branson. Founder of Virgin Galactic.
Elissa Butterfield. Former assistant to Musk.
Tim Buzza. Former VP of launch, SpaceX.
Jason Calacanis. Entrepreneur, Musk friend.
Gage Coffin. Former manufacturing engineer, Tesla.
Esther Crawford. Former director of product management, Twitter.
Larry David. Comedian and writer.
Steve Davis. President, The Boring Company.
Tejas Dharamsi. Software engineer, Twitter.
Thomas Dmytryk. Software engineer, Tesla.
John Doerr. Venture capitalist.
Kiko Dontchev. VP of launch, SpaceX.
Brian Dow. Former head of Tesla Energy.
Mickey Drexler. Former CEO of J.Crew and The Gap.

Phil Duan. Autopilot engineer, Tesla.

Martin Eberhard. Cofounder, Tesla.

Blair Effron. Investment banker.

Ira Ehrenpreis. Board member, Tesla.

Larry Ellison. Cofounder of Oracle.

Ashok Elluswamy. Director of Autopilot software, Tesla.

Ari Emanuel. CEO, Endeavor.

Navaid Farooq. Queen's University friend of Musk.

Nyame Farooq. Wife of Navaid Farooq.

Joe Fath. Portfolio manager, T. Rowe Price.

Lori Garver. Former deputy administrator of NASA.

Bill Gates. Cofounder of Microsoft.

Rory Gates. Son of Bill Gates.

David Gelles. Reporter, *New York Times*.

Bill Gerstenmaier. VP of flight reliability, SpaceX.

Kunal Girotra. Former head of Tesla Energy.

Juleanna Glover. Public relations consultant, Washington, DC.

Antonio Gracias. Friend of Musk and investor.

Michael Grimes. Managing director, Morgan Stanley.

Trip Harriss. Manager of launch site operations, SpaceX.

Demis Hassabis. Cofounder of DeepMind.

Amber Heard. Actress, former girlfriend of Musk.

Reid Hoffman. Cofounder of LinkedIn and PayPal.

Ken Howery. Cofounder of PayPal and Musk friend.

Lucas Hughes. Former finance director, SpaceX.

Jared Isaacman. Entrepreneur and Inspiration4 commander.

RJ Johnson. Former head of Tesla Energy.

Mark Juncosa. Musk top deputy at SpaceX.

Steve Jurvetson. Venture capitalist and Musk friend.

Nick Kalayjian. Former VP of engineering, Tesla.

Ro Khanna. California Democratic congressman.

Hans Koenigsmann. Longtime engineer, SpaceX.

Milan Kovac. Director of Autopilot software engineering, Tesla.

Andy Krebs. Former director of Starship civil engineering, SpaceX.

Joe Kuhn. Mechanical engineer, The Boring Company and Tesla.

Bill Lee. Venture capitalist and Musk friend.

Max Levchin. Cofounder of PayPal.

Jacob McKenzie. Senior director Raptor engineering, SpaceX.

Jon McNeill. Former president of Tesla.

Lars Moravy. VP of vehicle engineering, Tesla.

Michael Moritz. Venture capitalist.

Dave Morris. Senior design director, Tesla.

Rich Morris. VP of production and launch, SpaceX.

Marcus Mueller. Senior manager, Tesla Energy.

Tom Mueller. Founding employee and engine designer, SpaceX.

Andrew Musk. First cousin of Musk.

Christiana Musk. Wife of Kimbal Musk.

Elon Musk.

Errol Musk. Father of Musk.

Griffin Musk. Son of Musk.

James Musk. First cousin of Musk.

Justine Musk. First wife of Musk and mother of five of his children.

Kimbal Musk. Brother of Musk.

Maye Musk. Mother of Musk.

Tosca Musk. Sister of Musk.

Bill Nelson. Administrator, NASA.

Peter Nicholson. Former senior VP of Scotiabank and Musk mentor.

Ross Nordeen. Software engineer at Tesla and musketeer at Twitter.

Luke Nosek. Investor and friend of Musk.

Sam Patel. Director of Starship operations, SpaceX.

Chris Payne. Autopilot software engineer, Tesla.

Janet Petro. Director of the Kennedy Space Center, Cape Canaveral.

Joe Petrzelka. VP Starship engineering, SpaceX.

Henrik Pfister. Automobile designer.

Yoni Ramon. Director of security, Tesla.

Robin Ren. Close friend of Musk at Penn and former China head, Tesla.

Adeo Ressi. Close friend of Musk at Penn.

Bill Riley. Senior director, SpaceX.

Talulah Riley. Actress and second wife of Musk.

Peter Rive. First cousin of Musk.

Ben Rosen. Venture capitalist.

Yoel Roth. Former head of safety and moderation, Twitter.

David Sacks. PayPal cofounder, close friend of Musk, and investor.

Alan Salzman. Early investor in Tesla.

Ben San Souci. Software engineer, Twitter.

Joe Scarborough. Anchor, MSNBC.

DJ Seo. Cofounder of Neuralink.

Brad Sheftel. Partner of Antonio Gracias.

Gwynne Shotwell. President, SpaceX.

Dhaval Shroff. Software engineer, Tesla and Twitter musketeer.

Mark Soltys, principle launch engineer, SpaceX.

Alex Spiro. Musk lawyer.

Christopher Stanley. Senior VP security engineering, Tesla and SpaceX.

Robert Steel. Investment banker.

JB Straubel. Cofounder of Tesla.

Anand Swaminathan. Optimus engineer, Tesla.

Jessica Switzer. Former public relations advisor to Tesla.
Felix Sygulla. Optimus engineer, Tesla.
Marc Tarpenning. Cofounder of Tesla.
Sam Teller. Former chief of staff to Musk.
Peter Thiel. Cofounder of PayPal and investor.
Jim Vo. Manager of Starship build, SpaceX.
Franz von Holzhausen. Design chief, Tesla.
Tim Watkins. Partner of Antonio Gracias and Tesla SWAT team leader.
Bari Weiss. Journalist, *Free Press.*
Rodney Westmoreland. Director of infrastructure, Tesla.
Linda Yaccarino, Former NBC Universal ad sales head; CEO of Twitter.
Tim Zaman. AI engineer, Tesla Autopilot.
David Zaslav. CEO of Warner Bros. Discovery.
Shivon Zilis. Manager of Neuralink and mother of two of Musk's children.

Books

Eric Berger, *Liftoff* (William Morrow, 2021)
Max Chafkin, *The Contrarian* (Penguin, 2021)
Christian Davenport, *The Space Barons* (Public Affairs, 2018)
Tim Fernholz, *Rocket Billionaires* (Houghton Mifflin Harcourt, 2018)
Lori Garver, *Space Pirates* (Diversion, 2022)
Tim Higgins, *Power Play* (Doubleday, 2021)
Hamish McKenzie, *Insane Mode* (Dutton, 2018)
Maye Musk, *A Woman Makes a Plan* (Penguin, 2019)
Edward Niedermeyer, *Ludicrous* (BenBella, 2019)
Jimmy Soni, *The Founders* (Simon & Schuster, 2022)
Ashlee Vance, *Elon Musk* (Ecco, 2015)
Ashlee Vance, *When the Heavens Went on Sale* (Ecco, 2023)

Notes

Prologue: Author's interviews with Elon Musk, Kimbal Musk, Errol Musk, Maye Musk, Tosca Musk, Justine Musk, Talulah Riley, Claire Boucher (Grimes), Peter Thiel. Tom Junod, "Triumph of His Will," *Esquire*, Dec. 2012 (includes the quip about having no navel).

1. Adventurers: Author's interviews with Elon Musk, Maye Musk, Kimbal Musk, Tosca Musk, Errol Musk, Jared Birchall. Joseph Keating and Scott Haldeman, "Joshua N. Haldeman, DC: The Canadian Years," *Journal of the Canadian Chiropractic Association*, 1995; "Before Elon Musk Was Thinking about Mars," *Regina Leader-Post*, May 15, 2017; Joseph Keating, "Flying Chiros," *Dynamic Chiropractic*, Dec. 15, 2003; Nick Murray, "Elon Musk's Fascinating History with Moose Jaw," *Moose Jaw Independent*, Sept. 15, 2018; Joshua Haldeman, "We Fly Three Continents," *ICA International Review of Chiropractic*, Dec. 1954; Phillip de Wet, "Elon Musk's Family Once Owned an Emerald Mine in Zambia," *Business Insider*, Feb. 28, 2018; Phillip de Wet, "A Teenage Elon Musk Once Casually Sold His Father's Emeralds to Tiffany & Co.," *Business Insider*, Feb. 22, 2018; Jeremy Arnold, "Journalism and the Blood Emeralds Story," *Save Journalism*, Substack, Mar. 9, 2021; Vance, *Elon Musk*; Maye Musk, *A Woman*.

2. A Mind of His Own: Author's interviews with Maye Musk, Errol Musk, Elon Musk, Tosca Musk, Kimbal Musk. Neil Strauss, "The Architect of Tomorrow," *Rolling Stone*, Nov. 15, 2017; Elon Musk, TED Talk with Chris Anderson, Apr. 14, 2022; "Inter-galactic Family Feud," *Mail on Sunday*, Mar. 17, 2018; Vance, *Elon Musk*; Maye Musk, *A Woman*.

3. Life with Father: Author's interviews with Maye Musk, Errol Musk, Elon Musk, Tosca Musk, Kimbal Musk, Peter Rive. Elon Musk report cards from Waterkloof House Preparatory School, Glenashley Senior Primary School, Bryanston High School, and Pretoria Boys High School; Neil Strauss, "The Architect of Tomorrow"; Emily Lane Fox, "How Elon Musk's Mom (and Her Twin Sister) Raised the First Family of Tech," *Vanity Fair*, Oct. 21, 2015; Andrew Smith, "Emissary of the Future," *The Telegraph* (London), Jan. 8, 2014.

4. The Seeker: Author's interviews with Elon Musk, Kimbal Musk, Maye Musk, Errol Musk, Peter Rive. Elon Musk, *The Babylon Bee* podcast, Dec. 21, 2021; Tad Friend, "Plugged In," *The New Yorker*, Aug. 17, 2009; Maureen Dowd, "Blasting Off in Domestic Bliss," *New York Times*, July 25, 2020; Neil Strauss, "The Architect of Tomorrow"; Elon Musk, interview at the National Academies of Science, Engineering, and Medicine, Nov. 15, 2021.

5. Escape Velocity: Author's interviews with Elon Musk, Errol Musk, Kimbal Musk, Tosca Musk, Peter Rive.

6. Canada: Author's interviews with Elon Musk, Maye Musk, Tosca Musk. Postmedia News, "Before Elon Musk Was Thinking About Mars, He Was Doing Chores on a Saskatchewan Farm," *Regina Leader-Post*, May 15, 2017; Haley Steinberg, "The Education of Elon Musk," *Toronto Life*, Jan, 2023; Raffaele Panizza, "Interview with Maye Musk," *Vogue*, Oct. 12, 2017; Vance, *Elon Musk*.

7. Queen's: Author's interviews with Maye Musk, Tosca Musk, Kimbal Musk, Elon Musk, Navaid Farooq, Peter Nicholson. Robin Keats, "Rocket Man," *Queen's Alumni Review*, Vol. 1, 2013; Soni, *The Founders*; Vance, *Elon Musk*. Soni provided me his notes and other material.

8. Penn: Author's interview with Elon Musk, Adeo Ressi, Robin Ren, Kimbal Musk, Maye Musk. Alaina Levine, "Entrepreneur Elon Musk Talks about His Background in Physics," *APS News*, Oct. 2013; Soni, *The Founders*; Vance, *Elon Musk*.

9. Go West: Author's interviews with Elon Musk, Kimbal Musk, Robin Ren, Peter Nicholson. Phil Leggiere, "From Zip to X," *University of Pennsylvania Gazette*, Nov. 1999; Jennifer Gwynne, notes for auction items, rrauction.com, Aug. 2022.

10. Zip2: Author's interviews with Elon Musk, Kimbal Musk, Navaid Farooq, Nyame Farooq, Maye Musk, Errol Musk. Amit Katwala, "What's Driving Elon Musk?," *Wired UK*, Sept. 8, 2018; Elon Musk and Maurice J. Fitzgerald, "Interactive Network Directory Service with Integrated Maps and Directions," Patent US6148260A, filed on June 29, 1999; Max Chafkin, "Entrepreneur of the Year," *Inc.*, Dec. 1, 2007; Elon Musk, Stanford talk, Oct. 8 2003; Heidi Anderson, "Newspaperdom's New Superhero: Zip2," *Editor & Publisher*, Jan. 1996; Michael Gross, "Elon Musk 1.0," *Air Mail*, June 11, 2022; Maye Musk, *A Woman*; Vance, *Elon Musk*; Soni, *The Founders*.

11. Justine: Author's interviews with Justine Musk, Elon Musk, Maye Musk, Kimbal Musk, Navaid Farooq. Justine Musk, "I Was a Starter Wife," *Marie Claire*, Sept. 10, 2010.

12. X.com: Author's interviews with Elon Musk, Mike Moritz, Peter Thiel, Roelof Botha, Max Levchin, Reid Hoffman, Luke Nosek. Mark Gimein, "Elon Musk Is Poised to Become Silicon Valley's Next Big Thing," *Salon*, Aug. 17, 1999; Sarah Lacy, "Interview with Elon Musk," *Pando*, Apr. 15, 2009; Eric Jackson, *The PayPal Wars* (World Ahead, 2003); Chafkin, *The Contrarian*.

13. The Coup: Author's interviews with Elon Musk, Mike Moritz, Peter Thiel, Roelof Botha, Max Levchin, Reid Hoffman, Justine Musk, Kimbal Musk, Luke Nosek. Soni, *The Founders*; Vance, *Elon Musk*; Chafkin, *The Contrarian*.

14. Mars: Author's interviews with Elon Musk, Adeo Ressi, Navaid Farooq, Reid Hoffman. Dave Mosher, "Elon Musk Used to Fly a Russian Fighter Jet," *Business Insider*, Aug. 19, 2018; Elon Musk, "My Idea of Fun," *Fortune*, Oct. 6, 2003; M. G. Lord, "Rocket Man," *Los Angeles Magazine*, Oct. 1, 2007; Tom Junod, "Triumph of His Will," *Esquire*, Nov. 15, 2012; Richard Feloni, "Former SpaceX Exec Explains How Elon Musk Taught Himself Rocket Science," *Business Insider*, Oct. 23, 2014; Chris Anderson, "Elon Musk's Mission to Mars," *Wired*, Oct. 21, 2012; Elon Musk speech, Mars Society, Aug. 3, 2012; Elon Musk, "Risky Business," *IEEEE Spectrum*, May 30, 2009; Max Chafkin, "Entrepreneur of the Year," *Inc.*, Dec. 2007; Elon Musk, TED Talk, Apr. 2017; Davenport, *Space Barons*; Berger, *Liftoff*.

15. Rocket Man: Author's interviews with Elon Musk, Adeo Ressi. Amit Katwala, "What's Driving Elon Musk?," *Wired*, Sept. 8, 2018; Anderson, "Elon Musk's Mission to Mars"; Levine, "Entrepreneur Elon Musk Talks about His Background in Physics"; Junod, "Triumph of His Will."

16. Fathers and Sons: Author's interviews with Elon Musk, Kimbal Musk, Justine Musk, Maye Musk. Justine Musk, "I Was a Starter Wife"; Junod, "Triumph of His Will"; Strauss, "The Architect of Tomorrow."

17. Revving Up: Author's interviews with Tom Mueller, Elon Musk, Tim Buzza, Mark Juncosa. Jeremy Rosenberg, interview with Tom Mueller, KCET Public Radio, May 3, 2012; Michael Belfiore, "Behind the Scenes with the World's Most Ambitious Rocket Makers," *Popular Mechanics*, Sept. 1, 2009; Doug McInnis, "Rocket Man," *Loyola Marymount Alumni Magazine*, Aug. 31, 2011; Katwala, "What's Driving Elon Musk?"; Junod, "Triumph of His Will"; Davenport, *Space Barons*; Berger, *Liftoff*; Vance, *Elon Musk*.

18. Musk's Rules for Rocket-Building: Author's interviews with Tim Buzza, Tom Mueller, Elon Musk. Davenport, *Space Barons*; Berger, *Liftoff*; Vance, *Elon Musk*.

19. Mr. Musk Goes to Washington: Author's interviews with Gwynne Shotwell, Elon Musk, Tom Mueller, Hans Koenigsmann. Gwynne Shotwell, Graduation speech at Northwestern University, June 14, 2021; Chad Anderson, "Rethinking Public-Private Space Travel," *Space Policy*, Nov. 2013.

20. Founders: Author's interviews with Martin Eberhard, Marc Tarpenning, Elon Musk, JB Straubel, Ben Rosen. Michael Copeland, "Tesla's Wild Ride," *Fortune*, July 9, 2008; Drake Baer, "The Making of Tesla," *Business Insider*, Nov. 12, 2014; Higgins, *Power Play*; Vance, *Elon Musk*.

21. The Roadster: Author's interviews with Elon Musk, Martin Eberhard, Marc Tarpenning, JB Straubel, Kimbal Musk, Michael Moritz, John Doerr, Alan Salzman, Jessica Switzer, Mickey Drexler. Baer, "The Making of Tesla"; Joshua Davis, "Batteries Included," *Wired*, Aug. 1, 2006; Matthew Wald, "Zero to 60 in 4 Seconds," *New York Times* July 19, 2006; Copeland, "Tesla's Wild Ride"; Elon Musk, "The Secret Tesla Motors Master Plan," Tesla blog, Aug. 2, 2006; interview with Martin Eberhard, *Watt It Takes* podcast, Sept. 2021; Higgins, *Power Play*; Vance, *Elon Musk*; Niedermeyer, *Ludicrous*.

22. Kwaj: Author's interviews with Elon Musk, Gwynne Shotwell, Hans Koenigsmann, Tim Buzza. Berger, *Liftoff*. Berger reported the scramble to replace the faulty capacitors.

23. Two Strikes: Author's interviews with Elon Musk, Kimbal Musk, Hans Koenigsmann, Tom Mueller, Tim Buzza. Kimbal Musk, "Kwajalein Atoll and Rockets," blog posts for Mar. 2006, http://kwajrockets.blogspot.com/; Carl Hoffman, "Elon Musk Is Betting His Fortune on a Mission beyond Earth's Orbit," *Wired*, May 22, 2007; Brian Berger, "Pad Processing Error Doomed Falcon 1," *SpaceNews*, Apr. 10, 2006; Berger, *Liftoff*.

24. The SWAT Team: Author's interviews with Elon Musk, Martin Eberhard, JB Straubel, Antonio Gracias, Tim Watkins, Deepak Ahuja. Zak Edson, "Tesla Motors Case Study: Sotira Carbon Fiber Body Panel Ramp, May–Oct 2008," Valor Capital archives; Steven N. Kaplan et al., "Valor and Tesla Motors," Chicago Booth School of Business case study, 2017; Copeland, "Tesla's Wild Ride"; Baer, "The Making of Tesla"; Elon Musk interview, *Financial Times*, May 10, 2022; Higgins, *Power Play*.

25. Taking the Wheel: Author's interviews with Elon Musk, Antonio Gracias, Tim Watkins, Martin Eberhard, Marc Tarpenning, Michael Marks, Ira Ehrenpreis. Copeland, "Tesla's Wild Ride"; Gene Bylinksy, "Heroes of U.S. Manufacturing: Michael Marks," *Fortune*, Mar. 20, 2000; Higgins, *Power Play*.

26. Divorce: Author's interviews with Justine Musk, Elon Musk, Maye Musk, Kimbal Musk, Antonio Gracias. Justine Musk, "I Was a Starter Wife"; Justine Musk, TEDx Talk, Jan. 26, 2016; Justine Musk, "From the Head of Justine Musk," blog, justinemusk.com; Junod, "Triumph of His Will."

27. Talulah: Author's interviews with Talulah Riley, Elon Musk, Bill Lee.

28. Strike Three: Author's interviews with Tim Buzza, Hans Koenigsmann, Elon Musk, Tom Mueller. Berger, *Liftoff*; "SpaceX Stories," Elonx.net, Apr. 30, 2019; Elon Musk press phone call, Aug. 6, 2008; Carl Hoffman, "Now 0-for-3," *Wired*, Aug. 5, 2008. The launch took place August 3, 2008, Kwaj time, which was August 2 California time.

29. On the Brink: Author's interviews with Elon Musk, Kimbal Musk, Maye Musk, Antonio Gracias, Tim Watkins, Talulah Riley, Bill Lee, Mark Juncosa, Jason Calacanis. "P1 Arriving Now!," Tesla blog, Feb. 6, 2008; Scott Pelley, Elon Musk interview, *60 Minutes*, CBS, May 22, 2012.

30. The Fourth Launch: Author's interviews with Peter Thiel, Luke Nosek, David Sacks, Elon Musk, Tim Buzza, Tom Mueller, Kimbal Musk, Trip Harriss, Gwynne Shotwell. Ashlee Vance, *When the Heavens Went on Sale* (Ecco, 2023); Berger, *Liftoff*; Davenport, *Space Barons*.

31. Saving Tesla: Author's interviews with Elon Musk, Alan Salzman, Kimbal Musk, Ira Ehrenpreis, Deepak Ahuja, Ari Emanuel.

32. The Model S: Author's interviews with Henrik Pfister, Elon Musk, JB Straubel, Martin Eberhard, Nick Kalayjian, Franz von Holzhausen, Dave Morris, Lars Moravy, Drew Baglino. John Markoff, "Tesla Motors Files Suit against Competitor over Design Ideas," *New York Times*, Apr. 15, 2008; Chris Anderson, "The Shared Genius of Elon Musk and Steve Jobs," *Fortune*, Nov. 27, 2013; Charles Duhigg, "Dr. Elon & Mr. Musk," *Wired*, Dec. 13, 2018; Chuck Squatriglia, "First Look at Tesla's Stunning Model S," *Wired*, Mar. 26, 2009; Dan Neil, "Tesla S: A Model Citizen," *Los Angeles Times*, Apr. 29, 2009; Dan Neil, "To Elon Musk and the Model S: Congratulations," *Wall Street Journal*, June 29, 2012; Higgins, *Power Play*.

33. Private Space: Author's interviews with Elon Musk, Tom Mueller, Gwynne Shotwell, Tim Buzza, Lori Garver, Bill Nelson. Brian Mosdell, "Untold Stories from the Rocket Ranch," Kennedy Space Center archives, Mar. 5, 2015; Brian Mosdell, "SpaceX Stories: How SpaceX Built SLC-40 on a Shoestring Budget," *ElonX*, Apr. 15, 2019; Irene Klotz, "SpaceX Secret? Bash Bureaucracy, Simplify Technology," *Aviation Week & Space Technology*, June 15, 2009; Garver, *Space Pirates*; Berger, *Liftoff*; Davenport, *Space Barons*.

34. Falcon 9 Liftoff: Author's interviews with Tim Buzza, Elon Musk, Lori Garver. Brian Vastag, "SpaceX's Dragon Capsule Docks with International Space Station," *Washington Post*, May 25, 2012; Garver, *Space Pirates*; Berger, *Liftoff*; Davenport, *Space Barons*.

35. Marrying Talulah: Author's interviews with Talulah Riley, Elon Musk, Kimbal Musk, Bill Lee, Navaid Farooq. Hermione Eyre, "How to Marry a Billionaire," *The Evening Standard* (London), Apr. 10, 2012.

36. Manufacturing: Author's interviews with Elon Musk, Larry Ellison, Franz von Holzhausen, Dave Morris, JB Straubel. Angus MacKenzie, "Shocking Winner: Proof Positive That America Can Still Make (Great) Things," *Motor Trend*, Dec. 10, 2012; Peter Elkind, "Panasonic's Power Play," *Fortune*, Mar. 6, 2015; Vance, *Elon Musk*; Higgins, *Power Play*.

37. Musk and Bezos: Author's interviews with Jeff Bezos, Elon Musk, Bill Nelson, Tim Buzza. Dan Leone, "Musk Calls Out Blue Origin," *SpaceNews*, Sept. 25, 2013; Walter Isaacson, "In This Space Race, Elon Musk and Jeff Bezos Are Eager to Take You There," *New York Times*, Apr. 24, 2018; Jeff Bezos, *Invent and Wander* (Public Affairs/Harvard Business Review, 2021); Explorers Club 2014 dinner video, https://vimeo.com/119342003; Amanda Gordon, "Scene Last Night: Jeff Bezos Eats Gator, Elon Musk Space," *Bloomberg*, Mar. 17, 2014; Jeffrey P. Bezos, Gary Lai, and Sean R. Findlay, "Sea Landing of Space Launch Vehicles," Patent application US8678321B2, June 14, 2010; Trung Phan, Twitter thread, July 17, 2021; Davenport, *Space Barons*; Berger, *Liftoff*; Fernholz, *Rocket Billionaires*.

38. The Falcon Hears the Falconer: Author's interviews with Elon Musk, Sam Teller, Steve Jurvetson, Antonio Gracias, Mark Juncosa, Jeff Bezos, Kiko Dontchev. Calia Cofield, "Blue Origin Makes Historic Reusable Rocket Landing in Epic Test Flight," *Space.com*, Nov. 24, 2015; Davenport, *Space Barons*.

39. The Talulah Roller Coaster: Author's interviews with Talulah Riley, Elon Musk, Maye Musk, Kimbal Musk, Navaid Farooq, Bill Lee. Junod, "Force of His Will."

40. Artificial Intelligence: Author's interviews with Sam Altman, Demis Hassabis, Elon Musk, Reid Hoffman, Luke Nosek, Shivon Zilis. Steven Levy, "How Elon Musk and Y Combinator Plan to Stop Computers from Taking Over," *Backchannel*, Dec. 11, 2015; Cade Metz, "Inside OpenAI, Elon Musk's Wild Plan to Set Artificial Intelligence Free," *Wired*, Apr. 27, 2016; Maureen Dowd, "Elon Musk's Billion-Dollar Crusade to Stop the A.I. Apocalypse," *Vanity Fair*, Apr. 2017; Elon Musk talk, MIT Aeronautics and Astronautics Department's Centennial Symposium, Oct. 24, 2014; Chris Anderson interview with Elon Musk, TED Conference, Apr. 14, 2022.

41. The Launch of Autopilot: Author's interviews with Drew Baglino, Elon Musk, Omead Afshar, Sam Altman, Sam Teller. Alan Ohnsman, "Tesla CEO Talking with Google about 'Autopilot' Systems," *Bloomberg*, May 7, 2013; Joseph B. White, "Tesla Aims to Leapfrog Rivals," *Wall Street Journal*, Oct. 10, 2014; Jordan Golson and Dieter Bohn, "All New Tesla Cars Now Have Hardware for 'Full Self-Driving Capabilities' but Some Safety Features Will Be Disabled Initially," *The Verge*, Oct. 19, 2016; National Transportation Safety Board, "Collision between a Car Operating with Automated Vehicle Control Systems and a Tractor-Semitrailer Truck Near Williston, Florida on May 7, 2017," Sept. 12, 2017; Jack Stewart, "Elon Musk Says Every New Tesla Can Drive Itself," *Wired*, Oct. 19, 2016; Peter Valdes-Dapena, "You'll Be Able to Summon Your Driverless Tesla from Cross-country," CNN, Oct. 20, 2016; Niedermeyer, *Ludicrous*.

42. Solar: Author's interviews with Peter Rive, Elon Musk, Maye Musk, Errol Musk, Kimbal Musk, Drew Baglino, Sam Teller. Emily Jane Fox, "How Elon Musk's Mom (and Her Twin Sister) Raised the First Family of Tech," *Vanity Fair*, Oct. 21, 2015; Burt Helm, "Elon Musk, Lyndon Rive, and the Plan to Put Solar Panels on Every Roof in America," *Men's Journal*, July 2016 ; Eric Johnson, "From Santa Cruz to Solar City," *Hilltromper*, Nov. 20, 2015; Ronald D. White, "SolarCity CEO Lyndon Rive Built on a Bright Idea," *Los Angeles Times*, Sept. 13, 2013; Max Chafkin, "Entrepreneur of the Year"; Delaware Chancery Court, "Memorandum of opinion in re Tesla Motors stockholder litigation," C.A. No. 12711-VCS, Apr. 27, 2022; Austin Carr, "The Real Story behind Elon Musk's $2.6 Billion Acquisition of SolarCity," *Fast Company*, June 7, 2017; Austin Carr, "Inside Steel Pulse," *Fast Company*, June 9, 2017; Josh Dzieza, "Why Tesla's Battery for Your Home Should Terrify Utilities," *The Verge*, Feb. 13. 2015; Ivan Penn and Russ Mitchell, "Elon Musk Wants to Sell People Solar Roofs That Look Great," *Los Angeles Times*, Oct. 28, 2016.

43. The Boring Company: Author's interviews with Sam Teller, Steve Davis, Jon McNeil, Elon Musk, Joe Kuhn, Elissa Butterfield. Elon Musk, "Hyperloop Alpha," Tesla Blog, 2013; Max Chafkin, "Tunnel Vision," *Bloomberg*, Feb. 20, 2017.

44. Rocky Relationships: Author's interviews with Elon Musk, Juleanna Glover, Sam Teller, Peter Thiel, Amber Heard, Kimbal Musk, Tosca Musk, Maye Musk, Antonio Gracias, Jared Birchall. Joe Kernen, Donald Trump interview, CNBC, Jan. 22, 2020; Barbara Jones, "Inter-galactic Family Feud," *Mail on Sunday*, Mar. 17, 2018; Rob Crilly, "Elon Musk's Estranged Father, 72, Calls His Newborn Baby with Stepdaughter 'God's Plan,'" *The National Post* (Canada), Mar. 25, 2018; Strauss, "The Architect of Tomorrow."

45. Descent into the Dark: Author's interviews with Jon McNeill, Elon Musk, Kimbal Musk, Omead Afshar, Tim Watkins, Antonio Gracias, JB Straubel, Sam Teller, James Musk, Mark Juncosa, Jon McNeill, Gage Coffin. Duhigg, "Dr. Elon & Mr. Musk."

46. Fremont Factory Hell: Author's interviews with Elon Musk, Sam Teller, Omead Afshar, Nick Kalayjian, Tim Watkins, Antonio Gracias, JB Straubel, Mark Juncosa, Jon

McNeill, Sam Teller, Lars Moravy, Kimbal Musk, Rodney Westmoreland. Musk email to SpaceX employees, Sept. 18, 2021; Neal Boudette, "Inside Tesla's Audacious Push to Reinvent the Way Cars Are Made," *New York Times*, June 30, 2018; Austin Carr, "The Real Story," *Fast Company*, June 7, 2017; Strauss, "The Architect of Tomorrow"; Lora Kolodny, "Tesla Employees Say They Took Shortcuts," CNBC, July 15, 2019; Andrew Ross Sorkin, "Tesla's Elon Musk May Have Boldest Pay Plan in Corporate History," *New York Times*, Jan. 23, 2018; Tesla Schedule 14A, SEC filing, Jan. 21, 2018; Alex Adams, "Why Elon Musk's Compensation Plan Wouldn't Work for Most Executives," *Harvard Business Review*, Jan. 24, 2018; Ryan Kottenstette, "Elon Musk Wasn't Wrong about Automating the Model 3 Assembly Line, He Was Just Ahead of His Time," *TechCrunch*, Mar. 5, 2019; Elon Musk, TED Talk, Apr. 14, 2022; Alex Davies, "How Tesla Is Building Cars in Its Parking Lot," *Wired*, June 22, 2018; Boudette, "Inside Tesla's Audacious Push"; Higgins, *Power Play*. For a video of Musk explaining his algorithm, see Tim Dodd, "Starbase Tour," *Everyday Astronaut*, Aug. 2021.

47. Open-Loop Warning: Author's interviews with Kimbal Musk, Deepak Ahuja, Antonio Gracias, Elon Musk, Sam Teller, Joe Fath. Matt Robinson and Zeke Faux, "When Elon Musk Tried to Destroy a Tesla Whistleblower," *Bloomberg*, Mar. 13, 2019; Elon Musk email to Richard Stanton and reply, July 8, 2018; *Vernon Unsworth v. Elon Musk*, U.S. District Court, Central District of California, case 2:18 cv 8048, Sept. 17, 2018; Ryan Mac et al., "In a New Email, Elon Musk Accused a Cave Rescuer of Being a 'Child Rapist,'" *BuzzFeed*, Sept. 4, 2018; documents in support of summary judgment, *In re Tesla Inc. Securities Litigation*, U.S. District Court, Northern District California, motion filed Apr. 22, 2022; David Gelles, James B. Stewart, Jessica Silver-Greenberg, and Kate Kelly, "Elon Musk Details 'Excruciating' Personal Toll of Tesla," *New York Times*, Aug. 16, 2018; Dana Hull, "Weak Sauce," *Bloomberg*, Apr. 24, 2022; Jim Cramer, *Squawk on the Street*, CNBC, Aug. 8, 2018; James B. Stewart, "A Question for Tesla's Board: What Was Elon Musk's Mental State?," *New York Times*, Aug. 15, 2018; Elon Musk interview with Chris Anderson, TED, Apr. 14, 2022; Higgins, *Power Play*; McKenzie, *Insane Mode*.

48. Fallout: Author's interviews with Elon Musk, David Gelles, Juleanna Glover, Sam Teller, Gwynne Shotwell, Talulah Riley, JB Straubel, Jon McNeill, Kimbal Musk, Jared Birchall. *The Joe Rogan Experience* podcast, Sept. 7, 2018; David Gelles, "Interviewing Elon Musk," *New York Times*, Aug. 19, 2018.

49. Grimes: Author's interviews with Claire Boucher (Grimes), Elon Musk, Kimbal Musk, Maye Musk, Sam Teller. Azealia Banks, letter to Elon Musk, Aug. 19, 2018; Kate Taylor, "Azealia Banks Claims to Be at Elon Musk's House," *Business Insider*, Aug. 13, 2018; Maureen Dowd, "Elon Musk, Blasting Off in Domestic Bliss," *New York Times*, July 25, 2020.

50. Shanghai: Author's interviews with Robin Ren, Elon Musk.

51. Cybertruck: Author's interviews with Franz von Holzhausen, Elon Musk, Dave Morris. Stephanie Mlot, "Elon Musk Wants to Make Bond's Lotus Submarine Car a Reality," *PC Magazine*, Oct. 18, 2013.

52. Starlink: Author's interviews with Elon Musk, Mark Juncosa, Bill Riley, Sam Teller, Elissa Butterfield, Bill Gates.

53. Starship: Author's interviews with Elon Musk, Bill Riley, Sam Patel, Joe Petrzelka, Peter Nicholson, Elissa Butterfield, Jim Vo. Ryan d'Agostino, "Elon Musk: Why I'm Building the Starship out of Stainless Steel," *Popular Mechanics*, Jan. 22, 2019.

54. Autonomy Day: Author's interviews with Elon Musk, James Musk, Sam Teller, Franz von Holzhausen, Claire Boucher (Grimes), Omead Afshar, Shivon Zilis, Anand Swaminathan, Joe Fath.

55. Giga Texas: Author's interviews with Elon Musk, Omead Afshar, Lars Moravy.

56. Family Life: Author's interviews with Elon Musk, Claire Boucher (Grimes), Christiana Musk, Maye Musk, Kimbal Musk, Justine Musk, Ken Howery, Luke Nosek. Joe Rogan interview with Elon Musk, May 7, 2020; Rob Copeland, "Elon Musk Says He Lives in a $50,000 House," *Wall Street Journal*, Dec. 22, 2021.

57. Full Throttle: Author's interviews with Elon Musk, Kiko Dontchev, Kimbal Musk, Luke Nosek, Bill Riley, Rich Morris, Hans Koenigsmann, Gwynne Shotwell. Lex Fridman, podcast interview with Elon Musk, Dec 28, 2021; Joey Roulette, "SpaceX Ignored Last Minute Warnings from the FAA before December Launch," *The Verge*, June 15, 2021.

58. Bezos vs. Musk, Round 2: Author's interviews with Jeff Bezos, Elon Musk, Richard Branson. Christian Davenport, "Elon Musk Is Dominating the Space Race," *Washington Post*, Sept. 10, 2021; Richard Waters, "Interview with FT's Person of the Year," *Financial Times*, Dec. 15, 2021; Kara Swisher interview with Elon Musk, Code Conference, Sept. 28, 2021.

59. Starship Surge: Author's interviews with Bill Riley, Kiko Dontchev, Elon Musk, Sam Patel, Joe Petrzelka, Mark Juncosa, Gwynne Shotwell, Lucas Hughes, Sam Patel, Andy Krebs. Tim Dodd, "Starbase Tour," *Everyday Astronaut*, July 30, 2021.

60. Solar Surge: Author's interviews with Kunal Girotra, RJ Johnson, Brian Dow, Marcus Mueller, Elon Musk, Omead Afshar.

61. Nights Out: Author's interviews with Elon Musk, Maye Musk, Kimbal Musk,

Tosca Musk, Claire Boucher (Grimes), Bill Lee, Antonio Gracias. Arden Fanning Andrews, "The Making of Grimes's '*Dune*-esque' 2021 Met Gala Look," *Vogue*, Sept. 16, 2021.

62. Inspiration4: Author's interviews with Jared Isaacman, Elon Musk, Jehn Balajadia, Kiko Dontchev, Claire Boucher (Grimes), Bill Gerstenmaier, Hans Koenigsmann, Bill Nelson, Sam Patel.

63. Raptor Shake-up: Author's interviews with Elon Musk, Jacob McKenzie, Bill Riley, Joe Petrzelka, Lars Moravy, Jehn Balajadia.

64. Optimus Is Born: Author's interviews with Elon Musk, Franz von Holzhausen, Lars Moravy, Drew Baglino, Omead Afshar, Milan Kovac. Chris Anderson interview with Elon Musk, TED, Apr. 14, 2022.

65. Neuralink: Author's interviews with Elon Musk, Jon McNeill, Shivon Zilis, Sam Teller. Elon Musk, "An Integrated Brain-Machine Interface Platform with Thousands of Channels," *bioRxiv*, Aug. 2, 2019; Jeremy Kahn and Jonathan Vanian, "Inside Neuralink," *Fortune*, Jan. 29, 2022.

66. Vision Only: Author's interviews with Elon Musk, Lars Moravy, Omead Afshar, Franz von Holzhausen, Drew Baglino, Phil Duan, Dhaval Shroff. Cade Metz and Neal Boudette, "Inside Tesla as Elon Musk Pushed an Unflinching Vision for Self-Driving Cars," *New York Times*, Dec. 6, 2021; Emma Schwartz, Cade Metz, and Neal Boudette, "Elon Musk's Crash Course," FX/New York Times documentary, May 16, 2022; Niedermeyer, *Ludicrous*.

67. Money: Author's interviews with Elon Musk, Jared Birchall, Kimbal Musk, Christiana Musk, Claire Boucher (Grimes). Tesla Schedule 14A filing, Securities and Exchange Commission, Feb. 7, 2018; Kenrick Cai and Sergei Klebnikov, "Elon Musk Is Now the Richest Person in the World, Officially Surpassing Jeff Bezos," *Forbes*, Jan. 8, 2021. I use split-adjusted prices for the stock.

68. Father of the Year: Author's interviews with Shivon Zilis, Claire Boucher (Grimes), Tosca Musk, Elon Musk, Kimbal Musk, Maye Musk, Christiana Musk. Elon Musk interview with NPQ, Winter 2014; Devin Gordon, "Infamy Is Kind of Fun," *Vanity Fair*, Mar. 10, 2022; Ed Felsenthal, Molly Ball, Jeff Kluger, Alejandro de la Garza, and Walter Isaacson, "Person of the Year," *Time*, Dec. 13, 2021; Richard Waters, "Person of the Year," *Financial Times*, Dec. 15, 2021.

69. Politics: Author's interviews with Elon Musk, Kimbal Musk, Sam Teller, Jared Birchall, Claire Boucher (Grimes), Omead Afshar, Ken Howery, Luke Nosek, David Sacks. Dowd, "Elon Musk, Blasting Off in Domestic Bliss"; Strauss, "The Architect of Tomorrow"; Elon Musk interview with the *Babylon Bee*, Dec. 21, 2021; Rich McHugh, "A SpaceX Flight Attendant Said Elon Musk Exposed Himself and Propositioned Her for Sex," *Business Insider*, May 19, 2022; Dana Hull, "Biden's Praise for GM Overlooks Tesla's Actual EV Leadership," *Bloomberg*, Nov. 24, 2021; Dana Hull and Jennifer Jacobs, "Tesla, Who? Biden Can't Bring Himself to Say It," *Bloomberg*, Feb. 2, 2022; Ari Natter, Gabrielle Coppola, and Keith Laing, "Biden Snubs Tesla," *Bloomberg*, Aug. 5, 2021; Elon Musk interview with Kara Swisher, Code Conference, Sept. 28, 2021.

70. Ukraine: Author's interviews with Elon Musk, Gwynne Shotwell, Jared Birchall. Emails by Lauren Dreyer and text messages by Mykhailo Fedorov provided by Elon Musk. Christopher Miller, Mark Scott, and Bryan Bender, "UkraineX: How Elon Musk's Space Satellites Changed the War on the Ground," *Politico*, June 8, 2022; Cristiano Lima, "U.S. Quietly Paying Millions to Send Starlink Terminals to Ukraine," *Washington Post*, Apr. 8, 2022; Yaroslav Trofimov, Micah Maidenberg, and Drew FitzGerald, "Ukraine Leans on Elon Musk's Starlink in Fight against Russia," *Wall Street Journal*, July 16, 2022; Mehul Srivastava et al., "Ukrainian Forces Report Starlink Outages During Push against Russia," *Financial Times*, Oct. 7, 2022; Volodymyr Verbyany and Daryna Krasnolutska, "Ukraine to Get Thousands More Starlink Antennas," *Bloomberg*, Dec. 20, 2022; Adam Satariano, "Elon Musk Doesn't Want His Satellites to Run Ukraine's Drones," *New York Times*, Feb. 9, 2023; Joey Roulette, "SpaceX Curbed Ukraine's Use of Starlink," Reuters, Feb. 9, 2023.

71. Bill Gates: Author's interviews with Bill Gates, Rory Gates, Elon Musk, Omead Afshar, Jared Birchall, Claire Boucher (Grimes), Kimbal Musk. Rob Copeland, "Elon Musk's Inner Circle Rocked by Fight over His $230 Billion Fortune," *Wall Street Journal*, July 16, 2022; Sophie Alexander, "Elon Musk Enlisted Poker Star before Making $5.7 Billion Mystery Gift," *Bloomberg*, Feb. 15, 2022; Nicholas Kulish, "How a Scottish Moral Philosopher Got Elon Musk's Number," *New York Times*, Oct. 8, 2022; Melody Y. Guan, "Elon Musk, Superintelligence, and Maximizing Social Good," *Huffington Post*, Aug. 3, 2015.

72. Active Investor: Author's interviews with Elon Musk, Antonio Gracias, Omead Afshar, Kimbal Musk, Shivon Zilis, Bill Lee, Griffin Musk, Jared Birchall, Ken Howery, Luke Nosek. Tesla earnings call, Apr. 20, 2022; Matthew A. Winkler, "In Defense of Elon Musk's Managerial Excellence," *Bloomberg*, Apr. 18, 2022; text messages, https://www.documentcloud.org/documents/23112929-elon-musk-text-exhibits-twitter-v-musk; Lane Brown, "What Is Elon Musk?," *New York Magazine*, Aug. 8, 2022; Devin Gordon, "A Close Read of @elonmusk," *New York Magazine*, Aug. 12, 2022.

73. "I made an offer": Author's interviews with Elon Musk, Kimbal Musk, Larry Ellison, Navaid Farooq, Jared Birchall, Claire Boucher (Grimes), Chris Anderson.

Text messages, https://www.documentcloud.org/documents/23112929-elon-musk
-text-exhibits-twitter-v-musk; Rob Copeland, Georgia Wells, Rebecca Elliott, and
Liz Hoffman, "The Shadow Crew Who Encouraged Elon Musk's Twitter Takeover," *Wall Street Journal*, Apr. 29, 2022; Mike Isaac, Lauren Hirsch, and Anupreeta
Das, "Inside Elon Musk's Big Plans for Twitter," *New York Times*, May 6, 2022.

74. Hot and Cold: Author's interviews with Elon Musk, Larry Ellison, Kimbal
Musk, Robert Steel, Leslie Berland, Jared Birchall. Liz Hoffman, "Sam Bankman-
Fried, Elon Musk, and a Secret Text," *Semafor*, Nov. 23, 2022; Twitter town hall,
June 16, 2022.

75. Father's Day: Author's interviews with Elon Musk, Maye Musk, Justine Musk,
Kimbal Musk, Errol Musk, Jared Birchall, Talulah Riley, Griffin Musk, Christiana
Musk, Claire Boucher (Grimes), Omead Afshar, Shivon Zilis. Roula Khalaf, "Aren't
You Entertained?," *Financial Times*, Oct. 7, 2022; Julia Black, "Elon Musk Had Se-
cret Twins in 2022," *Business Insider*, July 6, 2022; Emily Smith and Lee Brown,
"Elon Musk Laughs Off Affair Rumors, Insists He Hasn't 'Had Sex in Ages,'" *New
York Post*, July 25, 2022; Alex Diaz, "Musk Be Kidding," *The Sun*, July 13, 2022; Errol
Musk, "Dad of a Genius," YouTube, 2022; Kirsten Grind and Emily Glazer, "Elon
Musk's Friendship with Sergey Brin Ruptured by Alleged Affair," *Wall Street Journal*,
July 24, 2022. Errol Musk often copied me on his emails to his son.

76. Starbase Shake-up: Author's interviews with Elon Musk, Sam Patel, Bill
Riley, Andy Krebs, Jonah Nolan, Mark Juncosa, Omead Afshar, Jake McKenzie,
Kiko Dontchev, Jared Isaacman, Sam Patel, Andy Krebs, Claire Boucher (Grimes),
Gwynne Shotwell. Dinner with Janet Petro, Lisa Watson-Morgan, Vanessa Wyche.

77. Optimus Prime: Author's interviews with Elon Musk, Franz von Holzhausen,
Lars Moravy.

78. Uncertainty: Author's interviews with Elon Musk, Jared Birchall, Alex Spiro,
Antonio Gracias, Robert Steel, Blair Effron, Ari Emanuel, Larry David, Joe Scarborough.

79. Optimus Unveiled: Author's interviews with Franz von Holzhausen, Elon
Musk, Steve Davis, Lars Moravy, Anand Swaminathan, Milan Kovac, Phil Duan,
Tim Zaman, Felix Sygulla, Anand Swaminathan, Ira Ehrenpreis, Jason Calacanis.

80. Robotaxi: Author's interviews with Elon Musk, Omead Afshar, Franz von Holzhausen, Lars Moravy, Drew Baglino.

81. "Let that sink in": Author's interviews with Elon Musk, Parag Agrawal, David
Sacks, Ben San Souci, Yoni Ramon, Esther Crawford, Leslie Berland.

82. The Takeover: Author's interviews with Elon Musk, Jared Birchall, Alex Spiro, Michael Grimes, Antonio Gracias, Brad Sheftel, David Sacks, Parag Agrawal, Tejas Dharamsi, Ro Khanna.

83. The Three Musketeers: Author's interviews with Elon Musk, James Musk, Andrew Musk, Dhaval Shroff, Ben San Souci, Chris Payne, Thomas Dmytryk, Yoni Ramon, Ross Nordeen, Kayvon Beykpour, Ben San Souci, Alex Spiro, Milan Kovac, Ashok Elluswamy, Tim Zaman, Phil Duan. Kate Conger, Mike Isaac, Ryan Mac, and Tiffany Hsu, "Two Weeks of Chaos," *New York Times*, Nov. 11, 2022.

84. Content Moderation: Author's interviews with Yoel Roth, David Sacks, Jason Calacanis, Elon Musk, Jared Birchall, Yoni Ramon. Cat Zakrzewski, Faiz Siddiqui, and Joseph Menn, "Musk's 'Free Speech' Agenda Dismantles Safety Work at Twitter," *Washington Post*, Nov. 22, 2022; Elon Musk, "Time 100: Kanye West," *Time*, Apr. 15, 2015; Steven Nelson and Natalie Musumeci, "Twitter Fact-Checker Has History of Politically Charged Posts," *New York Post*, May 27, 2020; Bari Weiss, "The Twitter Files Part Two," Twitter thread, Dec. 8, 2022.

85. Halloween: Author's interviews with Elon Musk, Maye Musk, Leslie Berland, Jason Calacanis, Yoel Roth.

86. Blue Checks: Author's interviews with Elon Musk, Yoel Roth, Alex Spiro, David Sacks, Jason Calacanis, Jared Birchall. Conger, Isaac, Mac, and Hsu, "Two Weeks of Chaos"; Zoë Schiffer, Casey Newton, and Alex Heath, "Extremely Hardcore," *The Verge* and *New York Magazine*, Jan. 17, 2023; Casey Newton and Zoë Schiffer, "Inside the Twitter Meltdown," *Platformer*, Nov. 10, 2022.

87. All In: Author's interviews with Elon Musk, Jared Birchall, Larry Ellison, Alex Spiro, James Musk, Andrew Musk, Ross Nordeen, Dhaval Shroff, David Sacks, Yoni Ramon. Gergely Orosz, "Twitter's Ongoing Cruel Treatment of Software Engineers," *Pragmatic Engineer*, Nov. 20, 2022; Alex Heath, "Elon Musk Says Twitter Is Done with Layoffs and Ready to Hire Again," *The Verge*, Nov. 21, 2022; Casey Newton and Zoë Schiffer, "The Only Constant at Elon Musk's Twitter Is Chaos," *The Verge*, Nov. 22, 2022; Schiffer, Newton, and Heath, "Extremely Hardcore."

88. Hardcore: Author's interviews with Elon Musk, Jared Birchall, Alex Spiro, James Musk, Andrew Musk, Ross Nordeen, Dhaval Shroff, David Sacks, Yoni Ramon Larry Ellison, employees at Apple. Schiffer, Newton, and Heath, "Extremely Hardcore."

89. Miracles: Author's interviews with Shivon Zilis, Jeremy Barenholtz, Elon Musk, DJ Seo, Ross Nordeen. Ashlee Vance, "Musk's Neuralink Hopes to Implant Computer in Human Brain in Six Months," *Bloomberg*, Nov. 30, 2022.

90. The Twitter Files: Author's interviews with Elon Musk, Bari Weiss, Nellie Bowles, Alex Spiro, Ross Nordeen. Matt Taibbi, "Note from San Francisco," *TK News*, Substack, Dec. 29, 2022; Matt Taibbi, Twitter File threads, *TK News*; Matt Taibbi, "America Needs Truth and Reconciliation on Russiagate," *TK News*, Jan. 12, 2023; Matt Taibbi, Twitter threads, Dec. 2022–Jan. 2023; Cathy Young, "Are the Twitter Files a Nothingburger?," *The Bulwark*, Dec. 14, 2022; Tim Miller, "No, You Do Not Have a Constitutional Right to Post Hunter Biden's Dick Pic on Twitter," *The Bulwark*, Dec. 3, 2022; Bari Weiss, "Our Reporting at Twitter," *The Free Press*, Dec. 15, 2022; Bari Weiss, Abigail Shrier, Michael Shellenberger, and Nellie Bowles, "Twitter's Secret Blacklists," *The Free Press*, Dec. 15, 2022; David Zweig, "How Twitter Rigged the COVID Debate," *The Free Press*, Dec 26, 2022; Freddie Sayers and Jay Bhattacharya, "What I Discovered at Twitter HQ," *unherd.com*, Dec. 26, 2022.

91. Rabbit Holes: Author's interviews with Elon Musk, Claire Boucher (Grimes), Kimbal Musk, James Musk, Ross Nordeen, Bari Weiss, Nellie Bowle, Yoel Roth, David Zaslav. Drew Harwell and Taylor Lorenz, "Musk Blamed a Twitter Account for an Alleged Stalker," *Washington Post*, Dec. 18, 2022; Drew Harwell, "QAnon, Adrift after Trump's Defeat, Finds New Life in Elon Musk's Twitter," *Washington Post*, Dec. 14, 2022; Yoel Roth, "Gay Data," University of Pennsylvania PhD dissertation, Nov. 30, 2016.

92. Christmas Capers: Author's interviews with Elon Musk, James Musk, Ross Nordeen, Kimbal Musk, Christiana Musk, Griffin Musk, David Agus.

93. AI for Cars: Author's interviews with Dhaval Shroff, James Musk, Elon Musk, Milan Kovac.

94. AI for Humans: Author's interviews with Elon Musk, Shivon Zilis, Bill Gates, Jared Birchall, Sam Altman, Demis Hassabis. Reed Albergotti, "The Secret History of Elon Musk, Sam Altman, and OpenAI," *Semafor*, Mar. 24, 2023; Kara Swisher, "Sam Altman on What Makes Him 'Super Nervous' about AI," *New York*, Mar. 23, 2023; Matt Taibbi, "Meet the Censored: Me?," Racket, Apr. 12, 2023; Tucker Carlson, interview with Elon Musk, Fox News, Apr. 17 and 18, 2023.

95. The Starship Launch: Author's interviews with Elon Musk, Maye Musk, Claire Boucher (Grimes), Mark Juncosa, Bill Riley, Shana Diez, Mark Soltys, Antonio Gracias, Jason Calacanis, Gwynne Shotwell, Hans Koenigsmann, Linda Yaccarino. Tim Higgins, "In 24 Hours, Elon Musk Reignited His Reputation for Risk," *Wall Street Journal*, Apr. 22, 2023; Damon Beres, "Elon Musk's Disastrous Week," *The Atlantic*, Apr. 20, 2023; George Packer, *Our Man* (Knopf, 2019). From Shakespeare's *Measure for Measure*: "They say best men are molded out of faults / And, for the most, become much more the better / For being a little bad."

Index

Photo Credits

Page 102   Courtesy of Kimbal Musk
Page 106   Gregg Segal
Page 111   Courtesy of SpaceX
Page 118   Courtesy of Gwynne Shotwell
Page 124   Top: Steve Jurvetson/Wikimedia Commons
            Bottom: Erin Lubin
Page 131   Courtesy of Tesla
Page 144   Photos courtesy of Hans Koenigsmann
Page 149   Photos courtesy of Hans Koenigsmann
Page 155   Courtesy of Tim Watkins
Page 162   Nicki Dugan Pogue/Wikimedia Commons
Page 168   Lauren Greenfield/Institute
Page 172   Nick Harvey/WireImage/Getty Images
Page 175   Courtesy of Hans Koenigsmann
Page 178   Courtesy of Hans Koenigsmann
Page 182   Photos courtesy of Hans Koenigsmann
Page 190   Courtesy of Navaid Farooq
Page 195   Left and right: Steve Jurvetson/Wikipedia Commons
Page 203   Official White House Photo by Chuck Kennedy
Page 209   Courtesy of Christopher Stanley
Page 213   Courtesy of Talulah Riley
Page 217   Top: Courtesy of YouTube.com
            Bottom: Courtesy of Sam Teller
Page 223   Courtesy of Trung Phan/Twitter
Page 229   Courtesy of Jehn Balajadia
Page 235   Photos courtesy of Navaid Farooq
Page 239   YouTube.com
Page 260   Top left and right: Courtesy of Amber Herd
            Bottom left: Gianluigi Guercia/AFP via Getty Images
            Bottom right: Brendan Smialowski /AFP via Getty Images
Page 267   Courtesy of Omead Afshar
Page 275   Courtesy of Sam Teller
Page 276   Top left: courtesy of Omead Afshar
            Top right and Bottom left: courtesy of Sam Teller
            Bottom right: Courtesy of Jehn Balajadia
Page 286   Courtesy of Omead Afshar
Page 287   Photos courtesy of Sam Teller
Page 295   Top: YouTube.com
            Bottom: Ryan David Brown/The New York Times/Redux

Page 305   Left: Courtesy of Grimes
               Right: Amy Sussman/WWD/Penske Media/Getty Images
Page 312   Courtesy of Robin Ren
Page 315   Courtesy of Sam Teller
Page 325   Right: Courtesy of Bill Riley
Page 340   Top left: Courtesy of Maye Musk
               Bottom: Martin Schoeller/August
Page 347   Top: Courtesy of SpaceX
               Bottom: Courtesy of Jehn Balajadia
Page 353   Left: Courtesy of Blue Origin
               Right: Courtesy of Elon Musk
Page 358   Top left: Courtesy of Andy Krebs
               Bottom left: Courtesy of Lucas Hughes
               Right: Nic Ansuini
Page 376   Left: Will Heath/NBC/NBCU Photo Bank via Getty Images
               Right: courtesy of Grimes
Page 382   Top: Courtesy of SpaceX
               Bottom: Courtesy of Kim Shiflett /NASA
Page 387   Bottom: Nic Ansuini
Page 393   Courtesy of Tesla
Page 398   Courtesy of Neuralink
Page 435   Imagine China/AP
Page 440   Left: Kevin Dietsch/Getty Images
               Right: Andrew Harrer/Bloomberg via Getty Images
Page 466   Bottom: Courtesy of Jared Birchall
Page 482   Photos courtesy of Tesla
Page 488   Top: The PhotOne/BACKGRID
               Bottom: Marlena Sloss/Bloomberg via Getty Images
Page 500   Courtesy of Milan Kovac
Page 501   Top: Courtesy of Omead Afshar
Page 506   Top: Courtesy of Elon Musk/Twitter
               Bottom: Courtesy of Jehn Balajadia
Page 511   Right: Courtesy of Jehn Balajadia
Page 523   Top left: Elon Musk/Twitter
               Top right: Courtesy of Twitter
               Bottom left: David Paul Morris/Bloomberg via Getty Images
               Bottom right: Duffy-Marie Arnoult/WireImage/Getty Images
Page 532   Top: Courtesy Elon Musk/Twitter
               Bottom: Courtesy of Maye Musk

Page 546   Top: Courtesy of Christopher Stanley
Page 561   Top: Courtesy of Neuralink
             Bottom: Courtesy of Jeremy Barenholtz
Page 565   Top: Wikimedia Commons
             Bottom: Samantha Bloom
Page 581   Photos courtesy of James Musk
Page 592   Courtesy of Dhaval Shroff

Front Endpaper: Courtesy of SpaceX
Back Endpaper: Courtesy of Tesla, Inc.

About the Author

Walter Isaacson has written biographies of Jennifer Doudna, Leonardo da Vinci, Steve Jobs, Albert Einstein, Henry Kissinger, and Benjamin Franklin. He is also the author of *The Innovators* and the coauthor of *The Wise Men*. He has been the editor of *Time*, the CEO of CNN, and the CEO of the Aspen Institute. He was awarded the National Humanities Medal in 2023. He is a professor at Tulane and lives with his wife in New Orleans.